Java EE 8 Recipes

A Problem-Solution Approach

Second Edition

Josh Juneau

Apress®

Java EE 8 Recipes

Josh Juneau
Hinckley, Illinois, USA

ISBN-13 (pbk): 978-1-4842-3593-5 ISBN-13 (electronic): 978-1-4842-3594-2
https://doi.org/10.1007/978-1-4842-3594-2

Library of Congress Control Number: 2018946699

Managing Director, Apress Media LLC: Welmoed Spahr
Acquisitions Editor: Jonathan Gennick
Development Editor: Laura Berendson
Coordinating Editor: Jill Balzano

Cover designed by eStudioCalamar

Cover image designed by Freepik (`www.freepik.com`)

Distributed to the book trade worldwide by Springer Science+Business Media New York, 233 Spring Street, 6th Floor, New York, NY 10013. Phone 1-800-SPRINGER, fax (201) 348-4505, e-mail `orders-ny@springer-sbm.com`, or visit `www.springeronline.com`. Apress Media, LLC is a California LLC and the sole member (owner) is Springer Science + Business Media Finance Inc (SSBM Finance Inc). SSBM Finance Inc is a **Delaware** corporation.

For information on translations, please e-mail `rights@apress.com`, or visit `http://www.apress.com/rights-permissions`.

Apress titles may be purchased in bulk for academic, corporate, or promotional use. eBook versions and licenses are also available for most titles. For more information, reference our Print and eBook Bulk Sales web page at `http://www.apress.com/bulk-sales`.

Any source code or other supplementary material referenced by the author in this book is available to readers on GitHub via the book's product page, located at `www.apress.com/9781484235935`. For more detailed information, please visit `http://www.apress.com/source-code`.

Printed on acid-free paper

This book is dedicated to my wife Angela, my five children: Kaitlyn, Jacob, Matthew, Zachary, and Lucas. You are my joy and inspiration. It is also dedicated to the many Java developers worldwide. I hope that these recipes can lead you to developing the sophisticated solutions of tomorrow.

—Josh Juneau

Contents

About the Author

Josh Juneau has been developing software and database systems for several years. Database application development and sophisticated web apps have been the focus of his career since the beginning. Early in his career, he became an Oracle database administrator and adopted the PL/SQL language for performing administrative tasks and developing applications for Oracle database. In an effort to build more complex solutions, he began to incorporate Java into his PL/SQL applications and later developed stand-alone and web applications with Java. Josh wrote his early Java web applications utilizing JDBC to work with backend databases. Later, he incorporated frameworks into his enterprise solutions, including Java EE, Spring, and JBoss Seam. Today, he primarily develops enterprise web solutions utilizing Java EE.

He extended his knowledge of the JVM by developing applications with other JVM languages such as Jython and Groovy. In 2006, Josh became the editor and publisher for the *Jython Monthly* newsletter. In late 2008, he began a podcast dedicated to the Jython programming language. Josh was the lead author for *The Definitive Guide to Jython, Oracle PL/SQL Recipes*, and *Java 7 Recipes*, which were published by Apress. Since then, he has continued to author Java-related books for Apress, including his most recent work entitled *Java 9 Recipes*. He is an avid contributor to Oracle's *Java Magazine*, and he speaks at Java User Groups and conferences when he has the opportunity.

He works as an application developer and systems analyst, and he is a contributor to the Chicago Java User Group. Josh is an Apache NetBeans committer and a Java Champion. He participates in the JCP and had been a part of the JSF expert group for the development of Java EE 8. Josh has a wonderful wife and five children with whom he loves to spend time. To hear more from Josh, follow his blog, which can be found at `http://jj- blogger.blogspot.com`. You can also follow him on Twitter via `@javajuneau`.

About the Technical Reviewer

Alex Bretet is a 35-year-old Frenchman who has been working in the software development industry since 2006. Specialized in Java environments (web and enterprise), he also has several projects with the Spring Framework. Currently based in Austria, he works as an international contractor for the bank and insurance industry.

To the new joiners and wannabe developers, he will never stress enough the importance of repetitively exposing oneself to new technological challenges on a private level. Particularly before and after graduation. Open source projects, entrepreneurial ideas, publications... all kinds of experience that can build confidence and your longer-term memory.

Acknowledgments

To my wife Angela: I am still amazed by you and always will be. Thanks again for helping to inspire me and keep me moving forward in my endeavors. You continue to be my rock, and I am so grateful for all you do.

To my children, Kaitlyn, Jacob, Matthew, Zachary, and Lucas—I love you all so much and I cherish every moment we have together. I hope that you'll find your passion in life and enjoy each day as much as I enjoy each day spending time with you. I wish I could slow time down...you are growing up too fast!

I want to thank my family for their continued support in my career. I also want to thank my co-workers for allowing me to guide the organization's application development efforts and build successful solutions to keep us moving forward.

To the folks at Apress—I thank you for providing me with the chance to share my knowledge with others, once again. I especially thank Jonathan Gennick for the continued support of my work and for providing the continued guidance to produce useful content for our readers. I also thank Jill Balzano for doing a great job coordinating this project and many of my others before it. To my technical reviewer, Alex Bretet, you have done an excellent job of solidifying the book content. Thanks again for your hard work and technical expertise. Lastly, I'd like to thank everyone else at Apress who had a hand in this book.

To the Java community—thanks again for helping to make the Java platform such an innovative and effective realm for application development. I especially want to thank those in the Java EE community who have a hand in helping to move things forward via EE4J, the Eclipse Working Group, Java EE Guardians, and other speakers, writers, and evangelists of Java EE and Jakarta EE. To the members of the Chicago Java Users Group, I want to thank you for helping Chicago be one of the best locations for Java expertise. I also want to thank my fellow members of the Java OffHeap podcast:—Freddy Guime, Bob Paulin, Michael Minella, and Jeff Palmer—you help me remain engaged in all of Java technologies and it is a privilege to have the opportunity to meet and discuss Java each month.

Introduction

The Java platform is one of the most widely used platforms for application development in the world. The platform is so popular that there are several different flavors of Java that can be used for developing applications that run on different mediums. From development of desktop, mobile, or web applications and hardware operating systems, Java can be utilized for development of just about any solution. As such, Java has become a very popular platform for development of web and enterprise applications, offering web services, reliability, security, and much more.

Java Enterprise Edition was originally released in 1999 as Java 2 Platform, Enterprise Edition (J2EE). Although several enterprise frameworks were available for development of reliable and secure applications on the Java platform, it made sense to standardize some solutions in order to minimize customization and help provide standards around Java Enterprise development to make it more prevalent in the industry. The platform originally included a terse number of specifications for standardization, including Java Servlet, JavaServer Pages, RMI, Java Database Connectivity (JDBC), Java Message Service API (JMS), Java Transaction API (JTA), and Enterprise JavaBeans. Early development of J2EE applications had a large learning curve, and it was cumbersome because it required lots of XML configuration. Even with these setbacks, it became popular among larger organizations and companies due to the prevalence of Java and its well-known security benefits. In 2001, J2EE 1.3 was released, adding more specifications to the platform, including the JavaServer Pages Standard Tag Library (JSTL), and Java Authentication and Authorization Service (JAAS). Other specifications, such as Java Servlet, also gained enhancements under the J2EE 1.3 release, making evolutionary enhancements to the platform. The release of J2EE 1.4 in 2003 marked a major milestone for Java Enterprise, as many new specifications were added to the platform, providing standards for even more Java technologies. The release of J2EE 1.4 marked the first iteration of Web Services for J2EE 1.1, JavaServer Faces (JSF), and Java APIs for XML solutions such as JAXP, JAXR, and more. Although the release of J2EE 1.4 included many specifications, it was still deemed as "difficult to learn," "cumbersome," and "not productive".

Over the next few years, J2EE was re-worked in an attempt to make it easier to learn and utilize for the construction of modern web applications. Although XML is an excellent means for configuration, it can be cumbersome and difficult to manage, so configuration was a big item that was being addressed for the next release. Technologies such as Enterprise JavaBeans (EJB) included some redundant characteristics, making EJB coding time-consuming and difficult to manage, so an overhaul of EJB was also in order. In May of 2006, Java EE 5 was released, leaving the J2EE acronym behind, and changing to simply Java EE instead. The Java EE 5 platform was significantly easier to use and maintain because features such as annotations were introduced, cutting down the amount of XML configuration significantly, as configuration could now be injected via annotations. EJBs were made easier to develop, and Java Persistence API (JPA) became a marketable technology for object-relational mapping. Java Enterprise Edition has since become a widely adopted and mature platform for enterprise development. Java EE 6 was released in 2009, making configuration and APIs even easier, and adding more specifications to the platform. Specifications such as Contexts and Dependency Injection and Bean Validation were introduced, vastly changing the landscape of the platform and streamlining development. Java EE 7 (released in 2013) continued to strengthen and modernize the platform, adding the WebSockets and JSON-P specifications. In the Java EE 7 release, specifications such as JSF and EJB were also enhanced, adding even more features to increase productivity and functionality and allowing them to work better for more modern web solutions.

What occurred next in the timeline was a definitive game changer for the Java EE platform. The Java EE 8 initiative had begun in 2015 and many of the specifications that make up the platform had begun to work. The focus of Java EE 8 was to continue to work toward Java SE 8 compatibility throughout the APIs and to continue making the APIs easier to use. There was also a focus on creating new specifications around making microservices easier to develop with Java EE. In late 2015, many of the specifications stopped moving forward, and there was a halt in progress across the board. A few specifications, such as JSF, CDI, and JSON-B, continued to progress, while many of the others stalled. During this stall, the community became concerned about the future of Java EE, and there was a perception that it was going to be dropped. Oracle was silent on the progress of Java EE 8 and uncertainty was in the air. It was during this same timeframe that the Java EE Guardians group was formed, with the focus on trying to make Oracle produce a statement about the future direction of the platform, and to make open source the platform rather than dropping it. Around that same time, the Microprofile project was started as a collaborative effort by a number of the Java EE container vendors, with the focus on providing a true Microservices profile for the Java EE platform.

In late 2016, Oracle changed the direction of Java EE 8 by removing some of the previously planned specification updates and adding others. There became a renewed effort to keep Java EE 8 moving forward in the hopes to produce a final release in 2017, working towards a better platform for producing microservices based applications. The Java EE 8 release was final in the fall of 2017, and it included updates to many of the specifications. However, even some of the specifications that were planned for enhancing microservices development were dropped in an effort to produce a timely release, including MVC and the Health Checking API.

In early Fall 2017 just before the release of Java EE 8, Oracle announced that they were going to open source Java EE. After a short while, it was announced that Oracle was going to contribute all of the Java EE sources (for each of the underlying specifications), along with all documentation and TCKs (Technology Compatibility Kits) to the Eclipse Foundation. In late 2017, the EE4J (Eclipse Enterprise for Java) project was formed, and the transfer of each specification began. In early 2018 it was voted that the new name for the platform under the open source EE4J project would become Jakarta EE. Once all of the specification sources, documentation, and TCKs were transferred, Jakarta EE was to release a 1.0, which was in parity with Java EE 8.

This book focuses on the Java EE 8 release, as well as the Jakarta EE initial release. As such, throughout this book, I will refer to the platform as Java EE 8. However, each of the recipes in this book also work with the initial release of Jakarta EE. The platform is covered as a whole, touching upon each most of the widely used specifications that make up Java EE. You will learn how to use each of the major specifications, making use of real-world examples and solutions. This book will cover APIs that have not been updated for Java EE 8, as well as those that have been enhanced, providing complete coverage for those who are newer to the platform. It also features recipes that cover the newest features of the platform, so that seasoned Java EE developers can skip those introductory concepts and delve into newer material.

I work with Java EE/Jakarta EE on a daily basis, and I have a deep passion for the technologies involved in the platform. I hope that this book increases your passion and productivity using the platform in its entirety.

Who This Book Is For

This book is intended for all those who are interested in learning Java Enterprise Edition (Java EE) development and/or already know Java EE but would like some information regarding the new features included in Java EE 8. Those who are new to Java EE development can read this book, and it will allow them to start from scratch to get up and running quickly. Intermediate and advanced Java developers who are looking to update their arsenal with the latest features that Java EE 8 has to offer can also read the book to quickly update and refresh their skillset.

How This Book Is Structured

This book is structured so that it does not have to be read from cover to cover. In fact, it is structured so that developers can choose which topic(s) they'd like to read about and jump right to them. Each recipe contains a problem to solve, one or more solutions to solve that problem, and a detailed explanation of how the solution works. Although some recipes may build on concepts that have been discussed in other recipes, they will contain the appropriate references so that the developer can find other related recipes that are beneficial to the solution. The book is designed to allow developers to get up and running quickly with a solution so that they can be home in time for dinner.

Conventions

Throughout the book, I've kept a consistent style for presenting Java code, SQL, command-line text, and results. Where pieces of code, SQL, reserved words, or code fragments are presented in the text, they are presented in fixed-width Courier font, such as this (working) example:

```
public class MyExample {
    public static void main(String[] args){
        System.out.println("Jakarta EE is excellent!");
    }
}
```

Downloading the Code

The code for the examples shown in this book is available on the Apress web site, `www.apress.com`. A link can be found on the book's information page under the Source Code/Downloads tab. This tab is located underneath the Related Titles section of the page.

Note The sources for this book may change over time, to provide new implementations that incorporate the most up-to-date features in Jakarta EE. That said, if any issues are found within the sources, please submit them via the Apress website "Errata" form, and code will be adjusted accordingly.

Configuring Database for the Book Sources

This book's sources have been developed using the Apache Derby database, which ships with NetBeans IDE and GlassFish. Please install and configure the database for use with the book sources prior to working with the sources. The database configuration involves creation of a database schema or user, as well as execution of the `create_database.sql` script (contained within the book sources) that goes along with the database of your choice. You must also place the appropriate database JDBC driver into the GlassFish `CLASSPATH`. You can do this by copying the `ojdbc6.jar` (Oracle) or `derbyclient.jar` (Apache Derby) JAR file into your Integrated Development Environment (IDE) project for the book sources, or into the `<GlassFish-Home>\glassfish5\domains\domain1\lib\ext` directory. If you're copying into the GlassFish `lib` directory, then once the JAR file has been copied into place, the GlassFish server will need to be restarted, if it is already running. If you're using Payara, the JAR file can be placed into the respective location.

Once the database has been installed/configured, and the SQL scripts contained within the book sources have been executed, log into the GlassFish administrative console and set up a database connection pool to work with the database of your choice. For more information, see Recipe 12-5.

After a connection pool has been configured, update the `persistence.xml` file that is contained within the book sources accordingly, so that the data source name aligns with the one you've assigned to the GlassFish JDBC resource.

Setting Up NetBeans Project

** Before setting up a NetBeans project for the book sources, install and configure GlassFish or Payara accordingly. For more information, see Recipe 12-1.

Note regarding dependencies This project depends on the use of the third-party PrimeFaces library. At the time of this book publication, the PrimeFaces 6.x was used and available for free download.

Perform the following steps to set up the NetBeans Maven Web project:

1. Open NetBeans IDE 8.2 or greater.
2. Choose the File ➤ New Project ➤ Maven ➤ Web Application menu option.
3. Title the project `JavaEE8Recipes` and choose a desired project location.
4. Server and settings:
   - If you have not yet registered your GlassFish server with NetBeans, click the Add button in this dialog and add the server. To do so, you will need to know the location of the GlassFish server on your file system.
   - Java EE Version: As of NetBeans 8.2, you only have the option to choose Java EE 7 Web.
5. Frameworks:
   - Select JavaServer Faces and then accept all defaults.
6. Click Finish.
7. Go to your file system and copy the contents from within the `JavaEE8Recipes-BookSources\NBProject\src` directory into your new NetBeans project `src` directory.
8. Add the required library dependencies to your project by right-clicking on the project and choosing the Properties option. Once the Properties dialog is open, select Libraries and add the following dependencies:
   - PrimeFaces 6.x
   - Database JDBC JAR file, if not already placed within the GlassFish `lib` directory

Testing Java EE Application Projects

This book will not delve into the world of testing Java EE application projects. Although testing is extremely important and essential for a project's success, it is far too big of a topic to fit into this book. That said, I want to get you pointed in the correct direction with my approach to testing Java EE application projects.

Note The recommendations made in this section have not been attempted with Jakarta EE since it was not available for testing at the time of this writing. However, since Jakarta EE 1.0 is assumed to be an open source replica of the Java EE 8 release, these recommendations should apply if you're using Jakarta EE 1.0, and perhaps for future versions of Jakarta EE as well.

Certainly testing is one of those objectives that meet the "more is better" mantra, so I believe it is important to take a multi-headed approach to testing. The most obvious testing is that you must test your application user interface and ensure that the application UI and business logic functions as expected during user testing. This is perhaps the easiest testing, as it only requires user-documented testing of each form within a web application. Before user testing can begin, functional testing and automated UI testing should take place. By functional testing, I mean using a framework such as JUnit to test the business logic of the application. Such tests can be configured to run each time a project is built and compiled. Automated UI testing can be achieved via the use of a testing API such as Arquillian, along with an add-on like Graphene. In fact, my approach is to utilize Arquillian for configuration and coordination of all unit tests via JUnit and also for orchestration of the automated UI testing via Graphene.

While this topic is too big to cover in this section, I want to point you to some online resources that you can use to get started with Arquillian testing of your Java EE application projects. It is important to gain a decent understanding of the Arquillian framework by reading through the documentation. One of the most difficult pieces of the puzzle is setting up the Maven POM file with the correct dependencies. For this reason, you will find a sample POM file dependency list for setting up Arquillian with Graphene extension in the sources for this book. Once the dependencies are set up, it is very easy to create tests that will be executed each time the project is built.

An Arquillian test file is simply a Java class that contains JUnit (or another testing framework) tests, that runs under the Arquillian harness. Harness allows one to set up a custom deployment package for each test class, packaging only the required dependencies for running the individual tests. The deployment package can then be deployed to a running application server container, or they can be deployed to an embedded container. In my experience, I've had the best luck deploying to an existing server...typically the same server that I develop against on my local machine.

The Graphene extension can be used to literally code the web interaction on a specific page of an application. You can code the completion of a web form, which is the pressing of a button, and test for a specified result.

Use the documentation found at the following links to get started with Arquillian and Selenum.

```
http://arquillian.org/guides/getting_started/
http://arquillian.org/guides/getting_started_rinse_and_repeat/
http://arquillian.org/guides/shrinkwrap_introduction/
http://arquillian.org/guides/functional_testing_using_graphene/
```

CHAPTER 1

Working with Servlets

Java servlets were the first technology for producing dynamic Java web applications. Sun Microsystems released the first Java Servlet specification in 1997. Since then it has undergone tremendous change, making it more powerful and easing development more with each release. The 3.0 version was released as part of Java EE 6 in December 2009.

Servlets are at the base of all Java EE applications. Although many developers use servlet frameworks such as Java Server Pages (JSP) and Java Server Faces (JSF), both of those technologies compile pages into Java servlets behind the scenes via the servlet container. That said, a fundamental knowledge of Java servlet technology could be very useful for any Java web developer.

Servlets are Java classes that conform to the Java Servlet API, which allows a Java class to respond to requests. Although servlets can respond to any type of request, they are most commonly written to respond to web-based requests. A servlet must be deployed to a Java servlet container in order to become usable. The Servlet API provides a number of objects that are used to enable the functionality of a servlet within a web container. Such objects include the request and response objects, `pageContext`, and a great deal of others, and when these objects are used properly, they enable a Java servlet to take care of just about any task a web-based application needs to perform. As mentioned, servlets can produce not only static content but also dynamic content. Since a servlet is written in Java, any valid Java code can be used within the body of the servlet class. This empowers Java servlets and allows them to interact with other Java classes, the web container, the underlying file server, and much more.

The Servlet 3.1 specification was released with Java EE 7, and it included many capabilities. Among the 3.1 features were support for HTTP 1.1 upgrade, non-blocking asynchronous I/O, and more. The Servlet 4.0 specification, which is part of Java EE 8, is a major revision, revolving around the major change from HTTP1.1 to HTTP/2. The updated version of the HTTP protocol brings forth many enhancements, including request/response multiplexing, server push, binary framing, and stream prioritization. Some of the functionality enhancements take place underneath the covers, meaning that there will be no API enhancements required to support. Other features, such as server push, expose new APIs for the developer.

This chapter will get you started developing and deploying servlets. To get started, you learn how to install Oracle's GlassFish application server and Payara server, which are both robust servlet containers, and each will enable you to deploy sophisticated Java enterprise applications. You learn the basics of developing servlets, how to use them with client web sessions, and how to link a servlet to another application. All the while, you learn to use standards from the latest release of the Java Servlet API, which modernizes servlet development and makes it much easier and more productive than in years past.

J. Juneau, *Java EE 8 Recipes*, https://doi.org/10.1007/978-1-4842-3594-2_1

■ **Note** You can run the examples in this chapter by deploying the `JavaEE8Recipes.war` file (contained in the sources) to a local Java EE application server container such as GlassFish v5 or Payara 5. You can also set up the NetBeans project entitled `JavaEE8Recipes` that is contained in the sources, build it, and deploy to GlassFish v5. Otherwise, you can run the examples in Chapter 1 stand-alone using the instructions provided in Recipe 1-3. If you deploy the `JavaEE8Recipes.war` file to a Java EE application server container, you can visit the following URL to load the examples for this chapter: `http://localhost:8080/JavaEE8Recipes/faces/chapter01/index.xhtml`.

1-1. Setting Up a Java Enterprise Environment

Problem

You want to set up an environment that you can use to deploy and run Java servlets and other Java enterprise technologies.

Solution #1

Download and install Oracle's GlassFish application server from the GlassFish website. The version used for this book is the open source edition, release 5.0, and it can be downloaded from `http://download.oracle.com/glassfish/` within the 5.0 directory. Navigate into the promoted directory and grab a copy of the `glassfish-5.0-x.zip`, where x determines the version. Decompress the downloaded files within a directory on your workstation. I will refer to that directory as `/JAVA_DEV/Glassfish`. The GlassFish distribution comes prepackaged with a domain so that developers can get up and running quickly. Once the `.zip` file has been unpacked, you can start the domain by opening a command prompt or terminal and starting GlassFish using the following statement:

```
/JAVA_DEV/Glassfish/bin/asadmin start-domain domain1
```

The domain will start, and it will be ready for use. You will see output from the server that looks similar to the following:

```
Waiting for domain1 to start ...........
Successfully started the domain : domain1
domain  Location: /PATH_TO_GLASSFISH/glassfish/domains/domain1
Log File: /PATH_TO_GLASSFISH/glassfish/domains/domain1/logs/server.log
Admin Port: 4848
Command start-domain executed successfully.
```

Solution #2

Download from the Payara website (`https://www.payara.fish/downloads`) and install Payara server. The Payara team has implemented the Payara 5 branch, which composes all of the Java EE 8 specification. To obtain Payara 5, download the archive and extract it to your drive. I refer to that directory as `/JAVA_DEV/Payara`. Once extracted, the default domain can be started by opening a command prompt or terminal and typing the following:

```
/JAVA_DEV/Payara/bin/asadmin start-domain domain1
```

Once invoked, the domain will start and it will become ready to use. The output will look as follows, very similar to that of GlassFish:

```
Waiting for domain1 to start .........
Successfully started the domain : domain1
domain  Location: /Java_Dev/payara/payara4.1.1.171.0.1/payara41/glassfish/domains/domain1
Log File: /Java_Dev/payara/payara4.1.1.171.0.1/payara41/glassfish/domains/domain1/logs/
server.log
Admin Port: 4848
Command start-domain executed successfully.
```

Once started, the domain can be stopped via the administrative console or from the command line:

```
/JAVA_DEV/Payara/bin/asadmin stop-domain domain1
```

■ **Note** Upon installation, Payara will not have an administrator password in-place. It is important to open the administrative console and set the administrator password immediately after install. Open a browser and navigate to `http://localhost:4848` to open the administrative console.

How It Works

The development of Java EE applications begins with a Java EE–compliant application server. A Java EE-compliant server contains all the essential components to provide a robust environment for deploying and hosting enterprise Java applications. The GlassFish application server is the reference implementation for Java EE. Payara also produces an implementation of the GlassFish server simply named Payara Server. For the purposes of this book, I will be using Payara open source edition. However, in a production environment, you may want to consider using the Payara licensed version so that technical support will be available if needed.

Installing GlassFish or Payara is very easy. The installation consists of downloading an archive and uncompressing it on your machine. Once you've completed this, the application server will use your locally installed Java development kit (JDK) when it is started. Once the server starts, you can open a browser and navigate to `http://localhost:4848` to gain access to the GlassFish or Payara administrative console. Most Java EE developers who deploy on GlassFish or Payara use the administrative console often for performing a multitude of administrative tasks. The administrative console provides developers with the tools needed to deploy web applications, register databases with Java Naming and Directory Interface (JNDI), set up security realms for a domain, and much more.

To access the GlassFish or Payara administrative console for the first time, use the user name of `admin` and the password of `adminadmin`. You should take some time to become familiar with the administrative console because the more you know about it, the easier it will be to maintain your Java EE environment. You should also note that Payara offers more options than GlassFish, as Payara has built many features onto the base GlassFish implementation, making Payara a robust and complete solution for production use.

Installing the GlassFish or Payara application servers is the first step toward developing Java applications for the enterprise. Other applications servers, such as JBoss, Apache TomEE, and WebLogic, are very well adopted for development and production use. GlassFish 5.0 offers an excellent environment for starting development with Java EE, whereas Payara 5 offers a solution that is easy to use and offers production-level support. Both servers offer open source options, and they are the reference implementation for Java EE 8.

1-2. Developing a Servlet

Problem

You want to develop a web page that enables you to include dynamic content.

Solution

Develop a Java servlet class and compile it to run within a Java servlet container. In this example, a simple servlet is created that will display some dynamic content to the web page. The following is the servlet code that contains the functionality for the servlet:

```
package org.javaee8ecipes.chapter01.recipe01_02;

import java.io.IOException;
import java.io.PrintWriter;
import javax.servlet.ServletException;
import javax.servlet.http.HttpServlet;
import javax.servlet.http.HttpServletRequest;
import javax.servlet.http.HttpServletResponse;

/**
 * Recipe 1-2: Developing a Servlet
 * @author juneau
 */
public class SimpleServlet extends HttpServlet {

    /**
     * Processes requests for both HTTP
     * <code>GET</code> and
     * <code>POST</code> methods.
     *
     * @param request servlet request
     * @param response servlet response
     * @throws ServletException if a servlet-specific error occurs
```

```
     * @throws IOException if an I/O error occurs
     */
    protected void processRequest(HttpServletRequest request, HttpServletResponse response)
            throws ServletException, IOException {
        response.setContentType("text/html;charset=UTF-8");
        PrintWriter out = response.getWriter();
        try {
           // Place page output here
            out.println("<html>");
            out.println("<head>");
            out.println("<title>Servlet SimpleServlet</title>");
            out.println("</head>");
            out.println("<body>");
            out.println("<h2>Servlet SimpleServlet at " + request.getContextPath() + "</h2>");
            out.println("<br/>Welcome to Java EE Recipes!");
            out.println("</body>");
            out.println("</html>");
        } finally {
            out.close();
        }
    }

   /**
     * Handles the HTTP GET
     *
     * @param request servlet request
     * @param response servlet response
     * @throws ServletException if a servlet-specific error occurs
     * @throws IOException if an I/O error occurs
     */
    @Override
    protected void doGet(HttpServletRequest request, HttpServletResponse response)
            throws ServletException, IOException {
        processRequest(request, response);
    }

    /**
     * Handles the HTTP POST
     *
     * @param request servlet request
     * @param response servlet response
     * @throws ServletException if a servlet-specific error occurs
     * @throws IOException if an I/O error occurs
     */
    @Override
    protected void doPost(HttpServletRequest request, HttpServletResponse response)
            throws ServletException, IOException {
        processRequest(request, response);
    }
```

```
    /**
     * Returns a short description of the servlet for documentation purposes.
     *
     * @return a String containing servlet description
     */
    @Override
    public String getServletInfo() {
        return "Short description";
    }// </editor-fold>
}
```

The following code is the web deployment descriptor (web.xml). This file is required for application deployment to a servlet container. It contains the servlet configuration and mapping that maps the servlet to a URL. The deployment descriptor must be placed within the WEB-INF folder, which is located at the web sources root. In Recipe 1-4, you will learn how to omit the servlet configuration and to map from the web.xml file to make servlet development, deployment, and maintenance easier.

```
<?xml version="1.0"?>
<web-app xmlns="http://java.sun.com/xml/ns/javaee"
    xmlns:xsi="http://www.w3.org/2001/XMLSchema-instance"
    xsi:schemaLocation="http://java.sun.com/xml/ns/javaee
        http://java.sun.com/xml/ns/javaee/web-app_3_0.xsd"
    version="3.0">

    <servlet>
        <servlet-name>SimpleServlet</servlet-name>
        <servlet-class>org.javaee8recipes.chapter01.recipe01_02.SimpleServlet</servlet-class>
    </servlet>
    <servlet-mapping>
        <servlet-name>SimpleServlet</servlet-name>
        <url-pattern>/SimpleServlet</url-pattern>
    </servlet-mapping>
                <welcome-file-list>
        <welcome-file> /SimpleServlet </welcome-file>
    </welcome-file-list>
</web-app>
```

■ **Note** Many web applications use a page named index.html or index.xhtml as their welcome file. There is nothing wrong with doing that, and as a matter of fact, it is the correct thing to do. The use of /SimpleServlet as the welcome file in this example is to make it easier to follow for demonstration purposes.

To compile the Java servlet, use the javac command-line utility. The following line was excerpted from the command line, and it compiles the SimpleServlet.java file into a class file. First, traverse into the directory containing the SimpleServlet.java file; then, execute the following:

```
javac -cp /JAVA_DEV/Glassfish/glassfish/modules/javax.servlet-api.jar SimpleServlet.java
```

Note that this command places the GlassFish javax.servlet-api.jar into the classpath for compilation. Once the servlet code has been compiled into a Java class file, it is ready to package for deployment.

■ **Note** You may want to consider installing a Java integrated development environment (IDE) to increase your development productivity. There are several very good IDEs available to developers, so be sure to choose one that contains the features you find most important and useful for development. As the author of this book on Java EE 8, I recommend installing NetBeans 8.2 or newer for development. NetBeans is an open source IDE that is maintained by Apache, and it includes support for all the cutting-edge features that the Java industry has to offer, including development with Java EE 8, JavaFX support, and more. To learn more about working with NetBeans and Java EE 8, see the appendix of this book.

How It Works

Java servlets provide developers with the flexibility to design applications using a request-response programming model. Servlets play a key role in the development of service-oriented and web application development on the Java platform. Different types of servlets can be created, and each of them is geared toward providing different functionality. The first type is known as GenericServlet, which provides services and functionality. The second type, HttpServlet, is a subclass of GenericServlet, and servlets of this type provide functionality and a response that uses HTTP. The solution to this recipe demonstrates the latter type of servlet because it displays a result for the user to see within a web browser.

Servlets conform to a lifecycle for processing requests and posting results. First, the Java servlet container calls the servlet's constructor. The constructor of every servlet must take no arguments. Next, the container calls the servlet init method, which is responsible for initializing the servlet. Once the servlet has been initialized, it is ready for use. At that point, the servlet can begin processing. Each servlet contains a service method, which handles the requests being made and dispatches them to the appropriate methods for request handling. Implementing the service method is optional. Finally, the container calls the servlet's destroy method, which takes care of finalizing the servlet and taking it out of service.

Every servlet class must implement the javax.servlet.Servlet interface or extend another class that does. In the solution to this recipe, the servlet named SimpleServlet extends the HttpServlet class, which provides methods for handling HTTP processes. In this scenario, a browser client request is sent from the container to the servlet; then the servlet service method dispatches the HttpServletRequest object to the appropriate method provided by HttpServlet. Namely, the HttpServlet class provides the doGet, doPut, doPost, and doDelete methods for working with an HTTP request. The most often used methods are doGet and doPost. The HttpServlet class is abstract, so it must be subclassed, and then an implementation can be provided for its methods. In the solution to this recipe, the doGet method is implemented, and the responsibility of processing is passed to the processRequest method, which writes a response to the browser using the PrintWriter. Table 1-1 describes each of the methods available to an HttpServlet.

Table 1-1. HttpServlet Methods

Method Name	Description
doGet	Used to process HTTP GET requests. Input sent to the servlet must be included in the URL address. For example: ?myName=Josh&myBook=JavaEE8Recipes.
doPost	Used to process HTTP POST requests. Input can be sent to the servlet within HTML form fields. See Recipe 1-6 for an example.
doPut	Used to process HTTP PUT requests.
doDelete	Used to process HTTP DELETE requests.
doHead	Used to process HTTP HEAD requests.
doOptions	Called by the container to allow OPTIONS request handling.
doTrace	Called by the container to handle TRACE requests.
getLastModified	Returns the time that the HttpServletRequest object was last modified.
init	Initializes the servlet.
destroy	Finalizes the servlet.
getServletInfo	Provides information regarding the servlet.

A servlet generally performs some processing in the implementation of its methods and then returns a response to the client. The HttpServletRequest object can be used to process arguments that are sent via the request. For instance, if an HTML form contains some input fields that are sent to the server, those fields would be contained within the HttpServletRequest object. The HttpServletResponse object is used to send responses to the client browser. Both the doGet and doPost methods within a servlet accept the same arguments, namely, the HttpServletRequest and HttpServletResponse objects.

■ **Note** The doGet method is used to intercept HTTP GET requests, and doPost is used to intercept HTTP POST requests. Generally, the doGet method is used to prepare a request before displaying for a client, and the doPost method is used to process a request and gather information from an HTML form.

In the solution to this recipe, both the doGet and doPost methods pass the HttpServletRequest and HttpServletResponse objects to the processRequest method for further processing. The HttpServletResponse object is used to set the content type of the response and to obtain a handle on the PrintWriter object in the processRequest method. The following lines of code show how this is done, assuming that the identifier referencing the HttpServletResponse object is response:

```
response.setContentType("text/html;charset=UTF-8");
PrintWriter out = response.getWriter();
```

A GenericServlet can be used for providing services to web applications. This type of servlet is oftentimes used for logging events because it implements the log method. A GenericServlet implements both the Servlet and ServletConfig interfaces, and to write a generic servlet, only the service method must be overridden.

1-3. Packaging, Compiling, and Deploying a Servlet

Problem

You have written a Java servlet and now want to package it and deploy it for use.

Solution

Compile the sources, set up a deployable application, and copy the contents into the server deployment directory. From the command line, use the `javac` command to compile the sources.

```
javac -cp /JAVA_DEV/Glassfish/glassfish/modules/javax.servlet-api.jar SimpleServlet.java
```

After the class has been compiled, deploy it along with the `web.xml` deployment descriptor, conforming to the appropriate directory structure.

QUICK START

To quickly get started with packaging, compiling, and deploying the example application for the servlet recipes in this chapter on GlassFish or other servlet containers such as Apache Tomcat, follow these steps:

1. Create a single application named `SimpleServlet` by making a directory named `SimpleServlet`.
2. Create the `WEB-INF`, `WEB-INF/classes` and `WEB-INF/lib` directories inside the newly created `SimpleServlet` directory.
3. Drag the Chapter 1 sources (beginning with the `org` directory) in the `WEB-INF/classes` directory you created, as well as the contents of the web folder, into the root of your `SimpleServlet` directory.
4. Copy the `web.xml` file that is in the source's `recipe01_02` directory into the `WEB-INF` directory you created.
5. Although not needed yet, download the JavaMail API code from GitHub (`https://github.com/javaee/javamail`) and copy the `mail.jar` file from the download into the `WEB-INF/lib` directory you created. This API will be used to send mail in future recipes.
6. Set your `CLASSPATH` to include the `mail.jar` file you downloaded in Step 5.

7. At the command prompt, change directories so that you are in the `classes` directory you created in Step 2. Compile each recipe with the command `javac org\javaee8recipes\chapter01\recipe1_x\*.java`, where x is equal to the recipe number.

8. Copy your `SimpleServlet` application directory to the `/JAVA_DEV/Glassfish/glassfish/domains/domain1/autodeploy` directory for GlassFish *or* the `/Tomcat/webapps` directory for Tomcat.

Test the application by launching a browser and going to `http://localhost:8080/SimpleServlet/servlet_name`, where `servlet_name` corresponds to the servlet name in each recipe. If you're using Tomcat, you may need to restart the server in order for the application to deploy. Alternatively, you can deploy the example application for this book, entitled `JavaEE8Recipes.war`, to an application server and launch a browser. Then navigate to `http://localhost:8080/JavaEE8Recipes/SimpleServlet` to test.

How It Works

To compile the sources, you can use your favorite Java IDE such as NetBeans or Eclipse, or you can use the command line. For the purposes of this recipe, I will use the latter. If you're using the command line, you must ensure you are using the `javac` command that is associated with the same Java release that you will be using to run your servlet container. In this example, we will say that the location of the Java SE 8 installation is at the following path:

```
/Library/Java/JavaVirtualMachines/1.8.0.jdk/Contents/Home
```

This path may differ in your environment if you are using a different operating system and/or installation location. To ensure you are using the Java runtime that is located at this path, set the `JAVA_HOME` environment variable equal to this path. On OS X and other UNIX-based operating systems, you can set the environment variable by opening the terminal and typing the following:

```
export JAVA_HOME=/Library/Java/JavaVirtualMachines/1.8.0.jdk/Contents/Home
```

If you are using Windows, use the `SET` command within the command line to set up the `JAVA_HOME` environment variable.

```
set JAVA_HOME=C:\your-java-se-path\
```

Next, compile your Java servlet sources, and be sure to include the `javax.servlet-api.jar` file that is packaged with your servlet container (use `servlet-api.jar` for Tomcat) in your `CLASSPATH`. You can set the `CLASSPATH` by using the `-cp` flag of the `javac` command. The following command should be executed at the command line from within the same directory that contains the sources. In this case, the source file is named `SimpleServlet.java`.

```
javac -cp /path_to_jar/javax.servlet-api.jar SimpleServlet.java
```

Next, package your application by creating a directory and naming it after your application. In this case, create a directory and name it `SimpleServlet`. Within that directory, create another directory named `WEB-INF`. Traverse into the `WEB-INF` directory, and create another directory named `classes`. Lastly, create directories within the `classes` directory in order to replicate your Java servlet package structure. For this recipe, the SimpleServlet.java class resides within the Java package org.javaee8recipes.chapter01.recipe01_02, so create a directory for each of those packages within the classes directory. Create another directory within WEB-INF and name it lib; any JAR files containing external libraries should be placed within the lib directory. In the end, your directory structure should resemble the following:

```
SimpleServlet
|_WEB-INF
        |_classes
              |_org
                    |_javaee8recipes
                                |_chapter01
                                        |_recipe01_02
        |_lib
```

Place your web.xml deployment descriptor within the WEB-INF directory and place the compiled SimpleServlet.class file in the recipe01_02 directory. The entire contents of the SimpleServlet directory can now be copied in the deployment directory for your application server container to deploy the application. Restart the application server if you're using Tomcat and visit the URL http://localhost:8080/SimpleServlet/SimpleServlet to see the servlet in action.

1-4. Registering Servlets Without WEB-XML

Problem

Registering servlets in the web.xml file is cumbersome, and you want to deploy servlets without modifying web.xml at all.

Solution

Use the @WebServlet annotation to annotate the servlet class and omit the web.xml registration. This will alleviate the need to modify the web.xml file each time a servlet is added to your application. The following adaptation of the SimpleServlet class that was used in Recipe 1-2 includes the @WebServlet annotation and demonstrates its use:

```
package org.javaee8recipes.chapter01.recipe01_04;

import java.io.IOException;
import java.io.PrintWriter;
import javax.servlet.ServletException;
import javax.servlet.annotation.WebServlet;
import javax.servlet.http.HttpServlet;
import javax.servlet.http.HttpServletRequest;
import javax.servlet.http.HttpServletResponse;

/**
 * Recipe 1-4: Registering Servlets Without WEB-XML
 * @author juneau
 */
```

```
@WebServlet(name = "SimpleServletNoDescriptor", urlPatterns = {"/
SimpleServletNoDescriptor"})
public class SimpleServletNoDescriptor extends HttpServlet {

    /**
     * Processes requests for both HTTP
     * <code>GET</code> and
     * <code>POST</code> methods.
     *
     * @param request servlet request
     * @param response servlet response
     * @throws ServletException if a servlet-specific error occurs
     * @throws IOException if an I/O error occurs
     */
    protected void processRequest(HttpServletRequest request, HttpServletResponse response)
            throws ServletException, IOException {
        response.setContentType("text/html;charset=UTF-8");
        PrintWriter out = response.getWriter();
        try {
            /*
             * TODO output your page here. You may use following sample code.
             */
            out.println("<html>");
            out.println("<head>");
            out.println("<title>Servlet SimpleServlet</title>");
            out.println("</head>");
            out.println("<body>");
            out.println("<h2>Servlet SimpleServlet at " + request.getContextPath() + "</h2>");
            out.println("<br/>Look ma, no WEB-XML!");
            out.println("</body>");
            out.println("</html>");
        } finally {
            out.close();
        }
    }

    /**
     * Handles the HTTP <code>GET</code> method.
     *
     * @param request servlet request
     * @param response servlet response
     * @throws ServletException if a servlet-specific error occurs
     * @throws IOException if an I/O error occurs
     */
    @Override
    protected void doGet(HttpServletRequest request, HttpServletResponse response)
            throws ServletException, IOException {
        processRequest(request, response);
    }
```

```
    /**
     * Handles the HTTP <code>POST</code> method.
     *
     * @param request servlet request
     * @param response servlet response
     * @throws ServletException if a servlet-specific error occurs
     * @throws IOException if an I/O error occurs
     */
    @Override
    protected void doPost(HttpServletRequest request, HttpServletResponse response)
            throws ServletException, IOException {
        processRequest(request, response);
    }

}
```

In the end, the servlet will be accessible via a URL in the same way that it would if the servlet were registered within `web.xml`.

■ **Note** Remove the existing servlet mapping within the `web.xml` file in order to use the `@WebServlet` annotation.

How It Works

There are a couple of ways to register servlets with a web container. The first way is to register them using the `web.xml` deployment descriptor, as demonstrated in Recipe 1-2. The second way to register them is to use the `@WebServlet` annotation. The Servlet 3.0 API introduced the `@WebServlet` annotation, which provides an easier technique to use for mapping a servlet to a URL. The `@WebServlet` annotation is placed before the declaration of a class, and it accepts the elements listed in Table 1-2.

Table 1-2. *@WebServlet Annotation Elements*

Element	Description
`description`	Description of the servlet
`displayName`	The display name of the servlet
`initParams`	Accepts list of `@WebInitParam` annotations
`largeIcon`	The large icon of the servlet
`loadOnStartup`	Load on startup order of the servlet
`name`	Servlet name
`smallIcon`	The small icon of the servlet
`urlPatterns`	URL patterns that invoke the servlet

In the solution to this recipe, the @WebServlet annotation maps the servlet class named SimpleServletNoDescriptor to the URL pattern of /SimpleServletNoDescriptor, and it also names the servlet SimpleServletNoDescriptor.

```
@WebServlet(name="SimpleServletNoDescriptor", urlPatterns={"/SimpleServletNoDescriptor"})
```

The new @WebServlet can be used rather than altering the web.xml file to register each servlet in an application. This provides ease of development and manageability. However, in some cases, it may make sense to continue using the deployment descriptor for servlet registration, such as if you do not want to recompile sources when a URL pattern changes. If you look at the web.xml listing in Recipe 1-2, you can see the following lines of XML, which map the servlet to a given URL and provide a name for the servlet. These lines of XML perform essentially the same function as the @WebServlet annotation in this recipe.

```
<servlet>
    <servlet-name>SimpleServletNoDescriptor</servlet-name>
    <servlet-class>org.javaee8recipes.chapter01.recipe01_04.SimpleServletNoDescriptor</
    servlet-class>
</servlet>
<servlet-mapping>
    <servlet-name>SimpleServletNoDescriptor</servlet-name>
    <url-pattern>/SimpleServletNoDescriptor</url-pattern>
</servlet-mapping>
```

1-5. Displaying Dynamic Content with a Servlet

Problem

You want to display some content to a web page that may change depending on server-side activity or user input.

Solution

Define a field within your servlet to contain the dynamic content that is to be displayed. Post the dynamic content on the page by appending the field containing it using the PrintWriter println method. The following example servlet declares a LocalDateTime field and updates it with the current date and time each time the page is loaded:

```
package org.javaee8recipes.chapter01.recipe01_05;

import java.io.IOException;
import java.io.PrintWriter;
import java.util.Date;
import javax.servlet.ServletException;
import javax.servlet.annotation.WebServlet;
import javax.servlet.http.HttpServlet;
import javax.servlet.http.HttpServletRequest;
import javax.servlet.http.HttpServletResponse;
```

```
/**
 * Recipe 1-5: Displaying Dynamic Content with a Servlet
 *
 * @author juneau
 */
@WebServlet(name = "CurrentDateAndTime", urlPatterns = {"/CurrentDateAndTime"})
public class CurrentDateAndTime extends HttpServlet {

    LocalDateTime currDateAndTime = LocalDateTime.now();

    /**
     * Processes requests for both HTTP
     * <code>GET</code> and
     * <code>POST</code> methods.
     *
     * @param request servlet request
     * @param response servlet response
     * @throws ServletException if a servlet-specific error occurs
     * @throws IOException if an I/O error occurs
     */
    protected void processRequest(HttpServletRequest request, HttpServletResponse response)
            throws ServletException, IOException {
        response.setContentType("text/html;charset=UTF-8");
        PrintWriter out = response.getWriter();
        try {
            out.println("<html>");
            out.println("<head>");
            out.println("<title>Servlet CurrentDateAndTime</title>");
            out.println("</head>");
            out.println("<body>");
            out.println("<h1>Servlet CurrentDateAndTime at " + request.getContextPath() +
            "</h1>");
            out.println("<br/>");
            synchronized(currDateAndTime){
              currDateAndTime = LocalDateTime.now();
              out.println("The current date and time is: " + currDateAndTime);
            }
            out.println("</body>");
            out.println("</html>");
        } finally {
            out.close();
        }
    }
/**
     * Handles the HTTP
     * <code>GET</code> method.
     *
     * @param request servlet request
     * @param response servlet response
     * @throws ServletException if a servlet-specific error occurs
     * @throws IOException if an I/O error occurs
     */
```

```
    @Override
    protected void doGet(HttpServletRequest request, HttpServletResponse response)
            throws ServletException, IOException {
        processRequest(request, response);
    }

    /**
     * Handles the HTTP
     * <code>POST</code> method.
     *
     * @param request servlet request
     * @param response servlet response
     * @throws ServletException if a servlet-specific error occurs
     * @throws IOException if an I/O error occurs
     */
    @Override
    protected void doPost(HttpServletRequest request, HttpServletResponse response)
            throws ServletException, IOException {
        processRequest(request, response);
    }
}
```

■ **Note** Servlets are multithreaded, and many client requests may be using a servlet concurrently. When a field is declared as a `Servlet` class member (not within a method) as you have done with `currDateAndTime`, you have to assure that only one client request can manipulate the field at any instance. You do this by synchronizing around the use of the field, as shown in the `processRequest()` method. You synchronize around the smallest block of code that is manageable in order to minimize latency.

```
synchronized( currDateAndTime ) {

    currDateAndTime = LocalDateTime.now();

    out.println("The current date and time is: " + currDateAndTime);

}
```

The resulting output from this servlet will be the current date and time.

How It Works

One of the reasons why Java servlets are so useful is because they allow dynamic content to be displayed on a web page. The content can be taken from the server itself, a database, another website, or many other web-accessible resources. Servlets are not static web pages; they are dynamic, and that is arguably their biggest strength.

In the solution to this recipe, a servlet is used to display the current time and date of the server. When the servlet is processed, the `doGet` method is called, which subsequently makes a call to the `processRequest` method, passing the `request` and `response` objects. Therefore, the `processRequest` method is where the bulk of the work occurs. The `processRequest` method creates a `PrintWriter` by calling the `response.getWriter` method, and the `PrintWriter` is used to display content on the resulting web page. Next, the current date and time are obtained from the server by creating a new `LocalDateTime` object and assigning it to the `currDateAndTime` field. Lastly, the `processRequest` method sends the web content through the `out.println` method, and the contents of the `currDateAndTime` field are concatenated to a string and sent to `out.println` as well. Each time the servlet is processed, it will display the current date and time at the time in which the servlet is invoked because a `LocalDateTime.now()` is invoked with each request.

This example just scratches the surface of what is possible with a Java servlet. Although displaying the current date and time is trivial, you could alter that logic to display the contents of any field contained within the servlet. Whether it be an `int` field that displays a calculation that was performed by the servlet container, or data that has been retrieved from a database into a field for displaying information, the possibilities are endless.

1-6. Handling Requests and Responses

Problem

You want to create a web form that accepts user input and then supply a response based on the input that has been received.

Solution

Create a standard HTML-based web form, and when the Submit button is clicked, invoke a servlet to process the end-user input and post a response. To examine this technique, you will see two different pieces of code. The following code is HTML that is used to generate the input form. This code exists within the file `recipe01_06.html`. Pay particular attention to the `<form>` and `<input>` tags. You will see that the form's `action` parameter lists a servlet name, `MathServlet`.

```
<html>
    <head>
    <title>Simple Math Servlet</title>
    </head>
    <body>
        <h1>This is a simple Math Servlet</h1>
        <form method="POST" action="MathServlet">
            <label for="numa">Enter Number A: </label>
            <input type="text" id="numa" name="numa"/><br><br>
                                    <label for="numb">Enter Number B: </label>
                                    <input type="text" id="numb" name="numb"/><br/><br/>
            <input type="submit" value="Submit Form"/>
            <input type="reset" value="Reset Form"/>
        </form>
    </body>
</html>
```

Next, take a look at the following code for a servlet named `MathServlet`. This is the Java code that receives the input from the HTML code listed earlier, processes it accordingly, and posts a response.

```
package org.javaee8recipes.chapter01.recipe01_06;

import java.io.IOException;
import java.io.PrintWriter;
import java.util.Date;

import javax.servlet.*;
import javax.servlet.annotation.WebServlet;
import javax.servlet.http.*;

/**
 * Recipe 1-6: Handling Requests and Responses
 */
// Uncomment the following line to run example stand-alone
//@WebServlet(name="SessionServlet", urlPatterns={"/MathServlet"})

// The following will allow the example to run within the context of the JavaEE8Recipes
example
// enterprise application (JavaEE8Recipes.war distro or Netbeans Project)
@WebServlet(name = "MathServlet", urlPatterns = {"/chapter01/MathServlet"})public class
MathServlet extends HttpServlet {

    public void doPost(HttpServletRequest req, HttpServletResponse res)
            throws IOException, ServletException {

        res.setContentType("text/html");

        // Store the input parameter values into Strings
        String numA = req.getParameter("numa");
        String numB = req.getParameter("numb");

        PrintWriter out = res.getWriter();
        out.println("<html><head>");
        out.println("<title>Test Math Servlet</title>");
        out.println("\t<style>body { font-family: 'Lucida Grande', "
                + "'Lucida Sans Unicode';font-size: 13px; }</style>");
        out.println("</head>");
        out.println("<body>");

        try {
            int solution = Integer.valueOf(numA) + Integer.valueOf(numB);

            /*
             * Display some response to the user
             */
            out.println("<p>Solution: "
                    + numA + " + " + numB + " = " + solution + "</p>");

        } catch (java.lang.NumberFormatException ex) {
            // Display error if an exception is raised
            out.println("<p>Please use numbers only...try again.</p>");
        }
```

```
        out.println("<br/><br/>");
        out.println("<a href='recipe1_6.html'>Add Two More Numbers</a>");
        out.println("</body></html>");

        out.close();
    }
}
```

Note To run the example, copy the previous HTML code into an HTML file within the web root of your `JavaEE8Recipes` application named `recipe1_6.html`, and then enter the following address into your browser: `http://localhost:8080/JavaEE8Recipes/recipe1_6.html`. This assumes you are using default port numbers for your application server installation. If you're using the NetBeans project that was packaged with the sources, you do not need to worry about copying the code, as everything is pre-configured.

How It Works

Servlets make it easy to create web applications that adhere to a request and response lifecycle. They have the ability to provide HTTP responses and process business logic within the same body of code. The ability to process business logic makes servlets much more powerful than standard HTML code. The solution to this recipe demonstrates a standard servlet structure for processing requests and sending responses. An HTML web form contains parameters that are sent to a servlet. The servlet then processes those parameters in some fashion and publishes a response that can be seen by the client. In the case of an `HttpServlet` object, the client is a web browser, and the response is a web page.

Values can be obtained from an HTML form by using HTML `<input>` tags embedded within an HTML `<form>`. In the solution to this recipe, two values are accepted as input, and they are referenced by their `id` attributes as `numa` and `numb`. There are two more `<input>` tags within the form; one of them is used to submit the values to the form `action`, and the other is used to reset the form fields to blank. The form action attribute is the name of the servlet that the form values will be passed to as parameters. In this case, the action attribute is set to `MathServlet`. The `<form>` tag also accepts a form-processing method, either `GET` or `POST`. In the example, the `POST` method is used because form data is being sent to the action; in this case, data is being sent to `MathServlet`. You could, of course, create an HTML form as detailed as you would like and then have that data sent to any servlet in the same manner. This example is relatively basic; it serves to give you an understanding of how the processing is performed.

The `<form>` action attribute states that the `MathServlet` should be used to process the values that are contained within the form. The `MathServlet` name is mapped back to the `MathServlet` class via the `web.xml` deployment descriptor or the `@WebServlet` annotation. Looking at the `MathServlet` code, you can see that a `doPost` method is implemented to handle the processing of the `POST` form values. The `doPost` method accepts `HttpServletRequest` and `HttpServletResponse` objects as arguments. The values contained with the HTML form are embodied within the `HttpServletRequest` object. To obtain those values, call the request object's `getParameter` method, passing the `id` of the input parameter you want to obtain. In the solution to this recipe, those values are obtained and stored within local `String` fields.

```
String numA = req.getParameter("numa");
String numB = req.getParameter("numb");
```

Once the values are obtained, they can be processed as needed. In this case, those String values are converted into int values, and then they are added together to generate a sum and stored into an int field. That field is then presented as a response on a resulting web page.

```
int solution = Integer.valueOf(numA) + Integer.valueOf(numB);
```

As mentioned, the HTML form could be much more complex, containing any number of <input> fields. Likewise, the servlet could perform more complex processing of those field values. This example is merely the tip of the iceberg, and the possibilities are without bounds. Servlet-based web frameworks such as JavaServer Pages and JavaServer Faces hide many of the complexities of passing form values to a servlet and processing a response. However, the same basic framework is used behind the scenes.

1-7. Listening for Servlet Container Events

Problem

You want to have the ability to listen for application startup and shutdown events.

Solution

Create a servlet context event listener to alert when the application has started up or when it has been shut down. The following solution demonstrates the code for a context listener, which will log application startup and shutdown events and send email alerting of such events:

```
package org.javaee8recipes.chapter01.recipe01_07;

import java.util.Properties;
import javax.mail.Message;
import javax.mail.Session;
import javax.mail.Transport;
import javax.mail.internet.InternetAddress;
import javax.mail.internet.MimeMessage;
import javax.servlet.ServletContextListener;
import javax.servlet.ServletContextEvent;
import javax.servlet.annotation.WebListener;

@WebListener
public class StartupShutdownListener implements ServletContextListener {

    public void contextInitialized(ServletContextEvent event) {
        System.out.println("Servlet startup...");
        System.out.println(event.getServletContext().getServerInfo());
        System.out.println(System.currentTimeMillis());
        sendEmail("Servlet context has initialized");
    }

    public void contextDestroyed(ServletContextEvent event) {
        System.out.println("Servlet shutdown...");
```

```
        System.out.println(event.getServletContext().getServerInfo());
        System.out.println(System.currentTimeMillis());
        // See error in server.log file if mail is unsuccessful
        sendEmail("Servlet context has been destroyed...");
    }

    /**
     * This implementation uses the GMail smtp server
     * @param message
     * @return
     */
    private boolean sendEmail(String message) {
       boolean result = false;
       String smtpHost = "smtp.gmail.com";
       String smtpUsername = "username";
       String smtpPassword = "password";
       String from = "fromaddress";
       String to = "toaddress";
       int smtpPort = 587;
       System.out.println("sending email...");
        try {
            // Send email here

            //Set the host smtp address
            Properties props = new Properties();
            props.put("mail.smtp.host", smtpHost);
            props.put("mail.smtp.auth", "true");
            props.put("mail.smtp.starttls.enable", "true");

            // create some properties and get the default Session
            Session session = Session.getInstance(props);

            // create a message
            Message msg = new MimeMessage(session);

            // set the from and to address
            InternetAddress addressFrom = new InternetAddress(from);
            msg.setFrom(addressFrom);
            InternetAddress[] address = new InternetAddress[1];
            address[0] = new InternetAddress(to);
            msg.setRecipients(Message.RecipientType.TO, address);
            msg.setSubject("Servlet container shutting down");
            // Append Footer
            msg.setContent(message, "text/plain");
            Transport transport = session.getTransport("smtp");
            transport.connect(smtpHost, smtpPort, smtpUsername, smtpPassword);

            Transport.send(msg);

            result = true;
        } catch (javax.mail.MessagingException ex) {
```

```
            ex.printStackTrace();
            result = false;
        }
        return result;
    }
}
```

■ **Note** To run this example, you may need additional external JARs in your CLASSPATH. Specifically, make sure you have mail.jar and javaee.jar.

How It Works

Sometimes it is useful to know when certain events occur within the application server container. This concept can be useful under many different circumstances, but most often it would be used for initializing an application upon startup or cleaning up after an application upon shutdown. A servlet listener can be registered with an application to indicate when it has been started up or shut down. Therefore, by listening for such events, the servlet has the opportunity to perform some actions when they occur.

To create a listener that performs actions based on a container event, you must develop a class that implements the ServletContextListener interface. The methods that need to be implemented are contextInitialized and contextDestroyed. Both of the methods accept a ServletContextEvent as an argument, and they are automatically called each time the servlet container is initialized or shut down, respectively. To register the listener with the container, you can use one of the following techniques:

- Utilize the @WebListener annotation, as demonstrated by the solution to this recipe.
- Register the listener within the web.xml application deployment descriptor.
- Use the addListener methods defined on ServletContext.

For example, to register this listener within web.xml, you need to add the following lines of XML:

```
<listener>
    <listener-class> org.javaee8recipes.chapter01.recipe01_07.StartupShutdown
Listener</listener-class>
</listener>
```

Neither way is better than the other. The only time that listener registration within the application deployment descriptor (web.xml) would be more helpful is if you had the need to disable the listener in some cases. On the other hand, to disable a listener when it is registered using @WebListener, you must remove the annotation and recompile the code. Altering the web deployment descriptor does not require any code to be recompiled.

There are many different listener types, and the interface that the class implements is what determines the listener type. For instance, in the solution to this recipe, the class implements the ServletContextListener interface. Doing so creates a listener for servlet context events. If, however, the class implements HttpSessionListener, it would be a listener for HTTP session events. The following is a complete listing of listener interfaces:

```
javax.servlet.ServletRequestListener
javax.servlet.ServletRequestAttrbuteListener
javax.servlet.ServletContextListener
```

```
javax.servlet.ServletContextAttributeListener
javax.servlet.http.HttpSessionListener
javax.servlet.http.HttpSessionAttributeListener
javax.servlet.http.HttpSessionIdListener
```

It is also possible to create a listener that implements multiple listener interfaces. To learn more about listening for different situations such as attribute changes, see Recipe 1-10.

1-8. Setting Initialization Parameters

Problem

A servlet you are writing requires the ability to accept one or more parameters to be set upon initialization.

Solution #1

Set the servlet initialization parameters using the `@WebInitParam` annotation. The following code sets an initialization parameter that is equal to a `String` value:

```
package org.javaee8recipes.chapter01.recipe01_08;

import java.io.IOException;
import java.io.PrintWriter;

import javax.servlet.*;
import javax.servlet.annotation.WebInitParam;
import javax.servlet.annotation.WebServlet;
import javax.servlet.http.*;

@WebServlet(name="SimpleServletCtx1", urlPatterns={"/SimpleServletCtx1"},
initParams={ @WebInitParam(name="name", value="Duke") })
public class SimpleServletCtx1 extends HttpServlet {

        @Override
    public void doGet(HttpServletRequest req, HttpServletResponse res)
        throws IOException, ServletException {

        res.setContentType("text/html");

        PrintWriter out = res.getWriter();

        /* Display some response to the user */

        out.println("<html><head>");
        out.println("<title>Simple Servlet Context Example</title>");
        out.println("\t<style>body { font-family: 'Lucida Grande', " +
            "'Lucida Sans Unicode';font-size: 13px; }</style>");
        out.println("</head>");
        out.println("<body>");
```

```
        out.println("<p>This is a simple servlet to demonstrate context!  Hello "
                            + getServletConfig().getInitParameter("name") + "</p>");

        out.println("</body></html>");
        out.close();
    }
}
```

To execute the example using the sources for this book, load the following URL into your web browser: `http://localhost:8080/JavaEE8Recipes/SimpleServletCtx1`. The resulting web page will display the following text:

```
This is a simple servlet to demonstrate context! Hello Duke
```

Solution #2

Place the `init` parameters inside the `web.xml` deployment descriptor file. The following lines are excerpted from the `web.xml` deployment descriptor for the `SimpleServlet` application. They include the initialization parameter names and values.

```
<web-app>
    <servlet>
        <servlet-name>SimpleServletCtx1</servlet-name>
        <servlet-class> org.javaee8recipes.chapter01.recipe01_08.SimpleServletCtx1
        </servlet-class>

        <init-param>
            <param-name>name</param-name>
            <param-value>Duke</param-value>
        </init-param>
    ...
    </servlet>
    ...
</web-app>
```

How It Works

Oftentimes there is a requirement to set initialization parameters for a servlet in order to initialize certain values. Servlets can accept any number of initialization parameters, and there are a couple of ways in which they can be set. The first solution is to annotate the servlet class with the `@WebInitParam` annotation, as demonstrated in Solution #1, and the second way to set an initialization parameter is to declare the parameter within the `web.xml` deployment descriptor, as demonstrated in Solution #2. Either way will work; however, the solution using `@WebInitParam` is based on the newer Java Servlet 3.0 API. Therefore, Solution #1 is the more contemporary approach, but Solution #2 remains valid for following an older model or using an older Java servlet release.

To use the `@WebInitParam` annotation, it must be embedded within the `@WebServlet` annotation. Therefore, the servlet must be registered with the web application via the `@WebServlet` annotation rather than within the `web.xml` file. For more information on registering a servlet via the `@WebServlet` annotation, see Recipe 1-4.

The @WebInitParam annotation accepts a name-value pair as an initialization parameter. In the solution to this recipe, the parameter name is name, and the value is Duke.

```
@WebInitParam(name="name", value="Duke")
```

Once set, the parameter can be used within code by calling getServletConfig().getInitializationParameter()and passing the name of the parameter, as shown in the following line of code:

```
out.println("<p>This is a simple servlet to demonstrate context! Hello "
                                  + getServletConfig().getInitParameter("name") + "</p>");
```

The annotations have the benefit of providing ease of development, and they also make it easier to maintain servlets as a single package rather than jumping back and forth between the servlet and the deployment descriptor. However, those benefits come at the cost of compilation because in order to change the value of an initialization parameter using the @WebInitParam annotation, you must recompile the code. Such is not the case when using the web.xml deployment descriptor. It is best to evaluate your application circumstances before committing to a standard for naming initialization parameters.

1-9. Filtering Web Requests

Problem

You want to invoke certain processing if a specified URL is used to access your application. For instance, if a specific URL were used to access your application, you would want to log the user's IP address.

Solution

Create a servlet filter that will be processed when the specified URL format is used to access the application. In this example, the filter will be executed when a URL conforming to the format of /* is used. This format pertains to any URL in the application. Therefore, any page will cause the servlet to be invoked.

```
package org.javaee8recipes.chapter01.recipe01_09;

import java.io.IOException;
import java.io.PrintWriter;
import java.util.Date;
import javax.servlet.*;
import javax.servlet.annotation.WebFilter;
import javax.servlet.http.*;

/**
 * Recipe 1-9: This filter obtains the IP address of the remote host and logs
 * it.
 *
* @author juneau
 */
```

```
@WebFilter("/*")
public class LoggingFilter implements Filter {

    private FilterConfig filterConf = null;

    public void init(FilterConfig filterConf) {
        this.filterConf = filterConf;
    }

    public void doFilter(ServletRequest request,
            ServletResponse response,
            FilterChain chain)
            throws IOException, ServletException {
        String userAddy = request.getRemoteHost();
        filterConf.getServletContext().log("Visitor User IP: " + userAddy);
        chain.doFilter(request, response);
    }

    @Override
    public void destroy() {
        throw new UnsupportedOperationException("Not supported yet.");
    }
}
```

The filter could contain any processing; the important thing to note is that this servlet is processed when a specified URL is used to access the application.

■ **Note** To invoke the filter, load a URL for the application with which the filter is associated. For the purposes of this example, load the following URL (for the previous recipe) to see the filter add text to the server log: `http://localhost:8080/JavaEE8Recipes/SimpleServletCtx1`

How It Works

Web filters are useful for preprocessing requests and invoking certain functionality when a given URL is visited. Rather than invoking a servlet that exists at a given URL directly, any filter that contains the same URL pattern will be invoked prior to the servlet. This can be helpful in many situations, perhaps the most useful for performing logging, authentication, or other services that occur in the background without user interaction.

Filters must implement the `javax.servlet.Filter` interface. Methods contained within this interface include `init`, `destroy`, and `doFilter`. The `init` and `destroy` methods are invoked by the container. The `doFilter` method is used to implement tasks for the filter class. As you can see from the solution to this recipe, the filter class has access to the `ServletRequest` and `ServletResponse` objects. This means the request can be captured, and information can be obtained from it. This also means the request can be modified if need be. For example, including the user name in the request after an authentication filter has been used.

If you want to chain filters or if more than one filter exists for a given URL pattern, they will be invoked in the order in which they are configured in the web.xml deployment descriptor. It is best to manually configure the filters if you are using more than one per URL pattern rather than using the @WebFilter annotation. To manually configure the web.xml file to include a filter, use the <filter> and <filter-mapping> XML elements along with their associated child element tags. The following excerpt from a web.xml configuration file shows how the filter that has been created for this recipe may be manually configured within the web.xml file:

```
<filter>
    <filter-name>LoggingFilter</filter-name>
    <filter-class>LoggingFilter</filter-class>
</filter>
<filter-mapping>
    <filter-name>LoggingFilter</filter-name>
    <url-pattern>/*</url-pattern>
</filter-mapping>
```

Of course, the @WebFilter annotation takes care of the configuration for you, so in this case the manual configuration is not required.

■ **Note** As of Servlet 3.1 API, if a filter invokes the next entity in the chain, each of the filter service methods must run in the same thread as all filters that apply to the servlet.

1-10. Listening for Attribute Changes

Problem

You want to have the ability to perform an action within a servlet when a servlet attribute is added, removed, or updated.

Solution

Generate an attribute listener servlet to listen for such events as attributes being added, removed, or modified, and invoke an action when these events occur. The following class demonstrates this technique by implementing HttpSessionAttributeListener and listening for attributes that are added, removed, or replaced within the HTTP session:

```
package org.javaee8recipes.chapter01.recipe01_10;

import javax.servlet.ServletContext;
import javax.servlet.ServletContextEvent;
import javax.servlet.ServletContextListener;
import javax.servlet.annotation.WebListener;
import javax.servlet.http.HttpSession;
import javax.servlet.http.HttpSessionAttributeListener;
import javax.servlet.http.HttpSessionBindingEvent;
```

```
/**
 * Recipe 1-10: Attribute Listener
 */
@WebListener
public final class AttributeListener implements ServletContextListener,
        HttpSessionAttributeListener {

    private ServletContext context = null;

    public void attributeAdded(HttpSessionBindingEvent se) {
        HttpSession session = se.getSession();
        String id = session.getId();
        String name = se.getName();
        String value = (String) se.getValue();
        String message = new StringBuffer("New attribute has been added to session: \n").
        append("Attribute Name: ").append(name).append("\n").append("Attribute Value:").
        append(value).toString();
        log(message);
    }

    public void attributeRemoved(HttpSessionBindingEvent se) {
        HttpSession session = se.getSession();
        String id = session.getId();
        String name = se.getName();
        if (name == null) {
            name = "Unknown";
        }
        String value = (String) se.getValue();
        String message = new StringBuffer("Attribute has been removed: \n")
        .append("Attribute Name: ").append(name).append("\n").append("Attribute Value:")
        .append(value).toString();
        log(message);
    }

    @Override
    public void attributeReplaced(HttpSessionBindingEvent se) {
        String name = se.getName();
        if (name == null) {
            name = "Unknown";
        }
        String value = (String) se.getValue();
        String message = new StringBuffer("Attribute has been replaced: \n ").append(name).
        toString();
        log(message);
    }

    private void log(String message) {
        if (context != null) {
            context.log("SessionListener: " + message);
```

```
        } else {
            System.out.println("SessionListener: " + message);
        }
    }

    @Override
    public void contextInitialized(ServletContextEvent event) {
        this.context = event.getServletContext();
        log("contextInitialized()");
    }

    @Override
    public void contextDestroyed(ServletContextEvent event) {
// Do something
    }
}
```

In this example, messages will be displayed within the server log file indicating when attributes have been added, removed, or replaced.

How It Works

In some situations, it can be useful to know when an attribute has been set or what an attribute value has been set to. The solution to this recipe demonstrates how to create an attribute listener in order to determine this information. To create a servlet listener, you must implement one or more of the servlet listener interfaces. To listen for HTTP session attribute changes, implement `HttpSessionAttributeListener`. In doing so, the listener will implement the `attributeAdded`, `attributeRemoved`, and `attributeReplaced` methods. Each of these methods accepts `HttpSessionBindingEvent` as an argument, and their implementation defines what will occur when an HTTP session attribute is added, removed, or changed, respectively.

In the solution to this recipe, you can see that each of the three methods listed in the previous paragraph contains a similar implementation. Within each method, the `HttpSessionBindingEvent` is interrogated and broken down into `String` values, which represent the ID, name, and value of the attribute that caused the listener to react. For instance, in the `attributeAdded` method, the session is obtained from `HttpSessionBindingEvent`, and then the session ID is retrieved via the use of `getSession`. The attribute information can be obtained directly from the `HttpSessionBindingEvent` using the `getId` and `getName` methods, as shown in the following lines of code:

```
HttpSession session = se.getSession();
String id = session.getId();
String name = se.getName();
String value = (String) se.getValue();
```

After these values are obtained, the application can do whatever it needs to do with them. In this recipe, the attribute ID, name, and session ID are simply logged and printed.

```
String message = new StringBuffer("New attribute has been added to session: \n")
.append("Attribute Name: ").append(name).append("\n")
.append("Attribute Value:").append(value).toString();
log(message);
```

The body of the attributeReplaced and attributeRemoved methods contain similar functionality. In the end, the same routine is used within each to obtain the attribute name and value, and then something is done with those values.

A few different options can be used to register the listener with the container. The @WebListener annotation is the easiest way to do so, and the only downfall to using it is that you will need to recompile code in order to remove the listener annotation if you ever need to do so. The listener can be registered within the web deployment descriptor, or it can be registered using one of the addListener methods contained in ServletContext.

Although the example in the recipe does not perform any life-changing events, it does demonstrate how to create and use an attribute listener. In the real world, such a listener could become handy if an application needed to capture the user name of everyone who logs in or needed to send an email whenever a specified attribute is set.

Note that it is possible to develop more sophisticated solutions using interfaces such as the ServletRequestAttributeListener or ServletContextAttributeListener, which can be useful for receiving events regarding ServletRequest or ServletContext attribute changes, respectively. For more information, refer to the JavaDoc https://javaee.github.io/javaee-spec/javadocs/javax/servlet/ServletContextAttributeListener.html.

1-11. Applying a Listener to a Session

Problem

You want to listen for sessions to be created and destroyed so that you can count how many active sessions your application currently contains as well as perform some initialization for each session.

Solution

Create a session listener and implement the sessionCreated and sessionDestroyed methods accordingly. In the following example, a servlet is used to keep track of active sessions. Each time someone works with the application, a counter has one added to it. Likewise, each time a person leaves the application, the counter goes down by one.

```
package org.javaee8recipes.chapter01.recipe01_11;

import javax.servlet.annotation.WebListener;
import javax.servlet.http.HttpSession;
import javax.servlet.http.HttpSessionEvent;
import javax.servlet.http.HttpSessionListener;

/**
 * Recipe 1-11: Applying a Listener to a Session
 *
 * @author juneau
 */
@WebListener
public class SessionListener implements HttpSessionListener {

    private int numberOfSessions;
```

```
    public SessionListener() {
        numberOfSessions = 0;
    }

    public int getNumberOfSessions() {
        return numberOfSessions;
    }

    @Override
    public void sessionCreated(HttpSessionEvent arg) {
        HttpSession session = arg.getSession();
        session.setMaxInactiveInterval(60);
        session.setAttribute("testAttr", "testVal");
        synchronized (this) {
            numberOfSessions++;
        }
        System.out.println("Session created, current count: " + numberOfSessions);
    }

    @Override
    public void sessionDestroyed(HttpSessionEvent arg) {
        HttpSession session = arg.getSession();
        synchronized (this) {
            numberOfSessions--;
        }
        System.out.println("Session destroyed, current count: " + numberOfSessions);
        System.out.println("The attribute value: " + session.getAttribute(("testAttr")));
    }
}
```

Each time a new visitor visits the application, a new session is started, and `testAttr` is set. When the session times out, it will be destroyed, and any attributes that have been set for the session will be removed.

How It Works

A meaningful way to track web application users is to place values in their `HttpSession` object. Using a Java servlet, session attributes can be set, which will exist for the life of the `HttpSession`. Once the session is invalidated, the attributes will be removed. To set up a session listener, create a Java servlet, annotate it with the `@WebListener` annotation, and implement `javax.servlet.http.HttpSessionListener`. Doing so will force the implementation of both the `sessionCreated` and `sessionDestroyed` methods, which is where the session magic occurs.

In the example to this recipe, the `sessionCreated` method first obtains a handle on the current `HttpSession` object by calling the `HttpSessionEvent` object's `getSession` method. The handle is assigned to an `HttpSession` variable named `session`. Now that you have that variable initialized with the `session` object, it can be used to set the time of life and place attributes that will live and die with the session's life. The first session configuration performed in the example is to set the maximum inactive life to 60 (seconds), after which time the servlet container will invalidate the session. Next an attribute named `testAttr` is set in the session and given a value of `testVal`.

```
HttpSession session = arg.getSession();
session.setMaxInactiveInterval(60);
session.setAttribute("testAttr", "testVal");
```

A field within the servlet named numberOfSessions is declared, and it is incremented each time a new session is started. Following the session.setAttribute() call, the counter is incremented within a synchronized statement. Finally, a message is printed to the server log indicating that a new session was created and providing the total active session count.

■ **Note** Placing the increment within the synchronized statement helps avoid concurrency issues with the field. For more information on Java synchronization and concurrency, see the online documentation at http://docs.oracle.com/javase/tutorial/essential/concurrency/locksync.html.

The sessionDestroyed method is called on a session once the maximum number of inactive seconds has passed. In this example, the method will be called after 60 seconds of inactivity. Within the sessionDestroyed method, another synchronization statement decrements the numberOfSessions field value by one, and then a couple of lines are printed to the server log indicating that a session has been destroyed and providing the new total number of active sessions.

Session listeners can be used to set cookies and perform other useful tactics to help manage a user's experience. They are easy to use and very powerful.

1-12. Managing Session Attributes

Problem

You want to maintain some information regarding an individual session on a per-session basis when a user visits your site.

Solution

Use session attributes to retain session-based information. To do so, use the HttpServletRequest object to obtain access to the session, and then use the getAttribute() and setAttribute() methods accordingly. In the following scenario, an HTML page is used to capture a user's email address, and then the email address is placed into a session attribute. The attribute is then used by Java servlets across different pages of the application in order to maintain state.

The following code demonstrates what the HTML form (recipe01_12.html) may look like in this scenario:

```
<html>
    <head>
        <title></title>
        <meta http-equiv="Content-Type" content="text/html; charset=UTF-8">
    </head>
    <body>
        <h1>Provide an email address to use with this transaction</h1>
        <br/>
        <form method="POST" action="SessionServlet">
            <input type="text" id="email" name="email"/>
            <br/>
            <input type="submit" value="Submit"/>
        </form>
    </body>
</html>
```

Next, the Java servlet named SessionServlet using a URL pattern of /SessionServlet is initiated when the form is submitted. Any form input values are passed to SessionServlet and processed accordingly.

```
package org.javaee8recipes.chapter01.recipe01_12;

import java.io.*;
import javax.servlet.*;
import javax.servlet.annotation.WebServlet;
import javax.servlet.http.*;

// Uncomment the following line to run example stand-alone
//@WebServlet(name="SessionServlet", urlPatterns={"/SessionServlet"})

// The following will allow the example to run within the context of the JavaEE8Recipes
example
// enterprise application (JavaEE8Recipes.war distro or Netbeans Project
@WebServlet(name="SessionServlet", urlPatterns={"/chapter01/SessionServlet"}) public class
SessionServlet extends HttpServlet {
  public void doPost (HttpServletRequest req, HttpServletResponse res)
       throws ServletException, IOException {

   // Obtain the Session object

      HttpSession session = req.getSession(true);

   // Set up a session attribute

      String email = (String)
      session.getAttribute ("session.email");
      if (email == null) {
          email = req.getParameter("email");
          session.setAttribute ("session.email", email);
      }
      String sessionId = session.getId();

      res.setContentType("text/html");
      PrintWriter out = res.getWriter();
      out.println("<html>");
      out.println("<head><title>Working with sessions</title></head>");
      out.println("<body>");
      out.println("<h1>Session Test</h1>");
      out.println ("Your email address is: " + email + "<br/><br/>");
      out.println ("Your session id: " + sessionId);
      out.println("</body></html>");
   }
}
```

In the end, the email address that was entered within the original HTML form was captured and used throughout the different pages in the application.

How It Works

Since the beginning of web development, session attributes have been used to retain important information regarding a user's session. This concept holds true when developing using Java servlets as well, and servlets make it easy to set and get the attribute values. All HttpServlet classes must implement doGet or doPost methods in order to process web application events. In doing so, these methods have access to the HttpServletRequest object as it is passed to them as an argument. An HttpSession object can be gleaned from the HttpServletRequest, and therefore, it can be used to retrieve and set attributes as needed.

In the solution to this recipe, an HTTP session attribute is used to store an email address. That address is then used throughout the application within different servlet classes by obtaining the session object and then retrieving the attribute value.

```
// Obtain the Session object
   HttpSession session = req.getSession(true);
// Set up a session attribute
   String email = (String)
   session.getAttribute ("session.email");
   if (email == null) {
       email = req.getParameter("email");
       session.setAttribute ("session.email", email);
   }
```

Any attributes will remain in the HttpSession object as long as the session remains valid. The session ID will remain consistent when traversing between pages. You can see that the solution to this recipe obtains and prints the current session ID for reference. Using attributes in the HttpSession is a good way to pass data around to maintain a session's state.

1-13. Downloading a File

Problem

You want to enable your servlet application to have the ability to download a given file.

Solution

Write a servlet that will accept the name and path of a chosen file and then read the file and stream it to the file requestor. The following web page can be used to select a file for the servlet to download. Although the following HTML (recipe 01_13.html) contains a statically typed file name, it could very well contain a dynamic list of files from a database or other source:

```
<!DOCTYPE html>
<html>
    <head>
        <title></title>
        <meta http-equiv="Content-Type" content="text/html; charset=UTF-8">
    </head>
```

```
    <body>
        <h1>Click on the link below to download the file.</h1>
        <br/>
        <a href="DownloadServlet?filename=downloadTest.txt">Download test file</a>
        <br/>

    </body>
</html>
```

■ **Note** For the example in this recipe, you can create and edit a file in your root directory next to the `WEB-INF` folder and name the file `downloadTest.txt` to see the servlet transfer the data to your browser client.

When a user clicks the link presented on the web page from the previous HTML, the following servlet will be used to download the given file by passing the `HttpServletRequest` and `HttpServletResponse` objects to it along with the file that should be downloaded:

```
package org.javaee8recipes.chapter01.recipe01_13;

import java.io.DataInputStream;
import java.io.File;
import java.io.FileInputStream;
import java.io.IOException;
import java.io.InputStream;
import java.io.PrintWriter;
import javax.servlet.ServletContext;
import javax.servlet.ServletException;
import javax.servlet.ServletOutputStream;
import javax.servlet.annotation.WebServlet;
import javax.servlet.http.HttpServlet;
import javax.servlet.http.HttpServletRequest;
import javax.servlet.http.HttpServletResponse;

/**
 * Recipe 1-13: Downloading a File
 *
 * @author juneau
 */
// Uncomment the following line to run example stand-alone
//@WebServlet(name = "DownloadServlet", urlPatterns = {"/DownloadServlet"})

// The following will allow the example to run within the context of the example
// enterprise application (JavaEE8Recipes.war distro or Netbeans Project)
@WebServlet(name = "DownloadServlet", urlPatterns = {"/chapter01/DownloadServlet"})
public class DownloadServlet extends HttpServlet {

    /**
     * Handles the HTTP
     * <code>GET</code> method.
     *
```

```
     * @param request servlet request
     * @param response servlet response
     * @throws ServletException if a servlet-specific error occurs
     * @throws IOException if an I/O error occurs
     */
    @Override
    protected void doGet(HttpServletRequest request, HttpServletResponse response)
            throws ServletException, IOException {
        // Read parameter from form that contains the file name to download
        String fileToDownload = request.getParameter("filename");
        // Call the download method with the given file
        System.err.println("Downloading file now...");
        doDownload(request, response, fileToDownload);
    }

    /**
     *  Sends a file to the output stream.
     *
     *  @param req The request
     *  @param resp The response
     *  @param original_filename The name the browser should receive.
     */
    private void doDownload( HttpServletRequest request, HttpServletResponse response,
                             String originalFile) throws IOException {
        final int BYTES = 1024;
        int                  length   = 0;
        ServletOutputStream outStream = response.getOutputStream();
        ServletContext      context   = getServletConfig().getServletContext();

        response.setContentType( (context.getMimeType( originalFile ) != null) ?
                context.getMimeType( originalFile ) : "text/plain" );
        response.setHeader( "Content-Disposition", "attachment; filename=\"" + originalFile
                             + "\"" );

        InputStream in = context.getResourceAsStream("/" + originalFile);
        byte[] bbuf = new byte[BYTES];

        while ((in != null) && ((length = in.read(bbuf)) != -1))
        {
            outStream.write(bbuf,0,length);
        }

        outStream.flush();
        outStream.close();
    }

    /**
     * Returns a short description of the servlet.
     *
     * @return a String containing servlet description
     */
```

```
    @Override
    public String getServletInfo() {
        return "Short description";
    }
}
```

The servlet will not produce a response; it will simply download the given file to the end user when the user clicks the link to download the file.

How It Works

Downloading files is an essential task for almost any web application. Performing the steps that are provided by this recipe will make it easy to achieve this task. The example in this recipe demonstrates an easy case in which users can visit a web page, click a file to download, and have the file retrieved from the server and copied to their machine. The HTML is very simplistic in this example, and it lists a URL link that invokes the servlet and passes the name of the file that is to be downloaded. When the user clicks the link, the name of the file is passed to /DownloadServlet as a parameter with the name filename. When the link is clicked, the servlet doGet method is invoked. The first task that is performed in the doGet method is to read the filename parameter from the invoking web page. That information is then passed to the doDownload method along with the HttpServletRequest and HttpServletResponse objects.

In the doDownload method, the ServletOutputStream is obtained from the HttpServletResponse object, and the ServletContext is obtained for later use. To download a file, the servlet must provide a response of the same type that matches that of the file to be downloaded. It must also indicate in the response header that an attachment is to be included. Therefore, the first tasks to be performed by the doDownload method involve setting up the HttpServletResponse appropriately.

```
response.setContentType( (context.getMimeType( originalFile ) != null) ?
                context.getMimeType( originalFile ) : "text/plain" );
response.setHeader( "Content-Disposition", "attachment; filename=\"" + originalFile + "\"" );
```

The file name, in this case originalFile, is used to obtain the MIME type of the file. If the MIME type of the file is null, then text/plain will be returned. The attachment is set up in the response header as well, by appending the file name as an attachment to the Content-Disposition. Next, the doDownload method obtains a reference to the file that is to be downloaded by calling the ServletContext getResourceAsStream method and passing the name of the file. This will return an InputStream object that can be used to read the contents of the indicated file. A byte buffer is then created, which will be used to obtain chunks of data from the file when it is being read. The final real task is to read the file contents and copy them to the output stream. This is done using a while loop, which will continue to read from the InputStream until everything has been processed. Chunks of data are read in and written to the output stream using the loop.

```
while ((in != null) && ((length = in.read(bbuf)) != -1))
{
    outStream.write(bbuf,0,length);
}
```

Lastly, the ServletOutputStream object's flush method is called to clear the contents, and it is then closed to release resources. The magic of downloading files using a Java servlet may be a bit obfuscated by this example, however, because a static file is being used as the download source in this example. In real life, the HTML page would probably contain a list of files that are contained within a database, and then when the user selects a file to download, the servlet will process that file accordingly, even extracting the file from the database if necessary.

1-14. Dispatching Requests

Problem

You want to write a servlet that hands off requests to other servlets based on the task that needs to be accomplished. Furthermore, you want the requests to be handed off without redirecting the client to another site, and therefore, the URL in the browser should not change.

Solution

Create a request dispatcher servlet, which will decide which task needs to be completed, and then send the request to an appropriate servlet to achieve that task. The following example demonstrates this concept via an HTML form that accepts two numbers from the user and allows the user to decide what type of mathematical evaluation should be performed by the server. The servlet processes the request by first determining which type of mathematical evaluation should be performed and then dispatching the request to the appropriate servlet to perform the task.

The following HTML form accepts two numbers from the user and allows them to choose which type of math to perform against the numbers:

```
<html>
    <head>
        <title></title>
        <meta http-equiv="Content-Type" content="text/html; charset=UTF-8">
    </head>
    <body>
        <h1>Request Dispatch Example</h1>
        <p>Perform a mathematical evaluation.  Insert two numbers to be evaluated and then
            choose the type of evaluation to perform.</p>
        <form method="POST" action="MathDispatcher">
            <label for="numa">Enter Number A: </label>
            <input type="text" id="numa" name="numa"/><br><br>
            <label for="numb">Enter Number B: </label>
            <input type="text" id="numb" name="numb"/><br/><br/>
            <select id="matheval" name="matheval">
                <option value="add">Add the numbers</option>
                <option value="subtract">Subtract the numbers</option>
                <option value="multiply">Multiply the numbers</option>
                <option value="divide">Divide the numbers</option>
            </select>
            <input type="submit" value="Submit Form"/>
            <input type="reset" value="Reset Form"/>
        </form>
    </body>
</html>
```

The next piece of code is the servlet, which will dispatch requests accordingly depending on the value of the matheval field:

```
package org.javaee8recipes.chapter01.recipe01_14;

import java.io.IOException;
import javax.servlet.RequestDispatcher;
import javax.servlet.ServletContext;
import javax.servlet.ServletException;
import javax.servlet.ServletRequest;
import javax.servlet.annotation.WebServlet;
import javax.servlet.http.HttpServlet;
import javax.servlet.http.HttpServletRequest;
import javax.servlet.http.HttpServletResponse;

/**
 *
 * @author juneau
 */
// Uncomment the following line to run example stand-alone
//@WebServlet(name = "MathDispatcher", urlPatterns = {"/MathDispatcher"})

// The following will allow the example to run within the context of the example
// enterprise application (JavaEE8Recipes.war distro or Netbeans Project)
@WebServlet(name = "MathDispatcher", urlPatterns = {"/chapter01/MathDispatcher"})
public class MathDispatcher extends HttpServlet {

    /**
     * Handles the HTTP
     * <code>POST</code> method.
     *
     * @param request servlet request
     * @param response servlet response
     * @throws ServletException if a servlet-specific error occurs
     * @throws IOException if an I/O error occurs
     */
    @Override
    protected void doPost(HttpServletRequest request, HttpServletResponse response)
            throws ServletException, IOException {
         System.out.println("In the servlet...");
        // Store the input parameter values into Strings
                String eval = request.getParameter("matheval");
                ServletContext sc = getServletConfig().getServletContext();
                RequestDispatcher rd = null;
                int evaluate = 0;
                int add = 0;
                int subtract = 1;
                int multiply = 2;
                int divide = 3;
                if(eval.equals("add"))
                    evaluate = add;
```

```
                if (eval.equals("subtract"))
                    evaluate = subtract;
                if (eval.equals("multiply"))
                    evaluate = multiply;
                if(eval.equals("divide")){
                    evaluate = divide;
                }
                switch(evaluate){
                    case(0): rd =  sc.getRequestDispatcher("/AddServlet");
                                 rd.forward(request, response);
                                 break;
                    case(1): rd =  sc.getRequestDispatcher("/SubtractServlet");
                                      rd.forward(request, response);
                                      break;
                    case(2): rd =  sc.getRequestDispatcher("/MultiplyServlet");
                                      rd.forward(request, response);
                                      break;
                    case(3): rd =  sc.getRequestDispatcher("/DivideServlet");
                                    rd.forward(request, response);
                                    break;
                }

    }

    /**
     * Returns a short description of the servlet.
     *
     * @return a String containing servlet description
     */
    @Override
    public String getServletInfo() {
        return "Short description";
    }
}
```

Next is an example of one of the servlets that the request will be dispatched to. The following is the code for the AddServlet, which will add the two numbers and return the sum to the user:

```
package org.javaee8recipes.chapter01.recipe01_14;

import java.io.IOException;
import java.io.PrintWriter;
import javax.servlet.ServletException;
import javax.servlet.annotation.WebServlet;
import javax.servlet.http.HttpServlet;
import javax.servlet.http.HttpServletRequest;
import javax.servlet.http.HttpServletResponse;

/**
 *
 * @author juneau
 */
```

```
// Uncomment the following line to run example stand-alone
//@WebServlet(name = "AddServlet", urlPatterns = {"/AddServlet"})

// The following will allow the example to run within the context of the example
// enterprise application (JavaEE8Recipes.war distro or Netbeans Project)
@WebServlet(name = "AddServlet", urlPatterns = {"/chapter01/AddServlet"})
public class AddServlet extends HttpServlet {

    /**
     * Processes requests for both HTTP
     * <code>GET</code> and
     * <code>POST</code> methods.
     *
     * @param request servlet request
     * @param response servlet response
     * @throws ServletException if a servlet-specific error occurs
     * @throws IOException if an I/O error occurs
     */
    protected void processRequest(HttpServletRequest request, HttpServletResponse response)
            throws ServletException, IOException {
        response.setContentType("text/html;charset=UTF-8");
        PrintWriter out = response.getWriter();
        // Store the input parameter values into Strings
                String numA = request.getParameter("numa");
                String numB = request.getParameter("numb");
                int sum = Integer.valueOf(numA) + Integer.valueOf(numB);
        try {
            out.println("<html>");
            out.println("<head>");
            out.println("<title>The Sum of the Numbers</title>");
            out.println("</head>");
            out.println("<body>");
            out.println("<h1>Sum: " + sum + "</h1>");
            out.println("<br/>");
            out.println("<a href=recipe01_14.html>Try Again</a>");
            out.println("</body>");
            out.println("</html>");
        } finally {
            out.close();
        }
    }

    /**
     * Handles the HTTP
     * <code>GET</code> method.
     *
     * @param request servlet request
     * @param response servlet response
     * @throws ServletException if a servlet-specific error occurs
     * @throws IOException if an I/O error occurs
     */
```

```
    @Override
    protected void doGet(HttpServletRequest request, HttpServletResponse response)
            throws ServletException, IOException {
        processRequest(request, response);
    }

    /**
     * Handles the HTTP
     * <code>POST</code> method.
     *
     * @param request servlet request
     * @param response servlet response
     * @throws ServletException if a servlet-specific error occurs
     * @throws IOException if an I/O error occurs
     */
    @Override
    protected void doPost(HttpServletRequest request, HttpServletResponse response)
            throws ServletException, IOException {
        processRequest(request, response);
    }

    /**
     * Returns a short description of the servlet.
     *
     * @return a String containing servlet description
     */
    @Override
    public String getServletInfo() {
        return "Short description";
    }
}
```

Each of the other servlets is very similar to AddServlet, except the mathematical evaluation is different. To see a full listing of the code, take a look at the sources for this book.

How It Works

Sometimes it is a good idea to hide the forwarding of requests from the end user. Other times it just makes sense to hand off a request from one servlet to another so that another type of processing can occur. These are just two examples of when it is handy to perform a request dispatch within a servlet. Forwarding a request versus dispatching a request is different because a forwarded request hands off the request on the client side, whereas a dispatched request hands off the request on the server side. The difference can be quite large since the end user has no idea of server-side dispatches, whereas the browser is redirected to a different URL when the request is forwarded on the client side.

Dispatching requests is an easy task. The facilities for doing so are built right into the ServletContext, so once you obtain a reference to ServletContext, you simply call the getRequestDispatcher method to obtain a RequestDispatcher object that can be used to dispatch the request. When calling the getRequestDispatcher method, pass a string containing the name of the servlet that you want to hand off the request to. You can actually obtain a RequestDisptacher object for any valid HTTP resource within the application by passing the appropriate URL for the resource in String format to the getRequestDispatcher method. Therefore, if you'd rather dispatch to a JSP or HTML page, you can do that as well. After a RequestDispatcher object has been obtained, invoke its forward method by passing the HttpServletRequest and HttpServletResponse objects to it. The forward method performs the task of handing off the request.

```
rd = sc.getRequestDispatcher("/AddServlet");
rd.forward(request, response);
```

In the case of the example in this recipe, you can dispatch requests to different servlets in order to perform a specific task. Once handed off, the servlet that has obtained the request is responsible for providing the response to the client. In this case, the servlet returns the result of the specified mathematical evaluation.

1-15. Redirecting to a Different Site

Problem

You need to redirect the browser to another URL when a specific URL within your application is visited.

Solution

Use the HttpServletResponse object's sendRedirect() method to redirect from the servlet to another URL. In the following example, when a URL that matches the /redirect pattern is used, then the servlet will redirect the browser to another site:

```
import java.io.IOException;
import javax.servlet.*;
import javax.servlet.annotation.WebServlet;
import javax.servlet.http.*;

@WebServlet(name="RedirectServlet", urlPatterns={"/redirect"})
public class RedirectServlet extends HttpServlet {

        @Override
    public void doGet(HttpServletRequest req, HttpServletResponse res)
        throws IOException, ServletException {
                String site = "http://www.apress.com";

        res.sendRedirect(site);
    }
}
```

In this example, the servlet will redirect to the www.apress.com website.

How It Works

There are some cases in which a web application needs to redirect traffic to another site or URL within the same or another application. For such cases, the HttpServletResponse sendRedirect method can be of use. The sendRedirect method accepts a URL in String format and then redirects the web browser to the given URL. The fact that sendRedirect accepts a string-based URL makes it easy to build dynamic URLs as well. For instance, some applications may redirect to a different URL based on certain parameters that are passed from a user. Dynamic generation of a URL in such cases may look something like the following:

```
String redirectUrl = null;
if(parameter.equals("SOME STRING")
    redirectUrl = "/" + urlPathA;
else
    redirectUrl = "/" + urlPathB;
res.sendRedirect(redirectUrl);
```

The sendRedirect() method can also come in handy for creating the control for web menus and other page items that can send web traffic to different locations.

■ **Note** This simple redirect, as opposed to servlet chaining, does not pass the HttpRequest object along to the target address.

1-16. Securely Maintaining State Within the Browser

Problem

You have the requirement to save a user's state within the browser for your application.

Solution

Use "HTTP only" browser cookies to save the state. In the following example, one servlet is used to place some session information into a cookie in the browser. Another servlet is then called, which reads the cookie information and displays it to the user. The following servlet demonstrates how to store a cookie in the browser using a Java servlet:

```
package org.javaee8recipes.chapter01.recipe01_16;

import java.io.IOException;
import java.io.PrintWriter;
import javax.servlet.ServletException;
import javax.servlet.annotation.WebServlet;
import javax.servlet.http.Cookie;
import javax.servlet.http.HttpServlet;
import javax.servlet.http.HttpServletRequest;
import javax.servlet.http.HttpServletResponse;

/**
 * Recipe 1-16: Securely Maintaining State Within the Browser
 * @author juneau
 */
@WebServlet(name = "SetCookieServlet", urlPatterns = {"/SetCookieServlet"})
public class SetCookieServlet extends HttpServlet {
```

```
    protected void processRequest(HttpServletRequest request, HttpServletResponse response)
            throws ServletException, IOException {
        response.setContentType("text/html;charset=UTF-8");
        PrintWriter out = response.getWriter();
        Cookie cookie = new Cookie("sessionId","12345");
        cookie.setHttpOnly(true);
        cookie.setMaxAge(-30);
        response.addCookie(cookie);
        try {
            out.println("<html>");
            out.println("<head>");
            out.println("<title>SetCookieServlet</title>");
            out.println("</head>");
            out.println("<body>");
            out.println("<h1>Servlet SetCookieServlet is setting a cookie into the browser
            </h1>");
            out.println("<br/><br/>");
            out.println("<a href='DisplayCookieServlet'>Display the cookie contents.</a>");
            out.println("</body>");
            out.println("</html>");
        } finally {
            out.close();
        }
    }

    @Override
    protected void doGet(HttpServletRequest request, HttpServletResponse response)
            throws ServletException, IOException {
        processRequest(request, response);
    }

    @Override
    protected void doPost(HttpServletRequest request, HttpServletResponse response)
            throws ServletException, IOException {
        processRequest(request, response);
    }

}
```

The next code listing demonstrates a servlet that reads the cookies in the browser and prints the contents:

```
package org.javaee8recipes.chapter01.recipe01_16;

import java.io.IOException;
import java.io.PrintWriter;
import javax.servlet.ServletException;
import javax.servlet.annotation.WebServlet;
import javax.servlet.http.Cookie;
import javax.servlet.http.HttpServlet;
import javax.servlet.http.HttpServletRequest;
import javax.servlet.http.HttpServletResponse;
```

```
/**
 * Recipe 1-16: Securely Maintaining State within the Browser
 * @author juneau
 */
@WebServlet(name = "DisplayCookieServlet", urlPatterns = {"/DisplayCookieServlet"})
public class DisplayCookieServlet extends HttpServlet {

    protected void processRequest(HttpServletRequest request, HttpServletResponse response)
            throws ServletException, IOException {
        response.setContentType("text/html;charset=UTF-8");
        PrintWriter out = response.getWriter();
        Cookie[] cookies = request.getCookies();

        try {
            out.println("<html>");
            out.println("<head>");
            out.println("<title>Display Cookies</title>");
            out.println("</head>");
            out.println("<body>");
            for(Cookie cookie:cookies){
                out.println("<p>");
                out.println("Cookie Name: " + cookie.getName());
                out.println("<br/>");
                out.println("Value: " + cookie.getValue());
                out.println("</p>");
            }
            out.println("</body>");
            out.println("</html>");
        } finally {
            out.close();
        }
    }

    @Override
    protected void doGet(HttpServletRequest request, HttpServletResponse response)
            throws ServletException, IOException {
        processRequest(request, response);
    }

    @Override
    protected void doPost(HttpServletRequest request, HttpServletResponse response)
            throws ServletException, IOException {
        processRequest(request, response);
    }

}
```

How It Works

Using cookies to store data in the browser is a technique that has been in practice for years. Since Servlet 3.0 API, the ability to mark a cookie as HTTP only has become available. This allows the cookie to be safeguarded against client-side scripting attacks, making the cookie more secure. Any standard servlet can create a cookie and place it into the current session. Similarly, any servlet that is contained within the same session can read or update a session's cookies values. In the example for this recipe, two servlets are used to demonstrate how cookies work. The first servlet that is listed is responsible for creating a new cookie and setting it into the browser session. The second servlet is responsible for displaying the contents of the cookie to the user.

To create a cookie, simply instantiate a new `javax.servlet.http.Cookie` object and assign a name and value to it. Passing both the name and value into the `Cookie` constructor at the time of instantiation can assign a name and value, or it can be done by passing values to the cookie's `setName` and `setValue` methods. Once the cookie has been instantiated, properties can be set that will help to configure the cookie. In the example to this recipe, the cookie's `setMaxAge` and `setHttpOnly` methods are called, setting the time of life for the cookie and ensuring that it will be guarded against client-side scripting. For a complete listing of cookie properties, refer to Table 1-3. Finally, the cookie is placed into the response by passing it to the response object's `addCookie` method.

```
Cookie cookie = new Cookie("sessionId","12345");
cookie.setHttpOnly(true);
cookie.setMaxAge(-30);
response.addCookie(cookie);
```

Table 1-3. *Cookie Property Methods*

Property	Description
`setComment`	Sets a comment to describe the cookie.
`setDomain`	Specifies the domain in which the cookie belongs.
`setHttpOnly`	Marks the cookie as HTTP only.
`setMaxAge`	Sets the maximum lifetime of the cookie. A negative value indicates that the cookie will expire when the session ends.
`setPath`	Specifies a path for the cookie to which the client should return it.
`setSecure`	Indicates that the cookie should be sent only using a secure protocol.
`setValue`	Assigns a value to the cookie.
`setVersion`	Specifies the version of the cookie protocol that the cookie will comply with.

The second servlet in the example, `DisplayCookieServlet`, is responsible for reading and displaying the session's cookies values. When `DisplayCookieServlet` is invoked, its `processRequest` method is called, which obtains the cookies within the `response` object by calling `response.getCookies()`and setting the result to an array of `Cookie` objects.

```
Cookie[] cookies = request.getCookies();
```

The cookie object array can now be iterated over in order to obtain each cookie and print its contents. The servlet does so by using a for loop and printing each cookie's name and value.

```
for(Cookie cookie:cookies){
        out.println("<p>");
        out.println("Cookie Name: " + cookie.getName());
        out.println("<br/>");
        out.println("Value: " + cookie.getValue());
        out.println("</p>");
}
```

1-17. Finalizing Servlet Tasks

Problem

There are some resources you want to have your servlet clean up once the servlet is no longer in use.

Solution

The solution to the problem is twofold. First, provide code for performing any cleanup within the servlet destroy method. Second, in the case that there are potentially long-running methods, code them so that you will become aware of a shutdown and, if necessary, halt and return so that the servlet can shut down cleanly. The following code excerpt is a small example of a destroy method. In this code, it is being used to initialize local variables and is setting the beingDestroyed boolean value to indicate that the servlet is shutting down.

```
...
    /**
     * Used to finalize the servlet
     */
    public void destroy() {
        // Tell the servlet it is shutting down
        setBeingDestroyed(true);
        // Perform any cleanup
        thisString = null;

    }
...
```

The code within the destroy method may successfully achieve a full cleanup of the servlet, but in the case where there may be a long-running task, then it must be notified of a shutdown. The following excerpt is a block of code that signifies a long-running task. The task should stop processing once the shutdown is indicated by the beingDestroyed value becoming true.

```
for (int x = 0; (x <= 100000 && !isBeingDestroyed()); x++) {
    doSomething();
}
```

■ **Note** If you want to perform cleanup prior to calling the `destroy` method, then create a `public`, `protected`, or `private` method that returns void and annotate it with `@PreDestroy`. The `@PreDestroy` annotation marks a method to be called prior to the component being removed from the container. This method must not throw a checked exception.

How It Works

The finalization of a servlet can be very important, especially if the servlet is using some resources that may lead to a memory leak, using a reusable resource such as a database connection, or needs to persist some values for another session. In such cases, it is a good idea to perform cleanup within the servlet `destroy` method. Every servlet contains a `destroy` method (which may be implemented to overload default behavior) that is initiated once the servlet container determines that a servlet should be taken out of service.

The `destroy` method is called once all of a servlet's service methods have stopped running. However, if there is a long-running service method, then a server grace period can be set that would cause any running service to be shut down when the grace period is reached. As mentioned earlier, the `destroy` method is the perfect place to clean up resources. However, the `destroy` method is also a good place to help clean up after long-running services. Cleanup can be done by setting a servlet-specific local variable to indicate that the servlet is being destroyed and by having the long-running service check the state of that variable periodically. If the variable indicates that the `destroy` method has been called, then it should stop executing.

1-18. Reading and Writing with Nonblocking I/O

Problem

You want to read and write I/O in an asynchronous, nonblocking manner.

Solution

Use the Non-Blocking I/O API that is part of the Servlet 3.1 release. To use the new technology, implement the new `ReadListener` interface when performing nonblocking reads, and implement the `WriteListener` interface for performing nonblocking writes. The implementation class can then be registered to a `ServletInputStream` or `ServletOutputStream` so that reads or writes can be performed when the listener finds that servlet content can be read or written without blocking.

The following sources are those of a `ReadListener` implementation that reside in the source file `org.javaee8recipes.chapter01.recipe01_18.AcmeReadListenerImpl.java`, and they demonstrate how to implement the `ReadListener`:

```
package org.javaee8recipes.chapter01.recipe01_18;

import java.io.IOException;
import java.util.logging.Level;
import java.util.logging.Logger;
import javax.servlet.AsyncContext;
import javax.servlet.ReadListener;
import javax.servlet.ServletInputStream;
```

```
public class AcmeReadListenerImpl implements ReadListener {

    private ServletInputStream is = null;
    private AsyncContext async = null;

    public AcmeReadListenerImpl(ServletInputStream in, AsyncContext ac) {
        this.is = in;
        this.async = ac;
        System.out.println("read listener initialized");
    }

    @Override
    public void onDataAvailable() {
        System.out.println("onDataAvailable");
        try {
            StringBuilder sb = new StringBuilder();
            int len = -1;
            byte b[] = new byte[1024];
            while (is.isReady()
                    && (len = is.read(b)) != -1) {
                String data = new String(b, 0, len);
                System.out.println(data);
            }
        } catch (IOException ex) {
            Logger.getLogger(AcmeReadListenerImpl.class.getName()).log(Level.SEVERE, null, ex);
        }
    }

    @Override
        public void onAllDataRead() {
        System.out.println("onAllDataRead");
        async.complete();

    }

    @Override
        public void onError(Throwable thrwbl) {
        System.out.println("Error: " + thrwbl);
        async.complete();
    }

}
```

Next, use the listener by registering it to a `ServletInputStream` (in the case of the `ReadListener`) or a `ServletOutputStream` (in the case of a `WriteListener`). For this example, I show a servlet that utilizes the `AcmeReadListenerImpl` class. The sources for the following class reside in the `org.javaee8recipes.chapter01.recipe01_18.AcmeReaderExample.java` file:

```
package org.javaee8recipes.chapter01.recipe01_18;

import java.io.IOException;
import java.io.InputStream;
import java.io.PrintWriter;
```

```
import java.util.concurrent.CountDownLatch;
import javax.servlet.AsyncContext;
import javax.servlet.ServletContext;
import javax.servlet.ServletException;
import javax.servlet.ServletInputStream;
import javax.servlet.ServletOutputStream;
import javax.servlet.annotation.WebServlet;
import javax.servlet.http.HttpServlet;
import javax.servlet.http.HttpServletRequest;
import javax.servlet.http.HttpServletResponse;

@WebServlet(urlPatterns = {"/AcmeReaderServlet"}, asyncSupported=true)
public class AcmeReaderServlet extends HttpServlet {

    protected void processRequest(HttpServletRequest request, HttpServletResponse response)
            throws ServletException, IOException {
        response.setContentType("text/html;charset=UTF-8");
        try (PrintWriter output = response.getWriter()) {
            String filename = "test.txt";
            ServletContext context = getServletContext();

            InputStream in = context.getResourceAsStream(filename);
            output.println("<html>");
            output.println("<head>");
            output.println("<title>Acme Reader</title>");
            output.println("</head>");
            output.println("<body>");
            output.println("<h1>Welcome to the Acme Reader Servlet</h1>");
            output.println("<br/><br/>");
            output.println("<p>Look at the server log to see data that was read
            asynchronously from a file<p>");
            AsyncContext asyncCtx = request.startAsync();
            ServletInputStream input = request.getInputStream();
            input.setReadListener(new AcmeReadListenerImpl(input, asyncCtx));

            output.println("</body>");
            output.println("</html>");
        } catch (Exception ex){
            System.out.println("Exception Occurred: " + ex);
        }
    }

  // Http Servlet Methods ...
...
}
```

The last piece of code that we need is the servlet that invokes the `AcmeReaderServlet`, passing the message that needs to be processed. In this example, a file from the server is passed to the `AcmeReaderServlet` as input, which then is asynchronously processed via the `AcmeReadListenerImpl` class. The following code is taken from `org.javaee8recipes.chapter01.recipe01_18.ReaderExample.java`.

```
package org.javaee8recipes.chapter01.recipe01_18;

import java.io.BufferedReader;
import java.io.BufferedWriter;
import java.io.IOException;
import java.io.InputStream;
import java.io.InputStreamReader;
import java.io.OutputStreamWriter;
import java.io.PrintWriter;
import java.net.HttpURLConnection;
import java.net.URL;
import java.util.logging.Level;
import java.util.logging.Logger;
import javax.servlet.ServletContext;
import javax.servlet.ServletException;
import javax.servlet.annotation.WebServlet;
import javax.servlet.http.HttpServlet;
import javax.servlet.http.HttpServletRequest;
import javax.servlet.http.HttpServletResponse;

@WebServlet(name = "ReaderExample", urlPatterns = {"/ReaderExample"})
public class ReaderExample extends HttpServlet {

    protected void processRequest(HttpServletRequest request, HttpServletResponse response)
            throws ServletException, IOException {
        response.setContentType("text/html;charset=UTF-8");
        String filename = "/WEB-INF/test.txt";
        ServletContext context = getServletContext();

        InputStream in = context.getResourceAsStream(filename);
        try (PrintWriter out = response.getWriter()) {
            String path = "http://"
                    + request.getServerName()
                    + ":"
                    + request.getServerPort()
                    + request.getContextPath()
                    + "/AcmeReaderServlet";
            out.println("<html>");
            out.println("<head>");
            out.println("<title>Intro to Java EE 7 - Servlet Reader Example</title>");
            out.println("</head>");
            out.println("<body>");
            out.println("<h1>Servlet ReaderExample at " + request.getContextPath() + "</h1>");
            out.println("Invoking the endpoint: " + path + "<br>");
            out.flush();
            URL url = new URL(path);
            HttpURLConnection conn = (HttpURLConnection) url.openConnection();
            conn.setChunkedStreamingMode(2);
            conn.setDoOutput(true);
            conn.connect();
```

```
            if (in != null) {
                InputStreamReader inreader = new InputStreamReader(in);
                BufferedReader reader = new BufferedReader(inreader);
                String text = "";
                out.println("Beginning Read");
                try (BufferedWriter output = new BufferedWriter(new OutputStreamWriter(conn.
                getOutputStream()))) {
                    out.println("got the output...beginning loop");
                    while ((text = reader.readLine()) != null) {
                        out.println("reading text: " + text);
                        out.flush();
                        output.write(text);

                        Thread.sleep(1000);
                        output.write("Ending example now..");
                        out.flush();
                    }
                    output.flush();
                    output.close();
                }
            }
            out.println("Review the Glassfish server log for messages...");
            out.println("</body>");
            out.println("</html>");
        } catch (InterruptedException | IOException ex) {
            Logger.getLogger(ReaderExample.class.getName()).log(Level.SEVERE, null, ex);
        }
    }

@Override
    protected void doGet(HttpServletRequest request, HttpServletResponse response)
            throws ServletException, IOException {
        processRequest(request, response);
    }

@Override
    protected void doPost(HttpServletRequest request, HttpServletResponse response)
            throws ServletException, IOException {
        processRequest(request, response);
    }

@Override
    public String getServletInfo() {
        return "Short description";
    }
}
```

When the servlet is visited, the asynchronous, nonblocking read of the `test.txt` file will occur, and its text will be displayed in the server log.

How It Works

Servlet technology has allowed only traditional (blocking) input/output during request processing since its inception. In the Servlet 3.1 release, the new Non-Blocking I/O API makes it possible for servlets to read or write without any blocking. This means other tasks can be performed at the same time that a read or write is occurring, without any wait. Such a solution opens a new realm of possibilities for servlets, making them much more flexible for use along with modern technologies such as the WebSockets protocol.

To implement a nonblocking I/O solution, new programming interfaces have been added to `ServletInputStream` and `ServletOutputStream`, as well as two event listeners: `ReadListener` and `WriteListener`. `ReadListener` and `WriteListener` interfaces make the servlet I/O processing occur in a nonblocking manner via callback methods that are invoked when servlet content can be read or written without blocking. Use the `ServletInputStream.setReadListener(ServletInputStream, AsyncContext)` method to register a `ReadListener` with a `ServletInputStream`, and use the I/O read `ServletInputStream.setWriteListener(ServletOutputStream, AsyncContext)` method for registering a `WriteListener`. The following lines of code demonstrate how to register a `ReadListener` implementation with a `ServletInputStream`:

```
AsyncContext context = request.startAsync();
ServletInputStream input = request.getInputStream();
input.setReadListener(new ReadListenerImpl(input, context));
```

■ **Note** In Servlet 3.0, `AsyncContext` was introduced to represent an execution context for an asynchronous operation that is initiated on a servlet request. To use the asynchronous context, a servlet should be annotated as a `@WebServlet`, and the `asyncSupported` attribute of the annotation must be set to `true`. The `@WebFilter` annotation also contains the `asyncSupported` attribute.

After a listener has been registered with a `ServletInputStream`, the status on a nonblocking read can be checked by calling the methods `ServletInputStream.isReady` and `ServletInputStream.isFinished`. For instance, a read can begin once the `ServletInputStream.isReady` method returns a `true`, as shown here:

```
while (is.isReady() && (b = input.read()) != -1)) {
    len = is.read(b);
    String data = new String(b, 0, len);
}
```

To create a `ReadListener` or `WriteListener`, three methods must be overridden: `onDataAvailable`, `onAllDataRead`, and `onError`. The `onDataAvailable` method is invoked when data is available to be read or written, `onAllDataRead` is invoked once all the data has been read or written, and `onError` is invoked if an error is encountered. The code for `AcmeReadListenerImpl` in the solution to this recipe demonstrates how to override these methods.

The `AsyncContext.complete` method is called in the `onAllDataRead` method to indicate that the read has been completed and to commit the response. This method is also called in the `onError` implementation so that the read will complete, so it is important to perform any cleanup within the body of the `onError` method to ensure that no resources are leaked, and so on.

To implement a `WriteListener`, use the new `ServletOutputStream.canWrite` method, which determines whether data can be written in a nonblocking fashion. A `WriteListener` implementation class must override a couple of methods: `onWritePossible` and `onError`. The `onWritePossible` method is invoked when a nonblocking write can occur. The write implementation should take place within the body of this method. The `onError` method is much the same as its `ReadListener` implementation counterpart, because it is invoked when an error occurs.

The following lines of code demonstrate how to register a `WriteListener` with a `ServletOutputStream`:

```
AsyncContext context = request.startAsync();
ServletOutputStream os = response.getOutputStream();
os.setWriteListener(new WriteListenerImpl(os, context));
```

The `WriteListener` implementation class must include overriding methods for `onWritePossible` and `onError`. The following is an example for a `WriteListener` implementation class:

```
import javax.servlet.AsyncContext;
import javax.servlet.ServletOutputStream;
import javax.servlet.WriteListener;

public class WriteListenerImpl implements WriteListener {

    ServletOutputStream os;
    AsyncContext context;

    public WriteListenerImpl(ServletOutputStream out, AsyncContext ctx){
        this.os = out;
        this.context = ctx;
        System.out.println("Write Listener Initialized");
    }

    @Override
    public void onWritePossible() {
        System.out.println("Now possible to write...");
        // Write implementation goes here...
    }

    @Override
    public void onError(Throwable thrwbl) {
        System.out.println("Error occurred");
        context.complete();
    }

}
```

■ **Note** In most cases, the `ReadListener` and `WriteListener` implementation classes can be embedded within the calling servlet. They have been broken out into separate classes for the examples in this book for demonstration purposes.

The new Non-Blocking I/O API helps bring the Servlet API into compliance with new web standards. The new API makes it possible to create web-based applications that perform well in an asynchronous fashion.

1-19. Pushing Resources from a Server to a Client

Problem

You want to push resources to your clients automatically when they visit a particular page within your web application.

Solution

Use the Servlet HTTP/2 Push API to push the resources before the page is loaded. This will cause all of the resources to be included with the single response, rather than multiple responses that used to be needed for HTTP 1.1 implementations. In the following example, a PushBuilder is created, and then a number of statically typed resources are pushed to the client prior to loading the page.

```
@WebServlet(name = "PushServlet", urlPatterns = {"/PushServlet"})
public class PushServlet extends HttpServlet {

    protected void processRequest(HttpServletRequest request, HttpServletResponse response)
            throws ServletException, IOException {
        response.setContentType("text/html;charset=UTF-8");
        try (PrintWriter out = response.getWriter()) {
            /* TODO output your page here. You may use following sample code. */
            out.println("<!DOCTYPE html>");
            out.println("<html>");
            out.println("<head>");
            out.println("<title>Servlet PushServlet</title>");
            out.println("</head>");
            out.println("<body>");
            out.println("<h1>Servlet PushServlet at " + request.getContextPath() + "!</h1>");
            out.println("</body>");
            out.println("</html>");
        }
    }

@Override
    protected void doGet(HttpServletRequest request, HttpServletResponse response)
            throws ServletException, IOException {
        System.out.println("In the servlet");
        if(request.getRequestURI().equals("/JavaEE8Recipes/PushServlet") && request.
        getPushBuilder() != null) {
            System.out.println("Pushing resources");
            PushBuilder builder =
            request.getPushBuilder().path("/resources/images/javaee9recipes.png");
            builder.path("/resources/images/javaee7recipes.png");
            builder.push();
        }       processRequest(request, response);
    }

. . .
}
```

How It Works

A significant problem with serving content from the web has always been the request and response lifecycle. HTTP 1.1 requires multiple TCP connections issuing parallel requests in order to load page content containing various resources such as JavaScript files and images. This can not only lead to significant performance issues, but also starves network resources. HTTP/2 is fundamentally different in that it is fully multiplexed, rather than being ordered and blocking. It also allows a single connection to be used for issuing requests in parallel, making performance much better and using much less network resource. Other differences for HTTP/2 include using header compression to help reduce overhead, and allowing servers to have the ability to push resources proactively to active clients. This last feature of HTTP/2 that was mentioned is covered by the example in this recipe, pushing resources from the server, rather than making the client fetch each required resource.

The `PushBuilder` interface was introduced with Servlet 4.0, which is part of the Java EE 8 platform. The `PushBuilder` is used to build a push request based on the `HttpServletRequest`. Once the `PushBuilder` is obtained, it can be used to add resources via the `path` method, which are subsequently pushed to the client while the target page is being processed. In the example, a couple PNG image resources are added using the `path` method. However, an application can be coded such that any resource that is required by a specified page can be pushed preemptively to the client and loaded into the browser cache. Once obtained, the `PushBuilder` can be used as many times as required. After all resources have been loaded, initiate the `PushBuilder.push()` method to perform the push action.

After the resources have been pushed, the invoked page will be loaded in an effort to process resources, determining which resources have already been cached and which need to be loaded from the server push. If a client browser already has the resource in the cache, it returns an `RST_STREAM` to indicate that the server does not need to end it.

CHAPTER 2

JavaServer Pages

The JavaServer Pages (JSP) web framework introduced a great productivity boost for Java web developers over the Java Servlet API. When the JSP technology was introduced in 1999, it was Sun's answer to PHP, which provided web developers with a quick way to create dynamic web content. JSPs contain a mix of XML and HTML but can also contain embedded Java code within scripting elements known as *scriptlets*. Indeed, JSPs are easy to learn and allow developers to quickly create dynamic content and use their favorite HTML editor to lay out nice-looking pages. JSP was introduced several years ago and still remains one of the most important Java web technologies available. Although JSP technology has changed over the years, there are still many applications using older JSP variations in the world today.

Over the years, the creation of dynamic web content has solidified, and the techniques used to develop web applications have become easier to maintain down the road. Whereas early JSP applications included a mixture of Java and XML markup within the pages, today the separation of markup from business logic is increasingly important. Newer releases of the JSP technology have accounted for these changes in the web space, and the most recent releases allow developers the flexibility to develop highly dynamic content without utilizing any embedded Java code but, instead, using markup and custom tags within pages.

This chapter shows you the ins and outs of JSP development. Starting with creating a simple JSP application, you learn how to develop applications using JSP technology from the ground up and harness the productivity and power that the technology has to offer. The chapter also brushes on advanced techniques such as the development of custom JSP tags and the invocation of Java functions utilizing conditional tags. Although entire books have been written on JSP, the recipes within this chapter lay a solid foundation on which you can begin to develop applications utilizing JSP.

Note Utilizing a Java integrated development environment (IDE) can significantly reduce development time, especially when working with Java web technologies such as JSP. To start learning how to create a JSP application using the NetBeans IDE, see the appendix of this book.

J. Juneau, *Java EE 8 Recipes*, https://doi.org/10.1007/978-1-4842-3594-2_2

2-1. Creating a Simple JSP Page

Problem

You want to develop a web page using HTML markup that enables you to include dynamic content.

Solution

Use JavaServer Pages to create a web page that combines standard markup with blocks of Java code that are embedded within the markup. The following JSP markup demonstrates how to include dynamic code in a page:

```
<%--
    Document    : recipe02_01
    Author      : juneau
--%>

<%@page contentType="text/html" pageEncoding="UTF-8"%>
<!DOCTYPE html>
<html>
    <head>
        <meta http-equiv="Content-Type" content="text/html; charset=UTF-8">
        <title>JSP Page Example</title>
    </head>
    <body>
        <jsp:useBean id="dateBean" scope="application" class="org.javaee8recipes.chapter02.
        recipe02_01.DateBean"/>
        <h1>Hello World!</h1>
        <br/>
        <p>
            The current date is: ${dateBean.currentDate}!
        </p>
    </body>
</html>
```

The previous JSP code uses a JavaBean to pull the current date into the page. The following Java code is the JavaBean that is used by the JSP code:

```
package org.javaee8recipes.chapter02.recipe02_01;

import java.util.Date;

/**
 * Recipe 2-1: Creating a Simple JSP Page
 * @author juneau
 */
public class DateBean {

    private Date currentDate = new Date();

    /**
     * @return the currentDate
     */
```

```
    public Date getCurrentDate() {
        return currentDate;
    }

    /**
     * @param currentDate the currentDate to set
     */
    public void setCurrentDate(Date currentDate) {
        this.currentDate = currentDate;
    }

}
```

The following output would result. Of course, the page will display the current date when you run the code.

```
Hello World!
The current date is: Fri Dec 23 10:41:07 CST 2016!
```

How It Works

The JavaServer Pages technology makes it easy to develop web pages that can utilize both static and dynamic web content by providing a set of tags and value expressions to expose dynamic Java fields to a web page. Using the JSP technology, a page developer can access the underlying JavaBeans classes to pass content between the client and the server. In the example within this recipe, a JSP page is used to display the current date and time, which is obtained from a JavaBean class on the server. Therefore, when a user visits the JSP page in a browser, the current time and date on the server will be displayed.

A JSP page should use a document extension of `.jsp` if it is a standard HTML-based JSP page. Other types of JSP pages contain different extensions; one of those is the JSP document type. A JSP document is an XML-based well-formed JSP page. You can learn more about JSP documents in Recipe 2-6. JSP pages can contain HTML markup, special JSP tags, page directives, JavaScript, embedded Java code, and more. This example contains the `<jsp:useBean>` tag, as well as a value expression to display the content of a field that is contained within the JavaBean. The `<jsp:useBean>` tag is used to include a reference to a Java class that will be referenced in the JSP page markup. In this case, the class that is referenced is named `org.javaee8recipes.chapter02.recipe02_01.DateBean`, and it will be referenced as `dateBean` within the page. For a full description of the `<jsp:useBean>` tag, reference Recipe 2-3.

```
<jsp:useBean id="dateBean" scope="application" class="org.javaee8recipes.chapter02.
recipe02_01.DateBean"/>
```

Since the `<jsp:useBean>` tag contains a reference to the `DateBean` Java class, the JSP page that includes the tag can use any public fields or methods that are contained within the class or private fields through public "getter" methods. This is demonstrated by using the Expression Language (EL) value expression, which is enclosed within the `${}` characters. To learn more about JSP EL expressions, see Recipe 2-4. In the example, the value of the JavaBean field named `currentDate` is displayed on the page. The value of the private field is retrieved automatically via the pubic "getter" method, `getCurrentDate`.

```
The current date is: ${dateBean.currentDate}!
```

LIFECYCLE OF A JSP PAGE

The lifecycle of a JSP page is very much the same as that of a Java servlet. This is because a JSP page is translated to a servlet (the `HttpJspBase` JSP servlet class) behind the scenes by a special servlet. When a request is sent to a JSP page, the special servlet checks to ensure that the JSP page's servlet is not older than the page itself. If it is, the JSP is retranslated into a servlet class and compiled. The JSP-to-servlet translation is automatic, which makes JSP very productive.

When a JSP page is translated, a servlet with a name such as `0002fjspname_jsp.java` is created, where `jspname` is the name of the JSP page. If errors result during the translation, they will be displayed when the JSP page response is displayed.

Different portions of the JSP page are treated differently during the translation to a Java servlet.

If the JSP page's servlet does not already exist, then the container does the following:

- Template data is translated into code.
- JSP scripting elements are inserted into the JSP page's servlet class.
- `<jsp:XXX .../>` elements are converted into method calls.

After translation, the lifecycle works similarly to the servlet lifecycle:

1. Loads the servlet class.
2. Instantiates the servlet class.
3. Initializes the servlet instance with a call to the `jspInit` method.

This recipe contains only beginning knowledge of what is possible with the JSP technology. To learn more regarding the technology and best practices when using JSP, continue reading the recipes in this chapter.

2-2. Embedding Java into a JSP Page

Problem

You want to embed some Java code into a standard JSP web page for dynamic content creation.

Solution

Use JSP scripting elements to embed Java code into the page and then display Java field content. The following JSP code demonstrates how to import the Java `Date` class and then use it to obtain the current date without using a server-side JavaBean class:

```
<%--
    Document   : recipe02_02
    Author     : juneau
--%>
```

```
<%@page import="java.util.Date"%>
<%@page contentType="text/html" pageEncoding="UTF-8"%>
<!DOCTYPE html>
<%! Date currDate = null; %>
<% currDate = new Date(); %>
<html>
    <head>
        <meta http-equiv="Content-Type" content="text/html; charset=UTF-8">
        <title>Recipe 2-2: Embedding Java into a JSP Page</title>
    </head>
    <body>
        <h1>Hello World!</h1>
        <br/>
        <br/>
        The current date and time is: <%= currDate %>

    </body>
</html>
```

This page will display the current system date from the server that hosts the JSP application.

How It Works

Using scripting elements within a JSP page allows you to embed Java code directly in a web page. However, it should be noted that this is not the best approach to web development. Scripting element programming used to be thought of as one of the best ways to code web applications using JSP technology. However, when it came time to perform maintenance activities on a JSP page or to introduce new developers to a code base that used scripting elements in JSP, nightmares ensued because in order to debug a problem, the developer had to search through scripts embedded within HTML, as well as Java classes themselves. Sometimes it is still nice to have the ability to embed Java code directly into a page, even if for nothing more than testing, so that is why I show how it is done in this recipe. A better approach would be to separate the business logic from the view code, which you saw in Recipe 2-1 and will also see in subsequent recipes.

In this example, the current date is pulled into the JSP page via the Java `Date` class. A new `Date` instance is assigned to a field that is named `currDate`. An `import` page directive is used to import the `java.util.Date` class into the JSP page using the following line:

```
<%@page import="java.util.Date"%>
```

The declaration of `currDate` is done within a declaration scripting element. Declaration scripting elements begin with the character sequence `<%!` and end with the character sequence `%>`. Excerpted from the example, the `currDate` field is declared in the following line of code:

```
<%! Date currDate = null; %>
```

Anything that is contained inside declarations goes directly to the `jspService()` method of the generated JSP servlet class, creating a global declaration for the entire servlet to use. Any variable or method can be declared within declarations' character sequences.

■ **Note** Declarations are executed only once for the JSP page, when it is initially converted into a servlet. If any code on the JSP page changes, it will be translated to a servlet again, and the declaration will be evaluated again at that time. If you want for code to be executed each time the JSP page is loaded by the browser, do not place it in a declaration.

In the example for this recipe, you can see that there are no JSP tags used to reference a server-side JavaBean class to create a new instance of the Date class, and that is because the instantiation is done right within the JSP code in between character sequences known as *scriptlets*, `<% %>`. Scriptlets basically have the same syntax as declarations, except that they do not include the exclamation point in the first character sequence. Scriptlets are used to embed any Java code that you want to have run each time the JSP is loaded, at request-processing time. At translation time, anything contained within a scriptlet is placed into a method named `_jspService` within the translated JSP servlet, and that method is executed with each request on the JSP page. Scriptlets are the most common place to use embedded Java in a JSP page. Since in this example you want the current date to be displayed each time the page is loaded, the new `Date` class is instantiated and assigned to the `currDate` variable within a scriptlet.

```
<% currDate = new Date(); %>
```

Later in the JSP page, the `currDate` field is displayed using an expression, which is enclosed using the <%= and %> character sequences. Expressions are used to display content, and anything that is contained within an expression is automatically converted to a string when a request is processed. After the string conversion, it is displayed as output on the page.

```
The current date and time is: <%= currDate %>
```

■ **Note** If the code within an expression is unable to be converted into a `String`, an exception will occur.

While embedding Java code in a JSP page is possible to do, it is frowned upon within the Java community since the Model-View-Controller (MVC) paradigm makes coding much cleaner. To learn more about coding JSP applications without using scripting elements, see the next example, Recipe 2-3.

2-3. Separating Business Logic from View Code

Problem

You want to separate the business logic from the code that is used to create a view within your web application.

Solution

Separate the business logic into a JavaBean class and use JSP tags to incorporate the logic into the view. In the following example, a JavaBean is referenced from within a JSP page, and one of the JavaBean fields is displayed on the page. Each time the page is refreshed, the field value is updated because the page calls the underlying JavaBean field's getter method, where the field is initialized.

The following JSP markup contains a reference to a JavaBean named RandomBean and displays a field from the bean on the page:

```
<%--
    Document   : recipe02_03
    Author     : juneau
--%>

<%@page contentType="text/html" pageEncoding="UTF-8"%>
<!DOCTYPE html>
<html>
    <head>
        <meta http-equiv="Content-Type" content="text/html; charset=UTF-8">
        <title>Recipe 2-3: Separating Business Logic from View Code</title>
    </head>
    <body>
        <jsp:useBean id="randomBean" scope="application" class="org.javaee8recipes.
        chapter02.recipe02_03.RandomBean"/>
        <h1>Display a Random Number</h1>
        <br/>
        <br/>
        <p>
            Your random number is ${randomBean.randomNumber}.  Refresh page to see another!
        </p>
    </body>
</html>
```

The next code is that of the JavaBean class referenced in the JSP code, known as RandomBean:

```
package org.javaee8recipes.chapter02.recipe02_03;

import java.util.Random;

/**
 * Recipe 2-3
 * @author juneau
 */
public class RandomBean {
    Random randomGenerator = new Random();
    private int randomNumber = 0;

    /**
     * @return the randomNumber
     */
    public int getRandomNumber() {
        randomNumber = randomGenerator.nextInt();
        return randomNumber;
    }

}
```

The resulting output for the page resembles the following, although the random number will be different every time the page is loaded:

```
Your random number is -1200578984. Refresh page to see another!
```

How It Works

Sometimes embedding Java code directly into a JSP page can be helpful, and it can satisfy the requirement. However, in most cases, it is a good idea to separate any Java code from markup code that is used to create the web view. Doing so makes maintenance easier, and it allows a page developer to focus on creating nice-looking web pages rather than wading through Java code. In some organizations, a Java developer can then write the server-side business logic code, and a web developer can focus on the view. In many organizations today, the same person is performing both tasks, and using the MVC methodology can help separate the logic and increase productivity.

In the early days of JSP, embedding Java directly into a JSP page was considered the best way to go, but as time went on, the MVC paradigm caught on, and JSP has been updated to follow suit. As a best practice, it is good to use JSP tags to separate Java code from page markup. In the example, the `<jsp:useBean>` element is used to reference a server-side JavaBean class so that the public fields and methods from that class, as well as private fields via public "getter" methods, can be incorporated into the JSP page. The `jsp:useBean` element requires that you provide an ID and a scope, along with a class name or a `beanName`. In the example, the `id` attribute is set to `randomBean`, and this `id` is used to reference the bean within the JSP page. The `scope` attribute is set to `application`, which means that the bean can be used from any JSP page within the application. Table 2-1 displays all the possible scopes and what they mean. The `class` attribute is set to the fully qualified name of the Java class that will be referenced via the name that is set with the `id` attribute, which in this case is `randomBean`.

Table 2-1. *jsp:useBean Element Scopes*

Scope	Description
`page` (default)	The bean can be used within the same JSP page that contains the `jsp:useBean` element.
`request`	The bean can be used from any JSP page processing the same request.
`session`	The bean can be used from any JSP page within the same session as the JSP page that contains the `jsp:useBean` element that created the bean. The page that creates the bean must have a page directive with `session="true"`.
`application`	The bean can be used from any JSP within the same application as the JSP page that created it.

After the `jsp:useBean` element has been added to a page, JavaBean properties can be used in the JSP page, and public methods can be called from the page. The example demonstrates how to display the value of a JavaBean property using the ${ } notation. Any variable that contains a "getter" and a "setter" method in the JavaBean can be accessed from a JSP page by referencing the class member field in between the ${ and } character sequences, better known as an Expression Language (EL) expression. To learn more about EL expressions, see Recipe 2-4. The following excerpt from the example demonstrates how to display the `randomNumber` field from the JavaBean:

```
Your random number is ${randomBean.randomNumber}. Refresh page to see another!
```

The key to separating business logic from view logic in the JSP technology is the `jsp:useBean` element. This will allow you to use JavaBean classes from within the JSP page, without embedding the code directly in the page. Separating business logic from view code can help make it easier to maintain code in the future and make the code easier to follow.

2-4. Yielding or Setting Values

Problem

You want to display values from a JavaBean in a JSP page. Furthermore, you want to have the ability to set values in a JSP page.

Solution

Expose the values from a JavaBean in a JSP page using EL expressions with the `${ bean.value }` syntax. In the following JSP code, a Java class by the name of `EasyBean` will be used to hold the value that is entered into a text field by a user. The value will then be read from the bean and displayed on the page using EL expressions.

The following code shows a JSP page that contains an input form and displays the value that is entered into the text box:

```
<%--
    Document   : recipe02_04
    Author     : juneau
--%>

<%@page contentType="text/html" pageEncoding="UTF-8"%>
<!DOCTYPE html>
<html>
    <head>
        <meta http-equiv="Content-Type" content="text/html; charset=UTF-8">
        <title>Recipe 2-4: Yielding or Setting Values</title>
    </head>
    <body>
        <jsp:useBean id="easyBean" scope="page" class="org.javaee8recipes.chapter02.
        recipe02_04.EasyBean"/>
        <jsp:setProperty name="easyBean" property="*"/>
        <form method="post">
        Use the input text box below to set the value, and then hit submit.
        <br/><br/>
        Set the field value:
        <input id="fieldValue" name="fieldValue" type="text" size="30"/>
        <br/>
        The value contained within the field is currently:
        <jsp:getProperty name="easyBean" property="fieldValue"/>

        <input type="submit">
        </form>
    </body>
</html>
```

Next, the JavaBean class, which is used to hold the value that is used by the page, looks like the following:

```
package org.javaee8recipes.chapter02.recipe02_04;

/**
 * Recipe 2-4: Yielding or Setting Values
 * @author juneau
 */
public class EasyBean implements java.io.Serializable {
    private String fieldValue;

    public EasyBean(){
        fieldValue = null;
    }

    /**
     * @return the fieldValue
     */
    public String getFieldValue() {
        return fieldValue;
    }

    /**
     * @param fieldValue the fieldValue to set
     */
    public void setFieldValue(String fieldValue) {
        this.fieldValue = fieldValue;
    }

}
```

This simple example demonstrates how to enter a value, "set" it into the JavaBean variable, and then display it on the page.

How It Works

Perhaps one of the most useful web constructs is the input form, which allows a user to enter information into text boxes or other input constructs on the page and submit them to a server for processing. JSP makes it easy to submit values from an HTML form, and it is equally easy to display data back onto a page. To do so, a field is declared in a Java class and accessor methods (aka, getters and setters) are provided so that other classes can save values to the field and obtain values that are currently stored in it. Sometimes Java classes that contain fields with accessor methods are referred to as JavaBean *classes*. The classes can also contain other methods that can be used to perform tasks, but it is a best practice to keep JavaBeans as simple as possible. JavaBean classes should also implement `java.io.Serializable` so that they can be easily stored as a byte stream and resurrected.

In the example for this recipe, a Java class named `EasyBean` contains a private field named `fieldValue`. The accessor methods `getFieldValue` and `setFieldValue` can be used to obtain and store the value in `fieldValue`, respectively. Those accessor methods are declared as public, and thus they can be used from another Java class or JSP page. The JSP page uses the `jsp:useBean` element to obtain a reference to the `EasyBean` class. The scope is set to `page` so that the class can be used only within the JSP page that contains the jsp:useBean element. Table 2-1, which can be found in the previous recipe, lists the different scopes available for use with the jsp:useBean element.

```
<jsp:useBean id="easyBean" scope="page" class="org.javaee8recipes.chapter02.recipe02_04.
EasyBean"/>
```

Next, an HTML form is defined in the JSP page with the POST method, and it contains an input field named fieldValue, which allows a user to enter a string of text that will be submitted as a request parameter when the form is submitted. Note that the form in the example does not have an action specified; this means that the same URL will be used for form submission, and the same JSP will be used for form submission and will be displayed again once the form is submitted. Since the JSP has a jsp:useBean element specified on the page, all request parameters will be sent to that bean when the page is submitted. The key to ensuring that the value entered into the fieldValue input text field is stored into the fieldValue variable within the Java class is using the jsp:setProperty element within the form. The jsp:setProperty element allows one or more properties to be set in a JavaBean class using the corresponding setter methods. In the example, <jsp:useBean> is used to instantiate the EasyBean Java class, and <jsp:setProperty> is used to set the value that is entered within the fieldValue input text box to the fieldValue variable within the EasyBean class. The jsp:setProperty name attribute must equal the value of the jsp:useBean id attribute. The jsp:setProperty property attribute can equal the name of the field within the Java class that you want to set in the bean, or it can be a wildcard * character to submit all input fields to the bean. The value attribute of jsp:setProperty can be used to specify a static value for the property. The following excerpt from the example shows how the jsp:setProperty tag is used:

```
<jsp:setProperty name="easyBean" property="*"/>
```

■ **Note** The ordering of the JSP elements is very important. <jsp:useBean> must come before <jsp:setProperty> because the jsp:useBean element is responsible for instantiating its corresponding Java class. Since the JSP page is executed from the top of the page downward, the bean would be unavailable for use to any elements prior to when jsp:useBean is specified.

When the user enters a value into the input field and submits the request, it is submitted as a request parameter to the Java class that corresponds to the jsp:useBean element for that page. There are a couple of different ways to display the data that has been populated in the JavaBean field. The example demonstrates how to use the jsp:getProperty element to display the value of the fieldValue variable. The <jsp:getProperty> element must specify a name attribute, which corresponds to the id of the Java class that was specified within the jsp:useBean element. It must also specify a property attribute, which corresponds to the name of the JavaBean property that you want to display. The following excerpt from the example demonstrates the use of the jsp:getProperty tag:

```
<jsp:getProperty name="easyBean" property="fieldValue"/>
```

It is also possible to display the value of a JavaBean property using EL expressions, using the id of specified in the jsp:useBean element, along with the property name. To try this, you can replace the jsp:getProperty element with the following EL expression:

```
${easyBean.fieldValue}
```

The JSP framework makes the development of web applications using Java technology much easier than using servlets. Input forms such as the one demonstrated in this example show how much more productive JSP is compared to standard servlet coding. As with anything, both servlets and JSP technology have their place in your toolbox. For creating simple data entry forms, JSP definitely takes the cake.

2-5. Invoking a Function in a Conditional Expression

Problem

You want to use a Java function to perform a conditional evaluation within your JSP. However, you do not want to embed Java code into your JSP page.

Solution

Code the function in a JavaBean class and then register the bean with the JSP via the `<jsp:useBean>` tag. You will then need to register the function within a tag library descriptor (TLD) so that it can be made usable on the JSP page via a tag. Finally, set up a page directive for the TLD in which the function is registered, and use the function tag within the page. In the example that follows, a JSP page will use a function to tell the user whether a given Java type is a primitive type. The user will enter a string value into a text box, and that value will be submitted to a JavaBean field. The contents of the field will then be compared against a list of Java primitive types to determine whether it is a match. If the value entered into the field is a primitive, a message will be displayed to the user.

The following code is the Java class that contains the implementation of the function, which is going to be used from within the JSP. The bean also contains a field that will be used from the JSP page for setting and getting the value that is entered by the user.

```
package org.javaee8recipes.chapter02.recipe02_05;

/**
 * Recipe 2-5: Invoking a Function in a Conditional Expression
 * @author juneau
 */
public class ConditionalClass implements java.io.Serializable {
    private String typename = null;
    public static String[] javaTypes = new String[8];

    public ConditionalClass(){
        javaTypes[0] = "byte";
        javaTypes[1] = "short";
        javaTypes[2] = "int";
        javaTypes[3] = "long";
        javaTypes[4] = "float";
        javaTypes[5] = "double";
        javaTypes[6] = "boolean";
        javaTypes[7] = "char";
    }

    public static boolean isPrimitive(String value){
        boolean returnValue = false;
        for(int x=0; x<=javaTypes.length-1; x++){
```

```
            if(javaTypes[x].equalsIgnoreCase(value)){
                returnValue = true;
            }
        }
        return returnValue;
    }

    /**
     * @return the typename
     */
    public String getTypename() {
        return typename;
    }

    /**
     * @param typename the typename to set
     */
    public void setTypename(String typename) {
        this.typename = typename;
    }
}
```

The field typename will be used from the JSP page to set the value that is entered by the user and to retrieve it for passing to the function named isPrimitive();, which is used to compare the given value to a list of Java primitives. Next is a listing of the TLD that is used to register the function so that it can be used as a tag within the JSP. For simplicity, the TLD file is named functions.tld.

```
<?xml version="1.0" encoding="UTF-8"?>
<taglib version="2.1" xmlns="http://java.sun.com/xml/ns/javaee"     xmlns:xsi="http://
www.w3.org/2001/XMLSchema-instance" xsi:schemaLocation="http://java.sun.com/xml/ns/javaee
http://java.sun.com/xml/ns/javaee/web-jsptaglibrary_2_1.xsd">
    <tlib-version>1.0</tlib-version>
    <short-name>fct</short-name>
    <uri>functions</uri>
    <function>
        <name>isPrimitive</name>
        <function-class>org.javaee8recipes.chapter02.recipe02_05.ConditionalClass</function-
class>
        <function-signature>boolean isPrimitive(java.lang.String)</function-signature>
    </function>
</taglib>
```

Last is the JSP code that contains the page directive for using the TLD and the conditional call to the function isPrimitive() via a tag:

```
<%--
    Document   : recipe02_05
    Author     : juneau
--%>
```

```
<%@page contentType="text/html" pageEncoding="UTF-8"%>
<!DOCTYPE html>
<%@ taglib uri="http://java.sun.com/jsp/jstl/core"
     prefix="c" %>
<%@ taglib uri="/WEB-INF/tlds/functions.tld" prefix="fct" %>
<html>
    <head>
        <meta http-equiv="Content-Type" content="text/html; charset=UTF-8">
        <title>Recipe 2-5: Invoking a Function in an Expression</title>
    </head>
    <body>

        <form method="get">
            <p>Name one of the primitive Java types:
                <input type="text" id="typename" name="typename" size="40"/>
            </p>
            <br/>
            <input type="submit">
        </form>
        <jsp:useBean id="conditionalBean" scope="page" class="org.javaee8recipes.chapter02.
        recipe02_05.ConditionalClass"/>
        <jsp:setProperty name="conditionalBean" property="typename"/>
        <c:if test="${fct:isPrimitive(conditionalBean.typename)}" >
            ${ conditionalBean.typename } is a primitive type.
        </c:if>

        <c:if test="${conditionalBean.typename ne null and !fct:isPrimitive(conditionalBean.
        typename)}" >
            ${ conditionalBean.typename } is not a primitive type.
        </c:if>
    </body>
</html>
```

Following the strategy used in this solution, you can create a conditional test that is usable via a JSP tag for your pages.

How It Works

You need to take a few different steps before a Java function can become accessible from a JSP page. One of the most commonly overlooked conditions is that the function must be declared with a `static` modifier in the Java class. In the example for this recipe, the function `isPrimitive` is declared as `static`, and it returns a boolean value indicating whether the user types the name of a Java primitive type.

The next step toward making a function accessible via a JSP page is to register it with a TLD. In the example, a TLD named `functions.tld` is created. If there is already a custom TLD in your application, then you could register the function with it rather than creating an additional one if you want. The TLD in this example has a `short-name` attribute of `fct`, which will be used from within JSP tags. To actually register the function, you must create a `function` element within the TLD, provide a function name, indicate the class that the function resides within, and, finally, specify the function signature.

```
<function>
    <name>isPrimitive</name>
    <function-class>org.javaee8recipes.chapter02.recipe02_05.ConditionalClass</function-class>
    <function-signature>boolean isPrimitive(java.lang.String)</function-signature>
</function>
```

The function is now ready for use within the JSP. To make the function accessible via the JSP, register the TLD that contains the function element by including a `taglib` directive specifying the `uri` and prefix for the TLD. The `uri` is the path to the TLD, and the prefix should match the name given in the `short-name` element of the TLD. The following excerpt from the JSP in this example shows the `taglib` directive:

```
<%@ taglib uri="/WEB-INF/tlds/functions.tld" prefix="fct" %>
```

The function will now be accessible via an EL expression within the JSP by specifying the `taglib` prefix along with the name of the function as it is registered in the TLD. The EL expression in the example calls the function, passing the `typename` parameter. The `isPrimitive` function is used to determine whether the text contained within the `typename` bean field is equal to one of the Java primitive types.

```
<c:if test="${fct:isPrimitive(conditionalBean.typename)}" >
```

The solution in this recipe also uses the Java Standard Tag Library (JSTL) core. Depending on the server environment being used, this may be a separate download. The JSTL provides an extension to the standard set of tags provided with the JSP API. For more information regarding JSTL, refer to the online documentation, which can be found at `www.oracle.com/technetwork/java/index-jsp-135995.html`.

The JSTL `<c:if>` tag can be used to test conditions, executing the markup between its opening and closing tags if the condition test returns a `true` value. Not surprisingly, the `<c:if>` tag includes a `test` attribute that specifies an EL expression that indicates the test that needs to be performed. In the example, the `isPrimitive` function is called within the EL expression, passing the bean value. If the test returns a true, then a message is printed indicating that the given value is equal to a Java primitive type. Another `<c:if>` test follows the first in the example, and this time it tests to ensure that the property value is not equal to `null` and that it is not a Java primitive type. Expression Language is used to determine whether the property value is equal to `null` via the `ne` expression. The `and` expression ties the first and second conditional expressions together within the EL expression, meaning that both of the expressions must evaluate to a `true` value in order for the condition to be met. If both conditions are met, then the value specified by the user is not a Java primitive type, and a corresponding message is printed.

```
<c:if test="${conditionalBean.typename ne null and !fct:isPrimitive(conditionalBean.
typename)}" >
            ${ conditionalBean.typename } is not a primitive type.
</c:if>
```

It takes only a few easy steps to create a conditional function for use within JSPs. First, in the JavaBean class, you must create a public static function, which returns a boolean value. Second, create a TLD, which will make the function available via a JSP tag. Lastly, use the custom tag from within the JSP page along with JSTL conditional test tags to display the content conditionally.

2-6. Creating a JSP Document

Problem

Rather than using standard HTML format, you want to ensure that your JSP code follows the XML standard and contains only valid HTML and JSP tags.

Solution

Create a JSP document rather than a standard JSP. A JSP document is an XML-based representation of a standard JSP document that conforms to the XML standard. The following JSP document contains the same code that is used in the JSP code for Recipe 2-5, but it uses the JSP document format instead. As you can see, not much is different because well-formed tags were already used to create the standard JSP document. The page is also saved with an extension of jspx rather than jsp.

```
<!--
    Document   : recipe02_06
    Author     : juneau
-->
<html xmlns:jsp="http://java.sun.com/JSP/Page" version="2.0"
      xmlns:c="http://java.sun.com/jsp/jstl/core"
      xmlns:fct="/WEB-INF/tlds/functions.tld">

    <jsp:directive.page contentType="text/html" pageEncoding="UTF-8"/>

    <body>
        <form method="get">
            <p>Name one of the primitive Java types:
                <input type="text" id="typename" name="typename" size="40"/>
            </p>
            <br/>
            <input type="submit"/>
        </form>
        <jsp:useBean id="conditionalBean" scope="request" class="org.javaee8recipes.
        chapter02.recipe02_05.ConditionalClass"/>
        <jsp:setProperty name="conditionalBean" property="typename"
                         value="${param.typename}" />
        <c:if test="${fct:isPrimitive(conditionalBean.typename)}" >
            ${ conditionalBean.typename } is a primitive type.
        </c:if>

        <c:if test="${fn.length(conditionalBean.typename) > 0 and !fct:isPrimitive(condition
        alBean.typename)}" >
            ${ conditionalBean.typename } is not a primitive type.
        </c:if>

    </body>
</html>
```

This JSP document will yield the same output as the one in Recipe 2-5. However, a well-formed document will be enforced, and this will exclude the use of scripting elements within the page.

How It Works

As foreshadowed in Recipe 2-3, separating business logic from markup code can be important for many reasons. Standard JSP pages can adhere to the MVC paradigm, but they are not forced into doing so. Sometimes it makes sense to enforce the separation of business logic, by strictly adhering to a well-formed XML document using only JSP tags to work with server-side Java classes. Well-formed means that there should be only one root element, and each starting tag must have a corresponding ending tag. Creating a JSP document is one answer because such documents enforce well-formed XML and do not allow scripting elements to be used within the JSP page. It is still possible to display the value of scripting expressions in the body of a JSP document using the `<jsp:expression/>` tag or value expressions, as demonstrated in Recipe 2-8.

Several JSP tags can be used to communicate with Java classes, perform JSP-specific functionality, and make markup easy to follow. As such, modern JSP-based applications should use well-formed JSP documents utilizing such JSP tags, rather than embedding scripting elements throughout markup. Table 2-2 describes what the different JSP tags do.

Table 2-2. *JSP Tags*

Tag	Description
`<jsp:attribute>`	Defines attributes for a JSP page.
`<jsp:body>`	Defines an element body.
`<jsp:declaration>`	Defines page declarations.
`<jsp:directive>`	Defines page includes and page directives.
`<jsp:doBody>`	Executes the body of the JSP tag that is used by the calling JSP page to invoke the tag.
`<jsp:element>`	Generates an XML element dynamically.
`<jsp:expression>`	Inserts the value of a scripting language expression, converted into a string.
`<jsp:forward>`	Forwards a request to another page. The new page can be HTML, JSP, or servlet.
`<jsp:getProperty>`	Obtains the value of a bean property and places it in the page.
`<jsp:include>`	Includes another JSP or web resource in the page.
`<jsp:invoke>`	Invokes a specified JSP fragment.
`<jsp:output>`	Specifies the document type declaration.
`<jsp:plugin>`	Executes an applet or bean with the specified plug-in.
`<jsp:root>`	Defines standard elements and tag library namespaces.
`<jsp:scriptlet>`	Embeds code fragments into a page if necessary.
`<jsp:setProperty>`	Sets specified value(s) into a bean property.
`<jsp:text>`	Encloses template data.
`<jsp:useBean>`	References and instantiates (if needed) a JavaBean class using a name and providing a scope.

Creating a well-formed JSP can lead to easier development, ease of maintenance, and better overall design. Since it is so important, the remaining recipes in this chapter use the JSP document format.

2-7. Embedding Expressions in EL

Problem

You want to use some conditional expressions and/or arithmetic within your JSP without embedding Java code using scripting elements.

Solution

Use EL expressions within JSP tags to perform conditional and/or arithmetic expressions. This solution will look at two examples of EL expressions. The first example demonstrates how to perform conditional logic using EL expressions. Note that the JSTL tag library is also used in this case, to conditionally display a message on the page if the expression results to true.

```
<!--
    Document   : recipe02_07a
    Author     : juneau
-->
<html xmlns:jsp="http://java.sun.com/JSP/Page"
      xmlns:c="http://java.sun.com/jsp/jstl/core"
      version="2.0">

    <jsp:directive.page contentType="text/html" pageEncoding="UTF-8"/>
    <head>
        <title>Recipe 2-7: Embedding Expressions in EL</title>
    </head>
    <body>
        <h1>Conditional Expressions</h1>
        <p>
            The following portion of the page will only display conditional
            expressions which result in a true value.
        </p>
        <c:if test="${1 + 1 == 2}">
            The conditional expression (1 + 1 == 2) results in TRUE.
            <br/>
        </c:if>

        <c:if test="${'x' == 'y'}">
            The conditional expression (x == y) results in TRUE.
            <br/>
        </c:if>

        <c:if test="${(100/10) gt 5}">
            The conditional expression ((100/10) > 5) results in TRUE.
            <br/>
        </c:if>

        <c:if test="${20 mod 3 eq 2}">
            The conditional expression (20 mod 3 eq 2) results in TRUE.
            <br/>
```

```
        </c:if>
    </body>
</html>
```

This JSP page will result in the following output being displayed:

```
...
The conditional expression (1 + 1 == 2) results in TRUE.
The conditional expression ((100/10) > 5) results in TRUE.
The conditional expression (20 mod 3 eq 2) results in TRUE.
...
```

Arithmetic expressions can also be evaluated using EL. The following JSP code demonstrates some examples of using arithmetic within EL:

```
<!--
    Document   : recipe02_07b
    Author     : juneau
-->
<html xmlns:jsp="http://java.sun.com/JSP/Page"
      xmlns:c="http://java.sun.com/jsp/jstl/core"
      version="2.0">

    <jsp:directive.page contentType="text/html" pageEncoding="UTF-8"/>
    <head>
        <title>Recipe 2-7: Embedding Expressions in EL</title>
    </head>
    <body>
        <jsp:useBean id="expBean" class="org.javaee8recipes.chapter02.recipe02_07.Expressions"/>
        <h1>Arithmetic Expressions</h1>
        <p>
            The following expressions demonstrate how to perform arithmetic using EL.
        </p>
        10 - 4 = ${10 - 4}
        <br/>
        85 / 15 = ${85 / 15}
        <br/>
        847 divided by 6 = ${847 div 6}
        <br/>
        ${expBean.num1} * ${expBean.num2} = ${expBean.num1 * expBean.num2}

    </body>

</html>
```

The preceding JSP will result in the following output being displayed:

```
...
10 - 4 = 6
85 / 15 = 5.666666666666667
847 divided by 6 = 141.16666666666666
5 * 634.324 = 3171.62
...
```

How It Works

The JSP technology makes it easy to work with expressions. Conditional page rendering can be performed using a combination of EL value expressions, which are enclosed within the ${ } character sequences and JSTL tags. Arithmetic expressions can also be performed using EL expressions. To make things easier, the Expression Language contains keywords or characters that can be used to help form expressions. The example for this recipe contains various expressions and conditional page rendering using the JSTL `<c:if>` tag.

In the first JSP page displayed in the example, there are some examples of conditional page rendering. To use the `<c:if>` tag to perform the conditional tests, you must be sure to import the JSTL tag library with the JSP page. To do so, add an `import` for the JSTL tag library and assign it to a character or string of characters. In the following excerpt from the recipe, the JSTL library is assigned to the character `c`:

```
<html xmlns:jsp="http://java.sun.com/JSP/Page"
      xmlns:c="http://java.sun.com/jsp/jstl/core"
      version="2.0">
```

An EL value expression is contained within the ${ and } character sequences. Anything within these characters will be treated as EL, and as such, the syntax must be correct, or the JSP page will not be able to compile into a servlet, and it will throw an error. All expressions using the ${ } syntax are evaluated immediately, and they are read-only expressions. That is, no expressions using this syntax can be used to set values into a JavaBean property. The JSP engine first evaluates the expression, and then it converts into a `String` and lastly returns the value to the tag handler. Four types of objects can be referenced within a value expression. Those are JavaBean components, collections, enumerated types, and implicit objects. If using a JavaBean component, the JavaBean must be registered with the JSP page using the `jsp:useBean` element (see Recipe 2-3 for details). Collections or enumerated types can also be referenced from a JavaBean that has been registered with the page. Implicit objects are those that allow access to page context, scoped variables, and other such objects. Table 2-3 lists different implicit objects that can be referenced from within EL expressions.

Table 2-3. *Implicit JSP Objects*

Object	Type	Description
`pageContext`	Context	Provides access to the context of the page and various subobjects
`servletContext`	Page context	Context for JSP page servlet and web components
`session`	Page context	Session object for the client
`request`	Page context	Request that invoked the execution of the page
`response`	Page context	Response that is returned by the JSP
`param`	N/A	Responsible for mapping parameter names to values
`paramValues`	N/A	Maps request parameter to an array of values
`header`	N/A	Responsible for mapping a header name to a value
`headerValues`	N/A	Maps header name to an array of values
`cookie`	N/A	Maps a cookie name to a single cookie
`initParam`	N/A	Maps a context initialization parameter to a value
`pageScope`	Scope	Maps page scope variables
`requestScope`	Scope	Maps request scope variables
`sessionScope`	Scope	Maps session scope variables
`applicationScope`	Scope	Maps application scope variables

The following are some examples of expressions that use JavaBean components, collections, enumerated types, and implicit objects:

```
// Displays the value of a variable named myVar within a JavaBean referenced as elTester
${ elTester.myVar }
// Does the same thing as the line above
${ elTester["myVar"] }

// Evaluates an Enumerated Type in which myEnum is an instance of MyEnum
${ myEnum == "myValue" }
// Reference a getter method of the Enum named getTestVal()
${ myEnum.testVal}

// References a collection named myCollection within the JavaBean referenced as elTester
${ elTester.myCollection }

// Obtain the parameter named "testParam"
${ param.testParam }  // Same as: request.getParameter("testParam")
// Obtain session attribute named "testAttr"
${ sessionScope.testAttr } // Same as: session.getAttribute("testAttr")
```

In the recipe example, the `<c:if>` tag is used to test a series of value expressions and conditionally display page content. The test attribute of `<c:if>` is used to register a test condition, and if the test condition returns a `true` result, then the content contained between the `<c:if>` starting and ending tags is displayed. The following excerpt from the example demonstrates how a test is performed:

```
<c:if test="${'x' == 'y'}">
        The conditional expression (x == y) results in TRUE.
        <br/>
   </c:if>
```

EL expressions can contain a series of reserved words that can be used to help evaluate the expression. For instance, the following expression utilizes the `gt` reserved word to return a value indicating whether the value returned from the calculation of 100/10 is greater than 5:

```
<c:if test="${(100/10) gt 5}">
        The conditional expression ((100/10) > 5) results in TRUE.
        <br/>
</c:if>
```

Table 2-4 lists all the JSP EL expression reserved words and their meanings.

Table 2-4. *EL Expression Reserved Words*

Reserved Word	Description
`and`	Combines expressions and returns `true` if all of them evaluate to `true`
`or`	Combines expressions and returns `true` if one of them evaluates to `true`
`not`	Negates an expression
`eq`	Equal
`ne`	Not equal
`lt`	Less than
`gt`	Greater than
`le`	Less than or equal
`ge`	Greater than or equal
`true`	True value
`false`	False value
`null`	Null value
`instanceof`	Used to test whether an object is an instance of another object
`empty`	Determines whether a list or collection is empty
`div`	Divided by
`mod`	Modulus

Arithmetic expressions are demonstrated by the second example in this recipe. The following arithmetic operators can be utilized within expressions:

- + (addition), - (binary and unary), * (multiplication), / and `div` (division), %, and `mod` (modulus)
- `and`, `&&`, `or`, `||`, `not`, `!`
- `==`, `!=`, `<`, `>`, `<=`, `>=`
- `X ? Y : Z` (ternary conditional)

Entire chapters of books have been written on the use of EL expressions within JSPs. This recipe only touches on the possibilities of using value expressions. The best way to get used to expressions is to create a test JSP page and experiment with the different options that are available.

2-8. Accessing Parameters in Multiple Pages

Problem

You want to access a parameter from within multiple pages of your web application.

Solution

Create an input form to submit parameters to the request object, and then utilize the request object to retrieve the values in another page. In the example that follows, a JSP page that contains an input form is used to pass values to another JSP page by setting the HTML form action attribute to the value of the JSP page that will utilize the parameters. In the case of this example, the receiving JSP page merely displays the parameter values, but other work could be performed as well.

The following JSP code demonstrates the use of an input form to save parameters into the request object and pass them to a page named recipe02_08b.jspx:

```
<!--
    Document   : recipe02_08a
    Author     : juneau
-->
<html xmlns:jsp="http://java.sun.com/JSP/Page"
      xmlns:c="http://java.sun.com/jsp/jstl/core"
      version="2.0">

    <jsp:directive.page contentType="text/html" pageEncoding="UTF-8"/>
    <head>
        <title>Recipe 2-8: Accessing Parameters in Multiple Pages </title>
    </head>
    <body>

        <h1>Passing Parameters</h1>
        <p>
            The following parameters will be passed to the next JSP.
        </p>
        <form method="get" action="recipe02_08b.jspx">
        Param 1: <input id="param1" name="param1" type="text" value="1"/>
        <br/>
        Param 2: <input id="param2" name="param2" type="text" value="2 + 0"/>
        <br/>
        Param 3: <input id="param3" name="param3" type="text" value="three"/>
        <br/>
        <input type="submit" value="Go to next page"/>
        </form>
    </body>

</html>
```

The next JSP code receives the parameters and displays their values:

```
<!--
    Document   : recipe02_08b
    Author     : juneau
-->
<html xmlns:jsp="http://java.sun.com/JSP/Page"
      xmlns:c="http://java.sun.com/jsp/jstl/core"
      version="2.0">

    <jsp:directive.page contentType="text/html" pageEncoding="UTF-8"/>
    <head>
        <title>Recipe 2-8: Accessing Parameters in Multiple Pages </title>
    </head>
    <body>

        <h1>Passing Parameters</h1>
        <p>
            The following parameters will were passed from the original JSP.
        </p>
        <form method="post" action="recipe02_08a.jspx">
        Param 1: <jsp:expression>request.getParameter("param1") </jsp:expression>
        <br/>
        Param 2: <jsp:expression> request.getParameter("param2") </jsp:expression>
        <br/>
        Param 3: <jsp:expression> request.getParameter("param3") </jsp:expression>
        <br/>
        OR using value expressions
        <br/>
        Param 1: ${ param.param1 }
        <br/>
        Param 2: ${ param.param2 }
        <br/>
        Param 3: ${ param.param3 }
        <br/>

        <input type="submit" value="Back to Page 1"/>
        </form>
    </body>

</html>
```

As you can see, a couple of variations can be used to display the parameter values. Both of the variations will display the same result.

How It Works

Request parameters are one of the most useful features of web applications. When a user enters some data into a web form and submits the form, the request contains the parameters that were entered into the form. Parameters can also be statically embedded in a web page or concatenated onto a URL and sent to a receiving servlet or JSP page. The data contained in request parameters can then be inserted into a database, redisplayed on another JSP page, used to perform a calculation, or a myriad of other possibilities. The JSP technology provides an easy mechanism for using request parameters in other JSP pages, and the example in this recipe demonstrates how to do just that.

■ **Note** Request parameters are always translated into `String` values.

Note that in the example, the first JSP page uses a simple HTML form to obtain values from a user and submit them to the request. Another JSP page named `recipe02_08b.jspx` is set as the form action attribute, so when the form is submitted, it will send the request to `recipe02_08b.jspx`. The input fields on the first JSP page specify both an `id` attribute and a `name` attribute, although only the `name` attribute is required. The name that is given to the input fields is the name that will be used to reference the value entered into it as a request parameter.

■ **Note** It is a good programming practice to always include an `id` attribute. The ID is useful for performing work with the DOM and for referencing elements via a scripting language such as JavaScript.

The receiving action, `recipe02_08b.jspx` in this example, can make a call to `response.getParameter()`, passing the name of a parameter (input field name) to obtain the value that was entered into its corresponding text field. To adhere to JSP document standards, the scriptlet containing the call to `response.getParameter()` must be enclosed in `<jsp:expression>` tags. The following excerpt demonstrates how this is done:

```
Param 1: <jsp:expression>request.getParameter("param1") </jsp:expression>
```

Optionally, an EL expression can contain a reference to the implicit `param` object and obtain the request parameter in the same way. When the expression `${param.param1}` is called, it is evaluated by the JSP engine, and it is translated into `response.getParameter("param1")`. The following excerpt demonstrates this use of EL expressions:

```
Param 1: ${ param.param1 }
```

Either technique will perform the same task; the named request parameter will be obtained and displayed on the page.

2-9. Creating a Custom JSP Tag

Problem

You want to create a JSP tag that provides custom functionality for your application.

Solution

Create a custom JSP tag using JSP 2.0 *simple tag support*. Suppose you want to create a custom tag that will insert a signature into the JSP where the tag is placed. The custom tag will print a default signature, but it will also accept an `authorName` attribute, which will include a given author's name to the signature if provided. To get started, you'll need to define a Java class that extends the SimpleTagSupport class. This class will provide the implementation for your tag. The following code is the implementation for a class named Signature, which provides the implementation for the custom tag.

■ **Note** To compile the following code, you need to add javax.servlet.jsp-api.jar to classpath:

```
cd recipe02_09

javac -cp ...\glassfish\modules\javax.servlet.jsp-api.jar *.java
```

```
package org.javaee8recipes.chapter02.recipe02_09;

import javax.servlet.jsp.JspException;
import javax.servlet.jsp.JspWriter;
import javax.servlet.jsp.PageContext;
import javax.servlet.jsp.tagext.SimpleTagSupport;

/**
 * Recipe 2-9: Creating a Custom JSP Tag
 * @author juneau
 */
public class Signature extends SimpleTagSupport {

    private String authorName = null;

    /**
     * @param authorName the authorName to set
     */
    public void setAuthorName(String authorName) {
        this.authorName = authorName;
    }

    @Override
    public void doTag() throws JspException {
        PageContext pageContext = (PageContext) getJspContext();
        JspWriter out = pageContext.getOut();

        try {
            if(authorName != null){
                out.println("Written by " + authorName);
                out.println("<br/>");
            }
            out.println("Published by Apress");

        } catch (Exception e) {
            System.out.println(e);
        }

    }
}
```

Next, a TLD needs to be created to map the `Signature` class tag implementation to a tag. The TLD that includes the custom tag mapping is listed here:

```
<?xml version="1.0" encoding="UTF-8"?>
<taglib version="2.1" xmlns="http://java.sun.com/xml/ns/javaee" xmlns:xsi="http://www.
w3.org/2001/XMLSchema-instance" xsi:schemaLocation="http://java.sun.com/xml/ns/javaee
http://java.sun.com/xml/ns/javaee/web-jsptaglibrary_2_1.xsd">
  <tlib-version>1.0</tlib-version>
  <short-name>cust</short-name>
  <uri>custom</uri>
  <tag>
   <name>signature</name>
   <tag-class>org.javaee8recipes.chapter02.recipe02_09.Signature</tag-class>
   <body-content>empty</body-content>
   <attribute>
       <name>authorName</name>
       <rtexprvalue>true</rtexprvalue>
       <required>false</required>
    </attribute>
 </tag>
</taglib>
```

Once the class implementation and the TLD are in place, the tag can be used from within a JSP page. The following JSP code is an example of using the custom tag on a page:

```
<!--
    Document   : recipe02_09
    Author     : juneau
-->
<html xmlns:jsp="http://java.sun.com/JSP/Page"
      xmlns:c="http://java.sun.com/jsp/jstl/core"
      xmlns:cust="custom"
      version="2.0">

    <jsp:directive.page contentType="text/html" pageEncoding="UTF-8"/>
    <head>
        <title>Recipe 2-9: Creating a Custom JSP Tag</title>
    </head>
    <body>

        <h1>Custom JSP Tag</h1>
        <p>
            The custom JSP tag is used as the footer for this page.
            <br/>
        </p>
        <cust:signature authorName="Josh Juneau"/>

    </body>

</html>
```

The custom tag output will now be displayed in place of the `cust:signature` element on the JSP page.

How It Works

One of the most useful new features of JSP 2.0 was the inclusion of the `SimpleTagSupport` class, which provides an easy way for developers to create custom tags. Prior to the 2.0 release, custom tag creation took a good deal of more work, because the developer had to provide much more code to implement the tag within the tag's implementation class. The `SimpleTagSupport` class takes care of much implementation for the developer so that the only thing left to do is implement the `doTag` method in order to provide an implementation for the custom tag.

In the example for this recipe, a custom tag is created that will print a signature on the JSP page in the position where the tag is located. To create a custom tag implementation, create a Java class that will extend the `SimpleTagSupport` class, and provide an implementation for the `doTag` method. The example class also contains a field named `authorName`, which will be mapped within the TLD as an attribute for the custom tag. In the `doTag` method, a handle on the JSP page context is obtained by calling the `getJspContext` method. `getJspContext` is a custom method that is implemented for you in `SimpleTagSupport` and makes it easy to get a hold of the JSP page context. Next, to provide the ability to write to the JSP output, a handle is obtained on the `JspWriter` by calling `PageContext`'s `getOut` method.

```
PageContext pageContext = (PageContext) getJspContext();
JspWriter out = pageContext.getOut();
```

The next lines within `doTag` provide the implementation for writing to the JSP output via a series of calls to `out.println`. Any content that is passed to `out.println` will be displayed on the page. Note that in the example, the `authorName` field is checked to see whether it contains a `null` value. If it does not contain a `null` value, then it is displayed on the page; otherwise, it is omitted. Therefore, if the tag within the JSP page contains a value for the `authorName` attribute, then it will be printed on the page. The `out.println` code is contained within a `try-catch` block in case any exceptions occur.

■ **Note** To allow your tag to accept scriptlets, you will need to use the *classic tag handlers*. The classic tag handlers existed before the JSP 2.0 era and can still be used today alongside the simple tag handlers. The simple tag handlers revolve around the `doTag()` method, whereas the classic tag handlers deal with a `doStartTag()` method and a `doEndTag()` method, as well as others. Since the simple tag handlers can be used alongside the classic tag handlers, it is possible to use some of the more complex classic tag methods, while utilizing simple tag methods in the same application. This eases the transition from the classic tag handlers to the simple tag handlers. For more information regarding the differences between the two APIs, see some online documentation by searching for the keywords *Simple vs. Classic Tag Handlers*.

That's it; the implementation for the tag is complete. To map the implementation class to the Document Object Model (DOM) via a tag name, a TLD must contain a mapping to the class. In the example, a TLD is created named `custom.tld`, and it contains the mapping for the class. The `short-name` element specifies the name that must be used within the JSP page to reference the tag. The `uri` element specifies the name of the TLD, and it is used from within the JSP page to reference the TLD file itself. The meat of the TLD is contained within the `tag` element. The `name` element is used to specify the name for the tag, and it will be used within a JSP page in combination with the `short-name` element to provide the complete tag name. The `tag-class` element provides the name of the class that implements the tag, and `body-content` specifies a value to indicate whether the body content for the JSP page will be made available for the tag implementation class. It is set to `empty` for this example. To specify an attribute for the tag, the `attribute` element must be added to the TLD, including the `name`, `rtexprvalue`, and `required` elements. The `name` element of attribute specifies the name of the attribute, rtexprvalue indicates whether the attribute can contain an EL expression, and required indicates whether the attribute is required.

To use the tag in a JSP page, the custom.tld TLD must be mapped to the page within the <html> element in a JSP document or a taglib directive within a standard JSP. The following lines show the difference between these two:

```
<!—JSP Document syntax -->
<html
xmlns:cust="custom"
. . .(more taglib directives) . . .>

<!—JSP syntax -->
<%@taglib prefix="cust" uri="custom" %>
```

To use the tag within the page, simply specify the TLD short-name along with the mapping name for the tag implementation and any attributes you want to provide.

```
<cust:signature authorName="Josh Juneau"/>
```

Creating custom tags within JSP is easier than it was in the past. Custom tags provide developers with the ability to define custom actions and/or content that can be made accessible from within a JSP page via a tag rather than scriptlets. Custom tags help developers follow the MVC architecture, separating code from business logic.

2-10. Including Other JSPs into a Page

Problem

Rather than coding the same header or footer into each JSP, you want to place the content for those page sections into a separate JSP page and then pull them into JSP pages by reference.

Solution

Use the <jsp:include> tag to embed other static or dynamic pages in your JSP page. The following example demonstrates the inclusion of two JSP pages within another. One of the JSP pages is used to formulate the header of the page, and another is used for the footer. The following page demonstrates the main JSP page, which includes two others using the <jsp:include> tag. The JSPX files named recipe02_10-header.jspx and recipe02_10-footer.jspx are included in the body of the main JSP page in order to provide the header and footer sections of the page.

```
<html xmlns:jsp="http://java.sun.com/JSP/Page"
      xmlns:c="http://java.sun.com/jsp/jstl/core"
      version="2.0">

    <jsp:directive.page contentType="text/html" pageEncoding="UTF-8"/>
    <head>
        <title>Recipe 2-10: Including Other JSPs into a Page</title>
    </head>
```

```
    <body>
        <jsp:include page="recipe02_10-header.jspx" />
        <h1>This is the body of the main JSP.</h1>
        <p>
            Both the header and footer for this page were created as separate JSPs.
        </p>
        <jsp:include page="recipe02_10-footer.jspx"/>

    </body>

</html>
```

Next is the JSP code that comprises the page header. It's nothing fancy but is a separate JSP page nonetheless.

```
<html xmlns:jsp="http://java.sun.com/JSP/Page" version="2.0">

    <jsp:directive.page contentType="text/html" pageEncoding="UTF-8"/>

    <p>This is the page header</p>
</html>
```

The following JSP code makes up the page footer:

```
<html xmlns:jsp="http://java.sun.com/JSP/Page" version="2.0">

    <jsp:directive.page contentType="text/html" pageEncoding="UTF-8"/>

    <p>This is the page footer</p>

</html>
```

In the end, these three pages create a single page that contains a header, a body, and a footer.

How It Works

Including other JSP pages helps increase developer productivity and reduces maintenance time. Using this technique, a developer can extract any JSP features that appear in multiple pages and place them into a separate JSP page. Doing so will allow a single point of maintenance when one of these features needs to be updated.

To include another page within a JSP page, use the `<jsp:include>` tag. The `<jsp:include>` tag allows embedding a static file or another web component. The tag includes a page attribute, which is used to specify the relative URL or an expression that results in another file or web component to include in the page.

■ **Note** The tag also has an optional `flush` attribute, which can be set to `true` or `false` to indicate whether the output buffer should be flushed prior to the page inclusion. The default value for the `flush` attribute is `false`.

Optionally, `<jsp:param>` clauses can be placed between the opening and closing `<jsp:include>` tags to pass one or more name-value pairs to the included resource if the resource is dynamic. An example of performing this technique would resemble something like the following lines of code. In the following lines, a parameter with a name of bookAuthor and a value of Juneau is passed to the header JSP page.

```
<jsp:include page="header.jspx">
    <jsp:param name="bookAuthor" value="Juneau"/>
</jsp:include>
```

The ability to include other content within a JSP page provides a means to encapsulate resources and static content. This allows developers to create content once and include it in many pages.

2-11. Creating an Input Form for a Database Record

Problem

You want to create a JSP page that will be used to input information that will be inserted as a database record.

Solution

Create an input form and use a Java servlet action method to insert the values into the database. This solution requires a JSP document and a Java servlet in order to complete the database input form. In the following example, an input form is created within a JSP document to populate records within a database table named RECIPES. When the user enters the information into the text fields on the form and clicks the Submit button, a servlet is called that performs the database insert transaction.

The following code is the JSP document that is used to create the input form for the database application:

```
<!--
    Document   : recipe02_11
    Author     : juneau
-->
<html xmlns:jsp="http://java.sun.com/JSP/Page"
      xmlns:c="http://java.sun.com/jsp/jstl/core"
      version="2.0">

    <jsp:directive.page contentType="text/html" pageEncoding="UTF-8"/>
    <head>
        <title>Recipe 2-11: Creating an Input Form for a Database Record </title>
    </head>
    <body>
        <h1>Recipe Input Form</h1>
        <p>
            Please insert recipe details using the text fields below.
        </p>
        ${ recipeBean.message }
        <form method="POST" action="/Javaee8recipes/RecipeServlet">
            Recipe Number: <input id="recipeNumber" name="recipeNumber" size="30"/>
            <br/>
```

```
            Recipe Name: <input id="name" name="name" size="30"/>
            <br/>
            Recipe Description: <input id="description" name="description" size="30"/>
            <br/>
            Recipe Text: <input id="text" name="text" size="30"/>
            <br/>
            <br/>
            <input type="submit"/>
        </form>
    </body>
</html>
```

Next is the code for a servlet named RecipeServlet. It is responsible for reading the request parameters from the JSP document input form and inserting the fields into the database.

```
package org.javaee8recipes.chapter02.recipe02_11;

import java.io.IOException;
import java.io.PrintWriter;
import java.sql.Connection;
import java.sql.PreparedStatement;
import java.sql.SQLException;
import javax.servlet.ServletException;
import javax.servlet.annotation.WebServlet;
import javax.servlet.http.HttpServlet;
import javax.servlet.http.HttpServletRequest;
import javax.servlet.http.HttpServletResponse;

/**
 * Recipe 2-11: Creating an Input Form for a Database Record
 * @author juneau
 */
@WebServlet(name = "RecipeServlet", urlPatterns = {"/RecipeServlet"})
public class RecipeServlet extends HttpServlet {

    /**
     * Processes requests for both HTTP
     * <code>GET</code> and
     * <code>POST</code> methods.
     *
     * @param request servlet request
     * @param response servlet response
     * @throws ServletException if a servlet-specific error occurs
     * @throws IOException if an I/O error occurs
     */
    protected void processRequest(HttpServletRequest request, HttpServletResponse response)
            throws ServletException, IOException {
        response.setContentType("text/html;charset=UTF-8");
        PrintWriter out = response.getWriter();
        int result = -1;
        try {
```

```
        /*
         * TODO Perform validation on the request parameters here
         */
        result = insertRow (request.getParameter("recipeNumber"),
                    request.getParameter("name"),
                    request.getParameter("description"),
                    request.getParameter("text"));
        out.println("<html>");
        out.println("<head>");
        out.println("<title>Servlet RecipeServlet</title>");
        out.println("</head>");
        out.println("<body>");
        out.println("<h1>Servlet RecipeServlet at " + request.getContextPath() + "</h1>");
        out.println("<br/><br/>");

        if(result > 0){
            out.println("<font color='green'>Record successfully inserted!</font>");
            out.println("<br/><br/><a href='/Javaee8recipes/chapter02/recipe02_11.
            jspx'>Insert another record</a>");
        } else {
            out.println("<font color='red'>Record NOT inserted!</font>");
            out.println("<br/><br/><a href='/Javaee8recipes/chapter02/recipe02_11.
            jspx'>Try Again</a>");
        }

        out.println("</body>");
        out.println("</html>");
    } finally {
        out.close();
    }
}

public int insertRow(String recipeNumber,
                      String name,
                      String description,
                      String text) {

    String sql = "INSERT INTO RECIPES VALUES(" +
                 "RECIPES_SEQ.NEXTVAL,?,?,?,?)";
    PreparedStatement stmt = null;
    int result = -1;
    try {
        CreateConnection createConn = new CreateConnection();
        Connection conn = createConn.getConnection();
        stmt = (PreparedStatement) conn.prepareStatement(sql);
        stmt.setString(1, recipeNumber);
        stmt.setString(2, name);
        stmt.setString(3, description);
        stmt.setString(4, text);
        // Returns row-count or 0 if not successful
```

```
            result = stmt.executeUpdate();
            if (result > 0){
                 System.out.println("-- Record created --");
            } else {
                System.out.println("!! Record NOT Created !!");
            }
        } catch (SQLException e) {
            e.printStackTrace();
        } finally {
            if (stmt != null) {
                try {
                    stmt.close();
                } catch (SQLException ex) {
                    ex.printStackTrace();
                }
            }

        }
        return result;
    }

    @Override
    protected void doGet(HttpServletRequest request, HttpServletResponse response)
            throws ServletException, IOException {
        processRequest(request, response);
    }

    @Override
    protected void doPost(HttpServletRequest request, HttpServletResponse response)
            throws ServletException, IOException {
        processRequest(request, response);
    }
}
```

If the request is successful, the record will be inserted into the database, and the user will be able to click a link to add another record. Of course, in a real-life application, you would want to code some validation using JavaScript either within the input form or within the server-side Java code to help ensure database integrity.

How It Works

A fundamental task to almost every enterprise application is the use of a database input form. Database input forms make it easy for end-users to populate database tables with data. When using JSP technology along with servlets, this operation can become fairly simple. As you have seen in the example to this recipe, writing a JSP input form is straightforward and can be coded using basic HTML. The key is to set up a Java servlet to receive a submitted request and process the records using the servlet. This provides an easy mechanism for separating web content from the application logic.

In the example, a JSP document named `recipe02_11.jspx` contains a standard HTML form with a method of `POST` and an action of `/Javaee8recipes/RecipeServlet`. The input form contains four fields, which map to database columns into which the data will eventually be inserted. The input tags contain the name of four corresponding fields (recipeNumber, name, description, and text), which will be passed to the form action when submitted. As you can see, the only reference to the Java code is the name of the servlet that is contained within the form action attribute.

The Java servlet named RecipeServlet is responsible for obtaining the request parameters that were submitted via the JSP document, validating them accordingly (not shown in the example), and inserting them into the database. When the page is submitted, RecipeServlet is invoked, and the request is sent to the doPost method since the HTML action method is POST. Both the doGet and doPost methods are really just wrapper methods for a processing method named processRequest, which is responsible for most of the work. The processRequest method is responsible for obtaining the request parameters, inserting them into the database, and sending a response to the client.

A PrintWriter object is declared and created by making a call to response.getWriter() first because this object will be used later to help form the response that is sent to the client. Next, an int value named result is set up and initialized to -1. This variable will be used for determining whether the SQL insert worked or failed. After those declarations, a try-catch block is opened, and the first line of the try block is a call to the insertRow method, passing the request parameters as values. The result variable is going to accept the int value that is returned from the execution of the insertRows method, indicating whether the insert was successful.

```
result = insertRow (request.getParameter("recipeNumber"),
                    request.getParameter("name"),
                    request.getParameter("description"),
                    request.getParameter("text"));
```

As such, an SQL insert statement is assigned to a string named sql, and it is set up using the PreparedStatement format. Each question mark in the SQL string corresponds to a parameter that will be substituted in the string when the SQL is executed.

```
String sql = "INSERT INTO RECIPES VALUES(" +
                   "RECIPES_SEQ.NEXTVAL,?,?,?,?)";
```

Next, the PreparedStatement and int values are initialized, and then a try-catch-finally block is opened, which will contain the SQL insert code. Within the block, a Connection object is created by calling a helper class named CreateConnection. If you want to read more about this helper class, you can read Chapter 7 on JDBC. For now, all you need to know is that CreateConnection will return a database connection that can then be used to work with the database. If for some reason the connection fails, the catch block will be executed, followed by the finally block. A PreparedStatement object is created from the successful connection, and the SQL string that contains the database insert is assigned to it. Each of the request parameter values, in turn, is then set as a parameter to the PreparedStatement. Lastly, the PreparedStatement's executeUpdate method is called, which performs an insert to the database. The return value of executeUpdate is assigned to the result variable and then returned to the processRequest method. Once the control is returned to processRequest, the servlet response is created using a series of PrintWriter statements. If the insert was successful, then a message indicating success is displayed. Likewise, if unsuccessful, then a message indicating failure is displayed.

Developing database input forms with JSP is fairly easy to do. To preserve the MVC structure, using a Java servlet for handing the request and database logic is the best choice.

2-12. Looping Through Database Records Within a Page

Problem

You want to display the records from a database table on your JSP page.

Solution

Encapsulate the database logic in a Java class and access it from the JSP page. Use the JSTL c:forEach element to iterate through the database rows and display them on the page. Two Java classes would be used for working with the data in this situation. One of the classes would represent the table, which you are querying from the database, and it would contain fields for each column in that table. Another JavaBean class would be used to contain the database business logic for querying the database.

The example for this recipe will display the first and last names of each author contained within the AUTHORS database table. The following code is used to create the JSP document that will display the data from the table using a standard HTML-based table along with the JSTL <c:forEach> tag to loop through the rows:

```
<!--
    Document   : recipe02_12
    Author     : juneau
-->
<html xmlns:jsp="http://java.sun.com/JSP/Page"
      xmlns:c="http://java.sun.com/jsp/jstl/core"
      version="2.0">

    <jsp:directive.page contentType="text/html" pageEncoding="UTF-8"/>
    <jsp:useBean id="authorBean" scope="session" class="org.javaee8recipes.chapter02.
    recipe02_12.AuthorBean"/>
    <head>
        <title>Recipe 2-12: Looping Through Database Records Within a Page </title>
    </head>
    <body>
        <h1>Authors</h1>
        <p>
            The authors from the books which Josh Juneau has worked on are printed below.
        </p>
        <table border="1">

        <c:forEach items="${authorBean.authorList }" var="author">
            <tr>
                <td> ${ author.first } ${ author.last }</td>
            </tr>
        </c:forEach>
        </table>
    </body>
</html>
```

As you can see, <c:forEach> is used to loop through the items contained within ${authorBean.authorList}. Each item within the list is an object of type Author. The following Java code is that of the Author class, which is used for holding the data contained within each table row:

```
package org.javaee8recipes.chapter02.recipe02_12;

/**
 *
 * @author juneau
 */
public class Author implements java.io.Serializable {
    private int id;
    private String first;
    private String last;

    public Author(){
        id = -1;
        first = null;
        last = null;
    }

    /**
     * @return the id
     */
    public int getId() {
        return id;
    }

    /**
     * @param id the id to set
     */
    public void setId(int id) {
        this.id = id;
    }

    /**
     * @return the first
     */
    public String getFirst() {
        return first;
    }

    /**
     * @param first the first to set
     */
    public void setFirst(String first) {
        this.first = first;
    }

    /**
     * @return the last
```

```
     */
    public String getLast() {
        return last;
    }

    /**
     * @param last the last to set
     */
    public void setLast(String last) {
        this.last = last;
    }
}
```

Lastly, the JSP document makes reference to a JavaBean named AuthorBean, which contains the business logic to query the data and return it as a list to the JSP page. The following code is contained in the AuthorBean class:

```
package org.javaee8recipes.chapter02.recipe02_12;

import java.sql.Connection;
import java.sql.PreparedStatement;
import java.sql.ResultSet;
import java.sql.SQLException;
import java.util.ArrayList;
import java.util.List;
import org.javaee8recipes.common.CreateConnection;

/**
 * Recipe 2-12: Looping Through Database Records Within a Page
 * @author juneau
 */
public class AuthorBean implements java.io.Serializable {

    public static Connection conn = null;
    private List authorList = null;

    public List queryAuthors(){
        String sql = "SELECT ID, FIRST, LAST FROM BOOK_AUTHOR";
        List<Author> authorList = new ArrayList<>();
        PreparedStatement stmt = null;
        ResultSet rs = null;
        int result = -1;
        try {
            CreateConnection createConn = new CreateConnection();
            conn = createConn.getConnection();
            stmt = (PreparedStatement) conn.prepareStatement(sql);

            // Returns row-count or 0 if not successful
             rs = stmt.executeQuery();
             while (rs.next()){
                 Author author = new Author();
                 author.setId(rs.getInt("ID"));
```

```
                author.setFirst((rs.getString("FIRST"));
                author.setLast(rs.getString("LAST"));
                authorList.add(author);
            }
        } catch (SQLException e) {
            e.printStackTrace();
        } finally {
            if (stmt != null) {
                try {
                    stmt.close();
                } catch (SQLException ex) {
                    ex.printStackTrace();
                }
            }

        }
        return authorList;
    }

    public List getAuthorList(){
        authorList = queryAuthors();
        return authorList;
    }
}
```

The names of the authors contained in the records in the table will be displayed on the page.

How It Works

Almost any enterprise application performs some sort of database querying. Oftentimes results from a database query are displayed in a table format. The example in this recipe demonstrates how to query a database and return the results to a JSP page for display in a standard HTML table. The JSP page in this example uses the JSTL `c:forEach` element to iterate through the results of the database query. Note that there is more than one way to develop this type of database query using JSP; however, the format demonstrated in this recipe is most recommended for use in a production enterprise environment.

As mentioned previously, the JSP page in this recipe uses a combination of the `jsp:useBean` element and the `c:forEach` element to iterate over the results of a database query. The logic for querying the database resides within a server-side JavaBean class that is referenced within the `jsp:useBean` element on the page. In the example, the JavaBean is named `AuthorBean`, and it is responsible for querying a database table named `AUTHORS` and populating a list of `Author` objects with the results of the query. When the `c:forEach` element is evaluated with the `items` attribute set to `${authorBean.authorList }`, it calls on the JavaBean method named `getAuthorList` because JSP expressions always append "get" to a method call behind the scenes and capitalizes the first letter of the method name within the call. When the `getAuthorList` method is called, the `authorList` field is populated via a call to `queryAuthors`. The `queryAuthors` method utilizes a Java Database Connectivity (JDBC) database call to obtain the authors from the `AUTHORS` table. A new `Author` object is created for each row returned by the database query, and each new `Author` object is, in turn, added to the `authorList`. In the end, the populated `authorList` contains a number of `Author` objects, and it is returned to the JSP page and iterated over utilizing the `c:forEach` element.

The `c:forEach` element contains an attribute named `var`, and this should be set equal to a string that will represent each element in the list that is being iterated over. The `var` is then used between the opening and closing `c:forEach` element tags to reference each element in the list, printing each author's first and last names.

This recipe provides some insight on how to combine the power of JSTL tags with other technologies such as JDBC to produce very useful results. To learn more about the different JSTL tags that are part of JSP, visit the online documentation at `www.oracle.com/technetwork/java/jstl-137486.html`. To learn more about JDBC, read Chapter 7 of this book.

2-13. Handling JSP Errors

Problem

You want to display a nicely formatted error page when a JSP page encounters an error.

Solution

Create a standard error page and forward control to the error page if an exception occurs within the JSP page. The following JSP document, in JSP format (not JSPX), demonstrates a standard error page to display when an error occurs within a JSP application. If an exception occurs within any JSP page in the application, the following error page will be displayed.

■ **Note** The example in the solution for this recipe uses the JSTL fmt library, which provides convenient access to formatting capabilities that allow for localization of text as well as date and number formatting. Text localization capabilities allow locales to be set so that text can be formatted into different languages, depending on the user locale. Tags used for date manipulation make it easy for developers to format dates and times within a JSP page and provide a way to parse dates and times for data input. Lastly, number-formatting tags provide a way to format and parse numeric data within pages. To learn more about the JSTL fmt tag library, refer to the online documentation at `https://docs.oracle.com/javaee/5/jstl/1.1/docs/tlddocs/`.

```
<%--
    Document   : recipe02_13_errorPage
    Author     : juneau
--%>

<%@page contentType="text/html" pageEncoding="UTF-8"%>
<%@ page isErrorPage="true" %>
<%@ taglib uri="http://java.sun.com/jsp/jstl/core"
     prefix="c" %>
<%@ taglib uri="http://java.sun.com/jsp/jstl/fmt"
     prefix="fmt" %>
<!DOCTYPE html>
<html>
    <head>
        <meta http-equiv="Content-Type" content="text/html; charset=UTF-8">
        <title>JSP Error Page</title>
    </head>
    <body>
        <h1>Error Encountered</h1>
        <br/>
        <br/>
```

```
        <p>
            The application has encountered the following error:
            <br/>
            <fmt:message key="ServerError"/>: ${pageContext.errorData.statusCode}

        </p>
    </body>
</html>
```

For example, the following JSP would create an error (`NullPointerException`) if the parameter designated as `param` is `null`. If this occurs, the indicated error page would be displayed.

```
<!--
    Document    : recipe02_13
    Author      : juneau
-->
<html xmlns:jsp="http://java.sun.com/JSP/Page"
      xmlns:c="http://java.sun.com/jsp/jstl/core"
      version="2.0">

    <jsp:directive.page contentType="text/html" pageEncoding="UTF-8"/>
    <jsp:directive.page errorPage="recipe02_13_errorPage.jsp"/>

    <head>
        <title>Recipe 2-13: Handling JSP Errors </title>
    </head>
    <body>
        <h1>There is an error on this page</h1>
        <p>
            This will produce an error:
            <jsp:scriptlet>
             if (request.getParameter("param").equals("value")) {
                System.out.println("test");
             }
            </jsp:scriptlet>
        </p>
    </body>

</html>
```

How It Works

One of the most annoying issues for users while working with applications is when an error is thrown. A nasty, long stack trace is often produced, and the user is left with no idea how to resolve the error. It is better to display a user-friendly error page when such an error occurs. The JSP technology allows an error page to be designated by adding a page directive to each JSP page that may produce an error. The directive should designate an error page that will be displayed if the page containing the directive produces an error.

The second JSP document in the solution to this recipe demonstrates a JSP page that will throw an error if the parameter being requested within the page is null. If this were to occur and there were no error page specified, then a NullPointerException error message would be displayed. However, this JSP indicates an error page by designating it within a page directive using the following syntax:

```
<jsp:directive.page errorPage="recipe02_13_errorPage.jsp"/>
```

When an error occurs on the example page, recipe02_13.errorPage.jsp is displayed. The first JSP document listed in the solution to this recipe contains the sources for the recipe02_13.errorPage.jsp page. It is flagged as an error page because it includes a page directive indicating as such:

```
<%@ page isErrorPage="true" %>
```

An error page is able to determine the error code, status, exception, and an array of other information by using the pageContext implicit object. In the example, the ${pageContext.errorData.statusCode} expression is used to display the status code of the exception. Table 2-5 displays the other possible pieces of information that can be gleaned from the pageContext object.

Table 2-5. *pageContext Implicit Object Exception Information*

Expression	Value
pageContext.errorData	Provides access to the error information
pageContext.exception	Returns the current value of the exception object
pageContext.errorData.requestURI	Returns the request URI
pageContext.errorData.servletName	Returns the name of the servlet invoked
pageContext.errorData.statusCode	Returns the error status code
pageContext.errorData.throwable	Returns the throwable that caused the error

Providing user-friendly error pages in any application can help create a more usable and overall more functional experience for the end-user. JSP and Java technology provide robust exception handling and mechanisms that can be used to help users and administrators alike when exceptions occur.

2-14. Disabling Scriptlets in Pages

Problem

You want to ensure that Java code cannot be embedded into JSP pages within your web application.

Solution

Set the scripting-invalid element within the web deployment descriptor to true. The following excerpt from a web.xml deployment descriptor demonstrates how to do so:

```
<jsp-config>
    <jsp-property-group>
        <scripting-invalid>true</scripting-invalid>
    </jsp-property-group>
</jsp-config>
```

How It Works

When working in an environment that encourages the use of the Model-View-Controller architecture, it can be useful to prohibit the use of scriptlets within JSP pages and documents. When JSP 2.1 was released, it provided solutions to help developers move Java code out of JSP pages and into server-side Java classes where it belonged. In the early years of JSP, pages were cluttered with scriptlets and markup. This made it difficult for developers to separate business logic from content, and it was hard to find good tools to help develop such pages effectively. JSP 2.1 introduced tags, which make it possible to eliminate the use of scriptlets within JSP pages, and this helps maintain the use of the MVC architecture.

To prohibit the use of scriptlets within JSP pages in an application, add the `jsp-config` element within the `web.xml` file of the application of which you want to enforce the rule. Add a subelement of `jsp-property-group` along with the `scripting-invalid` element. The value of the `scripting-invalid` element should be set to `true`.

2-15. Ignoring EL in Pages

Problem

You want to turn off EL expression translation within your JSP page so that older applications will be able to pass through expressions verbatim.

Solution #1

Escape the EL expressions within the page by using the \ character before any expressions. For instance, the following expressions will be ignored because the \ character appears before them:

```
\${elBean.myProperty}
\${2 + 4}
```

Solution #2

Configure a JSP property group within the `web.xml` file for the application. Within the `web.xml` file, a `<jsp-property-group>` element can contain child elements that characterize how the JSP page evaluates specified items. By including an `<el-ignored>true</el-ignored>` element, all EL within the application's JSP documents will be ignored and treated as literals. The following excerpt from `web.xml` demonstrates this feature:

```
<jsp-property-group>
     <el-ignored>true</el-ignored>
 </jsp-property-group>
```

Solution #3

Include a page directive including the `isELIgnored` attribute and set it to `true`. The following page directive can be placed at the top of a given JSP document to allow each EL expression to be treated as a literal:

```
<jsp:directive.page isELIgnored="true"/>
```

or in a standard JSP:

```
<%@ page isELIgnored="true" %>
```

How It Works

There may be a situation in which the evaluation of JSP EL expressions should be turned off. This occurs most often in cases of legacy applications using older versions of JSP technology; EL expressions were not yet available. There are a few different ways to turn off the evaluation of EL expressions, and this recipe demonstrates each of them.

In the first solution to this recipe, the escape technique is demonstrated. An EL expression can be escaped by placing the \ character directly before the expression, as shown in the example. Doing so will cause the JSP interpreter to treat the expression as a string literal, and the output on the page will be the expression itself, rather than its evaluation. The second solution to this recipe demonstrates adding a `jsp-property-group` to the `web.xml` deployment descriptor in order to ignore EL. All EL within an application will be ignored by including the `isELIgnored` element and providing a `true` value for it. Lastly, the final solution demonstrates how to ignore EL on a page-by-page basis by including a page directive with the `isELIgnored` attribute set to `true`.

Each of the different solutions for ignoring EL allows coverage to different parts of the application. The solution you choose should depend on how broadly you want to ignore EL throughout an application.

CHAPTER 3

The Basics of JavaServer Faces

In 2004 Sun Microsystems introduced a Java web framework called JavaServer Faces (JSF) in an effort to help simplify web application development. It is an evolution of the JavaServer Pages (JSP) framework, adding a more organized development lifecycle and the ability to more easily utilize modern web technologies. JSF uses XML files for view construction and uses Java classes for application logic, making it adhere to the Model-View-Controller (MVC) architecture. JSF is request-driven, and each request is processed by a special servlet named the `FacesServlet`. The `FacesServlet` is responsible for building the component trees, processing events, determining which view to process next, and rendering the response. JSF 1.*x* used a special resource file named the `faces-config.xml` file for specifying application details such as navigation rules, registering listeners, and so on. While the `faces-config.xml` file can still be used in JSF 2.*x*, the more modern releases of JSF have focused on being more easy to use, minimizing the amount of XML configuration, and utilizing annotations in place of XML where possible.

The framework is very powerful, including easy integration with technologies such as Ajax and making it effortless to develop dynamic content. JSF works well with databases, using RESTful data calls, JDBC, or EJB technology to work with the back end. JavaBeans, known as JSF *controller class* or *Controllers*, are used for application business logic and support the dynamic content in each view. They can adhere to different lifecycles, depending on the scope that is specified. Views can invoke methods within the beans to perform actions such as data manipulation and form processing. Properties can also be declared within the beans and exposed within the views, providing a convenient way to make dynamic content available within a view or pass request values. JSF allows developers to customize their applications with preexisting validation and conversion tags that can be used on components with the view to validate or convert data. It is also easy to build custom validators, as well as custom components that can be applied to components in a view.

This chapter includes recipes that will be useful for those who are getting started with JSF and also those who are looking to beef up their basic knowledge of the framework with some of the latest JSF techniques. You learn how to create controller classes, work with standard components, and handle page navigation. There are also recipes that cover useful techniques such as building custom validators and creating bookmarkable URLs. The recipes are refined to include the most current techniques and provide the most useful methodologies for using them. After studying the recipes in this chapter, you will be ready to build standard JSF applications, sprinkling in some custom features as well.

Note Many people prefer to work within an integrated development environment (IDE) for increased productivity. To get started learning how to create a new JSF project and manage it with the NetBeans IDE, see the appendix of this book.

J. Juneau, *Java EE 8 Recipes*, https://doi.org/10.1007/978-1-4842-3594-2_3

3-1. Writing a Simple JSF Application

Problem

You want to get up and running quickly by creating a simple JSF application.

Solution #1

Create a simple JSF web application that is composed of a single XHTML page and a single JSF controller class, along with the other required JSF configuration files. The application in this recipe simply displays a message that is initialized in a JSF controller class.

■ **Note** It is recommended that you utilize a Java IDE to make life easier. If you have not yet created a JSF application and are interested in learning how to create one from scratch with an IDE, see Solution #2 to this recipe. This book focuses on working with the Apache NetBeans IDE, a cutting-edge Java development environment that is usually one of the first to support new Java features. However, there are many excellent IDE choices. You can choose the IDE you prefer and follow along with its instructions for working with JSF.

Displaying a JSF Controller Field Value

The following code makes up the XHTML view that will be used to display the JSF controller field value:

```
<!DOCTYPE html PUBLIC "-//W3C//DTD XHTML 1.0 Strict//EN" "http://www.w3.org/TR/xhtml1/DTD/
xhtml1-strict.dtd">
<html xmlns="http://www.w3.org/1999/xhtml"
      xmlns:f="http://xmlns.jcp.org/jsf/core"
      xmlns:h="http://xmlns.jcp.org/jsf/html">
    <h:head>
        <meta http-equiv="Content-Type" content="text/html; charset=UTF-8"/>
        <title>Recipe 3-1:  A Simple JSF Application</title>
    </h:head>
    <h:body>
        <p>
            This simple application utilizes a request-scoped JSF controller class
            to display the message below.  If you change the message within the
            controller class's constructor and then recompile the application, the
            new message appears.
            <br/>
            <br/>
            #{helloWorldController.hello}
            <br/>
            or
            <br/>
            <h:outputText id="helloMessage" value="#{helloWorldController.hello}"/>
        </p>
    </h:body>
</html>
```

As you can see, the JSF page utilizes a JSF expression, #{helloWorldController.hello}. Much like JSP technology, a backing JavaBean, originally referred to as a *JSF managed bean*, but since JSF 2.0+ as the *controller class*, is referenced in the expression along with the field to expose.

Examining the JSF Controller

The following code is that of HelloWorldController, the JSF controller for this recipe example:

```
package org.javaee8recipes.chapter03.recipe03_01;

import java.io.Serializable;
import javax.annotation.PostConstruct;
import javax.inject.Named;
import javax.enterprise.context.RequestScoped;

/**
 * Recipe 3-1:  A Simple JSF Application
 * @author juneau
 */
@Named(value = "helloWorldController")
@RequestScoped
public class HelloWorldController implements Serializable {

    private String hello;

    /**
     * Creates a new instance of HelloWorldBean
     */
    public HelloWorldController() {

    }

    @PostConstruct
    public void init(){
        System.out.println ("Instantiated helloWorldController");
        hello = "Hello World";
    }

    /**
     * @return the hello
     */
    public String getHello() {
        return hello;
    }

    /**
     * @param hello the hello to set
     */
    public void setHello(String hello) {
        this.hello = hello;
    }
}
```

■ **Note** Prior to JSF 2.0, in order to enable the JSF servlet to translate the XHTML page, you needed to ensure that the `web.xml` file contained a servlet element indicating the `javax.faces.webapp.FacesServlet` class and its associated servlet-mapping URL. Since the release of JSF 2.0, if you're using a Servlet 3.*x* container, the `FacesServlet` is automatically mapped for you, so there is no requirement to adjust the `web.xml` configuration.

The listing that follows is an excerpt taken from the `web.xml` file for the sources to this book, and it demonstrates the features that must be added to the `web.xml` file in order to make the JSF application function properly in a Pre JSF 2.0 environment.

```
...
<servlet>
    <servlet-name>Faces Servlet</servlet-name>
    <servlet-class>javax.faces.webapp.FacesServlet</servlet-class>
    <load-on-startup>1</load-on-startup>
  </servlet>
  ...
  <servlet-mapping>
    <servlet-name>Faces Servlet</servlet-name>
    <url-pattern>/faces/*</url-pattern>
  </servlet-mapping>
...
  <welcome-file-list>
    <welcome-file>faces/index.xhtml</welcome-file>
  </welcome-file-list>
```

Let's take a deeper look at the `web.xml` configuration for a JSF application. It is not very complex, but a few elements could use some explanation. The `javax.faces.webapp.FacesServlet` servlet can optionally be declared within the `web.xml` file. If declared, the declaration must contain a `servlet-name`; the `servlet-class` element, which lists the fully qualified class name; and a `load-on-startup` value of `1` to ensure that the servlet is loaded when the application is started up by the container. The `web.xml` file must then map that servlet to a given URL within a `servlet-mapping` element. The `servlet-mapping` element must include the `servlet-name`, which is the same value as the `servlet-name` element that is contained in the servlet declaration, and a `url-pattern` element, which specifies the URL that will be used to map JSF pages with the servlet. When a URL is specified that contains the `/faces/` mapping, the `FacesServlet` will be used to translate the view.

To load the application in your browser, visit `http://localhost:8080/JavaEERecipes/faces/chapter03/recipe03_01.xhtml`, and you will see the following text:

```
Hello World
or
Hello World
```

This simple application utilizes a request-scoped JSF controller class to display this message. If you change the `"hello"` variable within the controller class's constructor and then recompile and run the application, the new message appears.

Solution #2

Use an IDE, such as NetBeans, to create a JSF application. To get started with NetBeans, first download the most recent release of NetBeans from the `https://netbeans.apache.org` website. The examples in this solution use NetBeans 8.x. For more information about downloading and installing NetBeans, see the appendix of this book. Once installed, create a new project by choosing the File ➤ New Project menu.

Follow the directions in the book's appendix (in the "Creating a NetBeans Java Web Project" section). The `index.xhtml` file will open in the editor, which will be the default landing page for your application. Modify the `index.xhtml` file by making the page the same as the JSF view that is listed in Solution #1's "Displaying JSF Controller Field Value" section. Once you're done, add the controller class to your application that will be used to supply the business logic for the `index.xhtml` page. To create the controller class, right-click the Source Packages navigation menu for your project and choose New ➤ JSF Controller Class from the context menu. This will open the New JSF Controller Class dialog (see Figure 3-1), which allows you to specify several options for your controller, including the name, location, and scope.

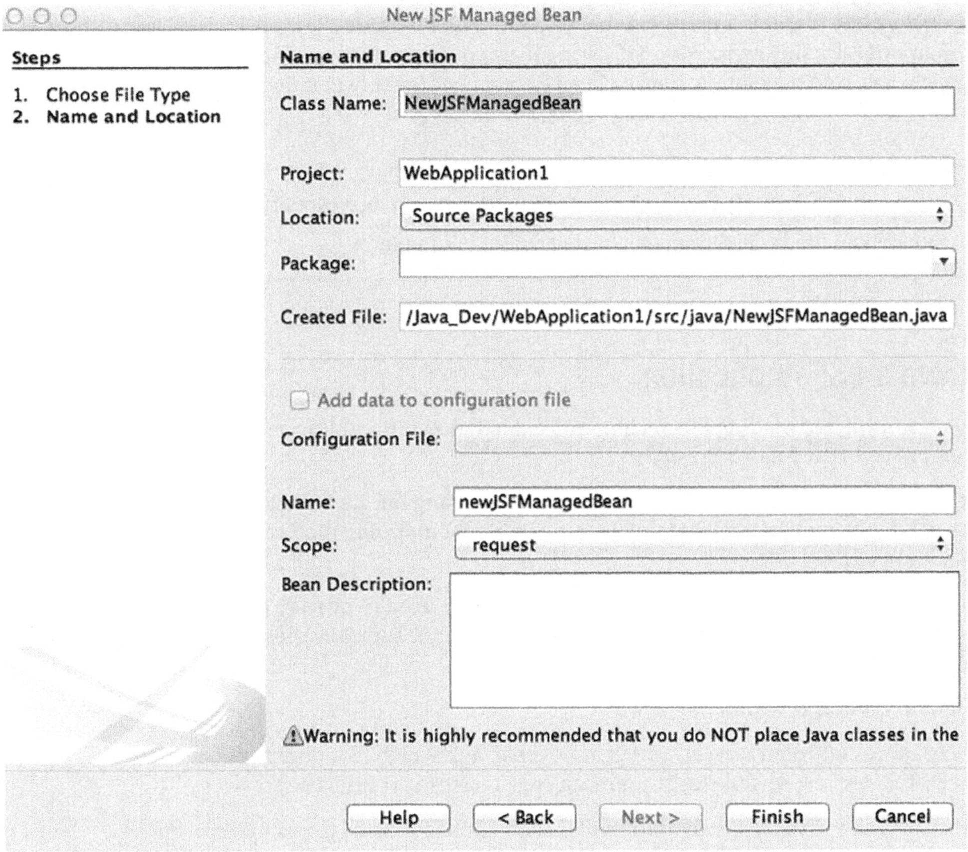

Figure 3-1. *New JSF controller class via the New JSF Controller Class dialog*

For the purposes of this recipe, change the name of the class to `HelloWorldController`, and leave the rest of the options at their defaults; then click Finish. Copy and paste the code from Solution #1's "Examining the JSF Controller" section into the newly created controller class. Once you're finished, right-click the application project from the Project navigation menu and choose Deploy to deploy your application.

To load the application in your browser, visit `http://localhost:8080/WebApplication1/faces/index.xhtml`, and you will see the following text:

```
Hello World
or
Hello World
```

This simple application utilizes a request-scoped JSF controller to display this message. If you change the "`hello`" variable in the controller's constructor and then recompile and run the application, the new message appears.

How It Works

This recipe merely scratches the surface of JSF, but it is meant as a starting point to guide you along the path of becoming a JSF expert. The example in this recipe demonstrates how closely related JSF and JSP technologies are. In fact, the main differences in the two view pages include the use of the JSF expression `#{}` rather than the standard JSP value expression `${}`, and the use of some JSF tags. Thanks to the JSP 2.0 unified expression language, Java web developers now have an easy transition between the two technologies, and they now share many of the same expression language features.

■ **Note** JSF 2.*x* can use the Facelets view technology to produce even more sophisticated and organized designs. To learn more about the Facelets view technology, refer to Chapter 4.

Breaking Down a JSF Application

Now for the real reason you are reading this recipe...the explanation for building a JSF application! A JSF application is comprised of the following parts:

- If it's using or maintaining JSF applications written using JSF 1.*x*, it includes the `web.xml` deployment descriptor that is responsible for mapping the `FacesServlet` instance to a URL path.
- One or more web pages on which JSF components are used to provide the page layout (may or may not utilize Facelets view technology). Typically these web pages are referred to as "views".
- JSF component tags within the views.
- One or more controller classes, which are simple, lightweight container-managed objects that are responsible for supporting page constructs and basic services.
- Optionally, one or more configuration files such as `faces-config.xml` that can be used to define navigation rules and configure beans and other custom objects.
- Optionally, supporting objects such as listeners, converters, or custom component.
- Optionally, custom tags for use on a JSF view.

LIFECYCLE OF A JSF APPLICATION

The JSF view processing lifecycle contains six stages. These stages are as follows:

1. Restore View
2. Apply Request Values
3. Process Validations
4. Update Model Values
5. Invoke Application
6. Render Response

Restore View is the first phase in the JSF lifecycle, and it is responsible for constructing the view. The component tree then applies the request parameters to each of the corresponding component values using the component tree's decode method. This occurs during the Apply Request Values phase. During this phase, any value conversion errors will be added to `FacesContext` for display as error messages during the Render Response phase. Next, all of the validations are processed. During the Process Validations phase, each component that has a registered validator is examined, and local values are compared to the validation rules. If any validation errors arise, the Render Response phase is entered, rendering the page with the corresponding validation errors.

If the Process Validations phase exits without errors, the Update Model Values phase begins. During this phase, controller class properties are set for each of the corresponding input components within the tree that contain local values. Once again, if any errors occur, then the Render Response phase is entered, rendering the page with the corresponding errors displayed. After the successful completion of the Update Model Values phase, the application-level events are handled during the Invoke Applications phase. Such events include page submits or redirects to other pages. Finally, the Render Response phase occurs, and the page is rendered to the user. If the application is using JSP pages, then the JSF implementation allows the JSP container to render the page.

The example in this recipe uses the minimum number of these parts. To run the example, you need to ensure that the `web.xml` file contains the proper JSF configuration if it's running in a pre-JSF 2.*x* environment. You need to have a controller declaring the field that is exposed on the JSF view along with the necessary accessor methods to make it work properly. And lastly, you need to have the XHTML JSF view page containing the JSF expression that exposes the field declared in the controller class.

A JSF controller class is a lightweight, container-managed object that is associated with a JSF page. The controller class is much like a JSP JavaBean in that it provides the application logic for a particular page so that Java code does not need to be embedded into the view code. Components (aka JSF tags) that are used within a JSF view are mapped to server-side fields and methods contained within the JSF controller. Controller classes are indeed the controllers for the page logic. In the example, the JSF controller class is named `HelloWorldController`, and a field named `hello` is declared, exposing itself to the public via the `getHello()` and `setHello()` methods. The JSF controller class is instantiated and initialized when a page that contains a reference to the bean is requested, and the controller class scope determines the lifespan of the bean. In the case of this example, the controller class contains a request scope, via the `@RequestScoped` annotation. Therefore, its lifespan is that of a single request, and it is re-instantiated each time a request is made. In this case, when the page in the example is reloaded. To learn more about the scope and annotations that are available for a controller class, see Recipe 3-2.

JSF technology utilizes a web view declaration framework known as Facelets. Facelets uses a special set of XML tags, similar in style to the standard JSF tags, to help build componentized web views. While this example does not use Facelets, it is a vital part of JSF view technology. Facelets pages typically use XHTML, which is an HTML page that is comprised of well-formed XML components. The example JSF view in this recipe is well-structured, and it contains two JSF EL expressions that are responsible for instantiating the controller class and displaying the content for the `hello` field. When the EL expression `#{helloWorldBean.hello}` is translated by the `FacesServlet`, it makes the call to the `HelloBeanController`'s `getHello()` method.

Lots of information was thrown at you in this introductory recipe. The simple example in this recipe provides a good starting point for working with JSF technology. Continue with the recipes in this chapter to gain a broader knowledge of each component that is used for developing JavaServer Faces web applications.

3-2. Writing a Controller Class

Problem

You want to use a server-side Java class from within your JSF application web pages.

Solution

Develop a JSF controller class, a lightweight container-managed component, which will provide the application logic for use within your JSF application web pages. The example in this recipe is comprised of a JSF view and a JSF controller class. The application calculates two numbers that are entered by the user and then adds, subtracts, multiplies, or divides them depending on the user's selection. The following code is the controller class that is responsible for declaring fields for each of the numbers that will be entered by the user, as well as a field for the result of the calculation. The controller class is also responsible for creating a list of `Strings` that will be displayed within an `h:selectOneMenu` element within the JSF view and retaining the value that is chosen by the user.

Although it may seem as though this controller class is doing a lot of work, it actually is very simple to make it happen! The controller class is really a beefed-up Plain Old Java Object (POJO) that includes some methods that can be called from JSF view components.

Controller Class

The following code is for the controller class that is used for the calculation example. The class is named `CalculationController`, and it is referenced as `calculationController` from within the JSF view. JSF uses convention over configuration for its naming conventions. By default, JSF views can contain EL that references a controller class by specifying the class name with the first character in lowercase.

```
package org.javaee8recipes.chapter03.recipe03_02;

import java.io.Serializable;
import java.util.ArrayList;
import java.util.List;
import javax.enterprise.context.SessionScoped;
import javax.faces.application.FacesMessage;
import javax.faces.context.FacesContext;
import javax.faces.model.SelectItem;
import javax.inject.Named;
```

```
/**
 * Recipe 3-2:  Writing a JSF controller class
 * @author juneau
 */

@Named
@SessionScoped
public class CalculationController implements Serializable {

    private int num1;
    private int num2;
    private int result;
    private String calculationType;
    private static final String ADDITION = "Addition";
    private static final String SUBTRACTION = "Subtraction";
    private static final String MULTIPLICATION = "Multiplication";
    private static final String DIVISION = "Division";
    List<SelectItem> calculationList;

    /**
     * Creates a new instance of CalculationController
     */
    public CalculationController() {
        // Initialize variables
        num1 = 0;
        num2 = 0;
        result = 0;
        calculationType = null;
        // Initialize the list of values for the SelectOneMenu
        populateCalculationList();
        System.out.println("initialized the bean!");
    }

    /**
     * @return the num1
     */
    public int getNum1() {
        return num1;
    }

    /**
     * @param num1 the num1 to set
     */
    public void setNum1(int num1) {
        this.num1 = num1;
    }

    /**
     * @return the num2
     */
```

```
    public int getNum2() {
        return num2;
    }

    /**
     * @param num2 the num2 to set
     */
    public void setNum2(int num2) {
        this.num2 = num2;
    }

        /**
     * @return the result
     */
    public int getResult() {
        return result;
    }

    /**
     * @param result the result to set
     */
    public void setResult(int result) {
        this.result = result;
    }

    /**
     * @return the calculationType
     */
    public String getCalculationType() {
        return calculationType;
    }

    /**
     * @param calculationType the calculationType to set
     */
    public void setCalculationType(String calculationType) {
        this.calculationType = calculationType;
    }

    public List<SelectItem> getCalculationList(){
        return calculationList;
    }

    private void populateCalculationList(){
        calculationList = new ArrayList<>();
        calculationList.add(new SelectItem(ADDITION));
        calculationList.add(new SelectItem(SUBTRACTION));
        calculationList.add(new SelectItem(MULTIPLICATION));
        calculationList.add(new SelectItem(DIVISION));
    }
```

```
    public void performCalculation() {
        switch (getCalculationType()) {
            case ADDITION:
                setResult(num1 + num2);
                break;
            case SUBTRACTION:
                setResult(num1 - num2);
                break;
            case MULTIPLICATION:
                setResult(num1 * num2);
                break;
            case DIVISION:
                try{
                    setResult(num1 / num2);
                } catch (Exception ex){
                    FacesMessage facesMsg = new FacesMessage(FacesMessage.SEVERITY_ERROR,
                    "Invalid Calculation", "Invalid Calculation");
                    FacesContext.getCurrentInstance().addMessage(null, facesMsg);
                }   break;
            default:
                break;
        }
    }
}
```

Next is the view that composes the web page, which is displayed to the user. The view is composed within an XHTML document and is well-formed XML.

JSF View

The view contains JSF components that are displayed as text boxes into which the user can enter information, a pick-list of different calculation types for the user to choose from, a component responsible for displaying the result of the calculation, and an h:commandButton component for submitting the form values.

```
<?xml version="1.0" encoding="UTF-8"?>
<!--
Book:  Java EE 8 Recipes
Recipe: 3-2 Writing a JSF Controller Class
Author: J. Juneau
-->
<!DOCTYPE html PUBLIC "-//W3C//DTD XHTML 1.0 Strict//EN" "http://www.w3.org/TR/xhtml1/DTD/
xhtml1-strict.dtd">
<html xmlns="http://www.w3.org/1999/xhtml"
      xmlns:f="http://xmlns.jcp.org/jsf/core"
      xmlns:h="http://xmlns.jcp.org/jsf/html">
    <h:head>
        <meta http-equiv="Content-Type" content="text/html; charset=UTF-8"/>
        <title>Recipe 3-2:  Writing a JSF Managed Bean</title>
    </h:head>
    <h:body>
        <f:view>
```

```
            <h2>Perform a Calculation</h2>
            <p>
                Use the following form to perform a calculation on two numbers.
                <br/>
                Enter
                the numbers in the two text fields below, and select a calculation to
                <br/>
                perform, then hit the Calculate button.
                <br/>
                <br/>
                <h:messages errorStyle="color: red" infoStyle="color: green"
                globalOnly="true"/>
                <br/>
                <h:form id="calulationForm">
                    Number1:
                    <h:inputText id="num1" value="#{calculationController.num1}"/>
                    <br/>
                    Number2:
                    <h:inputText id="num2" value="#{calculationController.num2}"/>
                    <br/>
                    <br/>
                    Calculation Type:
                    <h:selectOneMenu id="calculationType" value="#{calculationController.
                    calculationType}">
                        <f:selectItems value="#{calculationController.calculationList}"/>
                    </h:selectOneMenu>
                    <br/>
                    <br/>
                    Result:
                    <h:outputText id="result" value="#{calculationController.result}"/>
                    <br/>
                    <br/>
                    <h:commandButton action="#{calculationController.performCalculation()}"
value="Calculate"/>
                </h:form>
            </p>
        </f:view>
    </h:body>
</html>
```

The resulting JSF view looks like Figure 3-2 when displayed to the user.

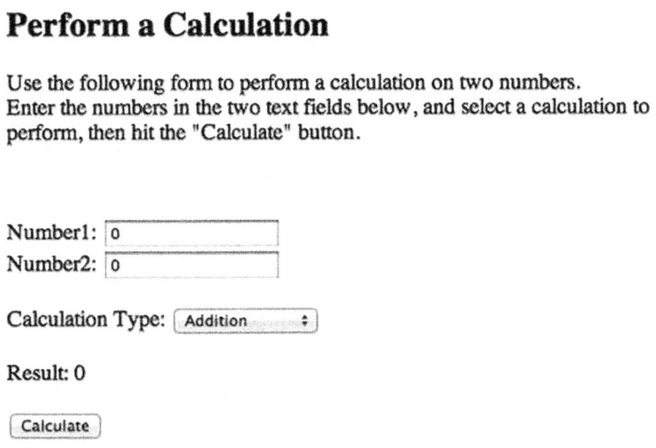

Perform a Calculation

Use the following form to perform a calculation on two numbers.
Enter the numbers in the two text fields below, and select a calculation to perform, then hit the "Calculate" button.

Number1: 0
Number2: 0

Calculation Type: Addition

Result: 0

Calculate

Figure 3-2. *Resulting JSF view page*

How It Works

The JSF controller class is responsible for providing the application logic for a JSF-based web application. Much like the JavaBean is to a JSP, the controller class is the backbone for a JSF view. They are also referred to as *backing beans* or *managed beans*, because there is typically one JSF controller class per each JSF view. Controller classes have changed a bit since the JSF technology was introduced. There used to be configuration required for each controller class in a `faces-config.xml` configuration file and also in the `web.xml` file for use with some application servers. Starting with the release of JSF 2.0, controller class became easier to use, and coding powerful JSF applications is easier than ever. This recipe focuses on newer controller class technology.

The example for this recipe demonstrates many of the most important features of a JSF controller class. The view components refer to the controller class as `calculationController`. By default, a JSF controller class can be referred to within a JSF view using the name of the bean class with a lowercase first letter. A controller class must be annotated with `@Named` in order to mark it as an injectable CDI bean. Using the `@Named` annotation, the string that is used to reference the bean from within a view can be changed. In the example, `calculationController` is also used as the name passed to the `@Named` annotation, but it could have easily been some other string. The `@Named` annotation should be placed before the class declaration.

```
@Named(value="calculationController")
```

Scopes

The bean in the example will be initialized when it is first accessed by a session and destroyed when the session is destroyed. It is a controller class that "lives" with the session. The scope of the bean is configured by an annotation on the class, just before the class declaration. There are different annotations that can be used for each available scope. In this case, the annotation is `@SessionScoped`, denoting that the controller class is session-scoped. All of the possible controller class scopes are listed in Table 3-1.

Table 3-1. *Controller Class Scopes*

Scope Annotation	Description
@ApplicationScoped	Specifies that a bean is application scoped. Initialized when the application is started up. Destroyed when the application is shut down. Controller classes with this scope are available to all application constructs within the same application.
@RequestScoped	Specifies that a bean is request scoped in a web application context. Initialized when an HTTP request to the bean is made and destroyed when the request is complete.
@SessionScoped	Specifies that a bean is session scoped in a web application context. Initialized when first accessed within a session. Destroyed when the session ends. Available to all servlet requests that are made within the same session.
@ConversationScoped	Specifies that a bean is conversation scoped. A conversation is a series of HTTP requests and responses that occur in a step-by-step manner, in order to complete a process. This application scope is specific to web application contexts. Initialized when a conversation is started and destroyed when the conversation ends. Controllers with this scope are available throughout the lifecycle of a conversation and belong to a single HTTP session. If the HTTP session ends, all conversation contexts that were created during the session are destroyed.
@Singleton	This is a pseudo-scope, meaning that it is not proxied as with other CDI scopes. This scope specifies that only one instance of the bean will exist for the entire application.
@Dependent	This is a pseudo-scope, meaning that it is not proxied as with other CDI scopes. Beans that use this scope behave differently than controller class containing any of the other scopes.
@TransactionScoped	Life of a bean annotated with this scope indicates that the lifespan will exist for the duration of an active transaction. The first time a CDI bean uses a controller with this annotation in a session, the same instance will be used throughout the transaction.
@FlowScoped	Beans of this scope are used in the context of a JSF flow. The bean will be instantiated the first time it is accessed in the scope of a flow, and it will be destroyed once the flow is complete.
@ViewScoped	This scope indicates that the bean will remain available throughout the life of the JSF view.

The @Named annotation specifies to the application server container that the class is a CDI bean. Prior to JSF 2.0, a controller class had to be declared in the faces-config.xml file, and they were annotated with @ManagedBean until JSF 2.2+. The addition of annotations has made JSF controller class XML configuration-free. It is important to note that the controller class implements java.io.Serializable; all controller classes should be specified as serializable so that they can be persisted to disk by the container if necessary.

Fields declared in a controller should be specified as private in order to adhere to object-oriented methodology. To make a field accessible to the public and usable from JSF views, accessor methods should be declared for it. Any field that has a corresponding "getter" and "setter" is known as a JSF controller class *property*. Properties are available for use within JSF views by utilizing lvalue JSF EL expressions, meaning that the expression is contained in the #{ and } character sequences and that it is readable and writable. lvalue expressions can specify targets, whereas rvalue expressions cannot. For instance, to access the field num1 that is declared in the controller class, the JSF view can use the #{calculationController.num1} expression, as you can see in the JSF view code for the example.

Any pubic method contained in a JSF controller class is accessible from within a JSF view using the same EL expression syntax, that is, by specifying `#{beanName.methodName}` as the expression. In the example to this recipe, the `performCalculation` method of the controller class is invoked from within the JSF view using an `h:commandButton` JSF component. The component action is equal to the EL expression that will invoke the JSF controller class method. To learn more about JSF components and how to use them in view, see Recipe 3-3 and Chapter 5.

```
<h:commandButton action="#{calculationController.performCalculation}" value="Calculate"/>
```

■ **Note** The input form tag for this example contains no `action` attribute. JSF forms do not contain action attributes since JSF components within the view are responsible for specifying the action method, rather than the form itself.

JSF controller classes are a fundamental part of the JSF web framework. They provide the means for developing dynamic, robust, and sophisticated web applications with the Java platform.

3-3. Building Sophisticated JSF Views with Components

Problem

You want to create a sophisticated user interface comprised of prebundled components.

Solution

Use the bundled JSF components in your JSF views. JSF components contain bundled application logic and view constructs, including styles and JavaScript actions, that can be used in applications by merely adding tags to a view. In the following example, several JSF components are used to create a view that displays the authors for an Apress book and allows for a new author to be added to the list. The following code is the XHTML for the JSF view:

```
<!DOCTYPE html PUBLIC "-//W3C//DTD XHTML 1.0 Strict//EN" "http://www.w3.org/TR/xhtml1/DTD/
xhtml1-strict.dtd">
<html xmlns="http://www.w3.org/1999/xhtml"
      xmlns:f="http://xmlns.jcp.org/jsf/core"
      xmlns:h="http://xmlns.jcp.org/jsf/html">
    <h:head>
        <meta http-equiv="Content-Type" content="text/html; charset=UTF-8"/>
        <title>Recipe 3-3: Building Sophisticated JSF Views with Components</title>
    </h:head>
    <h:body>
        <h:form id="componentForm">
            <h1>JSF Components, Creating a Sophisticated Page</h1>
            <p>
                The view for this page is made up entirely of JSF standard components.
                <br/>As you can see, there are many useful components bundled with JSF out
                of the box.
                <br/>
            </p>
```

```
            <p>Book Recommendation:  Java 9 Recipes
                <br/>
                <h:graphicImage id="java9recipes" library="image" name="java9recipes.png"/>
                <br/>

                <h:dataTable id="authorTable" value="#{authorController.authorList}"
                             var="author">
                    <f:facet name="header">
                        Java 9 Recipes Authors
                    </f:facet>
                    <h:column>
                    <h:outputText id="authorName" value="#{author.first} #{author.last}"/>
                    </h:column>
                </h:dataTable>
                <br/>
                <br/>
                <p>
                    Use the following form to add an author to the list.
                </p>
                <h:outputLabel for="newAuthorFirst" value="New Author First Name: "/>
                <h:inputText id="newAuthorFirst" value="#{authorController.newAuthorLast}"/>
                <br/>
                <h:outputLabel for="newAuthorLast" value="New Author Last Name: "/>
                <h:inputText id="newAuthorLast" value="#{authorController.newAuthorLast}"/>
                <br/>
                <h:inputTextarea id="bio" cols="20" rows="5"
                                 value="#{authorController.bio}"/>
                <br/>
                <br/>
                <h:commandButton id="addAuthor" action="#{authorController.addAuthor}"
                                 value="Add Author"/>
                <br/>
                <br/>

            </p>
        </h:form>
    </h:body>
</html>
```

This example utilizes a JSF controller class named AuthorController. The controller class declares a handful of properties that are exposed in the view, and it also declares and populates a list of authors that is displayed on the page in a JSF h:dataTable component.

```
package org.javaee8recipes.chapter03.recipe03_03;

import java.io.Serializable;
import java.util.ArrayList;
import java.util.List;
import javax.enterprise.context.SessionScoped;
import javax.inject.Named;
```

```
@Named(value = "authorController")
@SessionScoped
public class AuthorController implements Serializable {

    private String newAuthorFirst;
    private String newAuthorLast;
    private String bio;
    private List<Author> authorList;

    /**
     * Creates a new instance of RecipeController
     */
    public AuthorController() {
        populateAuthorList();
    }

    private void populateAuthorList(){
        System.out.println("initializing authors");
        authorList = new ArrayList<>();
        authorList.add(new Author("Josh", "Juneau", null));
        authorList.add(new Author("Carl", "Dea", null));
        authorList.add(new Author("Mark", "Beaty", null));
        authorList.add(new Author("John", "O'Conner", null));
        authorList.add(new Author("Freddy", "Guime", null));
        System.out.println("AuthorList size:" +authorList.size());

    }

    public void addAuthor() {
        getAuthorList().add(
                new Author(this.getNewAuthorFirst(),
                           this.getNewAuthorLast(),
                           this.getBio()));
    }

    /**
     * @return the authorList
     */
    public List<Author> getAuthorList() {
        return authorList;
    }

    /**
     * @param authorList the authorList to set
     */
    public void setAuthorList(List<Author> authorList) {
        this.authorList = authorList;
    }

    /**
     * @return the newAuthorFirst
     */
```

```
    public String getNewAuthorFirst() {
        return newAuthorFirst;
    }

    /**
     * @param newAuthorFirst the newAuthorFirst to set
     */
    public void setNewAuthorFirst(String newAuthorFirst) {
        this.newAuthorFirst = newAuthorFirst;
    }

    /**
     * @return the newAuthorLast
     */
    public String getNewAuthorLast() {
        return newAuthorLast;
    }

    /**
     * @param newAuthorLast the newAuthorLast to set
     */
    public void setNewAuthorLast(String newAuthorLast) {
        this.newAuthorLast = newAuthorLast;
    }

    /**
     * @return the bio
     */
    public String getBio() {
        return bio;
    }

    /**
     * @param bio the bio to set
     */
    public void setBio(String bio) {
        this.bio = bio;
    }
}
```

Finally, the Author class is used to hold instances of Author objects that are loaded into the authorList. The following code is for the Author class:

```
package org.javaee8recipes.chapter03.recipe03_03;

/**
 * Recipe 3-3
 * @author juneau
 */
public class Author implements java.io.Serializable {
    private String first;
    private String last;
    private String bio;
```

```
    public Author(){
        this.first = null;
        this.last = null;
        this.bio = null;
    }

    public Author(String first, String last, String bio){
        this.first = first;
        this.last = last;
        this.bio = bio;
    }
    /**
     * @return the first
     */
    public String getFirst() {
        return first;
    }

    /**
     * @param first the first to set
     */
    public void setFirst(String first) {
        this.first = first;
    }

    /**
     * @return the last
     */
    public String getLast() {
        return last;
    }

    /**
     * @param last the last to set
     */
    public void setLast(String last) {
        this.last = last;
    }

    /**
     * @return the bio
     */
    public String getBio() {
        return bio;
    }

    /**
     * @param bio the bio to set
     */
    public void setBio(String bio) {
        this.bio = bio;
    }
}
```

The resulting web page will resemble the page shown in Figure 3-3.

JSF Components, Creating a Sophisticated Page

**The view for this page is made up entirely of JSF standard components.
As you can see, there are many useful components bundled with JSF out of the box.**

Book Recommendation: Java 9 Recipes

Java 9 Recipes

apress

Java 9 Recipes Authors
Josh Juneau
Carl Dea
Mark Beaty
John O'Conner
Freddy Guime

Use the following form to add an author to the list.

New Author First Name:
New Author Last Name:

Add Author

Figure 3-3. *Sophisticated JSF view example*

How It Works

JSF views are comprised of well-formed XML, being a mixture of HTML and JSF component tags. Any well-formed HTML can be used in a JSF view, but the components are the means by which JSF communicates with controller class instances. There are components shipped with JSF that can be used for adding images to views, text areas, buttons, check boxes, and much more. Moreover, there are several very good component libraries that include additional JSF components, which can be used within your applications. This recipe is meant to give you an overall understanding of JSF components and how they work. You can learn more details regarding JSF components and the use of external component libraries by reading the recipes in Chapter 5.

The first step toward using a component in a JSF view is to declare the tag library on the page. This is done within the HTML element at the top of the page. The example in this recipe declares both the JSF core component library and the JSF HTML component library within the HTML element near the top of the page. These two libraries are standard JSF component libraries that should be declared in every JSF view.

```
...
<html xmlns="http://www.w3.org/1999/xhtml"
      xmlns:f="http://xmlns.jcp.org/jsf/core"
      xmlns:h="http://xmlns.jcp.org/jsf/html">
...
```

Once a library is declared, a component from within that library can be used in the view by specifying the library namespace, along with the component you want to use. For instance, to specify an HTML element for displaying text, use the JSF `h:outputText` component tag, along with the various component attributes.

Prior to JSF 2.0, it was important to enclose a JSF view along with all of the components in the `f:view` tag. As of JSF 2.0, the tag is no longer required because the underlying Facelets view technology is part of every JSF view by default, so it takes care of specifying the view automatically. However, the `f:view` element can still be useful for specifying locale, content type, or encoding. See the online documentation for more information regarding the use of those features: `https://javaserverfaces.github.io/docs/2.3/vdldoc/index.html`.

The `<h:head>` and `<h:body>` tags can be used to specify the header and body for a JSF web view. However, using the standard HTML `<head>` and `<body>` tags is fine also. Some Java IDEs will automatically use `<h:head>` and `<h:body>` in place of the standard HTML tags when writing JSF views. An important note is that you must enclose any content that will be treated as an HTML input form with the `<h:form>` JSF tag. This tag encloses a JSF form and renders an HTML form using a `POST` method if none is specified. No `action` attribute is required for a JSF form tag because the JSF controller class action is invoked using one of the JSF action components such as `h:commandButton` or `h:commandLink`.

■ **Tip** Always specify an `id` for the `h:form` tag because the form `id` is added as a prefix to all JSF component tag `ids` when the page is rendered. For instance, if a form `id` of `myform` contained a component tag with an `id` of `mytag`, the component `id` will be rendered as `myform:mytag`. If you do not specify an `id`, then one will be generated for you automatically. If you want to use JavaScript to work with any of the page components, you will need to have an `id` specified for `h:form`, or you will never be able to access them programmatically.

■ **Note** This recipe provides a quick overview of a handful of the standard JSF components. For an in-depth explanation of JSF components and their usage, see Chapter 4.

The standard JSF component library contains a variety of components, and a few of them are utilized in the example. The h:graphicImage tag can be used to place an image on the page and utilize a JSF controller class if needed. The h:graphicImage tag is rendered into an HTML component, and as with all of the other JSF components, it accepts JSF EL expressions in its attributes, which allows for the rendering of dynamic images. In this recipe, a static image is specified with the url attribute, but an expression could also be used, using a JSF controller class field. The library attribute is used to specify the directory in which the resource, in this case an image, resides.

```
<h:graphicImage id="java9recipes" library="image" name="java9recipes.png"/>
```

The h:outputLabel tag is useful for reading controller class properties and displaying their values when the view is rendered. They are rendered as a label for a corresponding field within the view. The example utilizes static values for the h:outputLabel component, but they could include JSF expressions if needed. The h:outputText component is also useful for reading controller class properties and displaying their values. This component renders basic text on the page. The difference between h:outputLabel and h:outputText is that they are rendered into different HTML tags. Both components can accept JSF controller class expressions for their value attributes.

In the example, a couple of text fields are displayed on the page using the h:inputText component, which renders an input field. The value attribute for h:inputText can be set to a JSF controller class field, which binds the text field to the corresponding controller class property. For instance, the example includes an h:inputText component with a value of #{authorController.newAuthorFirst}, which binds the component to the newAuthorFirst property in the AuthorController class. If the field contains a value, then a value will be present within a text field when the page is rendered. If a value is entered into the corresponding text field and the form is submitted, the value will be set into the newAuthorFirst field using its setter method. The h:inputText tag allows for both reading and writing of controller class properties because it uses lvalue JSF EL expressions. The h:inputTextarea tag is very similar to h:inputText in that it works the same way, but it renders a text area rather instead of a text field.

The h:commandButton component is used to render a submit button on a page. Its action attribute can be set to a JSF controller class method. When the button is pressed, the corresponding controller class method will be executed, and the form will be submitted. The request will be sent to the FacesServlet controller, and any properties on the page will be set. See Recipe 3-1 for more details regarding the JSF lifecycle. The h:commandButton used in the example has an action attribute of #{authorController.addAuthor}, which will invoke the addAuthor method within the AuthorController class. As you can see from the method, when invoked it will add a new Author object to the authorList, utilizing the values that were populated in the corresponding h:inputText components for the newAuthorFirst, newAuthorLast, and bio fields. The following excerpt from the example's JSF view lists the h:commandButton component:

```
<h:commandButton id="addAuthor" action="#{authorController.addAuthor}"
                                value="Add Author"/>
```

The last component in the example that bears some explanation is the h:dataTable. This JSF component is rendered into an HTML table, and it enables developers to dynamically populate tables with collections of data from a controller class. In the example, the h:dataTable value attribute is set to the controller class property of #{authorController.authorList}, which maps to an instance list that is populated with Author objects. The dataTable var attribute contains a string that will be used to reference the different objects contained in each row of the table. In the example, the var attribute is set to author, so referencing #{author.first} in the dataTable will return the value for the current Author object's first property. The dataTable in the example effectively prints out the first and last names of each Author object within the authorList. This is just a quick overview of how the JSF dataTable component works. For more details, refer to Recipe 3-12.

As you work more with constructing JSF views, you will become very familiar with the component library. The tags will become second nature, and you will be able to construct highly sophisticated views for your application. Adding external JSF component libraries into the mix along with using Ajax for updating components is the real icing on the cake! You will learn more about spreading the icing on the cake and creating beautiful and user-friendly views in Chapter 5!

3-4. Displaying Messages in JSF Pages

Problem

You have the requirement to display an information message on the screen for your application users.

Solution

Add the h:messages component to your JSF view and create messages as needed within the view's controller class using FacesMessage objects. The following JSF view contains an h:messages component tag that will render any messages that were registered with FacesContext within the corresponding page's controller class. It also includes an h:message component that is bound to an h:inputText field. The h:message component can display messages that are specific to the corresponding text field.

```
<!DOCTYPE html PUBLIC "-//W3C//DTD XHTML 1.0 Strict//EN" "http://www.w3.org/TR/xhtml1/DTD/
xhtml1-strict.dtd">
<html xmlns="http://www.w3.org/1999/xhtml"
      xmlns:f="http://xmlns.jcp.org/jsf/core"
      xmlns:h="http://xmlns.jcp.org/jsf/html">
    <h:head>
        <meta http-equiv="Content-Type" content="text/html; charset=UTF-8"/>
        <title>Recipe 3-4: Displaying Messages in JSF Pages</title>
    </h:head>
    <h:body>
        <h:form id="componentForm">
            <h1>JSF Messages</h1>
            <p>
                This page contains a JSF message component below.  It will display
                messages from a JSF managed bean once the bean has been initialized.
            </p>
            <h:messages errorStyle="color: red" infoStyle="color: green" globalOnly="true"/>
            <br/>
            <br/>
            Enter the word Java here:
            <h:inputText id="javaText" value="#{messageController.javaText}"/>
            <h:message for="javaText"  errorStyle="color: red" infoStyle="color: green"/>
            <br/><br/>
            <h:commandButton id="addMessage" action="#{messageController.newMessage}"
                             value="New Message"/>

        </h:form>
    </h:body>
</html>
```

The controller class in this example is named MessageController. It will create a JSF message upon initialization, and then each time the newMessage method is invoked, another message will be displayed. Also, if the text *java* is entered into the text field that corresponds to the h:inputText tag, then a success message will be displayed for that component. Otherwise, if a different value is entered into that field or if the field is left blank, then an error message will be displayed. The following listing is that of MessageController:

```
package org.javaee8recipes.chapter03.recipe03_04;

import java.util.Date;
import javax.enterprise.context.SessionScoped;
import javax.faces.application.FacesMessage;
import javax.faces.context.FacesContext;
import javax.inject.Named;

@Named
@SessionScoped
public class MessageController implements java.io.Serializable {
    int hitCounter = 0;
    private String javaText;

    /**
     * Creates a new instance of MessageController
     */
    public MessageController() {
        javaText = null;
        FacesMessage facesMsg = new FacesMessage(FacesMessage.SEVERITY_INFO, "Managed Bean
        Initialized", null);

        FacesContext.getCurrentInstance().addMessage(null, facesMsg);
    }

    public void newMessage(){
        String hitMessage = null;
        hitCounter++;
        if(hitCounter > 1){
            hitMessage = hitCounter + " times";
        } else {
            hitMessage = hitCounter + " time";
        }

        Date currDate = new Date();
        FacesMessage facesMsg = new FacesMessage(FacesMessage.SEVERITY_ERROR,
                "You've pressed that button " + hitMessage + "!  The current date and time:
"

                + currDate, null);
        FacesContext.getCurrentInstance().addMessage(null, facesMsg);

        if (getJavaText().equalsIgnoreCase("java")){
            FacesMessage javaTextMsg = new FacesMessage(FacesMessage.SEVERITY_INFO,
                "Good Job, that is the correct text!", null);
```

```
            FacesContext.getCurrentInstance().addMessage("componentForm:javaText",
            javaTextMsg);
        } else {
            FacesMessage javaTextMsg = new FacesMessage(FacesMessage.SEVERITY_ERROR,
                "Sorry, that is NOT the correct text!", null);
            FacesContext.getCurrentInstance().addMessage("componentForm:javaText",
            javaTextMsg);
        }
    }

    /**
     * @return the javaText
     */
    public String getJavaText() {
        return javaText;
    }

    /**
     * @param javaText the javaText to set
     */
    public void setJavaText(String javaText) {
        this.javaText = javaText;
    }
}
```

The message will be displayed on the page in red text if it is an error message and in green text if it is an informational message. In this example, the initialization message is printed green, and the update message is printed in red.

How It Works

It is always a good idea to relay messages to application users, especially in the event that some action needs to be taken by the user. The JSF framework provides an easy API that allows messages to be added to a view from the JSF controller class. To use the API, add the `h:message` component to a view for displaying messages that are bound to specific components and add the `h:messages` component to a view for displaying messages that are not bound to specific components. The `h:message` component contains a number of attributes that can be used to customize message output and other things. It can be bound to a component within the same view by specifying that component's `id` in the `for` attribute of `h:message`. The most important attributes for the `h:message` component are as follows:

- `id`: Specifies a unique identifier for the component
- `rendered`: Specifies whether the message is rendered
- `errorStyle`: Specifies the CSS styles to be applied to error messages
- `errorClass`: Indicates the CSS class to apply to error messages
- `infoStyle`: Specifies the CSS styles to be applied to informational messages
- `infoClass`: Indicates the CSS class to apply to informational messages
- `for`: Specifies the component for which the message belongs

For a list of all attributes available for the h:message component, refer to the online documentation. In the example for this recipe, the h:message component is bound to the h:inputText component with an id of javaText. When the page is submitted, the newMessage method in the MessageController class is invoked. That method is used in this example for generating messages to display on the page. If the text entered in the javaText property matches Java, then a successful message will be printed on the page. To create a message, an instance of the javax.faces.application.FacesMessage class is generated, passing three parameters that correspond to message severity, message summary, and message detail. A FacesMessage object can be created without passing any parameters, but usually it is more productive to pass the message into the constructor at the time of instantiation. The general format for creating a FacesMessage object is as follows:

```
new FacesMessage(FacesMessage.severity severity, String summary, String detail)
```

Passing a static field from the FacesMessage class specifies the message severity. Table 3-2 shows the possible message severity values along with their descriptions.

Table 3-2. *FacesMessage Severity Values*

Severity	Description
SEVERITY_ERROR	Indicates that an error has occurred
SEVERITY_FATAL	Indicates that a serious error has occurred
SEVERITY_INFO	Indicates an informational message rather than an error
SEVERITY_WARN	Indicates that an error may have occurred

In the example, if the value entered for the javaText property equals Java, then an informational message is created. Otherwise, an error message is created. In either case, once the message is created, then it needs to be passed into the current context using FacesContext.getCurrentInstance().addMessage(String componentId, FacesMessage message). In the example, the method is called, passing a component ID of componentForm:javaText. This refers to the component within the JSF view that has an ID of javaText (h:inputText component). The componentForm identifier belongs to the form (h:form component) that contains the h:inputText component, so in reality the h:inputText component is nested within the h:form component. To reference a nested component, combine component IDs using a colon as a delimiter. The following is an excerpt from the example, demonstrating how to create a message and send it to the h:message component:

```
FacesMessage javaTextMsg = new FacesMessage(FacesMessage.SEVERITY_ERROR,
                "Sorry, that is NOT the correct text!", null);
FacesContext.getCurrentInstance().addMessage("componentForm:javaText", javaTextMsg);
```

The h:messages component can be used for displaying all messages that pertain to a view, or it can be used for displaying only non-component-related messages by using the globalOnly attribute. All other attributes for h:messages are very similar to the h:message component. By indicating a true value for the globalOnly attribute, you are telling the component to ignore any component-specific messages. Therefore, any FacesMessage that is sent to a specific component will not be displayed by h:messages. In the example, the message that is displayed by h:messages is generated in the same manner as the component-specific message, with the exception of specifying a specific component to which the message belongs. The following excerpt demonstrates sending an error message to the h:messages component. Note that the last argument that is sent to the FacesMessage call is a null value. This argument should be the clientId specification, and by setting it to null, you are indicating that there is no specified client identifier. Therefore, the message should be a global message rather than tied to a specific component.

```
FacesMessage facesMsg = new FacesMessage(FacesMessage.SEVERITY_ERROR,
                "You've pressed that button " + hitMessage + "!  The current date and time:
"
                + currDate, null);
FacesContext.getCurrentInstance().addMessage(null, facesMsg);
```

Displaying the appropriate message at the right time in an application is very important. By utilizing FacesMessages objects and displaying them using either the h:message or h:messages component, you can ensure that your application users will be well informed of the application state.

3-5. Updating Messages Without Recompiling

Problem

Rather than hard-coding messages into your controller classes, you want to specify the messages in a properties file so that they can be edited on the fly.

Solution

Create a resource bundle or properties file and specify your messages within it. Then retrieve the messages from the bundle and add them to the FacesMessages objects rather than hard-coding a String value. In the example that follows, a resource bundle is used to specify a message that is to be displayed on a page. If you need to change the message at any time, simply modify the resource bundle and reload the page in the browser without the need to redeploy the entire application or change any code.

The following code is for a JSF view that contains the h:messages component for displaying the message from a corresponding controller class:

```
<!DOCTYPE html PUBLIC "-//W3C//DTD XHTML 1.0 Strict//EN" "http://www.w3.org/TR/xhtml1/DTD/
xhtml1-strict.dtd">
<html xmlns="http://www.w3.org/1999/xhtml"
      xmlns:f="http://xmlns.jcp.org/jsf/core"
      xmlns:h="http://xmlns.jcp.org/jsf/html">
    <h:head>
        <meta http-equiv="Content-Type" content="text/html; charset=UTF-8"/>
        <title>Recipe 3-5: Specifying Updatable Messages</title>
    </h:head>
    <h:body>
        <h:form id="componentForm">
            <h1>Utilizing a resource bundle</h1>
            <p>
                The message below is displayed from a resource bundle.  The h:outputText
                component has been added to the page only to instantiate the bean for this
                example.  To change
                the message, simply modify the corresponding message within the bundle
                and then refresh the page.
            </p>
            <h:outputText id="exampleProperty" value="#{exampleController.
            exampleProperty}"/>
            <br/>
```

```
            <h:messages errorStyle="color: red" infoStyle="color: green" globalOnly="true"/>
        </h:form>
    </h:body>
</html>
```

Next, the controller class is responsible for creating the message and sending it to the h:messages component via the FacesContext. The following source is for ExampleController, which is the controller class for the JSF view in this example:

```
package org.javaee8recipes.chapter03.recipe03_05;

import java.util.ResourceBundle;
import javax.enterprise.context.RequestScoped;

import javax.faces.application.FacesMessage;
import javax.faces.context.FacesContext;
import javax.inject.Named;

/**
 * Recipe 3-5
 * @author juneau
 */
@Named(value="exampleController")
@RequestScoped
public class ExampleController {
    private String exampleProperty;

    /**
     * Creates a new instance of ExampleController
     */
    public ExampleController() {
        exampleProperty = "Used to instantiate the bean.";
        FacesMessage facesMsg = new FacesMessage(FacesMessage.SEVERITY_INFO,
                ResourceBundle.getBundle("/org/javaeerecipes/chapter03/Bundle").
                getString("ExampleMessage"), null);
        FacesContext.getCurrentInstance().addMessage(null, facesMsg);
    }

    /**
     * @return the exampleProperty
     */
    public String getExampleProperty() {
        return exampleProperty;
    }

    /**
     * @param exampleProperty the exampleProperty to set
     */
    public void setExampleProperty(String exampleProperty) {
        this.exampleProperty = exampleProperty;
    }
}
```

The resource bundle, which contains the message, is read by the controller class to obtain the message. If you want to update the message, you can do so without recompiling any code.

```
# This file is an example resource bundle
ExampleMessage=This message can be changed by updating the message bundle!
```

When the page is loaded, the `h:outputText` component instantiates `ExampleController`, which in turn creates the `FacesMessage` objects that are used to display the message on the screen.

How It Works

Oftentimes it is useful to have the ability to update custom system or user messages rather than hard-coding them. This could be useful in the case that some custom information that is contained in a particular message may have the possibility of changing in the future. It'd be nice to simply update the message in text format rather than editing the code, recompiling, and redeploying your application. It is possible to create updateable messages using a resource bundle. A resource bundle is simply a properties file, which contains name-value pairs. When adding custom messages to a bundle, name the message appropriately and then add the custom message as the value portion of the property. An application can then look up the property by name and utilize its value. In this case, the value is a string that will be used to create a `FacesMessage` instance.

In the example, the bundle contains a property named `ExampleMessage`, along with a corresponding value. When the JSF view is loaded into the browser, the `ExampleController` class is instantiated, causing its constructor to be executed. A `FacesMessage` instance is created, generating a message of type `FacesMessage.SEVERITY_INFO`, and it reads the resource bundle and obtains the value for the `ExampleMessage` property. The following excerpt demonstrates how to obtain a specified message value from the resource bundle:

```
ResourceBundle.getBundle("/org/javaee8recipes/chapter03/Bundle").
getString("ExampleMessage"), null);
```

After the message is created, it is added to the current instance of `FacesContext` and, subsequently, displayed on the page when it is rendered. Using a resource bundle to specify your messages can make life much easier because you'll no longer be required to recompile code in order to update such messages.

3-6. Navigating Based Upon Conditions

Problem

Your JSF application contains multiple pages, and you want to set up navigation between them.

Solution

Utilize one of the following techniques for performing navigation within JSF applications:

- Utilize explicit navigation through the use of a JSF controller class method along with a corresponding `faces-config.xml` configuration file to control the navigation for your application.
- Use implicit navigation for specifying the next view to render from within the controller class, returning the name of the view in String format from an action method.
- Use implicit navigation by specifying the name of the view to render as the `action` attribute of a component tag, bypassing the controller class altogether.

The example in this recipe consists of four JSF views, and each one contains h:commandButton components that invoke navigation to another view. The h:commandButton components are linked to controller class methods that are present in the view's corresponding controller class named NavigationController. The first view listed here contains two h:commandButton components, each of which invokes a method within the controller class named NavigationController. The first button utilizes explicit JSF navigation, and the second uses implicit navigation.

```
<?xml version="1.0" encoding="UTF-8"?>
<!DOCTYPE html PUBLIC "-//W3C//DTD XHTML 1.0 Strict//EN" "http://www.w3.org/TR/xhtml1/DTD/
xhtml1-strict.dtd">
<html xmlns="http://www.w3.org/1999/xhtml"
      xmlns:f="http://xmlns.jcp.org/jsf/core"
      xmlns:h="http://xmlns.jcp.org/jsf/html">
    <h:head>
        <meta http-equiv="Content-Type" content="text/html; charset=UTF-8"/>
        <title>Recipe 3-6/title>
    </h:head>
    <h:body>
        <h:form id="componentForm">
            <h1>JSF Navigation - Page 1</h1>
            <p>
                Clicking the submit button below will take you to Page #2.
            </p>

            <br/>
            <h:commandButton id="navButton" action="#{navigationController.pageTwo}"
                             value="Go To Page 2"/>
            <br/>
            <br/>
            <h:commandButton id="navButton2" action="#{navigationController.nextPage}"
                             value="Implicitly Navigate to Page 3"/>

        </h:form>
    </h:body>
</html>
```

The source for the second JSF view is very similar, except that a different controller class method is specified in the action attribute of the view's h:commandButton component.

```
<?xml version="1.0" encoding="UTF-8"?>
<!DOCTYPE html PUBLIC "-//W3C//DTD XHTML 1.0 Strict//EN" "http://www.w3.org/TR/xhtml1/DTD/
xhtml1-strict.dtd">
<html xmlns="http://www.w3.org/1999/xhtml"
      xmlns:f="http://xmlns.jcp.org/jsf/core"
      xmlns:h="http://xmlns.jcp.org/jsf/html">
    <h:head>
        <meta http-equiv="Content-Type" content="text/html; charset=UTF-8"/>
        <title>Recipe 3-6 JSF Navigation</title>
    </h:head>
    <h:body>
        <h:form id="componentForm">
            <h1>JSF Navigation - Page 2</h1>
```

```
            <p>
                Clicking the submit button below will take you to Page #1.
            </p>

            <br/>
            <h:commandButton id="navButton" action="#{navigationController.pageOne}"
                             value="Go To Page 1"/>
        </h:form>
    </h:body>
</html>
```

The third JSF view contains an h:commandButton component that invokes a controller class action and utilizes conditional navigation, rendering pages depending on a conditional outcome in faces-config.xml.

```
<?xml version="1.0" encoding="UTF-8"?>
<!DOCTYPE html PUBLIC "-//W3C//DTD XHTML 1.0 Strict//EN" "http://www.w3.org/TR/xhtml1/DTD/
xhtml1-strict.dtd">
<html xmlns="http://www.w3.org/1999/xhtml"
      xmlns:f="http://xmlns.jcp.org/jsf/core"
      xmlns:h="http://xmlns.jcp.org/jsf/html">
    <h:head>
        <meta http-equiv="Content-Type" content="text/html; charset=UTF-8"/>
        <title>Recipe 3-6 JSF Navigation</title>
    </h:head>
    <h:body>
        <h:form id="componentForm">
            <h1>JSF Navigation - Page 3</h1>
            <p>
                The button below will utilize conditional navigation to take a user
                to the next page.  The application will use authentication to test
                conditional navigation.
            </p>

            <br/>
            <h:commandButton id="loginButton" action="#{navigationController.login}"
                             value="Login Action"/>
        </h:form>
    </h:body>
</html>
```

Lastly, the fourth JSF view in the navigational example application contains an h:commandButton that invokes a method and uses implicit navigation to return to the third JSF view, specifying the view name within the action attribute directly and bypassing the controller class altogether.

```
<?xml version="1.0" encoding="UTF-8"?>

<!DOCTYPE html PUBLIC "-//W3C//DTD XHTML 1.0 Strict//EN" "http://www.w3.org/TR/xhtml1/DTD/
xhtml1-strict.dtd">
<html xmlns="http://www.w3.org/1999/xhtml"
      xmlns:f="http://xmlns.jcp.org/jsf/core"
      xmlns:h="http://xmlns.jcp.org/jsf/html">
```

```
    <h:head>
        <meta http-equiv="Content-Type" content="text/html; charset=UTF-8"/>
        <title>Recipe 3-6 JSF Navigation</title>
    </h:head>
    <h:body>
        <h:form id="componentForm">
            <h1>JSF Navigation - Page 4</h1>
            <p>
                Clicking the submit button below will take you to Page #1 using conditional
                navigation rules.
            </p>

            <br/>
            <h:commandButton id="navButton2" action="recipe03_06c"
                             value="Implicitly Navigate to Page 3"/>
        </h:form>
    </h:body>
</html>
```

Now let's look at the source listing for NavigationController. It contains the methods that are specified within each page's h:commandButton action attribute. Some of the methods return a String value, and others do not. However, after the methods are invoked, then the FacesServlet processes the request, and the faces-config.xml configuration file is traversed, if needed, to determine the next view to render.

```
package org.javaee8recipes.chapter03.recipe03_06;

import javax.inject.Named;
import javax.enterprise.context.RequestScoped;

/**
 * Recipe 3-6
 * @author juneau
 */
@Named(value = "navigationController")
@RequestScoped
public class NavigationController implements java.io.Serializable{

    private boolean authenticated = false;

    /**
     * Creates a new instance of NavigationController
     */
    public NavigationController() {
    }

    public String pageOne(){
        return "PAGE_1";
    }

    public String pageTwo(){
        return "PAGE_2";
    }
```

```
    /**
     * Utilizing implicit navigation, a page name can be returned from an
     * action method rather than listing a navigation-rule within faces-config.xml
     * @return
     */
    public String nextPage(){
        // Perform some task, then implicitly list a page to render

        return "recipe03_06c";
    }

    /**
     * Demonstrates the use of conditional navigation
     */
    public void login(){
        // Perform some tasks, if needed, and then return boolean
        setAuthenticated(true);
        System.out.println("Here");
    }

    /**
     * @return the authenticated
     */
    public boolean isAuthenticated() {
        return authenticated;
    }

    /**
     * @param authenticated the authenticated to set
     */
    public void setAuthenticated(boolean authenticated) {
        this.authenticated = authenticated;
    }
}
```

At the heart of navigation is the `faces-config.xml` file. It specifies which view should be displayed after a corresponding outcome. Two of the `navigation-rules` use standard JSF navigation, and the last `navigation-rule` uses conditional navigation.

```
<?xml version='1.0' encoding='UTF-8'?>

<!-- =========== FULL CONFIGURATION FILE ================================== -->

<faces-config version="2.3"
              xmlns="http://xmlns.jcp.org/xml/ns/javaee"
              xmlns:xsi="http://www.w3.org/2001/XMLSchema-instance"
              xsi:schemaLocation="http://xmlns.jcp.org/xml/ns/javaee http://xmlns.jcp.org/
              xml/ns/javaee/web-facesconfig_2_3.xsd">
    <navigation-rule>
        <from-view-id>/chapter03/recipe03_06a.xhtml</from-view-id>
        <navigation-case>
```

```
            <from-outcome>PAGE_2/from-outcome>
            <to-view-id>/chapter03/recipe03_06b.xhtml</to-view-id>
        </navigation-case>
    </navigation-rule>

    <navigation-rule>
        <from-view-id>/chapter03/recipe03_06b.xhtml</from-view-id>
        <navigation-case>
            <from-outcome>PAGE_1</from-outcome>
            <to-view-id>/chapter03/recipe03_06a.xhtml</to-view-id>
        </navigation-case>
    </navigation-rule>

    <navigation-rule>
        <navigation-case>
            <from-action>#{navigationController.login}</from-action>
            <if>#{navigationController.authenticated}</if>
            <to-view-id>/chapter03/recipe03_06d.xhtml</to-view-id>
            <redirect/>
        </navigation-case>
    </navigation-rule>
</faces-config>
```

How It Works

One of the most daunting tasks when building a web application is to determine the overall page navigation. Many web frameworks have instituted XML configuration files for organizing page navigation. This is one technique used by the JavaServer Faces web framework, and the navigational XML is placed in a JSF application's `faces-config.xml` configuration file. When it's using standard navigation, JSF utilizes navigation rules to determine which view to render based on the outcome of page actions. If it's using standard JSF navigation, when a page action occurs, the controller class method that is associated with the action can return a `String` value. That value is then evaluated using the navigational rules that are defined in the `faces-config.xml` file and used to determine which page to render next.

The standard navigation infrastructure works well in most cases, but in some instances it makes more sense to directly list the next page to be rendered within the controller class, rather than making a navigation rule in the configuration file. When a controller class action is invoked, it can return the name of a view, without the `.xhtml` suffix. Such navigation was introduced with the release of JSF 2.0, and it is known as *implicit navigation*. As shown in the fourth example for the solution, you can also perform implicit navigation by specifying the name of a view without the suffix for an `action` attribute of the component tag.

Yet another type of navigation was introduced with JSF 2.0, taking navigation to the next level by allowing the use of JSF EL expressions in the `faces-config.xml` navigation rules. Conditional navigation allows for an `<if>` element to be specified within the navigational rule, which corresponds to a JSF EL condition. If the condition evaluates to `true`, then the specified view is rendered.

Navigation rules are constructed in XML residing within the `faces-config.xml` descriptor, and each rule has a root element of `navigation-rule`. Within each rule construct, the `from-view-id` element should contain the name of the view from which the action method was invoked. A series of `navigation-cases` should follow the `from-view-id` element. Each `navigation-case` contains a `from-outcome` element, which should be set to a `String` value corresponding to the `String` value that is returned from a subsequent action method. For instance, when the `pageOne` method is invoked in the example, the `String "PAGE_1"` is returned, and it should be specified within the `from-outcome` element within a `navigation-case` in the `faces-config.xml` file. Lastly, the `to-view-id` element should follow the `from-outcome` element within the navigation-case, and it should specify which view to render if the string in from-outcome is returned from the action method. The following excerpt shows the standard navigation rule that allows for navigation from page 1 to page 2 of the application:

```
<navigation-rule>
        <from-view-id>/chapter03/recipe03_06a.xhtml</from-view-id>
        <navigation-case>
            <from-outcome>PAGE_1</from-outcome>
            <to-view-id>/chapter03/recipe03_06b.xhtml</to-view-id>
        </navigation-case>
</navigation-rule>
```

Implicit navigation does not require any XML navigation rules to be declared. The action method that is invoked via an h:commandButton returns a String that is equal to the name of the view that should be rendered next. In the example, the second h:commandButton on view 1 invokes the nextPage controller class method, which returns the name of the next view that should be rendered.

```
public String nextPage(){
        // Perform some task, then implicitly list a page to render

        return "recipe03_06c";
}
```

If you want to use implicit navigation, you can bypass the controller class altogether and specify the name of the view that you want to render directly within the action attribute of h:commandButton or h:commandLink. The fourth JSF view in the example demonstrates this technique.

The third view in the example, named recipe03_05c.xhtml, demonstrates conditional navigation. Its h:commandButton action invokes the login method within the NavigationController class. That method does not contain much business logic in this example, but it does set the bean's authenticated field equal to true. Imagine that someone entered an incorrect password and failed to authenticate; in such a case, the authenticated field would be set to false. After the login method is executed, the faces-config.xml file is parsed to determine the next view to render, and the conditional navigation rule utilizes JSF EL to specify the navigation condition. The from-action element is set equal to the JSF EL that is used to invoke the login method, and an <if> element is specified, referencing the navigationController.authenticated field via JSF EL. If that field is equal to true, then the view specified within the to-view-id element will be rendered. Note that the <redirect/> is required to tell JSF to redirect to the view listed in the <to-view-id> element since JSF uses a redirect rather than a forward.

```
<navigation-rule>
        <navigation-case>
            <from-action>#{navigationController.login}</from-action>
            <if>#{navigationController.authenticated}</if>
            <to-view-id>/chapter03/recipe03_06d.xhtml</to-view-id>
            <redirect/>
        </navigation-case>
    </navigation-rule>
</faces-config>
```

Standard JSF navigation allows enough flexibility for most cases, and its architecture is much more sophisticated than other web frameworks. However, in JSF 2.0, two new navigational techniques known as *implicit* and *conditional navigation* were introduced. With the addition of the new techniques, JSF navigation is more robust and easier to manage.

3-7. Validating User Input

Problem

You want to add the ability for your application to validate any data that is entered into a JSF form.

Solution

Register a JSF validator on any text field components or other input components that need to be validated. Use predefined JSF validators where applicable and create custom validator classes when needed. The example for this recipe utilizes predefined validators for two h:inputText components in order to ensure that the values entered into them are of proper length. A custom validator is added to a third text field, and it is responsible for ensuring that the text contains a specified string. The three fields make up an employee input form, and when an employee is entered and the data validates successfully, a new Employee object is created and added to a list of employees. An h:dataTable element in the view is used to display the list of employees if there are any. This is perhaps not the most true-to-life example, but you can apply the basic philosophy to validate real-world needs in your own applications.

The following listing is for the JSF view that constructs the employee input form, including the validation tags for each input text field:

```
<html xmlns="http://www.w3.org/1999/xhtml"
      xmlns:f="http://xmlns.jcp.org/jsf/core"
      xmlns:h="http://xmlns.jcp.org/jsf/html">
    <h:head>
        <meta http-equiv="Content-Type" content="text/html; charset=UTF-8"/>
        <title>Recipe 3-7: Validating Data</title>
    </h:head>
    <h:body>
        <h:form id="employeeForm">
            <h1>Java Developer Employee Information</h1>
            <br/>
            <h:messages globalOnly="true" errorStyle="color: red" infoStyle="color: green"/>
            <br/>
            <h:dataTable id="empTable" var="emp"
                         border="1" value="#{employeeController.employeeList}"
                         rendered="#{employeeController.employeeList.size() > 0}">
                <f:facet name="header">
                    Current Employees
                </f:facet>
                <h:column id="empNameCol">
                    <f:facet name="header">Employee</f:facet>
                    <h:outputText id="empName" value="#{emp.employeeFirst} #{emp.
                    employeeLast}"/>
                </h:column>
                <h:column id="titleCol">
                    <f:facet name="header">Title</f:facet>
                    <h:outputText id="title" value="#{emp.employeeTitle}"/>
                </h:column>
```

```
            </h:dataTable>
            <p>
                Please use the form below to insert employee information.
            </p>
            <h:panelGrid columns="3">
                <h:outputLabel for="employeeFirst" value="First: " />
                <h:inputText id="employeeFirst" value="#{employeeController.employeeFirst}">
                    <f:validateLength minimum="3" maximum="30"/>
                </h:inputText>
                <h:message for="employeeFirst" errorStyle="color:red"/>

                <h:outputLabel for="employeeLast" value="Last: "  />
                <h:inputText id="employeeLast" value="#{employeeController.employeeLast}">
                    <f:validateLength minimum="3" maximum="30"/>
                </h:inputText>
                <h:message for="employeeLast" errorStyle="color:red"/>

                <h:outputLabel for="employeeTitle" value="Title (Must be a Java Position): "/>
                <h:inputText id="employeeTitle" value="#{employeeController.employeeTitle}">
                    <f:validator validatorId="employeeTitleValidate" />
                </h:inputText>
                <h:message for="employeeTitle" errorStyle="color:red"/>

            </h:panelGrid>
            <h:commandButton id="employeeInsert" action="#{employeeController.
            insertEmployee}"
                             value="Insert Employee"/>
        </h:form>
    </h:body>
</html>
```

The third h:inputText component in the view utilizes a custom validator. The f:validator tag is used to specify a custom validator, and its validatorId attribute is used to specify a corresponding validator class. The following listing is the Java code for a class named EmployeeTitleValidate, the custom validation class for the text field:

```
package org.javaee8recipes.chapter03.recipe03_07;

import java.util.Date;
import java.util.Locale;
import java.util.ResourceBundle;
import javax.faces.application.FacesMessage;
import javax.faces.component.UIComponent;
import javax.faces.context.FacesContext;
import javax.faces.validator.FacesValidator;
import javax.faces.validator.Validator;
import javax.faces.validator.ValidatorException;

/**
 *
 * @author juneau
 */
```

```
@FacesValidator("employeeTitleValidate")
public class EmployeeTitleValidate implements Validator {

    @Override
    public void validate(FacesContext facesContext, UIComponent uiComponent, Object value)
            throws ValidatorException {

        checkTitle(value);

    }

    private void checkTitle(Object value) {
        String title = value.toString();
        if (!title.contains("Java")) {
            String messageText = "Title does not include the word Java";
            throw new ValidatorException(new FacesMessage(FacesMessage.SEVERITY_ERROR,
                    messageText, messageText));
        }
    }
}
```

■ **Note** As of JSF 2.3, it is possible to inject resources such as into validator classes. User-generated validator classes are also injectable into other resources.

Now let's look at the JSF controller class for the JSF view that contains the validation tags. The controller class is named EmployeeController, and the action method, insertEmployee, is used to add new Employee objects containing valid data to an ArrayList.

```
package org.javaee8recipes.chapter03.recipe03_07;

import java.io.Serializable;
import java.util.ArrayList;
import java.util.List;
import javax.enterprise.context.SessionScoped;

import javax.faces.application.FacesMessage;
import javax.faces.context.FacesContext;
import javax.inject.Named;

@Named(value="employeeController")
@SessionScoped
public class EmployeeController implements Serializable {

    private String employeeFirst;
    private String employeeLast;
    private String employeeTitle;
```

```
private List <Employee> employeeList;

public EmployeeController(){
    employeeFirst = null;
    employeeLast = null;
    employeeTitle = null;
    employeeList = new ArrayList();
}

public void insertEmployee(){
    Employee emp = new Employee(employeeFirst,
                                employeeLast,
                                employeeTitle);
    employeeList.add(emp);
    FacesMessage facesMsg = new FacesMessage(FacesMessage.SEVERITY_INFO, "Employee
    Successfully Added", null);
    FacesContext.getCurrentInstance().addMessage(null, facesMsg);
}

/**
 * @return the employeeFirst
 */
public String getEmployeeFirst() {
    return employeeFirst;
}

/**
 * @param employeeFirst the employeeFirst to set
 */
public void setEmployeeFirst(String employeeFirst) {
    this.employeeFirst = employeeFirst;
}

/**
 * @return the employeeLast
 */
public String getEmployeeLast() {
    return employeeLast;
}

/**
 * @param employeeLast the employeeLast to set
 */
public void setEmployeeLast(String employeeLast) {
    this.employeeLast = employeeLast;
}

/**
 * @return the employeeTitle
 */
```

```
    public String getEmployeeTitle() {
        return employeeTitle;
    }

    /**
     * @param employeeTitle the employeeTitle to set
     */
    public void setEmployeeTitle(String employeeTitle) {
        this.employeeTitle = employeeTitle;
    }

    /**
     * @return the employeeList
     */
    public List <Employee> getEmployeeList() {
        return employeeList;
    }

    /**
     * @param employeeList the employeeList to set
     */
    public void setEmployeeList(List <Employee> employeeList) {
        this.employeeList = employeeList;
    }
}
```

In the end, the validators will raise exceptions if a user attempts to enter an employee first or last name using an invalid length or a title that does not contain the word *Java*. When user input validation fails, error messages are displayed next to the components containing the invalid entries.

How It Works

The JSF framework contains many features that make it more convenient for developers to customize their applications. Validators are one of those features, because they can be used to solidify application data and ensure data is correct before storing in a database or other data store. The JSF framework ships with a good deal of validators that are already implemented. To use these predefined validators, simply embed the appropriate validator tag within a component tag in a view to validate that component's data values. Sometimes there are cases where the standard validators will not do the trick. In such cases, JSF provides a means for developing custom validator classes that can be used from within a view in the same manner as the predefined validators.

In the example for this recipe, two of the `h:inputText` components contain standard JSF validators used to validate the length of the values entered. The `f:validateLength` tag can be embedded into a component for string-length validation, and the tag's `minimum` and `maximum` attributes can be populated with the minimum and maximum string length, respectively. As mentioned previously, JSF ships with a good number of these predefined validators. All that the developer is required to do is embed the validator tags in the components that they want to validate. Table 3-3 lists all standard validator tags and what they do. For a detailed look at each of the validator attributes, see the online documentation.

Table 3-3. *Standard Validators*

Validator Tag	Description
validateLength	Checks the length of a string
validateLongRange	Checks the range of a numeric value
validateDoubleRange	Checks the range of a floating-point value
validateRequired	Ensures the input field is not empty (also an alternative to using the required attribute on an input field component tag)
validateRegex	Validates the component against a given regular expression pattern

Oftentimes, there is a need for some other type of validation to take place for a specified component. In such cases, developing a custom validator class may be the best choice. Many developers shy away from writing their own validators because it seems to be a daunting task at first glance. However, JSF 2.0 took great strides toward making custom validator classes easier to write and understand.

To create a custom validator class, implement the `javax.faces.validator.Validator` class. Annotate the validator class with the `@FacesValidator` annotation, specifying the string you want to use for registering your validator within the `f:validator` tag. In the example, the name used to reference the validator class is `employeeTitleValidate`. The only requirement is that the validator class overrides the `validate` method, which is where the custom validation takes place. The validate method contains the following signature:

```
public void validate(FacesContext facesContext, UIComponent uiComponent, Object value)
            throws ValidatorException
```

Utilizing the parameters that are passed into the method, you can obtain the current `FacesContext`, a handle on the component being validated, as well as the component's value. In the example, a helper method is called from within the `validate` method, and it is used to check the component's value and ensure that the word *Java* is contained somewhere within it. If it does not validate successfully, a `ValidatorException` is created and thrown. The message that is placed within the `ValidatorException` is what will appear next to the component being validated if the validation fails. The following excerpt from the validation class demonstrates creating and throwing a `ValidatorException`:

```
throw new ValidatorException(new FacesMessage(FacesMessage.SEVERITY_ERROR,
                    messageText, messageText));
```

So, when does the validation occur? That is the key to the validator, isn't it? The answer is immediately, before the request is sent to the controller class action method. Any validation occurs during the *process validation* phase, and if one or more components being validated within a view throw a `ValidatorException`, then the processing stops, and the request is not sent to the action method. When the user clicks the Submit button, the validation takes place first, and if everything is okay, then the request is passed to the action method.

■ **Note** A means of validating that an input component simply contains a value is to use the `required` attribute. The `required` attribute of input component tags can be set to `true` in order to force a value to be entered for that component.

The validation of components in a JSF view using standard validators can really save a developer some time and increase the usability and precision of an application's data. The ability to create custom validators allows validation to be performed for any scenario. Be constructive, use validation on all of your application's input forms, and create custom validators to perform validation using unique techniques. Your application users will appreciate it!

3-8. Evaluating Page Expressions Immediately

Problem

You want to have some of your JSF component values evaluated immediately, rather than waiting until the form is submitted.

Solution

Specify `true` for the component tag's `immediate` attribute, and also specify the component's onchange attribute and set it equal to `submit()`. This will cause the input form to be submitted immediately when the value for the component is changed, and JSF will skip the render response phase when doing so and execute all components that specify an `immediate` attribute set to `true` during the Apply Request Values JSF lifecycle phase. The example for this recipe uses an employee form. Instead of waiting until the form is submitted, the first and last `h:inputText` components will be evaluated and validated during the Apply Request Values phase immediately when their values change. The following source is for the JSF view named `recipe03_08.xhtml`:

```
<html xmlns="http://www.w3.org/1999/xhtml"
      xmlns:f="http://xmlns.jcp.org/jsf/core"
      xmlns:h="http://xmlns.jcp.org/jsf/html">
    <h:head>
        <meta http-equiv="Content-Type" content="text/html; charset=UTF-8"/>
        <title>Recipe 3-8 Immediate View Evaluation</title>
    </h:head>
    <h:body>
        <h:form id="employeeForm">
            <h1>Java Developer Employee Information</h1>
            <br/>
            <h:messages globalOnly="true" errorStyle="color: red" infoStyle="color: green"/>
            <br/>
            <h:dataTable id="empTable" var="emp"
                         border="1" value="#{employeeController.employeeList}"
                         rendered="#{employeeController.employeeList.size() > 0}">
                <f:facet name="header">
                    Current Employees
                </f:facet>
                <h:column id="empNameCol">
                    <f:facet name="header">Employee</f:facet>
                    <h:outputText id="empName" value="#{emp.employeeFirst} #{emp.
                    employeeLast}"/>
                </h:column>
                <h:column id="titleCol">
                    <f:facet name="header">Title</f:facet>
```

```
                <h:outputText id="title" value="#{emp.employeeTitle}"/>
            </h:column>

        </h:dataTable>
        <p style="width: 40%;">
            Please use the form below to insert employee information. The first and
            last text fields will result in immediate evaluation during the apply
            request
            values phase, whereas the text field
            in the middle will result in standard evaluation and be validated during
            the invoke application phase.
            <br/><br/>
            To test, try inserting just one character in the first text field
            and then tab to the next field.  You should see an immediate result.
        </p>
        <h:panelGrid columns="3">
            <h:outputLabel for="employeeFirst" value="First: " />
            <h:inputText id="employeeFirst" immediate="true" onchange="submit()"
            value="#{employeeController.employeeFirst}">
                <f:validateLength minimum="3" maximum="30"/>
            </h:inputText>
            <h:message for="employeeFirst" errorStyle="color:red"/>

            <h:outputLabel for="employeeLast" value="Last: "  />
            <h:inputText id="employeeLast" value="#{employeeController.employeeLast}">
                <f:validateLength minimum="3" maximum="30"/>
            </h:inputText>
            <h:message for="employeeLast" errorStyle="color:red"/>

            <h:outputLabel for="employeeTitle" value="Title (Must be a Java Position): "/>
            <h:inputText id="employeeTitle" immediate="true"
            value="#{employeeController.employeeTitle}">
                <f:validator validatorId="employeeTitleValidate" />
            </h:inputText>
            <h:message for="employeeTitle" errorStyle="color:red"/>

        </h:panelGrid>
        <h:commandButton id="employeeInsert" action="#{employeeController.
        insertEmployee}"
                         value="Insert Employee"/>
    </h:form>
  </h:body>
</html>
```

As you can see, the h:inputText components with ids of employeeFirst and employeeTitle specify both the immediate="true" and the onchange="submit()" attributes. These two attributes cause the components to be validated immediately rather than when the h:commandButton action is invoked.

How It Works

Event handling that occurs immediately can be useful in cases where you do not want to validate the entire form in order to process input but, rather, when you want chosen components to be validated immediately. As mentioned in Recipe 3-1, when a JSF view is processed, a number of phases are executed. As such, when a form is submitted, the Invoke Application phase initiates the event handlers for view components, and validation occurs. When the `immediate` attribute for a component is set to `true`, the event handlers for that component execute during the Apply Request Values phase, which occurs before the Process Validation phase, where component validation normally occurs. This allows for an immediate validation response for the specified components, resulting in immediate error messages if needed.

As mentioned previously, specify the `immediate` attribute for a component and set it to `true` if you want to have that component evaluated immediately. This will cause the component to be evaluated and validated during the Apply Request Values phase. The real fun comes into play when you also specify the `onclick` attribute and set it equal to `submit()`, causing the form to be submitted when the value for the component changes. Specifying attributes as such will cause any component in the view that has an `immediate` attribute set to `true` to be validated when the component value changes.

■ **Note** The immediate attribute can also be useful when used on a `commandButton` component in such instances where you do not want any form processing to take place, such as if you want to set up a Cancel button or another button to bypass form processing.

3-9. Passing Page Parameters to Methods

Problem

You want to pass parameters to controller class methods from within a JSF view via Expression Language (EL).

Solution

Use a standard JSF EL expression to invoke a controller class method and enclose the parameters that you want to pass to the method within parentheses. In the example for this recipe, an `h:dataTable` component is used to display a list of `Author` objects in a view. Each row in the `h:dataTable` contains an `h:commandLink` component, which invokes a JSF controller class method when selected. The `h:commandLink` displays the current row's author name and invokes the `AuthorController` class `displayAuthor` method when clicked, passing the last name for the author being displayed in the current row. In the `displayAuthor` method, the list of authors is traversed, finding the element that contains the same last name as the parameter, which is passed into the method. The current author is then displayed in a subsequent page, which is rendered using implicit navigation.

The following source is for the JSF view entitled `recipe03_09a.xhtml`, which displays the list of authors using an `h:dataTable` component:

```
<html xmlns="http://www.w3.org/1999/xhtml"
      xmlns:f="http://xmlns.jcp.org/jsf/core"
      xmlns:h="http://xmlns.jcp.org/jsf/html">
    <h:head>
        <meta http-equiv="Content-Type" content="text/html; charset=UTF-8"/>
        <title>Recipe 3-9: Passing Page Parameters to Methods</title>
```

```
    </h:head>
    <h:body>
        <h:form id="componentForm">
            <h1>Author List</h1>
            <p>
                Below is the list of authors.  Click on the author's last name
                for more information regarding the author.
            </p>

            <h:graphicImage id="java9recipes" style="width: 10%; height: 20%"
            library="image" name="java9recipes.png"/>
            <br/>
            <h:dataTable id="authorTable" border="1" value="#{authorTableController.
            authorList}"
                         var="author">
                <f:facet name="header">
                    Java 9 Recipes Authors
                </f:facet>
                <h:column>
                <h:commandLink id="authorName" action="#{authorTableController.
                displayAuthor(author.last)}"
                               value="#{author.first} #{author.last}"/>
                </h:column>
            </h:dataTable>
            <br/>
            <br/>

        </h:form>
    </h:body>
</html>
```

The next listing is that of the controller class controller for the preceding JSF view. The controller class populates an `ArrayList` with `Author` objects upon instantiation.

```
package org.javaee8recipes.chapter03.recipe03_09;

import java.io.Serializable;
import java.util.ArrayList;
import java.util.List;
import javax.enterprise.context.SessionScoped;
import javax.inject.Named;

@Named(value = "authorTableController")
@SessionScoped
public class AuthorController implements Serializable {

    private List<Author> authorList = null;
    private final String juneauBio = "This is Josh Juneau's Bio";
    private final String deaBio = "This is Carl Dea's Bio";
    private final String beatyBio = "This is Mark Beaty's Bio";
    private final String oConnerBio = "This is John O'Connor's Bio";
    private final String guimeBio = "This is Freddy Guime's Bio";
```

```
    private Author current;
    private String authorLast;
    /**
     * Creates a new instance of RecipeController
     */
    public AuthorController() {
        super();
        authorLast = null;
        populateAuthorList();
    }

    private void populateAuthorList() {

        if(authorList == null){
            System.out.println("initializng authors list");
            authorList = new ArrayList<>();
            authorList.add(new Author("Josh", "Juneau", juneauBio));
            authorList.add(new Author("Carl", "Dea", deaBio));
            authorList.add(new Author("Mark", "Beaty", beatyBio));
            authorList.add(new Author("John", "O'Conner", oConnerBio));
            authorList.add(new Author("Freddy", "Guime", guimeBio));
        }
    }

    public String displayAuthor(String last){
        for(Author author:authorList){
            if(author.getLast().equals(last)){
                current = author;
                break;
            }
        }
        return "recipe03_09b";
    }

    /**
     * @return the authorList
     */
    public List getAuthorList() {
        System.out.println("Getting the authorlist =>" + authorList.size());
        return authorList;
    }

    /**
     * @return the current
     */
    public Author getCurrent() {
        return current;
    }

    /**
     * @param current the current to set
     */
```

```
    public void setCurrent(Author current) {
        this.current = current;
    }

    /**
     * @return the authorLast
     */
    public String getAuthorLast() {
        return authorLast;
    }

    /**
     * @param authorLast the authorLast to set
     */
    public void setAuthorLast(String authorLast) {
        displayAuthor(authorLast);
    }
}
```

The Author class is the same Author Plain Old Java Object (POJO) that was utilized in Recipe 3-3. For the source of the Author class, refer to that recipe. Lastly, the following code is for a JSF view entitled recipe03_09b.xhtml, the detail view for each author. When an author name is clicked from the h:dataTable component in the first view, the component's corresponding controller class method is invoked, and then this view is rendered to display the selected author's information.

```
<html xmlns="http://www.w3.org/1999/xhtml"
      xmlns:f="http://xmlns.jcp.org/jsf/core"
      xmlns:h="http://xmlns.jcp.org/jsf/html">
    <h:head>
        <meta http-equiv="Content-Type" content="text/html; charset=UTF-8"/>
        <title>Recipe 3-9: Passing Page Parameters to Methods</title>
    </h:head>
    <h:body>
        <h:form id="componentForm">
            <h1>#{authorTableController.current.first} #{authorTableController.current.
            last}</h1>
            <p>
                <h:graphicImage id="java9recipes" library="image" style="width: 10%; height:
                20%" name="java9recipes.png"/>
                <br/>
                #{authorTableController.current.bio}
            </p>

            <h:link value="Go Back to List" outcome="recipe03_09a"/>

        </h:form>
    </h:body>
</html>
```

How It Works

The release of JSF 2.0 contained many enhancements that made the life of JSF developers much easier than before. The ability to pass parameters to controller class methods from within JSF views is one such enhancement. As you can see from the example for this recipe, it is possible to pass parameters to a method within a JSF EL construct in the same manner that you would call any method with parameters in Java: by enclosing the argument(s) within parentheses after the method name. It cannot get much simpler than that!

Let's look at the lines of code that make this example hum. The first JSF view displays a table of author names, and each name is displayed using an h:commandLink component. The value attribute for the h:commandLink component is set to the author name, and the action attribute is set to the JSF EL, which invokes a controller class action method named displayAuthor. Notice that within the call to the controller class method, the EL for the author's last name is passed as a String parameter.

```
<h:dataTable id="authorTable" border="1" value="#{authorTableController.authorList}"
                         var="author">
        <f:facet name="header">
                    Java 9Recipes Authors
        </f:facet>
        <h:column>
                <h:commandLink id="authorName" action="#{authorTableController.
                displayAuthor(author.last)}"
                               value="#{author.first} #{author.last}"/>
        </h:column>
 </h:dataTable>
```

The displayAuthor method in the controller class accepts a String parameter value, which is the author's last name, and then finds an Author object within the list of authors that contains the same last name. When it's found, a class field named current is set equal to the Author object for the matching List element. The subsequent JSF view then displays content utilizing the current Author information.

Prior to JSF 2.0, developers were unable to pass parameters to controller class methods from within a view. This made it a bit more difficult to perform such techniques and usually involved a bit more code.

3-10. Using Operators and Reserved Words in Expressions

Problem

You want to perform some arithmetic and combine expressions within your JSF views.

Solution

JSF EL expressions can contain arithmetic using standard arithmetic operators. It is also possible to combine two or more expressions utilizing some of JSF ELs reserved words. In the following example, some JSF EL expressions are used to display mathematical results on a page. Both the usage of arithmetic and reserved words are used in the expressions.

```
<html xmlns="http://www.w3.org/1999/xhtml"
      xmlns:f="http://xmlns.jcp.org/jsf/core"
      xmlns:h="http://xmlns.jcp.org/jsf/html"
      xmlns:c="http://xmlns.jcp.org/jsp/jstl/core">
    <h:head>
```

```
        <meta http-equiv="Content-Type" content="text/html; charset=UTF-8"/>
        <title>Recipe 3-10: Arithmetic and Reserved Words</title>
    </h:head>
    <h:body>
        <h:form id="componentForm">
            <h1>JSF Arithmetic and Reserved Words in EL</h1>
            <p>
                The following examples use JSF EL to perform some arithmetic.
            </p>
            1 + 1 = #{1 + 1}
            <br/>
            <h:outputText value="20 / 5 = #{20 / 5}"/>
            <br/>

            <h:outputText rendered="#{1 + 1 eq 2}" value="1 + 1 DOES equal 2"/>
            <br/>
            <h:outputText rendered="#{5 * 4 != 20}" value="Is 5 * 4 equal to 20?"/>
            <br/>
            <h:outputText rendered="#{5 * 5 eq 25 and 1 + 1 eq 2}" value="Combining some
            expressions"/>
            <br/>
            <c:if test="#{evaluationController.expr1()}">
                This will be displayed if expr1() evaluates to true.
            </c:if>
            <br/>
            <c:if test="#{evaluationController.expr2() or evaluationController.field1}">
                This will be displayed if expr2() or field1 evaluates to true.
            </c:if>
        </h:form>
    </h:body>
</html>
```

Some of the expressions contain controller class references for a bean named EvaluationController. The listing for this controller class is as follows:

```
package org.javaee8recipes.chapter03.recipe03_10;

import javax.enterprise.context.RequestScoped;
import javax.inject.Named;

/**
 * Recipe 3-10
 * @author juneau
 */
@Named(value = "evaluationController")
@RequestScoped
public class EvaluationController {

    private boolean field1 = true;
```

```
    /**
     * Creates a new instance of EvaluationController
     */
    public EvaluationController() {
    }

    public boolean expr1(){
        return true;
    }

    public boolean expr2(){
        return false;
    }

    /**
     * @return the field1
     */
    public boolean isField1() {
        return field1;
    }

    /**
     * @param field1 the field1 to set
     */
    public void setField1(boolean field1) {
        this.field1 = field1;
    }
}
```

The resulting page will look as follows:

```
The following examples use JSF EL to perform some arithmetic.
1 + 1 = 2
20 / 5 = 4.0
1 + 1 DOES equal 2

Combining some expressions
This will be displayed if expr1() evaluates to true.
This will be displayed if expr1() or field1 evaluates to true.
```

How It Works

It is possible to use standard arithmetic and combine expressions using reserved words within JSF EL expressions. All standard arithmetic operators are valid in EL, but a couple of things are different. For instance, instead of writing an expression such as `#{1 + 1 = 2}`, you could use the eq reserved characters so that the expression reads `#{1 + 1 eq 2}`. Similarly, the != symbol could be used to specify that some value is not equal to another value, but rather, in this example, the ne reserved word is used. Table 3-4 describes all such reserved words.

Table 3-4. *JSF EL Reserved Words*

Reserved Word	Description
`and`	Combines two or more expressions
`div`	Used to divide
`empty`	Used to refer to an empty list
`eq`	Equal to
`false`	Boolean false
`ge`	Greater than or equal to
`gt`	Greater than
`instanceof`	Used to evaluate whether an object is an instance of another
`le`	Less than or equal
`lt`	Less than
`mod`	Modulus
`ne`	Not equal
`not`	Used for negation
`null`	Evaluates a null value
`or`	Combines two or more expressions
`true`	Boolean true

Table 3-5 lists the available operators that can be used within JSF EL expressions, in order of precedence.

Table 3-5. *Operators for Use in Expressions*

<table>
<tr><th>Operator</th></tr>
<tr><td>[]</td></tr>
<tr><td>()</td></tr>
<tr><td>- (unary), not, !, empty</td></tr>
<tr><td>*, /, div, %, mod</td></tr>
<tr><td>+, - (binary)</td></tr>
<tr><td><, >, <=, >=, lt, gt, le, ge</td></tr>
<tr><td>==, !, eq, ne</td></tr>
<tr><td>&&, and</td></tr>
<tr><td>||, or</td></tr>
<tr><td>?, :</td></tr>
</table>

3-11. Creating Bookmarkable URLs

Problem

You want to enable your application to allow URLs that will be linked to display specific objects. For instance, you want to use a GET URL such as `http://myserver.com/JavaEERecipes/chapter03/chapter03_11.xhtml?last=juneau` in order to display a page containing information on the author with the specified last name.

Solution

Add view parameters to a JSF view for which you want to create a bookmarkable URL by defining the parameter in an `f:viewParam` tag, which is a subtag of the `f:metadata` tag. Doing so will allow a page to become accessible via a URL that contains request parameters, which can be used for record identification. In this example, the view contains a view parameter, via the `f:viewParam` tag, that allows for the specification of an author's last name when the view is requested. In the following example, the controller class that was created in Recipe 3-9 has been modified to include a new property named `authorLast` in order to accommodate the new view parameter.

The sources for the view named `recipe03_11.xhtml` are listed next. They are very similar to the view named `recipe03_09b.xhtml`, except that they include an `f:viewParam` element, which is enclosed between opening and closing `f:metadata` elements.

```
<html xmlns="http://www.w3.org/1999/xhtml"
      xmlns:f="http://xmlns.jcp.org/jsf/core"
      xmlns:h="http://xmlns.jcp.org/jsf/html">
    <h:head>
        <meta http-equiv="Content-Type" content="text/html; charset=UTF-8"/>
        <title>Recipe 3-11: Creating Bookmarkable URLs</title>

    </h:head>
    <h:body>

        <f:metadata>
            <f:viewParam name="authorLast" value="#{authorTableController.authorLast}"/>
        </f:metadata>
        <h:form id="componentForm">
            <h1>#{authorTableController.current.first} #{authorTableController.current.
            last}</h1>
            <p>
                <h:graphicImage id="java9recipes" library="image" style="width: 10%; height:
                20%" name="java9recipes.png"/>
                <br/>
                #{authorTableController.current.bio}
            </p>

            <h:link value="Go Back to List" outcome="recipe03_09a"/>

        </h:form>

    </h:body>
</html>
```

The code for the AuthorController class that's pertinent to this example is listed next:

```
...
public class AuthorController implements Serializable {

    ...
    private String authorLast;
    ...

    /**
     * @return the authorLast
     */
    public String getAuthorLast() {
        return authorLast;
    }

    /**
     * @param authorLast the authorLast to set
     */
    public void setAuthorLast(String authorLast) {
        displayAuthor(authorLast);
    }
}
```

As mentioned previously, a property named `authorLast` has been included in this controller. This property makes it possible for the JSF view listed in the example to accept a request parameter named `authorLast` via a `GET` URL and pass it to the bean when the page is requested. In the end, the URL for accessing the view and requesting the details for the author Josh Juneau would be as follows:

```
http://my-server.com/JavaEERecipes/chapter03/chapter03_11.xhtml?authorLast=Juneau
```

How It Works

In the past, JSF applications had a weakness in that they used to require a launch view, which created an entry point for accessing the application. This gave the application a view that would set up an initial state for the application session. While this concept is nice because each user session would begin with an initialized application state, it prevented the ability for records to be linked directly via a URL. Sometimes it is very useful to have the ability to link a view to a URL that contains request parameters so that records matching the given parameters can be returned to the view without further user interaction; for instance, say a website included information regarding a book and wanted to include a URL to find out more about the book's author. It's much nicer to directly link to a view containing that author's information rather than redirecting the user to a website that requires them to perform a manual search for the author. Such URLs are also known as *bookmarkable* URLs because the URL contains all of the state that is required to make the request. Therefore, they allow the user of a web application to bookmark the URL for direct access to a specific point in an application.

JSF 2.0 introduced the ability to include view parameters, adding the ability for views to accept request parameters. Utilizing a `GET`-based URL, a request parameter can be appended to the end along with its value, and a view containing the new view parameter can then pass the parameter to a controller class before the response is rendered. The bean can then accept the parameter value and query a database or search through some other collection of data to find a record that matches the given value before rendering the response.

To include one or more view parameters within a view, you must add an opening and closing f:metadata element to the view and embed the number of f:viewParam elements between them. The f:viewParam element includes two attributes that must have values, those being the name and value attributes. The name attribute specifies the name of the request parameter as you would like it to appear within the bookmarkable URL, and the value attribute specifies the controller class field that should be mapped to that request parameter. In the example for this recipe, the JSF view contains a view parameter named authorLast, and the associated authorLast field within the controller class contains a setter method, which is invoked when the page is requested. The following excerpt from the view demonstrates the lines for adding the metadata and view parameter:

```
<f:metadata>
    <f:viewParam name="authorLast" value="#{authorTableController.authorLast}"/>
</f:metadata>
```

With the addition of the view parameter, the page can be requested with a URL containing the authorLast request parameter as follows:

```
http://my-server.com/JavaEERecipes/chapter03/chapter03_11.xhtml?authorLast=Juneau
```

When the page is requested, the view parameter's value invokes the setAuthorLast method in the controller class, which then searches for an author record that contains a last name equal to the given request parameter value.

```
...
public void setAuthorLast(String authorLast) {
        displayAuthor(authorLast);
    }
...
```

The addition of view parameters to JSF 2.0 has made it easy to create bookmarkable URLs. This allows applications to be more flexible and produce results immediately without requiring a user to navigate through several pages before producing a result.

3-12. Displaying Lists of Objects

Problem

You want to display a list of objects in your rendered JSF page.

Solution

Use a JSF h:dataTable component to display the list objects, iterating over each object in the list and displaying the specified values. The h:dataTable component is very customizable and can be configured to display content in a variety of layouts. The following JSF view contains two h:dataTable components that are used to display the authors for the *Java 9 Recipes* book using controller classes developed in previous recipes. The first table in the view is straightforward and displays the names of each author. It has been formatted to display alternating row colors. The second table contains two rows for each corresponding list element, displaying the author names on the first row and their bios on the second.

```
<html xmlns="http://www.w3.org/1999/xhtml"
      xmlns:f="http://xmlns.jcp.org/jsf/core"
      xmlns:h="http://xmlns.jcp.org/jsf/html">
    <h:head>
        <meta http-equiv="Content-Type" content="text/html; charset=UTF-8"/>
        <title>Recipe 3-12: Displaying Lists of Objects</title>

        <link href="#{facesContext.externalContext.requestContextPath}/css/styles.css"
              rel="stylesheet" type="text/css" />

    </h:head>
    <h:body>

        <h:form id="componentForm">
            <p>

                <h:graphicImage id="java9recipes" style="width: 10%; height: 20%"
                library="image" name="java9recipes.png"/>
                <br/>
                #{authorTableController.current.bio}
            </p>

            <h:dataTable id="authorTable" border="1"
                         value="#{authorTableController.authorList}"
                         styleClass="authorTable"
                         rowClasses="authorTableOdd, authorTableEven"
                         var="author">
                <f:facet name="header">
                    Java 9 Recipes Authors
                </f:facet>
                <h:column>
                <h:outputText id="authorName" value="#{author.first} #{author.last}"/>
                </h:column>
            </h:dataTable>
            <br/><br/>
            <h:dataTable id="authorTable2" border="1" value="#{authorTableController.
            authorList}"
                         var="author" width="500px;">
                <f:facet name="header">
                    Java 9 Recipes Authors
                </f:facet>
                <h:column>
                    <h:panelGrid columns="2" border="1" width="100%">
                        <h:outputText id="authorFirst" value="#{author.first}" style="width:
                        50%"/>
                        <h:outputText id="authorLast" value="#{author.last}"
                        style="width:50%"/>
```

```
                    </h:panelGrid>
                    <h:outputText id="authorBio" value="#{author.bio}"/>
                </h:column>
            </h:dataTable>

        </h:form>

    </h:body>
</html>
```

The example utilizes a cascading style sheet to help format the colors on the table. The source for the style sheet is as follows:

```
.authorTable{
        border-collapse:collapse;
}
.authorTableOdd{
        text-align:center;
        background:none repeat scroll 0 0 #CCFFFF;
        border-top:1px solid #BBBBBB;
}

.authorTableEven{
        text-align:center;
        background:none repeat scroll 0 0 #99CCFF;
        border-top:1px solid #BBBBBB;
}
```

The resulting page should look similar to Figure 3-4.

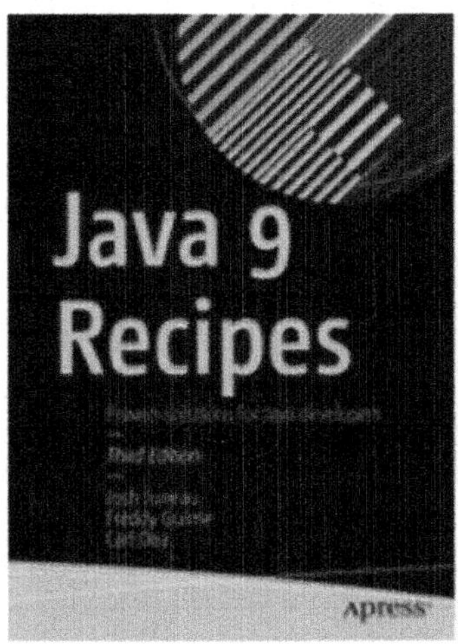

Java 9 Recipes Authors
Josh Juneau
Carl Dea
Mark Beaty
John O'Conner
Freddy Guime

Java 9 Recipes Authors	
Josh	Juneau
This is Josh Juneau's Bio	
Carl	Dea
This is Carl Dea's Bio	
Mark	Beaty
This is Mark Beaty's Bio	
John	O'Conner
This is John O'Connor's Bio	
Freddy	Guime
This is Freddy Guime's Bio	

Figure 3-4. *JSF DataTable component examples*

How It Works

A JSF `h:dataTable` component can be used to display lists of objects in a page. When rendered, an HTML table is constructed, populating the cells of the table with the data for each list element or record of data. The `h:dataTable` can iterate over a collection of data, laying it out in a columnar format including column headers and the ability to customize the look using Cascading Style Sheets (CSS). The component contains a number of important attributes, as listed in Table 3-6. Perhaps the most important of them are the `value` and `var` attributes. The `value` attribute specifies the collection of data to iterate, and the `var` attribute lists a `String` that will be used to reference each individual row of the table. The collection usually comes from the controller class, such as in the example for this recipe. The legal data types for the `value` attribute are `Array`, `DataModel`, `List`, and `Result`. The `var` attribute is used in each column to reference a specific field in an object for the corresponding row.

Table 3-6. *DataTable Attributes*

Attribute	Description
`id`	ID for the component
`border`	An integer indicating border thickness; 0 is default
`bgcolor`	Background color of table
`cellpadding`	Padding between the cell wall and its contents
`cellspacing`	Spacing within the cells
`width`	Overall width of the table, specified in pixels or percentages
`first`	The first entry in the collection to display
`rows`	Total number of rows to display
`styleClass`, `captionClass`, `headerClass`, `footerClass`, `rowClasses`, `columnClasses`	CSS attributes
`rendered`	Boolean value indicating whether the component will be rendered

The `h:dataTable` can contain any number of columns, and each is specified within the `h:dataTable` component in the JSF view. The `h:column` nested element encloses the output for each column. A column can contain just about any valid component or HTML, even embedded `dataTables`. An `h:column` normally does not have any attributes specified, but it always contains an expression or hard-coded value for display.

```
<h:column>my column value</h:column>
```

or

```
<h:column>#{myTable.myColValue}</h:column>
```

Normally, columns in an HTML table contain headers. You can add headers to the `h:dataTable` or individual columns by embedding an `f:facet` element within the `h:dataTable` and outside of the column specifications or within each `h:column` by specifying the name attribute as `header`. The `f:facet` element can also specify caption for the name attribute in order to add a caption to the table. The following excerpt from the example demonstrates an h:dataTable that includes each of these features:

```
<h:dataTable id="authorTable" border="1"
                        value="#{authorTableController.authorList}"
                        styleClass="authorTable"
                        rowClasses="authorTableOdd, authorTableEven"
                        var="author">
    <f:facet name="header">
        Java 9 Recipes Authors
    </f:facet>
    <h:column>
        <h:outputText id="authorName" value="#{author.first} #{author.last}"/>
    </h:column>
</h:dataTable>
```

In the example, you can see that the h:dataTable value attribute is listed as #{authorTableController.authorList}, a list of Author objects declared in the controller class. The var attribute establishes a variable named author that refers to the current author who is being processed from the author list. The author variable can then be accessed from within each h:column, displaying the data associated with the current list element.

An important piece of the puzzle to help make tables easier to read and follow is the CSS that can be used to style the table. The h:dataTable supports various attributes that allow you to apply externally defined CSS classes to your table, specifically, the styleClass, captionClass, headerClass, footerClass, rowClasses, and columnClasses attributes. Each of them can contain a CSS class specification for formatting. The example demonstrates this feature.

3-13. Developing with HTML5

Problem

You would like to develop your view composed using standard HTML5 markup, rather than JSF tags. Furthermore, you would like to take advantage of the JSF lifecycle and the managed bean/controller class architecture.

Solution

Utilize the HTML-friendly markup for use within JSF views. By using HTML5 within JSF views directly, you can take advantage of the entire JSF stack while coding views in pure HTML5. To use this solution, HTML5 tags have the ability to access the JSF infrastructure via the use of a new taglib URI specification jsf="http://xmlns.jcp.org/jsf", which can be utilized within JSF views beginning with JSF 2.2 and beyond. In views that specify the new taglib URI, HTML tags can utilize attributes that expose the underlying JSF architecture.

In the following example view, HTML5 tags are used to compose an input form that is backed by a JSF managed bean. To visit the sources for this example, visit the recipe03_13.xhtml view in the sources for the book.

```
<?xml version="1.0" encoding="UTF-8"?>
<!DOCTYPE html PUBLIC "-//W3C//DTD XHTML 1.0 Strict//EN" "http://www.w3.org/TR/xhtml1/DTD/
xhtml1-strict.dtd">
```

```
<html xmlns="http://www.w3.org/1999/xhtml"
      xmlns:jsf="http://xmlns.jcp.org/jsf">
    <head jsf:id="head">
        <meta http-equiv="Content-Type" content="text/html; charset=UTF-8"/>

    </head>
    <body jsf:id="body">
        <form jsf:id="form" jsf:prependId="false">
            <input type="email" jsf:id="value1" value="#{ajaxBean.value1}">
            </input>
            <br/><br/>
            <input type="text" jsf:id="value2" value="#{ajaxBean.value2}">

            </input>
            <br/>
            <br/>
            <input type="submit" jsf:id="status" jsf:value="#{ajaxBean.status}"
                   jsf:action="#{ajaxBean.process()}" value="Process"/>
            <label for="status">Message: </label>
            <output jsf:id="status">#{ajaxBean.status}</output>
        </form>
    </body>
</html>
```

■ **Note** This feature is only available to views written in Facelets. It is not available to views written in JSP.

How It Works

The JSF 2.2 release includes the ability to utilize HTML5 markup within JSF views. As a matter of fact, the markup is not limited to HTML5; it can also include HTML4, and so on. The addition of a new `taglib` URI makes this possible, because it allows existing HTML tags to be bound to the JSF lifecycle via the use of new namespace attributes. It is now possible to develop entire JSF views without using any JSF tags at all.

To utilize the new namespace attributes, your JSF view must import the `taglib` URI `jsf="http://xmlns.jcp.org/jsf"`. The new `taglib` can then be referenced as attributes within existing HTML tags, setting the underlying JSF attributes that are referenced. For instance, to utilize an HTML input tag with JSF, you would add the `jsf:id` attribute and set it equal to the JSF ID that you want to assign to that component. You would then set an attribute of `jsf:value` equal to the managed bean value.

■ **Note** There is no need to import the `http://xmlns.jcp.org/jsf/html taglib` because you are no longer utilizing JSF component tags in the view.

The syntax provides several benefits for web developers. Although not all web developers are familiar with JSF component tags, HTML tags are well known. By utilizing the syntax, JSF and HTML developers alike can create web views that utilize the power of JSF along with the flexibility of HTML. The syntax also makes it easier to bind HTML tags with JavaScript, if needed. You no longer need to worry about JSF view IDs getting in the way when working with HTML and JavaScript. With the addition of new JSF `taglib` namespace for use with HTML tags, both JSF and HTML alike have been improved.

3-14. Creating Page Templates

Problem

You want to make each of the JSF views in your application follow the same structure. Moreover, you want to have the ability to reuse the same layout for each view.

Solution

Create a page template using the Facelets view definition language. Facelets ships as part of JavaServer Faces, and you can use it to create highly sophisticated layouts for your views in a proficient manner. The template demonstrated in this recipe will be used to define the standard layout for all pages within an application. The demo application for this chapter is for a bookstore website. The site will display a number of book titles on the left side of the screen, a header at the top, a footer at the bottom, and a main view in the middle. When a book title is clicked in the left menu, the middle view changes, displaying the list of authors for the selected book.

To create a template, you must first develop a new XHTML view file and then add the appropriate HTML/JSF/XML markup to it. Content from other views will displace the `ui:insert` elements in the template once the template has been applied to one or more JSF views. The following source is that of a template named `custom_template.xhtml`; this is the template that will be used for all views in the application:

```
<html xmlns="http://www.w3.org/1999/xhtml"
      xmlns:ui="http://xmlns.jcp.org/jsf/facelets"
      xmlns:h="http://xmlns.jcp.org/jsf/html">

    <h:head>
        <meta http-equiv="Content-Type" content="text/html; charset=UTF-8" />
        <h:outputStylesheet library="css" name="default.css"/>
        <h:outputStylesheet library="css" name="cssLayout.css"/>
        <h:outputStylesheet library="css" name="styles.css"/>
        <title>#{faceletsAuthorController.storeName}</title>
    </h:head>

    <h:body>

        <div id="top">
            <h2>#{faceletsAuthorController.storeName}</h2>
        </div>
        <div>
            <div id="left">
                <h:form id="navForm">
                    <h:commandLink action="#{faceletsAuthorController.
                    populateJavaRecipesAuthorList}" >Java 9 Recipes</h:commandLink>
                    <br/>
                    <br/>
```

```
                    <h:commandLink action="#{faceletsAuthorController.populateJavaEERecipesA
                    uthorList}">Java EE 8 Recipes </h:commandLink>
                </h:form>
            </div>
            <div id="content" class="left_content">
                <ui:insert name="content">Content</ui:insert>
            </div>
        </div>
        <div id="bottom" style="position: absolute;width: 100%;bottom: 20px;">
            Written by Josh Juneau, Apress Author
        </div>

    </h:body>

</html>
```

The template defines the overall structure for the application views. However, it uses a CSS style sheet to declare the formatting for each of the `<div>` elements within the template. The style sheet, entitled `default.css`, should be contained within a `resources` directory in the application so that it will be accessible to the views. Refer to Recipe 3-16 for more details on the `resources` directory.

■ **Note** The CSS style sheets can be automatically generated for you if you're using the NetBeans IDE.

There are also a couple of JSF EL expressions utilized within the template. The EL references a JSF controller by the name of `AuthorController`, which is referenced by `faceletsAuthorController`. While the source for this class is very important for the overall application, you'll wait to look at that code until Recipe 3-15 since it does not play a role in the application template layout.

How It Works

To create a unified application experience, all of the views should be coherent in that they look similar and function in a uniform fashion. The idea of developing web page templates has been around for a number of years, but unfortunately many template implementations contain duplicate markup on every application page. While duplicating the same layout for every separate web page works, it creates a maintenance nightmare. What happens when there is a need to update a single link within the page header? Such a conundrum would cause a developer to visit and manually update every web page of an application if the template was duplicated on every page. The Facelets view definition language provides a robust solution for the development of view templates, and it is one of the major bonuses of working with the JSF technology.

Facelets provides the ability for a single template to be applied to one or more views within an application. This means a developer can create one view that constructs the header, footer, and other portions of the template, and then this view can be applied to any number of other views that are responsible for containing the main view content. This technique mitigates issues such as changing a single link within the page header, because now the template can be updated with the new link, and every other view within the application will automatically reflect the change.

To create a template using Facelets, create an XHTML view, declare the required namespaces, and then add HTML, JSF, and Facelets tags accordingly to design the layout you desire. The template can be thought of as an "outer shell" for a web view, in that it can contain any number of other views within it. Likewise, any number of JSF views can have the same template applied, so the overall look and feel of the application will remain constant. Figure 3-5 provides a visual demonstrating the concept of an application template.

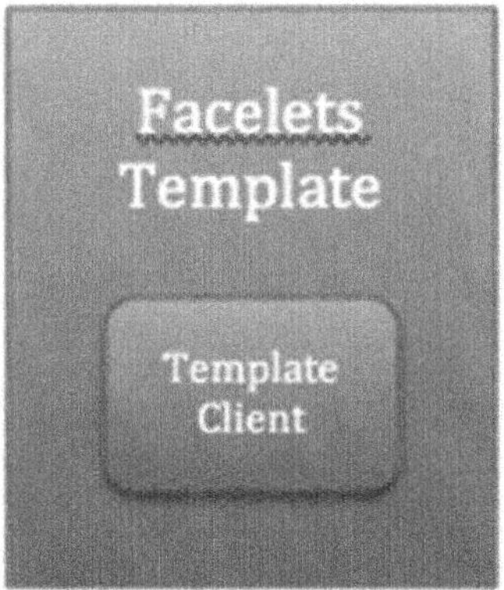

Figure 3-5. *Visual representation of a Facelets template and client*

You may have noticed from the view listing in the solution to this recipe that there are some tags toting the `ui:` prefix. Those are the Facelets tags that are responsible for controlling the view layout. To utilize these Facelets tags, you'll need to declare the XML namespace for the Facelets tag library in the `<html>` element in the template. Note that the XML namespace for the standard JSF tag libraries is also specified here.

```
<html xmlns="http://www.w3.org/1999/xhtml"
      xmlns:ui="http://xmlns.jcp.org/jsf/facelets"
      xmlns:h="http://xmlns.jcp.org/jsf/html">
...
```

■ **Note** The Facelets template must include the `<html>`, `<head>`, or `<h:head>`, and `<body>` or `<h:body>`, elements because they define the overall layout for each view that uses it. Each view that uses a Facelets template is known as a *composition*. One template can be used by multiple compositions or views. In actuality, everything outside of the `<ui:composition>` opening and closing tags in a composition is ignored. You'll learn more about that in the next recipe!

Facelets contains a number of special tags that can be used to help control page flow and layout. Table 3-7 in Recipe 3-15 lists the Facelets tags that are useful for controlling page flow and layout. The only Facelets tag that is used within the template for this recipe example is `ui:insert`. The `ui:insert` tag contains a `name` attribute, which is set to the name of the corresponding `ui:define` element that will be included in the view. Looking at the source for this recipe, you can see the following `ui:insert` tag:

```
<ui:insert name="content">Content</ui:insert>
```

If a view that uses the template, aka the template client, specifies a `ui:define` tag with the same `name` as the `ui:insert name`, then any content that is placed between the opening and closing `ui:define` tags will be inserted into the view in that location. However, if the template client does not contain a `ui:define` tag with the same name as the `ui:insert` tag, the content between the opening and closing `ui:insert` tags in the template will be displayed.

Templates can be created via an IDE, such as NetBeans, to provide a more visual representation of the layout you are trying to achieve. To create a Facelets template from within NetBeans, right-click the project folder into which you want to place the template and select New ➤ Other from the contextual menu to open the New File window. Once that's open, select JavaServer Faces from the Category menu and then Facelets Template from within the file types, as shown in Figure 3-6.

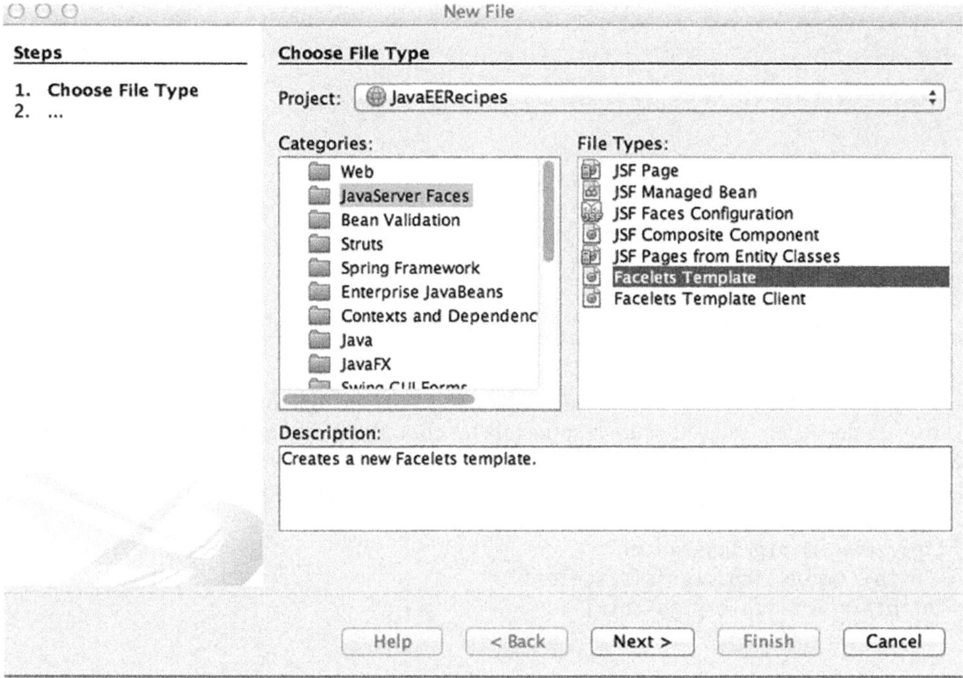

Figure 3-6. *Creating a Facelets template from within NetBeans*

After you've selected the Facelets Template file type, click the Next button to open the New Facelets Template window (see Figure 3-7). This window allows you to select the overall layout that you want to compose for your application views, as well as choose the location and name for the template.

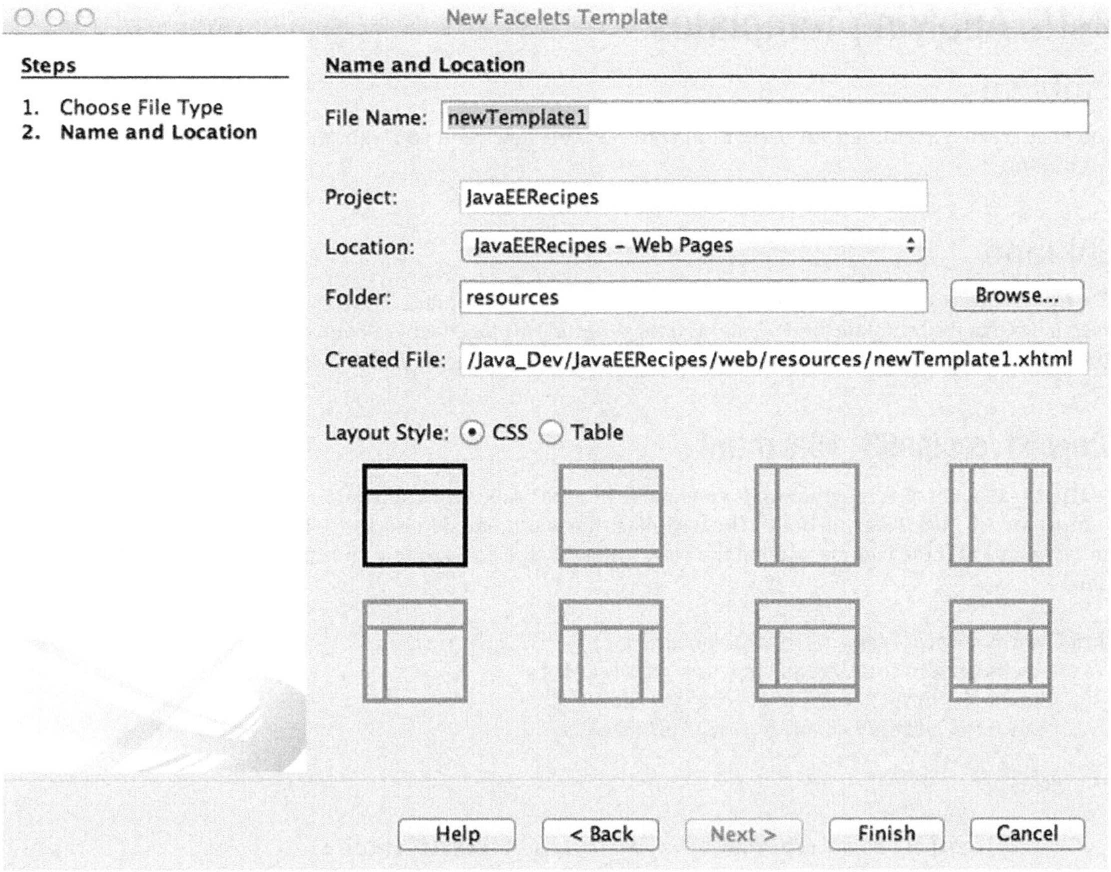

Figure 3-7. *New Facelets Template window in NetBeans*

After you've selected the layout of your choice and filled in the other options, the template will be opened within the NetBeans code editor, and you can begin to apply the template to JSF view clients (see Recipe 3-15). Using a wizard such as the one offered by NetBeans can help since you can choose a visual representation of the template at creation time.

In summary, a Facelets template consists of HTML and JSF markup, and it is used to define a page layout. Sections of the template can specify where page content will be displayed through the `ui:insert` tag. Any areas in the template that contain a `ui:insert` tag can have content inserted into them from a template client.

3-15. Applying Templates

Problem

You have created a template for use within your JSF web views and you want to apply it to the views of your application.

Solution

Use the `ui:composition` tag in each view that will utilize the template. The `ui:composition` tag should be used to invoke the template, and `ui:define` tags should be placed where content should be inserted. The following listings demonstrate how Facelets templates are applied to various views.

View #1: recipe03_15a.xhtml

`recipe03_15a.xhtml` is the markup for a view within the bookstore application that is used to display the authors for the *Java 9 Recipes* book. The template that was created in Recipe 3-14 is applied to the view, and individual `ui:define` tags are used in the view to specify the content that should be inserted into the page/view.

```
<html xmlns="http://www.w3.org/1999/xhtml"
      xmlns:ui="http://xmlns.jcp.org/jsf/facelets"
      xmlns:f="http://xmlns.jcp.org/jsf/core"
      xmlns:h="http://xmlns.jcp.org/jsf/html">

    <body>

        <ui:composition template="./layout/custom_template.xhtml">

            <ui:define name="top">

            </ui:define>

            <ui:define name="left">

            </ui:define>

            <ui:define name="content">
                <h:form id="componentForm">
                    <h1>Author List for Java 9 Recipes</h1>
                    <p>
                        Below is the list of authors.  Click on the author's last name
                        for more information regarding the author.
                    </p>

                    <h:graphicImage id="javarecipes" style="width: 100px; height: 120px"
                    library="image" name="java9recipes.png"/>
                    <br/>
                    <h:dataTable id="authorTable" border="1" value="#{faceletsAuthorControl
                    ler.authorList}"
```

```
                              var="author">
                    <f:facet name="header">
                        Java 9 Recipes Authors
                    </f:facet>
                    <h:column>
                        <h:commandLink id="authorName" action="#{faceletsAuthorControll
                        er.displayAuthor(author.last)}"
                                       value="#{author.first} #{author.last}"/>
                    </h:column>
                </h:dataTable>
                <br/>
                <br/>

            </h:form>
        </ui:define>

        <ui:define name="bottom">
            bottom
        </ui:define>

    </ui:composition>

</body>
</html>
```

View #2: recipe03_015b.xhtml

recipe03_15b.xhtml contains the sources for the second view within the bookstore application. It is used to list the authors for the *Java EE 8 Recipes* book. Again, note that the template has been applied to the view by specifying the template attribute within the ui:composition tag.

```
<html xmlns="http://www.w3.org/1999/xhtml"
      xmlns:ui="http://xmlns.jcp.org/jsf/facelets"
      xmlns:f="http://xmlns.jcp.org/jsf/core"
      xmlns:h="http://xmlns.jcp.org/jsf/html">

    <body>

        <ui:composition template="./layout/custom_template.xhtml">

            <ui:define name="top">

            </ui:define>

            <ui:define name="left">

            </ui:define>

            <ui:define name="content">
                <h:form id="componentForm">
                    <h1>Author List for Java EE 8 Recipes</h1>
```

```
                <p>
                    Below is the list of authors.  Click on the author's last name
                    for more information regarding the author.
                </p>

                <h:graphicImage id="javarecipes" library="image" style="width: 100px;
                height: 120px" name="java9recipes.png"/>
                <br/>
                <h:dataTable id="authorTable" border="1" value="#{faceletsAuthorControl
                ler.authorList}"
                             var="author">
                    <f:facet name="header">
                        Java 9 Recipes Authors
                    </f:facet>
                    <h:column>
                        <h:commandLink id="authorName" action="#{faceletsAuthorControll
                        er.displayAuthor(author.last)}"
                                       value="#{author.first} #{author.last}"/>
                    </h:column>
                </h:dataTable>
                <br/>
                <br/>

            </h:form>
        </ui:define>

        <ui:define name="bottom">
            bottom
        </ui:define>

    </ui:composition>

  </body>
</html>
```

View #3: recipe03_15c.xhtml

Recipe03_15c.xhtml contains the sources for another view listing that is part of the bookstore application. This view is responsible for displaying the individual author detail. Again, the template is applied to this page.

```
<html xmlns="http://www.w3.org/1999/xhtml"
      xmlns:f="http://xmlns.jcp.org/jsf/core"
      xmlns:ui="http://xmlns.jcp.org/jsf/facelets"
      xmlns:h="http://xmlns.jcp.org/jsf/html">
    <h:head>
        <meta http-equiv="Content-Type" content="text/html; charset=UTF-8"/>
        <title>Recipe 3-15: Facelets Page Template</title>
    </h:head>
    <h:body>
```

```
        <ui:composition template="./layout/custom_template.xhtml">

            <ui:define name="top">

            </ui:define>

            <ui:define name="left">

            </ui:define>

            <ui:define name="content">
                <h:form id="componentForm">
                    <h1>#{faceletsAuthorController.current.first}
                    #{faceletsAuthorController.current.last}</h1>
                    <p>
                        <h:graphicImage id="java9recipes" library="image" style="width:
                        100px; height: 120px" name="java9recipes.png"/>
                        <br/>
                        #{faceletsAuthorController.current.bio}
                    </p>
                </h:form>
            </ui:define>

            <ui:define name="bottom">
                bottom
            </ui:define>

        </ui:composition>
    </h:body>
</html>
```

Managed Bean Controller: AuthorController

Of course, all the business logic and navigation is occurring from within a JSF controller class. AuthorController is the bean that handles all the logic for the bookstore application. Note that the @Named annotation specifies a String value of faceletsAuthorController, which is used to reference the bean from within the views.

```
package org.javaee8recipes.chapter03.recipe03_15;

import java.io.Serializable;
import java.util.ArrayList;
import java.util.List;
import javax.annotation.PostConstruct;
import javax.enterprise.context.SessionScoped;
import javax.inject.Named;

@Named(value = "faceletsAuthorController")
@SessionScoped

public class AuthorController implements Serializable {

    private List<Author> authorList;
    private String storeName = "Acme Bookstore";
```

```
    private final String juneauBio =
            "Josh Juneau has been developing software"
            + " since the mid-1990s. PL/SQL development and database programming"
            + " was the focus of his career in the beginning, but as his skills developed,"
            + " he began to use Java and later shifted to it as a primary base for his"
            + " application development. Josh has worked with Java in the form of graphical"
            + " user interface, web, and command-line programming for several years. "
            + "During his tenure as a Java developer, he has worked with many frameworks"
            + " such as JSF, EJB, and JBoss Seam. At the same time, Josh has extended his"
            + " knowledge of the Java Virtual Machine (JVM) by learning and developing
            applications"
            + " with other JVM languages such as Jython and Groovy. His interest in
            learning"
            + " new languages that run on the JVM led to his interest in Jython. Since 2006,"
            + " Josh has been the editor and publisher for the Jython Monthly newsletter. "
            + "In late 2008, he began a podcast dedicated to the Jython programming
            language.";
    private final String deaBio = "This is Carl Dea's Bio";
    private final String beatyBio = "This is Mark Beaty's Bio";
    private final String oConnerBio = "This is John O'Connor's Bio";
    private final String guimeBio = "This is Freddy Guime's Bio";
    private Author current;
    private String authorLast;

    /**
     * Creates a new instance of RecipeController
     */
    public AuthorController() {

    }

    /**
     * Methods that are annotated with @PostConstruct are invoked when the
     * controller class is created.
     */
    @PostConstruct
    public void init(){
        populateJavaRecipesAuthorList();
    }

    public String populateJavaRecipesAuthorList() {

        authorList = null;

        authorList = new ArrayList<>();
        authorList.add(new Author("Josh", "Juneau", juneauBio));
        authorList.add(new Author("Carl", "Dea", deaBio));
        authorList.add(new Author("Mark", "Beaty", beatyBio));
        authorList.add(new Author("John", "O'Conner", oConnerBio));
        authorList.add(new Author("Freddy", "Guime", guimeBio));
        return "recipe04_01a";
    }
```

```
public String populateJavaEERecipesAuthorList() {
    System.out.println("initializng authors list");
    authorList = new ArrayList<>();
    authorList.add(new Author("Josh", "Juneau", juneauBio));
    return "recipe04_01b";

}

public String displayAuthor(String last) {
    for (Author author : authorList) {
        if (author.getLast().equals(last)) {
            current = author;
        }
    }
    return "recipe04_01c";
}

/**
 * @return the authorList
 */
public List getAuthorList() {
    return authorList;
}

/**
 * @return the current
 */
public Author getCurrent() {
    return current;
}

/**
 * @param current the current to set
 */
public void setCurrent(Author current) {
    this.current = current;
}

/**
 * @return the authorLast
 */
public String getAuthorLast() {
    return authorLast;
}

/**
 * @param authorLast the authorLast to set
 */
public void setAuthorLast(String authorLast) {
    this.authorLast = authorLast;
}
```

```
    /**
     * @return the storeName
     */
    public String getStoreName() {
        return storeName;
    }

    /**
     * @param storeName the storeName to set
     */
    public void setStoreName(String storeName) {
        this.storeName = storeName;
    }
}
```

In the end, the overall application will look like Figure 3-8. To run the application from the sources, deploy the WAR file distribution to your application server, and then load the following URL into your browser: `http://your-server:port_number/JavaEERecipes/faces/chapter03/chapter03_15a.xhtml`.

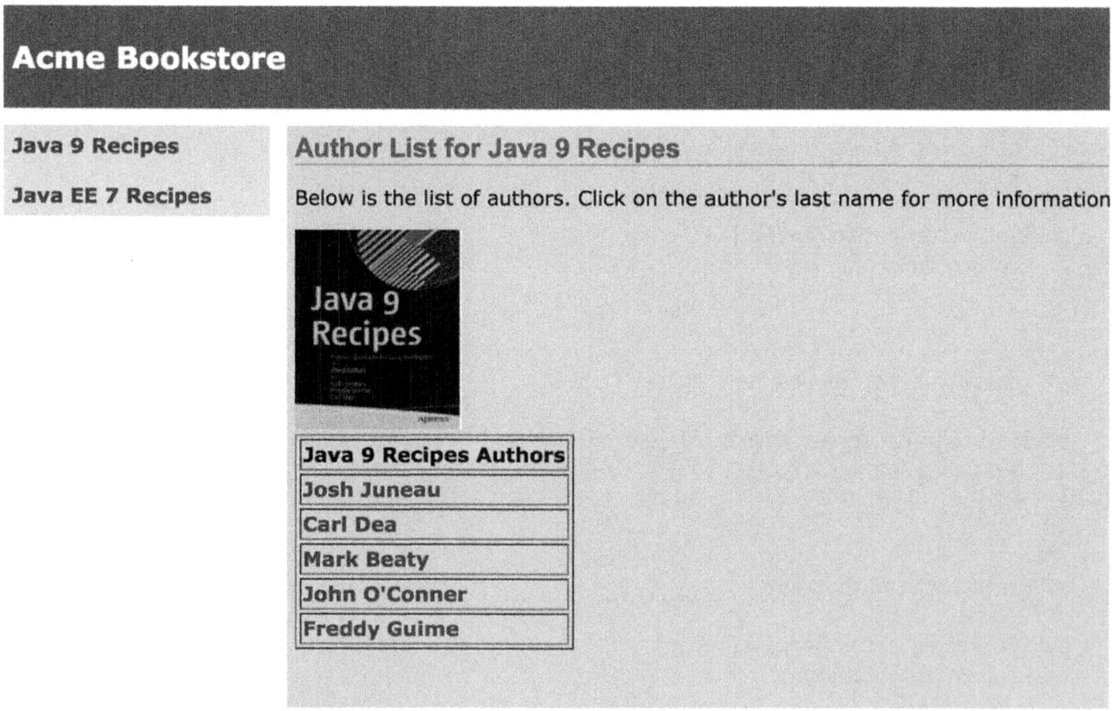

Figure 3-8. *Application using Facelets template*

How It Works

Applying a Facelets template to individual views in a JSF application is quite easy. Views that use a template are known as *template clients*. As mentioned in Recipe 3-14, a view template can specify individual `ui:insert` tags, along with the `name` attribute, in any location on the template where view content could be inserted. The `name` attribute within the `ui:insert` tag will pair up with the `name` attribute within the `ui:define` tag in the template client in order to determine what content is inserted.

■ **Note** As noted in Recipe 3-14, each view that uses a Facelets template can be referred to as a *composition*. It can also be referred to as a *template client*. It is important to note that a template client, or composition, contains an opening and closing `<ui:composition>` tag. Everything outside of those tags is actually ignored at rendering time because the template body is used instead. You can also omit the `<html>` tags within a template client and just open and close the view using the `<ui:composition>` tags instead. See the "Opening/Closing Template Clients with <ui:composition>" sidebar for an example.

OPENING/CLOSING TEMPLATE CLIENTS WITH <UI:COMPOSITION>

It is common to see template client views using opening and closing `<html>` tags, as demonstrated with the example views in the solution to this recipe. However, since everything outside of the `<ui:composition>` tags is ignored at rendering time, you can omit those tags completely. It is sometimes useful to open and close a template client with the `<ui:composition>` tag. However, some page editors will be unable to work with the code or errors will be displayed because the view does not include the `<html>` element at its root. Here's an example of using `<ui:composition>` as the opening and closing elements of a template client:

```
<ui:composition xmlns="http://www.w3.org/1999/xhtml"
      xmlns:ui="http://xmlns.jcp.org/jsf/facelets"
      xmlns:f="http://xmlns.jcp.org/jsf/core"
      xmlns:h=http://xmlns.jcp.org/jsf/html
      template="./layout/custom_template.xhtml">

<<same as code per the view samples in the solution to this recipe>>

 </ui:composition>
```

Use the technique that suits your application the best! Remember, JSF and Facelets will treat each view the same, and you can save a few lines of code specifying `<ui:composition>` as the root.

Applying Templates

A template can be applied to a view by specifying it within the template attribute within the view's `ui:composition` tag. For instance, all the views in this example specify the same template, as you can see in the following excerpt:

```
<ui:composition template="./layout/custom_template.xhtml">
```

The name of the template in the example is `custom_template.xhtml`, and the path to the template is `./layout/`. The `ui:composition` tag should encapsulate all other markup in a Facelets view. All views that are to use the template must specify the `ui:composition` tag. A number of other useful Facelets template tags come along with Facelets, as described in Table 3-7.

Table 3-7. *Facelets Page Control and Template Tags*

Tag	Description
`ui:component`	Defines a template component and specifies a file name for the component
`ui:composition`	Defines a page composition and encapsulates all other JSF markup
`ui:debug`	Creates a debug component, which captures debugging information, namely, the state of the component tree and the scoped variables in the application, when the component is rendered
`ui:define`	Defines content that is inserted into a page by a template
`ui:decorate`	Decorates pieces of a page
`ui:fragment`	Defines a template fragment, much like `ui:component`, except that all content outside of tag is not disregarded
`ui:include`	Allows another XHTML page to be encapsulated and reused within a view
`ui:insert`	Inserts content into a template
`ui:param`	Passes parameters to an included file or template
`ui:repeat`	Iterates over a collection of data
`ui:remove`	Removes content from a page

The `ui:define` tag encloses content that will be inserted into the template at the location of the template's `ui:insert` tags. The `ui:define` tag is matched to a template's `ui:insert` tag based on the value of the `name` attribute that is common to each tag. As you can see from the first view listing in this example, the first `ui:define` tag specifies `top` for the `name` attribute, and this will correspond to the template `ui:insert` tag with a `name` attribute equal to `top`. But the template does not specify such a tag! That is okay; there does not have to be a one-to-one match between the `ui:define` and `ui:insert` tags. A view can specify any number of `ui:define` tags, and if they do not correspond to any of the `ui:insert` tags in the template, then they are ignored. Likewise, a template can specify any number of `ui:insert` tags, and if they do not correspond to a `ui:define` tag in the template client view, then the content that is defined in the template in that location will be displayed.

Looking at the same view, another `ui:define` tag contains a `name` attribute value equal to `content`, and this tag does correspond with a `ui:insert` tag in the template that also has a `name` attribute value of `content`. The following excerpt is taken from the template, and it shows the `ui:insert` tag that corresponds to the view's `ui:define` tag with the same `name` attribute. You can see the full listing for the template in Recipe 3-14.

```
<div id="content" class="left_content">
        <ui:insert name="content">Content</ui:insert>
</div>
```

The following excerpt, taken from recipe04_01a.xhtml, is the corresponding ui:define tag that will be inserted into the template at this location:

```
<ui:define name="content">
        <h:form id="componentForm">
            <h1>Author List for Java 9 Recipes</h1>
            <p>
                Below is the list of authors.  Click on the author's last name
                for more information regarding the author.
            </p>

            <h:graphicImage id="javarecipes" style="width: 10%; height: 20%" library="image"
            name="java9recipes.png"/>
            <br/>
            <h:dataTable id="authorTable" border="1" value="#{faceletsAuthorController.
            authorList}"
                         var="author">
                <f:facet name="header">
                    Java 9 Recipes Authors
                </f:facet>
                <h:column>
                    <h:commandLink id="authorName" action="#{faceletsAuthorController.
                    displayAuthor(author.last)}"
                                   value="#{author.first} #{author.last}"/>
                </h:column>
            </h:dataTable>
            <br/>
            <br/>

        </h:form>
    </ui:define>
```

As you can see, it can be very powerful to define a view template that can be applied to several views in an application. Facelets templating provides a very powerful solution for defining such a template, allowing for consistent page layout and reusable page code.

3-16. Adding Resources into the Mix

Problem

You want to include resources, such as CSS, images, and JavaScript code, within your views that are accessible for use from every view within your application. For instance, rather than hard-coding a URL to an image, you want to reference the image location and have the application dynamically create the URL to the image location at runtime.

Solution

Create a resource directory and, optionally, subfolders within the resources directory to contain the resources that your application will utilize. Any CSS files, images, and so on, that are placed within subdirectories in the resources folder can be referenced within a JSF view via a JSF component's library attribute, rather than specifying the full path to the resource. In the following example, a cascading style sheet is used to style the table of authors within the application. For this recipe, you will use the styles.css sheet that was applied to the h:dataTable in an earlier recipe. The style sheet declaration will reside in the custom_template.xhtml template, and you will use an h:outputStylesheet component rather than a <link> tag. As a matter of fact, all of the <link> tags will be removed and replaced with h:outputStylesheet components to take advantage of the resources folder. The directory structure should look like Figure 3-9 when set up correctly.

Figure 3-9. *Utilizing the resources directory*

The following listing is the updated custom_template.xhtml, because it now utilizes the h:outputStylesheet component rather than the <link> tag. Note that the library attribute is specified as css.

```
<html xmlns="http://www.w3.org/1999/xhtml"
      xmlns:ui="http://xmlns.jcp.org/jsf/facelets"
      xmlns:f="http://xmlns.jcp.org/jsf/core"
      xmlns:h="http://xmlns.jcp.org/jsf/html">

    <body>

        <ui:composition template="./layout/custom_template.xhtml">

            <ui:define name="content">
                <h:form id="componentForm">
                    <h1>Author List for Java 9 Recipes</h1>
                    <p>
                        Below is the list of authors.  Click on the author's last name
                        for more information regarding the author.
                    </p>

                    <h:graphicImage id="javarecipes"
                                    library="image" style="width: 100px; height: 120px"
                                    name="java9recipes.png"/>
                    <br/>
```

```
                <h:dataTable id="authorTable" border="1" value="#{faceletsAuthorControl
                ler.authorList}"
                             styleClass="authorTable"
                             rowClasses="authorTableOdd, authorTableEven"
                             var="author">
                    <f:facet name="header">
                        Java 9 Recipes Authors
                    </f:facet>
                    <h:column>
                        <h:commandLink id="authorName" action="#{faceletsAuthorController.
                        displayAuthor(author.last)}"
                                       value="#{author.first} #{author.last}"/>
                    </h:column>
                </h:dataTable>
                <br/>
                <br/>

            </h:form>
        </ui:define>

    </ui:composition>

  </body>
</html>
```

The h:dataTable component that is used to list the authors within the views of the Acme Bookstore application can now use the styles that are listed in styles.css. The following excerpt from the XHTML document named recipe03_16.xhtml demonstrates the h:dataTable component with the styles applied:

```
<h:dataTable id="authorTable" border="1" value="#{faceletsAuthorController.authorList}"
                              styleClass="authorTable"
                              rowClasses="authorTableOdd, authorTableEven"
                              var="author">
        <f:facet name="header">
             Java 9 Recipes Authors
        </f:facet>
        <h:column>
                <h:commandLink id="authorName"
                    action="#{faceletsAuthorController.displayAuthor(author.last)}"
                     value="#{author.first} #{author.last}"/>
        </h:column>
    </h:dataTable>
```

The table should now look like Figure 3-10 when rendered on a page.

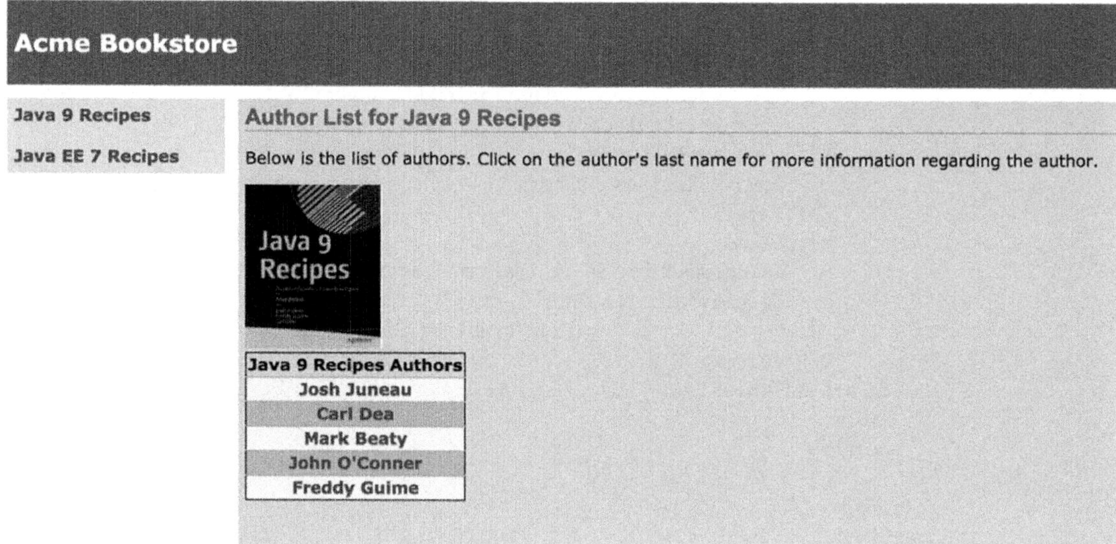

Figure 3-10. *Author table with styles applied*

How It Works

It is easy to add a resource to a JSF application because there is no need to worry about referring to a static path when declaring the resources. Since the release of JSF 2.0, the `resources` folder can be used to list subfolders, also known as *libraries*, into which the resources can be placed. The JSF components that can use resources now have the `library` attribute baked into them. This allows a specific library to be specified for such components so that the component will know where to find the resources that it requires.

To use the new `resources` folder, create a folder at the root of an application's web directory and name it `resources`. That `resources` folder can then contain subfolders, which will become the libraries that can be utilized within the JSF components. For instance, subfolders can be named `css` and `images`, and then those names can be specified for the `library` attribute of JSF components that utilize such resources. In the example, cascading style sheets are placed into the `resources/css` folder, and then they are referenced utilizing the `h:outputStylesheet` component and specifying the `css` library as follows:

```
<h:outputStylesheet library="css" name="default.css"/>
```

Other resources can be placed in such libraries. The `h:graphicImage` component also contains the `library` attribute, so the images for the books can be moved into a folder named `resources/image`, and then the `h:graphicImage` tag can reference the image as such:

```
<h:graphicImage id="javarecipes"
                              library="image" style="width: 100px; height: 120px"
                              name="java9recipes.png"/>
```

It has always been a challenge referencing resource files from the pages of a web application. To do so, a developer needs to know the exact path to the resource, and sometimes the path can be broken if folder names are changed or if the application is deployed in a different server environment. The use of the resources folder in JSF 2.0 along with the new library attribute has greatly reduced the complexity of managing such resources.

3-17. Handling Variable-Length Data

Problem

You are interested in iterating over a collection of data using a technique other than an h:dataTable component because you want to use standard HTML table markup for each row and column of the table.

Solution

Use the Facelets ui:repeat tag for iterating over a collection of data rather than the h:dataTable component. Doing so allows for the same style of collection iteration, but it does not force the use of the h:dataTable component elements. For this recipe, the Acme Bookstore application has been rewritten so that it now contains the ability to list each author's books separately on their bio page. When an author name is chosen from the book listing or when an author is searched, then the bio page will appear, and the author's bio is displayed along with each of the books that the author has written.

■ **Note** The example for this recipe has been rewritten to make the application more robust. A new Book class has been created so that each book is now its own object. The Author class has been rewritten so that one or more Book objects can now be added to each Author object. The AuthorController has been rewritten so that the new Book and Author objects can be used to populate the author listing tables, and a new method has been added that allows for the initialization of each Book and Author object. To use the new classes, the application template (custom_template_neworg.xhtml), search component (search_neworg.xhtml), and each of the application have been rewritten. Refer to the sources in the org.javaee8recipes.chapter03.recipe03_17 package and the recipe's corresponding XHTML documents for complete listings.

The ui:repeat tag is used to iterate over a collection of the selected author's books within the author bio view, named recipe04_05c.xhtml. The author bio page can be reached by selecting an author from a listing of authors or searching for an author using the search component. The following code shows the view, recipe03_17c.xhtml, which is the bio view:

```
<html xmlns="http://www.w3.org/1999/xhtml"
      xmlns:f="http://xmlns.jcp.org/jsf/core"
      xmlns:ui="http://xmlns.jcp.org/jsf/facelets"
      xmlns:h="http://xmlns.jcp.org/jsf/html">
    <h:head>
        <meta http-equiv="Content-Type" content="text/html; charset=UTF-8"/>
        <title>Recipe 3-17: Facelets Page Template</title>
    </h:head>
    <h:body>
        <ui:composition template="./layout_enhanced/custom_template_search_neworg.xhtml">
            <ui:define name="content">
                <h:form id="componentForm">
```

```
                <h1>#{uiRepeatAuthorController.current.first}
                #{uiRepeatAuthorController.current.last}</h1>
                <p>
                    #{uiRepeatAuthorController.current.bio}
                </p>

                <br/>
                <h1>Author's Books</h1>

                <table>
                <ui:repeat id="bookList" var="book" value="#{uiRepeatAuthorController.
                current.books}">
                    <tr>
                        <td>
                            <h:graphicImage id="bookImage"
                                            library="image"
                                            style="width: 100px; height: 120px"
                                            name="#{book.image}"/>
                        </td>
                    </tr>
                    <tr>
                        <td>
                            <strong>#{book.title}</strong>
                        </td>
                    </tr>
                </ui:repeat>
                </table>
            </h:form>
        </ui:define>

    </ui:composition>
  </h:body>
</html>
```

Each Author object contains a list of books that an author has written, and when the bio page is rendered, it looks like Figure 3-11, displaying the list of books that the author has written using the ui:repeat tag.

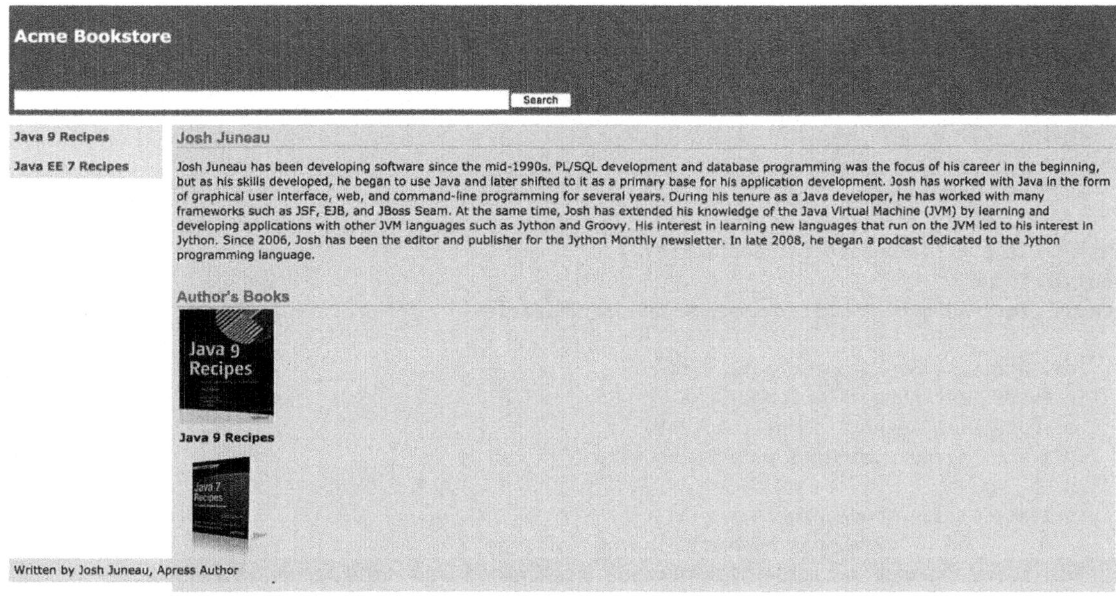

***Figure 3-11.** Displaying a collection of objects with ui:repeat*

How It Works

The Facelets `ui:repeat` tag is a nice alternative to the `h:dataTable` component if you need to have more control over the HTML table that is rendered. The `h:dataTable` component is powerful in that it makes it easy to iterate over a collection of objects and display them in a page. However, sometimes it is useful to control the layout a bit more, and `ui:repeat` provides that level of control.

The `ui:repeat` tag has a handful of attributes that need to be specified in order to bind the tag to a collection of data within a managed bean. Specifically, the `value` and `var` attributes, much like those of the `h:dataTable` component, are used to specify the collection to iterate over and the variable that will be used to refer to a single object within the collection, respectively. In the example, the `value` attribute is set to `#{uiRepeatAuthorController.current.books}`, which is a collection of `Book` objects that is attached to the currently selected `Author`, and the `var` attribute is set to the value `book`.

The markup and JSF tags placed between the opening and closing `ui:repeat` tags will be processed for each iteration over the collection of objects. In the example, two table rows are placed inside `ui:repeat`; one row contains the book cover image, and the other contains the name of the book. The `Book` object fields are referenced within `ui:repeat` using the value of the `var` attribute, `book`.

In the example for this recipe, the views that display the complete author list for each of the books use a list named `authorList`. The `authorList` is declared within the `AuthorController` managed bean and populated with `Author` objects. When an author is selected from the list, the `displayAuthor` method within `AuthorController` is invoked, which populates the current `Author` object. Let's look at the `AuthorController` for this recipe, which has been rewritten since its use in previous recipes.

```
package org.javaee8recipes.chapter03.recipe03_17;

import java.io.Serializable;
import java.util.ArrayList;
import java.util.List;
import javax.annotation.PostConstruct;
```

```
import javax.enterprise.context.SessionScoped;
import javax.inject.Named;

/**
 * Recipe 3-17
 *
 * @author juneau
 */
@Named(value = "uiRepeatAuthorController")
@SessionScoped
public class AuthorController implements Serializable {

    private List<Book> authorBookList;
    private List<Author> authorList;
    private List<Author> completeAuthorList;
    private String storeName = "Acme Bookstore";

    private String juneauBio =
            "Josh Juneau has been developing software"
            + " since the mid-1990s. PL/SQL development and database programming"
            + " was the focus of his career in the beginning, but as his skills developed,"
            + " he began to use Java and later shifted to it as a primary base for his"
            + " application development. Josh has worked with Java in the form of graphical"
            + " user interface, web, and command-line programming for several years. "
            + "During his tenure as a Java developer, he has worked with many frameworks"
            + " such as JSF, EJB, and JBoss Seam. At the same time, Josh has extended his"
            + " knowledge of the Java Virtual Machine (JVM) by learning and developing
            applications"
            + " with other JVM languages such as Jython and Groovy. His interest in
            learning"
            + " new languages that run on the JVM led to his interest in Jython. Since 2006,"
            + " Josh has been the editor and publisher for the Jython Monthly newsletter. "
            + "In late 2008, he began a podcast dedicated to the Jython programming
            language.";
    private String deaBio = "This is Carl Dea's Bio";
    private String beatyBio = "This is Mark Beaty's Bio";
    private String oConnerBio = "This is John O'Connor's Bio";
    private String guimeBio = "This is Freddy Guime's Bio";
    private Author current;
    private String authorLast;

    /**
     * Creates a new instance of RecipeController
     */
    public AuthorController() {

    }

    @PostConstruct
    public void init(){
        populateAuthors();
```

```
    populateJavaRecipesAuthorList();
    populateCompleteAuthorList();
}
private void populateAuthors(){
    Book book1 = new Book("Java 9 Recipes", "java9recipes.png");
    Book book2 = new Book("Java EE 8 Recipes", "javaee8recipes.png");
    Book book3 = new Book("Java FX 2.0: Introduction By Example", "javafx.png");
    authorBookList = new ArrayList<Author>();

    Author author1 = new Author("Josh", "Juneau", juneauBio);
    author1.addBook(book1);
    author1.addBook(book2);
    authorBookList.add(author1);

    Author author2 = new Author("Carl", "Dea", deaBio);
    author2.addBook(book1);
    author2.addBook(book3);
    authorBookList.add(author2);

    Author author3 = new Author("Mark", "Beaty", beatyBio);
    author3.addBook(book1);
    authorBookList.add(author3);

    Author author4 = new Author("John", "O'Conner", oConnerBio);
    author4.addBook(book1);
    authorBookList.add(author4);

    Author author5 = new Author("Freddy", "Guime", guimeBio);
    author5.addBook(book1);
    authorBookList.add(author5);
}

/**
 * Searches through all Author objects and populates the authorList
 * with only those authors who were involved with the Java 9 Recipes book
 * @return
 */
public String populateJavaRecipesAuthorList() {
    authorList = new ArrayList<>();
    for(Author author:authorBookList){
        List<Book>books = author.getBooks();
        for(Book book:books){
            if(book.getTitle().equals("Java 9 Recipes")){
                authorList.add(author);
            }
        }
    }

    return "recipe04_05a";
}
```

```
/**
 * Searches through all Author objects and populates the authorList
 * with only those authors who were involved with the Java EE 8 Recipes book
 * @return
 */
public String populateJavaEERecipesAuthorList() {
    authorList = new ArrayList<>();
    for(Author author:authorBookList){
        List<Book>books = author.getBooks();
        for(Book book:books){
            if(book.getTitle().equals("Java EE 8 Recipes")){
                authorList.add(author);
            }
        }
    }
    return "recipe04_05b";

}

/**
 * Populates completeAuthorList with each existing Author object
 * @return
 */
private void populateCompleteAuthorList() {
    completeAuthorList = new ArrayList();
    for(Author author:authorBookList){
        completeAuthorList.add(author);
    }

}

public String displayAuthor(String last) {
    for (Author author : authorList) {
        if (author.getLast().equals(last)) {
            current = author;
        }
    }
    return "recipe04_05c";
}

/**
 * @return the authorList
 */
public List getauthorList() {
    return authorList;
}

/**
 * @return the current
 */
public Author getCurrent() {
    return current;
}
```

```
    /**
     * @param current the current to set
     */
    public void setCurrent(Author current) {
        this.current = current;
    }

    /**
     * @return the authorLast
     */
    public String getAuthorLast() {
        return authorLast;
    }

    /**
     * @param authorLast the authorLast to set
     */
    public void setAuthorLast(String authorLast) {
        displayAuthor(authorLast);
    }

    /**
     * @return the storeName
     */
    public String getStoreName() {
        return storeName;
    }

    /**
     * @param storeName the storeName to set
     */
    public void setStoreName(String storeName) {
        this.storeName = storeName;
    }

    /**
     * @return the completeAuthorList
     */
    public List<Author> getCompleteAuthorList() {
        return completeAuthorList;
    }

    /**
     * @param completeAuthorList the completeAuthorList to set
     */
    public void setCompleteAuthorList(List<Author> completeAuthorList) {
        this.completeAuthorList = completeAuthorList;
    }
}
```

When displayAuthor is invoked, the current Author object is populated with the currently selected author, and the bio page is rendered. The bio page source is listed in the solution to this recipe. Each Author object contains a list of Book objects that correspond to the books that a particular author has written. The ui:repeat tag is used to iterate over this list of books.

The ui:repeat tag can be effective in various use cases. When you're deciding to use h:dataTable or ui:repeat, it is best to determine whether customization is going to be imperative. For those situations where more control is desired, ui:repeat is certainly the best choice.

3-18. Invoking Controller Class Actions on Lifecycle Phase Events

Problem

You want to automatically invoke a controller class action when a specific JSF lifecycle phase event occurs. For instance, when a view is loading, you want to invoke a controller class action that performs a conditional verification based on the user who is visiting the page.

Solution

Utilize a JSF view action by adding the f:viewAction facet to the JSF view. Use the facet to specify the controller class action to invoke, as well as when to invoke the action. In the following excerpt from the chapter03/recipe03_18.xhtml view, a controller class method action named validateUser is invoked:

```
<f:metadata>
        <f:viewAction action="#{viewActionManagedBean.validateUser()}"/>
</f:metadata>
```

How It Works

In JSF 2.1 and prior, it was difficult to invoke action methods within a controller class unless they were bound to a command component. Sometimes it makes sense to invoke a method when the page is loading, after the page has been fully loaded, and so on. In the past, this was done by using a preRenderView event listener, which invokes a method contained in a managed before the view is rendered. Utilization of the preRenderView event listener works, but it does not provide the level of control that is required to invoke a method during different phases of the view lifecycle. The preRenderView also requires developers to programmatically check the request type and work with the navigation handler.

In the JSF 2.2 release, a new technique can be used to invoke action methods in a controller class during specified lifecycle events that occur within the view. A new tag, f:viewAction, can be bound to a view, and it can be incorporated into the JSF lifecycle in both non-JSF (initial) and JSF (postback) requests. To use the tag, it must be a child of the metadata facet. View parameters can be specified within the metadata facet as well, and they will become available from within the controller class when the action method is invoked.

In the example, the action method named validateUser is invoked using the viewAction. In the example method, a string is returned, which enables implicit navigation based on the action method results. If null is returned, the navigation handler is invoked, but the same view will be rendered again so long as there are no navigation condition expressions that change the navigation. If a string-based view name is returned, then the navigation handler will render that view once the method has completed. This can come in handy for situations such as authentication handling, where an action method is used to check the user's role and then the appropriate view is rendered based on the authenticated user role.

```
public String validateUser() {
        String viewName;
        System.out.println("Look in the server log to see this message");
        // Here we would perform validation based upon the user visiting the
        // site to ensure that they had the appropriate permissions to view
        // the selected view.  For the purposes of this example, this
        // conditional logic is just a prototype.
        if (visitor.isAdmin()){
            // visit the current page
            viewName = null;
            System.out.println("Current User is an Admin");
        } else {
            viewName = "notAdmin";
            System.out.println("Current User is NOT an Admin");
        }
        return viewName;
    }
```

As mentioned previously, `f:viewAction` facet can be customized to allow the action method to be invoked at different stages within the view lifecycle. By default, the `viewAction` will be initiated before postback because the specified action method is expected to execute whether the request was Faces or non-Faces. However, this can be changed by setting the `onPostback` attribute of the `f:viewAction` tag to `true`.

```
<f:viewAction action="#{viewActionManagedBean.validateUser()}" onPostback="true"/>
```

If you need to get even more granular and invoke a view action during specified lifecycle phase, it is possible by setting the `phase` attribute to the phase required. Table 3-8 specifies the different phases along with their phase value.

Table 3-8. *JSF Lifecycle Phases*

Phase	Tag Value
Restore View	RESTORE_VIEW
Apply Request Values	APPLY_REQUEST_VALUES
Process Validations	PROCESS_VALIDATIONS
Update Model Values	UPDATE_MODEL_VALUES
Invoke Application	INVOKE_APPLICATION
Render Response	RENDER_RESPONSE

The following example demonstrates the `f:viewAction` facet that will cause the action to be invoked during the Process Validations phase:

```
<f:viewAction action="#{viewActionManagedBean.validateUser()}"
                phase="PROCESS_VALIDATIONS"/>
```

CHAPTER 4

JavaServer Faces Standard Components

The JSF framework allows developers to build applications utilizing a series of views, and each view consists of a series of components. The framework is kind of like a puzzle in that each piece must fit into its particular place in order to make things work smoothly. Components are just another piece of the puzzle. Components are the building blocks that make up JSF views. One of the strengths of using the JSF framework is the abundance of components that are available for use in views. To developers, components can be tags that are placed within the XHTML views. Components resemble standard HTML tags; they contain a number of attributes, an opening tag and a closing tag, and sometimes components that are to be embedded inside of others. Components can also be written in Java code, and their tags can be bound to Java code that resides in a JSF managed bean (aka, *controller class*).

A number of components come standard with the JSF framework. The recipes in this chapter cover the standard components in detail and provide examples that will allow you to begin using components in your applications right away.

This chapter focuses on the JSF standard component library, and toward the end it features some recipes showing how to use external component libraries. The example in this chapter grows from the first recipe throughout each recipe to the final recipe. In the end, a newsletter page for the Acme Bookstore will be complete and full-featured.

Before tackling the recipes, though, the following section provides a brief overview of the standard JSF components and associated common component tags. This will help you get the most out of the recipes.

Component and Tag Primer

Table 4-1 lists the components that are available with a clean install of the JSF framework.

J. Juneau, *Java EE 8 Recipes*, https://doi.org/10.1007/978-1-4842-3594-2_4

Table 4-1. JSF HTML Components

Component	Tag	Description
UIColumn	h:column	Represents a column of data in the dataTable component
UICommand	h:commandButton	Submits a form
	h:commandLink	Links pages or actions
h:commandScript	Provides ability to call an arbitrary server-side method via Ajax from a JSF view	
UIData	h:dataTable	Represents a table used for iterating over collections of data
UIForm	h:form	Represents an input form
UIGraphic	h:graphicImage	Displays an image
UIInput	h:inputHidden	Includes a hidden variable in a form
	h:inputSecret	Allows text entry without displaying the actual text
	h:inputText	Allows text entry
	h:inputTextarea	Allows multiline text entry
UIOutcomeTarget	h:link	Links to another page or location
UIMessage	h:message	Displays a localized message
UIMessages	h:messages	Displays localized messages
UIOutput	h:outputFormat	Displays a formatted localized message
	h:outputLabel	Displays a label for a specified field
	h:outputLink	Links to another page or location
UIPanel	h:panelGrid	Displays a table
	h:panelGroup	Groups components
UISelectBoolean	h:selectBooleanCheckbox	Displays a boolean choice
UISelectItem	h:selectItem	Represents one item in a list of items for selection
UISelectItems	h:selectItems	Represents a list of items for selection
UISelectMany	h:selectManyCheckbox	Displays a group of check boxes that allow multiple user choices
	h:selectManyListbox	Allows a user to select multiple items from a list
	h:selectManyMenu	Allows a user to select multiple items from a drop-down menu
UISelectOne	h:selectOneListbox	Allows a user to select a single item from a list
	h:selectOneMenu	Allows a user to select a single item from a drop-down menu
	h:selectOneRadio	Allows a user to select one item from a set

JSF provides a number of core tags that can be used to provide more functionality for the components. For example, these tags can be embedded inside JSF component tags and specify rules that can be used to convert the values that are displayed or used as input for the component. Other uses of the core tags are to provide a list of options for a select component, validate input, and provide action and event listeners. Table 4-2 describes the JSF core tags.

Table 4-2. *JSF Core Tags*

Tag	Function
`f:actionListener`	Registers an action listener method with a component
`f:phaseListener`	Registers a `PhaseListener` to a page
`f:setPropertyActionListener`	Registers a special form submittal action listener
`f:valueChangeListener`	Registers a value change listener with a component
`f:converter`	Registers an arbitrary converter with a component
`f:convertDateTime`	Registers a `DateTimeConverter` instance with a component
`f:convertNumber`	Registers a `NumberConverter` with a component
`f:facet`	Adds a nested component to particular enclosing parents
`f:metadata`	Registers a particular facet with a parent component
`f:selectItem`	Encapsulates one item in a list
`f:selectItems`	Encapsulates all items of a list
`f:websocket`	Provides ability to receive messages into a view via WebSockets
`f:validateDoubleRange`	Registers a `DoubleRangeValidator` with a component
`f:validateLength`	Registers a `LengthValidator` with a component
`f:validateLongRange`	Registers a `LongRangeValidator` with a component
`f:validator`	Registers a custom validator with a component
`f:validateRegex`	Registers a `RegExValidator` with a component (JSF 2.0)
`f:validateBean`	Delegates validation of a local value to a `BeanValidator` (JSF 2.0)
`f:validateWholeBean`	Delegates validation of an entire bean or class
`f:validateRequired`	Ensures that a value is present in a parent component

■ **Note** The common sources and the completed classes to run the application for Chapter 4 are contained in the `org.javaee8recipes.chapter04` package, and one or more recipes throughout this chapter will utilize classes contained in that package.

Common Component Tag Attributes

Each standard JSF component tag contains a set of attributes that must be specified in order to uniquely identify it from the others, register the component to a managed bean, and so on. There is a set of attributes that are common across each component tag, and this section lists those attributes, along with a description of each. *All attributes besides* `id` *can be specified using JSF EL.*

- `binding`: A managed bean property can be specified for this attribute, and it can be used to bind the tag to a component instance within a managed bean. Doing so allows you to programmatically control the component from within the managed bean.
- `id`: This attribute can be set to uniquely identify the component. If you do not specify a value for the `id` attribute, then JSF will automatically generate one. Each component within a view must have a unique `id` attribute, or an error will be generated when the page is rendered. *I recommend you manually specify a value for the* `id` *attribute on each component tag, because then it will be easy to statically reference the tag from a scripting language or a managed bean if needed. If you let JSF automatically populate this attribute, it may be different each time, and you will never be able to statically reference the tag from a scripting language.*
- `immediate`: This attribute can be set to true for input and command components in order to force the processing of validations, conversions, and events when the request parameter values are applied.
- `rendered`: The rendered attribute can be used to specify whether the component should be rendered. This attribute is typically specified as a JSF EL expression that is bound to a managed bean property yielding a boolean result. The EL expression must be an `rvalue` expression, meaning that it is read-only and cannot set a value.
- `style`: This attribute allows a CSS style to be applied to the component. The specified style will be applied when the component is rendered as output.
- `styleClass`: This attribute allows a CSS style class to be applied to the component. The specified style will be applied when the component is rendered as output.
- `value`: This attribute identifies the value of a given component. For some components, the `value` attribute is used to bind the tag to a managed bean property. In this case, the value specified for the component will be read from, or set within, the managed bean property. Other components, such as the `commandButton` component, use the `value` attribute to specify a label for the given component.

Common JavaScript Component Tags

Table 4-3 lists a number of attributes that are shared by many of the components, which enable JavaScript functionality to interact with the component.

Table 4-3. *Common Component Attributes*

Attribute	Description
onblur	JavaScript code that should be executed when the component loses focus.
onchange	JavaScript code that should be executed when the component loses focus and the value changes.
ondblclick	JavaScript code that should be executed when the component has been clicked twice.
onfocus	JavaScript code that should be executed when the component gains focus.
onkeydown	JavaScript code that should be executed when user presses a key down and the component is in focus.
onkeypress	JavaScript code that should be executed when user presses a key and the component is in focus.
onkeyup	JavaScript code that should be executed when key press is completed and the component is in focus.
onmousedown	JavaScript code that should be executed when user clicks the mouse button and the component is in focus.
onmouseout	JavaScript code that should be executed when user moves mouse away from the component.
onmouseover	JavaScript code that should be executed when user moves mouse onto the component.
onmousemove	JavaScript code that should be executed when user moves mouse within the component.
onmouseup	JavaScript code that should be executed when mouse button click is completed and the component is in focus.
onselect	JavaScript code that should be executed when the component is selected by user.

Binding Components to Properties

All JSF components can be bound to managed bean properties. Do so by declaring a property for the type of component you want to bind within the managed bean and then by referencing that property using the component's binding attribute. For instance, the following `dataTable` component is bound to a managed bean property and then manipulated from within the bean.

In the view:

```
<h:dataTable id="myTable" binding="#{myBean.myTable}" value="#{myBean.myTableCollection}"/>
```

In the bean:

```
// Provide getter and setter methods for this property
private javax.faces.component.UIData myTable;
...
myTable.setRendered(true);
...
```

Binding can prove to be very useful in some cases, especially when you need to manipulate the state of a component programmatically before re-rendering the view.

4-1. Creating an Input Form

Problem

You want to add input fields to a form within your application.

Solution

Create an input form by enclosing child input components within a parent `form` component. There are four JSF components that will allow for text entry as input. Those components are `inputText`, `inputSecret`, `inputHidden`, and `inputTextarea`. Any or all of these components can be placed within a `form` component in order to create an input form that accepts text entry.

In the example for this recipe, you will create an input form that will be used to sign up for the Acme Bookstore newsletter. The users will be able to enter their first and last names, an email address, a password, and a short description of their interests.

The View: recipe04_01.xhtml

The following code is for the view `recipe04_01.xhtml`, which constructs the layout for the input form:

```
<html xmlns="http://www.w3.org/1999/xhtml"
      xmlns:ui="http://xmlns.jcp.org/jsf/facelets"
      xmlns:f="http://xmlns.jcp.org/jsf/core"
      xmlns:h="http://xmlns.jcp.org/jsf/html">

    <body>

        <ui:composition template="layout/custom_template_search.xhtml">
            <ui:define name="content">
                <h:messages globalOnly="true"  errorStyle="color: red" infoStyle="color:
                green"/>
                <h:form id="contactForm">
                    <h1>Subscribe to Newsletter</h1>
                    <p>
                        Enter your information below in order to be added to the Acme
                        Bookstore newsletter.
                    </p>

                    <br/>
                    <label for="first">First: </label>
                    <h:inputText id="first" size="40" value="#{contactController1.current.
                    first}"/>
                    <br/>
                    <label for="last">Last: </label>
                    <h:inputText id="last" size="40" value="#{contactController1.current.
                    last}"/>
                    <br/>
```

```
                <label for="email">Email: </label>
                <h:inputText id="email" size="40" value="#{contactController1.current.
                email}"/>
                <br/>
                <label for="password">Enter a password for site access:</label>
                <h:inputSecret id="password" size="40" value="#{contactController1.
                current.password}"/>
                <br/><br/>
                <label for="description">Enter your book interests</label>
                <br/>
                <h:inputTextarea id="description" rows="5" cols="100"
                value="#{contactController1.current.description}"/>
                <br/>
                <h:commandButton id="contactSubmit" action="#{contactController1.
                subscribe}" value="Save"/>
            </h:form>
        </ui:define>
    </ui:composition>

    </body>
</html>
```

■ **Note** As you can see from the example, HTML can be mixed together with JSF component tags. An HTML label tag is used to specify a label for each input component in this recipe. In Recipe 4-3, you will learn about the JSF component that is used to render a label.

To learn more about how the commandButton component works, see Recipe 4-2.

Managed Bean: ContactController.java

Each view that contains an input form needs to have an associated managed bean, right? The managed bean in this case is RequestScoped, and the name of the bean class is ContactController. An excerpt from the listing for the ContactController class is as follows:

```
import java.util.*;
import javax.enterprise.context.RequestScoped;
import javax.faces.application.FacesMessage;
import javax.faces.component.UIComponent;
import javax.faces.context.FacesContext;
import javax.faces.event.ValueChangeEvent;
import javax.faces.model.SelectItem;
import javax.faces.validator.ValidatorException;
import javax.inject.Inject;
import javax.inject.Named;
```

```
/**
 * Chapter 4
 *
 * @author juneau
 */
@RequestScoped
@Named(value = "contactController")
public class ContactController implements java.io.Serializable {
    private Contact current;

    /**
     * Creates a new instance of ContactController
     */
    public ContactController() {

    }

    /**
     * Obtain the current instance of the Contact object
     * @return Contact
     */
    public Contact getCurrent(){
        if (current == null){
            current = new Contact();
        }
        return current;
    }

    /**
     * Adds a subscriber to the newsletter
     * @return String
     */
    public String subscribe(){
        // No implementation yet, will add to a database table in Chapter 7
        FacesMessage facesMsg = new FacesMessage(FacesMessage.SEVERITY_INFO,
                "Successfully Subscribed to Newsletter for " + getCurrent().getEmail(),
                 null);
        FacesContext.getCurrentInstance().addMessage(null, facesMsg);
        return "SUBSCRIBE";
    }

    /**
     * Navigational method
     * @return String
     */
    public String add(){
        return "ADD_SUBSCRIBER";
    }
}
```

■ **Note** At this time, nothing happens when the Submit button is clicked other than a nice "Success" message being displayed on the screen. Later in the book, we will revisit the subscribe method and add the code for creating a record within an underlying database. The input screen should look like Figure 4-1 when rendered.

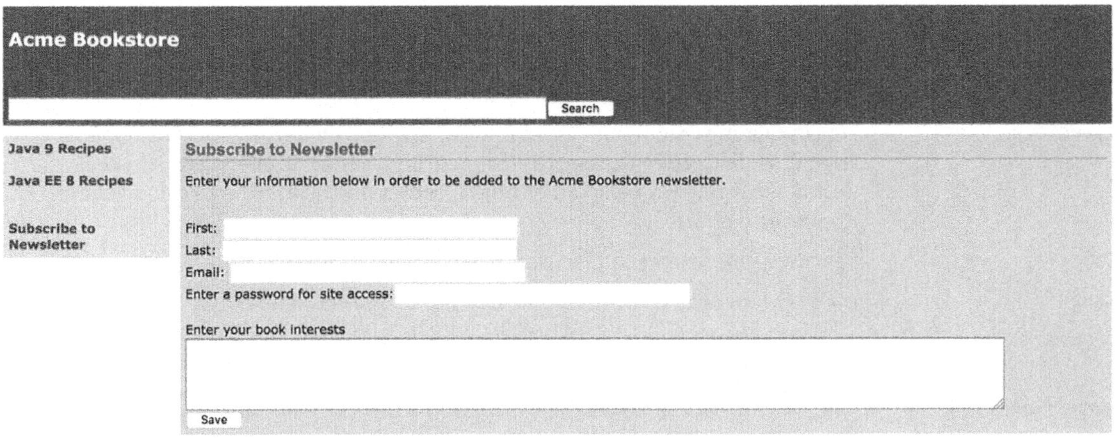

Figure 4-1. *JSF input form for subscribing to the Acme Bookstore newsletter*

How It Works

The JavaServer Faces framework ships with a slew of standard components that can be utilized within JSF views. There are four standard components that can be used for capturing text input: `inputText`, `inputSecret`, `inputHidden`, and `inputTextarea`. These component tags, as well as all of the other standard JSF component tags, share a common set of attributes and some attributes that are unique to each specific tag. To learn more about the common attributes, see the related section in the introduction to this chapter. In this recipe, I go over the specifics for each of these input components. The `form` component, specified via the `h:form` tag, is used to create an input form within a JSF view. Each component that is to be processed within the form should be enclosed between the opening and closing `h:form` tags. Each `form` typically contains at least one command component, such as a `commandButton`. A view can contain more than one `form` component, and only those components that are contained within the `form` will be processed when the `form` is submitted.

■ **Note** I recommend you always specify the `id` attribute for each component. Most importantly, specify the `id` attribute for the `form` component. If you do not specify the `id` attribute for a given JSF component, then one will be automatically generated for you. The automatic generation of JSF component `id`s prohibits the ability to statically reference a component from within a scripting language, such as JavaScript, or a managed bean. For instance, in the example for this recipe, the `form id` attribute is set to `contactForm`, and the first `inputText` component `id` is set to `first`. This allows you to reference the component statically by appending the `form id` to the component `id` from a scripting language or managed bean. In the case of the example, you'd reference the first component as `contactForm:first`.

Each of the input tags support the list of attributes that is shown in Table 4-4, in addition to those already listed as common component attributes in the introduction to this chapter.

***Table 4-4.** Input Component Tag Attributes*

Attribute	Description
converter	Allows a converter to be applied to the component's data.
converterMessage	Specifies a message that will be displayed when a registered converter fails.
dir	Specifies the direction of text displayed by the component. *(*LTR *is used to indicate left-to-right, and* RTL *is used to indicate right-to-left.)*
immediate	Flag indicating that, if this component is activated by the user, notifications should be delivered to interested listeners and actions immediately (that is, during the Apply Request Values phase) rather than waiting until the Invoke Application phase.
label	Specifies a name that can be used for component identification.
lang	Allows a language code to be specified for the rendered markup.
required	Accepts a boolean to indicate whether the user must enter a value for the given component.
requiredMessage	Specifies an error message to be displayed if the user does not enter a value for a *required* component.
validator	Allows a validator to be applied to the component.
valueChangeListener	Allows a managed bean method to be bound for event-handling purposes. The method will be called when there is a change made to the component.

The inputText component is used to generate a single-line text box within a rendered page. The inputText component value attribute is most commonly bound to a managed bean property so that the values of the property can be retrieved or set when a form is processed. In the recipe example, the first inputText component is bound to the managed bean property named first. The EL expression #{contactController1.current.first} is specified for the component value, so if the managed bean's first property contains a value, then it will be displayed in the inputText component. Likewise, when the form is submitted, then any value that has been entered within the component will be saved within the first property in the managed bean.

The inputSecret component generates a single-line text box within a rendered page, and when text is entered into the component, then it is not displayed; rather, asterisks are displayed in place of each character typed. This component makes it possible for a user to enter private text, such as a password, without it being displayed on the screen for others to read. The inputSecret component works identically to the inputText component, other than hiding the text with asterisks. In the example, the value of the inputSecret component is bound to a managed bean property named password via the #{contactController1.current.password} EL expression.

The inputTextarea component is used to generate a multiline text box within a rendered page. As such, this component has a couple of additional attributes that can be used to indicate how large the text area should be. The inputTextarea has the rows and cols attributes, which allow a developer to specify how many rows (height) and how many columns (wide) of space the component should take up on the page, respectively. Other than those two attributes, the inputTextarea component works in much the same manner as the inputText component. In the example, the value attribute of the inputTextarea component is specified as #{contactController1.current.description}, so the description property will be populated with the contents of the component when the form is submitted.

The input component I have not yet discussed is the inputHidden component. This component is used to place a hidden input field into the form. It works in the same manner as the inputText component, except that it is not rendered on the page for the user to see. The value for an inputHidden component can be bound to a managed bean property in the same way as the other components. You can use such a component for passing a hidden token to and from a form.

As you can see, the days of passing and receiving request parameters within JSP pages are over. Utilizing the JSF standard input components, it is possible to bind values to managed bean properties using JSF EL expressions. This makes it much easier for developers to submit values from an input form for processing. Rather than retrieving parameters from a page, assigning them to variables, and then processing, the JSF framework takes care of that overhead for you. Although I have not covered the usage of all input component attributes within this recipe, I will cover more in the recipes that follow as I build upon the Acme Bookstore newsletter subscription page.

4-2. Invoking Actions from Within a Page

Problem

You want to trigger a server-side method to be invoked from a button or link on one of your application pages.

Solution

Utilize the commandButton or commandLink components within your view to invoke action methods within a managed bean controller. The command components allow for the user invocation of actions within managed beans. Command components bind buttons and links on a page directly to action methods, allowing developers to spend more time thinking about the development of the application and less time thinking about the Java servlet-processing lifecycle.

In the example for this recipe, a button and a link are added to the newsletter page for the Acme Bookstore. The button that will be added to the page will be used to submit the input form for processing, and the link will allow users to log in to the application and manage their subscriptions and bookstore accounts.

■ **Note** This recipe will not cover any authentication or security features; it focuses only on invoking actions within managed beans. For more information regarding authentication, see Chapter 14.

The View: recipe04_02.xhtml

The following code is for the newsletter subscription view including the command components. The sources are for the file named recipe04_02.xhtml.

```
<html xmlns="http://www.w3.org/1999/xhtml"
      xmlns:ui="http://xmlns.jcp.org/jsf/facelets"
      xmlns:f="http://xmlns.jcp.org/jsf/core"
      xmlns:h="http://xmlns.jcp.org/jsf/html">
```

```
    <body>

        <ui:composition template="layout/custom_template_search.xhtml">
            <ui:define name="content">
                <h:messages globalOnly="true"  errorStyle="color: red" infoStyle="color:
                green"/>
                <h:form id="contactForm">
                    <h1>Subscribe to Newsletter</h1>
                    <p>
                        Enter your information below in order to be added to the Acme
                        Bookstore newsletter.
                    </p>

                    <br/>
                    <label for="first">First: </label>
                    <h:inputText id="first" size="40" value="#{contactController.current.
                    first}"/>
                    <br/>
                    <label for="last">Last: </label>
                    <h:inputText id="last" size="40" value="#{contactController.current.
                    last}"/>
                    <br/>
                    <label for="email">Email: </label>
                    <h:inputText id="email" size="40" value="#{contactController.current.
                    email}"/>
                    <br/>
                    <label for="password">Enter a password for site access:</label>
                    <h:inputSecret id="password" size="40" value="#{contactController.
                    current.password}"/>
                    <br/><br/>
                    <label for="description">Enter your book interests</label>
                    <br/>
                    <h:inputTextarea id="description" rows="5" cols="100"
                    value="#{contactController.current.description}"/>
                    <br/>
                    <h:commandButton id="contactSubmit" action="#{contactController.
                    subscribe}" value="Save"/>
                    <br/><br/>
                    <h:commandLink  id="manageAccount" action="#{contactController.manage}"
                    value="Manage Subscription"/>
                </h:form>
            </ui:define>
        </ui:composition>

    </body>
</html>
```

Managed Bean: ContactController.java

The managed bean that contains the action methods is named `ContactController`, which was created in Recipe 4-1. The following code excerpt is taken from the `ContactController` class, and it shows the updates that have been made to the methods for this recipe.

■ **Note** The complete implementation of `ContactController` resides in the `org.javaee8recipes.chapter05` package.

```
...
    /**
     * Adds a subscriber to the newsletter
     * @return String
     */
    public String subscribe(){
        // Using a list implementation for now,
        // but will add to a database table in Chapter 7

        // Add the current contact to the subscription list
        subscriptionController.getSubscriptionList().add(current);
        FacesMessage facesMsg = new FacesMessage(FacesMessage.SEVERITY_INFO,
                "Successfully Subscribed to Newsletter for " + getCurrent().getEmail(), null);
        FacesContext.getCurrentInstance().addMessage(null, facesMsg);
        return "SUBSCRIBE";
    }

    /**
     * Navigational method
     * @return String
     */
    public String add(){
        return "ADD_SUBSCRIBER";
    }

    /**
     * This method will allow a user to navigate to the manageAccount view.
     * This method will be moved into another managed bean that focuses on
     * authentication later on.
     * @return
     */
    public String manage(){
        return "/chapter04/manageAccount";
    }
...
```

When the view is rendered, the resulting page looks like Figure 4-2.

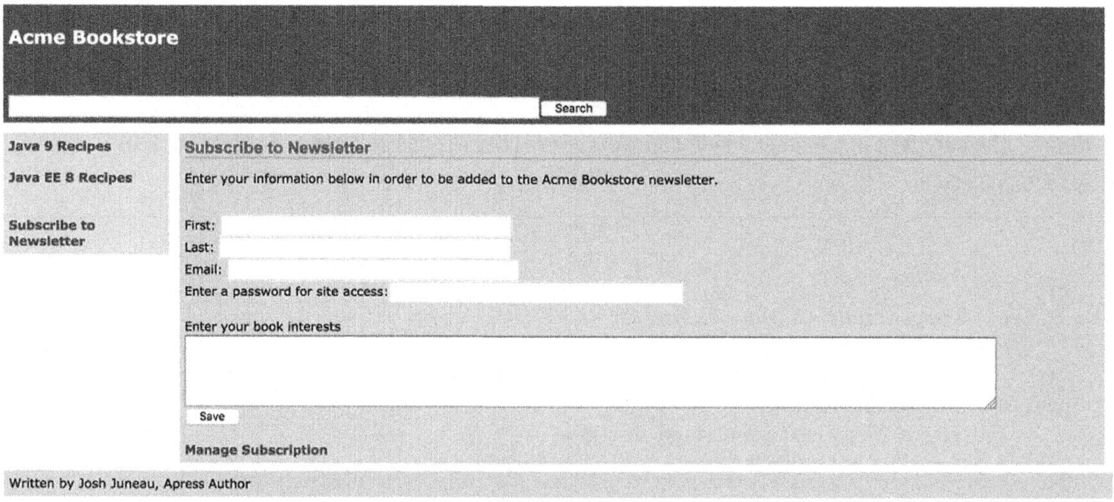

Figure 4-2. *Utilizing command components within a view*

How It Works

The command components make JSF vastly different from using JSP technology. In many of the other technologies, form actions are used to handle request parameters and perform any required business logic with them. With the JSF command components, Java methods can be bound directly to a button or a link and invoked when the components are activated (button or link clicked). In the example for this recipe, both the `commandButton` and `commandLink` components are utilized. The `commandButton` component is used to submit the form request parameters for processing, and the `commandLink` component is bound to an action method that performs a redirect to another application page.

The command components have a handful of attributes that are of note. Those attributes, along with a description of each, are listed in Table 4-5 and Table 4-6.

Table 4-5. *commandButton Component Additional Attributes*

Attribute	Description
`action`	EL that specifies a managed bean action method that will be invoked when the user activates the component.
`actionListener`	EL that specifies a managed bean action method that will be notified when this component is activated. The action method should be public and accept an `ActionEvent` parameter, with a return type of `void`.
`class`	CSS style class that can be applied to the component.
`dir`	Direction indication for text (`LTR`: left-to-right; `RTL`: right-to-left).
`disabled`	A Boolean to indicate whether the component is disabled.
`image`	Absolute or relative URL to an image that will be displayed on the button.

(*continued*)

Table 4-5. *(continued)*

Attribute	Description
immediate	Flag indicating that, if this component is activated by the user, notifications should be delivered to interested listeners and actions immediately (that is, during the Apply Request Values phase) rather than waiting until the Invoke Application phase.
label	Name for the component.
lang	Code for the language used for generating the component markup.
readonly	Boolean indicating whether the component is read only.
rendererType	Identifier of renderer instance.
tabindex	Index value indicating number of tab button presses it takes to bring the component into focus.
title	Tooltip that will be displayed when the mouse hovers over component.
transient	Boolean indicating whether component should be included in the state of the component tree.
type	Indicates type of button to create. Values are submit (default), reset, and button.

Table 4-6. *commandLink Component Additional Attributes*

Attribute	Description
action	EL that specifies a managed bean action method that will be invoked when the user activates the component.
accessKey	Access key value that will transfer the focus to the component.
cords	Position and shape of the hotspot on the screen.
dir	Direction indication for text (LTR: left-to-right; RTL: right-to-left).
disabled	Specifies a boolean to indicate whether the component is disabled.
hreflang	Language code of the resource designated by the hyperlink.
immediate	Flag indicating that, if this component is activated by the user, notifications should be delivered to interested listeners and actions immediately (that is, during the Apply Request Values phase) rather than waiting until the Invoke Application phase.
lang	Code for the language used for generating the component markup.
rel	Relationship from the current document to the anchor specified by the hyperlink.
rev	Reverse anchor specified by this hyperlink to the current document.
shape	Shape of the hotspot on the screen.
tabindex	Index value indicating number of tab button presses it takes to bring the component into focus.
target	Name of a frame where the resource retrieved via the hyperlink will be displayed.
title	Tooltip that will be displayed when the mouse hovers over component.
type	Indicates type of button to create. Values are submit (default), reset, and button.
charset	Character encoding of the resource designated by the hyperlink.

The commandButton and commandLink components in the example to this recipe specify only a minimum number of attributes. That is, they both specify id, action, and value attributes. The id attribute is used to uniquely identify each of the components. The action attribute is set to the JSF EL, which binds the components to their managed bean action methods. The commandButton component has an action attribute of #{contactController.subscribe}, which means that the ContactController class's subscribe method will be invoked when the button on the page is clicked. The commandLink has an action attribute of #{contactController.manage}, which means that the ContactController class's manage method will be invoked when the link is clicked. Each of the components also specifies a value attribute, which is set to the text that is displayed on the button or link when rendered.

As you can see, only a handful of the available attributes are used in the example. However, the components can be customized using the additional attributes that are available. For instance, an actionListener method can be specified, which will bind a managed bean method to the component, and that method will be invoked when the component is activated. JavaScript functions can be specified for each of the attributes beginning with the word on, providing the ability to produce client-side functionality.

Command components vastly changed the landscape of Java web application development. They allow the incorporation of direct Java method access from within user pages and provide an easy means for processing request parameters.

4-3. Displaying Output

Problem

You want to display text from a managed bean property in your application pages.

Solution

Incorporate JSF output components into your views. Output components are used to display static or dynamic text on a page, as well as the results of expression language arithmetic. The standard JSF component library contains five components that render output: outputLabel, outputText, outputFormat, outputLink, and link. The Acme Bookstore utilizes each of these components in the bookstore newsletter application façade.

The View: recipe05_03.xhtml

In the following example, the newsletter subscription view has been rewritten to utilize some of the output components:

```
<html xmlns="http://www.w3.org/1999/xhtml"
      xmlns:ui="http://xmlns.jcp.org/jsf/facelets"
      xmlns:f="http://xmlns.jcp.org/jsf/core"
      xmlns:h="http://xmlns.jcp.org/jsf/html">

    <body>

        <ui:composition template="layout/custom_template_search.xhtml">
            <ui:define name="content">
                <h:messages globalOnly="true"  errorStyle="color: red" infoStyle="color:
                green"/>
                <h:form id="contactForm">
```

```
                <h1>Subscribe to Newsletter</h1>
                <p>
                    <h:outputText  id="newsletterSubscriptionDesc"
                                  value="#{contactController.newsletterDescription}"/>
                </p>

                <br/>
                <h:outputLabel for="first" value="First: "/>
                <h:inputText id="first" size="40" value="#{contactController.current.
                first}">
                    <f:validateRequired/>
                    <f:validateLength minimum="2" maximum="40"/>
                </h:inputText>
                <br/>
                <h:outputLabel for="last" value="Last: "/>
                <h:inputText id="last" size="40" value="#{contactController.current.last}">
                    <f:validateRequired/>
                    <f:validateLength minimum="2" maximum="40"/>
                </h:inputText>
                <br/>
                <h:outputLabel for="email" value="Email: "/>
                <h:inputText id="email" size="40" value="#{contactController.current.
                email}">
                    <f:validateRequired/>
                    <f:validateRegex pattern=""/>
                </h:inputText>

                <br/>
                <h:outputLabel for="password" value="Enter a password for site access: "/>
                <h:inputSecret id="password" size="40" value="#{contactController.
                current.password}">
                    <f:validateRegex pattern=""/>
                </h:inputSecret>
                <br/><br/>
                <h:outputLabel  for="description" value="Enter your book interests"/>
                <br/>
                <h:inputTextarea id="description" rows="5" cols="100"
                value="#{contactController.current.description}"/>
                <br/>
                <h:commandButton id="contactSubmit" action="#{contactController.
                subscribe}" value="Save"/>
                <br/><br/>
                <h:commandLink id="manageAccount" action="#{contactController.manage}"
                value="Manage Subscription"/>
                <br/><br/>
            </h:form>
        </ui:define>
    </ui:composition>

  </body>
</html>
```

Managed Bean: ContactController.java

The ContactController managed bean has been modified throughout the recipes in this chapter to incorporate new functionality as the recipes move forward. In this recipe, a new property has been added to the ContactController that contains the description of the newsletter.

■ **Note** The hard-coded newsletter description is not a good idea for use in a production application. It is used in this example for demonstration purposes only. For a production application, utilization of resource bundles or database storage would be a more viable approach for storing strings of text.

The following source excerpt from the ContactController class shows the code that is of interest in this example:

```
...
    private String newsletterDescription;

    public ContactController() {
        current = null;
        newsletterDescription = "Enter your information below in order to be " +
                "added to the Acme Bookstore newsletter.";
    }
...
    public String getNewsletterDescription() {
        return newsletterDescription;
    }

    public void setNewsletterDescription(String newsletterDescription) {
        this.newsletterDescription = newsletterDescription;
    }
...
```

The resulting page looks like Figure 4-3. Note that the text is the same, because it is merely reading the same text from a managed bean property. Also note that there is now an additional link added to the bottom of the page, which reads Home.

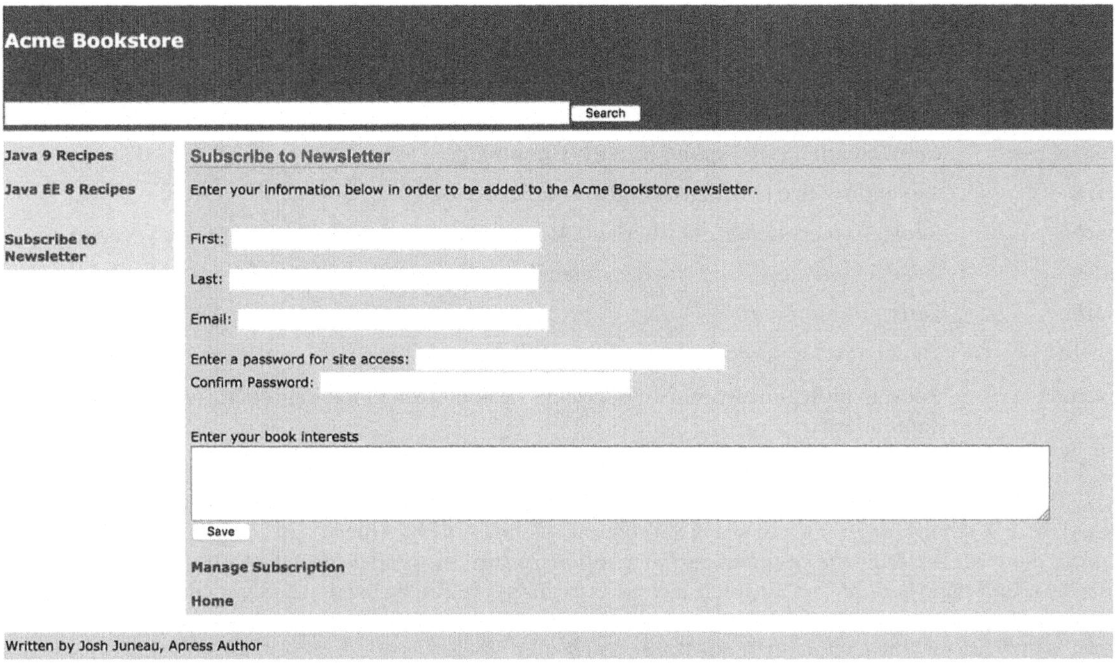

Figure 4-3. *Utilizing output components within a view*

How It Works

Output components can be used to display output that is generated in a managed bean or to render a link to another resource. They can be useful in many cases for displaying dynamic output to a web view. The example for this recipe demonstrates three out of the five output component types: `outputText`, `outputLink`, and `outputLabel`. Each of the components shares a common set of attributes, which are listed in Table 4-7.

■ **Note** The `outputText` component has become a bit less important since the release of JSF 2.0 because the Facelets view definition language implicitly wraps inline content with a similar output component. Therefore, the use of the `outputText` tag within JSF 2.0 is necessary only if you want to utilize some of the tag attributes for rendering, JavaScript invocation, or the like.

Table 4-7. Common Output Component Attributes (Not Listed in Introduction)

Attribute	Description
class	CSS class for styling
converter	Converter that is registered with the component
dir	Direction of text (LTR: left-to-right; RTL: right-to-left)
escape	Boolean value to indicate whether XML- and HTML-sensitive characters are escaped
lang	Code for language used when generating markup for the component
parent	Parent component
title	Tooltip text for the component
transient	Boolean indicating whether component should be included in the state of the component tree

The outputText component in the example contains a value of #{contactController.newsletterDescription}, which displays the contents of the newsletterDescription property within ContactController. Only the common output component attributes can be specified within the h:outputText tag. Therefore, an attribute such as class or style can be used to apply styles to the text displayed by the component. If the component contains HTML or XML, the escape attribute can be set to true to indicate that the characters should be escaped.

The outputFormat component shares the same set of attributes as the outputText component. The outputFormat component can be used to render parameterized text. Therefore, if you require the ability to alter different portions of a string of text, you can do so via the use of JSF parameters (via the f:param tag). For example, suppose you wanted to list the name of books that someone has purchased from the Acme Bookstore; you could use the outputFormat component like in the following example:

```
<h:outputFormat value="Cart contains the books {0}, {1}, {2}"/>
    <f:param value="Java 9 Recipes"/>
    <f:param value="JavaFX 2.0: Introduction by Example"/>
    <f:param value="Java EE 8 Recipes"/>
</h:outputFormat>
```

The outputLink and outputLabel components can each specify a number of other attributes that are not available to the previously discussed output components. The additional attributes are listed in Table 4-8 (outputLink) and Table 4-9 (outputLabel). The outputLink component can be used to create an anchor or link that will redirect an application user to another page when the link is clicked. In the example, the outputLink component is used to redirect a user to a view named home.xhtml. The value for the outputLink component can be set to a static page name, as per the example, or it can contain a JSF EL expression corresponding to a managed bean property. It is also possible to pass parameters to another page using the outputLink component by nesting f:param tags between opening and closing h:outputLink tags as follows:

```
<h:outputLink id="homeLink" value="home.xhtml">
    <h:outputText value="User Home Page"/>
    <f:param name="username" value="#{contactController.current.email}"/>
 </h:outputLink>
```

The previous example would produce a link with the text *User Home Page* when rendered on the page. It would produce the following HTML link, where `emailAddress` corresponds to the EL expression of `#{contactController.current.email}`:

```
<a href="home.xhtml?username=emailAddress">Home Page</a>
```

Similarly, rather than displaying a link as text on the page, an image can be used by embedding a `graphicImage` component (see Recipe 4-6 for details).

The `outputLabel` component renders an HTML `<label>` tag, and it can be used in much the same way as the `outputText` component. In the example, the `outputLabel` component values are all using static text, but they could also utilize JSF EL expressions to use managed bean property values if that is more suitable for the application.

Table 4-8. *outputLink Additional Attributes*

Attribute	Description
`accessKey`	Access key value that will transfer the focus to the component.
`binding`	`ValueExpresssion` linking this component to a property in a backing bean.
`charset`	The character encoding of the resource designated by this hyperlink.
`cords`	Position and shape of the hotspot on the screen.
`dir`	Direction indication for text (`LTR`: left-to-right; `RTL`: right-to-left).
`disabled`	Specifies a boolean to indicate whether the component is disabled.
`fragment`	Identifier for the page fragment that should be brought into focus when the target page is rendered.
`hreflang`	Language code of the resource designated by the hyperlink.
`lang`	Code for the language used for generating the component markup.
`rel`	Relationship from the current document to the anchor specified by the hyperlink.
`rev`	Reverse anchor specified by this hyperlink to the current document.
`shape`	Shape of the hotspot on the screen.
`tabindex`	Index value indicating number of Tab button presses it takes to bring the component into focus.
`target`	Name of a frame where the resource retrieved via the hyperlink will be displayed.
`title`	Tooltip that will be displayed when the mouse hovers over component.
`type`	Type of button to create. Values are `submit` (default), `reset`, and `button`.

Table 4-9. outputLabel Additional Attributes

Attribute	Description
accessKey	Access key value that will transfer the focus to the component.
binding	ValueExpresssion linking this component to a property in a backing bean.
dir	Direction indication for text (LTR: left-to-right; RTL: right-to-left).
escape	Flag indicating that characters that are sensitive in HTML and XML markup must be escaped.
for	Client identifier of the component for which this element is a label.
lang	Code for the language used for generating the component markup.
tabindex	Index value indicating number of Tab button presses it takes to bring the component into focus.
title	Tooltip that will be displayed when the mouse hovers over a component.
type	Type of button to create. Values are submit (default), reset, and button.

The last output component that I'll cover in this recipe is the link component. It was introduced to JSF in release 2.0, and it makes the task of adding links to a page just a bit easier. The outputLink and link components produce similar results, but link has just a couple of different attributes that make it react a bit differently. The value attribute of the h:link tag specifies the label or text that should be used when the link is rendered on the page, and the outcome attribute specifies the page that should be linked to. The following example of the link component produces the same output as the outputLink component in the example for this recipe:

```
<h:link id=""homeLink"" value=""Home"" outcome=""home""/>
```

Parameters and images can also embedded within the h:link tag, in the same manner as with outputLink. The link component also contains some custom attributes, as listed in Table 4-10.

Table 4-10. link Component Additional Attributes

Attribute	Description
charset	Character encoding of the resource that is designated by the hyperlink.
cords	Position and shape of the hotspot on the screen, usually used when generating maps or images containing multiple links.
disabled	Flag to indicate that the component should never receive focus.
fragment	Identifier for the page fragment that should be brought into focus when the link is clicked. The identifier is appended to the # character.
hreflang	Language of the resource designated by this link.
includeviewparams	Boolean indicating whether to include page parameters when redirecting.
outcome	Logical outcome used to resolve a navigational case.
rel	Relationship from the current document to the resource specified by link.
rev	Reverse link from the anchor specified from this link to the current document.
shape	Shape of the hotspot on the screen.
target	Name of the frame in which the resource linked to is to be displayed.
type	Content type of resource that is linked to.

This recipe provided a high-level overview of the JSF standard output components. In JSF 2.0+, it is important to note that you can simply include a JSF EL expression without using an output component to display text in a page. However, these components can still be quite useful under certain circumstances, making them an important set of components to have in your arsenal.

4-4. Adding Form Validation

Problem

To ensure that valid data is being submitted via your form, you need to incorporate some validation on your input fields.

Solution #1

Utilize prebuilt JSF validator tags on the view's input components where possible. JSF ships with a handful of prebuilt validators that can be applied to components within a view by embedding the validator tag within the component you want to validate. The following code excerpt is taken from a JSF view that defines the layout for the newsletter subscription page of the Acme Bookstore application. The sources can be found in the view named `recipe04_04.xhtml`, and the excerpt demonstrates applying prebuilt validators to some `inputText` components.

```
...
<h:outputLabel for="first" value="First: "/>
<h:inputText id="first" size="40" value="#{contactController.current.first}">
    <f:validateLength minimum="1" maximum="40"/>
 </h:inputText>
<br/>
<h:message id="firstError"
                   for="first"
                   errorStyle="color:red"/>
<br/>
<h:outputLabel for="last" value="Last: "/>
<h:inputText id="last" size="40" value="#{contactController.current.last}">
    <f:validateLength minimum="1" maximum="40"/>
</h:inputText>
<br/>
<h:message id="lastError"
                    for="last"
                    errorStyle="color:red"/>
<br/>
...
```

In the preceding code excerpt, you can see that the `f:validateLength` validator tags have been embedded in different `inputText` components. When the form is submitted, these validators will be applied to the values in the `inputText` component fields and will return an error message if the constraints have not been met.

Solution #2

Utilize JSF bean validation by annotating managed bean fields with validation annotations. It is possible to perform validation from within the managed bean by annotating the property field declaration with the validation annotations that are needed. When the form is submitted, the bean validation will be performed.

■ **Note** An f:validateBean tag can be embedded within the component in the view if you're using validationGroups in order to delegate the validation of the local value to the Bean Validation API. If you're using f:validateBean, the validationGroups attribute will serve as a filter that instructs which constraints should be enforced.

The following code excerpt is taken from the JSF view that defines the layout for the newsletter subscription page of the Acme Bookstore application. The sources can be found in the view named recipe04_04.xhtml.

```
...
<h:outputLabel for="email" value="Email: "/>
<h:inputText id="email" size="40" value="#{contactController.current.email}"/>
<br/>
<h:message id="emailError"
                     for="email"
                     errorStyle="color:red"/>
...
```

Next is an excerpt from the ContactController managed bean that demonstrates applying a validator annotation to the email property field declaration:

```
...
@Pattern(regexp = "[a-zA-Z0-9]+@[a-zA-Z0-9]+\\.[a-zA-Z0-9]+", message = "Email format is invalid.")
    private String email;
...
```

When the form is submitted, the validation on the email field will occur. If the value entered into the inputText component does not validate against the regular expression noted in the annotation, the message will be displayed within the corresponding messages component.

Solution #3

Create a custom validator method within a managed bean and register that method with an input component by specifying the appropriate EL for the component's validator attribute. The following code excerpt is taken from the JSF view that defines the layout for the newsletter subscription page of the Acme Bookstore application. The sources can be found in the view named recipe04_04.xhtml, and the excerpt demonstrates a custom validator method to a component by specifying it for the validator attribute.

```
...
<h:outputLabel for="password" value="Enter a password for site access: "/>
<h:inputSecret id="password" size="40" redisplay="true" value="#{contactController.current.
password}"/>
<br/>
<h:outputLabel for="passwordConfirm" value="Confirm Password: "/>
<h:inputSecret id="passwordConfirm" size="40" redisplay="true"
                         validator="#{contactController.validatePassword}"/>
<br/>
<h:message id="passwordConfirmError"
                     for="passwordConfirm"
                     style="color:red"/>
...
```

■ **Note** If you are thinking outside of the box, you'll see that the previous code fragment would be an excellent choice for creating into a composite component! If a composite component is created, it would be as simple as adding a tag such as `<custom:passwordValidate>` to your form. See Recipe 4-4 for more details on developing composite components.

The `validator` attribute specifies the `validatePassword` method within the `ContactController` managed bean. The following excerpt is taken from `ContactController`, and it shows the validator method's implementation:

```
...
/**
     * Custom validator to ensure that password field contents match
     * @param context
     * @param component
     * @param value
     */
    public void validatePassword(FacesContext context,
                                 UIComponent component,
                                 Object value){
        Map map = context.getExternalContext().getRequestParameterMap();
        String passwordText = (String) map.get(("contactForm:password"));
        String confirmPassword = value.toString();

        if (!passwordText.equals(confirmPassword)) {
            throw new ValidatorException(new FacesMessage("Passwords do not match"));
        }
    }
...
```

When the form is submitted, the `validatePassword` method will be invoked during the Process Validations phase. The method will read the values of both the `password` and `passwordConfirm` fields, and an exception will be thrown if they do not match. For example, if the input form for the newsletter subscription page is submitted without any values, then the page should be re-rendered and look like Figure 4-4.

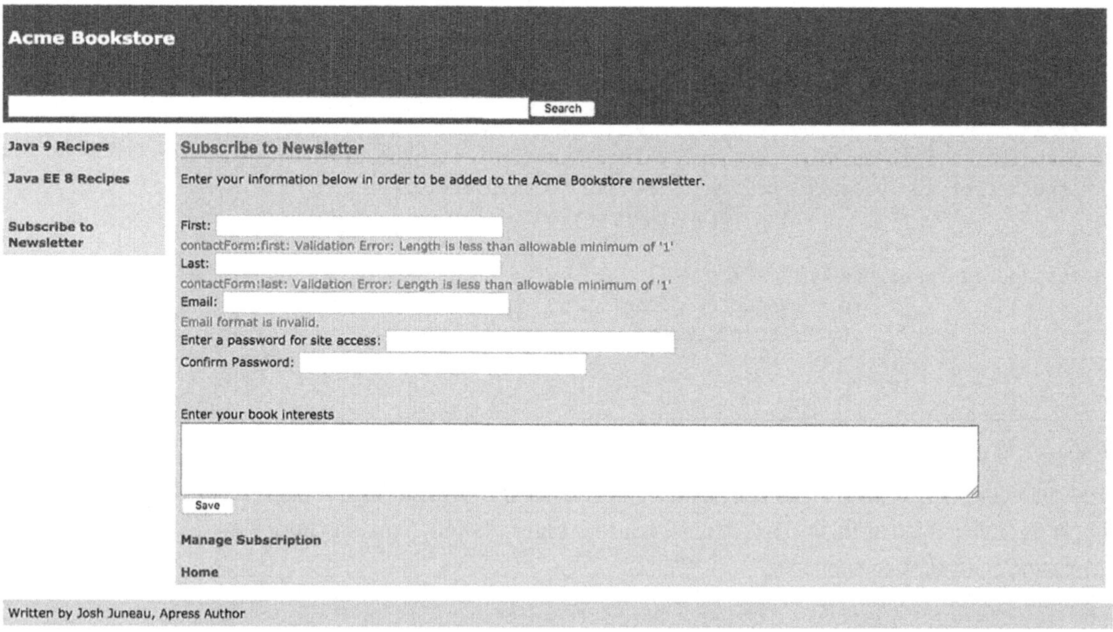

***Figure 4-4.** Validation errors on input fields*

How It Works

There are a few different ways to apply validation to form input fields. The easiest way to apply validation to an input component is to utilize the prebuilt validator tags that ship with JSF. There are prebuilt tags for validating data for a specified length, range, and so on. See Table 4-2 in the introduction to this chapter for the complete list of validator tags. You can also choose to apply validation to input components using bean validation. Bean validation requires validation annotations to be placed on the property declaration within the managed bean. Yet another possible way to perform validation is to create a custom validation method and specify the method within the input component's `validator` attribute. This section will provide a brief overview of each prebuilt validation tag, cover the basics of bean validation, and demonstrate how to build a custom validation method.

■ **Note** It is possible to create a class that implements the `Validator` interface to perform validation. For more information, see Recipe 3-7.

No matter which validation solution you choose to implement, the validation occurs during the Process Validations phase of the JSF lifecycle. When a form is submitted, via a command component or an Ajax request, all validators that are registered on the components within the tree are processed. The rules that are specified within the attributes of the component are compared against the local value for the component. At this point, if any of the validations fails, the messages are returned to the corresponding `message` components and displayed to the user.

To utilize the prebuilt validation tags, they must be embedded between opening and closing input component tag and specify attributes according to the validation parameters you want to set. In Solution #1 for this recipe, you learned how to use the `f:validateLength` validator tag, which allows validation of component data for a specified length. The `minimum` and `maximum` attributes are set to the minimum string length and maximum string length, respectively.

The f:validateLongRange validator can be used to check the range of a numeric value that has been entered. The minimum and maximum attributes of f:validateLongRange are used to determine whether the value entered falls within the lower and upper bounds, respectively.

Similar to f:validateLongRange is the f:validateDoubleRange validator, which is used to validate the range of a floating-point value. Again, the minimum and maximum attributes of f:validateDoubleRange are used to determine whether the value entered falls within the lower and upper bounds, respectively.

New with the release of JSF 2.0 was the f:validateRequired validator, which is used to ensure that an input field is not empty. No attributes are needed with this validator; simply embed it within a component tag to ensure that the component will not contain an empty value.

Another new validator that shipped with the JSF 2.0 release was the f:validateRegex validator. This validator uses a regular expression pattern to determine whether the value entered matches the specified pattern. The validator's pattern attribute is used to specify the regular expression pattern, as shown in the example for Solution #1 to this recipe.

In Solution #2, JSF bean validation is demonstrated, which was also a new feature of the JSF 2.0 release. Bean validation allows you to annotate a managed bean field with constraint annotations that indicate the type of validation that should be performed. The validation automatically occurs on the annotated fields when a form is submitted that contains input components referencing them. A handful of standard constraint annotations can be applied to bean fields, as listed in Table 4-11. Each annotation accepts different attributes; see the online documentation at http://docs.oracle.com/javaee/6/api/ for more details.

Table 4-11. *Constraint Annotations Used for Bean Validation*

Annotation	Description
@AssertFalse	The annotated element must be false.
@AssertTrue	The annotated element must be true.
@DecimalMax	The annotated element must be a decimal that has a value less than or equal to the specified maximum.
@DecimalMin	The annotated element must be a decimal that has a value greater than or equal to the specified minimum.
@Digits	The annotated element must be a number within the accepted range.
@Email	The annotated element must adhere to the format of an email address.
@Future	The annotated element must be a date in the future.
@Max	The annotated element must be a number that has a value less than or equal to the specified maximum.
@Min	The annotated element must be a number that has a value greater than or equal to the specified minimum.
@Negative	The annotated element must be a negative number.
@NotBlank	The annotated element must not be null or blank after removing any trailing or leading whitespace.
@NotEmpty	The annotated element must not be null or empty.
@NotNull	The annotated element must not be null.
@Null	The annotated element must be null.
@Past	The annotated element must be a date in the past.

(*continued*)

Table 4-11. (*continued*)

Annotation	Description
`@Pattern`	The annotated element must match the pattern specified in the regular annotation's regular expression.
`@Positive`	The annotated element must be a positive number.
`@Size`	The annotated element must be between the specified boundaries

When using bean validation, the input component that references an annotated bean field can contain an `f:validateBean` tag to customize behavior. The `f:validateBean` tag's `validationGroups` annotation can be used to specify validation groups that can be used for validating the component. For instance, such a solution may resemble something like the following:

```
<h:inputText id="email" value="#{contactController.email}">
    <f:validateBean validationGroups="org.javaee8recipes.validation.groups.EmailGroup"/>
</h:inputText>
```

■ **Note** Validation groups define a subset of constraints that can be applied for validation. A validation group is represented by an empty Java interface. The interface name can then be applied to annotation constraints within a bean class in order to assign such constraints to a particular group. For instance, the following field that is annotated with `@Size` specifies a group of `EmailGroup.class`:

```
@Size(min=2, max=30, groups=Email.class)

private String email;
```

When utilizing the `f:validateBean` tag, any constraint annotations that are contained in the specified group will be applied to the field for validation.

When you're using bean validation, a custom error message can be displayed if the validation for a field fails. To add a custom message, include the `message` attribute in the annotation, along with the error message that you want to have displayed. As a best practice, error messages should be pulled from a message bundle so that they can be updated without the need to change code.

The example for Solution #3 demonstrates the use of a custom validator method in order to perform validation on an input component. The input component's `validator` attribute can reference a managed bean method that has no return type and accepts a `FacesContext`, a `UIComponent`, and an `Object`. The method can utilize the parameters to gain access to the current `FacesContext`, the `UIComponent` that is being validated, and the current value that is contained in the object, respectively. The validation logic can throw a `javax.faces.validator.ValidatorException` if the value does not pass validation and then return a message to the user via the exception. In the example, the method named `validatePassword` is used to compare the two password field contents to ensure that they match. The first two lines of code within the method are used to obtain the value of the component with the `id` of `password` and save it into a local variable. The actual validation logic compares that value against the incoming parameter's `Object` value, which is the current value of the component being validated, to determine whether there is a match. If not, then a `ValidationException` is thrown with a corresponding message. That message will then be displayed within the `messages` component that corresponds to the component being validated.

As mentioned at the beginning of this recipe, there are a few ways to validate input. None of them is any better than the other; their usage depends on the needs of your application. If you are going to be changing validation patterns often, then you may want to stick with the prebuilt validator tags so that you do not need to recompile code in order to change the validation. On the other hand, if you know that your validation will not change, then it may be easier for you to work with the bean validation technique. Whatever the case, validation can be made even easier with Ajax, and that topic is covered in Chapter 5.

4-5. Adding Select Lists to Pages

Problem

You want to provide a list of options to choose from for some of the input fields on your page.

Solution

Use the JSF `selectOneMenu`, `selectManyMenu`, `selectOneListbox`, or `selectManyListbox` component, depending on the type of list your application requires. Each of these selection components allows for either one or many selections to be made from a particular set of values. The example for this recipe adds to the newsletter subscription page of the Acme Bookstore. The bookstore application will allow the customers to select their occupation from a drop-down list and to select one or more newsletters to which they would like to subscribe from a multiple-select list. Since they'll be selecting only a single option for their occupation, a `selectOneMenu` is used. However, since multiple newsletter selections can be made, a `selectManyListbox` is the best choice.

The View: recipe04_05.xhtml

The following excerpt is taken from the JSF view named `recipe04_05.xhtml`, and it demonstrates the usage of these components:

```
...
<h:outputLabel for="occupation" value="Occupation: "/>
<h:selectOneMenu id="occupation" value="#{contactController.current.occupation}">
    <f:selectItem itemLabel="" itemValue=""/>
    <f:selectItems value="#{contactController.occupationList}"/>
</h:selectOneMenu>
<br/><br/>
<h:outputLabel for="newsletterList" value="Newsletters:"/>
<h:selectManyListbox id="newsletterList" value="#{contactController.current.
newsletterList}">
    <f:selectItems value="#{contactController.allNewsletters}"/>
</h:selectManyListbox>
...
```

Managed Bean: ContactController.java

The components are bound to properties in the `ContactController` managed bean. The following excerpt, taken from `ContactController`, shows the declaration of the properties, along with their corresponding accessor methods:

```
...
// Declaration of the managed bean properties
private List<String> occupationList;
private Map<String, Object> allNewsletters;
...
// Example of populating the object
private void populateOccupationList(){
        occupationList = new ArrayList();
        occupationList.add("Author");
        occupationList.add("IT Professional");
}

// Example of populating the object
private void populateNewsletterList(){
    newsletterList = new LinkedHashMap<String,Object>();
    newsletterList.put("Java 9 Recipes Weekly", "Java");
    newsletterList.put("JavaFX Weekly", "FX");
    newsletterList.put("Oracle PL/SQL Weekly", "Oracle");
    newsletterList.put("New Books Weekly", "New Books");
}

...
/**
    * @return the occupationList
    */
public List<String> getOccupationList() {
    return occupationList;
}

/**
    * @param occupationList the occupationList to set
    */
public void setOccupationList(List<String> occupationList) {
    this.occupationList = occupationList;
}

/**
    * @return the newsletterList
    */
public Map<String,Object> getNewsletterList() {
    return newsletterList;
}
```

```
/**
    * @param newsletterList the newsletterList to set
    */
public void setNewsletterList(Map<String,Object> newsletterList) {
    this.newsletterList = newsletterList;
}
...
```

The newly updated newsletter subscription page should look like Figure 4-5.

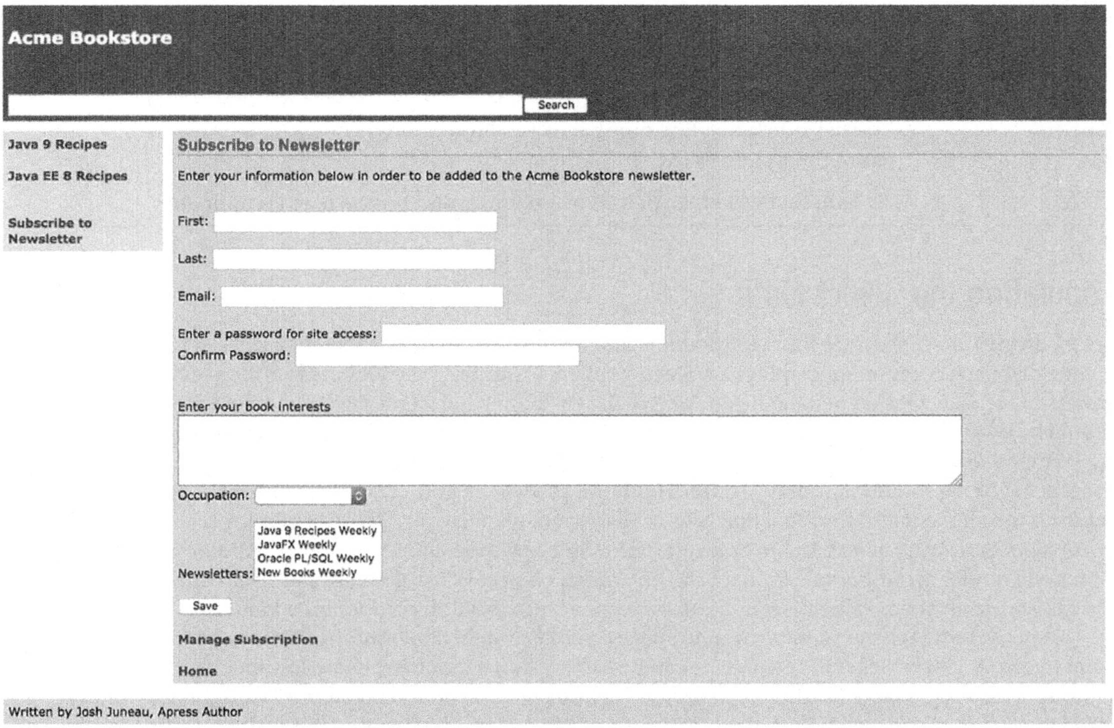

Figure 4-5. Selection components including lists of values

How It Works

To ensure data integrity, it is always a good idea to include input components that are prepopulated with data if possible. Doing so ensures that users are not entering free-text values of varying varieties into text boxes, and it also gives the user a convenient choice of options. Utilizing selection components provides the user with a list of values to choose from, allowing one or more selections to be made. The standard JSF component library ships with four input components that accept lists of data from which a user can choose one or more selections. The selection components are `selectOneListbox`, `selectManyListbox`, `selectOneMenu`, and `selectManyMenu`. Each of these components shares a common set of attributes. Those common attributes that were not already displayed in Table 4-2 are listed in Table 4-12.

Table 4-12. *Select Component Attributes*

Attribute	Description
accesskey	Access key that, when pressed, transfers focus to the component
dir	Direction indication for text (LTR: left-to-right; RTL: right-to-left)
disabled	Boolean value to indicate whether the component is disabled
disabledClass	CSS style class to apply to the rendered label on disabled options
enabledClass	CSS style class to apply to the rendered label on enabled options
label	Localized user-presentable name for the component
lang	Code describing the language used in the generate markup for the component
size	Number of available options to be shown at all times (selectManyListbox)
tabindex	Index value indicating number of Tab button presses it takes to bring the component into focus
title	Tooltip that will be displayed when the mouse hovers over component

Populating the Select Lists

Before diving into each of the four components and a brief description of how they work, it is important to note that each component displays a collection of data, and the `f:selectItem` or `f:selectItems` tags are used to specify that set of data. If you want to list each data item separately, then the `f:selectItem` tag should be used. One `f:selectItem` tag represents one element in the collection of values. The `f:selectItem` tag contains several attributes, but I cover only some of the important ones in this discussion. Every `f:selectItem` tag should minimally contain both the `itemValue` and `itemLabel` attributes, specifying the value for the element and the label that is to be displayed, respectively. These attributes accept a JSF EL expression, or a string of text. In the example, both the `itemValue` and `itemLabel` attributes are left blank, which will render an empty selection for the first menu choice. When the user selects an option from the list, the `itemValue` attribute value is set into the corresponding selection component's value.

The `f:selectItems` tag can be used to specify a collection of data that should be used for the component. A `List` of `SelectItem` objects can be built within a managed bean and specified for the `f:selectItems` tag. Much like the `f:selectItem` tag, several attributes can be used with this tag, and I'll cover the essential ones here. Both the `itemValue` and `itemLabel` attributes can also be specified for the `f:selectItems` tag, corresponding to a `List` or `Map` of values, and a string label, respectively. However, most often, the `value` attribute is specified, referencing a managed bean property that contains a `Collection` or array of objects. The `Collection` or array can contain any valid Java object, and in the example a `LinkedHashMap` is used to populate the `newsletterList` property. It is possible to populate individual `SelectItem` objects and then load them into a `List` for use with the `f:selectItems` tag. The following lines of code show how to populate a collection of newsletters:

```
private void populateNewsletterList() {
        allNewsletters = new LinkedHashMap<String, Object>();
        allNewsletters.put("Java 9 Recipes Weekly", "Java");
        allNewsletters.put("JavaFX Weekly", "FX");
        allNewsletters.put("Oracle PL/SQL Weekly", "Oracle");
        allNewsletters.put("New Books Weekly", "New Books");
    }
```

Regarding Each Component Type

The selectOneMenu is probably the most commonly used selection component, and it renders a collection of data into a drop-down list. The user can select one entry from the menu, and the selected entry will be set into the managed bean property that is specified for the value attribute of the component. In the example to this recipe, the value is set to #{contactController.current.occupation}, so when an entry from the list is selected, then it will be set into the currently selected Contact object's occupation field.

The selectOneListbox allows a user to select one value from a list of data. The user can see at least a few of the entries within the list within a box on the screen and can select one of the options from the list box. The selectOneListbox contains an additional attribute named collectionType, which allows the type of collection to be specified using a literal value.

Both the selectManyMenu and selectManyListbox components allow the user to choose more than one option in the selection list. The example demonstrates how to use a selectManyListbox component, allowing the user to choose more than one newsletter from the list. The main difference when using one of these components is that the managed bean property value for the component must be able to accept more than one value. In the example, the selectManyListbox component value references the Contact class's newsletterList field. The newsletterList field is declared as a List of String objects, so when the user selects more than one value from the newsletterList, all of the choices can be stored in the current Contact object.

In the example for this recipe, two components are used to display lists of options for selection. One of the components allows a user to select one value from the collection and displays the options in a drop-down list, and the other allows a user to select more than one value and displays the options within a list box.

4-6. Adding Graphics to Your Pages

Problem

You want to incorporate a graphic into your site template or other select application pages.

Solution

Place the images that you want to display into a library in your application's resources folder, and then use the graphicImage component to display them. The book.xhtml view for the Acme Bookstore application contains an image of each book in the store. To render the image, the book image name is populated from the image field of the Book managed bean. The following code excerpt taken from book.xhtml demonstrates how to use the h:graphicImage tag:

```
<h:graphicImage id="bookImage" library="image"
            style="width: 100px; height: 120px" name="#{book.image}"/>
```

How It Works

Since the inception of JSF, the graphicImage component has been used to display images. Using the library attribute of the graphicImage component, a JSF view can reference an image resource without needing to specify a fully qualified path to the image file. In the solution to this recipe, the value specified for the library attribute is image, meaning that the image can be found in the resource\image folder. It also provides the convenience of accepting JSF EL in attributes as needed so that images can be dynamically loaded based upon the current values in the corresponding managed bean properties. The graphicImage component makes it easy to display images, both dynamically and statically.

The h:graphicImage tag supports a number of attributes, above and beyond the standard JSF component attributes, as listed in Table 4-13.

Table 4-13. *graphicImage Component-Specific Attributes*

Attribute	Description
alt	Alternate textual description of the element rendered by the component
dir	Direction indication for text (LTR: left-to-right; RTL: right-to-left)
height	Overrides the height of the image
ismap	Boolean indicating whether the image is to be used as a server-side image map
lang	Code describing the language used in the generated markup for the component
longdesc	URI to a long description of the image represented by the element
title	Advisory title information about the markup elements generated by the component
usemap	Name of a client-side image map for which this element provides the image
width	Overrides the width of the image

When the page is rendered in the example to this recipe, the image that resides within the application's resources/image directory that corresponds to the name attribute on the tag will be displayed. If the user selects a different book from the menu, then that book's image will be displayed using the same graphicImage component, because the name specified for the image can be changed depending on the currently selected book object in the managed bean.

By utilizing a graphicImage in your views, you enable your images to take on the dynamic characteristics of standard JSF components.

4-7. Adding Check Boxes to a View

Problem

You need to add check box fields to an application view.

Solution

Utilize the selectOneCheckbox and selectManyCheckbox components within the view. These components allow you to specify a boolean value as input by simply checking a box for a true value and deselecting the check box for a false value.

The View: recipe04_07.xhtml

The following code excerpt is taken from the view named recipe04_07.xhtml, and it demonstrates the use of these components:

```
...
<h:outputLabel for="notifyme" value="Would you like to receive other promotional email?"/>
<h:selectBooleanCheckbox id="notifyme"
value="#{contactController.current.receiveNotifications}"/>
```

```
<br/><br/>
<h:outputLabel for="notificationTypes"
                          value="What type of notifications are you interested in
receiving?"/>
<h:selectManyCheckbox id="notifyTypes" value="#{contactController.current.
notificationType}">
    <f:selectItems value="#{contactController.notificationTypes}"/>
</h:selectManyCheckbox>
...
```

Managed Bean Controllers

Each of the components is bound to a Contact object, so when the form is submitted, the current Contact object will receive the data if valid. The following listing contains excerpts from the updated Contact class, an object that is used to hold the contact's information. For the complete listing, see the Contact.java sources in the org.javaee8recipes.chapter04 packages in the sources.

```
...
private boolean receiveNotifications;
private Map<String, Object> notificationType;
...

/**
    * @return the receiveNotifications
    */
public boolean isReceiveNotifications() {
    return receiveNotifications;
}

/**
    * @param receiveNotifications the receiveNotifications to set
    */
public void setReceiveNotifications(boolean receiveNotifications) {
    this.receiveNotifications = receiveNotifications;
}

/**
     * @return the notificationTypes
     */
    public Map<String, Object> getNotificationTypes() {
        return notificationTypes;
    }

    /**
     * @param notificationTypes the notificationTypes to set
     */
    public void setNotificationTypes(Map<String, Object> notificationTypes) {
        this.notificationTypes = notificationTypes;
    }
```

The last piece of the puzzle is the list of notification types that are bound to the `f:selectItems` tag that is embedded within the `h:selectManyCheckbox` component. These are bound to a property named `notificationTypes` in the `ContactController` managed bean. The following listing contains the relevant excerpts from that class.

```
...
// Declaration
private Map<String, Object> notificationTypes;
...
// Population occurs within the constructor, calling the populateNotificationTypes method
/**
    * Creates a new instance of ContactController
    */
public ContactController() {
    current = null;
    passwordConfirm = null;
    newsletterDescription = "Enter your information below in order to be " +
            "added to the Acme Bookstore newsletter.";
    populateOccupationList();
    populateNewsletterList();
    populateNotificationTypes();

}

private void populateNotificationTypes() {
        notificationTypes = new HashMap<>();
        notificationTypes.put("Product Updates", "1");
        notificationTypes.put("Best Seller Alerts","2");
        notificationTypes.put("Spam", "3");

    }
...
```

The resulting newsletter subscription input screen for the Acme Bookstore application, including the new check box components, will look like Figure 4-6.

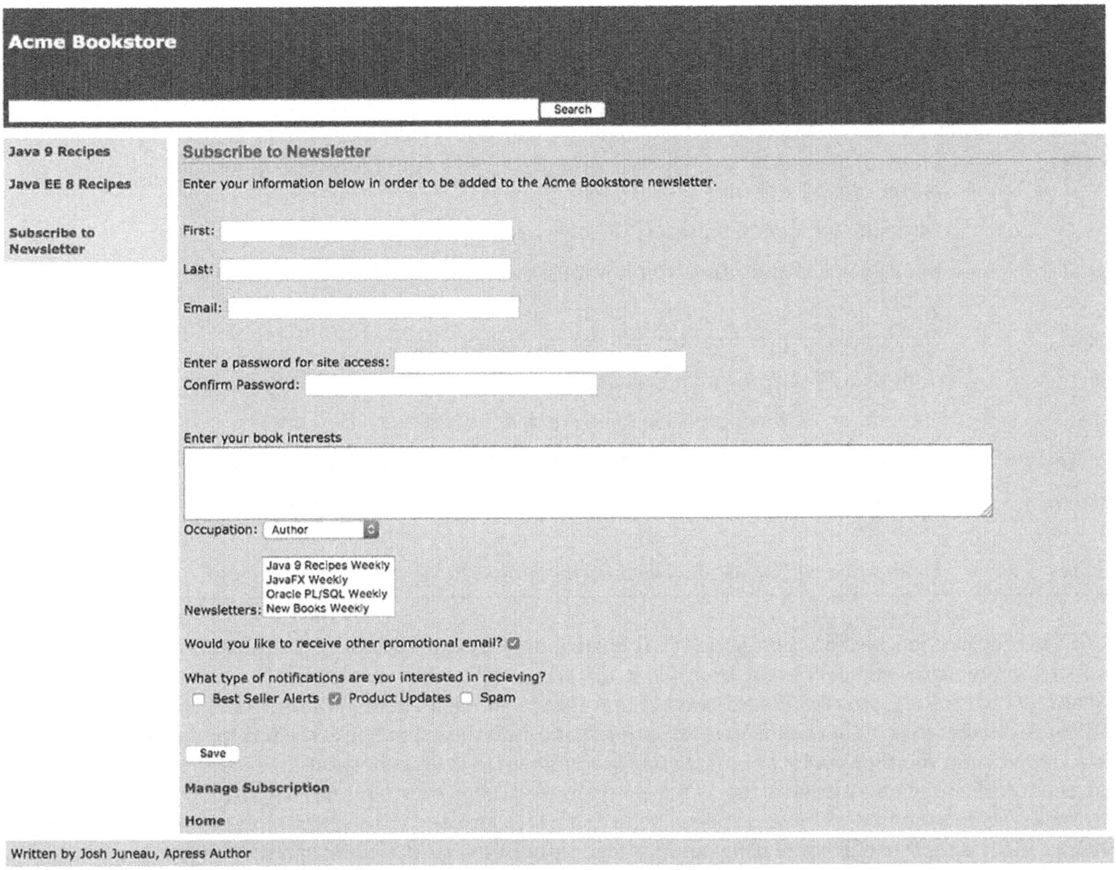

Figure 4-6. *Incorporating check boxes into your pages*

How It Works

Check boxes are very common in applications because they provide an easy means for users to enter boolean values. The box is either checked or not, and a checked box relates to a `true` value, leaving an unchecked box relating to a `false` value. The JSF standard component library ships with a couple of different check box selection components, namely, the `selectBooleanCheckbox` and the `selectManyCheckbox`. The `selectBooleanCheckbox` renders a single HTML input element with `type="checkbox"` on the page, whereas the `selectManyCheckbox` component renders multiple HTML input elements with `type="checkbox"`. As with all JSF components, the check box selection components share a standard set of attributes above and beyond the common JSF component attributes, which are listed in Table 4-14.

Table 4-14. *Check Box Selection Component Attributes*

Attribute	Description
accessKey	Access key that, when pressed, transfers focus to the element
border	Width of the border to be drawn around the table containing the options list (selectManyCheckbox)
dir	Direction indication for text (LTR: left-to-right; RTL: right-to-left)
disabled	Boolean value indicating whether the element must receive focus or be included in a submit
label	Localized user presentable name for the component
lang	Code describing the language used in the generated markup for the component
layout	Orientation of the options list to be created (selectManyCheckbox)
readonly	Boolean indicating whether the component is read-only
tabindex	Index value indicating number of Tab button presses it takes to bring the component into focus
title	Tooltip that will be displayed when the mouse hovers over a component

A selectBooleanCheckbox component value attribute EL expression should correspond to a boolean property in the managed bean. In the example to this recipe, the selectBooleanCheckbox value is set to #{contactController.current.receiveNotifications}, a boolean field in the current Contact object that indicates whether the contact wants to receive notifications. If the user checks the box for the component, then the value for the receiveNotifications field will be set to true; otherwise, it will be set to false. The value attribute is the only attribute that is required for use. However, oftentimes the valueChangeListener attribute is set to a method within a managed bean that will be invoked if the value for the component value changes. This is most useful when using an Ajax form submit so that the client can see the results of a ValueChangeEvent immediately, rather than after the form is re-rendered. To learn more about working with valueChangeListeners, see Chapter 5.

The selectManyCheckbox component displays one or more check boxes on a page. The value attribute for this component should correspond to a string array. Each check box contained within the component has a corresponding String value. Now you are probably thinking to yourself, what does a string have to do with a boolean value? In fact, each string in the array corresponds to a check box on the page, and when a box is checked, the string that corresponds to that box is added to the array. If no boxes are checked, then there are no strings added to the array. Therefore, the presence of the string signifies that the check box corresponding to that string value has been checked.

To add check boxes, individual f:selectItem tags can be used for each check box, or a collection of check boxes can be added using the f:selectItems tag. If you're using f:selectItem, then the itemValue attribute is set to the String value that corresponds to that check box, and the itemLabel attribute is set to the check box label. In the example, the f:selectItems tag is used to populate check boxes for the component. The f:selectItems tag in the example contains a value attribute that is set to #{contactController.notificationTypes}, which corresponds to the notificationTypes field in the ContactController class. If you take a look at the notificationTypes field, you will see that it is declared as a Map<String, Object>, and each element in the array will correspond to a check box. When the ContactController class is instantiated, the populateNotificationTypes method is called, which populates the map with the values for each check box. The following listing is that of the populateNotificationTypes method. Each element in the map corresponds to a check box.

```
private void populateNotificationTypes() {
        notificationTypes = new HashMap<>();
        notificationTypes.put("Product Updates", "1");
        notificationTypes.put("Best Seller Alerts","2");
        notificationTypes.put("Spam", "3");

    }
```

Check boxes make it easy for users to indicate a `true` or `false` (checked or unchecked) value for a given option. The JSF check box selection components help organize content on a page, and they provide a good means of ensuring data integrity since the user does not have to enter free text.

4-8. Adding Radio Buttons to a View

Problem

You want to display a set of items on a page in the form of radio buttons and allow the user to select only one of them.

Solution

Use radio buttons on your page to provide the user the option of selecting one item from a set. Radio buttons are often a nice solution when you want to display all options on the screen at once but allow only one selection. For this recipe, the Acme Bookstore wants to add a radio button on the newsletter subscription page to determine whether the subscriber is male or female.

The View: recipe04_08.xhtml

The following excerpt is taken from the JSF view named `recipe04_08.xhtml`, and it demonstrates the `selectOneRadio` component:

```
...
<h:outputLabel for="gender" value="Gender: "/>
<h:selectOneRadio id="gender" value="#{contactController.current.gender}">
    <f:selectItem itemValue="M" itemLabel="Male"/>
    <f:selectItem itemValue="F" itemLabel="Female"/>
</h:selectOneRadio>
<br/><br/>
<h:message id="genderError"
           for="gender"
           errorStyle="color:red"/>
<br/>
...
```

Managed Bean

The component is bound to a managed bean property named gender that has been added to the Contact class. The following listing contains excerpts from the Contact class, which show the updates for incorporating the new field:

```
...
private String gender;
...
/**
    * @return the gender
    */
public String getGender() {
    return gender;
}

/**
    * @param gender the gender to set
    */
public void setGender(String gender) {
    this.gender = gender;
}
...
```

When the selectOneRadio component is rendered on the screen, it adds a radio button for each of the available options. The updated Acme Bookstore newsletter page looks like that in Figure 4-7.

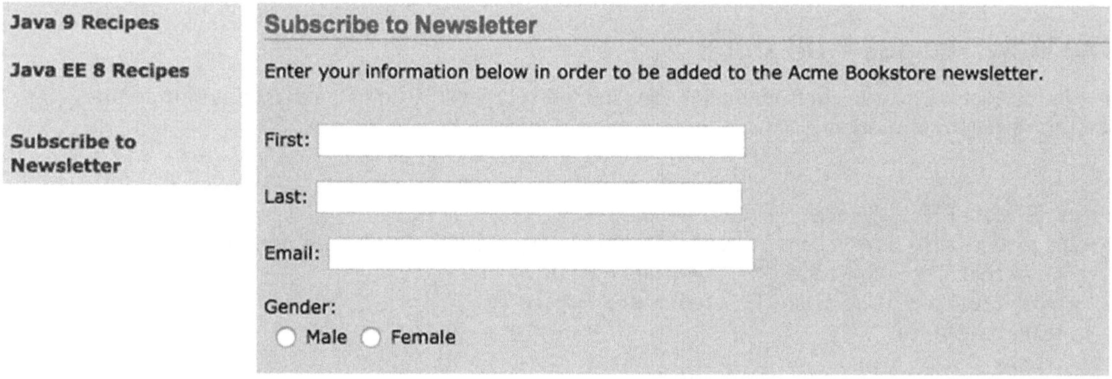

Java 9 Recipes

Java EE 8 Recipes

Subscribe to Newsletter

Subscribe to Newsletter

Enter your information below in order to be added to the Acme Bookstore newsletter.

First:

Last:

Email:

Gender:

Male Female

Figure 4-7. *Using a selectOneRadio component*

How It Works

Radio buttons are very similar to check boxes in that they provide the user with an on or off value for a designated page value. The value added to using radio buttons is that they make it easy to display several options on the screen at once and allow the user to select only one of them. If a user tries to select a different option, then the currently selected item becomes unselected, forcing the user to select only one option. The JSF selectOneRadio component is used to render radio buttons on a page, and the component works in much the same manner as the selectManyCheckbox (see Recipe 4-7).

The selectOneRadio shares all of the same attributes as the selectBooleanCheckbox component. See Table 4-14 for a listing of those attributes. The selectOneRadio component also contains a number of additional attributes, as listed in Table 4-15.

Table 4-15. *selectOneRadio Attributes (in Addition to Those Listed in Table 4-14)*

Attribute	Description
disabledClass	CSS style class to apply to the rendered label on disabled options.
group	Specifies a group of radio buttons to which the component belongs.
enabledClass	CSS style class to apply to the rendered label on enabled options.

To use the selectOneRadio component, the value attribute should be set to a string. In the example, the value for the selectOneRadio component is set to the gender field in the current Contact object. When one of the radio buttons is selected, the String value corresponding to that button will be set into the field value. The radio buttons are populated using either the f:selectItem tag or the f:selectItems tag, much like the selectManyCheckbox component (see Recipe 4-7). In the example, two f:selectItem tags are used to add two radio buttons to the component; the itemValue attribute is the string that will be submitted for the selected button, and the itemLabel attribute is the string that is displayed next to the corresponding button.

If you want to use an f:selectItems tag to populate a collection of radio buttons, the f:selectItems value attribute should be set to a managed bean property that is declared as a string array, a map, or a list of SelectItem objects. To see an example, review the example for the selectManyCheckbox component in Recipe 4-7.

■ **Note** In JSF 2.3, the group attribute was added to the component. This attribute allows radio buttons to be placed in a view individually, while still having the ability to share selection with all other buttons of the same group.

Radio buttons are an easy way to display multiple options to a user and allow them to select one. If you understand how a selectManyCheckbox component works, then the selectOneRadio is very similar.

4-9. Displaying a Collection of Data

Problem

You are interested in displaying a collection of data in one of your JSF application pages.

Solution

Utilize a dataTable component to display a collection of data. A dataTable component can be used to iterate over a collection of data, providing a handle for each row object so that column data can be interrogated if need be or simply displayed. For this example, the book page is being updated to display the table of contents for a chosen book. The table of contents will be displayed in a dataTable component, which has been customized for readability.

The View: recipe04_09.xhtml

The following listing is that of the view named `recipe04_09.xhtml`, which is an incomplete snapshot of the `book.xhtml` view:

```
<html xmlns="http://www.w3.org/1999/xhtml"
      xmlns:ui="http://xmlns.jcp.org/jsf/facelets"
      xmlns:f="http://xmlns.jcp.org/jsf/core"
      xmlns:h="http://xmlns.jcp.org/jsf/html">
<h:head>
        <meta http-equiv="Content-Type" content="text/html; charset=UTF-8"/>
        <title>Acme Bookstore</title>
    </h:head>
    <h:body>
        <ui:composition template="./layout/custom_template_search.xhtml">

            <ui:define name="content">
                <h:form id="componentForm">
                    <h1>Author List for #{ch4AuthorController.currentBook.title}</h1>
                    <p>
                        Below is the list of authors. Click on the author's last name
                        for more information regarding the author.
                    </p>

                    <h:graphicImage id="javarecipes" library="image"
                                    style="width: 100px; height: 120px"
                                    name="#{ch4AuthorController.currentBook.image}"/>
                    <br/>
                    <h:dataTable  id="authorTable" border="1"
                           value="#{ch4AuthorController.authorList}"
                                 var="author">
                        <f:facet name="header">
                            #{ch4AuthorController.currentBook.title} Authors
                        </f:facet>
                        <h:column >
                            <h:commandLink id="authorName" action="#{ch4AuthorController.
                            displayAuthor(author.last)}"
                                           value="#{author.first} #{author.last}"/>
                        </h:column>
                    </h:dataTable>
                    <br/><br/>
                    <h:dataTable id="bookDetail" border="1"
                                 value="#{ch4AuthorController.currentBook.chapters}"
                                 var="book" style="width:100%"
                                 rowClasses="tocTableOdd, tocTableEven"
                                 columnClasses="col1">
                        <f:facet name="header">
                            #{ch4AuthorController.currentBook.title} Details
                        </f:facet>
```

```
                        <h:column >
                            <f:facet name="header">
                                Chapter
                            </f:facet>
                            <h:outputText value="#{book.chapterNumber}"/>
                        </h:column>
                        <h:column>
                            <f:facet name="header">
                                Title
                            </f:facet>
                            <h:outputText value="#{book.title}"/>
                        </h:column>

                    </h:dataTable>
                    <br/>
                    <br/>

                </h:form>
            </ui:define>

        </ui:composition>

    </h:body>
</html>
```

CSS

The dataTable utilizes some CSS style classes in order to make it easier to read. The following excerpt is taken from the Acme Bookstore application style sheet named styles.css, and it contains the styles utilized by the table. The styles.css sheet is linked to the view because it is declared as a resource within the template.

```
.tocTableOdd{
    background: #c0c0c0;
}

.tocTableEven{
    background: #e0e0e0;
}

.col1{
    text-indent: 15px;
    font-weight: bold;
}
```

■ **Note** In JSF 2.3, the `dataTable` has a new `rowClass` attribute, which accepts EL to access the current row. Therefore, something like the following is possible:

```
<h:dataTable id="bookDetail" border="1"

    value="#{ch4AuthorController.currentBook.chapters}"

    var="book" style="width:100%"

    rowClass="#{book eq 'Java EE 8 Recipes'? style1:style2}"

    columnClasses="col1">
```

The `h:column` had a new `styleClass` attribute added in JSF 2.3. This attribute allows you to apply a specified style to an individual column.

Managed Bean

To accommodate the new table, a class named `Chapter` has been added to the application. The `Chapter` class is an object that will contain the chapter number, the title, and a description of each chapter. There is to be one `Chapter` object instantiated for each chapter in every book. To view the listing, see the `org.javaee8recipes.chapter04.Chapter` class in the sources. To populate the `Chapter` objects for each book, the `AuthorController` managed bean has been updated. The following excerpt is taken from the `AuthorController` managed bean, and it shows how the chapters are populated into the Book objects.

■ **Note** The example demonstrates hard-coding of strings within Java classes. This is generally a bad idea, and the use of a database or resource bundle for obtaining strings is a better fit for enterprise applications. This code is for demonstration purposes only; to learn more about using databases to store strings, refer to Part II or Part III of this book.

```
...
public void populateAuthors(){
...
    Book book1 = new Book("Java 9 Recipes", "java9recipes.png");
    book1 = addChapters1(book1);
...
}
...
private Book addChapters1(Book book){
    Chapter chapter1 = new Chapter(1, "Getting Started with Java 7", null);
    Chapter chapter2 = new Chapter(2, "Strings", null);
    Chapter chapter3 = new Chapter(3, "Numbers and Dates", null);
    Chapter chapter4 = new Chapter(4, "Data Structures, Conditionals, and Iteration", null);
    Chapter chapter5 = new Chapter(5, "Input and Output", null);
```

```
    Chapter chapter6 = new Chapter(6, "Exceptions, Logging, and Debugging", null);
    Chapter chapter7 = new Chapter(7, "Object Oriented Java", null);
    Chapter chapter8 = new Chapter(8, "Concurrency", null);
    Chapter chapter9 = new Chapter(9, "Debugging and Unit Testing", null);
    Chapter chapter10 = new Chapter(10, "Unicode, Internationalization, and Currency Codes",
    null);
    Chapter chapter11 = new Chapter(11, "Working with Databases (JDBC)", null);
    Chapter chapter12 = new Chapter(12, "Java 2D Graphics and Media", null);
    Chapter chapter13 = new Chapter(13, "Java 3D", null);
    Chapter chapter14 = new Chapter(14, "Swing API", null);
    Chapter chapter15 = new Chapter(15, "JavaFX Fundamentals", null);
    Chapter chapter16 = new Chapter(16, "Graphics with JavaFX", null);
    Chapter chapter17 = new Chapter(17, "Media with JavaFX", null);
    Chapter chapter18 = new Chapter(18, "Working with Servlets", null);
    Chapter chapter19 = new Chapter(19, "Applets", null);
    Chapter chapter20 = new Chapter(20, "JavaFX on the Web", null);
    Chapter chapter21 = new Chapter(21, "Email", null);
    Chapter chapter22 = new Chapter(22, "XML and Web Services", null);
    Chapter chapter23 = new Chapter(23, "Networking", null);
    List <Chapter> chapterList = new ArrayList();
    chapterList.add(chapter1);
    chapterList.add(chapter2);
    chapterList.add(chapter3);
    chapterList.add(chapter4);
    chapterList.add(chapter5);
    chapterList.add(chapter6);
    chapterList.add(chapter7);
    chapterList.add(chapter8);
    chapterList.add(chapter9);
    chapterList.add(chapter10);
    chapterList.add(chapter11);
    chapterList.add(chapter12);
    chapterList.add(chapter13);
    chapterList.add(chapter14);
    chapterList.add(chapter15);
    chapterList.add(chapter16);
    chapterList.add(chapter17);
    chapterList.add(chapter18);
    chapterList.add(chapter19);
    chapterList.add(chapter20);
    chapterList.add(chapter21);
    chapterList.add(chapter22);
    chapterList.add(chapter23);
    book.setChapters(chapterList);
    return book;

}
...
```

The resulting table of contents on the book page will look like Figure 4-8.

Java 7 Recipes Details	
Chapter	**Title**
1	Getting Started with Java 7
2	Strings
3	Numbers and Dates
4	Data Structures, Conditionals, and Iteration
5	Input and Output
6	Exceptions, Logging, and Debugging
7	Object Oriented Java
8	Concurrency
9	Debugging and Unit Testing
10	Unicode, Internationalization, and Currency Codes
11	Working with Databases (JDBC)
12	Java 2D Graphics and Media
13	Java 3D
14	Swing API
15	JavaFX Fundamentals
16	Graphics with JavaFX
17	Media with JavaFX
18	Working with Servlets
19	Applets
20	JavaFX on the Web
21	Email
22	XML and Web Services
23	Networking

Figure 4-8. *Using a dataTable component*

How It Works

The JSF `dataTable` component can be used to display collections of data in a uniform fashion. The `dataTable` component is easy to work with, and it allows the flexibility to work with each field within a data collection. There are other means of displaying collections of data, such as the `ui-repeat` Facelets tag or the use of a `panelGrid` component, but a `dataTable` makes a developer's life easy if the table does not need to be customized to the *n*th degree.

The `dataTable` component contains various attributes that can be used to customize the look and feel of the table, as well as some behavioral characteristics. Each of those attributes is listed in Table 4-16. Each `dataTable` also contains `column` components, which are declared within a `dataTable` component using the `h:column` tag. As with any other JSF tag, there are many attributes that correspond to the `h:column` tag, as listed in Table 4-17.

Table 4-16. dataTable Attributes

Attribute	Description
bgcolor	Name or code of the background color for the table.
bodyrows	Comma-separated list of row indices for which a new <tbody> element should be started.
border	Width (pixels) of the border to be drawn around the table.
captionClass	Space-separated list of CSS style classes that will be applied to any caption generated for the table.
captionStyle	CSS style to be applied when the caption is rendered.
cellpadding	Definition of how much space the user agent should leave between the border of each cell and its contents.
cellspacing	Definition of how much space the user agent should leave between the left side of the table and the leftmost column, the top of the table and the top of the top side of the topmost row, and so on, for the right and bottom of the table. This also specifies how much space to leave between cells.
columnClasses	Comma-delimited list of CSS styles that will be applied to the columns of the table. A space-separated list of classes can also be specified for any individual column.
columns	Number of columns to render before starting a new row.
dir	Direction indication for text (LTR: left-to-right; RTL: right-to-left).
footerClass	Space-separated list of CSS style classes that will be applied to any footer generated for the table.
frame	Code specifying which sides of the frame surrounding the table will be visible.
headerClass	Space-separated list of CSS style classes that will be applied to any header generated for the table.
lang	Code describing the language used in the generated markup for the component.
rowClass	Accepts EL to access rows, and can be used to apply CSS style classes to specified rows.
rowClasses	Comma-delimited list of CSS style classes that will be applied to the rows of the table. A space-separated list of classes may also be specified for each individual row.
rules	Code specifying which rules will appear between the cells of the table. Valid values include none, groups, rows, cols, and all.
summary	Summary of the table's purpose and structure for user agents rendering to nonvisual media.
title	Advisory title information about markup elements generated for the component.
width	Width of the entire table.

Table 4-17. h:column Attributes

Attribute	Description
footerClass	CSS class that will be applied to the column footer
headerClass	CSS class that will be applied to the column header
styleClass	Allows CSS class to be applied to the individual column

The easiest way to describe the dataTable is to walk through an example. The solution to this recipe contains a JSF view, in which there are two dataTable components utilized. The first dataTable has an id attribute of authorTable, and the second has an id attribute of bookTable. You are most interested in the second dataTable, whose id attribute equals bookTable, although the first dataTable functions in much the same way. The bookTable component is used to iterate over a collection of Chapter objects and display the corresponding chapter number and title for the currently selected book. The value attribute of the dataTable is set to #{ch4AuthorController.currentBook.chapters}, which corresponds to a List<String> property within the AuthorController managed bean. A dataTable can iterate over many different collection types, including a list, DataModel, and array. Beginning with the release of JSF 2.2, the common Collection interface also became supported. The var attribute of the dataTable component is used to specify a handle that allows access to the collection data at the row level. This means you can hone in on a specific field of the data collection if needed. The dataTable tag does not display anything on its own; it must have column components embedded within it in order to display the content. Each h:column tag within a dataTable correlates to a single column of the resulting table when it is rendered. For instance, if you look at the first h:column tag within the dataTable that has an id of bookDetail, it has an embedded outputText component, which specifies a value of #{book.chapterNumber}. This specific column is used to display the chapter number, which is a field within the Chapter object that correlates to the currentBook object's chapters List.

A column component can contain any valid JSF component, or it can contain plain JSF EL correlating to a data field within the collection. If you look at the dataTable that has an id attribute of authorTable, you will see that a commandLink component is used within one of the columns. Oftentimes such is the case, because you may want to link to the currently selected row's data from within a table cell. The dataTable with an id of authorTable contains a good example of doing just that. The commandLink in the table contains an action attribute that specifies a method within the AuthorController class, and the currently selected row's value, lastName, is passed to the method as a parameter. The underlying method uses that parameter to retrieve all the data for the selected row and display it in a different view.

```
<h:commandLink id="authorName" action="#{ch4AuthorController.displayAuthor(author.last)}"
                              value="#{author.first} #{author.last}"/>
```

To place a header or footer on the table, you must embed a facet into the table using an f:facet tag. The f:facet tag contains a number of typical JSF component attributes, but one that stands out for this component is the name attribute. The name attribute is used to specify what type of facet the tag is, and in the case of the dataTable those names are header and footer. To create the table header or footer, simply embed the f:facet tag, specifying the name of the facet (type of facet to create) inside the dataTable component.

■ **Note** A unique data type that can be used for a dataTable collection is the DataModel. To have the ability to display row numbers, use a DataModel.

The dataTable component can be extremely useful in situations when you need to display a collection of data. One of the pitfalls to using the dataTable is that it does not provide an overabundance of customizability. However, it is very possible to extend the functionality of the dataTable to suit one's need. There are plenty of third-party component libraries that do just that; they provide extended dataTables that feature sorting, row expansion, inline editing, and so forth. To learn more about using these custom dataTable components, see Chapter 7.

4-10. Utilizing Custom JSF Component Libraries

Problem

You want to include components from an external JSF library in your application pages.

Solution

Obtain the latest stable version of the JSF component library that you'd like to utilize and configure it for use in your application. This recipe will cover the configuration of the PrimeFaces component library, which contains a number of customized components that can add a great deal of functionality to your applications. To download the PrimeFaces library, visit the site `www.primefaces.org`. PrimeFaces and some other component libraries can be used together within a single JSF application, allowing you to utilize multiple third-party libraries if needed.

If you're downloading the libraries via the JAR files, add them to your JSF application by adding the component library JAR file to the `WEB-INF/lib` directory in your application's web source directory. If you're using Maven, add the specified library's Maven coordinates to your POM file. Note that you may also need to include additional JAR files with your application in order to utilize external libraries. For instance, the PrimeFaces library recommends that you also include external libraries such as `commons-collections.jar` and `commons-beanutils.jar`, among others. See each library's documentation for complete details on each external JARs or maven dependencies that need to be included in your application in order to gain full functionality.

After the libraries have been added, you can begin to utilize the library's components in your application by declaring their corresponding tag libraries within the application views in which you want to use them. The following tag declarations are used to allow usage PrimeFaces 5+ components within a JSF view:

```
xmlns:p="http://www.primefaces.org/ui"
```

How It Works

The JSF standard component library contains a vast number of components for use within applications. However, many individuals and organizations require the use of more customized components and components that build on the functionality of the standard components. Utilizing a third-party JSF component library is very easy and usually involves nothing more than downloading the distribution, including the recommended JAR files or maven dependencies within your application, and referencing the tag libraries from within the views. However, it is best to take care when utilizing more than one third-party JSF component library in the same application, because there may be some compatibility issues/conflicts that arise between them.

Once you have followed the procedures outlined in the solution to this recipe, you will be able to begin adding components from the PrimeFaces library into your views. The library includes exciting components such as the `autoComplete` component, which renders an input text box that will automatically complete a string of text when the user begins to type. While I will not delve into any details of the components in this chapter, you will begin using them within Chapter 5.

4-11. Implementing File Uploading

Problem

You want to add a file upload component to your application.

Solution

Use the JSF file upload component to create an Ajax or non-Ajax-based file upload system for your application. To utilize the `inputFile` component, it must be placed within a JSF form that has an `enctype` set to `multipart/form-data` and does not specify an `id` attribute. The `h:form` element contains the attributes `enctype` and `prependId`, which can be used to specify these requirements, respectively. A JSF command component or the `f:ajax` tag should be set to an action method within the managed bean that will save the file to disk.

The following JSF view demonstrates the use of the `inputFile` component in a non-Ajax solution:

```
<h:form prependId="false" enctype="multipart/form-data">
    Choose a file to upload to the server:    <br/>
     <h:inputFile id="uploadFile" value="#{ajaxBean.file}"/>
    <br/>    <h:commandButton action="#{ajaxBean.uploadFile()}" value="Upload File"/></h:form>
```

The sources for the `uploadFile` method that is invoked via the `commandButton` are as follows:

```
public void uploadFile() {

        try(InputStream is = file.getInputStream();) {
            byte[] b = new byte[1024];
            is.read(b);
            String fileName = file.getName();
            FileOutputStream os = new FileOutputStream("/Java_Dev/" + fileName);

        } catch (IOException ex) {
            Logger.getLogger(AjaxBean.class.getName()).log(Level.SEVERE, null, ex);
        }
}
```

Note that in the example, the path `/Java_Dev/` indicates an operating system path or directory to which the uploaded file will be saved.

How It Works

JSF 2.2 included a new file upload component that relies on new Servlet 3.1 file upload support. The file upload support can be Ajax-enabled or non-Ajax-enabled. The `inputFile` component can be used with or without the `f:ajax` tag, so files can be uploaded with a page refresh (non-Ajax) or without (Ajax).

The following line of code demonstrates how to set the attributes for a form containing an `inputFile` component:

```
<h:form prependId="false" enctype="multipart/form-data">
```

The `value` attribute of the `inputFile` component is set to a variable of type `javax.servlet.http.Part` within the `AjaxBean` managed bean, and the `commandButton` has an action set to the managed bean's `uploadFile` method. To make the solution utilize Ajax, simply embed an `f:ajax` tag into the `commandButton`, which invokes the underlying managed bean method.

The addition of a native file upload component to JSF is much welcomed. For years now, JSF developers have had to rely on third-party libraries to handle file-uploading procedures. The scope of components that requires third-party integration is becoming narrower, and the default JSF component toolset is becoming complete enough to be the only requirement for standard enterprise applications.

CHAPTER 5

Advanced JavaServer Faces and Ajax

A task that can be run in the background, independent of other running tasks, is known as an *asynchronous* task. JavaScript is the most popular modern browser language that is used to implement asynchronous tasking in web applications. Ajax is a set of technologies that allows you to perform asynchronous tasks using JavaScript in the background, sending responses from the client browser to the server, and then sending a response back to the client. That response is used to update the page's Document Object Model (DOM). Enhancing an application to use such asynchronous requests and responses can greatly improve the overall user experience. The typical web applications from years past included a series of web pages, including buttons that were used to navigate from one page to the next. The browser had to refreshed to repaint each new page, and when a user was finished with the next page, they'd click another button or link to go to a subsequent page, and so on.

The days of page reloads are long gone, and client-side asynchronous processing is now the norm. Ajax technology has overtaken the industry of web application development, and users now expect to experience a richer and more desktop-like experience when using a web application.

The JSF framework allows developers to create rich user experiences via the use of technologies such as Ajax and HTML5. Much of the implementation detail behind these technologies can be abstracted away from the JSF developer using JSF components. As such, the developer needs to worry only about how to use a JSF component tag and relate it to a server-side property.

This chapter delves into using Ajax with the JSF web framework. Along the way, you will learn how to spruce up applications and make the user interface richer and more user friendly so that it behaves more like that of a desktop application. You'll also learn how to listen to different component phases and system events, allowing further customization of application functionality.

Note This chapter contains examples using the third-party component library PrimeFaces. It is recommended to use the most recent releases of third-party libraries in order to ensure that your application contains stable and secure sources.

J. Juneau, *Java EE 8 Recipes*, https://doi.org/10.1007/978-1-4842-3594-2_5

5-1. Validating Input with Ajax

Problem

You want to validate the values that are entered into text fields of a form, but you want them to be evaluated immediately, rather than after the form is submitted.

Solution

Perform validation on the field(s) by embedding the `f:ajax` tag within each component whose values you want to validate. Specify appropriate values for the `event` and `render` attributes so that the Ajax validation will occur when the field(s) loses focus, and any validation errors will be identified immediately. The following listing is the JSF view for the newsletter subscription page of the Acme Bookstore application. It has been updated to utilize Ajax validation so that the validation occurs immediately, without the need to submit the form before corresponding errors are displayed.

```
<ui:composition xmlns="http://www.w3.org/1999/xhtml"
                xmlns:ui="http://xmlns.jcp.org/jsf/facelets"
                xmlns:f="http://xmlns.jcp.org/jsf/core"
                xmlns:h="http://xmlns.jcp.org/jsf/html"

                template="layout/custom_template_search.xhtml">
    <ui:define name="content">
        <h:messages globalOnly="true"  errorStyle="color: red" infoStyle="color: green"/>
        <h:form id="contactForm">
            <h1>Subscribe to Newsletter</h1>
            <p>
                <h:outputText id="newsletterSubscriptionDesc"
                              value="#{ch5ContactController.newsletterDescription}"/>
            </p>

            <br />
            <h:panelGrid columns="2" bgcolor="" border="0">
                <h:panelGroup>
                    <h:outputLabel for="first" value="First: "/>
                    <h:inputText id="first" size="40" value="#{ch5ContactController.current.
                    first}">
                        <f:validateLength minimum="1" maximum="40"/>
                        <f:ajax event="blur" render="firstError"/>
                    </h:inputText>
                </h:panelGroup>
                <h:panelGroup>

                    <h:outputLabel for="last" value="Last: "/>
                    <h:inputText id="last" size="40" value="#{ch5ContactController.current.
                    last}">
                        <f:validateLength minimum="1" maximum="40"/>
                        <f:ajax event="blur" render="lastError"/>
                    </h:inputText>
                </h:panelGroup>
```

```
    <h:message id="firstError"
               for="first"
               errorStyle="color:red"/>

    <h:message id="lastError"
               for="last"
               errorStyle="color:red"/>
    <h:panelGroup>
        <h:outputLabel for="email" value="Email: "/>
        <h:inputText id="email" size="40" value="#{ch5ContactController.current.
        email}">
            <f:ajax event="blur" render="emailError"/>
        </h:inputText>
    </h:panelGroup>
    <h:panelGroup/>
    <h:message id="emailError"
               for="email"
               errorStyle="color:red"/>
    <h:panelGroup/>

    <h:selectOneRadio title="Gender" id="gender" value="#{ch5ContactController.
    current.gender}">
        <f:selectItem  itemValue="M" itemLabel="Male"/>
        <f:selectItem itemValue="F" itemLabel="Female"/>
    </h:selectOneRadio>
    <h:panelGroup>
        <h:outputLabel for="occupation" value="Occupation: "/>
        <h:selectOneMenu id="occupation" value="#{ch5ContactController.current.
        occupation}">
            <f:selectItems value="#{ch5ContactController.occupationList}"/>
        </h:selectOneMenu>
    </h:panelGroup>
    <h:message id="genderError"
               for="gender"
               errorStyle="color:red"/>

</h:panelGrid>
<br />
<h:outputLabel for="description" value="Enter your book interests"/>
<br />
<h:inputTextarea id="description" rows="5" cols="75"
value="#{ch5ContactController.current.description}"/>

<br />
<h:panelGrid columns="2">
    <h:outputLabel for="password" value="Enter a password for site access: "/>
    <h:inputSecret id="password" size="40" value="#{ch5ContactController.
    current.password}">
        <f:validateRequired/>
        <f:ajax event="blur" render="passwordError"/>
    </h:inputSecret>
```

```
        <h:outputLabel for="passwordConfirm" value="Confirm Password: "/>
        <h:inputSecret id="passwordConfirm" size="40" value="#{ch5ContactController.
        passwordConfirm}"
                       validator="#{ch5ContactController.validatePassword}">
            <f:ajax event="blur" render="passwordConfirmError"/>
        </h:inputSecret>
    </h:panelGrid>
    <h:message id="passwordError"
               for="password"
               style="color:red"/>
    <br />
    <h:message id="passwordConfirmError"
               for="passwordConfirm"
               style="color:red"/>
    <br />
    <hr/>
    <br />

    <h:panelGrid columns="3">
        <h:panelGroup>
            <h:outputLabel for="newsletterList" value="Newsletters:" style=" "/>
            <h:selectManyListbox id="newsletterList" value="#{ch5ContactController.
            current.newsletterList}">
                <f:selectItems value="#{ch5ContactController.newsletterList}"/>
            </h:selectManyListbox>
        </h:panelGroup>
        <h:panelGroup/>
        <h:panelGroup>
            <h:panelGrid columns="1">
                <h:panelGroup>
                    <h:outputLabel for="notifyme" value="Would you like to receive
                    other promotional email?"/>
                    <h:selectBooleanCheckbox id="notifyme" value="#{ch5Contact
                    Controller.current.receiveNotifications}"/>
                </h:panelGroup>
                <h:panelGroup/>
                <hr/>
                <h:panelGroup/>
                <h:panelGroup>
                    <h:outputLabel for="notificationTypes" value="What type of
                    notifications are you interested in receiving?"/>
                    <br />
                    <h:selectManyCheckbox id="notifyTypes" value="#{ch5Contact
                    Controller.current.notificationType}">
                        <f:selectItems value="#{ch5ContactController.notification
                        Types}"/>
                    </h:selectManyCheckbox>
                </h:panelGroup>
            </h:panelGrid>
        </h:panelGroup>
```

```
            </h:panelGrid>
            <hr/>
            <br />

            <h:commandButton id="contactSubmit" action="#{ch5ContactController.subscribe}"
            value="Save"/>
            <h:panelGrid  columns="2" width="400px;">
                <h:commandLink id="manageAccount" action="#{ch5ContactController.manage}"
                value="Manage Subscription"/>

                <h:outputLink id="homeLink" value="home.xhtml">Home</h:outputLink>
            </h:panelGrid>
        </h:form>
    </ui:define>
</ui:composition>
```

Once the input components have been "Ajaxified" by embedding the `f:ajax` tag within them, then tabbing through the fields (causing the `onBlur` event to occur for each field) will result in a form that resembles Figure 5-1.

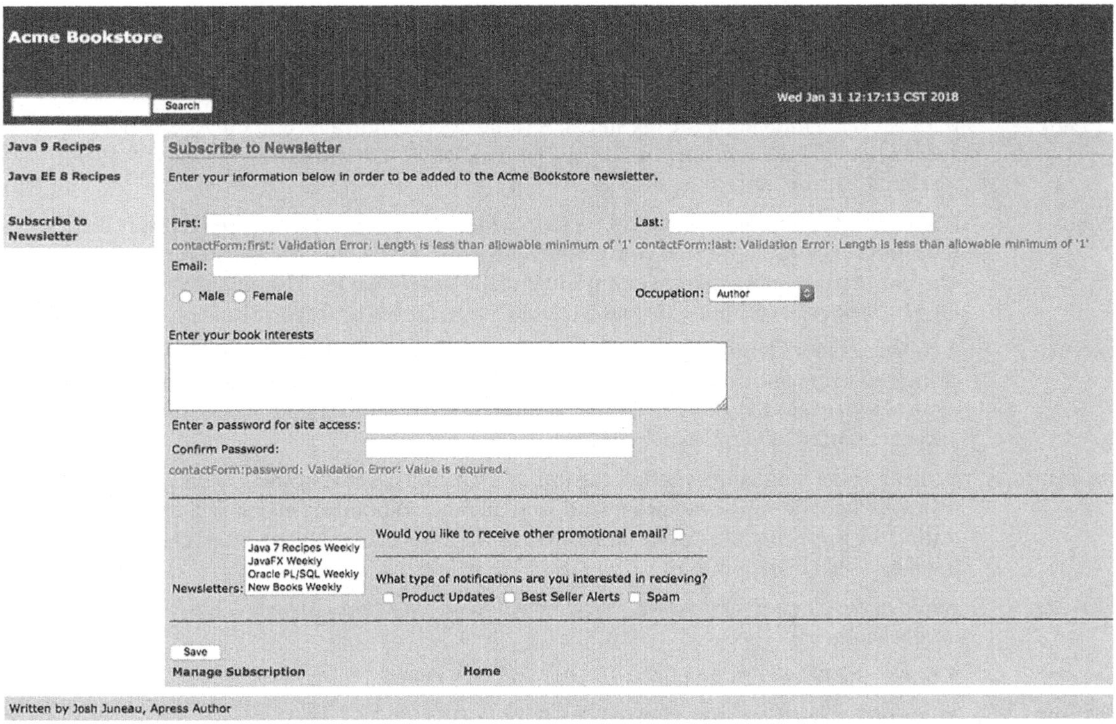

Figure 5-1. *Ajax validation using the f:ajax tag*

How It Works

In releases of JSF prior to 2.0, performing immediate validation required the manual coding of JavaScript or a third-party component library. The `f:ajax` tag was added to the JSF arsenal with the release of 2.0, bringing with it the power to easily add immediate validation (and other asynchronous processes) to JSF views using standard or third-party components. The `f:ajax` tag can be embedded within any JSF input component in order to immediately enhance the component, adding Ajax capabilities to it. This provides many benefits to the developer in that there is no longer a need to manually code JavaScript to perform client-side validation. It also allows validation to occur on the server (in Java code within a JSF managed bean) asynchronously, providing seamless interaction between the client and server and generating an immediate response to the client. The result is a rich Internet application that behaves in much the same manner as a native desktop application. Validation can now occur instantaneously in front of an end user's eyes without the need to perform several page submits in order to repair all of the possible issues.

To use the `f:ajax` tag, simply embed it within any JSF component. There are a number of attributes that can be specified with `f:ajax`, as described in Table 5-1. If an attribute is not specified, the default values are substituted. It is quite possible to include no attributes in an `f:ajax` tag, and if this is done, then the default attribute values for the component in which the `f:ajax` tag is embedded will take effect.

Table 5-1. *f:ajax Tag Attributes*

Attribute	Description
`delay`	A value that is specified in milliseconds, corresponding to the amount of delay between sending Ajax requests from the client-side queue to the server. The value `none` can be specified to disable this feature.
`disabled`	Boolean value indicating the tag status. A value of `true` indicates that the Ajax behavior should not be rendered, and a value of `false` indicates that the Ajax behavior should be rendered. The default value is `false`.
`event`	A `String` that identifies the type of event to which the Ajax action will apply. If specified, it must be one of the supported component events. The default value is the event that triggers the Ajax request for the parent component of the Ajax behavior. The default event is `action` for `ActionSource` components and is `valueChange` for `EditableValueHolder` components.
`execute`	A collection that identifies a list of components to be executed on the server. A space-delimited string of component identifiers can be specified as the value for this attribute, or a `ValueExpression` (JSF EL) can be specified. The default value is `@this`, meaning the parent component of the Ajax behavior.
`immediate`	Boolean value indicating whether the input values are processed early in the lifecycle. If its' `true`, then the values are processed, and their corresponding events will be broadcast during the Apply Request Values phase; otherwise, the events will be broadcast during the Invoke Applications phase.
`listener`	Name of the listener method that is called when an `AjaxBehaviorEvent` has been broadcast for the listener.
`onevent`	Name of the JavaScript function used to handle UI events.
`onerror`	Name of the JavaScript function used to handle errors.
`resetValues`	If true, then this particular Ajax transaction will reset the values.
`render`	Collection that identifies the components to be rendered on the client when the Ajax behavior is complete. A space-delimited string of component identifiers can be specified as the value for this attribute, or a `ValueExpression` (JSF EL) can be specified. The default value is `@none`, meaning that no components will be rendered when the Ajax behavior is complete.

The execute and render attributes of the f:ajax tag can specify a number of keywords to indicate which components are executed on the server for the Ajax behavior or which are rendered again after the Ajax behavior is complete, respectively. Table 5-2 lists the values that can be specified for these two attributes.

Table 5-2. *f:ajax Tag execute and render Attribute Values*

Attribute Value	Description
@all	All component identifiers
@form	The form that encloses the component
@none	No component identifiers (default for render attribute)
@this	The Ajax behavior parent component
@child(n)	The nth child of base component
@composite	Closest composite component ancestor of base component
@id(id)	All component descendants of base component with the specified id
@namingcontainer	Closest NamingContainer ancestor of base component
@next	Next component in view after base component
@parent	Parent of base component
@previous	Previous component to the base component
@root	UIViewRoot
Component IDs	Space-separated list of individual component identifiers
JSF EL	Expression that resolves to a collection of string identifiers

In the example for this recipe, an f:ajax tag has been embedded inside many of the input components within the form. Each of those components has been Ajaxified, in that the data entered as the value for the components will now have the ability to be processed using the JavaScript resource library associated with JSF. Behind the scenes, the jsf.ajax.request() method of the JavaScript resource library will collect the data for each component that has been Ajaxified and post the request to the JavaServer Faces lifecycle. In effect, the data is sent to the managed bean property without submitting the page in a traditional fashion. Notice that the event attribute specifies a JavaScript event that will be used to trigger the Ajax behavior.

The JavaScript events that can be specified for the event attribute are those same JavaScript event attributes that are available on the parent component's tag, but the on prefix has been removed. For instance, if you want to perform an Ajax behavior on an inputText component when it loses focus, you would specify blur for the f:ajax event attribute rather than onBlur. Applying this concept to the example, when a user leaves the first or last name field, they will be validated using their associated f:validate tags immediately because the f:ajax tag has been embedded in them and the event on the f:ajax tag is specified as blur. When the Ajax behavior (the validation in this case) is complete, then the components whose identifiers are specified in the f:ajax render attribute will be re-rendered. In the case of the first and last inputText fields, their associated message components will be re-rendered, displaying any errors that may have occurred during validation.

UTILIZING AN ACTION LISTENER

It is possible to bind an action listener to an `f:ajax` tag so that when the invoking action occurs, the listener method is invoked. Why would you want to bind an action listener? There are any reasons to do so. For instance, suppose you wanted to capture the text that a user is typing into a text field. You could do so by binding an action method within a managed bean to the listener attribute of an `inputText` field's corresponding `f:ajax` tag and then obtaining the current component's value from the `AjaxBehaviorEvent` object within the action method. For instance, suppose that you wanted to test a password for complexity and display a corresponding message indicating whether a password was strong enough. The `inputSecret` component for the password could be modified to include an `f:ajax` tag with an event specification of `keyup` and a listener specified as `#{ch5ContactController.passwordStrength}`, such as the following listing demonstrates.

Within the view:

```
<h:outputLabel for="password" value="Enter a password for site access: "/>
<h:inputSecret id="password" size="40"
       value="#{ch5ContactController.current.password}">
    <f:validateRequired/>
    <f:ajax event="keyup" listener="#{ch5ContactController.passwordStrength}"
                                            render="passwordStrengthMessage"/>
</h:inputSecret>
...
```

Within the managed bean:

```
public void passwordStrength(AjaxBehaviorEvent event){
        UIInput password = (UIInput) event.getComponent();
        boolean isStrong = false;
        String input = password.getValue().toString();

        if(input.matches("((?=.*\\d)(?=.*[a-z])(?=.*[A-Z]).{6,})")) {
            isStrong = true;
        }

        if(isStrong == true){
            setPasswordStrengthMessage("Password is strong");
        } else {
            setPasswordStrengthMessage("Password is weak");
        }
    }
```

The code in this example would create a listener event that, when a user types a value, would check the present entry to determine whether it met the given criteria for a secure password. A message would then be displayed to the user to let them know whether the password was secure.

Using the f:ajax tag makes it easy to add Ajax behavior to a JSF component. Before the f:ajax tag, special third-party JavaScript libraries were often used to incorporate similar behaviors within JSF views. f:ajax adds the benefit of allowing the developer to choose between using Ajax behaviors, without the need for coding a single line of JavaScript.

5-2. Submitting Pages Without Page Reloads

Problem

You want to enable your input form to have the ability to submit input fields for processing without reloading the page. In essence, you want your web application input form to react more like that of a desktop application rather than navigating from page to page in order to process data.

Solution

Embed an <f:ajax/> tag within the command component in the view so that the managed bean action is invoked without the page being submitted. Enable f:ajax to update the messages component in the view so that any errors or success messages that result from the processing can be displayed. In this example, the newsletter subscription page for the Acme Bookstore will be changed so that the form is submitted using Ajax, and the commandLink component is processed without submitting the form in a traditional manner. The following excerpt from the newsletter subscription form sources from recipe05_02.xhtml, which demonstrates how to add Ajax functionality to the action components within the form:

```
<h:commandButton id="contactSubmit" action="#{ch5ContactController.subscribe}"
                 value="Save">
    <f:ajax event="action" execute="@form" render="@all"/>
</h:commandButton>
<h:panelGrid  columns="2" width="400px;">
```

When the button or link is clicked, JavaScript will be used in the background to process the request so that the results will be displayed immediately without needing to refresh the page.

How It Works

The user experience for web applications has traditionally involved a point, click, and page refresh mantra. While this type of experience is not particularly a bad one, it is not as nice as the immediate response that is oftentimes presented within a native desktop application. The use of Ajax within web applications has helped create a more unified user experience, allowing a web application the ability to produce an "immediate" response much like that of a native desktop application. Field validation (covered in Recipe 5-1) is a great candidate for immediate feedback, but another area where immediate responses work well is when forms are being submitted.

The f:ajax tag can be embedded in an action component in order to invoke the corresponding action method using JavaScript behind the scenes. The f:ajax tag contains a number of attributes, covered in Table 5-1 (see Recipe 5-1), that can be used to invoke Ajax behavior given a specified event and re-render view components when that Ajax behavior is complete. Refer to Table 5-2 to see the values that can be specified for the execute and render attributes of the f:ajax tag.

In the example for this recipe, the commandButton component with an identifier of contactSubmit contains an f:ajax tag that specifies the event attribute as action, the execute attribute as @form, and the render attribute as @all. This means that when the button is invoked, the ch5ContactController.subscribe method will be called asynchronously using JavaScript, and it will send all the input component values from the form to the server (managed bean) for processing. When the Ajax behavior (subscribe method) is complete, all of the components in the view will be re-rendered. By re-rendering all the components in the view, this allows those message components to display any messages that have been queued up as a result of failed validation or a successful form submission. It is possible to process or render only specified components during an Ajax behavior; to learn more about doing so, see Recipe 5-3.

■ **Note** Note that the event attribute has a default value of action when the f:ajax tag is embedded in a UICommand component. However, it is specified in the code for this example for consistency.

Adding Ajax actions to a page has been simplified since the addition of the f:ajax tag with the 2.0 release of JSF. Validation and page actions are easy to process asynchronously by utilizing a single tag, f:ajax, to incorporate Ajax functionality into any JSF component.

5-3. Making Partial-Page Updates

Problem

You want to execute only a section of a page using an Ajax event and then render the corresponding section's components when the Ajax behavior is complete.

Solution

Use the f:ajax tag to add Ajax functionality to the components that you want to execute and render when the Ajax behavior is completed. Specify only the component identifiers corresponding to those components, or @form, @this, or one of the other execute keywords, for the f:ajax tag execute attribute. Likewise, specify only the component identifiers for the corresponding message components in the render attribute.

Suppose that the Acme Bookstore wants to execute the submission of the newsletter subscription form values and update the form's global message only when the submission is complete. The following commandButton component would execute only the form in which it is placed and the component corresponding to the identifier newsletterSubscriptionMsgs:

```
<h:commandButton id="contactSubmit" action="#{ch5ContactController.subscribe}" value="Save">
    <f:ajax event="action" execute="@form" render="newsletterSubscriptionMsgs"/>
</h:commandButton>
```

When the button is clicked, the current form component values will be processed with the request, and the ContactController managed bean's subscribe method will be invoked. Once the subscribe method is complete, the component in the form that contains an identifier of newsletterSubscriptionMsgs (in this case, a messages component) will be re-rendered.

■ **Note** In the case of the newsletter subscription form for the Acme Bookstore, a partial-page render upon completion is a bad idea. This is because the form will never be submitted if the values within the form do not validate correctly. In this case, if some of the form values do not validate correctly, then nothing will be displayed on the page when the Save button is clicked because the `subscribe` method will never be invoked. If the `f:ajax` tag's `render` attribute is set to `@all`, then all of the components that failed validation will have a corresponding error message that is displayed. This example should demonstrate how important it is to process the appropriate portions of the page for the result you are trying to achieve.

How It Works

The `f:ajax` tag makes it simple to perform partial-page updates. To do so, specify the identifiers for those components that you want to execute for the `f:ajax execute` attribute. As mentioned in the example for this recipe, suppose you want to execute only a portion of a page, rather than all of the components on the given page. You could do so by identifying the components that you want to execute within the view, specifying them within the `f:ajax execute` attribute, and then rendering the corresponding message components when the Ajax behavior was completed. If nothing is specified for an `f:ajax` execute attribute, then the `f:ajax` tag must be embedded inside a component, in which case the parent component would be executed. Such is the default behavior for the `f:ajax execute` attribute. In the example, the `execute` attribute of the `f:ajax` tag specifies the `@form` keyword, rather than a specific component `id`. As mentioned previously, a number of keywords can be specified for both the `execute` and `render` attributes of the `f:ajax` tag. Those keywords are listed in Table 5-2, which describes that the `@form` keyword indicates that all components in the same form as the given `f:ajax` tag will be executed when the Ajax behavior occurs. Therefore, all fields within the newsletter subscription form in this example will be sent to the managed bean for processing when the button is clicked.

The same holds true for the `render` attribute, and once the Ajax behavior has completed, any component specified for the `render` attribute of the `f:ajax` tag will be re-rendered. Thus, if a validation occurs when a component is being processed because of the result of an `f:ajax` method call, a corresponding validation failure message can be displayed on the page after the validation fails. Any component can be rendered again, and the same keywords that can be specified for the `execute` attribute can also be used for the `render` attribute. In the example, the `newsletterSubscriptonMsgs` component is rendered once the Ajax behavior is completed.

Partial-page updates, a common use of the `f:ajax` tag, are easy to implement and can enhance the functionality and usability of an application. Later in this chapter you learn how to utilize some third-party component libraries to perform partial-page updates, creating highly usable interfaces for editing data and the like.

5-4. Applying Ajax Functionality to a Group of Components

Problem

You want to apply Ajax functionality to a group of input components, rather than to each component separately.

Solution

Enclose any components to which you want to apply Ajax functionality within an `f:ajax` tag. The `f:ajax` tag can be the parent to one or more JSF components, in which case each of the child components inherits the given Ajax behavior. Applying Ajax functionality to multiple components is demonstrated in the following code listing. In the example, the newsletter subscription view of the Acme Bookstore application is adjusted so that each of the `inputText` components that contains a validator is enclosed by a single `f:ajax` tag. Given that each of the `inputText` components is embodied in the same `f:ajax` tag, the `f:ajax` `render` attribute has been set to specify the `message` component for each of the corresponding `inputText` fields in the group.

```
<html xmlns="http://www.w3.org/1999/xhtml"
      xmlns:ui="http://xmlns.jcp.org/jsf/facelets"
      xmlns:f="http://xmlns.jcp.org/jsf/core"
      xmlns:h="http://xmlns.jcp.org/jsf/html">

    <body>

        <ui:composition template="layout/custom_template_search.xhtml">
            <ui:define name="content">
                <h:form id="contactForm">
                    <h1>Subscribe to Newsletter</h1>
                    <p>
                        <h:outputText id="newsletterSubscriptionDesc"
                                      value="#{ch5ContactController.newsletter
                                      Description}"/>
                    </p>

                    <br/>
                    <h:messages id="newsletterSubscriptionMsgs" globalOnly=
                    "true"  errorStyle="color: red" infoStyle="color: green"/>
                    <br/>
                    <f:ajax event="blur" render="firstError lastError emailError genderError
                    passwordError passwordConfirmError">
                    <h:panelGrid columns="2" bgcolor="" border="0">
                        <h:panelGroup>
                            <h:outputLabel for="first" value="First: "/>
                            <h:inputText id="first" size="40" value="#{ch5ContactController.
                            current.first}">
                                <f:validateLength minimum="1" maximum="40"/>

                            </h:inputText>
                        </h:panelGroup>
                        <h:panelGroup>

                            <h:outputLabel for="last" value="Last: "/>
                            <h:inputText id="last" size="40" value="#{ch5ContactController.
                            current.last}">
                                <f:validateLength minimum="1" maximum="40"/>

                            </h:inputText>
                        </h:panelGroup>
```

```
    <h:message id="firstError"
               for="first"
               errorStyle="color:red"/>

    <h:message id="lastError"
               for="last"
               errorStyle="color:red"/>
    <h:panelGroup>
        <h:outputLabel for="email" value="Email: "/>
        <h:inputText id="email" size="40" value="#{ch5ContactController.
        current.email}">

        </h:inputText>
    </h:panelGroup>
    <h:panelGroup/>
    <h:message id="emailError"
               for="email"
               errorStyle="color:red"/>
    <h:panelGroup/>

    <h:selectOneRadio title="Gender" id="gender" value="#{ch5Contact
    Controller.current.gender}">
        <f:selectItem  itemValue="M" itemLabel="Male"/>
        <f:selectItem itemValue="F" itemLabel="Female"/>
    </h:selectOneRadio>
    <h:panelGroup>
        <h:outputLabel for="occupation" value="Occupation: "/>
        <h:selectOneMenu id="occupation" value="#{ch5ContactController.
        current.occupation}">
            <f:selectItems value="#{ch5ContactController.occupation
            List}"/>
        </h:selectOneMenu>
    </h:panelGroup>
    <h:message id="genderError"
               for="gender"
               errorStyle="color:red"/>

</h:panelGrid>
<br/>
<h:outputLabel for="description" value="Enter your book interests"/>
<br/>
<h:inputTextarea id="description" rows="5" cols="75" value="#{ch5Contact
Controller.current.description}"/>

<br/>
<h:panelGrid columns="2">
    <h:outputLabel for="password" value="Enter a password for site
    access: "/>
    <h:inputSecret id="password" size="40" value="#{ch5Contact
    Controller.current.password}">
        <f:validateRequired/>
```

```
                <f:ajax event="keyup" listener="#{ch5ContactController.
                passwordStrength}" render="passwordStrengthMessage"/>
            </h:inputSecret>

            <h:outputLabel for="passwordConfirm" value="Confirm Password: "/>
            <h:inputSecret id="passwordConfirm" size="40" value="#{ch5Contact
            Controller.passwordConfirm}"
                           validator="#{ch5ContactController.validatePassword}">

            </h:inputSecret>
        </h:panelGrid>
        <h:panelGroup>
            <h:outputText id="passwordStrengthMessage" value="#{ch5Contact
            Controller.passwordStrengthMessage}"/>
            <h:message id="passwordError"
                    for="password"
                    style="color:red"/>
        </h:panelGroup>
        <br/>
        <h:message id="passwordConfirmError"
                   for="passwordConfirm"
                   style="color:red"/>
        <br/>
        <hr/>
        <br/>

        <h:panelGrid columns="3">
            <h:panelGroup>
                <h:outputLabel for="newsletterList" value="Newsletters:
                " style=" "/>
                <h:selectManyListbox id="newsletterList" value="#{ch5Contact
                Controller.current.newsletterList}">
                    <f:selectItems value="#{ch5ContactController.
                    newsletterList}"/>
                </h:selectManyListbox>
            </h:panelGroup>
            <h:panelGroup/>
            <h:panelGroup>
                <h:panelGrid columns="1">
                    <h:panelGroup>
                        <h:outputLabel for="notifyme" value="Would you like to
                        receive other promotional email?"/>
                       <h:selectBooleanCheckbox id="notifyme" value="#{ch5Contact
                       Controller.current.receiveNotifications}"/>
                    </h:panelGroup>
                    <h:panelGroup/>
                    <hr/>
                    <h:panelGroup/>
                    <h:panelGroup>
                        <h:outputLabel for="notificationTypes" value="What type
                        of notifications are you interested in receiving?"/>
```

```
                                    <br/>
                                    <h:selectManyCheckbox id="notifyTypes" value="#{ch5Contact
                                    Controller.current.notificationType}">
                                        <f:selectItems value="#{ch5ContactController.
                                        notificationTypes}"/>
                                    </h:selectManyCheckbox>
                                </h:panelGroup>
                            </h:panelGrid>
                        </h:panelGroup>
                    </h:panelGrid>
                    <hr/>
                    <br/>
                    </f:ajax>
                    <h:commandButton id="contactSubmit" action="#{ch5ContactController.
                    subscribe}" value="Save">
                        <f:ajax event="action" execute="@form" render="@all"/>
                    </h:commandButton>
                    <h:panelGrid  columns="2" width="400px;">
                        <h:commandLink id="manageAccount" action="#{ch5ContactController.
                        manage}" value="Manage Subscription">
                            <f:ajax event="action" execute="@this" render="@all"/>
                        </h:commandLink>
                        <h:outputLink id="homeLink" value="home.xhtml">Home</h:outputLink>
                    </h:panelGrid>
                </h:form>
            </ui:define>
        </ui:composition>

    </body>
</html>
```

When the page is rendered, each component will react separately given their associated validations. That is, if validation fails for one component, only the message component that corresponds with the component failing validation will be displayed, although each component identified within the f:ajax render attribute will be re-rendered.

■ **Note** As a result of specifying a global f:ajax tag, the password component can now execute two Ajax requests. One of the Ajax requests for the field is responsible for validating to ensure that the field is not blank, and the other is responsible for ensuring that the given password string is strong.

How It Works

Grouping multiple components with the same Ajax behavior has its benefits. For one, if the behavior needs to be adjusted for any reason, you change can now be made to the Ajax behavior, and each of the components in the group can benefit from the single adjustment. However, the f:ajax tag is smart enough to enable each component to still utilize separate functionality, such as validation or actions, so each can still have their own customized Ajax behavior. To group components under a single f:ajax tag, they must be added to the view as sub-elements of the `f:ajax` tag. That is, any child components must be enclosed between the opening and closing `f:ajax` tags. All of the enclosed components will then use Ajax to send requests to the server using JavaScript in an asynchronous fashion.

In the example for this recipe, a handful of the `inputText` components within the newsletter subscription view have been embodied inside an `f:ajax` tag so that their values will be validated using server-side bean validation when they lose focus. The `f:ajax` tag that is used to group the components has an `event` attribute set to `blur`, and its `render` attribute contains the `String`-based identifier for each of the `message` components corresponding to the components that are included in the group. The space-separated list of component `ids` is used to re-render each of the message components when the Ajax behavior is complete, displaying any errors that occur as a result of the validation.

5-5. Custom Processing of Ajax Functionality

Problem

You want to customize the Ajax processing for JSF components within a view in your application.

Solution

Write the JavaScript that will be used for processing your request and utilize the `jsf.ajax.request()` function along with one of the standard JavaScript event-handling attributes for a JSF component. The following example is the JSF view for the newsletter subscription page for the Acme Bookstore application. All of the `f:ajax` tags that were previously used for validating `inputText` fields (see Recipe 5-1) have been removed, and the `onblur` attribute of each `inputText` component has been set to use the `jsf.ajax.request()` method in order to Ajaxify the component. The following excerpt is taken from the view named `recipe05_05.xhtml`, representing the updated newsletter subscription JSF view:

```
...
                    <h:outputScript name="jsf.js" library="javax.faces" target="head"/>
                    <h1>Subscribe to Newsletter</h1>
                    <p>
                        <h:outputText id="newsletterSubscriptionDesc"
                                      value="#{ch5ContactController.newsletter
                                      Description}"/>
                    </p>

                    <br/>
                    <h:messages id="newsletterSubscriptionMsgs" globalOnly="true"
                    errorStyle="color: red" infoStyle="color: green"/>
                    <br/>

                    <h:panelGrid columns="2" bgcolor="" border="0">
                        <h:panelGroup>
                            <h:outputLabel for="first" value="First: "/>
                            <h:inputText id="first" size="40" value="#{ch5ContactController.
                            current.first}"
                                         onblur="jsf.ajax.request(this, event,
                                         {execute: 'first', render: 'firstError'});
                                         return false;">
```

```
                <f:validateLength minimum="1" maximum="40"/>
            </h:inputText>
        </h:panelGroup>
        <h:panelGroup>
            <h:outputLabel for="last" value="Last: "/>
            <h:inputText id="last" size="40" value="#{ch5ContactController.
            current.last}"
                         onblur="jsf.ajax.request(this, event, {execute:
                         'last', render: 'lastError'});
                         return false;">
                <f:validateLength minimum="1" maximum="40"/>
            </h:inputText>
        </h:panelGroup>

        <h:message id="firstError"
                   for="first"
                   errorStyle="color:red"/>

        <h:message id="lastError"
                   for="last"
                   errorStyle="color:red"/>
        <h:panelGroup>
            <h:outputLabel for="email" value="Email: "/>
            <h:inputText id="email" size="40" value="#{ch5ContactController.
            current.email}"
                         onblur="jsf.ajax.request(this, event,
                         {execute: 'email', render: 'emailError'});
                         return false;"/>
        </h:panelGroup>
        <h:panelGroup/>
        <h:message id="emailError"
                   for="email"
                   errorStyle="color:red"/>
        <h:panelGroup/>
...
```

■ **Note** The `<h:panelGroup/>` tag is used to add a placeholder panel group to the grid for spacing purposes.

Using this technique, the `inputText` components that specify Ajax behavior for the `onblur` event will asynchronously have their values validated when they lose focus. If any custom JavaScript code needs to be used, it can be added to the same inline JavaScript call to `jsf.ajax.request()`.

■ **Note** Method calls cannot be made using the `jsf.ajax.request()` technique, so it is not possible to invoke a listener explicitly with the Ajax request. However, it should be noted that the `commandScript` component that was introduced with the release of JSF 2.3 can invoke server-side methods via JavaScript. See Recipe 5-19 for more details.

How It Works

The JavaScript API method `jsf.ajax.request()`, a JSF 2.*x* feature, can be accessed directly by a Facelets application, enabling a developer to have slightly more control than using the `f:ajax` tag. Behind the scenes, the `f:ajax` tag is converted into a call to `jsf.ajax.request()`, sending the parameters as specified via the tag's attributes. To use this technique, you must include the `jsf.js` library within the view. A JSF `outputScript` tag should be included in the view, specifying `jsf.js` as the script name and `javax.faces` as the `library`. The `jsf.js` script within this example will be placed in the head of the view, which is done by specifying head for the `target` attribute of the `outputScript` tag. The following excerpt from the example demonstrates what the tag should look like:

```
<h:outputScript name="jsf.js" library="javax.faces" target="head"/>
```

■ **Note** To avoid nested IDs, it is a good idea to specify the `h:form` attribute of `prependId="false"` when using `jsf.ajax.request()` manually. For instance, the form tag should look as follows:

```
<h:form prependId=”false”>
```

The `jsf.ajax.request()` method can be called inline, as is the case with the example for this recipe, and it can be invoked from within any of the JavaScript `event` attributes of a given component. The format for calling the JavaScript method is as follows:

```
jsf.ajax.request(component, event,{execute:'id or keyword', render:'id or keyword'});
```

Usually when the request is made using an inline call, the `this` keyword is specified for the first parameter, signifying that the current component should be passed. The `event` keyword is passed as the second parameter, and it passes with it the current event that is occurring against the component. Lastly, a map of name-value pairs is passed, specifying the `execute` and `render` attributes along with the component identifiers or keywords that should be executed and rendered after the execution completes, respectively. For a list of the valid keywords that can be used, refer to Table 5-2.

■ **Note** You can also utilize the `jsf.ajax.request` method from within a managed bean by specifying the `@ResourceDependency` annotation as follows:

```
@ResourceDependency(name="jsf.js" library="javax.faces" target="head")
```

The majority of developers will never need to utilize a manual call to the JSF JavaScript API. However, if the need ever arises, calling the `jsf.ajax.request()` method is fairly straightforward.

5-6. Custom Conversion of Input Values

Problem

You want to automatically convert the values of some input text in a way such that that it better conforms to the needs of your application. However, the conversion that you want to perform is outside the scope of those conversions that are available via the JSF standard converter library.

Solution

Create a custom converter class containing the logic that is required for converting the values, and then apply that converter to the `inputText` components as needed. For this example, the Acme Bookstore has decided that it would like all first and last names in the subscriber list to appear in uppercase. The store would also like all email addresses in lowercase. Therefore, a custom converter will be developed to perform the string conversion automatically behind the scenes.

The following listing is for the conversion class, `LowerConverter`, which accepts values from registered components and returns a formatted `String` value in lowercase:

```
import javax.faces.component.UIComponent;
import javax.faces.context.FacesContext;
import javax.faces.convert.Converter;
import javax.faces.convert.FacesConverter;

/**
 *
 * @author juneau
 */
@FacesConverter("org.javaee8recipes.converter.LowerConverter")
public class LowerConverter implements Converter {

    @Override
    public Object getAsObject(FacesContext context, UIComponent component,
            String value) {
        // Return String value in lowercase
        return value.toString().toLowerCase();
    }

    @Override
    public String getAsString(FacesContext context, UIComponent component,
            Object value) {

        // Return String value
        return value.toString().toLowerCase();

    }
}
```

The code that is used to create the uppercase converter is very similar, except that the `getAsObject` and `getAsString` methods use different `String` functions to return the uppercase values. The sources reside in a class named `org.javaee8recipes.chapter5.converter.UpperConverter`, and they are nearly identical to the `LowerConverter` class with the exception of calling the `toUpperCase()` method, rather than `toLowerCase()`.

Now that the conversion classes have been built, it is time to apply the converters to the JSF components where applicable. The following excerpt is taken from the newsletter subscription page of the Acme Bookstore application, and it demonstrates the use of the converters for the first, last, and email input components.

```
...
<h:panelGroup>
    <h:outputLabel for="first" value="First: "/>
    <h:inputText id="first" size="40" value="#{ch5ContactController.current.first}">
        <f:validateLength minimum="1" maximum="40"/>
        <f:converter converterId="org.javaee8recipes.converter.UpperConverter"/>
    </h:inputText>
</h:panelGroup>
<h:panelGroup>

    <h:outputLabel for="last" value="Last: "/>
    <h:inputText id="last" size="40" value="#{ch5ContactController.current.last}">
        <f:validateLength minimum="1" maximum="40"/>
        <f:converter converterId="org.javaee8recipes.converter.UpperConverter"/>
    </h:inputText>
</h:panelGroup>

<h:message id="firstError"
           for="first"
           errorStyle="color:red"/>

<h:message id="lastError"
           for="last"
           errorStyle="color:red"/>
<h:panelGroup>
    <h:outputLabel for="email" value="Email: "/>
    <h:inputText id="email" size="40" value="#{ch5ContactController.current.email}">
        <f:converter converterId="org.javaee8recipes.converter.LowerConverter"/>
    </h:inputText>
</h:panelGroup>
<h:panelGroup/>
<h:message id="emailError"
           for="email"
           errorStyle="color:red"/>
<h:panelGroup/>
...
```

Now if a user types in lowercase for the first or last name or in uppercase for the email field, the values will automatically be converted during the Apply Request Values phase.

How It Works

How many times have you seen an application's data become unmanageable because of inconsistencies? Maybe you have seen some records where a particular field contains a value in lowercase and other records contain the same value in uppercase...maybe even a mixture of cases! Applying conversion to data before it is persisted (usually in a database) is the best way to ensure data integrity. As you may have read about in Chapter 4, the JSF framework ships with a library of standard converters that can be applied to JSF components in order to convert data into a manageable format. While the standard converters will do the job for most applications, there may be situations when custom converters are needed in order to manipulate values into a manageable format for your application. In such cases, JSF custom converter classes can be used to develop the custom conversion logic; they are very easy to develop and apply to JSF components with minimal configuration.

■ **Note** Beginning with JSF 2.2, converters and validators can be used as injection targets. For information regarding injection of classes, see Chapter 13.

To develop a custom converter class, you must implement the `javax.faces.convert.Converter` interface, overriding two methods: `getAsString` and `getAsObject`. The `getAsString` method should accept three parameters: `FacesContext`, `UIComponent`, and a string. It should perform the desired conversion and return the converted value in `String` format. In the case of the `LowerConverter` example, simply applying `toLowerCase()` to the string and returning it is all the functionality you require. The `getAsObject` method should accept the same parameters as the `getAsString` method, and it should also apply the desired conversion and then return an object of any type. In the case of `LowerConverter`, you return a string in lowercase, just like the `getAsString` method. If you follow along and look through the same methods in `UpperConverter`, the opposite conversion is applied, returning an uppercase string.

To make a converter class available for use within a view, you must annotate the class by applying `@FacesConverter` to the class declaration. Pass a string into the annotation, being the string-based fully qualified name of the converter class. The `UpperConverter @FacesConverter` annotation reads as follows:

```
@FacesConverter("org.javaee8recipes.converter.UpperConverter")
```

Once the converter class has been written and annotated as required, the converter can be used just like a standard JSF converter tag. The logic contained in the converter can be much more complex than that which is demonstrated in this example, and given the wide variety of prebuilt converters, a custom converter usually does contain complex conversion logic.

■ **Note** As of JSF 2.3, converters, validators, and behaviors are now injectable into targets. This would allow one to utilize a converter from within another managed bean, if needed. To inject a converter that was created in this recipe, you'd do the following within a managed bean.

```
@Inject

@FacesConverter(value="LowerConverter", managed=true)

private FacesConverter lowerConverter ;
```

It is also possible to inject resources into converters, validators, and behaviors. As such, one can inject other managed beans or CDI injectables into a `FacesConverter` implementation, utilizing functionality as needed.

5-7. Maintaining Managed Bean Scopes for a Session

Problem

Your application has the requirement to maintain some managed beans that are retained for the entire session and others that are retained only for a single request.

Solution

Develop using the proper JSF managed bean scope that your situation requires. Managed beans utilize annotations to determine how long they are retained, so if your application needs to maintain state within a managed bean for a certain time frame, the scope can be set by annotating the managed bean class accordingly. In this example, you will be adding a shopping cart to the Acme Bookstore website. The cart will be maintained for the lifetime of a browser session, so if a book is added to the cart, then it will remain there until the current session ends. This recipe builds on those concepts that were covered in Recipe 3-2 because it demonstrates how to use SessionScoped managed beans.

Let's take a look at the JSF views that are being used for the shopping cart implementation. You are adding a couple of views to the application and modifying one view to accommodate the navigational buttons for the cart. The following excerpt is taken from the book view, which is displayed when a user clicks one of the book titles from the left menu. You are adding buttons to the bottom of the page to add the book to the cart and to view the current cart contents. To view the sources in entirety, see the view located in the sources: web/chapter05/book.xhtml.

```
...
<h:panelGrid columns="2" width="45%">
    <h:commandButton id="addToCart" action="#{ch5CartController.addToCart}"
                value="Add to Cart">
                          <f:ajax render="shoppingCartMsgs"/>
    </h:commandButton>
    <h:commandButton id="viewCart" action="#{ch5CartController.viewCart}"
                value="View Cart">
    </h:commandButton>
</h:panelGrid>
...
```

The two buttons that have been added to the book view reference a new class, referred to as ch5CartController, although the name of the class is CartController. The CartController class is a JSF managed bean that contains the shopping cart implementation.

■ **Note** Throughout the sources for this book, CDI bean names will change, although the class names will remain the same as those used in other chapter source packages. This is because the classes are being modified for each particular chapter to demonstrate different functionality, and we must reference each CDI bean by a different CDI bean name. However, the class names will remain the same so that you can see that the same class used in other chapters is simply being modified for use with different examples throughout the book.

The new buttons in the book view are used to add the current book title to the shopping cart and to view the cart. At this time, the shopping cart is a list of `Item` objects, and each `Item` object contains a `Book` object and a quantity. The sources for the `Item` class can be seen in the next listing:

```
package org.javaee8recipes.chapter05;

/**
 * Object to hold a single cart item
 * @author juneau
 */
public class Item implements java.io.Serializable {
    private Book book = null;
    private int quantity = 0;

    public Item(Book book, int qty){
        this.book = book;
        this.quantity = qty;
    }

    /**
     * @return the book
     */
    public Book getBook() {
        return book;
    }

    /**
     * @param book the book to set
     */
    public void setBook(Book book) {
        this.book = book;
    }

    /**
     * @return the quantity
     */
    public int getQuantity() {
        return quantity;
    }

    /**
     * @param quantity the quantity to set
     */
    public void setQuantity(int quantity) {
        this.quantity = quantity;
    }

}
```

For the new shopping cart implementation, the Book class has been updated to include a description field; to see the sources for the Book class, refer to `src/org/javaeerecipes/chapter05/Book.java`. The most important class in this example is the `CartController` managed bean. The sources for this class are listed here:

```
package org.javaee8recipes.chapter05;

import java.io.Serializable;
import javax.enterprise.context.SessionScoped;

import javax.faces.application.FacesMessage;

import javax.faces.component.UIOutput;
import javax.faces.context.FacesContext;
import javax.faces.event.ComponentSystemEvent;
import javax.inject.Inject;
import javax.inject.Named;

/**
 * Chapter 5
 *
 * @author juneau
 */
@SessionScoped
@Named("ch5CartController")
public class CartController implements Serializable {

    private Cart cart = null;
    private Item currentBook = null;

    @Inject
    private AuthorController authorController;

    /**
     * Creates a new instance of CartController
     */
    public CartController() {
    }

    public String addToCart() {
        if (getCart() == null) {
            cart = new Cart();
            getCart().addBook(getAuthorController().getCurrentBook(), 1);
        } else {
            System.out.println("adding book to cart...");
            getCart().addBook(getAuthorController().getCurrentBook(),
                    searchCart(getAuthorController().getCurrentBook().getTitle()) + 1);
        }
```

```
        FacesMessage facesMsg = new FacesMessage(FacesMessage.SEVERITY_INFO,
                "Successfully Updated Cart", null);
        FacesContext.getCurrentInstance().addMessage(null, facesMsg);
        return null;
    }

    /**
     * Determines if a book is already in the shopping cart
     *
     * @param title
     * @return
     */
    public int searchCart(String title) {
        int count = 0;

        for (Item item : getCart().getBooks()) {
            if (item.getBook().getTitle().equals(title)) {
                count++;
            }
        }
        return count;
    }

    public String viewCart() {
        if (cart == null) {
            FacesMessage facesMsg = new FacesMessage(FacesMessage.SEVERITY_INFO,
                    "No books in cart...", null);
            FacesContext.getCurrentInstance().addMessage(null, facesMsg);
        }

        return "/chapter05/cart";
    }

    public String continueShopping() {
        return "/chapter05/book";
    }

    public String editItem(String title) {
        for (Item item : cart.getBooks()) {
            if (item.getBook().getTitle().equals(title)) {
                currentBook = item;
            }
        }
        return "/chapter05/reviewItem";

    }

    public String updateCart(String title) {
        Item foundItem = null;
        if (currentBook.getQuantity() == 0) {
            for (Item item : cart.getBooks()) {
```

```
                if (item.getBook().getTitle().equals(title)) {
                    foundItem = item;
                }
            }
        }
        cart.getBooks().remove(foundItem);
        FacesMessage facesMsg = new FacesMessage(FacesMessage.SEVERITY_INFO,
                "Successfully Updated Cart", null);
        FacesContext.getCurrentInstance().addMessage(null, facesMsg);
        return "/chapter05/cart";
    }

    /**
     * @return the cart
     */
    public Cart getCart() {
        return cart;
    }

    /**
     * @param cart the cart to set
     */
    public void setCart(Cart cart) {
        this.cart = cart;
    }

    /**
     * @return the currentBook
     */
    public Item getCurrentBook() {
        return currentBook;
    }

    /**
     * @param currentBook the currentBook to set
     */
    public void setCurrentBook(Item currentBook) {
        this.currentBook = currentBook;
    }

    public void isBookInCart(ComponentSystemEvent event) {
        UIOutput output = (UIOutput) event.getComponent();
        if (cart != null) {
            if (searchCart(getAuthorController().getCurrentBook().getTitle()) > 0) {
                output.setValue("This book is currently in your cart.");
            } else {
                output.setValue("This book is not in your cart.");
            }
        } else {
            output.setValue("This book is not in your cart.");
        }
    }
```

```
    public void updateRowData(RowEditEvent event){
        Item book = (Item) event.getObject();
        // Do something with the edits...save to list or update database
    }

    /**
     * @return the authorController
     */
    public AuthorController getAuthorController() {
        return authorController;
    }

    /**
     * @param authorController the authorController to set
     */
    public void setAuthorController(AuthorController authorController) {
        this.authorController = authorController;
    }
}
```

There is another class that has been added to the application in order to accommodate the shopping cart. The Cart class is an object that is used to hold the list of books in the shopping cart. The listing for the Cart class is as follows:

```
public class Cart implements java.io.Serializable {
    // List containing book objects
    private List<Item> books = null;

    public Cart(){
        books = null;
    }

    /**
     * @return the books
     */
    public List <Item> getBooks() {
        return books;
    }

    /**
     * @param books the books to set
     */
    public void setBooks(List books) {
        this.books = books;
    }

    /**
     * Utility method to add a book and quantity
     */
```

```
    public void addBook(Book title, int qty){
        if (books == null){
            books = new ArrayList();
        }
        books.add(new Item(title, qty));
    }
}
```

Lastly, let's take a look at the views that are used to display the contents of the shopping cart. The cart view is used to display the Cart object contents. The contents are displayed using a dataTable component, and each row in the table contains a commandLink that can be clicked to edit that item's quantity. The cart.xhtml listing is as follows:

```
<html xmlns="http://www.w3.org/1999/xhtml"
      xmlns:f="http://xmlns.jcp.org/jsf/core"
      xmlns:ui="http://xmlns.jcp.org/jsf/facelets"
      xmlns:h="http://xmlns.jcp.org/jsf/html"
      xmlns:p="http://primefaces.org/ui">
    <h:head>
        <meta http-equiv="Content-Type" content="text/html; charset=UTF-8"/>
        <title>Acme Bookstore</title>
    </h:head>
    <h:body>
        <ui:composition template="./layout/custom_template_search.xhtml">
            <ui:define name="content">
                <h:form id="shoppingCartForm">
                    <h1>Shopping Cart Contents</h1>
                    <p>
                        Below are the contents of your cart.
                    </p>
                    <h:messages id="cartMessage" globalOnly="true"
                            errorStyle="color: red" infoStyle="color: green"/>
                    <br/>
                    <p:dialog id="updateDialog" widgetVar="updateDlg"
                            modal="true"
                            height="40" resizable="false"
                            closable="false" showHeader="false" >

                        <h:graphicImage id="loading" library="image" name="ajaxloading.gif"/>
                    </p:dialog>
                    <p:dataTable id="cartTable" value="#{ch5CartController.cart.books}"
                    var="book"
                             rendered="#{ch5CartController.cart.books ne null}">
                        <p:ajax id="rowEditAjax" event="rowEdit" update="@this"
                            listener="#{ch5CartController.updateRowData}"
                            onstart="updateDlg.show();"
                            oncomplete="updateDlg.hide();"
                            onerror="updateDlg.hide();"/>
```

```
                <p:column id="title" headerText="Title">
                    <p:commandLink value="#{book.book.title}" ajax="false"
                                   action="#{ch5CartController.editItem
                                   (book.book.title)}"/>
                </p:column>
                <p:column id="quantity" headerText="Quantity">
                    <p:cellEditor>
                        <f:facet name="output">
                            <h:inputText readonly="true" size="10" value="#{book.
                            quantity}"/>
                        </f:facet>
                        <f:facet name="input">
                            <h:inputText id="bookQty" size="10" value="#{book.
                            quantity}"/>
                            </f:facet>
                    </p:cellEditor>
                </p:column>
                <p:column id="edit" headerText="Edit">
                    <p:rowEditor />
                </p:column>

            </p:dataTable>

            <h:outputText id="emptyCart" value="No items currently in cart."
                          rendered="#{ch5CartController.cart.books eq null}"/>
            <br/>
            <h:commandLink id="continueLink" action="#{ch5CartController.
            continueShopping}" value="Continue Shopping"/>
        </h:form>
    </ui:define>
    </ui:composition>
    </h:body>
</html>
```

The cart view will look like Figure 5-2 when it is rendered.

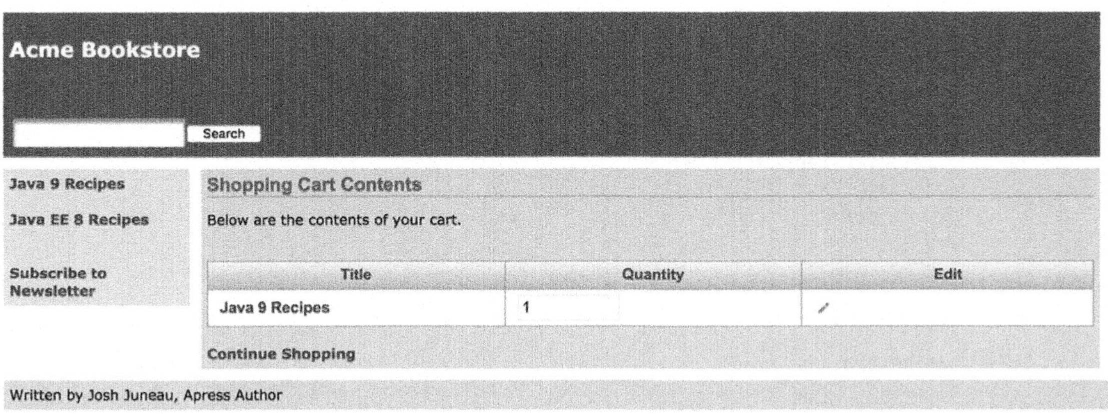

Figure 5-2. *Shopping cart view*

Finally, when the edit link is clicked, the current book selection quantity can be edited. The view for editing the shopping cart items is named reviewItem.xhtml, and the sources are as follows:

```
<html xmlns="http://www.w3.org/1999/xhtml"
      xmlns:ui="http://xmlns.jcp.org/jsf/facelets"
      xmlns:h="http://xmlns.jcp.org/jsf/html">
    <h:head>
        <meta http-equiv="Content-Type" content="text/html; charset=UTF-8"/>
        <title>Acme Bookstore</title>
    </h:head>
    <h:body>
        <ui:composition template="./layout/custom_template_search.xhtml">

            <ui:define name="content">
                <h:form id="bookForm">
                    <h1>Review Item</h1>
                    <br/>
                    <h:messages id="reviewMsg" globalOnly="true"
                                errorStyle="color: red" infoStyle="color: green"/>
                    <br/>

                    #{ch5CartController.currentBook.book.title}
                    <br/>
                    <h:graphicImage    id="javarecipes" library="image"
                                       style="width: 100px; height: 120px"
                                       name="#{ch5CartController.currentBook.book.image}"/>
                    <br/>
                    <h:outputLabel for="quantity" value="Quantity: "/>
                    <h:inputText id="quantity"
                                 value="#{ch5CartController.currentBook.quantity}">

                    </h:inputText>
                    <br/>
                    <h:panelGrid columns="2">
                        <h:commandButton id="updateCart" action="#{ch5CartController.update
                        Cart(ch5CartController.currentBook.book.title)}"
                                         value="Update"/>

                        <h:commandButton id="viewCart" action="#{ch5CartController.
                        viewCart}" value="Back To Cart">
                        </h:commandButton>
                    </h:panelGrid>
                    <br/>
                    <br/>

                </h:form>
            </ui:define>

        </ui:composition>

    </h:body>
</html>
```

Figure 5-3 demonstrates how the item review form will look once it is rendered.

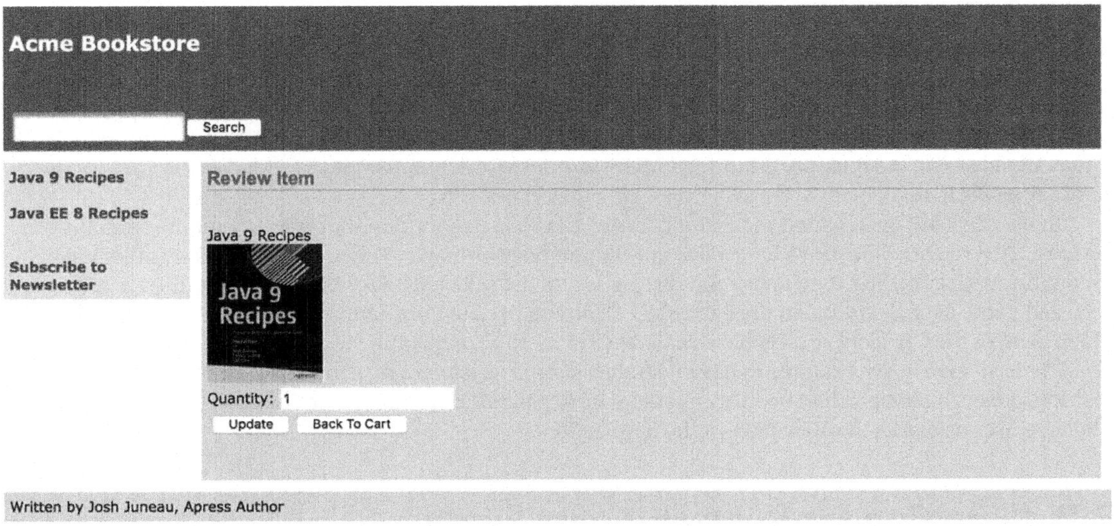

Figure 5-3. *Review cart item*

■ **Note** The session scope is not the best implementation for a shopping cart because it ties the managed bean contents to a particular browser session. What happens when the user needs to leave for a few minutes and then comes back to the browser to see that the session has expired or the browser has been closed? A more functional scope for handling this situation is the `Conversation` scope, which is covered in Chapter 13. For the most optimal solution, you would implement authentication into an account, which would then store the user's session that could be used for retrieval at a later time, if needed.

How It Works

Annotating the managed bean class with the CDI scope annotation corresponding to how long you need your managed bean to remain valid controls scope. Typically, one or more JSF views belong to a corresponding managed bean controller. *CDI scope* refers to how long a JSF view value needs to be retained in a browser session. Sometimes the value can be reset after a request is placed, and other times the value needs to be retained across several pages. Table 3-1 in Chapter 3 lists the annotations.

■ **Note** Be aware that two different sets of annotations are available for use with Java EE 8 applications. To apply a scope to a JSF managed bean, be sure you import the correct annotation class, or your results may vary. Typically, the classes you need to be importing for managing the JSF CDI bean scopes reside in the `javax.enterprise.context` package.

In this example, you will focus on the use of the @SessionScoped annotation. The shopping cart managed bean, CartController, has been annotated with @SessionScoped, so it becomes instantiated when a new session begins, and values that are stored in the bean are maintained throughout the client session. When someone visits the Acme Bookstore and decides to add a book to their shopping cart, they click the commandButton labeled Add to Cart on the book view. When this occurs, the addToCart method in the CartController is invoked, and if a Cart instance has not yet been created, then a new instance of Cart is instantiated. After that, the currently selected Book object is added to the cart. If the Cart instance already exists, then the Book objects in the Cart are traversed to make sure that the book does not already exist. If it does already exist, the quantity is bumped up by 1; otherwise, a quantity of 1 is added to the Cart for the currently selected book.

After a book has been added to the Cart, a user can elect to continue shopping or edit the contents of the Cart. This is where the @SessionScoped annotation does its magic. The user can go to any other page within the application and then revisit the cart view, and the selected Book object and quantity are still persisted. If the user elects to edit the Cart object, she can update the quantity by clicking the Update button, which invokes the CartController class's updateCart method, adjusting the quantity accordingly.

This is an exhaustive example to demonstrate a simple task, marking a managed bean as @ SessionScoped. If the bean had been annotated with @RequestScoped, then the Cart contents would be lost when the user navigates to a new page in the application.

5-8. Listening for System-Level Events

Problem

You want to invoke a method in your application whenever a system-level event occurs.

Solution

Create a system event listener class by implementing the SystemEventListener interface and overriding the processEvent(SystemEvent event) and isListenerForSource(Object source) methods. Implement these methods accordingly to perform the desired event processing. The following code listing is for a class named BookstoreAppListener, and it is invoked when the application is started up or when it is shutting down:

```
package org.javaee8recipes.chapter05.recipe05_08;

import javax.faces.application.Application;
import javax.faces.event.*;

/**
 * Recipe 5-8: System Event Listener
 * @author juneau
 */
public class BookstoreAppListener implements SystemEventListener {

    @Override
    public void processEvent(SystemEvent event) throws AbortProcessingException {
        if(event instanceof PostConstructApplicationEvent){
            System.out.println("The application has been constructed...");
        }
```

```
        if(event instanceof PreDestroyApplicationEvent){
            System.out.println("The application is being destroyed...");
        }
    }

    @Override
    public boolean isListenerForSource(Object source) {
        return(source instanceof Application);
    }

}
```

Next, the system event listener must be registered in the faces-config.xml file. The following excerpt is taken from the faces-config.xml file for the Acme Bookstore application:

```
...
<application>

                <system-event-listener>
                                <system-event-listener-class>
                                                org.javaee8recipes.chapter05.recipe05_08.
                                                BookstoreAppListener
                                 </system-event-listener-class>
                                 <system-event-class>
                                                javax.faces.event.PostConstructApplicationEvent
                                 </system-event-class
                </system-event-listener>

                <system-event-listener>
                                <system-event-listener-class>
                                                org.javaee8recipes.chapter05.recipe05_08.
                                                BookstoreAppListener
                                </system-event-listener-class>
                                <system-event-class>
                                                javax.faces.event.PreDestroyApplicationEvent
                                </system-event-class
        </system-event-listener>

    </application>
...
```

When the application is started, the message "The application has been constructed..." will be displayed in the server log. When the application is shutting down, the message "The application is being destroyed..." will be displayed in the server log.

How It Works

The ability to perform tasks when an application starts up can sometimes be useful. For instance, let's say you'd like to have an email sent to the application administrator each time the application starts. You can do this by performing the task of sending an email in a class that implements the SystemEventListener interface. A class that implements SystemEventListener must then override two methods, processEvent(SystemEvent event) and isListenerForSource(Object source). The processEvent method is where the real action occurs, because it is the method into which your custom code should be placed. Whenever a system event occurs, the processEvent method is invoked. In this method, you will need to perform a check to determine what type of event has occurred so that you can process only those events that are pertinent. To determine the event that has occurred, perform an instanceof check on the SystemEvent object. In the example, there are two if statements used to determine the type of event that is occurring and to print a different message for each. If the event type is of PostConstructApplicationEvent, then that means the application is being constructed. Otherwise, if the event type is of PreDestroyApplicationEvent, the application is about to be destroyed. The PostConstructApplicationEvent event is called just after the application has been constructed, and PreDestroyApplicationEvent is called just prior to the application destruction.

The other method that must be overridden within the SystemEventListener class is named isListenerForSource. This method must return true if this listener instance is interested in receiving events from the instance referenced by the source parameter. Since the example class is built to listen for system events for the application, a true value is returned if the source parameter is an instance of Application.

After the system event listener class has been written, it needs to be registered with the application. In the example, you want to listen for both the PostConstructApplicationEvent and the PreDestroyApplicationEvent, so there needs to be a system-event-listener element added to the faces-config.xml file for each of these events. Within the system-event-listener element, specify the name of the event listener class within a system-event-listener-class element and the name of the event within a system-event-class element.

■ **Note** As of JSF 2.3, there is now a PostRenderView event. This event is invoked after a view has been completely rendered.

5-9. Listening for Component Events

Problem

You want to invoke a listener method when a specified component event is occurring. For instance, you want to listen for a component render event.

Solution

Embed an f:event tag in the component for which you want to listen for events. The f:event tag allows components to invoke managed bean listener methods based on the current component state. For instance, if a component is being rendered or validated, a specified listener method could be invoked. In the example for this recipe, an outputText component is added to the book view of the Acme Bookstore application to specify whether the current book is in the user's shopping cart. When the outputText component is being rendered, a component listener is invoked that checks the current state of the cart to see whether the book is contained within it. If it is in the cart, then the outputText component will render a message stating so; if not, then the outputText component will render a message stating that it is not in the cart.

The following excerpt is taken from a view named recipe05_09.xhtml, a derivative of the book view for the application. It demonstrates the use of the f:event tag in a component. Note that the outputText component contains no value attribute because the value will be set within the event listener.

```
...
<h:outputText id="isInCart" style="font-style: italic; color: ">
    <f:event type="preRenderComponent" listener="#{ch5CartController.isBookInCart}"/>
</h:outputText>
...
```

The CartController class contains a method named isBookInCart. The f:event tag in the view references this listener method via the CartController managed bean name, ch5CartController. The listener method is responsible for constructing the text that will be displayed in the outputText component.

```
public void isBookInCart(ComponentSystemEvent event) {
        UIOutput output = (UIOutput) event.getComponent();
        if (cart != null) {
            if (searchCart(authorController.getCurrentBook().getTitle()) > 0) {
                output.setValue("This book is currently in your cart.");
            } else {
                output.setValue("This book is not in your cart.");
            }
        } else {
            output.setValue("This book is not in your cart.");
        }
    }
```

How It Works

Everything that occurs within JSF applications is governed by the JSF application lifecycle. As part of the lifecycle, JSF components go through different phases throughout their lifetimes. Listeners can be added to JSF components to perform different tasks when a given phase is beginning or ending. There are two pieces to the puzzle for creating a component listener: the tag that is embedded within the component for which your listener will perform tasks and the listener method itself. To add a listener to a component, the f:event tag should be embedded within the opening and closing tags of the component that will be interrogated. The f:event tag contains a handful of attributes, but only two of them are mandatory for use: type and listener. The type attribute specifies the type of event that will be listened for, and the listener attribute specifies the managed bean listener method that will be invoked when that event occurs. The valid values that could be specified for the name attribute are preRenderComponent, postAddToView, preValidate, and postValidate. In addition to these event values, any Java class that extends javax.faces.event.ComponentSystemEvent can also be specified for the name attribute.

The listener method must accept a ComponentSystemEvent object. In the example, the listener checks to see whether the shopping cart is null, and if it is, a message indicating an empty cart will be set for the outputText component's value. Otherwise, if the cart is not empty, then the method looks through the list of books in the cart to see whether the currently selected book is in the cart. A message indicating whether the book is in the cart is then added to the value of the outputText component. Via the listener, the actual value of the component was manipulated. Such a technique could be used in various ways to alter components to suit the needs of the situation.

5-10. Invoking a Managed Bean Action on Render

Problem

You want to invoke an application-specific action when a JSF view is rendered.

Solution

Add an f:metadata tag to the head of your view and then embed a viewAction component within it, specifying the action method you want to invoke. This technique can be handy for executing backend code prior to loading a page. As such, this technique can also be used to replace the f:event tag in order to create a bookmarkable URL. In this example, the Acme Bookstore author bio page has been updated so that it can be directly linked to, passing an author's last name as a view parameter via the URL. The viewAction component is executed before the view is rendered, invoking the business logic to search for the requested author by last name and to populate the view components with the found author's information.

The following listing is for recipe05_10.xhtml, and it can be invoked by visiting a URL such as http://your-server:8080/JavaEERecipes/faces/chapter05/recipe05_10.xhtml?authorLast=juneau:

```
<ui:composition xmlns="http://www.w3.org/1999/xhtml"
                xmlns:f="http://xmlns.jcp.org/jsf/core"
                xmlns:ui="http://xmlns.jcp.org/jsf/facelets"
                xmlns:h="http://xmlns.jcp.org/jsf/html"
                template="./layout/custom_template_search.xhtml">
    <f:metadata>
        <f:viewParam name="authorLast" value="#{ch5AuthorController.authorLast}"/>
        <f:viewAction action="#{ch5AuthorController.findAuthor}" />
    </f:metadata>

    <ui:define name="content">
        <h:form id="componentForm">
            <h1>#{ch5AuthorController.current.first} #{ch5AuthorController.current.last}</h1>
            <p>
                #{ch5AuthorController.current.bio}
            </p>

            <br/>
            <h1>Author's Books</h1>
            <ui:repeat id="bookList" var="book" value="#{ch5AuthorController.current.books}">
                <tr>
                    <td>
                        <h:graphicImage id="bookImage"
                                        library="image"
                                        style="width: 100px; height: 120px" name="#{book.
                                        image}"/>
                    </td>
                </tr>
                <tr>
                    <td>
                        <strong>#{book.title}</strong>
                    </td>
```

```
                </tr>
            </ui:repeat>
        </h:form>
    </ui:define>

</ui:composition>
```

The next piece of code is an excerpt from the AuthorController managed bean class. This method is the implementation for the action method that is specified within the viewAction component. This method is responsible for finding the author by last name and loading the current Author object with the found object.

```
public void findAuthor(){
        if (this.authorLast != null){
            for(Author author:authorList){
                if(author.getLast().equalsIgnoreCase(authorLast)){
                    this.current = author;
                }
            }
        } else {
            FacesContext facesContext = FacesContext.getCurrentInstance();
            facesContext.addMessage(null,
                new FacesMessage("No last name specified."));

        }
    }
```

How It Works

The viewAction component was added to JSF in release 2.2, and with it comes the ability to perform evaluations before a page is rendered. The viewAction component is very similar to f:event, except for some notable differences.

- The view action timing is controllable.
- The same context as the GET request can be used for the action.
- Both the initial and postback requests are supported since the view action is incorporated into the JSF lifecycle.
- viewAction supports both implicit and explicit navigation.

The viewAction component contains a number of attributes, as described in Table 5-3.

Table 5-3. viewAction Component Attributes

Attribute	Description
action	Method expression representing the application action to invoke when this component is activated by the user
onPostback	Boolean value to indicate whether the action should operate on postback (default: false)
if	Boolean value to indicate whether the component should be enabled (default: true)
immediate	Boolean value to indicate whether notifications should be delivered to interested listeners and actions immediately, during the Apply Requests Values phase
phase	String that specifies the phase in which the action invocation should occur using the name of the phase constraint in the PhaseId class (default: INVOKE_APPLICATION)

In the example for this recipe, the viewAction component is used to invoke a managed bean method, which searches for the author whose last name equals that which is contained within the authorLast property. An action method must accept no parameters, and it must return a string, which is then passed to the NavigationHandler for the application.

5-11. Asynchronously Updating Components

Problem

You want to provide periodic, asynchronous updates to portions of your view so that the users do not have to refresh the page in order to see the most up-to-date information.

Solution

Utilize an Ajax polling component (available from a third-party JSF component library) to poll the data asynchronously and re-render display components with the updated data without any user interaction. In this example, the site template for the Acme Bookstore application has been updated to include the current time and date. The clock will be updated each second so that, from a user's point of view, it resembles a digital clock.

The following code is that of the view template entitled chapter05/layout/custom_template_search.xhtml, and it demonstrates how to use the PrimeFaces poll component:

```
<html xmlns="http://www.w3.org/1999/xhtml"
      xmlns:ui="http://xmlns.jcp.org/jsf/facelets"
      xmlns:h="http://xmlns.jcp.org/jsf/html"
      xmlns:f="http://xmlns.jcp.org/jsf/core"
      xmlns:p="http://primefaces.org/ui"
      xmlns:s="http://xmlns.jcp.org/jsf/composite/components/util">

    <h:head>
        <meta http-equiv="Content-Type" content="text/html; charset=UTF-8" />
        <h:outputStylesheet library="css" name="default.css"/>
        <h:outputStylesheet library="css" name="cssLayout.css"/>
        <h:outputStylesheet library="css" name="styles.css"/>
```

```
        <title>#{ch5AuthorController.storeName}</title>
    </h:head>

    <h:body>
        <div id="top">
            <h2>#{ch5AuthorController.storeName}</h2>
            <br/>
            <h:panelGrid width="100%" columns="2">
                <s:search id="searchAuthor"/>

                <h:form>
                <p:poll id="poll" interval="1" update="dayAndTime"/>

                <h:outputText id="dayAndTime" value="#{bookstoreController.dayAndTime}"/>
                </h:form>
            </h:panelGrid>
        </div>
        <div id="content">
            <div id="left">
                <h:form id="navForm">
                    <h:commandLink action="#{ch5AuthorController.populateJavaRecipes
                    AuthorList}" >Java 9 Recipes</h:commandLink>
                    <br/>
                    <br/>
                    <h:commandLink action="#{ch5AuthorController.populateJavaEERecipesAuthor
                    List}">Java EE 8 Recipes </h:commandLink>
                    <br/>
                    <br/>
                    <br/>
                    <h:commandLink action="#{ch5ContactController.add()}">Subscribe to
                    Newsletter</h:commandLink>
                </h:form>
            </div>
            <div id="content" class="left_content">
                <ui:insert name="content">Content</ui:insert>
            </div>
        </div>
        <div id="bottom" >
            Written by Josh Juneau, Apress Author
        </div>

    </h:body>

</html>
```

Here's the class:

```
package org.javaee8recipes.jpa.jsf;

import java.util.Date;
import javax.enterprise.context.ApplicationScoped;
import javax.inject.Named;
```

```
/**
 *
 * @author juneau
 */
@Named("bookstoreController")
@ApplicationScoped
public class BookstoreController {

    private Date dayAndTime = null;

    /**
     * Creates a new instance of BookstoreController
     */
    public BookstoreController() {
    }

    /**
     * @return the dayAndTime
     */
    public Date getDayAndTime() {
        dayAndTime = new Date();
        return dayAndTime;
    }

    /**
     * @param dayAndTime the dayAndTime to set
     */
    public void setDayAndTime(Date dayAndTime) {
        this.dayAndTime = dayAndTime;
    }
}
```

The date and time will appear on the right side of the header for the bookstore. The resulting solution should resemble that in Figure 5-4.

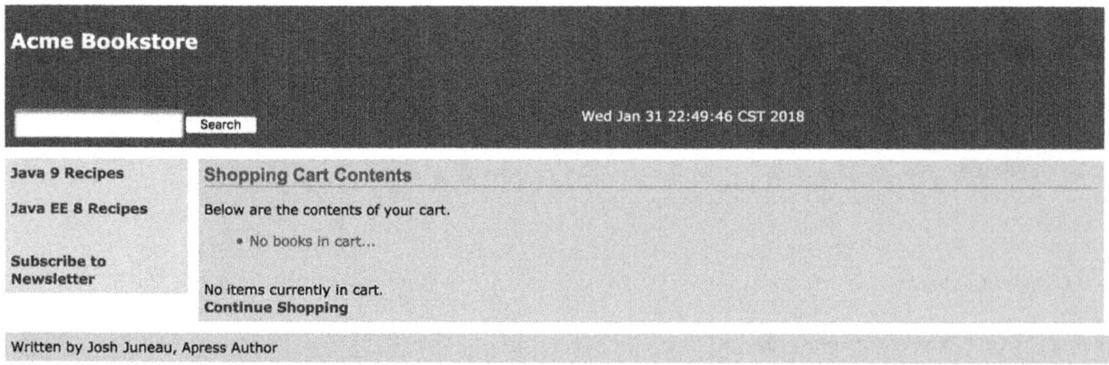

Figure 5-4. *Ajax poll component used to update date/time*

How It Works

The poll component of the PrimeFaces JSF component library can be used to update a specified portion of a view asynchronously on a timed interval. This can make website content more dynamic because features can refresh in real time without any user interaction. For instance, the poll component would work well for a stock market graph to asynchronously update the graph every minute or so. In the example for this recipe, the PrimeFaces poll component is used to display the current time and date in the Acme Bookstore application, updating the time every second.

For starters, you must ensure you have installed the PrimeFaces component library to utilize the poll component. To learn more about installing a third-party component library, see Recipe 5-11. Both PrimeFaces and RichFaces have a poll component, so you can take your pick of which to use. Neither is better than the other, but you may choose one over the other based on the library that you like to use best. After the library has been installed, you must add the namespace for the taglib reference to each page in which the components will be utilized. In the example, the xmlns:p="http://primefaces.org/ui" namespace is added to the <html> tag. After the namespace has been referenced in the view, the PrimeFaces components can be added to the view.

The poll component can be added to a view by including a tag that uses the p prefix, therefore, p:poll. To utilize the p:poll tag, you must set an update interval. This can be done by setting the interval attribute to a numerical value, which defines an interval in seconds between the previous response and the next request. In the example, the interval is set to 1 and, therefore, every second. The update attribute of the poll component is used to specify which component(s) to update each time the specified interval of time goes by. It is really as easy as that. In the example, the update attribute is set to the component identifier of dayAndTime. If you look down a few lines in the code, you can see that dayAndTime is actually an outputText component that is used to display the current contents of the dayAndTime property within the BookstoreController managed bean via the EL #{bookstoreController.dayAndTime}. Diving into the code for the managed bean, it is easy to see that each time the dayAndTime property is obtained, it is set equal to a new Date() object. A new Date() object contains the current time and date at the time of instantiation. Therefore, the date and time will always remain current.

The poll component is just one simplistic example of how third-party component libraries can assist in the development of more dynamic applications. Although the poll component is not very complex or difficult to use, it provides a large amount of functionality for an application view in just one line of code. I recommend you download the latest user guides for both the RichFaces and PrimeFaces component libraries and read about all the components that are available. If you have a basic understanding of what is available, it will help you formulate a plan for the development of your application when starting your next project.

5-12. Developing JSF Components Containing HTML5

Problem

You are interested in adding some HTML5 component functionality into your web application.

Solution

Create a composite component for JSF using the HTML5 component of your choice. For this example, an HTML5 video component will be constructed into a JSF composite component. The composite component will declare attributes, which will be passed through to the HTML5 video component in a seamless manner.

The first listing is that of the composite component, which resides in the resources/components/html5/video.xhtml file of the sources for this book.

```
<?xml version='1.0' encoding='UTF-8' ?>
<!DOCTYPE html PUBLIC "-//W3C//DTD XHTML 1.0 Transitional//EN" "http://www.w3.org/TR/xhtml1/
DTD/xhtml1-transitional.dtd">
<html xmlns="http://www.w3.org/1999/xhtml"
      xmlns:h="http://xmlns.jcp.org/jsf/html"
      xmlns:cc="http://xmlns.jcp.org/jsf/composite">

    <!-- INTERFACE -->
    <cc:interface>
        <cc:attribute name="id"/>
        <cc:attribute name="width" default="450"/>
        <cc:attribute name="height" default="300"/>
        <cc:attribute name="controls" default="controls"/>
        <cc:attribute name="library" default="movie"/>
        <cc:attribute name="source"/>
        <cc:attribute name="type" default="video/mp4"/>
    </cc:interface>

    <!-- IMPLEMENTATION -->
    <cc:implementation>
        <video width="#{cc.attrs.width}" height="#{cc.attrs.height}" controls="#{cc.attrs.
        controls}">
            <source src="#{cc.attrs.source}" type="#{cc.attrs.type}" />

              Your browser does not support the video tag.
        </video>
    </cc:implementation>
</html>
```

To keep an aesthetically pleasing look to your pages, you will place a video component in the Acme Bookstore view named recipe05_12.xhtml. And the view that uses the component will look as follows:

```
<!DOCTYPE html PUBLIC "-//W3C//DTD XHTML 1.0 Transitional//EN" "http://www.w3.org/TR/xhtml1/
DTD/xhtml1-transitional.dtd">
<html xmlns="http://www.w3.org/1999/xhtml"
      xmlns:ui="http://xmlns.jcp.org/jsf/facelets"
      xmlns:h5="http://xmlns.jcp.org/jsf/composite/components/html5">
    <head>
    </head>

    <body>

        <ui:composition template="layout/custom_template_search.xhtml">
            <ui:define name="content">

                <h1>Bear Movie</h1>
                <p>
                    <h5:video id="myvideo" width="300"
                              source="http://www.w3schools.com/html5/movie.mp4"/>
                </p>
```

```
            </ui:define>
        </ui:composition>

    </body>
</html>
```

When the view is rendered, the user will see a page that resembles Figure 5-5.

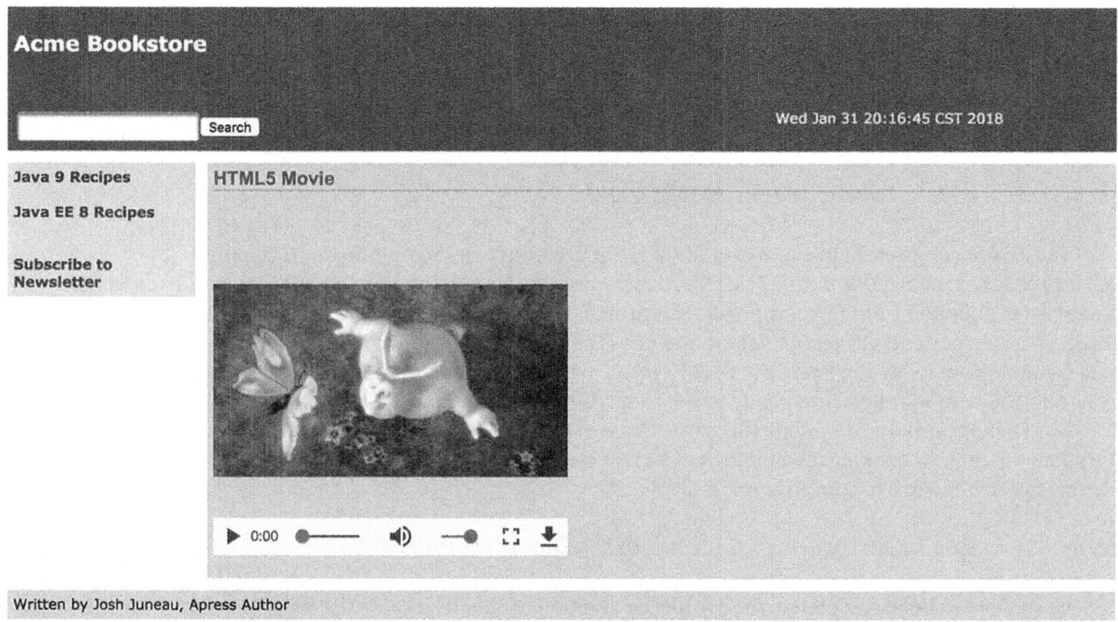

Figure 5-5. *Using HTML5 components within JSF 2 composite components*

How It Works

The use of HTML5 has become prevalent across the Web over the past few years. It is becoming the standard markup for producing web components that contain rich user interfaces. The JSF 2.2 release is being aligned with HTML5 so that the two technologies can coexist within the same views seamlessly. Prior to JSF 2.2, this was still a possible option, but some issues still may have been encountered when attempting to utilize some of the HTML5 components.

In the example for this recipe, an HTML5 component is embedded in a JSF composite component, and the result is a JSF-based video component that has the ability to accept the same attributes as the HTML5 `video` component and configure default attributes where possible. If you have not yet reviewed how to create composite components, go to Recipe 4-4 and review the content there. The following are the major differences between the example in Recipe 4-4 and this recipe:

- HTML5 is specifically used in this recipe, and it is not in Recipe 4-4.
- No server-side code is written for this composite component.

The composite component is placed in the `resources/components/html5` folder, so it will be made available for use in the application views automatically. All that is required for use within a client view is the definition of the `taglib` namespace in the `html` element. The name of the XHTML file that contains the composite component markup is `video.xhtml`, and it defines the namespace for the JSF composite component library inside the `<html>` element.

```
xmlns:cc="http://xmlns.jcp.org/jsf/composite"
```

The HTML5 `video` component accepts a number of attributes, and each of these is made available to the resulting JSF composite component by adding an interface to the component. This is done by supplying the opening and closing `cc:interface` tags, and each of the attributes that are to be made available for use with the composite component should be declared between the opening and closing tags. Each attribute is declared by adding a `cc:attribute` tag, along with the name of the attribute and a default value if needed. Here, you can see that the `width` attribute for the component will default to `450px` if the user does not specify a width:

```
<cc:attribute name="width" default="450"/>
```

The actual component implementation takes place between the opening and closing `cc:implementation` tags, and the HTML5 `video` component is placed there. As you can see, each of the attributes is obtained from the composite component's interface, so any of the attributes specified for the composite component will accept values and pass them through to their corresponding attributes within the `video` component using the `#{cc.attrs.X}` syntax, where `X` is the name of the attribute that is being passed. That's it...the component is now ready to be used within a view.

To use the component, specify the namespace to the `taglib` within the client view's `<html>` element, and then the tag will be made available. As you can see in the example, the namespace given to the `taglib` for this JSF HTML5 `video` component is `h5`:

```
xmlns:h5="http://xmlns.jcp.org/jsf/composite/components/html5"
```

Once that has been completed, the composite component can be used in the same manner as any standard JSF component or one from a third-party library. HTML5 can add exciting features to your web applications, and I expect the number of JSF custom components utilizing HTML5 (a mix of JavaScript and markup) to increase.

5-13. Listening to JSF Phases

Problem

You want to invoke a method in your application each time a particular JSF phase event occurs.

Solution

Create a class that implements the `javax.faces.event.PhaseListener` interface, and then implement the class's `beforePhase`, `afterPhase`, and `getPhaseId` methods to suit the needs of your application. The following class demonstrates the creation of a `PhaseListener`:

```
package org.javaee8recipes.chapter05;

import javax.faces.context.FacesContext;
import javax.faces.event.PhaseEvent;
import javax.faces.event.PhaseId;
```

```
public class BookstorePhaseListener implements javax.faces.event.PhaseListener {

    @Override
    public void beforePhase(PhaseEvent event) {
        FacesContext.getCurrentInstance().getExternalContext().log("Before the Phase - "
                + event.getPhaseId());
    }

    @Override
    public void afterPhase(PhaseEvent event) {
        FacesContext.getCurrentInstance().getExternalContext().log("After the Phase - "
                + event.getPhaseId());
    }

    @Override
    public PhaseId getPhaseId() {
        return PhaseId.ANY_PHASE;
    }
}
```

Any view that wants to use the PhaseListener should then be registered with the listener by adding an f:phaseListener tag to the view as follows:

```
<f:phaseListener type="org.javaee8recipes.chapter05.BookstorePhaseListener" />
```

In the end, when the application is launched and any view containing the f:phaseListener tag shown previously is rendered, a series of events will be published to the server log such as the following whenever a component is accessed:

```
INFO: PWC1412: WebModule[null] ServletContext.log():Before the Phase - APPLY_REQUEST_VALUES 2
INFO: PWC1412: WebModule[null] ServletContext.log():Before the Phase - APPLY_REQUEST_VALUES 2
INFO: PWC1412: WebModule[null] ServletContext.log():After  the Phase - APPLY_REQUEST_VALUES 2
INFO: PWC1412: WebModule[null] ServletContext.log():After  the Phase - APPLY_REQUEST_VALUES 2
INFO: PWC1412: WebModule[null] ServletContext.log():Before the Phase - PROCESS_VALIDATIONS 3
INFO: PWC1412: WebModule[null] ServletContext.log():Before the Phase - PROCESS_VALIDATIONS 3
INFO: PWC1412: WebModule[null] ServletContext.log():After  the Phase - PROCESS_VALIDATIONS 3
INFO: PWC1412: WebModule[null] ServletContext.log():After  the Phase - PROCESS_VALIDATIONS 3
INFO: PWC1412: WebModule[null] ServletContext.log():Before the Phase - RENDER_RESPONSE 5
INFO: PWC1412: WebModule[null] ServletContext.log():Before the Phase - RENDER_RESPONSE 5
INFO: PWC1412: WebModule[null] ServletContext.log():After  the Phase - RENDER_RESPONSE 5
INFO: PWC1412: WebModule[null] ServletContext.log():After  the Phase - RENDER_RESPONSE 5
```

■ **Note** For more detail regarding the lifecycle phases of a JSF application, visit the online documentation at http://docs.oracle.com/javaee/7/tutorial/doc/bnaqq.html.

How It Works

It is possible to listen to individual phases for each of the components in a view. Sometimes developers want to do this so that they can customize the component activity during these phases. A custom class can implement the `PhaseListener` interface in order to perform this level of scrutiny against components in your views. The class can then override the `beforePhase` and `afterPhase` methods to implement custom tasks that will be performed prior to or after the phase of your choice.

To create a `PhaseListener` class, implement the `javax.faces.event.PhaseListener` interface. Doing so will force you to implement the abstract methods: `beforePhase`, `afterPhase`, and `getPhaseId`. The `getPhaseId` method returns the phase that the listener will fire its actions against. In the example, the `getPhaseId` returns `PhaseId.ANY_PHASE`, which will cause the listener to be invoked before and after each phase. There are static identifiers for each of the other phases too, so you can cause the `PhaseListener` to invoke its actions only when a specific phase is occurring. Specifically, the other options are `APPLY_REQUEST_VALUES`, `INVOKE_APPLICATION`, `PROCESS_VALIDATIONS`, `RENDER_RESPONSE`, `RESTORE_VIEW`, and `UPDATE_MODEL_VALUES`.

The `beforePhase` method takes a `PhaseEvent` object, and it is invoked before the phase that is returned by the `getPhaseId` method. Therefore, in the case of the example, the `beforePhase` method will be fired before any phase occurs. The example simply prints out to the server log which phase is currently beginning.

The `afterPhase` method also takes a `PhaseEvent` object, and it is invoked after the phase that is returned by the `getPhaseId` method occurs. Therefore, in the case of the example, the `afterPhase` method will be fired after any phase occurs. The example prints out to the server log the phase that has just ended.

To register a view with the `PhaseListener`, you need to add an `f:phaseListener` tag to it and set the tag's `type` attribute to the `PhaseListener` class that you have created. Doing so will register the listener with the view such that when the view is rendered, the `PhaseListener` will kick in and begin listening for the phases that are specified by the `getPhaseId` method.

5-14. Adding Auto-Completion to Text Fields

Problem

You want to add auto-completion to a text field so that when the user of your application begins to type, possible entries are displayed and made selectable via a drop-down list.

Solution

Utilize a third-party component library and add an autocomplete text field to your application. For this example, the search box that is used for querying books and authors within the example Acme Bookstore application will be adjusted so that it auto-populates with text when a user starts typing. The following code is that of the custom search component view named `search.xhtml`, contained within the `web/resources/components/util` directory of the JavaEE8Recipes NetBeans project bundle. It has been updated to utilize a PrimeFaces `autoComplete` component as opposed to standard `inputText`.

■ **Note** This source comprises a JSF composite component. To learn more about JSF composite components, refer to online documentation at `https://docs.oracle.com/javaee/7/tutorial/jsf-facelets005.htm`.

```
<?xml version='1.0' encoding='UTF-8' ?>
<!DOCTYPE html PUBLIC "-//W3C//DTD XHTML 1.0 Transitional//EN" "http://www.w3.org/TR/xhtml1/
DTD/xhtml1-transitional.dtd">
<html xmlns="http://www.w3.org/1999/xhtml"
      xmlns:h="http://xmlns.jcp.org/jsf/html"
      xmlns:composite="http://xmlns.jcp.org/jsf/composite"
      xmlns:p="http://primefaces.org/ui">

    <!-- INTERFACE -->
    <composite:interface>
        <composite:attribute name="searchAction" default="#{bookstoreSearchController.search
        Authors(ch5AuthorController.completeAuthorList)}"
                    method-signature="java.lang.String action(java.util.List)"/>
    </composite:interface>

    <!-- IMPLEMENTATION -->
    <composite:implementation>
        <h:form id="searchForm">
            <h:outputText id="error" value="#{bookstoreSearchController.errorText}"/>
            <br/>
            <!-- implementation without autocomplete is commented -->
            <!--h:inputText id="searchText" styleClass="searchBox" size="75" value="#{book
            storeSearchController.searchText}"/-->

            <p:autoComplete id="searchText" value="#{bookstoreSearchController.searchText}"
                    completeMethod="#{ch5AuthorController.complete(bookstoreSearch
                    Controller.searchText)}"/>
            <h:commandButton id="searchButton" value="Search" action="#{cc.attrs.
            searchAction}"/>

        </h:form>
    </composite:implementation>
</html>
```

Note that the autoComplete component contains a value attribute, which is set to the searchText property of the BookstoreSearchController managed bean, and a completeMethod attribute, which is used to specify the name of the method to use for autocompletion of the text. In this case, the method is named complete, and it resides in the AuthorController class. The following excerpt of code shows the complete method, which is excerpted from the AuthorController class (contained in the sources for Chapter 5):

```
    /**
     * Auto-completes author names from the authorBookList
     *
     * @param text
     * @return
     */
    public List<String> complete(String text){
        List<String> results = new ArrayList();
        // This should print each time you type a letter in the autocomplete box
        System.out.println("completing: " + text);
        for (Author author:authorBookList){
```

```
            if(author.getLast().toUpperCase().contains(text.toUpperCase())){
                results.add(author.getLast().toUpperCase() + " " + author.getFirst().toUpper
                Case());
            }
        }
        return results;
    }
```

■ **Note** The searching logic in this application is suitable for smaller datasets. For larger datasets, a different approach would likely be used, such as a fully featured search engine solution.

When the component is rendered on the page and the user begins to type, then a drop-down list of matching author names will appear, allowing the user to choose one from the list. The drop-down list will resemble Figure 5-6.

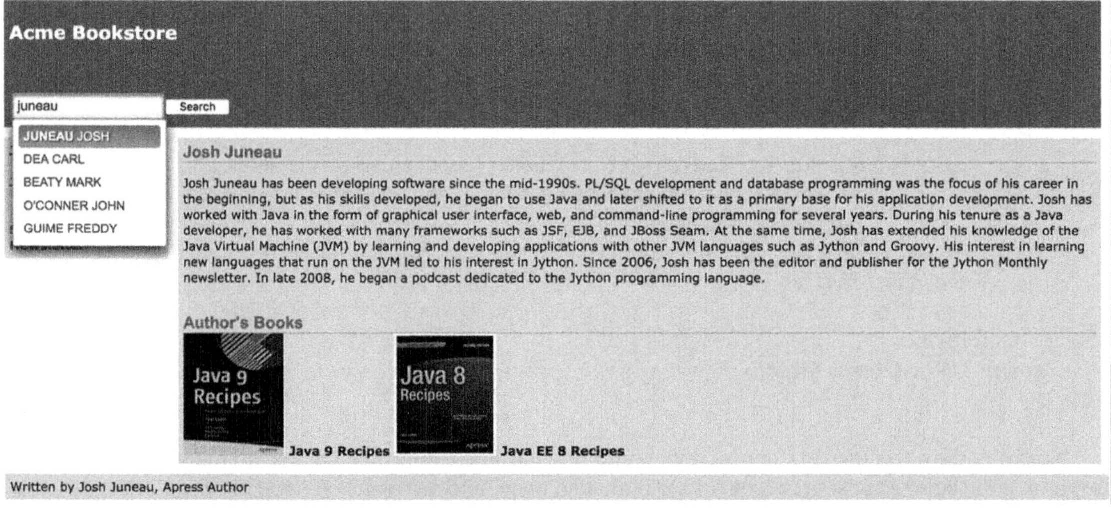

***Figure 5-6.** The PrimeFaces autoComplete component*

How It Works

The autocomplete text box is one of the most sought after components for anyone looking to build a web input form. It is an ingenious invention because it helps the users choose from a list of available options, while narrowing down that list as the user types characters. In the end, the user will be less likely to enter invalid data since a selection list is made available while typing, and this will decrease the likelihood for invalid data. Unfortunately, the standard JSF component library does not ship with an autocomplete component, but luckily there are several available for use from other third-party libraries. This recipe covers use of the PrimeFaces `autoComplete` component. The PrimeFaces `autoComplete` component provides a myriad of choices to the developer, and a handful of them will be covered here. For complete documentation regarding the `autoComplete` component, visit the PrimeFaces online documentation.

To use the PrimeFaces component, the namespace must be declared for the PrimeFaces tag library within the view where the autoComplete component will be used. In the example, the namespace is declared as p, so the autoComplete tag is written as p:autoComplete. The example uses only three attributes, and two of them are essential for the use of the component. The first attribute is id, which is the unique identifier for the component within the view. Next is the value attribute, which is set to a managed bean property where the ending value will be stored. The value attribute for the autoComplete component is analogous to the value attribute of an inputText component. The final attribute used in the example is completeMethod, which is set to the managed bean method used to perform the autocompletion of the text.

The completeMethod is where the real work occurs, because this is where the text that has been entered into the component is compared against a list of values to determine which of the list elements are possible choices for the autoComplete component value. A list of strings is returned from the completeMethod, and the values of the list will be displayed in a drop-down menu below the component when the results are returned. The completeMethod is executed each time the user presses another key, and the text that has been entered into the component thus far is sent to the method each time for evaluation. In the example, the text is compared to the author's last name, and any author whose last name contains the text that has been entered will be added to the return list. Oftentimes the text from the component is compared against database table record values, as opposed to list elements, but the list demonstrates the technique fine too.

Those pieces of the puzzle that have been addressed already are the only essential pieces for making the autoComplete component function as expected. However, the PrimeFaces autoComplete component has a variety of attributes that can be used to customize the functionality of the autoComplete component. For instance, the component contains a minQueryLength attribute that can specify the minimum number of characters that need to be typed before the completeMethod will be invoked. The effect attribute can specify a range of different effects to apply to the autocomplete animation. The forceSelection attribute can be set to true to force a user to make a selection, and so forth. As mentioned previously, for a complete set of documentation covering the PrimeFaces autoComplete component, along with each of its attributes, refer to the online documentation at www.primefaces.org.

The ability to autocomplete a user's text entry while they are typing the characters provides a wide variety of benefits to an application. First, the data integrity of the application can benefit from the use of standard entries that are displayed via the autocomplete feature, as opposed to freehand text entries from many different users. Second, autocomplete solutions provide a more unified user experience, allowing the user to choose from an available list of options rather than guessing what the entry should contain.

5-15. Developing Custom Constraint Annotations

Problem

You want to create an annotation that can be applied to a managed bean property to perform bean validation.

Solution

Create a custom annotation class, specifying the properties you want the annotation to accept, and create a validator class that will perform the actual validation on the property. In this example, you'll create a constraint annotation that can be used to validate the length of an inputSecret component value, that is, the length of a password. The following code is for a class named PasswordLength, which creates the annotation that will be used for validating the password length:

```
package org.javaee8recipes.chapter05.annotation;

import static java.lang.annotation.ElementType.*;
import static java.lang.annotation.RetentionPolicy.*;
```

```
import java.lang.annotation.Documented;
import java.lang.annotation.Retention;
import java.lang.annotation.Target;

import javax.validation.Constraint;
import javax.validation.Payload;
import org.javaee8recipes.chapter05.validator.CheckPasswordValidator;

@Target( { METHOD, FIELD, ANNOTATION_TYPE })
@Retention(RUNTIME)
@Constraint(validatedBy = CheckPasswordValidator.class)
@Documented
public @interface PasswordLength {

    String message() default "{org.javaee8recipes.constraints.password}";

     * @return password length
     */
    int passwordLength();

}
```

Note that in the annotation class there is a reference to the CheckPasswordValidator class, which is where the actual validation takes place. The validator class for the annotation contains the logic for performing the actual validation, and the sources for the CheckPasswordValidator class are as follows:

```
package org.javaee8recipes.chapter05.validator;

import javax.validation.ConstraintValidator;
import javax.validation.ConstraintValidatorContext;
import org.javaee8recipes.chapter05.annotation.PasswordLength;

/**
 * Custom validation class to ensure password is long enough
 * @author juneau
 */
public class CheckPasswordValidator implements
        ConstraintValidator<PasswordLength, Object> {
    private int passwordLength;

    private String password;
    @Override
    public void initialize(PasswordLength constraintAnnotation) {
        // Initialize implementation here
        passwordLength = constraintAnnotation.passwordLength();
    }

    @Override
    public boolean isValid(Object value, ConstraintValidatorContext context) {
        boolean returnValue = false;
        if (value.toString().length() >= passwordLength){
```

```
            returnValue = true;
        } else {
            returnValue = false;
        }
        return returnValue;
    }
}
```

To use the annotation, place it before a field declaration just as with standard bean validation.

```
@PasswordLength(passwordLength=8)
    private String password;
```

How It Works

Annotations can be placed before a class, method, variable, package, or parameter declaration to indicate that it be treated in a different manner than a standard class or method. Annotations have been referred to as *syntactic metadata*, and they change the way that a piece of code functions at runtime. To create an annotation, you must create a piece of code that is very similar to a standard Java interface. At a glance, the main feature that separates a standard interface from an annotation is the `@` character. It is prefixed on the `interface` keyword. However, they have many differences, and special guidelines must be followed when creating them.

The name of the annotation when it is in use will be the same as the name of the `@interface` that is used to create the annotation. In the example, the annotation being created has a signature of `@interface PasswordLength`, and later the annotation will be used by specifying `@PasswordLength`, along with any parameters that go along with it. Annotations can contain method declarations, but the declaration must not contain any parameters. Method declarations should not contain any `throws` clauses, and the return types of method declarations should be one of the following:

- String
- Class
- Enum
- Primitive
- Array

Annotations can contain special annotations themselves that can be used only in the context of annotations. Those annotations are `@Target`, `@Retention`, `@Constraint`, `@Documented`, and `@Inherited`. I briefly cover each of these annotation types, but it is important to note that custom constraint annotations require the `@Constraint` annotation to be placed before the `@interface` declaration, whereas other types of annotations do not.

The `@Target` annotation is used to signify which program elements can use the annotation. Table 5-4 describes the options that can be used in the `@Target` annotation.

Table 5-4. *@Target Annotation Values*

Value	Description
TYPE	The annotation can be placed on a class, interface, or enum.
FIELD	The annotation can be placed on a class member field.
METHOD	The annotation can be placed on a method.
PARAMETER	The annotation can be placed on a method parameter.
CONSTRUCTOR	The annotation can be placed on a constructor.
LOCAL_VARIABLE	The annotation can be placed on a local variable or a catch clause.
ANNOTATION_TYPE	The annotation can be placed on an annotation type.
PACKAGE	The annotation can be placed on a Java package.

For the purposes of creating a constraint annotation, the @Target annotation usually contains the following, as in the example to this recipe:

```
@Target( { METHOD, FIELD, ANNOTATION_TYPE })
```

The @Retention annotation is used to indicate how long the annotation will be retained. The options are class, source, and runtime. Table 5-5 describes these three types of retention.

Table 5-5. *Annotation Retention Values*

Value	Description
class	The annotation is discarded during the class load.
source	The annotation is discarded after compilation.
runtime	The annotation is never discarded, and is available for reflection at runtime.

The @Documentation annotation can be added to ensure that the @interface is added to the JavaDoc for the specific project that it is contained within. The @Constraint annotation is used to declare which constraint class will be used for testing the validity of the value contained within the field being annotated. In the example, the @Constraint annotation contains a validatedBy parameter value of CheckPasswordValidator.class, and this signifies that the CheckPasswordValidator class will be used to validate the value. You will take a more in-depth look at the CheckPasswordValidator class in a moment.

The last annotation that can be specified in an @interface declaration is @Inherited. This is used to allow the annotation to inherit properties of another class. In other words, if the @Inherited annotation is placed on an @interface declaration, then the properties of an annotation that has been placed on a class can be inherited by another class, which extends it. Therefore, if ClassA contains your custom annotation and the @Inherited annotation has been specified in the declaration of the custom annotation, then if ClassB extends ClassA, it also inherits the properties of the custom annotation.

To briefly explain the annotation member elements and methods, both the message() and passwordLength() elements are exposed for use with the annotation, so a developer can specify @PasswordLength(message="some message" passwordLength=5), for instance. You can add any number of elements to the annotation, utilizing any data type that makes sense for your annotation requirements, although most of the time an int or String data type is specified. In the case of the validation annotation, you may want to expose one or more of the elements within the validator class. I show you how to do that after a brief explanation of how the validator class works.

■ **Note** Any member element in an annotation `@interface` can contain a default value by specifying the keyword default and specifying the default value afterward. Doing so would enable a developer to use the annotation without specifying the element when using the annotation.

The last piece of the puzzle for developing a custom validator annotation is the validator class itself. The validator class must implement `ConstraintValidator`. In the validator class, override the `initialize` and `isValid` methods for the implementation. The `initialize` method accepts an object of the annotation type that you created. In the example, you can see that the `initialize` method accepts a `PasswordLength` object. The `initialize` method is where you set up all the local fields that will be needed to validate the contents of the field that the annotation has been placed on. In the example, a couple of member fields have been declared: `passwordLength` and `password`. The `passwordLength` field is set to the value specified by the annotation element that is exposed to the developer. To capture this value, in the `initialize` method, the annotation object is used to obtain the value. In the example, `passswordLength` is set equal to `constraintAnnotation.passwordLength()`. The `isValid` method is then invoked, and the actual value that is contained in the annotated managed bean property is passed into this method. This is where the actual validation occurs. The `isValid` method should return a boolean value indicating whether the value is valid. In the example, if the value is greater than or equal to the `passwordLength` field value, then it is valid, and `isValue` returns a true value.

Although there are a few pieces, it isn't difficult to create a custom validation annotation once you've done it a time or two. There are some good use cases for developing custom annotations, so they make for a good tool to have in your arsenal.

5-16. Developing a Page Flow

Problem

You want to develop a flow of pages in your application that share information with one another.

Solution

Define a page flow using the faces flow technology that was introduced in JSF 2.2. The faces flow solution allows a defined set of views to be interrelated with one another to share a common set of data, and views outside of the flow do not have access to the flow's data. Flows also have their own set of navigational logic, so they are almost like a subprogram within an application. To enable an application to utilize faces flow, a `<flow-definition>` section should be added to the `faces-config.xml` file. The section can be empty, because the navigational logic can instead reside in a separate configuration file for the flow. The following `faces-config.xml` file demonstrates how to enable faces flow for an application:

```
<faces-config version="2.3"
       xmlns="http://xmlns.jcp.org/xml/ns/javaee"
       xmlns:xsi="http://www.w3.org/2001/XMLSchema-instance"
       xsi:schemaLocation="http://xmlns.jcp.org/xml/ns/javaee
       http://xmlns.jcp.org/xml/ns/javaee/web-facesconfig_2_3.xsd">
 ...
<flow-definition>
    </flow-definition>
     ...
</faces-config>
```

The views belonging to a flow should be separated from the rest of the application views and placed into a folder at the root of the application's web directory. The folder containing the flow views should be named the same as the flow identifier. Navigation and configuration code is contained within a separate XML configuration file that resides within the flow view directory, and the file is named `flowname-flow.xml`, where `flowname` is the flow identifier. The following configuration file demonstrates the configuration for a very basic flow identified by `exampleFlow`. You can find more information regarding the different elements that can be used within the flow configuration in the "How It Works" section.

```
<faces-config version="2.2" xmlns="http://xmlns.jcp.org/xml/ns/javaee"
              xmlns:xsi="http://www.w3.org/2001/XMLSchema-instance"
              xsi:schemaLocation="
       http://xmlns.jcp.org/xml/ns/javaee
       http://xmlns.jcp.org/xml/ns/javaee/web-facesconfig_2_2.xsd">

    <flow-definition id="exampleFlow">

    </flow-definition>

</faces-config>
```

The views belonging to the flow should reside in the flow folder alongside the flow configuration file. Each of the views can access a managed bean that is dedicated to facilitating the flow. The flows share a context that begins when the flow is accessed and ends when the flow exits. The following view demonstrates the entry point to a flow named `exampleFlow`. This example view can be found in the book sources in the file `recipes05_16.xhtml`.

```
<ui:composition xmlns:ui="http://xmlns.jcp.org/jsf/facelets"
                xmlns:f="http://xmlns.jcp.org/jsf/core"
                xmlns:h="http://xmlns.jcp.org/jsf/html"
                template="layout/custom_template_search.xhtml">
    <ui:define name="content">
        <h:messages globalOnly="true"  errorStyle="color: red" infoStyle="color: green"/>
        <h:form id="flowForm">
            <p>
                Faces Flow Example
            </p>
            <h:commandButton value="Begin Flow" action="exampleFlow"/>
            <h:commandButton value="Stay Here" action="stay"/>

        </h:form>
    </ui:define>
</ui:composition>
```

Next, let's take a look at a view that is accessing the managed bean that is dedicated to the flow. In the following view, the managed bean named `FlowBean` is accessed to invoke a method, which will return an implicit navigational string directing the application to the next view in the flow. Notice that this view also accesses the `facesContext.application.flowHandler`, which I discuss more in the "How It Works" section.

```
<h:body>
        <f:view>
            <h:form>
        <p>
            This is the first view of the flow.
            <br/><br/>
            Flow ID: #{facesContext.application.flowHandler.currentFlow.id}
            <br/>
            <h:commandLink value="Go to another view in the flow" action="#{flowBean.nav
            Method()}"/>
        </p>
            </h:form>
        </f:view>
    </h:body>
```

Each subsequent view in the flow can also access the resources of the flow's managed bean. Lastly, you'll look at the code that is contained in `org.javaee8recipes.chapter05.FlowBean`, which is the managed bean that is dedicated to the flow.

```
import javax.faces.flow.FlowScoped;
import javax.inject.Named;

@Named
@FlowScoped("exampleFlow")
public class FlowBean implements java.io.Serializable {

    private String flowValue;
    private String parameter1;
    /**
     * Creates a new instance of FlowBean
     */
    public FlowBean() {
    }

    /**
     * Initializes the flow
     */

    public void initializeIt(){
        System.out.println("Initialize the flow...");
    }
    /**
     * Finalizes the flow
     */

    public void finalizeIt(){
        System.out.println("Finalize the flow...");
    }
```

```
    public String navMethod(){
        return "intermediateFlow";
    }

    public String testMethod(){
        return "intermediate";
    }

    public String endFlow(){
        return "endingFlow";
    }

    /**
     * @return the flowValue
     */
    public String getFlowValue() {
        return flowValue;
    }

    /**
     * @param flowValue the flowValue to set
     */
    public void setFlowValue(String flowValue) {
        this.flowValue = flowValue;
    }

    /**
     * @return the parameter1
     */
    public String getParameter1() {
        return parameter1;
    }

    /**
     * @param parameter1 the parameter1 to set
     */
    public void setParameter1(String parameter1) {
        this.parameter1 = parameter1;
    }
}
```

This solution provided a quick overview of the files that are required for creating a flow in a JSF application. In the next section, I cover the features in more detail.

How It Works

The concept of session management has been a difficult feat to tackle since the beginning of web applications. A *web flow* refers to a grouping of web views that are related and must have the ability to share information with each view within the flow. Many web frameworks have attempted to tackle this issue by creating different solutions that would facilitate the sharing of data across multiple views. Oftentimes, a mixture of session variables, request parameters, and cookies are used as a patchwork solution.

Since JSF 2.2, a solution has been adopted for binding multiple JSF views to each other, allowing them to share information among each other. This solution is referenced as *faces flow*; and it allows a group of interrelated views to belong to a *flow instance*, and information can be shared across all the views belonging to a flow instance. Flows contain separate navigation that pertains to the flow itself and not the entire application. As such, flow navigation can be defined in an XML format or via code. A flow contains a single point of entry, and it can be called from any point within an application.

Defining a Flow

As mentioned in the solution to this recipe, the `faces-config.xml` file for a JSF application that will utilize the flow feature must contain a `<flow-definition>` section. This section of the `faces-config.xml` file can contain information specific to one or more flows residing in an application. However, for the purposes of this recipe, the solution utilizes a separate XML configuration file for use with the flow. Either way will work; the syntax does vary just a bit because the XML configuration file that is flow-specific uses a new JSF `taglib` for accessing the flow-specific configuration tags.

To learn more about using the `faces-config.xml` file for flow configuration, refer to the online documentation (`https://docs.oracle.com/javaee/7/tutorial/jsf-configure003.htm`). Even if a flow is not using the `faces-config.xml` file for defining the flow configuration, the `<flow-definition>` section must exist to tell the JSF runtime that flows are utilized in the application.

The flow-specific configuration file and all flow-related views should reside within the same folder, at the root of the application's web directory. The name of the folder should be the same as the flow identifier. As mentioned in the solution, the flow configuration file should be named `flowname-flow.xml`, where `flowname` is the same as the flow identifier.

The Flow Managed Bean

A flow contains its own managed bean annotated as `@FlowScoped`, which differs from `@SessionScoped` because the data can be accessed only by other views (`ViewNodes`) belonging to the flow. The `@FlowScoped` annotation relies on Contexts and Dependency Injection (CDI), because `FlowScoped` is a CDI scope that causes the runtime to consider classes with the `@FlowScoped` annotation to be in the scope of the specified flow. A `@FlowScoped` bean maintains a lifecycle that begins and ends with a flow instance. Multiple flow instances can exist for a single application, and if a user begins a flow within one browser tab and then opens another, a new flow instance will begin in the new tab. This solution resolves many lingering issues around sessions and new-age browsers that allow users to open multiple tabs. To maintain separate flow instances, the `ClientId` is used by JSF to differentiate among multiple instances.

Each flow can contain an `initializer` and a `finalizer` (that is, a method that will be invoked when a flow is entered and a method that will be invoked when a flow is exited, respectively). To declare an initializer, specify a child element named `<initializer>` in the flow configuration `<flow-definition>`. The initializer element can be an EL expression that declares the managed bean initializer method, as such:

```
...
<initializer>#{flowBean.initializeIt}></initializer>
...
```

Similarly, a `<finalizer>` element can be specified within the flow configuration to define the method that will be called when the flow is exited. The following demonstrates how to set the finalizer to an EL expression declaring the managed bean finalizer method:

```
...
<finalizer>#{flowBean.finalizeIt}></finalizer>
...
```

Flows can contain method calls and variable values that are accessible only via the flow nodes. These methods and variables should be placed in the FlowScoped bean and used the same as standard managed bean methods and variables. The main difference is that any method or variable that is defined within a FlowScoped bean is available only for a single flow instance.

Navigating Flow View Nodes

Flows contain their own navigational rules, which can be defined within the faces-config.xml file or the individual flow configuration files. These rules can be straightforward and produce a page-by-page navigation, or they can include conditional logic. There are a series of elements that can be specified within the navigation rules, which will facilitate conditional navigation. Table 5-6 lists the different elements, along with an explanation of what they do.

Table 5-6. *Flow Navigational Elements*

Element	Description
view	Navigates to a standard JSF view.
switch	Represents one or more EL expressions that conditionally evaluate to true or false. If true, then navigation occurs to the specified view node.
flow-return	Outcome determined by the caller of the flow.
flow-call	Represents a call to another flow; creates a nested flow.
method-call	Arbitrary method call that can invoke a method that returns a navigational outcome.

The following navigational sequence is an example of a flow navigation that contains conditional logic using the elements listed in Table 5-6:

```
<flow-definition>

    <start-node>exampleFlow</j:start-node>

    <switch id="startNode">
        <navigation-case>
            <if>#{flowBean.someCondition}</if>
                <from-outcome>newView</from-outcome>
        </navigation-case>
     </switch>

     <view id="oneFlow">
          <vdl-document>oneFlow.xhtml</vdl-document>
     </view>

     <flow-return id="exit">
          <navigation-case>
              <from-outcome>exitFlow</from-outcome>
          </navigation-case>
     </flow-return>

     <finalizer>#{flowBean.finalizeIt}</finalizer>

 </flow-definition>
```

Flow EL

Flows contain a new EL variable named facesFlowScope. This variable is associated with the current flow, and it is a map that can be used for storing arbitrary values for use within a flow. The key-value pairs can be stored and read via a JSF view or through Java code in a managed bean. For example, to display the content for a particular map key, you could use the following:

```
The content for the key is:  #{facesFlowScope.myKey}
```

5-17. Constructing a JSF View in Pure HTML5

Problem

You want to utilize HTML5 tags instead of JSF components, but you still want to utilize JSF and all of its capabilities in your application.

Solution

Utilize the HTML-friendly markup for use within JSF views. By using HTML5 within JSF views directly, you can take advantage of the entire JSF stack while coding views in pure HTML5. To use this solution, HTML5 tags have the ability to access the JSF infrastructure via the use of a new taglib URI specification jsf="http://xmlns.jcp.org/jsf", which can be utilized within JSF views beginning with JSF 2.2 and beyond. In views that specify the new taglib URI, HTML tags can utilize attributes that expose the underlying JSF architecture.

In the following example view, HTML5 tags are used to compose an input form that is backed by a JSF managed bean. To visit the sources for this example, visit the recipe05_17.xhtml view within the sources for the book.

```
<?xml version="1.0" encoding="UTF-8"?>
<!DOCTYPE html PUBLIC "-//W3C//DTD XHTML 1.0 Strict//EN" "http://www.w3.org/TR/xhtml1/DTD/
xhtml1-strict.dtd">
<html xmlns="http://www.w3.org/1999/xhtml"
      xmlns:f="http://xmlns.jcp.org/jsf/core"
      xmlns:jsf="http://xmlns.jcp.org/jsf">
    <head jsf:id="head">
        <meta http-equiv="Content-Type" content="text/html; charset=UTF-8"/>

    </head>
    <body jsf:id="body">
        <form jsf:id="form" jsf:prependId="false">
            <input type="email" jsf:id="value1" value="#{ajaxBean.value1}">
            </input>
            <br/><br/>
            <input type="text" jsf:id="value2" value="#{ajaxBean.value2}">

            </input>
            <br/>
            <br/>
            <input type="submit" jsf:id="status" jsf:value="#{ajaxBean.status}"
                   jsf:action="#{ajaxBean.process()}" value="Process"/>
```

```
            <label for="status">Message: </label>
            <output jsf:id="status">#{ajaxBean.status}</output>
        </form>
    </body>
</html>
```

■ **Note** This feature is only available to views written in Facelets. It is not available to views written in JSP.

How It Works

The JSF 2.2 release includes the ability to utilize HTML5 markup within JSF views. As a matter of fact, the markup is not limited to HTML5; it can also include HTML4, and so on. The addition of a new `taglib` URI makes this possible, because it allows existing HTML tags to be bound to the JSF lifecycle via the use of new namespace attributes. It is now possible to develop entire JSF views without using any JSF tags at all.

To utilize the new namespace attributes, your JSF view must import the new `taglib` URI `jsf="http://xmlns.jcp.org/jsf"`. The new `taglib` can then be referenced as attributes in existing HTML tags, setting the underlying JSF attributes that are referenced. For instance, to utilize an HTML input tag with JSF, you would add the `jsf:id` attribute and set it equal to the JSF ID that you want to assign to that component. You would then set an attribute of `jsf:value` equal to the managed bean value.

■ **Note** There is no need to import the `http://xmlns.jcp.org/jsf/html taglib` because you are no longer utilizing JSF component tags in the view.

The new syntax provides several benefits for web developers. Although not all web developers are familiar with JSF component tags, HTML tags are well known. Utilizing the new syntax, both JSF and HTML developers alike can create web views that utilize the power of JSF along with the flexibility of HTML. The new syntax also makes it easier to bind HTML tags with JavaScript, if needed. You no longer need to worry about JSF view IDs getting in the way when working with HTML and JavaScript. With the addition of new JSF `taglib` namespace for use with HTML tags, both JSF and HTML alike have been improved.

5-18. Invoking Server-Side Methods via Ajax

Problem

You want to invoke a server-side managed bean method from an Ajax component or JavaScript.

Solution

Utilize the h:commandScript component, which was newly introduced in JSF 2.3. The following excerpt demonstrates how to call a managed bean method using this new component. In the example, a JavaScript function invokes a managed bean method via the use of the h:commandScript. The JavaScript is invoked when the view is loaded. The following code is that from the simple view:

```
<?xml version="1.0" encoding="UTF-8"?>
<!DOCTYPE html PUBLIC "-//W3C//DTD XHTML 1.0 Strict//EN" "http://www.w3.org/TR/xhtml1/DTD/
xhtml1-strict.dtd">
<html xmlns="http://www.w3.org/1999/xhtml"
      xmlns:h="http://xmlns.jcp.org/jsf/html"
      xmlns:jsf="http://xmlns.jcp.org/jsf">
    <head jsf:id="head">
        <meta http-equiv="Content-Type" content="text/html; charset=UTF-8"/>

    </head>
    <h:body>
        <h:form>
            <h:commandScript name="serverCounter" autoRun="true"
action="#{bookstoreController.increaseCounter}"
                             render="counterMessage"/>
            <h:outputText id="counterMessage" value="This site has had
#{bookstoreController.counter} visitors."/>
        </h:form>
    </h:body>
</html>
```

In the view, you can see that the h:commandScript name attribute is set to serverCounter. This is the same as the function named that is invoked in the JavaScript function entitled initiateCounter(). The h:commandScript action attribute is set to invoke bookstoreController.increaseCounter. The following code shows the BookstoreController class, which is an ApplicationScoped bean that contains a property named counter. The increaseCounter() method simply increases the integer that is stored in the counter property by one.

```
import java.util.Date;
import javax.enterprise.context.ApplicationScoped;
import javax.inject.Named;

@Named("bookstoreController")
@ApplicationScoped
public class BookstoreController {

    private Date dayAndTime = null;

    private int counter;

    /**
     * Creates a new instance of BookstoreController
     */
```

```
    public BookstoreController() {
        init();
    }

    public void init(){
        setCounter(0);
    }

    public void increaseCounter(){
        counter++;
    }

    /**
     * @return the dayAndTime
     */
    public Date getDayAndTime() {
        dayAndTime = new Date();
        return dayAndTime;
    }

    /**
     * @param dayAndTime the dayAndTime to set
     */
    public void setDayAndTime(Date dayAndTime) {
        this.dayAndTime = dayAndTime;
    }

    /**
     * @return the counter
     */
    public int getCounter() {
        return counter;
    }

    /**
     * @param counter the counter to set
     */
    public void setCounter(int counter) {
        this.counter = counter;
    }
}
```

The resulting page looks like the one in Figure 5-7.

Press me This site has had 5 visitors.

Figure 5-7. View utilizing h:commandScript

How It Works

The `h:commandScript` component was a new addition to JSF 2.3, and it provides a means to invoke a server-side method from JavaScript or from a JavaScript event. The component contains a small number of attributes, as seen in Table 5-7.

Table 5-7. Key commandScript Attributes

Attribute	Description
`action`	Binds to the action method that is invoked in the managed bean.
`actionListener`	Binds to a listener that is invoked in the managed bean.
`autoRun`	Indicates whether the component should be invoked on page load.
`execute`	A space-separated list of client identifiers of components that participate in the "execute" portion of the Request Processing Lifecycle
`name`	Name of the JavaScript function to be initiated. This is the name that will be used to reference the component from within the JavaScript namespace.

As seen from the table, the `name` attribute is used to reference the component from a JavaScript call. Therefore, if the component is to be called upon from within a JavaScript method, then the component's name attribute should be referenced. Calling upon the name will initiate the action or `actionListener` of the component, which thereby invokes the server-side method call. The `autoRun` attribute, demonstrated in this recipe, is used to indicate whether the component should be invoked when the view is loaded.

For years, there has been no standard way of calling upon a server side method from JavaScript within a JSF view. Many third-party libraries added support for this type of interaction, including PrimeFaces and OmniFaces.

5-19. Broadcasting Messages from the Server to All Clients

Problem

Your organization has constructed a Java EE application and it is in use by a number of clients. You want to have the ability to send a message from the server and have that message distributed to all of the clients at once.

Solution

Use the f:websocket tag, which was new with the release of JSF 2.3, to send a message to all listening clients. The following example includes a client view, which contains a text box, a send button, and an f:websocket tag. The user can type a message into the text box and click the Send button, and the typed message will be sent to all other clients that are currently listening on the same channel.

```
<html xmlns="http://www.w3.org/1999/xhtml"
      xmlns:ui="http://xmlns.jcp.org/jsf/facelets"
      xmlns:f="http://xmlns.jcp.org/jsf/core"
      xmlns:h="http://xmlns.jcp.org/jsf/html">
    <head>
    </head>

    <body>

        <ui:composition template="layout/custom_template_search.xhtml">
            <ui:define name="content">
                <h:messages globalOnly="true"  errorStyle="color: red" infoStyle="color:
                green"/>
                <h:form id="webSocketForm">
                    <script type="text/javascript">
                        function messageListener(message) {
                            document.getElementById("messageDiv").innerHTML += message +
                            "<br/>";
                        }
                    </script>
                    <p>
                        Websocket Integration Example
                    </p>
                    <p>
                        Enter text into the box below and press send button.  This will send
                        a message to all connected clients.
                    </p>
                    <h:inputText id="websocketMessageText" value="#{bookstoreController.
                    messageText}"/>
                    <br/>
                    <h:commandButton id="sendMessage" action="#{bookstoreController.
                    sendMessage}" value="Send">
                        <f:ajax/>
                    </h:commandButton>
                    <br/>
                    <f:websocket channel="messagePusher" onmessage="messageListener" />

                    <div id="messageDiv"/>
                </h:form>
            </ui:define>
        </ui:composition>
    </body>
</html>
```

The following code shows the server-side code behind the `messagePusher` channel and the `bookstoreController.sendMessage()` method.

```
import java.util.Date;
import javax.enterprise.context.ApplicationScoped;
import javax.faces.push.Push;
import javax.faces.push.PushContext;
import javax.inject.Inject;
import javax.inject.Named;

@Named("bookstoreController")
@ApplicationScoped
public class BookstoreController {

    private Date dayAndTime = null;

    private int counter;

    @Inject
    @Push(channel="messagePusher")
    private PushContext push;

    private String messageText;
. . .
/**
     * Initiates a notification to all Websocket clients.  This method is used
     * for example 5-19.
     */
    public void sendMessage(){
        System.out.println("sending message");
        push.send(messageText);
        messageText = null;
    }
. . .
}
```

The resulting solution looks like the following. If you type and click Send, all listening clients (on the same view) will receive the message.

How It Works

WebSockets has become a standard protocol for client and server communication. There are a couple of different ways in which to implement WebSocket solutions. You can utilize a framework such as Atmosphere to develop WebSockets, or since the release of Java EE 7, native WebSocket support can be utilized. Both approaches are supported by the JSF WebSocket support. The support that is included JSF 2.3 supports both implementation, so it provides some flexibility. To enable this support, you must specify the `javax.faces.ENABLE_WEBSOCKET_ENDPOINT` context parameter in the `web.xml` deployment descriptor with a value of `true`, as follows:

```
<context-param>
    <param-name>javax.faces.ENABLE_WEBSOCKET_ENDPOINT</param-name>
    <param-value>true</param-value>
</context-param>
```

The f:websocket tag enables support for WebSockets within JSF client views. The tag includes a required channel attribute, which is a ValueExpression used to list the channel on which the WebSocket client will listen. The tag also includes a required onmessage attribute, which is also a ValueExpression and it is used to list the name of a JavaScript function that is to be executed when the WebSocket message is received. In the example, you can see that the channel is set to messagePusher, meaning that the server must send message(s) to the channel named messagePusher in order to successfully send to this client. The message attribute is set to messageListener, and if you look at the JavaScript source that has been added to the view, you can see that it contains a function named messageListener. This function is executed when the message is received. In this example, the function merely prints a message to the div with an ID of messageDiv in the view. The signature of the JavaScript function in this example accepts the message only. However, a JavaScript function could also accept a channel name and event argument, if needed.

The f:websocket tag contains a number of other useful attributes as well. While optional, the following parameters may be of use in certain circumstances:

- onclose: Specify a JavaScript function to invoke when the message is closed.
- scope: Specify a limit as to where messages are propagated. If set to session, this attribute limits the messages to all client views with the same WebSocket channel in the current session only.
- port: Specify the TCP port number other than the HTTP port, if needed.

Now let's look at the server-side implementation. The solution to this recipe uses a new PushContext, which is injected into an ApplicationScoped bean. This PushContext sends the message to all listening clients, and it can be injected into any CDI bean by including the @Push annotation, along with the context. The name of the channel can be specified via an optional channel attribute on the @Push annotation; otherwise it will assume the same name as the PushContext identifier. In the example, the PushContext is simply named "push". This is the channel on which all clients must listen.

To send a message, call upon the send() method of the PushContext, passing the message to be broadcast. The message will be encoded as JSON and delivered to the message argument of the JavaScript function on the client that corresponds to the function named in the f:websocket onmessage attribute. The message can be composed of any number of containers, including a plain string, list, map, object, etc.

The addition of the f:websocket tag and PushContext provides support for multiple WebSocket implementations in an easy-to-use API.

5-20. Programmatically Searching for Components

Problem

You want to use expression language (EL) or Java code to find a particular component or a set of components in a JSF view. There are a number of reasons why you may want to obtain access to components, such as invoking the component programmatically or referencing from another component within the view.

Solution #1

Use the JSF component search framework via the use of expression language or programmatically from Java code. In the following example, a JSF panelGrid component is updated via expression language using key JSF search terms. The f:ajax tag contains a render attribute that specifies @parent, indicating that the parent component should be re-rendered once the Ajax process is complete.

```
<h:panelGrid columns="2">
                <h:outputLabel for="password" value="Enter a password for site access: "/>
                <h:inputSecret id="password" size="40" value="#{ch5ContactController.
                 current.password}">
                    <f:validateRequired/>
                    <f:ajax event="blur" render="@parent"/>
                </h:inputSecret>
                <h:panelGroup/>
                <h:message id="passwordError"
                       for="password"
                       style="color:red"/>

                <h:outputLabel for="passwordConfirm" value="Confirm Password: "/>
                <h:inputSecret id="passwordConfirm" size="40" value="#{ch5ContactController.
                 passwordConfirm}"
                              validator="#{ch5ContactController.validatePassword}">
                    <f:ajax   event="blur" render="@parent"/>
                </h:inputSecret>
                <h:panelGroup/>
                <h:message id="passwordConfirmError"
                       for="passwordConfirm"
                       style="color:red"/>
            </h:panelGrid>
```

Solution #2

Utilize the programmatic API to search for components from within a server-side CDI managed bean. In the following solution, a button from a JSF view invokes an action method in the CDI bean. The action method merely demonstrates the programmatic search expression API. In the action method, a component is looked up by explicit ID.

```
public void findById() {
        FacesContext context = FacesContext.getCurrentInstance();
        SearchExpressionContext searchContext =
            SearchExpressionContext.createSearchExpressionContext(context, context.
            getViewRoot());

        context.getApplication()
               .getSearchExpressionHandler()
               .resolveComponent(
                  searchContext,
                  "passwordConfirm",
                  (ctx, target) -> out.print(target.getId()));
    }
```

How It Works

For years, JSF developers had difficulty referencing JSF components within a view by ID. There are a couple of problems that can be encountered if you're attempting to simply look up a component by ID. First, if an ID is not explicitly assigned to a JSF component, then the `FacesServlet` assigns one automatically. In this situation, the ID is unknown until runtime, and therefore it is almost impossible to reference the component using EL or from within Java code. Second, even if a JSF component is assigned a static ID, then the nesting architecture of JSF views and the JSF component tree causes the IDs of each parent components to be prepended to the ID of the child component. This can result in long and sometimes difficult to determine component IDs. Moreover, even if a specified component is easy to identify by prepending parent IDs, some components, such as those nested in tables, will still have dynamic IDs assigned at runtime.

There have been a number of third-party libraries that have developed solutions to combat this problem. OmniFaces and PrimeFaces are some of the most widely used. The addition of the JSF search expression API to JSF proper significantly reduces the work that needs to be done in order to gain access to JSF components within a view. This is especially the case in the event that a component is nested deep within other components in a view, or part of a `dataTable`, as mentioned previously. The search expression API allows you to utilize keywords to help search the component tree in a dynamic manner, rather than hard-coding static IDs that may change down the road.

Prior to JSF 2.3, there were four abstract search keywords that could be used to obtain reference to components, those being `@all`, `@this`, `@form`, and `@none`. Moreover, you could only perform EL search expressions in the `f:ajax` tag. This was quite a limitation, and JSF 2.3 greatly expands this functionality. The following features have been added to the search expression API (see Table 5-8):

Table 5-8. *New Search Keywords*

Keyword	Description
`@child(n)`	The nth child of the base component
`@composite`	Nearest composite component of the base
`@id(id)`	Nearest descendant of base component with an `id` matching specified value
`@namingcontainer`	Nearest naming container of base component
`@next`	Next component in view following the base component
`@parent`	Parent of the base component
`@previous`	Previous component to the base
`@root`	The `UIViewRoot`

- Keywords and search expressions can be used programmatically
- Many more keywords have been added
- Keywords accept arguments
- Keywords are extendible and can be chained

The solution demonstrates how to find components using the `@parent` keyword, but any of the others can be used and strung together in order to find desired components. Another new feature in JSF 2.3 is the programmatic search expression API. This makes it possible to gain access to components from within managed beans. The second listing in the solution demonstrates how to use the programmatic API. To use the API, first create a `SearchExpressionContext`, which will later be passed as a parameter to help find the component. Second, call on the `FacesContext` to gain reference to the application via `getApplication()`, and then invoke `getSearchExpressionHandler().resolveComponent()`, passing the `SearchExpressionContext`, the search expression string, and the function to call when the component is found. This can be used to search for any component via a programmatic API.

CHAPTER 6

The MVC Framework

Java EE has progressed over the years from a servlet-centric platform to one that provides a number of different options for building web and enterprise applications. In the early days of Java EE, in those days referred to as J2EE, one would focus on developing servlets for building the frontend, as well as the integration and business layers. Things got a bit more dynamic when JavaServer Pages (JSP) came to fruition, as developers could begin to divide the workload between groups that would focus on the HTML markup, and those who would focus on the application logic. JavaServer Faces took it one step further by adhering to the Model-View-Controller pattern, whereby code logic was separated from page markup, creating three different tiers. This pattern makes development more logical and long-term maintenance much easier.

Although JSF provides a robust and mature environment for development of enterprise applications, the framework is somewhat rigid, in that you must adhere to the JavaServer Faces philosophies. One example is that JSF contains a lifecycle that must be followed. One can choose to bypass certain phases of that lifecycle, but in the end there is still some level of control given to the Faces servlet. The MVC framework, introduced during the same timeframe as Java EE 8 was being developed, takes the Model-View-Controller focus one step further. It allows developers to adhere to the three-tier architecture without forcing certain behavior.

MVC was originally intended to be included with Java EE 8 under JSR 371, but later in an effort to minimize the number of new specifications for inclusion, it was removed from the platform. However, Oracle handed off the ownership of MVC 1.0 to the community, which later transferred the specification to the Eclipse Foundation. The reference implementation for MVC is Ozark, and the sources reside on GitHub in the location `https://github.com/mvc-spec/ozark`.

Throughout this chapter, I discuss the configuration for an MVC application, including how to develop controllers, models, and views, and how to tie it all together. The framework was built on top of JAX-RS, so many of the key components are the same. Therefore, you learn a bit about the fundamentals of the JAX-RS API in this chapter as well. Although not officially part of Java EE 8, MVC is a key new framework for building applications on the Java EE platform. As I always state, if you have more tools in the shed, you will be able to accomplish a larger variety of tasks. The same holds true about application development, and frameworks such as JSF are great for development of some applications, but MVC may be even better for developing others.

After reading this chapter, you will have a better understanding of the differences that MVC 1.0 has to offer. You should be able to dive in developing with the MVC 1.0 framework after reading, as I walk through the development of an MVC application from start to finish, using the Apache NetBeans IDE for development.

J. Juneau, *Java EE 8 Recipes*, https://doi.org/10.1007/978-1-4842-3594-2_6

6-1. Configuring an Application for the MVC Framework

Problem

You want to create an MVC application project. Therefore, you need to configure the project to work with the MVC API.

Solution

Add the appropriate configuration files to the project and configure JAX-RS accordingly. In this chapter, I cover the use of Maven as the project build system, but you could easily configure using another build system, such as Gradle. Configuration of an MVC 1.0 application is very much similar to that of an application that uses the JAX-RS specification. To begin, let's create a new project in Apache NetBeans. Create a Maven Web Application project and name it `BookStore`, as shown in Figure 6-1.

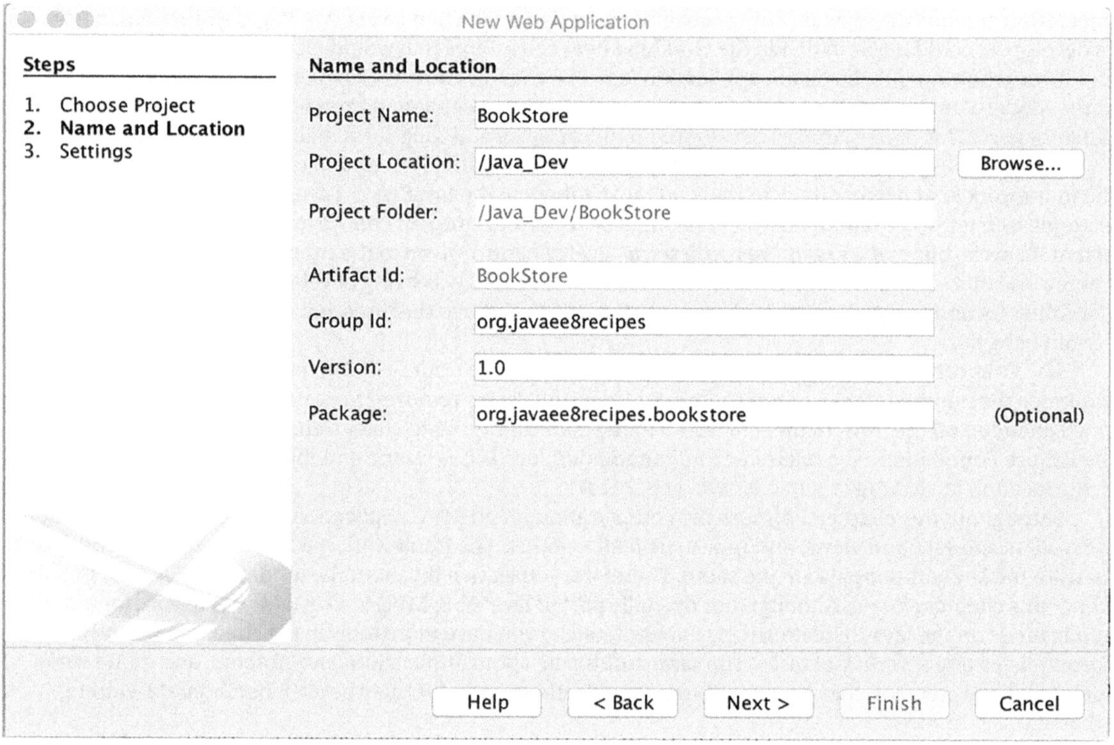

Figure 6-1. *New Maven web application*

Next, be sure to choose a Java EE 7 or Java EE 8 compliant application server for deployment, and then select Java EE 7 or Java EE 8 as the Java EE version. Click Finish to create the project. Once the project has been created, generate a `beans.xml` file. To do this, right-click on the project, click New, `beans.xml` (CDI Configuration File), accept the defaults to create it within `WEB-INF`, and keep the name as `beans.xml`. Click Finish.

Next, add the required dependencies to the POM file. To do so, right-click on the project and choose Open POM from the contextual menu. Once the POM file opens, add the dependencies for the MVC-API and Ozark, as follows:

```
<dependency>
    <groupId>javax.mvc</groupId>
    <artifactId>javax.mvc-api</artifactId>
    <version>1.0-edr2</version>
    <scope>provided</scope>
</dependency>
<dependency>
    <groupId>org.glassfish.ozark</groupId>
    <artifactId>ozark</artifactId>
    <version>1.0.0-m02</version>
    <scope>provided</scope>
</dependency>
```

Lastly, the application will need to be configured for use with JAX-RS. To do this, create an `ApplicationConfig` class within the `org.javaee8recipes.bookstore` package (see Figure 6-2).

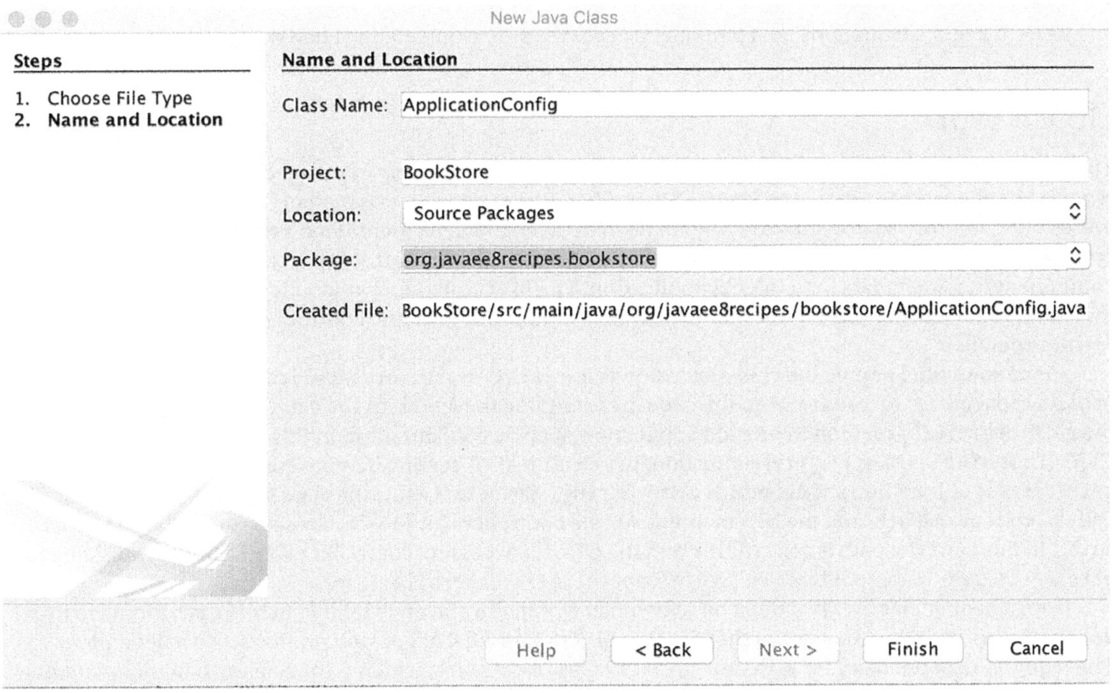

Figure 6-2. *Create ApplicationConfig class*

The ApplicationConfig class is used to map the RESTful web services to a URI. The @ApplicationPath annotation is used to configure the path for URI. The following code shows the sources for this class.

```
import java.util.HashMap;
import java.util.Map;
import javax.mvc.security.Csrf;
import javax.ws.rs.ApplicationPath;
import javax.ws.rs.core.Application;

@ApplicationPath("controller")
public class ApplicationConfig extends Application {

    @Override
    public Map<String, Object> getProperties() {
        final Map<String, Object> map = new HashMap<>();
        map.put(Csrf.CSRF_PROTECTION, Csrf.CsrfOptions.EXPLICIT);
        return map;
    }

}
```

Once these configurations are complete, you are ready to begin coding an MVC application.

How It Works

The MVC 1.0 framework requires a number of easy configurations made to a project in order to pull in the required dependencies, and to configure CDI and JAX-RS properly. In this recipe, I showed how to make these configurations, so now let's see why we need to make them. As mentioned previously, the JAX-RS configuration should reside within a class that extends javax.ws.rs.core.Application, which defines components and metadata for a JAX-RS application. The MVC 1.0 framework builds on the JAX-RS API, so this configuration is mandatory in order to provide the ability to generate controller classes (see Recipe 6-3 for more details).

In the solution, I named the class that extends the javax.ws.rs.core.Application class ApplicationConfig. As you see from the code, by extending the Application class, we can override the getProperties() method to provide application-specific configuration. In this case, I added CSRF (Cross-Site Request Forgery) protection, which is an MVC security feature (see Recipe 6-8). The getProperties() method should return a Map<String, Object>. Lastly, the class should be annotated with @ApplicationPath, and the URI mapping for the controllers (or JAX-RS classes) should be passed as a string. In this case, the path is controller and the URL for accessing controller classes should translate to http://<<server_name:port>>/BookStore/controller/<<controller-name>>.

The dependencies for MVC must be referenced within the Maven POM file. In this case, there are two dependencies, with the expectation that the Java EE 7 or Java EE 8 full or web profile is also a dependency. The required dependencies for MVC are javax.mvc-api and ozark, which is the reference implementation. Lastly, ensure that you create a beans.xml configuration file for CDI. This configuration file allows you to specify how CDI beans are discovered. For the purposes of this example, accept the default discovery mode of annotated, as follows:

```
<?xml version="1.0" encoding="UTF-8"?>
<beans xmlns="http://xmlns.jcp.org/xml/ns/javaee"
       xmlns:xsi="http://www.w3.org/2001/XMLSchema-instance"
```

```
        xsi:schemaLocation="http://xmlns.jcp.org/xml/ns/javaee
        http://xmlns.jcp.org/xml/ns/javaee/beans_1_1.xsd"
        bean-discovery-mode="annotated">
</beans>
```

This recipe walks through the configurations required to create an MVC 1.0 project. In the following recipes, I cover how to build the project into a fully-functional web application.

6-2. Making Data Available for the Application

Problem

You need to obtain existing data for your application, and you'd like to easily make the data available for your web views.

Solution #1

Utilize the Java Persistence API (JPA) along with Enterprise JavaBeans (EJBs) to provide data to your application. First, create entity classes that will map each of your database tables to a corresponding Java object. See Chapter 8 for more details on generating entity classes. For the purposes of the application that is being developed for this chapter, entity classes will be generated for a number of the tables being used throughout this book. In this solution, only a single entity class will be generated in order to demonstrate. However, if you look at the sources for the example application then you will find an entity class for each of the tables that are used within the application.

Since the application will be used for the purposes of an online bookstore, the database tables that are used along with the application pertain to authors and books. In this solution, we will generate the entity class for the AUTHOR database table. As a brief primer, an entity class maps each column of a database table to a corresponding class member. The following code is for the BookAuthor entity class.

```
package org.javaee8recipes.bookstore.entity;

import java.io.Serializable;
import java.math.BigDecimal;
import java.util.List;
import java.util.Set;
import javax.persistence.*;
import javax.validation.constraints.NotNull;
import javax.validation.constraints.Size;

@Entity
@Table(name = "BOOK_AUTHOR")
public class BookAuthor implements Serializable {

    private static final long serialVersionUID = 1L;
    @Id
    @Basic(optional = false)
    @Column(name = "ID")
    private BigDecimal id;
    @Size(max = 30)
    @Column(name = "LASTNAME")
```

```
    private String last;
    @Size(max = 30)
    @Column(name = "FIRSTNAME")
    private String first;
    @Lob
    @Column(name = "BIO")
    private String bio;
    @ManyToMany
    @JoinTable(name="AUTHOR_WORK",
            joinColumns=
            @JoinColumn(name="AUTHOR_ID", referencedColumnName="ID"),
            inverseJoinColumns=
            @JoinColumn(name="BOOK_ID", referencedColumnName="ID"))
    private Set<Book> books;

    public BookAuthor() {
    }

    public BookAuthor(BigDecimal id) {
        this.id = id;
    }

    public BigDecimal getId() {
        return id;
    }

    public void setId(BigDecimal id) {
        this.id = id;
    }

    public String getLast() {
        return last;
    }

    public void setLast(String last) {
        this.last = last;
    }

    public String getFirst() {
        return first;
    }

    public void setFirst(String first) {
        this.first = first;
    }

    public String getBio() {
        return bio;
    }
```

```
    public void setBio(String bio) {
        this.bio = bio;
    }

    public Set<Book> getBooks() {
        return books;
    }

    public void setBooks(Set<Book> books) {
        this.books = books;
    }

    @Override
    public int hashCode() {
        int hash = 0;
        hash += (id != null ? id.hashCode() : 0);
        return hash;
    }

    @Override
    public boolean equals(Object object) {
        if (!(object instanceof BookAuthor)) {
            return false;
        }
        BookAuthor other = (BookAuthor) object;
        if ((this.id == null && other.id != null) || (this.id != null && !this.
        id.equals(other.id))) {
            return false;
        }
        return true;
    }

    @Override
    public String toString() {
        return "org.javaee8recipes.bookstore.entity.BookAuthor[ id=" + id + " ]";
    }
}
```

Once the entity classes for each database table have been created, develop EJB façade (session bean) classes for each of them. To do this, first generate a package to hold all of the EJB session bean classes. In this case, create a package named `org.javaeerecipes.bookstore.session`. Next, create a session bean class for each of the entity classes that have been created. To create the session bean for the `BookAuthor` class, create a class within the newly created package, or if you're using NetBeans then right-click on the new package and select New ➤ Session Beans from Entity Classes. Name the bean `BookAuthorFacade`. If you're using Apache NetBeans, two classes will be generated, one of them is an abstract class named `AbstractFacade`. This abstract class will be extended by each of the session beans that are created for the application. It contains a set of common methods that can be used throughout all of the session beans. If you're creating a session bean from scratch, you need to create these methods for each bean or use a similar technique to provide a common implementation for beans to use, similar to the `AbstractFacade`.

No matter which technique you choose, you need to generate a persistence unit for your application. This is an XML configuration file that is used to hold connection configuration for your database. Typically, the persistence unit contains Java Naming and Directory Interface (JNDI) information for connecting to a datasource that has been defined within an application server container. In this case, create a persistence unit by right-clicking on your project and choosing Create Persistence Unit. Choose an existing datasource that has been configured for your database within Apache NetBeans.

The following code is that of the `AbstractFacade`, which is automatically generated by Apache NetBeans.

```
package org.javaee8recipes.bookstore.session;

import java.util.List;
import javax.persistence.EntityManager;

public abstract class AbstractFacade<T> {

    private Class<T> entityClass;

    public AbstractFacade(Class<T> entityClass) {
        this.entityClass = entityClass;
    }

    protected abstract EntityManager getEntityManager();

    public void create(T entity) {
        getEntityManager().persist(entity);
    }

    public void edit(T entity) {
        getEntityManager().merge(entity);
    }

    public void remove(T entity) {
        getEntityManager().remove(getEntityManager().merge(entity));
    }

    public T find(Object id) {
        return getEntityManager().find(entityClass, id);
    }

    public List<T> findAll() {
        javax.persistence.criteria.CriteriaQuery cq = getEntityManager().
        getCriteriaBuilder().createQuery();
        cq.select(cq.from(entityClass));
        return getEntityManager().createQuery(cq).getResultList();
    }

    public List<T> findRange(int[] range) {
        javax.persistence.criteria.CriteriaQuery cq = getEntityManager().
        getCriteriaBuilder().createQuery();
        cq.select(cq.from(entityClass));
        javax.persistence.Query q = getEntityManager().createQuery(cq);
```

```
        q.setMaxResults(range[1] - range[0] + 1);
        q.setFirstResult(range[0]);
        return q.getResultList();
    }

    public int count() {
        javax.persistence.criteria.CriteriaQuery cq = getEntityManager().
        getCriteriaBuilder().createQuery();
        javax.persistence.criteria.Root<T> rt = cq.from(entityClass);
        cq.select(getEntityManager().getCriteriaBuilder().count(rt));
        javax.persistence.Query q = getEntityManager().createQuery(cq);
        return ((Long) q.getSingleResult()).intValue();
    }

}
```

Next, let's take a look at the code that is generated for the BookAuthorFacade. This code is also automatically generated by Apache NetBeans, or it could be manually created if you want.

```
@Stateless
public class BookAuthorFacade extends AbstractFacade<BookAuthor> {

    @PersistenceContext(unitName = "org.javaee8recipes_BookStore_war_1.0PU")
    private EntityManager em;

    @Override
    protected EntityManager getEntityManager() {
        return em;
    }

    public BookAuthorFacade() {
        super(BookAuthor.class);
    }

}
```

Solution #2

Utilize RESTful web services to obtain data for your application. As mentioned in Solution #1, create entity classes that will map each of your database tables to a corresponding Java object. Once the entity classes have been created, develop REST service classes for each of them. If you're using an IDE such as Apache NetBeans, it will only take a few clicks to generate these RESTful web services, as most IDEs provide an auto-generation option. Otherwise, simply create a Plain Old Java Object (POJO) and annotate it accordingly to develop a RESTful service class.

To begin, create a new package and name it `org.javaee8recipes.bookstore.service`. Next, create the RESTful class inside the newly created package. In Apache NetBeans IDE, right-click on the package and select New ➤ Web Services ➤ RESTful Web Services from Entity Classes. Then choose Next. The New RESTful Web Services from Entity Classes dialog is shown. Select the `org.javaee8bookstore.entity.BookAuthor` class. On the next screen, change the Resource Package to `org.javaee8recipes.bookstore.service`, as shown in Figure 6-3. Lastly, click Finish to create the class.

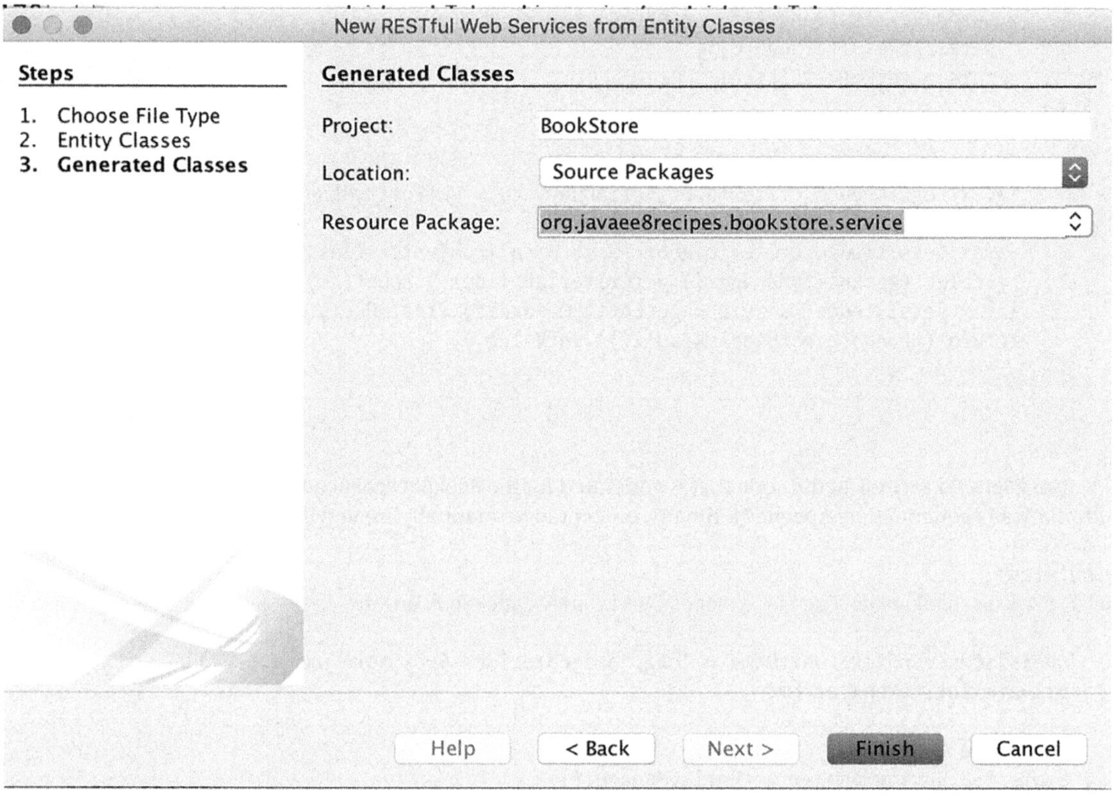

Figure 6-3. *Creating a RESTful web service from an entity class in Apache NetBeans IDE*

Similar to creation of an EJB, creation of a RESTful web service provides methods that can be used to perform create, read, update, and delete actions against a database. Furthermore, since these methods are annotated as REST services, they can be invoked via a REST client. The following code shows the RESTful web service class for the `BookAuthor` entity. This class is named `BookAuthorFacadeREST` by NetBeans IDE, or you can name it differently if you're generating it from scratch.

```
package org.javaee8recipes.bookstore.service;

import java.math.BigDecimal;
import java.util.List;
import javax.ejb.Stateless;
import javax.persistence.EntityManager;
import javax.persistence.PersistenceContext;
import javax.ws.rs.Consumes;
import javax.ws.rs.DELETE;
import javax.ws.rs.GET;
import javax.ws.rs.POST;
import javax.ws.rs.PUT;
import javax.ws.rs.Path;
import javax.ws.rs.PathParam;
import javax.ws.rs.Produces;
```

```
import javax.ws.rs.core.MediaType;
import org.javaee8recipes.bookstore.entity.BookAuthor;

/**
 *
 * @author Juneau
 */
@Stateless
@Path("org.javaee8recipes.bookstore.entity.bookauthor")
public class BookAuthorFacadeREST extends AbstractFacade<BookAuthor> {

    @PersistenceContext(unitName = "org.javaee8recipes_BookStore_war_1.0PU")
    private EntityManager em;

    public BookAuthorFacadeREST() {
        super(BookAuthor.class);
    }

    @POST
    @Override
    @Consumes({MediaType.APPLICATION_XML, MediaType.APPLICATION_JSON})
    public void create(BookAuthor entity) {
        super.create(entity);
    }

    @PUT
    @Path("{id}")
    @Consumes({MediaType.APPLICATION_XML, MediaType.APPLICATION_JSON})
    public void edit(@PathParam("id") BigDecimal id, BookAuthor entity) {
        super.edit(entity);
    }

    @DELETE
    @Path("{id}")
    public void remove(@PathParam("id") BigDecimal id) {
        super.remove(super.find(id));
    }

    @GET
    @Path("{id}")
    @Produces({MediaType.APPLICATION_XML, MediaType.APPLICATION_JSON})
    public BookAuthor find(@PathParam("id") BigDecimal id) {
        return super.find(id);
    }

    @GET
    @Override
    @Produces({MediaType.APPLICATION_XML, MediaType.APPLICATION_JSON})
    public List<BookAuthor> findAll() {
        return super.findAll();
    }
```

```
    @GET
    @Path("{from}/{to}")
    @Produces({MediaType.APPLICATION_XML, MediaType.APPLICATION_JSON})
    public List<BookAuthor> findRange(@PathParam("from") Integer from, @PathParam("to")
    Integer to) {
        return super.findRange(new int[]{from, to});
    }

    @GET
    @Path("count")
    @Produces(MediaType.TEXT_PLAIN)
    public String countREST() {
        return String.valueOf(super.count());
    }

    @Override
    protected EntityManager getEntityManager() {
        return em;
    }

}
```

To learn more about generating RESTful web services and the respective annotations, see Chapter 16. Once a RESTful web service has been created, it can be called upon from other applications to obtain data in various formats, being XML, JSON, plaintext, or some other medium. An MVC application can utilize a JAX-RS client to call upon RESTful web services to obtain data for the application. This can be achieved by generating a service class that contains the JAX-RS client and web service calls to obtain the data.

To begin, create a class within the `org.javaee8recipes.bookstore.service` package and name it `BookAuthorService`. This will be a session scoped CDI bean (see Chapter 13 for details on CDI), which will create a client upon bean construction, and then load data for use within the application, as needed. In the next recipe, which covers MVC controllers, I demonstrate how to call upon this service class from within a controller class to obtain data. The following code shows the finished product for the `BookAuthorService` class.

```
package org.javaee8recipes.bookstore.service;

import java.util.List;
import javax.annotation.PostConstruct;
import javax.ejb.EJB;
import javax.enterprise.context.SessionScoped;
import javax.ws.rs.client.Client;
import javax.ws.rs.client.ClientBuilder;
import javax.ws.rs.core.GenericType;
import org.javaee8recipes.bookstore.entity.BookAuthor;

@SessionScoped
public class BookAuthorService implements java.io.Serializable {
    Client jaxRsClient;
    private List<BookAuthor> bookAuthorList;
```

```
    String hostUri = "http://localhost:8080/BookStore/bookstore";

    public BookAuthorService(){

    }

    @PostConstruct
    public void init(){
        // Construct a JAX-RS Client
        jaxRsClient = ClientBuilder.newClient();
        loadData();
    }

    private void loadData(){

        bookAuthorList = jaxRsClient.target(hostUri + "/org.javaee8recipes.bookstore.entity.
        bookauthor/findAll")
                .request("application/xml")
                .get(new GenericType<List<BookAuthor>>() {
                }
                );
    }

    /**
     * @return the bookAuthorList
     */
    public List<BookAuthor> getBookAuthorList() {
        if(bookAuthorList == null){
             loadData();
        }
        return bookAuthorList;
    }

    /**
     * @param bookAuthorList
     */
    public void setBookAuthorList(List<BookAuthor> bookAuthorList) {
        this.bookAuthorList = bookAuthorList;
    }
}
```

The service class can be used to load the data and obtain the set of data for our application. This class could be modified at a later time to provide RESTful web service methods for creating, updating, and removing data, as needed.

How It Works

Most enterprise applications do some work with data. MVC applications are no different, as data typically plays an important role. The way to obtain data for an MVC application is very much the same as it would be for many other Java web applications, and RESTful web services or EJBs are some great options. Keep in mind that these are not the only options for pulling data into an MVC application. Since the MVC framework provides a very fluid design pattern, it allows the developer to make many choices along the way. To that end, one could certainly use another methodology such as JDBC or a home grown Data Access Object (DAO) to orchestrate work with the database. This recipe shows two of the most standard approaches.

In Solution #1, I showed how one could create entity classes based on existing (or new) database tables, and then write an EJB façade used in tandem with the entity classes to work with the data. This is, by far, one of the most standard approaches for coercing data into Java objects, dating back to the J2EE days. Back in the days of J2EE, developers were required to write heavyweight EJB solutions and lots of XML in order to pull off the same feat that can be resolved nowadays using simple POJOs with annotations.

The use of EJBs goes hand-in-hand with the use of entity classes for mapping database tables to Java objects. To learn more about the use of entity classes, refer to Chapter 8 where object relational mapping is discussed. Once an entity class has been constructed, it is easy to create an EJB that can be used to work with the entity class to orchestrate the data. Since Chapter 9 is dedicated to the use of EJBs, you can look there for more information on creating and using them. The point of this particular recipe is to show how to use these options within an MVC application. You can bind the use of EJBs with the MVC controller classes to obtain data and manipulate it, as needed. In the next recipe, you learn more about MVC controller classes.

Solution #2 also shows how to use entity classes for mapping Java object to database tables, but instead use RESTful service classes to obtain the data. The solution demonstrates how to create the RESTful web services that will provide the data, and it also shows how to create a JAX-RS client service class that can be used to call upon the RESTful web services to obtain data. Most likely with these two JAX-RS solutions, the JAX-RS web service and the JAX-RS client will not be part of the same application. Typically, one application or microservice will obtain the data from the database and provide it to other consumers via the JAX-RS web service, and other applications or microservices will act as consumers, using JAX-RS clients to obtain the data from the web service. I only demonstrated both the web service and the client in this application for the purposes of demonstration.

Since Chapter 16 covers RESTful web services in entirety, I will point you to that chapter for more information. Let's focus on how we can glean the data from the web services using a JAX-RS client for our MVC application. Typically, an MVC controller (see the next recipe) will call upon the JAX-RS client to obtain the data for the application. In Solution #2, a simple client is created to obtain the list of `BookAuthor` entities from the web service and load them into a local List. The `BookAuthorService` class is a session scoped CDI bean, so it is annotated with `@SessionScoped` (`javax.enterprise.context.SessionScoped`). Since this class may need to be saved to disk to save the session data, it must be made serializable. Next, declare a `javax.ws.rs.client.Client` and a `List<BookAuthor>` so that the client can be created and the list of `BookAuthor` objects can be stored in the session. The class should create the client and load the data when the bean is created, so one of the methods should be annotated with `@PostConstruct` so that it is automatically invoked upon bean construction.

In this case, the `init()` method is invoked upon construction, allowing the client to make a RESTful service call to the `org.javaee8recipes.bookstore.entity.bookauthor` web service to obtain all of the records and store them into the `bookAuthorList`.

Although this recipe does not directly pertain to the MVC application methodology, it is an important piece of the puzzle for obtaining data for use with the application. In the next recipe, I dive directly into the MVC controller class, which is the heart of the business logic for an MVC application.

6-3. Writing a Controller Class

Problem

You would like to orchestrate the navigation and business logic for an MVC application.

Solution

Develop MVC controller classes to provide the business logic and navigation logic behind the application. To get started, create a new package in which to store the controllers for the application. In this example, I've named the package `org.javaee8recipes.bookstore.controller`. Also create a package to hold classes that will be used as objects for transporting data within the application. Name this package `org.javaee8recipes.bookstore.container`. Before the controller class can be created, a container needs to be created within the newly created `org.javaee8recipes.bookstore.container` package. Name it `BookAuthorContainer`. This class is merely a `SessionScoped` CDI bean that will be used to hold instances of the `BookAuthor` objects and expose them to the web views of the application. The sources for `BookAuthorContainer` should look as follows:

```
package org.javaee8recipes.bookstore.container;

import java.util.List;
import javax.enterprise.context.SessionScoped;
import javax.inject.Inject;
import javax.inject.Named;
import org.javaee8recipes.bookstore.entity.BookAuthor;

@Named
@SessionScoped
public class BookAuthorContainer implements java.io.Serializable {

    private BookAuthor bookAuthor;

    private List<BookAuthor> bookAuthorList;

    public BookAuthorContainer(){

    }

    public BookAuthor getBookAuthor() {
        return bookAuthor;
    }

    public void setBookAuthor(BookAuthor bookAuthor) {
        this.bookAuthor = bookAuthor;
    }

    public List<BookAuthor> getBookAuthorList() {
        return bookAuthorList;
    }
```

```
    public void setBookAuthorList(List<BookAuthor> bookAuthorList) {
        this.bookAuthorList = bookAuthorList;
    }

}
```

Next, create a class named BookAuthorController inside of the `org.javaee8recipes.bookstore.controller` package and annotate the controller class with the `@Path("/bookAuthor")` and `@Controller` annotations. Next, create a public method with a return type of `String` and name it `loadBookAuthors`, accepting no arguments. Annotate the method with `@GET` and within this method query data for loading the BookAuthor list, and return a string of `"bookAuthor.jsp"`. The following sources show the code for the BookAuthorController class.

```
import java.util.List;
import javax.inject.Inject;
import javax.ws.rs.Path;
import javax.mvc.annotation.Controller;
import javax.ws.rs.GET;
import org.javaee8recipes.bookstore.entity.BookAuthor;
import org.javaee8recipes.bookstore.service.BookAuthorService;

@Path("/bookAuthor")
@Controller()
public class BookAuthorController {

    @Inject
    private BookAuthorService bookAuthorService;

    public BookAuthorController(){
    }

    @GET
    public String getBookAuthors(){
        // obtain list of authors
        return "bookAuthor.jsp";
    }
}
```

If a URI containing the path indicated by the `@Path` annotation is loaded, the `bookAuthor.jsp` view will be loaded.

How It Works

An MVC controller class is used to bind business logic to the view and process requests and responses. Controller classes are CDI controllers that contain a number of JAX-RS annotations, as the MVC controller façade is based on the JAX-RS API. Every controller class is indicated as such via the `javax.mvc.annotation.Controller` annotation. The `javax.ws.rs.Path` annotation is applied at the controller class level to indicate which URI will be used to access controller class methods via the web application. For instance, this controller class can be accessible via a URI matching the following format since there is only one method:

```
http://<<hostname>>:<<port>>/BookStore/bookAuthor/
```

It is important to note that the controller class is annotated like a JAX-RS class. Controllers in the MVC framework are implemented using the same annotations that are used to implement a JAX-RS RESTful web service class. That said, when the URI is used to access the application, the BookAuthor CDI controller is invoked due to the application path being /BookStore/, and the matching @Path annotation specifying /bookAuthor as the matching path. When invoked, the GET requests are handled by the getBookAuthors() method, as it is annotated with @GET without a specified path. The @GET annotation is used indicate an HTTP GET method. Since this particular controller only has one controller method annotated with @GET, the default path is going to invoke the single method. If there were more than one method in the controller, each method would also need to be annotated with @Path to indicate the sub-path to invoke each method in turn. An MVC controller should utilize other HTTP methods such as @PUT and @POST for inserting or updating records in a database.

In the example, when the getBookAuthors() method is invoked, the BookAuthorService is called upon, invoking the getBookAuthorList() method and loading the local bookAuthors list. Next, load data into a list that will be accessible via the view. The data loading processes are omitted from this recipe, but they are covered in greater detail in Recipe 6-4.

The last important detail to note is that the return value from the getBookAuthorList() method is the next view that will be rendered when the response is returned. The default return type for a Controller method is Text/HTML, but that can be changed via the @Produces annotation. A string returned from a controller method is the view path. In this case, the bookAuthor.jsp view is next to be loaded. It is possible to provide navigation to the next view in a number of different ways, and returning the name of the next view is the first technique.

A controller method can also have a return type of void, and in such cases the method must be annotated with @View("returnViewName"). As seen here, the string-based view name is passed as an attribute to the annotation. This technique makes it easy to differentiate navigational logic from business logic.

```
@GET
@View("bookAuthor.jsp")
public void getBookAuthors(){
    //obtain authors
}
```

The next technique involves returning a Viewable, which would look like the following lines of code. A Viewable provides flexibility, especially when you want to implement a non-standard view engine.

```
@GET
public Viewable getBookAuthors(){
    //obtain authors
    return new Viewable("bookAuthor.jsp");
}
```

The final technique for controlling navigation is to return a JAX-RS Response object, which provides a lot of information since it can include different response codes depending on certain situations.

```
@GET
public Response getBookAuthors(){
    // obtain authors
    return Response.status(Response.Status.OK).entity("bookAuthor.jsp").build();
}
```

As mentioned previously, MVC controller classes are very much the same as JAX-RS web service classes, in that they use common annotations. In the example, the controller class is utilized as an MVC controller only, but it is possible for a controller class to become a hybrid class, which also contains JAX-RS methods. To do this, move the `@Controller` annotation to each MVC method, rather than at the class level itself. The `javax.mvc.annotation.View` annotation can also be applied at either class or method level. As mentioned previously, it points to the view for the controller method.

The MVC controller method defines the business logic for an MVC application. Controllers utilize JAX-RS annotations and provide plumbing for the request response lifecycle. Lastly, controllers are responsible for returning responses including data to application views.

6-4. Using a Model to Expose Data to a View

Problem

You want to obtain data from a datasource and make it available for use within an application view.

Solution

Inject and use the Models API from within your controller class. In the following example, the method `getBookAuthors()`, which is invoked when the URI path to the controller is accessed, obtains data from a web service (see Recipe 6-2 for more information) and populates data for use in a view using a model.

```
import java.util.List;
import javax.inject.Inject;
import javax.mvc.Models;
import javax.ws.rs.Path;
import javax.mvc.annotation.Controller;
import javax.ws.rs.GET;
import org.javaee8recipes.bookstore.entity.BookAuthor;
import org.javaee8recipes.bookstore.service.BookAuthorService;

@Path("/bookAuthor")
@Controller()
public class BookAuthorController {

    @Inject
    private Models models;

    @Inject
    private BookAuthorService bookAuthorService;

    public BookAuthorController(){
    }

    @GET
    public String getBookAuthors(){
        List<BookAuthor> bookAuthors = bookAuthorService.getBookAuthorList();
        models.put("bookauthors", bookAuthors);
        return "bookAuthor.jsp";
    }
}
```

The JSP view markup that is contained within the bookAuthor.jsp JSP view looks like the following:

```
<%@ page contentType="text/html;charset=UTF-8" language="java" %>
<%@ taglib prefix="c" uri="http://java.sun.com/jsp/jstl/core" %>
<!DOCTYPE html>
<html>
    <head>
        <meta http-equiv="Content-Type" content="text/html; charset=UTF-8">
        <title>Example of MVC Using JSP for View</title>
    </head>
    <body>
        <h1>Book Authors</h1>
        <table class="table table-striped">
                <colgroup>
                    <col style="width: 80%;" />
                </colgroup>
                <thead>
                    <tr>
                        <th class="text-left">Author</th>
                    </tr>
                </thead>
                <tbody>
                    <c:forEach var="bookAuthor" items="${bookauthors}">
                        <tr>

                            <td class="text-center">
                                ${bookAuthor.last}
                            </td>

                        </tr>
                    </c:forEach>
                </tbody>
            </table>
    </body>
</html>
```

Given the sample dataset, the results of the simple view will look like that in Figure 6-4.

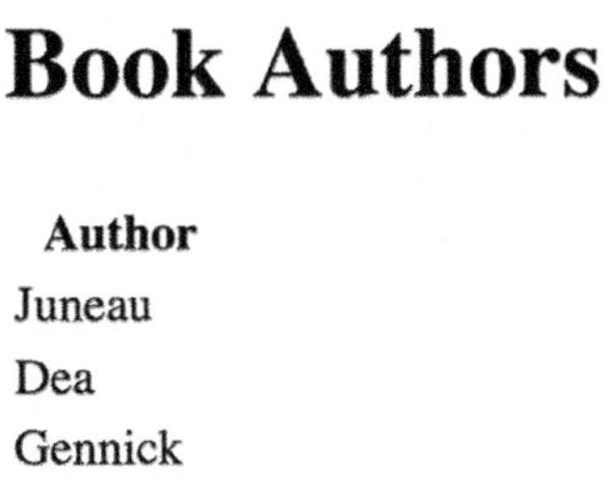

Book Authors

Author

Juneau

Dea

Gennick

Figure 6-4. *Example of bookAuthor.jsp results*

How It Works

The Models API must be included in every implementation of the MVC framework. Essentially, the Models API provides a `javax.mvc.Models` map, which is used to store a dataset with a key identifier as a key/value pair that is exposed to the next rendered view. The `HashMap` for the Models API adheres to the following format:

```
Map<String, Object> model = new HashMap<String, Object>();
```

In the example, the Models map is injected into the controller class using CDI `@Inject`. Once injected, the model can be used to store data for exposure. A `List<BookAuthor>` is placed into the Models map as follows:

```
models.put("bookauthors", bookAuthors);
```

The model is exposed to the view via the `bookauthors` key. In the example JSP view, the `${bookauthors}` expression is used within a JSTL `c:if` tag to display the records in a table.

```
<c:forEach var="bookAuthor" items="${bookauthors}">
    <tr>

        <td class="text-center">
            ${bookAuthor.last}
        </td>

    </tr>
</c:forEach>
```

Every implementation of the MVC framework must include the Models API. As seen in the example, the API is very easy to utilize. However, it is not the preferred method for exposing data, as CDI is preferred. Recipe 6-5 delves into utilizing CDI beans for exposing data.

6-5. Utilizing CDI for Exposing Data

Problem

You are interested in exposing data from a controller into a view, but you prefer not use the MVC Models to do so. Instead, you'd like to harness the power of CDI to expose data to views.

Solution

Utilize CDI models to return data to the view. The use of CDI is the preferred technique for exposing data to views. In this recipe, a CDI bean is injected into the controller, and then it is utilized to store data. This CDI bean is session scoped, so the data that is placed within the bean will last the entire web session. The following code is that of the CDI bean used to expose the data:

```
import java.util.List;
import javax.enterprise.context.SessionScoped;
import javax.inject.Named;
import org.javaee8recipes.bookstore.entity.Book;
```

```
@Named
@SessionScoped
public class BookContainer implements java.io.Serializable {

    private Book book;

    private List<Book> bookList;

    public BookContainer(){

    }

    public Book getBook() {
        return book;
    }

    public void setBook(Book book) {
        this.book = book;
    }

    public List<Book> getBookList() {
        return bookList;
    }

    public void setBookList(List<Book> bookList) {
        this.bookList = bookList;
    }
}
```

Next, the controller class utilizes the CDI bean to store data and make it available to the view.

```
@Path("/book")
@Controller()
public class BookController {
    @Inject
    private BookContainer bookContainer;

    public BookController() {
    }

    /**
     * Queries all books using the <code>BookService</code>
     * and returns to the <code>book.jsp</code> JSP page.
     * @return
     */
    @GET
    public String getBooks(){
        Book book = new Book();
        book.setTitle("Java EE 8 Recipes");
        bookContainer.setBook(book);
        return "book.jsp";
}
```

The following markup is that of the book.jsp view. As you can see from the example, the view simply displays the name of the book that was loaded into the CDI bean.

```
<%@page contentType="text/html" pageEncoding="UTF-8"%>
<!DOCTYPE html>
<html>
    <head>
        <meta http-equiv="Content-Type" content="text/html; charset=UTF-8">
        <title>Java EE 8 Recipes: Recipe 6-5</title>
    </head>
    <body>
        <h1>Book List</h1>
        The book that was loaded in BookController:  ${bookContainer.book.title}
    </body>
</html>
```

How It Works

The preferred technique for exposing data to the web views of an MVC application is to utilize Contexts and Dependency Injection (CDI) beans. CDI is a specification that binds many of the Java EE technologies together. CDI is a large specification that includes many details, but in-depth explanations of the specification are out of scope for this recipe. For more details on CDI, refer to Chapter 13. One of the functions of CDI is to wire beans together, effectively making it possible for data and scope to be shared between classes and between the backend and front-facing views of an application.

For the purposes of the MVC framework, one of the core focuses is the ability to share contextual objects between the backend code and the frontend views. In this simple example, the CDI bean is merely a SessionScoped container named BookContainer. As shown in the code, the BookContainer class is annotated with @Named, which marks the class as a CDI bean and makes it available for injection into other classes using the class name with the first letter in lowercase. In this case, the bean will be injectable via the name bookContainer. The @Named annotation does accept a string-based alias, which can be used to call upon the class at injection time from a view. The BookContainer class is also annotated with @SessionScoped, which defines the scope of the bean. The other available scope possibilities are @RequestScoped, @ApplicationScoped, and @ConversationScoped.

The BookController utilizes a contextual proxy to the bean by injecting an instance of it using the @Inject annotation. The bean is used within the getBooks() method, as it accepts a Book instance for which the title and description have been populated. It is also possible to define different class fields within the CDI bean and populate them with data directly to expose it to a view or other class. Once the data has been populated, the BookController bean can be accessed from a view using expression language, or the same instance of the bean can be injected into another class and made accessible. In this example, the controller method getBooks() simply returns the name of the next view to be loaded, books.jsp. The books.jsp JSP view accesses the title of the book by referring to the bean via the injection name ${bookController.book.title}.

CDI can be very powerful for managing contextual instances of classes within a Java EE application. Using CDI to expose data to a view within an MVC application brings forth the same functionality as the use of the Models API, and it also allows data to be utilized in other classes, if needed.

6-6. Supplying Message Feedback to the User

Problem

You want to display feedback to a user after a transaction occurs.

Solution

Utilize CDI beans to easily provide feedback to users in the form of messages displayed on-screen. In the following scenario, all books in a bookstore are loaded and displayed in the `book.jsp` view. A `RequestScoped` CDI bean entitled `Messages` is used to encapsulate the logic for storing informative or error messages. In the controller class, a message indicating the number of books that are loaded is set into the bean using the info field. This bean is then available for display in the view.

First, here is a look at the CDI bean named `Messages`:

```
import javax.enterprise.context.RequestScoped;
import javax.inject.Named;
import java.util.ArrayList;
import java.util.Collections;
import java.util.List;

/**
 * This class encapsulates messages displayed to the users. There can be a
 * single info message and multiple error messages. Controllers can use this
 * class to queue messages for rendering. The class shows how named CDI beans
 * can be used as a model for the view. Whether to to include some class like
 * this in the spec is not decided yet.
 */
@Named
@RequestScoped
public class Messages {

  private String info;

  private final List<String> errors = new ArrayList<>();

  public Messages addError(String error) {
    errors.add(error);
    return this;
  }

  public List<String> getErrors() {
    return Collections.unmodifiableList(errors);
  }

  public String getInfo() {
    return info;
  }
```

```
  public void setInfo(String info) {
    this.info = info;
  }

}
```

The code for the controller class used to load the book listing and provide the message is as follows:

```
@Inject
private Messages messages;
. . .
@GET
@Path("/books")
public String displayBookListing() {
    bookList = bookService.getBookList();
    bookContainer.setBookList(bookList);
    messages.setInfo("There are " + bookList.size() + " books in the library.");
    return "book.jsp";
}
```

The subsequent book.jsp view markup is as follows:

```
<%@page contentType="text/html" pageEncoding="UTF-8"%>
<!DOCTYPE html>
<html>
    <head>
        <meta http-equiv="Content-Type" content="text/html; charset=UTF-8">
        <link href="${pageContext.request.contextPath}/webjars/bootstrap/3.3.4/dist/css/
        bootstrap.css" rel="stylesheet">
        <script src="${pageContext.request.contextPath}/webjars/bootstrap/3.3.4/dist/js/
        bootstrap.js"></script>
        <title>Java EE 8 Recipes</title>
    </head>
    <body>
        <h1>Book List</h1>
        The book that was loaded in BookController:  ${bookContainer.book.title}
        <br/><br/>
        <c:if test="${messages.info != null}">
                <div class="alert alert-success" role="alert">
                    ${messages.info}
                </div>
            </c:if>
            <c:if test="${not empty messages.errors}">
                <div class="alert alert-danger" role="alert">
                    <ul class="list-unstyled">
                        <c:forEach var="error" items="${messages.errors}">
                            <li>${error}</li>
                            </c:forEach>
                    </ul>
                </div>
            </c:if>
        <br/>
```

```
        <table class="table table-striped">
                <colgroup>
                    <col style="width: 80%;" />
                </colgroup>
                <thead>
                    <tr>
                        <th class="text-left">Book</th>
                    </tr>
                </thead>
                <tbody>
                <c:forEach var="book" items="${bookContainer.bookList}">
                        <tr>

                            <td class="text-center">
                                ${book.title}
                            </td>

                        </tr>
                    </c:forEach>
                </tbody>
            </table>
  </body>
</html>
```

How It Works

CDI beans can be leveraged to easily display messages from a controller. As seen in Recipe 6-5, the CDI bean can be injected into a controller class, data can be set into the controller, and then it can be made available in subsequent views. In the example for this recipe, a message containing the number of books within the `bookList` is created as a string, and then it is assigned to the info field of the `Messages` bean.

```
messages.setInfo("There are " + bookList.size() + " books in the library.");
```

When the `book.jsp` view is loaded, the message is displayed within the view using expression language in the `${messages.info}` format. In the view, a `<c:if>` tag is used to conditionally display the informative message if it exists, or the error message exists then it will be displayed instead. If users are seeing an error message, it usually helps to have that message stand out in red text, or bold text. If a user is seeing helpful information in a message, it may be helpful to see that message in green text or something of the like. In such cases, the MVC framework can leverage existing JavaScript APIs to provide appropriate message formatting. The example utilizes the Bootstrap JavaScript library to display messages nicely depending on type (see Figure 6-5).

Book Listing

There are 2 books in the library.

Book

Java 9 Recipes

Java EE 7 Recipes

Figure 6-5. *Messages displayed nicely using Bootstrap*

6-7. Inserting and Updating Data

Problem

You want to utilize a form to insert or update data.

Solution

Create controller methods that are annotated with @PUT or @POST, depending on whether the methods will be utilized for inserting or updating, respectively. The following markup, excerpted from book.jsp, contains a form that is used to create a new book record. Make note that in the following example, that the action invoked upon submit will initiate the RESTful web service that contains the "/create" path.

```
<form action="${pageContext.request.contextPath}/bookstore/book/create" method="POST"
class="form-inline">
                 <div class="panel panel-default">
                    <div class="panel-heading">
                        <h3 class="panel-title">Book Information</h3>
                    </div>
                    <div class="panel-body">
                        <div class="form-group">
                            <label for="subject">Title</label>
                            <input type="text" class="form-control" id="title" name="title"
                            placeholder="Title"
                                   value="${book.title}" autofocus>
                        </div>

                    </div>
                </div>

                <br/><br/>
                <div class="form-group">
                    <label for="description">Description:</label>
                    <br/>
                    <textarea cols="100" rows="4" class="form-control" id="description"
                    name="description" placeholder="Description">
```

```
                    ${book.description}
                </textarea>
            </div>
            <br/><br/>
            <button type="submit" class="btn btn-primary">Create</button>
        </form>
```

The submit action in the form invokes the controller method named `createItem()`, which obtains data that was submitted via a form and utilizes JAX-RS to insert into the database.

```
@POST
@Path("/create")
@Controller
public String createItem(@BeanParam @Valid Book form) {
    // Create new book

    // Obtain issue list to count records for ID population
    bookList = bookService.getBookList();
    form.setId(new BigDecimal(bookList.size() + 1));
    Book entity = new Book();
    entity.setId(form.getId());
    entity.setTitle(form.getTitle());
    entity.setDescription(form.getDescription());

    bookService.create(entity);

    return displayBookListing();
}
```

Once the method has been executed, the book listing is refreshed because the final line of `createItem()` invokes `displayBookListing()`, which executes the code as follows:

```
@GET
@Path("/books")
public String displayBookListing() {
    bookList = bookService.getBookList();
    bookContainer.setBookList(bookList);
    messages.setInfo("There are " + bookList.size() + " books in the library.");
    System.out.println("Issue count: " + bookList.size());
    return "book.jsp";
}
```

The resulting view, `book.jsp`, will display the newly created book in the listing of books, as seen in the previous recipe in Figure 6-1.

How It Works

The overall mantra of the MVC framework is complete control and ease of use. This example demonstrates exactly those ideals, as it demonstrates how the entire request-processing lifecycle is handled by the developer, and the framework makes it easy to achieve. In order to create or update data, an HTML form is used to submit form data to a controller method. In this case, the form is written in JSP markup, and the submit action invokes a RESTful controller method entitled createItem(). The createItem() method contains a signature that returns a string for the next view to render after completion, and it accepts a parameter of type Book. Note that the parameter is annotated with @BeanParam and @Valid. The @BeanParam annotation indicates that the Book class contains some form parameter annotations to specify for fields. Specifically in this case, the Book entity class contains the following:

```
public class Book implements Serializable {
    private static final long serialVersionUID = 1L;
    // @Max(value=?)  @Min(value=?)//if you know range of your decimal fields consider using
    these annotations to enforce field validation
    @Id
    @GeneratedValue(strategy = GenerationType.SEQUENCE,
            generator = "book_s_generator")
    @SequenceGenerator(name = "book_s_generator", sequenceName = "book_s", allocationSize = 1)
    @Basic(optional = false)
   // @NotNull
    @Column(name = "ID")
    private BigDecimal id;
    //@Size(max = 150)
    @FormParam(value="title")
    @Column(name = "TITLE")
    protected String title;
    //@Size(max = 500)
    @Column(name = "IMAGE")
    private String image;
    @FormParam(value="description")
    @Lob
    @Column(name = "DESCRIPTION")
    private String description;
```

Therefore, the @BeanParam annotation will introspect the Book object for injection annotations and set it appropriately. The @Valid annotation, which indicates that bean validation processing, should be invoked for this object. At method invocation time (form submit), the bean validation will take place and help to prevent erroneous data from being submitted.

Once initiated, the book listing is obtained from the BookService, which will be used to count the number of books. This number is used to increment a number to produce the primary key for the new record being created. The new Book entity is then created, values are set accordingly, and then the create() method is called to persist the data. Once persisted, the database is queried again via the call to displayBookListing(), and then the response is returned and the book.jsp view is displayed.

6-8. Applying a Different View Engine

Problem

Rather than utilizing a standard MVC view engine, you'd like to use another view type that is either already supported or not yet officially supported.

Solution #1

Use another view engine that has already been implemented for the MVC framework. There have been many different view engines already generated that are ready for use, and this example demonstrates Facelets. Since Facelets ships with MVC 1.0, it is easy to add to a project. In order to do so, modify the `web.xml` to contain the Faces servlet mapping by adding the following:

```
 <servlet>
    <servlet-name>Faces Servlet</servlet-name>
    <servlet-class>javax.faces.webapp.FacesServlet</servlet-class>
    <load-on-startup>1</load-on-startup>
</servlet>
<servlet-mapping>
    <servlet-name>Faces Servlet</servlet-name>
    <url-pattern>*.xhtml</url-pattern>
</servlet-mapping>
```

Next, simply use the `.xhtml` views within the application. The following method in `BookController` sends a response to `hello.xhtml`, which is written in Facelets.

```
<?xml version="1.0" encoding="UTF-8"?>
<!DOCTYPE html PUBLIC "-//W3C//DTD XHTML 1.0 Transitional//EN" "http://www.w3.org/TR/xhtml1/
DTD/xhtml1-transitional.dtd">
<html xmlns="http://www.w3.org/1999/xhtml"
      xmlns:h="http://xmlns.jcp.org/jsf/html"
      xmlns:c="http://java.sun.com/jsp/jstl/core">
    <h:head>
        <title>Facelets View</title>
        <meta name="viewport" content="width=device-width, initial-scale=1.0"/>
    </h:head>
    <h:body>
        <h:dataTable var="book" value="#{bookContainer.bookList}">
            <h:column>
                ${book.title}
            </h:column>
        </h:dataTable>
    </h:body>
</html>
```

Solution #2

Generate a new view engine by implementing the `javax.mvc.ViewEngine` interface and incorporating logic to load and process the views of your choice. A `ViewEngine` is responsible for finding and loading views for an application, preparing models, and rendering views to return control to the client. In the following code, a `ViewEngine` has been implemented for the Pebble templating engine (`http://www.mitchellbosecke.com/pebble/home`).

```
package org.javaee8recipes.bookstore.engine;

import com.mitchellbosecke.pebble.PebbleEngine;
import com.mitchellbosecke.pebble.error.PebbleException;
```

```
import com.mitchellbosecke.pebble.template.PebbleTemplate;
import java.io.IOException;
import java.io.StringWriter;
import java.io.Writer;
import java.net.URL;
import javax.enterprise.context.ApplicationScoped;
import javax.inject.Inject;
import javax.mvc.engine.ViewEngine;
import javax.mvc.engine.ViewEngineContext;
import javax.mvc.engine.ViewEngineException;
import javax.servlet.ServletContext;

@ApplicationScoped
public class PebbleViewEngine implements ViewEngine {

    @Inject
    private ServletContext servletContext;

    @Override
    public boolean supports(String view) {
        return view.endsWith(".html");
    }

    @Override
    public void processView(ViewEngineContext context) throws ViewEngineException {

        try {

            String viewName = "/WEB-INF/views/" + context.getView();
            URL template = servletContext.getResource(viewName);

            PebbleEngine engine = new PebbleEngine.Builder()
                    .loader(new ServletLoader(servletContext)).build();

            PebbleTemplate compiledTemplate = engine.getTemplate(viewName);

            Writer writer = new StringWriter();

            compiledTemplate.evaluate(writer, context.getModels());

            context.getResponse().getWriter().write(writer.toString());

        } catch (IOException|PebbleException e) {
            throw new IllegalStateException(e);
        }

    }
}
```

Once the ViewEngine is created, simply begin generating views (or templates) using the markup for your view engine. The following sources are taken from the simple view pebbleTest.html:

```
<!DOCTYPE html>
<html>
        <head>
                <title>{{ websiteTitle }}</title>
        </head>
        <body>
                {{ content }}
        </body>
</html>
```

How It Works

The MVC framework is very flexible, allowing the developer to customize just about any functionality. One area where this comes in very handy is the choice of view (template) engine. Utilizing the ViewEngine interface, a developer can easily create a new ViewEngine to support just about any templating engine available. There are also a number of template engines that have already been implemented, supporting many of the most well-known templating engines in use. For example, there are engines available for download from Maven Central (http://search.maven.org/#search%7Cga%7C1%7Cg%3A%22com.oracle.ozark.ext%22), including the following:

- Thymeleaf
- Apache Velocity
- Mustache
- Handlebars
- Freemarker

In order to utilize one or more of these engines (yes, you can use more than one in a single application), download the artifact from Maven Central and include in your project. Then you can simply begin using the template engine of your choice, so long as the template pages adhere to the format that is specified within the ViewEngine implementation. In Solution #1, the Facelets view engine is used by simply modifying the web.xml to include a mapping to the Faces servlet when a view file containing the suffix of .xhtml is loaded. The ViewEngine implementation for Facelets is automatically invoked when views containing that suffix are loaded, so no additional configuration is needed.

If you're interested in creating a new custom view engine, simply implement the ViewEngine interface. In Solution #2, a ViewEngine implementation for the Pebble templating engine is created. To implement this interface, you must override two methods, supports() and processView(). The supports() method is used to determine the path or file extension that must be supported by this engine. In this case, any file with the .html suffix will utilize the PebbleViewEngine. The processView() method is where much of the customization will occur, as this is where each view engine will perform customized processing in order to render the view.

In this example, the view name is first determined by calling upon the `context.getView()` method and appending the returned name to the String based view path. Next, the `PebbleEngine` is created by utilizing the `PebbleEngine` builder API to load the injected `ServletContext`. This essentially allows the `PebbleEngine` to gain access to the views within the application. Once created, the engine is used to compile the currently visited view, returning a `PebbleTemplate`. Finally, the compiled template is evaluated using a `StringWriter` and passing in any Model values from the `ViewEngineContext`. Therefore, if anything has been loaded into via the Models API in the controller, then it is evaluated at this time and merged with the view. Lastly, the response writer is used to render the view.

The MVC framework makes it very easy to leverage different templating engines, making it a great choice for use with teams that have frontend developers familiar with different engines. Not only is it easy to swap different engines into applications where it makes sense, but it provides the flexibility to choose the one that suits your team and your project the best.

CHAPTER 7

JDBC

The Java Database Connectivity (JDBC) API is a standard for accessing relational database management systems (RDBMSs) via Java. It has been in use for years and can be used when developing all types of Java applications, including desktop, stand-alone, and web. Almost every nontrivial application utilizes an RDBMS for storing and retrieving data. Therefore, it is important for application developers of all types to learn how to work with JDBC.

Enterprise application development has proven to be more productive for developers when working directly with Java objects as opposed to database access. While the JDBC API is still very mainstream for the development of enterprise applications, many developers have begun to adopt object-relational mapping programming interfaces as a standard. One of the easiest ways to map Java objects to database tables is to encapsulate JDBC logic into classes containing private methods for performing database access and exposing those methods using public methods that work with objects instead of SQL. This chapter contains recipes to demonstrate the technique of abstracting JDBC logic from ordinary business logic, sometimes referred to as creating data access objects.

The JDBC 4.2 release, included with Java SE 8, introduced some new features into the JDBC API to make working with databases a bit easier, and this chapter includes a recipe that covers one of those new features as well, which is the use of the `REF_CURSOR`. For a full list of the new features and enhancements with the JDBC 4.2 release, visit the online documentation at `http://docs.oracle.com/javase/8/docs/technotes/guides/jdbc/jdbc_42.html`. After reviewing the recipes included in this chapter, you should be comfortable using JDBC in your Java web applications.

Note The Acme Bookstore application has been completely rewritten for this chapter in order to utilize an Oracle database rather than simple Java lists of data. Run the `create_database.sql` script in your database prior to working with the examples from this chapter. Also, you need to provide the necessary database connection properties for your database in the `db_props.properties` file and/or in the code examples for this chapter. If you are utilizing another database vendor, you should be able to adjust the SQL accordingly to work with that database. To access the Acme Bookstore application utilizing the database, be sure to deploy the JavaEE8Recipes web application to your GlassFish or Payara application server and visit the URL `http://localhost:8080/JavaEE8Recipes/faces/chapter07/home.xhtml`. This chapter will typically reference GlassFish server, although most of the references will be the same for Payara server.

J. Juneau, *Java EE 8 Recipes*, https://doi.org/10.1007/978-1-4842-3594-2_7

7-1. Obtaining Database Drivers and Adding Them to the CLASSPATH

Problem

You need to have the ability to utilize a database from your application, so you need to obtain drivers and configure the databases for your application.

Solution

Download the appropriate drivers for the database that you will be working with and add them to the CLASSPATH for your application. In this solution, I assume you are going to develop an enterprise-level web application and deploy it to the GlassFish application server. The application will utilize Oracle Database for persistence. In this case, you need to download the most current Oracle database driver for Java Database Connectivity (JDBC). At the time of this writing, the driver is `ojdbc8.jar`, but you can find the latest online at `http://www.oracle.com/technetwork/indexes/downloads/index.html`. The driver for your application may be different, depending on which database you plan to use. For instance, to work with a PostgreSQL database, you need to download the driver from the location `https://jdbc.postgresql.org/`.

Once you have downloaded the required drivers for your database, add them to the application CLASSPATH. If you're using an IDE, you can adjust the project properties for your application project accordingly to include the JAR that contains your database driver. If you are working from the command line or terminal, you can add the driver to your CLASSPATH by issuing one of the following commands, depending upon the OS platform you are using.

Use the following on UNIX-based systems or OS X:

```
export CLASSPATH=/path-to-jar/ojdbc8.jar
```

Use the following on Windows:

```
set CLASSPATH=C:\path-to-jar\ojdbc8.jar
```

You should now be able to work with the database from your application, but in order to deploy to the GlassFish application server, you need to make the database driver available for GlassFish. You can do this by copying the JAR containing the database driver into the GlassFish `lib` directory. The database driver JAR should be placed in a domain rather than at the application server level. Therefore, if your domain is named `domain1` (the default), then the path to where the JAR should be placed would be as follows:

```
/GlassFish_Home/glassfish4/glassfish/domains/domain1/lib/databases
```

Restart the application server instance, and you are ready to deploy your database application.

How It Works

The first step to working with any database from an application is to configure the database driver for the specific vendor of your choice. Whether you decide to use MySQL, PostgreSQL, Oracle, Microsoft SQL, or another database, most enterprise-level databases have a JDBC driver available. This driver must be added to the application CLASSPATH and integrated development environment (IDE) project CLASSPATH if you're using one. If working from the command line or terminal, you need to set the CLASSPATH each time you open a new session. If you're using an IDE, your settings can usually be saved so that you need to configure them only one time. After the driver for your database has been added to the application or project CLASSPATH, you are ready to begin working with the database.

When it comes time to deploy the application to a server, you need to ensure that the server has access to the database driver. You can simply add the driver JAR for your database to the domain's lib directory and restart the server. Once you've done this, then you can either deploy your JDBC-based application or set up a database connection pool for your database. See Recipe 7-2 for more information on how to connect to your database from within an application using standard JDBC connectivity or how to set up a JDBC connection pool via the GlassFish application server.

7-2. Connecting to a Database

Problem

You need to connect to a database so that your application can perform database transactions.

Solution #1

Perform a JDBC connection to the database from within your application. Do this by creating a new Connection object and then loading the driver that you need to use for your particular database. Once the Connection object is ready, call its getConnection() method. The following code demonstrates how to obtain a connection to an Oracle database:

```
public final static class OracleConnection {

    private String hostname = "myHost";
    private String port = "1521";
    private String database = "myDatabase";
    private String username = "user";
    private String password = "password";

    public static Connection getConnection() throws SQLException {
        Connection conn = null;
        String jdbcUrl = "jdbc:oracle:thin:@" + this.hostname + ":"
                + this.port + ":" + this.database;
        conn = DriverManager.getConnection(jdbcUrl, username, password);
        System.out.println("Successfully connected");
        return conn;
    }
}
```

The method portrayed in this example returns a Connection object that is ready to be used for database access.

Solution #2

Configure a database connection pool within an application server and connect to it from your application. Use a DataSource object to create a connection pool. The DataSource object must have been properly implemented and deployed to an application server environment. After a DataSource object has been implemented and deployed, it can be used by an application to obtain a connection to a database.

■ **Note** A *connection pool* is a cluster of identical database connections that are allocated by the application server (container-managed connection pool) to be utilized by applications for individual client sessions.

To create a connection pool using the GlassFish administrative console, first log in to the console by visiting `http://localhost:4848` (assuming you are on the same machine as the server and that your GlassFish installation is using the default port numbers). Once you have successfully logged in to the console, click the JDBC menu under Resources, and then expand the JDBC Connection Pools menu, as shown in Figure 7-1.

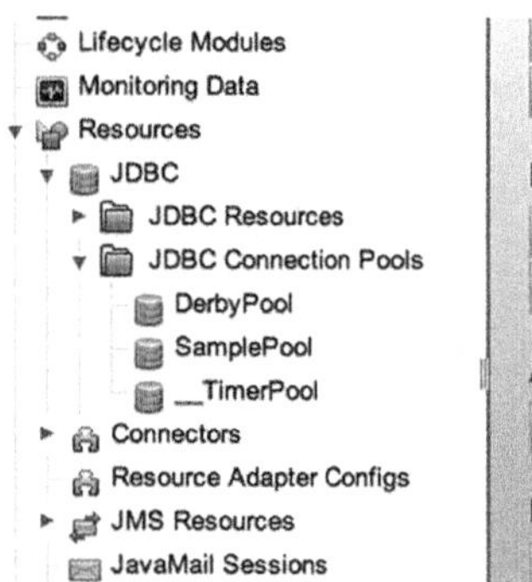

***Figure 7-1.** Displaying the JDBC Connection Pools from the GlassFish administrative console*

Click the New button on the JDBC Connection Pools screen, and it will then navigate you to the New JDBC Connection Pool (Step 1 of 2) screen. There, you can name the pool, select a resource type, and select a database driver vendor. For this example, I am using Oracle Database 11gR2. Therefore, the entries should be specified like those shown in Figure 7-2, although you could change the pool name to something you like better.

New JDBC Connection Pool (Step 1 of 2)

Identify the general settings for the connection pool.

Next Cancel

* Indicates required field

General Settings

Pool Name: * OraclePool

Resource Type:

Must be specified if the datasource class implements more than 1 of the interface.

Database Driver Vendor: Oracle

Select or enter a database driver vendor

Introspect: **Enabled**

If enabled, data source or driver implementation class names will enable introspection.

***Figure 7-2.** Creating a GlassFish JDBC connection pool*

When the next screen opens, it should automatically contain the mappings for your Oracle database `DataSource` class name as `oracle.jdbc.pool.OracleDataSource`. If it does not look like Figure 7-3, then you may not yet have the `ojdbc8.jar` database driver in the application server `lib` directory. Be sure to check the Enabled check box next to the Ping option.

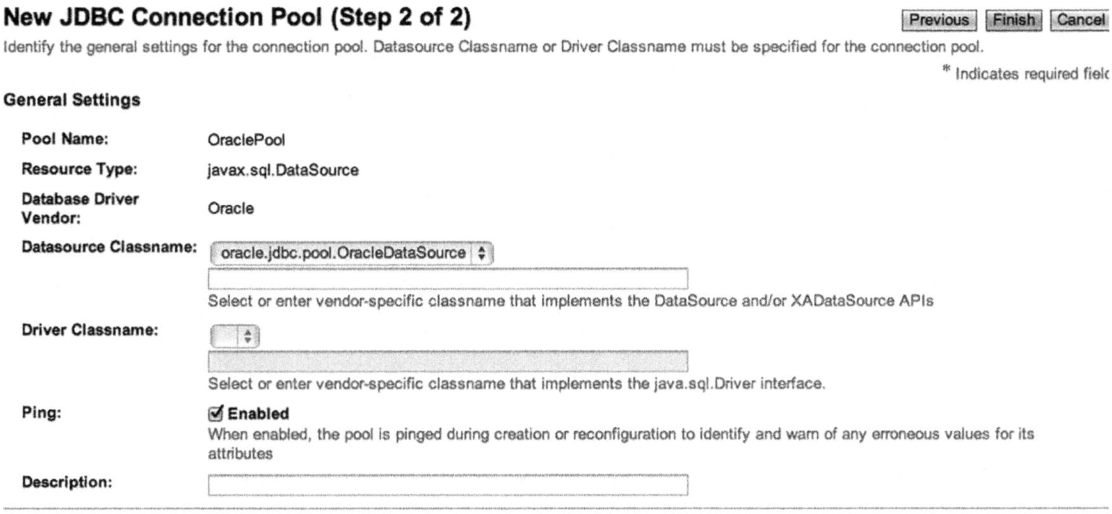

Figure 7-3. *The data source class name automatically populates*

Lastly, go down to the bottom of the second screen and check all the properties within the Additional Properties table with the exception of User, Password, and URL. Specify the information for these properties according to the database you will be connecting against, as shown in Figure 7-4. Once you populated them accordingly, click the Finish button.

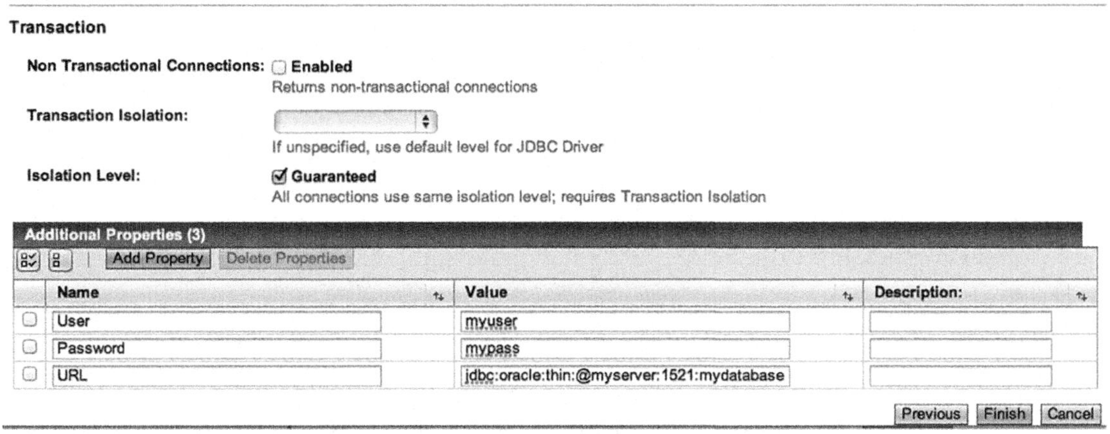

Figure 7-4. *Populating the additional properties for your database*

After clicking Finish, you should see a message indicating that the "ping" has succeeded. Now you can set up your JDBC resource by clicking the JDBC Resources menu within the left tree menu. When the JDBC Resources screen appears, click the New button. Enter a JNDI name for your resource, beginning with `jdbc/`, and then select the pool name for the database connection pool you just created. The screen should resemble Figure 7-5. Once you've populated it accordingly, click the OK button to complete the creation of the resource.

■ **Note** JNDI is the communication technology that allows applications to communicate with services by name within an application server container.

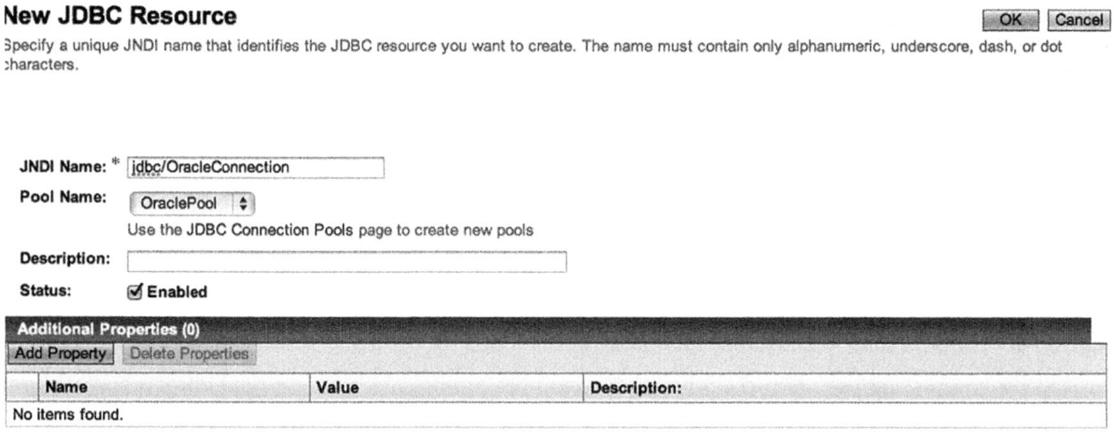

New JDBC Resource OK Cancel

Specify a unique JNDI name that identifies the JDBC resource you want to create. The name must contain only alphanumeric, underscore, dash, or dot characters.

JNDI Name: * jdbc/OracleConnection

Pool Name: OraclePool

Use the JDBC Connection Pools page to create new pools

Description:

Status: ☑ **Enabled**

Additional Properties (0)

Add Property Delete Properties

Name	Value	Description:
No items found.		

Figure 7-5. *Creating a JDBC resource*

You can use the following code to obtain a database connection via a `DataSource` object:

```
public static Connection getDSConnection() {
    Connection conn = null;
    try {
        Context ctx = new InitialContext();
        DataSource ds = (DataSource)ctx.lookup("jdbc/OracleConnection");
        conn = ds.getConnection();
    } catch (NamingException | SQLException ex) {
        ex.printStackTrace();
    }
        return conn;
 }
```

Notice that the only information required in the `DataSource` implementation is the name of a valid `DataSource` object. All the information that is required to obtain a connection with the database is managed in the application server.

How It Works

You have a couple of options for creating database connections for use within Java applications. If you are writing a stand-alone or desktop application, usually a standard JDBC connection is the best choice. However, if you're working with an enterprise-level or web-based application, DataSource objects may be the right choice. Solution #1 for this recipe covers the former option, and it is the easiest way to create a database connection in a stand-alone environment. I cover the creation of a JDBC connection via Solution #1 first.

Once you've determined which database you are going to use, you need to obtain the correct driver for the database vendor and release of your choice. See Recipe 7-1 for more information on obtaining a driver and placing it in your CLASSPATH for use. Once you have the JAR file in your application CLASSPATH, you can use a JDBC DriverManager to obtain a connection to the database. As of JDBC version 4.0, drivers that are contained within the CLASSPATH are automatically loaded into the DriverManager object. If you are using a JDBC version prior to 4.0, the driver will have to be manually loaded.

To obtain a connection to your database using the DriverManager, you need to pass a String containing the JDBC URL to it. The JDBC URL consists of the database vendor name, along with the name of the server that hosts the database, the name of the database, the database port number, and a valid database user name and password that has access to the schema you want to work with. Many times, the values used to create the JDBC URL can be obtained from a properties file so that the values can be easily changed if needed. To learn more about using a properties file to store connection values, see Recipe 7-4. The code that is used to create the JDBC URL for Solution #1 looks like the following:

```
String jdbcUrl = "jdbc:oracle:thin:@" + this.hostname + ":" +
this.port + ":" + this.database;
```

Once all the variables have been substituted into the string, it will look something like the following:

```
jdbc:oracle:thin:@hostname:1521:database
```

Once the JDBC URL has been created, it can be passed to the DriverManager.getConnection() method to obtain a java.sql.Connection object. If incorrect information has been passed to the getConnection method, a java.sql.SQLException will be thrown; otherwise, a valid Connection object will be returned.

■ **Note** The prefix of the jdbcurl connection string in the example, jdbc:oracle:thin, indicates that you will be using the Oracle drivers, which are located in the ojdbc8.jar. DriverManager makes the association.

If you're running on an application server, such as GlassFish, the preferred way to obtain a connection is to use a DataSource. To work with a DataSource object, you need to have an application server to deploy it to. Any compliant Java application server—such as Apache TomEE, GlassFish, Oracle WebLogic, or Jboss——will work. Most of the application servers contain an administrative web interface that can be used to easily deploy a DataSource object, such as demonstrated via GlassFish in Solution #2 to this recipe. However, you can manually deploy a DataSource object by using code that will look like the following:

```
org.javaee8recipes.chapter7.recipe07_02.FakeDataSourceDriver ds =
new org.javaee8recipes.chapter7.recipe07_02.FakeDataSourceDriver();
ds.setServerName("my-server");
ds.setDatabaseName("JavaEE8Recipes");
ds.setDescription("Database connection for Java EE 8 Recipes");
```

This code instantiates a new DataSource driver class, and then it sets properties based on the database you want to register. DataSource code such as that demonstrated here is typically used when registering a DataSource in an application server or with access to a JNDI server. Application servers usually do this work behind the scenes if you are using a web-based administration tool to deploy a DataSource. Most database vendors will supply a DataSource driver along with their JDBC drivers, so if the correct JAR resides within the application or server CLASSPATH, it should be recognized and available for use. Once a DataSource has been instantiated and configured, the next step is to register the DataSource with a JNDI naming service.

The following code demonstrates the registration of a DataSource with JNDI:

```
try {
    Context ctx = new InitialContext();
    DataSource ds =
    (DataSource) ctx.bind("jdbc/OracleConnection");
} catch (NamingException ex) {
    ex.printStackTrace();
}
```

Once the DataSource has been deployed, any application that has been deployed to the same application server will have access to it. The beauty of working with a DataSource object is that your application code doesn't need to know any connection information, such as user credentials, for the database; it needs to know only the name of the DataSource. By convention, the name of the DataSource begins with a jdbc/ prefix, followed by an identifier. To look up the DataSource object, an InitialContext is used. The InitialContext looks at all the DataSources available within the application server, and it returns a valid DataSource if it is found; otherwise, it will throw a java.naming.NamingException exception. In Solution #2, you can see that the InitialContext returns an object that must be cast as a DataSource.

```
Context ctx = new InitialContext();
DataSource ds = (DataSource)ctx.lookup("jdbc/OracleConnection");
```

If the DataSource is a connection pool cache, the application server will send one of the available connections in the pool when an application requests it. The following line of code returns a Connection object from the DataSource:

```
conn = ds.getConnection();
```

Of course, if no valid connection can be obtained, a java.sql.SQLException is thrown. The DataSource technique is preferred over manually specifying all details and passing to the DriverManager because database connection information is stored in only one place: the application server, not within each application. Once a valid DataSource is deployed, it can be used by many applications.

After a valid connection has been obtained by your application, it can be used to work with the database. To learn more about working with the database using a Connection object, see the recipes in this chapter regarding working with the database.

7-3. Handling Database Connection Exceptions

Problem

A database activity in your application has thrown an exception. You need to handle that SQL exception so your application does not crash.

Solution

Use a `try-catch` block to capture and handle any SQL exceptions that are thrown by your JDBC connection or SQL queries. The following code demonstrates how to implement a `try-catch` block in order to capture SQL exceptions:

```
try {
// perform database tasks
} catch (java.sql.SQLException){
// perform exception handling
}
```

How It Works

A standard `try-catch` block can be used to catch `java.sql.Connection` or `java.sql.SQLException` exceptions. Your code will not compile if these exceptions are not handled, and it is a good idea to handle them in order to prevent your application from crashing if one of these exceptions is thrown. Almost any work that is performed against a `java.sql.Connection` object will need to perform error handling to ensure that database exceptions are handled correctly. In fact, nested `try-catch` blocks are often required to handle all the possible exceptions. You need to ensure that connections are closed once work has been performed and the `Connection` object is no longer used. Similarly, it is a good idea to close `java.sql.Statement` objects for memory allocation cleanup.

Because `Statement` and `Connection` objects need to be closed, it is common to see `try-catch-finally` blocks used to ensure that all resources have been tended to as needed. It is not unlikely that you will see JDBC code that resembles the following style:

```
try {
    // perform database tasks
} catch (java.sql.SQLException ex) {
    // perform exception handling
} finally {
    try {
    // close Connection and Statement objects
    } catch (java.sql.SQLException ex){
    // perform exception handling
    }
}
```

As shown in the previous pseudo-code, nested `try-catch` blocks are often required in order to clean up unused resources. Proper exception handling sometimes makes JDBC code rather laborious to write, but it will also ensure that an application requiring database access will not fail, causing data to be lost.

7-4. Simplifying Connection Management

Problem

Your application requires the use of a database. To work with the database, you need to open a connection. Rather than code the logic to open a database connection every time you need to access the database, you want to simplify the connection process.

Solution

Write a class to handle all the connection management within your application. Doing so will allow you to call that class in order to obtain a connection, rather than setting up a new Connection object each time you need access to the database. Perform the following steps to set up a connection management environment for your JDBC application:

1. Create a class named CreateConnection.java that will encapsulate all the connection logic for your application.
2. Create a properties file to store your connection information. Place the file in a designated location so that the CreateConnection class can load it.
3. Use the CreateConnection class to obtain your database connections.

■ **Note** If you're utilizing an application server, you can handle a similar solution via a container-managed connection pool. However, if the application is not deployed to an application server container, then building a connection management utility such as the one in this solution is a good alternative.

The following code shows the org.javaee8recipes.chapter07.CreateConnection class that can be used for centralized connection management:

```
package org.javaee8recipes.chapter07;

import java.io.File;
import java.io.FileInputStream;
import java.io.FileNotFoundException;
import java.io.IOException;
import java.io.InputStream;
import java.nio.file.FileSystems;
import java.nio.file.Files;
import java.sql.Connection;
import java.sql.DriverManager;
import java.sql.SQLException;
import java.util.Properties;
import javax.naming.Context;
import javax.naming.InitialContext;
import javax.naming.NamingException;
import javax.sql.DataSource;

public final class CreateConnection {

    static Properties props = new Properties();
    static String hostname = null;
    static String port = null;
    static String database = null;
    static String username = null;
    static String password = null;
    static String jndi = null;
```

```
public CreateConnection() {

}

public static void loadProperties() {
    // Return if the host has already been loaded
    if(hostname != null){
        return;
    }

    try(InputStream in = Files.newInputStream(FileSystems.getDefault().getPath(System.
    getProperty("user.dir")
                + File.separator + "db_props.properties"));) {
        // Looks for properties file in the root of the src directory in Netbeans project

        System.out.println(FileSystems.getDefault().getPath(System.getProperty("user.dir")
                + File.separator + "db_props.properties"));
        props.load(in);

    } catch (IOException ex) {
        ex.printStackTrace();
    }

    hostname = props.getProperty("host_name");
    port = props.getProperty("port_number");
    database = props.getProperty("db_name");
    username = props.getProperty("username");
    password = props.getProperty("password");
    jndi = props.getProperty("jndi");
    System.out.println(hostname);
}

/**
 * Demonstrates obtaining a connection via DriverManager
 *
 * @return
 * @throws SQLException
 */
public static Connection getConnection() throws SQLException {
    Connection conn = null;
    String jdbcUrl = "jdbc:oracle:thin:@" + hostname + ":"
            + port + ":" + database;
    conn = DriverManager.getConnection(jdbcUrl, username, password);
    System.out.println("Successfully connected");
    return conn;
}

/**
 * Demonstrates obtaining a connection via a DataSource object
 *
 * @return
 */
```

```
    public static Connection getDSConnection() {
        Connection conn = null;
        try {
            Context ctx = new InitialContext();
            DataSource ds = (DataSource) ctx.lookup(jndi);
            conn = ds.getConnection();
        } catch (NamingException | SQLException ex) {
            ex.printStackTrace();
        }
        return conn;
    }

    public static void main(String[] args) {
        Connection conn = null;
        try {
            CreateConnection.loadProperties();
            System.out.println("Beginning connection..");
            conn = CreateConnection.getConnection();
            //performDbTask();
        } catch (java.sql.SQLException ex) {
            System.out.println(ex);
        } finally {
            if (conn != null) {
                try {
                    conn.close();
                } catch (SQLException ex) {
                    ex.printStackTrace();
                }
            }
        }

    }
}
```

Next, the following lines of code are an example of what should be contained in the properties file that is used for obtaining a connection to the database. For this example, the properties file is named db_props.properties.

```
host_name=your_db_server_name
db_name=your_db_name
username=db_username
password=db_username_password
port_number=db_port_number
jndi=jndi_connection_string
```

Finally, use the CreateConnection class to obtain connections for your application. The following code demonstrates this concept:

```
Connection conn = null;
try {
     CreateConnection.loadProperties();
     System.out.println("Beginning connection..");
```

```
        conn = CreateConnection.getConnection();
        //performDbTask();
    } catch (java.sql.SQLException ex) {
        System.out.println(ex);
    } finally {
        if (conn != null) {
            try {
                conn.close();
            } catch (SQLException ex) {
                ex.printStackTrace();
            }
        }
    }
```

■ **Note** You could update this code to use the `try-with-resources` syntax in order to get rid of the `finally` block requirement. However, I'm showing this syntax to demonstrate how to ensure that a `Connection` object is closed, if you're not using `try-with-resources`.

To run the code for testing, execute the `org.javaee8recipes.chapter07.CreateConnection.java` class because it contains a main method for testing purposes.

How It Works

Obtaining a connection within a database application can be code intensive. Moreover, the process can be prone to error if you retype the code each time you need to obtain a connection. By encapsulating database connection logic within a single class, you can reuse the same connection code each time you require a connection to the database. This increases your productivity, reduces the chances of typing errors, and enhances manageability because if you have to make a change, it can occur in one place rather than in several different locations.

Creating a strategic connection methodology is beneficial to you and others who might need to maintain your code in the future. Although data sources are the preferred technique for managing database connections when using an application server or JNDI, the solution to this recipe demonstrates how to use standard JDBC `DriverManager` connections. One of the security implications of using the `DriverManager` is that you will need to store the database credentials somewhere for use by the application. It is not safe to store those credentials in plain text anywhere, and it is also not safe to embed them in application code, which might be decompiled at some point in the future. As seen in the solution, a properties file that resides on disk is used to store the database credentials. Assume that this properties file will be encrypted at some point before deployment to a server.

As shown in the solution, the code reads the database credentials, host name, database name, and port number from the properties file. That information is then pieced together to form a JDBC URL that can be used by `DriverManager` to obtain a connection to the database. Once obtained, that connection can be used anywhere and then closed. Similarly, if you're using a `DataSource` that has been deployed to an application server, the properties file can be used to store the JNDI connection. That is the only piece of information that is needed to obtain a connection to the database using the `DataSource`. To the developer, the only difference between the two types of connections would be the method name that is called in order to obtain the `Connection` object, those being `getDSConnection` or `getConnection` in the example.

You could develop a JDBC application so that the code that is used to obtain a connection needs to be hard-coded throughout. Instead, this solution enables all the code for obtaining a connection to be encapsulated by a single class so that the developer does not need to worry about it. Such a technique also allows the code to be more maintainable. For instance, if the application were originally deployed using the `DriverManager` but then later had the ability to use a `DataSource`, very little code would need to be changed.

7-5. Querying a Database

Problem

You have a table that contains authors within the company database, and you want to query that table to retrieve the records.

Solution

Obtain a JDBC connection using one of the techniques covered in Recipe 7-2 or Recipe 7-4; then use the `java.sql.Connection` object to create a `Statement` object. A `java.sql.Statement` object contains the `executeQuery` method, which can be used to parse a string of text and use it to query a database. Once you've executed the query, you can retrieve the results of the query into a `ResultSet` object. The following example, excerpted from the `org.javaee8recipes.chapter07.dao.AuthorDAO` class, queries a database table named `BOOK_AUTHOR` and prints the results to the server log:

```
public void queryBookAuthor() {
        String qry = "select id, first, last, bio from book_author";
        CreateConnection.loadProperties();
        try (Connection conn = CreateConnection.getConnection();
                Statement stmt = conn.createStatement();
                ResultSet rs = stmt.executeQuery(qry);) {

            while (rs.next()) {
                int author_id = rs.getInt("ID");
                String first_name = rs.getString("FIRST");
                String last_name = rs.getString("LAST");
                String bio = rs.getString("BIO");
                System.out.println(author_id + "\t" + first_name
                        + " " + last_name + "\t" + bio);
            }
        } catch (SQLException e) {
            e.printStackTrace();
        }

    }
```

Executing this method against the database schema that ships with this book will produce the following results, considering that the `BIO` column is `null` for each author record:

```
Successfully connected
2     JOSH JUNEAU     null
3     CARL DEA     null
4     MARK BEATY     null
5     FREDDY GUIME     null
6     OCONNER JOHN     null
```

How It Works

One of the most commonly performed operations against a database is a query. Performing database queries using JDBC is quite easy, although there is a bit of boilerplate code that needs to be used each time a query is executed. First, you need to obtain a Connection object for the database and schema that you want to run the query against. You can do this by using one of the solutions in Recipe 7-2. Next, you need to form a query and store it in String format. The CreateConnection properties are then loaded via a call to the loadProperties method, which ensures that the db_props.properties file is used to populate database connection information. Next, a try-with-resources clause is used to create the objects that are necessary for querying the database. Since the objects are instantiated within the try-with-resources, then they will be closed automatically once they are no longer being used. The Connection object is then used to create a Statement. Your query String will be passed to the Statement object's executeQuery method in order to actually query the database.

```
String qry = "select id, first, last, bio from book_author";
        CreateConnection.loadProperties();
        try (Connection conn = CreateConnection.getConnection();
                Statement stmt = conn.createStatement();
                ResultSet rs = stmt.executeQuery(qry);) {
...
```

As you can see, the Statement object's executeQuery method accepts a string and returns a ResultSet object. The ResultSet object makes it easy to work with the query results so that you can obtain the information you need in any order. If you look at the next line of code, a while loop is created on the ResultSet object. This loop will continue to call the ResultSet object's next method, obtaining the next row that is returned from the query with each iteration. In this case, the ResultSet object is named rs, so while rs.next() returns true, the loop will continue to be processed. Once all the returned rows have been processed, rs.next() will return a false to indicate that there are no more rows to be processed.

Within the while loop, each returned row is processed. The ResultSet object is parsed to obtain the values of the given column names with each pass. Notice that if the column is expected to return a string, you must call the ResultSet getString method, passing the column name in String format. Similarly, if the column is expected to return an int, you'd call the ResultSet getInt method, passing the column name in String format. The same holds true for the other data types. These methods will return the corresponding column values. In the example in the solution to this recipe, those values are stored into local variables.

```
int author_id = rs.getInt("ID");
String first_name = rs.getString("FIRST");
String last_name = rs.getString("LAST");
String bio = rs.getString("BIO");
```

Once the column value has been obtained, you can do what you want to do with the values you have stored within local variables. In this case, they are printed using the System.out() method. Notice that there is a try-catch-finally block used in this example. A java.sql.SQLException could be thrown when attempting to query a database (for instance, if the Connection object has not been properly obtained or if the database tables that you are trying to query do not exist). You must provide exception handling to handle errors in these situations. Therefore, all database-processing code should be placed within a try block. The catch block then handles a SQLException, so if it is thrown, the exception will be handled using the code within the catch block. Sounds easy enough, right? It is, but you must do it each time you perform a database query. That means lots of boilerplate code. Inside the finally block, you will see that the Statement and Connection objects are closed if they are not equal to null.

■ **Note** Performing these tasks also incurs the overhead of handling `java.sql.SQLException` when it is thrown. They might occur if an attempt is made to close a `null` object. It is always a good idea to close statements and connections if they are open. This will help ensure that the system can reallocate resources as needed and act respectfully on the database. It is important to close connections as soon as possible so that other processes can reuse them.

7-6. Performing CRUD Operations

Problem

You need to have the ability to perform standard database operations from within your enterprise application. That is, you need to have the ability to Create, Retrieve, Update, and Delete (CRUD) database records.

Solution

Create a `Connection` object and obtain a database connection using one of the solutions provided in Recipe 7-2; then perform the CRUD operation using a `java.sql.Statement` object that is obtained from the `java.sql.Connection` object. The following code, taken from `org.javaee8recipes.chapter07.recipe07_06.AuthorDAOStandard.java`, demonstrates how to perform each of the CRUD operations against the BOOK_AUTHOR table using JDBC, with the exception of the query (retrieve) since that is already covered in Recipe 7-5.

■ **Note** This recipe demonstrates the use of string concatenation for creating SQL statements without the use of `PreparedStatement` objects. This is not a safe practice because the variables could potentially contain malicious values that may compromise your database. The solution to this recipe demonstrates the practice of creating SQL statements using string concatenation so that you can see the different options that are available. For information on using `PreparedStatement` objects and a safer alternative to string concatenation, see Recipe 7-7.

```
/**
     * Create a book author.
     *
     * @param first
     * @param last
     * @param bio
     */
    private void performCreate(String first, String last, String bio) {
        String sql = "INSERT INTO BOOK_AUTHOR VALUES("
                + "BOOK_AUTHOR_S.NEXTVAL, "
                + "'" + last.toUpperCase() + "', "
                + "'" + first.toUpperCase() + "', "
                + "'" + bio.toUpperCase() + "')";
        try (Connection conn = CreateConnection.getConnection();
                PreparedStatement stmt = conn.prepareStatement(sql)) {
```

```
            // Returns row-count or 0 if not successful
            int result = stmt.executeUpdate();
            if (result > 0) {
                System.out.println("-- Record created --");
            } else {
                System.out.println("!! Record NOT Created !!");
            }
        } catch (SQLException e) {
            e.printStackTrace();
        }
    }

    private void performUpdate(String first, String last, String bio) {
        String sql = "UPDATE BOOK_AUTHOR "
                + "SET bio = '" + bio.toUpperCase() + "' "
                + "WHERE last = '" + last.toUpperCase() + "' "
                + "AND first = '" + first.toUpperCase() + "'";
        try (Connection conn = CreateConnection.getConnection();
                PreparedStatement stmt = conn.prepareStatement(sql)) {
            int result = stmt.executeUpdate();
            if (result > 0) {
                System.out.println("-- Record Updated --");

            } else {
                System.out.println("!! Record NOT Updated !!");
            }
        } catch (SQLException e) {
            e.printStackTrace();
        }
    }

    private void performDelete(String first, String last) {
        String sql = "DELETE FROM BOOK_AUTHOR WHERE LAST = '" + last.toUpperCase() + "' "
                + "AND FIRST = '" + first.toUpperCase() + "'";
        try (Connection conn = CreateConnection.getConnection();
                PreparedStatement stmt = conn.prepareStatement(sql)) {
            int result = stmt.executeUpdate();
            if (result > 0) {
                System.out.println("-- Record Deleted --");
            } else {
                System.out.println("!! Record NOT Deleted!!");
            }
        } catch (SQLException e) {
            e.printStackTrace();
        }
    }
```

■ **Note** If you follow the code, you will notice that whenever a string of data is passed to the database, it is first changed to uppercase by calling the `toUpperCase` method on it. This is to help maintain a standard uppercase format for all data within the database.

Executing the following main method will produce the results that follow:

```
public static void main(String[] args) {
        AuthorDAO authorDao = new AuthorDAO();
        authorDao.queryBookAuthor();
        authorDao.performCreate("Joe", "Blow", "N/A");
        authorDao.performUpdate("Joe", "Blow", "Joes Bio");
        authorDao.queryBookAuthor();
        authorDao.performDelete("Joe", "Blow");
}
```

The results from running the main method should be similar to the following:

```
Successfully connected
2     JOSH JUNEAU    null
3     CARL DEA    null
4     MARK BEATY    null
5     FREDDY GUIME    null
6     OCONNER JOHN    null
Successfully connected
-- Record created --

Successfully connected
-- Record Updated --
Successfully connected
2     JOSH JUNEAU    null
3     CARL DEA    null
4     MARK BEATY    null
5     FREDDY GUIME    null
6     OCONNER JOHN    null
105     JOE BLOW    JOES BIO

Successfully connected
-- Record Deleted --
```

How It Works

The same basic code format is used for performing just about every database task. The format is as follows:

1. Obtain a connection to the database within the `try` clause.
2. Create a statement from the connection within the `try` clause.
3. Perform a database task with the statement.
4. Do something with the results of the database task.
5. Close the statement (and database connection if you're finished using it). This step is done automatically if you're using the `try-with-resources` clause, as demonstrated in the solution to this recipe.

The main difference between performing a query using JDBC and using Data Manipulation Language (DML) is that you will call different methods on the `Statement` object, depending on which operation you want to perform. To perform a query, you need to call the `Statement executeQuery` method. To perform DML tasks, such as insert, update, and delete, call the `executeUpdate` method.

The `performCreate` method in the solution to this recipe demonstrates the operation of inserting a record into a database. To insert a record in the database, you construct a SQL insert statement in `String` format. To perform the insert, pass the SQL string to the `Statement` object's `executeUpdate` method. If the insert is performed, an `int` value will be returned that specifies the number or rows that have been inserted. If the insert operation is not performed successfully, either a zero will be returned or a `SQLException` will be thrown, indicating a problem with the statement or database connection.

The `performUpdate` method in the solution to this recipe demonstrates the operation of updating record(s) within a database table. First, you will construct a SQL update statement in `String` format. Next, to perform the update operation, you will pass the SQL string to the `Statement` object's `executeUpdate` method. If the update is successfully performed, an `int` value will be returned, which specifies the number of records that were updated. If the update operation is not performed successfully, either a zero will be returned or a `SQLException` will be thrown, indicating a problem with the statement or database connection.

The last database operation that is covered in the solution is the delete operation. The `performDelete` method in the solution to this recipe demonstrates how to delete records from the database. First, you construct a SQL delete statement in `String` format. Next, to execute the deletion, you pass the SQL string to the `Statement` object's `executeUpdate` method. If the deletion is successful, an `int` value specifying the number of rows deleted will be returned. Otherwise, if the deletion fails, a zero will be returned, or a `SQLException` will be thrown, indicating a problem with the statement or database connection.

Almost every database application uses at least one of the CRUD operations at some point. This is foundational JDBC that you need to know if you are working with databases within Java applications. Even if you will not work directly with the JDBC API, it is good to know these basics.

7-7. Preventing SQL Injection

Problem

Your application performs database tasks. To reduce the chances of a SQL injection attack, you need to ensure that no unfiltered `Strings` of text are being appended to SQL statements and executed against the database.

■ **Tip** Prepared statements provide more than just protection against SQL injection attacks. They also provide a way to centralize and better control the SQL used within an application and optimize performance benefits. Instead of creating multiple and possibly different versions of the same query, you can create the query once as a prepared statement and invoke it from many different places in your code. Any change to the query logic needs to happen only at the point that you prepare the statement.

■ **Note** There have been data access objects (DAOs) created for each database table used by the Acme Bookstore application for this recipe. The DAO classes are used to perform CRUD operations against each of the tables for the Acme Bookstore application. The CRUD operations utilize `PreparedStatements` in order to add security and enhance the performance of the application.

Solution

Utilize PreparedStatements for performing the database tasks. PreparedStatements send a precompiled SQL statement to the DBMS rather than a clear-text string. The following code demonstrates how to perform a database query and a database update using a java.sql.PreparedStatement object. The following code excerpts are taken from a new data access object named org.javaee8recipes.chapter07.dao.AuthorDAO, which utilizes PreparedStatement objects rather than String concatenation for executing SQL statements:

```
...
   /**
     * Queries the database for a particular author based upon ID and returns
     * the Author object if found.
     *
     * @param id
     * @return
     */
    public Author performFind(int id) {
        String qry = "SELECT ID, LAST, FIRST, BIO "
                + "FROM BOOK_AUTHOR "
                + "WHERE ID = ?";

        Author author = null;
        CreateConnection.loadProperties();
        try (Connection conn = CreateConnection.getConnection();
                PreparedStatement stmt = conn.prepareStatement(qry)) {
            stmt.setInt(1, id);
            try (ResultSet rs = stmt.executeQuery();) {

                if (rs.next()) {
                    int author_id = rs.getInt("ID");
                    String first_name = rs.getString("FIRST");
                    String last_name = rs.getString("LAST");
                    String bio = rs.getString("BIO");
                    author = new Author(author_id,
                            first_name,
                            last_name,
                            bio);
                }
            }
        } catch (SQLException e) {
            e.printStackTrace();
        }
        return author;

    }

    /**
     * Queries the database for a particular author based upon first and last
     * name and returns a list of Author objects if found.
     *
     * @param id
```

```
     * @return
     */
    public List<Author> performFind(String first, String last) {
        String qry = "SELECT ID, LAST, FIRST, BIO "
                + "FROM BOOK_AUTHOR "
                + "WHERE LAST = ? "
                + "AND FIRST = ?";

        List authorList = new ArrayList();
        try (Connection conn = CreateConnection.getConnection();
                PreparedStatement stmt = conn.prepareStatement(qry)) {
            stmt.setString(1, last.toUpperCase());
            stmt.setString(2, first.toUpperCase());
            try (ResultSet rs = stmt.executeQuery();) {

                while (rs.next()) {
                    int author_id = rs.getInt("ID");
                    String first_name = rs.getString("FIRST");
                    String last_name = rs.getString("LAST");
                    String bio = rs.getString("BIO");
                    Author author = new Author(author_id,
                            first_name,
                            last_name,
                            bio);
                    authorList.add(author);
                }
            }
        } catch (SQLException e) {
            e.printStackTrace();
        }
        return authorList;

    }

    /**
     *
     * @param first
     * @param last
     * @param bio
     */
    private void performCreate(String first, String last, String bio) {
        String sql = "INSERT INTO BOOK_AUTHOR VALUES("
                + "BOOK_AUTHOR_S.NEXTVAL, ?, ?, ?)";
        try (Connection conn = CreateConnection.getConnection();
                PreparedStatement stmt = conn.prepareStatement(sql)) {
            stmt.setString(1, last.toUpperCase());
            stmt.setString(2, first.toUpperCase());
            stmt.setString(3, bio.toUpperCase());
```

```
                // Returns row-count or 0 if not successful
                int result = stmt.executeUpdate();
                if (result > 0) {
                    System.out.println("-- Record created --");
                } else {
                    System.out.println("!! Record NOT Created !!");
                }

        } catch (SQLException e) {
            e.printStackTrace();
        }
    }

    private void performUpdate(int id, String first, String last, String bio) {
        String sql = "UPDATE BOOK_AUTHOR "
                + "SET bio = ?,"
                + "    last = ?,"
                + "    first = ? "
                + "WHERE ID = ?";
        try (Connection conn = CreateConnection.getConnection();
                PreparedStatement stmt = conn.prepareStatement(sql)) {
            stmt.setString(1, bio.toUpperCase());
            stmt.setString(2, last.toUpperCase());
            stmt.setString(3, first.toUpperCase());
            stmt.setInt(4, id);

                int result = stmt.executeUpdate();
                if (result > 0) {
                    System.out.println("-- Record Updated --");

                } else {
                    System.out.println("!! Record NOT Updated !!");
                }

        } catch (SQLException e) {
            e.printStackTrace();
        }
    }

    private void performDelete(int id) {
        String sql = "DELETE FROM BOOK_AUTHOR WHERE ID = ?";
        try (Connection conn = CreateConnection.getConnection();
                PreparedStatement stmt = conn.prepareStatement(sql)) {
            stmt.setInt(1, id);

                int result = stmt.executeUpdate();
                if (result > 0) {
                    System.out.println("-- Record Deleted --");
```

```
                } else {
                    System.out.println("!! Record NOT Deleted!!");
                }

        } catch (SQLException e) {
            e.printStackTrace();
        }
    }
...
```

The methods displayed previously exhibit the use of PreparedStatement objects rather than using standard JDBC Statement objects and String concatenation for appending variables into SQL statements.

How It Works

While standard JDBC statements will get the job done, the harsh reality is that they can be insecure and difficult to work with. For instance, bad things can occur if a dynamic SQL statement is used to query a database and a user-accepted string is assigned to a variable and concatenated with the intended SQL string. In most ordinary cases, the user-accepted string would be concatenated, and the SQL string would be used to query the database as expected. However, an attacker could decide to place malicious code inside the string (aka *SQL injection*), which would then be inadvertently sent to the database using a standard Statement object. Using PreparedStatements prevents malicious strings from being concatenated into a SQL string and passed to the DBMS. PreparedStatements use substitution variables rather than concatenation to make SQL strings dynamic. They are also precompiled, which means that a valid SQL string is formed prior to the SQL being sent to the DBMS. Moreover, PreparedStatements can help your application perform better because if the same SQL has to be run more than one time, it has to be compiled only once per session. After that, the substitution variables are interchangeable, but the PreparedStatement can execute the SQL very quickly.

Let's look at how a PreparedStatement works in practice. If you look at the example in the solution to this recipe, you can see that the database table BOOK_AUTHOR is being queried in the performFind method, sending the author's ID as a substitution variable and retrieving the results for the matching record. The SQL string looks like the following:

```
String qry = "SELECT ID, LAST, FIRST, BIO "
                    + "FROM BOOK_AUTHOR "
                    + "WHERE ID = ?";
```

Everything looks standard with the SQL text except for the question mark (?) at the end of the string. Placing a question mark within a string of SQL signifies that a substitution variable will be used in place of that question mark when the SQL is executed.

The next step for using a PreparedStatement is to declare a variable of type PreparedStatement. You can see this with the following line of code:

```
PreparedStatement stmt = null;
```

Now that a PreparedStatement has been declared, it can be put to use. However, using a PreparedStatement may or may not cause an exception to be thrown. Therefore, any use of a PreparedStatement should occur in a try-catch block so that any exceptions can be handled gracefully. For instance, exceptions can occur if the database connection is unavailable for some reason or if the SQL string is invalid. Rather than crashing an application because of such issues, it is best to handle the exceptions wisely within a catch block. The following try-catch block includes the code that is necessary to send the SQL string to the database and retrieve results:

```
try (Connection conn = CreateConnection.getConnection();
        PreparedStatement stmt = conn.prepareStatement(qry)) {
    stmt.setInt(1, id);
    try (ResultSet rs = stmt.executeQuery();) {
    if (rs.next()) {
        int author_id = rs.getInt("ID");
        String first_name = rs.getString("FIRST");
        String last_name = rs.getString("LAST");
        String bio = rs.getString("BIO");
        author = new Author(author_id,
                            first_name,
                            last_name,
                            bio);
    }
  }
} catch (SQLException e) {
    e.printStackTrace();
}
```

First, you can see that the Connection object is used to instantiate a PreparedStatement object. The SQL string is passed to the PreparedStatement object's constructor upon creation. Next, the PreparedStatement object is used to set values for any substitution variables that have been placed into the SQL string. As you can see, the PreparedStatement setString method is used in the example to set the substitution variable at position 1 equal to the contents of the id variable. The positioning of the substitution variable is associated with the placement of the question mark (?) within the SQL string. The first question mark within the string is assigned to the first position, the second one is assigned to the second position, and so forth. If there were more than one substitution variable to be assigned, there would be more than one call to the PreparedStatement setter methods, assigning each of the variables until each one has been accounted for. PreparedStatements can accept substitution variables of many different data types. For instance, if a Date value were being assigned to a substitution variable, a call to the setDate(position, variable) method would be in order. See the online documentation or your IDE's code completion for a complete set of methods that can be used for assigning substitution variables using PreparedStatement objects.

It is also possible to utilized named parameters, rather than indexes. To use this technique, provide a name prefixed with a colon for each substitution variable, rather than a question mark. The following lines of code demonstrate named parameters.

```
String qry = "SELECT ID, LAST, FIRST, BIO "
              + "FROM BOOK_AUTHOR "
              + "WHERE LAST = :last "
              + "AND FIRST = :first";
```

```
        List authorList = new ArrayList();
        try (Connection conn = CreateConnection.getConnection();
                PreparedStatement stmt = conn.prepareStatement(qry)) {
            stmt.setString("last", last.toUpperCase());
            stmt.setString("first", first.toUpperCase());
            try (ResultSet rs = stmt.executeQuery();) {
. . .
```

Once all the variables have been assigned, the SQL string can be executed. The PreparedStatement object contains an executeQuery method that is used to execute a SQL string that represents a query.

The executeQuery method returns a ResultSet object, which contains the results that have been fetched from the database for the particular SQL query. Next, the ResultSet can be traversed to obtain the values retrieved from the database. There are two different ways to retrieve the results from the ResultSet. Positional assignments can be used to retrieve the results by calling the ResultSet object's corresponding getter methods and passing the position of the column value, or the String identifier of the column value that you want to obtain can be passed to the getter methods. If passing the position, it is determined by the order in which the column names appear within the SQL string. In the example, String-based column identifiers are used to obtain the values. As you can see from the example, passing the column identifier to the appropriate getter method will retrieve the value. When the record values from the ResultSet are obtained, they are stored into local variables. Once all the variables have been collected for a particular author, they are stored into an Author object, which will eventually be returned from the method. Of course, if the substitution variable is not set correctly or if there is an issue with the SQL string, an exception will be thrown. This would cause the code that is contained within the catch block to be executed.

If you do not use the try-with-resources clause, as demonstrated in the solution, you should be sure to clean up after using PreparedStatements by closing the statement when you are finished using it. It is a good practice to put all the cleanup code within a finally block to be sure that it is executed even if an exception is thrown. For example, a finally block that is used to clean up unused Statement and Connection objects may look like the following:

```
finally {
    if (stmt != null) {
        try {
            stmt.close();
        } catch (SQLException ex) {
            ex.printStackTrace();
        }

    }
    if (conn != null) {
        try {
            conn.close();
            conn = null;
        } catch (SQLException ex) {
            ex.printStackTrace();
        }
    }
    return author;

}
```

You can see that the PreparedStatement object that was instantiated, stmt, is checked to see whether it is NULL. If not, it is closed by calling the close method. Working through the code in the solution to this recipe, you can see that similar code is used to process database insert, update, and delete statements. The only difference in those cases is that the PreparedStatement executeUpdate method is called rather than the executeQuery method. The executeUpdate method will return an int value representing the number of rows affected by the SQL statement.

The use of PreparedStatement objects is preferred over JDBC Statement objects. This is because they are more secure and perform better. They can also make your code easier to follow and easier to maintain.

7-8. Utilizing Java Objects for Database Access

Problem

Your application works with an underlying database for storing and retrieving data. You would prefer to code your business logic using Java objects, rather than working directly with JDBC and SQL for performing database activities.

Solution

Create a Data Access Object (DAO) for each database table that will be used to perform the mundane JDBC and SQL work. Within the DAO, create façade methods that accept Java objects to represent a single record of data for the database table for which the DAO has been created. Use the Java objects to pass record data to and from the DAO, while the DAO breaks the objects apart and utilizes the data fields within standard SQL statements.

The following class excerpts demonstrate a data access object for the AUTHOR database table, which is used for storing book author data (a main method has been included merely for testing purposes within this DAO).

■ **Note** For the full source listing, refer to the org.javaee8recipes.chapter07.dao.AuthorDAO class, located in the Javaee8recipes NetBeans project. Repetitive portions of the sources (finally blocks) have been removed from the following listing for brevity.

```
...
public class AuthorDAO implements java.io.Serializable {

    public AuthorDAO() {
    }

    public void queryBookAuthor() {
        String qry = "select id, first, last, bio from book_author";
        CreateConnection.loadProperties();
        try (Connection conn = CreateConnection.getConnection();
                Statement stmt = conn.createStatement();
                ResultSet rs = stmt.executeQuery(qry);) {

            while (rs.next()) {
                int author_id = rs.getInt("ID");
                String first_name = rs.getString("FIRST");
```

```
            String last_name = rs.getString("LAST");
            String bio = rs.getString("BIO");
            System.out.println(author_id + "\t" + first_name
                    + " " + last_name + "\t" + bio);
        }
    } catch (SQLException e) {
        e.printStackTrace();
    }

}

public List<Author> obtainCompleteAuthorList() {
    String qry = "select id, first, last, bio from book_author";
    List<Author> authors = new ArrayList();
    CreateConnection.loadProperties();
    try (Connection conn = CreateConnection.getConnection();
            Statement stmt = conn.createStatement();
            ResultSet rs = stmt.executeQuery(qry);) {
        while (rs.next()) {
            int author_id = rs.getInt("ID");
            String first_name = rs.getString("FIRST");
            String last_name = rs.getString("LAST");
            String bio = rs.getString("BIO");
            Author author = new Author(author_id, first_name,
                    last_name, bio);
            authors.add(author);
        }
    } catch (SQLException e) {
        e.printStackTrace();
    }
    return authors;
}

/**
 * Queries the database for a particular author based upon ID and returns
 * the Author object if found.
 *
 * @param id
 * @return
 */
public Author performFind(int id) {
    String qry = "SELECT ID, LAST, FIRST, BIO "
            + "FROM BOOK_AUTHOR "
            + "WHERE ID = ?";

    Author author = null;
    CreateConnection.loadProperties();
    try (Connection conn = CreateConnection.getConnection();
            PreparedStatement stmt = conn.prepareStatement(qry)) {
        stmt.setInt(1, id);
        try (ResultSet rs = stmt.executeQuery();) {
```

```
            if (rs.next()) {
                int author_id = rs.getInt("ID");
                String first_name = rs.getString("FIRST");
                String last_name = rs.getString("LAST");
                String bio = rs.getString("BIO");
                author = new Author(author_id,
                        first_name,
                        last_name,
                        bio);
            }
        }
    } catch (SQLException e) {
        e.printStackTrace();
    }
    return author;

}

/**
 * Queries the database for a particular author based upon first and last
 * name and returns a list of Author objects if found.
 *
 * @param id
 * @return
 */
public List<Author> performFind(String first, String last) {
    String qry = "SELECT ID, LAST, FIRST, BIO "
            + "FROM BOOK_AUTHOR "
            + "WHERE LAST = ? "
            + "AND FIRST = ?";

    List authorList = new ArrayList();
    try (Connection conn = CreateConnection.getConnection();
            PreparedStatement stmt = conn.prepareStatement(qry)) {
        stmt.setString(1, last.toUpperCase());
        stmt.setString(2, first.toUpperCase());
        try (ResultSet rs = stmt.executeQuery();) {

            while (rs.next()) {
                int author_id = rs.getInt("ID");
                String first_name = rs.getString("FIRST");
                String last_name = rs.getString("LAST");
                String bio = rs.getString("BIO");
                Author author = new Author(author_id,
                        first_name,
                        last_name,
                        bio);
                authorList.add(author);
            }
        }
```

```
    } catch (SQLException e) {
        e.printStackTrace();
    }
    return authorList;

}

/**
 *
 * @param first
 * @param last
 * @param bio
 */
private void performCreate(String first, String last, String bio) {
    String sql = "INSERT INTO BOOK_AUTHOR VALUES("
            + "BOOK_AUTHOR_S.NEXTVAL, ?, ?, ?)";
    try (Connection conn = CreateConnection.getConnection();
            PreparedStatement stmt = conn.prepareStatement(sql)) {
        stmt.setString(1, last.toUpperCase());
        stmt.setString(2, first.toUpperCase());
        stmt.setString(3, bio.toUpperCase());

            // Returns row-count or 0 if not successful
            int result = stmt.executeUpdate();
            if (result > 0) {
                System.out.println("-- Record created --");
            } else {
                System.out.println("!! Record NOT Created !!");
            }

    } catch (SQLException e) {
        e.printStackTrace();
    }
}

private void performUpdate(int id, String first, String last, String bio) {
    String sql = "UPDATE BOOK_AUTHOR "
            + "SET bio = ?,"
            + "    last = ?,"
            + "    first = ? "
            + "WHERE ID = ?";
    try (Connection conn = CreateConnection.getConnection();
            PreparedStatement stmt = conn.prepareStatement(sql)) {
        stmt.setString(1, bio.toUpperCase());
        stmt.setString(2, last.toUpperCase());
        stmt.setString(3, first.toUpperCase());
        stmt.setInt(4, id);

            int result = stmt.executeUpdate();
            if (result > 0) {
                System.out.println("-- Record Updated --");
```

```
                } else {
                    System.out.println("!! Record NOT Updated !!");
                }

        } catch (SQLException e) {
            e.printStackTrace();
        }
    }

    private void performDelete(int id) {
        String sql = "DELETE FROM BOOK_AUTHOR WHERE ID = ?";
        try (Connection conn = CreateConnection.getConnection();
                PreparedStatement stmt = conn.prepareStatement(sql)) {
            stmt.setInt(1, id);

                int result = stmt.executeUpdate();
                if (result > 0) {
                    System.out.println("-- Record Deleted --");
                } else {
                    System.out.println("!! Record NOT Deleted!!");
                }

        } catch (SQLException e) {
            e.printStackTrace();
        }
    }

    /**
     * Returns the next ID in the BOOK_AUTHOR_S sequence
     *
     * @return
     */
    public int getNextId() {
        String qry = "select book_author_s.currval as ID from dual";

        int returnId = -1;
        CreateConnection.loadProperties();
        try (Connection conn = CreateConnection.getConnection();
                Statement stmt = conn.createStatement();
                ResultSet rs = stmt.executeQuery(qry);) {

            while (rs.next()) {
                int author_id = rs.getInt("ID");
                returnId = author_id + 1;
            }
        } catch (SQLException e) {
            e.printStackTrace();
        }
        return returnId;

    }
```

```
    /**
     * Facade method for inserting Author objects into the BOOK_AUTHOR table
     *
     * @param author
     */
    public void insert(Author author) {
        performCreate(author.getFirst(),
                author.getLast(),
                author.getBio());
    }

    /**
     * Facade method for updating Author objects in the BOOK_AUTHOR table
     *
     * @param author
     */
    public void update(Author author) {
        this.performUpdate(author.getId(), author.getFirst(), author.getLast(), author.
        getBio());
    }

    /**
     * Facade method for deleting Author objects from the BOOK_AUTHOR table
     *
     * @param args
     */
    public void delete(Author author) {
        performDelete(author.getId());
    }

    public static void main(String[] args) {
        AuthorDAO authorDao = new AuthorDAO();
        authorDao.queryBookAuthor();
        authorDao.performCreate("Joe", "Blow", "N/A");

        // Find any author named Joe Blow and store in authList
        List<Author> authList = authorDao.performFind("Joe", "Blow");
        // Update the BIO for any author named Joe Blow
        for (Author auth : authList) {
            auth.setBio("New Bio");
            authorDao.update(auth);
        }
        authorDao.queryBookAuthor();

        // Delete any author named Joe Blow
        for (Author auth : authList) {
            authorDao.delete(auth);
        }
    }
}
```

How It Works

It can be advantageous for developers to separate different types of work into different classes within an application code base. In the same way that you separate web views from Java code within a Java web application, you should also separate JDBC from classes that are used to perform business logic. Have you ever had to maintain or debug a class that was riddled with business logic and SQL statements? It can be a nightmare! Simplifying code by breaking it down into smaller, more manageable pieces can oftentimes make maintenance and debugging much easier on a developer. The idea of separating JDBC and database-specific code from other business logic within an application falls within this same concept. Creating data access objects that are used solely for accessing the database can allow developers to code against Java objects rather than database tables.

A DAO is not a standard Java enterprise object. There is no framework that is used for creating DAOs. A DAO is simply a class that contains all of the JDBC code that is relevant for working with a single database table for your application. If there are 20 database tables that are required for use, then there should be that same number of DAOs. A DAO should contain minimally eight different methods. There should be at least one method for each of the four possible database transactions that could take place, those being `CREATE`, `READ`, `UPDATE`, and `DELETE`. These methods would contain specific JDBC code for connecting to the database, performing JDBC calls, and then closing the connection. The DAO should also contain four façade methods that will be used directly by classes containing the business logic. These methods should accept Java objects that correspond to the database table for which the DAO was written, and they should break down the object into separate fields and pass them to the JDBC methods to perform the actual database transaction.

In the solution to this recipe, the `AuthorDAO` class contains more than eight methods. This is because there is more than one way to search for author records within the database, and therefore, there is more than one find method within the class. A couple of different `performFind` methods are available, each with a different method signature. These methods allow one to find an author based upon ID or by name. Once a matching author record is found in the database, the values for that record are retrieved using standard JDBC methods, and they are stored into the corresponding fields within a new `Author` object. In the end, either a list of `Author` objects or a single `Author` object is returned to the caller. These finder methods contain public modifiers, so a managed bean can call them directly to retrieve a list of `Author` objects or a single `Author` object.

The `performCreate`, `performUpdate`, and `performDelete` methods are private, and therefore they can be accessed only by other methods within the same class. A CDI managed bean should not work directly with these private methods, nor will it be allowed to do so. Instead, there are public methods named insert, update, and delete, which are to be used by the CDI managed beans in order to access the private methods. The insert, update, and delete methods accept `Author` objects, and they perform the task of breaking down the `Author` object by field and passing the appropriate fields to their corresponding private methods in order to perform database activities. For instance, a bean can call the `AuthorDAO` insert method, passing an `Author` object. The insert method then calls the `performCreate` method, passing the fields of the `Author` object in their respective positions. Each of the CRUD operations can be performed in the same manner, allowing the business logic to interact directly with `Author` objects rather than deal with SQL.

7-9. Navigating Data with Scrollable ResultSets

Problem

You have queried the database and obtained some results. You want to store those results in an object that will allow you to traverse forward and backward through the results, updating values as needed.

Solution

Create a scrollable ResultSet object, and then you will have the ability to read the next, first, last, and previous records. Using a scrollable ResultSet allows the results of a query to be fetched in any direction so that the data can be retrieved as needed. The following method, taken from the org.javaee8recipes.chapter07.dao.ChapterDAO class, demonstrates the creation of a scrollable ResultSet object:

```
private void queryBookChapters() {
        String sql = "SELECT ID, CHAPTER_NUMBER, TITLE, DESCRIPTION "
                + "FROM CHAPTER";

        int id = 0;
        int chapterNumber = 0;
        String title;

        CreateConnection.loadProperties();
        try (Connection conn = CreateConnection.getConnection();
                PreparedStatement stmt = conn.prepareStatement(sql,
                   ResultSet.TYPE_SCROLL_INSENSITIVE,
                        ResultSet.CONCUR_READ_ONLY);
                ResultSet rs = stmt.executeQuery();) {

            rs.first();
            id = rs.getInt("ID");
            chapterNumber = rs.getInt("CHAPTER_NUMBER");
            title = rs.getString("TITLE");
            System.out.println(id + " - " + chapterNumber + ": " + title);

            rs.next();
            id = rs.getInt("ID");
            chapterNumber = rs.getInt("CHAPTER_NUMBER");
            title = rs.getString("TITLE");
            System.out.println(id + " - " + chapterNumber + ": " + title);

            rs.last();
            id = rs.getInt("ID");
            chapterNumber = rs.getInt("CHAPTER_NUMBER");
            title = rs.getString("TITLE");
            System.out.println(id + " - " + chapterNumber + ": " + title);

            rs.previous();
            id = rs.getInt("ID");
            chapterNumber = rs.getInt("CHAPTER_NUMBER");
            title = rs.getString("TITLE");
            System.out.println(id + " - " + chapterNumber + ": " + title);

        } catch (SQLException ex) {
            ex.printStackTrace();
        }
    }
```

Executing this method will result in the following output using the data that resides in the CHAPTER table (your results will vary depending on the contents of the table in your database):

```
1 - 1: Getting Started with Java 7
2 - 2: Strings
18 - 18: JavaFX in the Enterprise
17 - 17: HTML5 APIs
```

How It Works

Ordinary ResultSet objects allow results to be fetched in a forward direction. That is, an application can process a default ResultSet object from the first record retrieved forward to the last. Sometimes an application requires more functionality when it comes to traversing a ResultSet. For instance, let's say you want to write an application that allows for someone to display the first or last record that was retrieved or perhaps page forward or backward through results. You could not do this very easily using a standard ResultSet. However, by creating a scrollable ResultSet, you can easily move backward and forward through the results.

To create a scrollable ResultSet, you must first create an instance of a Statement or PreparedStatement that has the ability to create a scrollable ResultSet. That is, when creating the Statement, you must pass the ResultSet scroll type constant value to the Connection object's createStatement method. Likewise, you must pass the scroll type constant value to the Connection object's prepareStatement method when using a PreparedStatement. Three different scroll type constants can be used. Table 7-1 displays those three constants.

***Table 7-1.** ResultSet Scroll Type Constants*

Constant	Description
ResultSet.TYPE_FORWARD_ONLY	Default type; allows forward movement only.
ResultSet.TYPE_SCROLL_INSENSITIVE	Allows forward and backward movement. Not sensitive to ResultSet updates.
ResultSet.TYPE_SCROLL_SENSITIVE	Allows forward and backward movement. Sensitive to ResultSet updates.

You must also pass a ResultSet concurrency constant to advise whether the ResultSet is intended to be updatable. The default is ResultSet.CONCUR_READ_ONLY, which means that the ResultSet is not updatable. The other concurrency type is ResultSet.CONCUR_UPDATABLE, which signifies an updatable ResultSet object.

In the solution to this recipe, a PreparedStatement object is used, and the code to create a PreparedStatement object that has the ability to generate a scrollable ResultSet looks like the following line:

```
pstmt = conn.prepareStatement(sql, ResultSet.TYPE_SCROLL_INSENSITIVE,
ResultSet.CONCUR_READ_ONLY);
```

Once the PreparedStatement has been created as such, a scrollable ResultSet is returned. You can traverse in several different directions using a scrollable ResultSet by calling the ResultSet methods indicating the direction you want to move or the placement that you want to be. The following line of code will retrieve the first record within the ResultSet:

```
ResultSet rs = pstmt.executeQuery();
rs.first();
```

The solution to this recipe demonstrates a few different scroll directions. Specifically, you can see that the ResultSet first, next, last, and previous methods are called in order to move to different positions within the ResultSet. For a complete reference to the ResultSet object, see the online documentation at http://download.oracle.com/javase/9/docs/api/java/sql/ResultSet.html.

Scrollable ResultSet objects have a niche in application development. They are one of those niceties that are there when you need them, but they are also something you might not need very often.

7-10. Calling PL/SQL Stored Procedures

Problem

Some logic that is required for your application is written as a stored procedure residing in the database. You require the ability to invoke the stored procedure from within your application.

Solution

The following block of code shows the PL/SQL that is required to create the stored procedure that will be called by Java. The functionality of this stored procedure is very minor; it simply accepts a value and assigns that value to an OUT parameter so that the program can display it.

```
create or replace procedure dummy_proc (text IN VARCHAR2,
msg OUT VARCHAR2) as
begin
-- Do something, in this case the IN parameter value is assigned to the OUT parameter
msg :=text;
end;
```

The CallableStatement in the following code executes this stored procedure that is contained within the database, passing the necessary parameters. The results of the OUT parameter are then displayed to the user.

```
CallableStatement cs = null;
try {
    cs = conn.prepareCall("{call DUMMY_PROC(?,?)}");
    cs.setString(1, "This is a test");
    cs.registerOutParameter(2, Types.VARCHAR);
    cs.executeQuery();
    System.out.println(cs.getString(2));
} catch (SQLException ex){
    ex.printStackTrace();
}
```

Running the example class for this recipe will display the following output, which is the same as the input. This is because the DUMMY_PROC procedure simply assigns the contents of the IN parameter to the OUT parameter.

```
This is a test
```

How It Works

It is not uncommon for an application to use database stored procedures for logic that can be executed directly within the database. To call a database stored procedure from Java, you must create a CallableStatement object, rather than using a PreparedStatement. In the solution to this recipe, a CallableStatement is used to invoke a stored procedure named DUMMY_PROC. The syntax for instantiating the CallableStatement is similar to that of using a PreparedStatement. Use the Connection object's prepareCall method, passing the call to the stored procedure. The solution to this recipe demonstrates one technique for making a stored procedure call, that is, enclosing it in curly braces: {}.

```
cs = conn.prepareCall("{call DUMMY_PROC(?,?)}");
```

Once the CallableStatement has been instantiated, it can be used just like a PreparedStatement for setting the values of parameters. However, if a parameter is registered within the database stored procedure as an OUT parameter, you must call a special method, registerOutParameter, passing the parameter position and database type of the OUT parameter that you want to register. In the solution to this recipe, the OUT parameter is in the second position, and it has a VARCHAR type.

```
cs.registerOutParameter(2, Types.VARCHAR);
```

To execute the stored procedure, call the executeQuery method on the CallableStatement. Once this has been done, you can see the value of the OUT parameter by making a call to the CallableStatement getXXX method that corresponds to the data type:

```
System.out.println(cs.getString(2));
```

A NOTE REGARDING STORED FUNCTIONS

Calling a stored database function is essentially the same as calling a stored procedure. However, the syntax to prepareCall() is slightly modified. To call a stored function, change the call within the curly braces to entail a returned value using a ? character. For instance, suppose that a function named DUMMY_FUNC accepted one parameter and returned a value. The following code would be used to make the call and return the value:

```
cs = conn.prepareCall("{? = call DUMMY_FUNC(?)}");
cs.registerOutParameter(1, Types.VARCHAR);
cs.setString(2, "This is a test");
cs.execute();
```

A call to cs.getString(1) would then retrieve the returned value.

7-11. Querying and Storing Large Objects

Problem

The application you are developing requires the storage of strings of text that can include an unlimited number of characters.

Solution

Because the size of the strings that need to be stored is unlimited, it is best to use a character large object (CLOB) data type to store the data. The code in the following example demonstrates how to load a CLOB into the database and how to query it. The following excerpts are two methods from the org.javaee8recipes.chapter7.dao.ChapterDAO class.

Let's look at how to read a CLOB column value from the database. The readClob method queries the database, reading the CHAPTER_NUMBER, TITLE, and DESCRIPTION columns from the CHAPTER database table. The length of the DESCRIPTION, which is the CLOB column, is printed to the command line along with the chapter number, title, and description.

```
public void readClob() {
        String qry = "select chapter_number, title, description from chapter";
        Clob theClob = null;
        CreateConnection.loadProperties();
        try (Connection conn = CreateConnection.getConnection();
                PreparedStatement stmt = conn.prepareStatement(qry)) {

            try (ResultSet rs = stmt.executeQuery();) {
                while (rs.next()) {
                    int chapterNumber = rs.getInt(1);
                    String title = rs.getString(2);
                    theClob = rs.getClob(3);
                    System.out.println("Clob length: " + theClob.length());
                    System.out.println(chapterNumber + " - " + title + ": ");
                    java.io.InputStream in =
                            theClob.getAsciiStream();
                    int i;
                    while ((i = in.read()) > -1) {
                        System.out.print((char) i);
                    }
                    System.out.println();
                }
            }
        } catch (IOException ex) {
            ex.printStackTrace();
        } catch (SQLException ex) {
            ex.printStackTrace();
        }
    }
```

The resulting output from running the method would look similar to the following, depending on which records are stored in the database:

```
Clob length: 19
1 - Getting Started with Java 7:
chapter description
Clob length: 19
2 - Strings:
chapter description
Clob length: 19
```

```
3 - Numbers and Dates:
chapter description
Clob length: 19
4 - Data Structures, Conditionals, and Iteration:
chapter description
Clob length: 19
5 - Input and Output:
chapter description
Clob length: 19
6 - Exceptions, Logging, and Debugging:
chapter description
Clob length: 19
7 - Object-Oriented Java:
chapter description
Clob length: 19
8 - Concurrency:
chapter description
Clob length: 19
9 - Debugging and Unit Testing:
chapter description
Clob length: 19
10 - Unicode, Internationalization, and Currency Codes:
chapter description
```

What about inserting CLOB values into the database? The next method accepts values for each field within a record of the CHAPTER table, and it constructs the CLOB contents and lastly performs the insert.

```
private void performCreate(int chapterNumber, int bookId, String title, String description)
{
        String sql = "INSERT INTO CHAPTER VALUES("
                + "CHAPTER_S.NEXTVAL, ?, ?, ?, ?)";

        Clob textClob = null;
        CreateConnection.loadProperties();
        try (Connection conn = CreateConnection.getConnection();
                PreparedStatement stmt = conn.prepareStatement(sql)) {

            textClob = conn.createClob();
            textClob.setString(1, description);

            stmt.setInt(1, chapterNumber);
            stmt.setString(2, title.toUpperCase());
            stmt.setClob(3, textClob);
            stmt.setInt(4, bookId);
            // Returns row-count or 0 if not successful
            int result = stmt.executeUpdate();
            if (result > 0) {
                System.out.println("-- Record created --");
            } else {
                System.out.println("!! Record NOT Created !!");
            }
```

```
        } catch (SQLException e) {
            e.printStackTrace();
        }
    }
```

How It Works

If your application requires the storage of string values, you need to know how large those strings might possibly become. Most databases have an upper boundary when it comes to the storage size of VARCHAR fields. For instance, Oracle Database has an upper boundary of 4,000 bytes, and anything exceeding that length will be cut off. If you have large amounts of text that need to be stored, use a CLOB field in the database.

A CLOB is handled a bit differently from a string in Java code. In fact, it is actually a bit odd to work with the first couple of times you use it because you have to create a CLOB from a Connection.

■ **Note** In reality, CLOBs and BLOBs (binary large objects) are not stored in the Oracle table where they are defined. Instead, a large object (LOB) locator is stored in the table column. Oracle might place the CLOB in a separate file on the database server. When Java creates the Clob object, it can be used to hold data for update to a specific LOB location in the database or to retrieve the data from a specific LOB location within the database.

Let's look at the performCreate method that is contained in the solution to this recipe. As you can see, a Clob object is created using the Connection object's createClob method. Once the Clob has been created, you set its contents using the setString method by passing the position, which indicates where to place the String, and the String of text itself:

```
textClob = conn.createClob();
textClob.setString(1, "This will be the recipe text in clob format");
```

Once you have created and populated the Clob, you simply pass it to the database using the PreparedStatement setClob method. In the case of this example, the PreparedStatement performs a database insert into the CHAPTER table by calling the executeUpdate method as usual. Querying a Clob is fairly straightforward as well. As you can see in the readClob method that is contained in the solution to this recipe, a PreparedStatement query is set up, and the results are retrieved in a ResultSet. The only difference between using a Clob and a String is that you must load the Clob into a Clob type. Calling the Clob object's getString method will pass you a strange-looking String of text that denotes a Clob object. Therefore, calling the Clob object's getAsciiStream method will return the actual data that is stored in the Clob. This technique is used in the solution to this recipe.

Although Clobs are fairly easy to use, they take a couple of extra steps to prepare. It is best to plan your applications accordingly and try to estimate whether the database fields you are using might need to be CLOBs because of size restrictions. Proper planning will prevent you from going back and changing standard string-based code to work with Clobs later.

7-12. Caching Data for Use When Disconnected

Problem

You want to work with data from a DBMS when you are in a disconnected state. That is, you are working on a device that is not connected to the database, and you still want to have the ability to work with a set of data as though you are connected. For instance, you are working in an area with an intermittent connection. You want the ability to query, insert, update, and delete data, even though there is no connection available. Once a connection becomes available, you want to have your device synchronize any database changes that have been made while disconnected.

Solution

Use a `CachedRowSet` object to store the data that you want to work with while offline. This will afford your application the ability to work with data as though it were connected to a database. Once your connection is restored or you connect to the database, synchronize the data that has been changed within the `CachedRowSet` with the database repository. The following example class demonstrates the usage of a `CachedRowSet`. In this scenario, the `main` method executes the example. Suppose there was no `main` method, though, and that another application on a portable device invoked the methods of this class.

Follow the code in the example and consider the possibility of working with the results that are stored within the `CachedRowSet` while not connected to the database. For instance, suppose you began some work in the office while connected to the network and are now outside of the office, where the network is spotty and you cannot maintain a constant connection to the database.

```
import java.sql.Connection;
import java.sql.PreparedStatement;
import java.sql.ResultSet;
import java.sql.SQLException;
import javax.sql.rowset.CachedRowSet;
import javax.sql.rowset.RowSetFactory;
import javax.sql.rowset.RowSetProvider;
import javax.sql.rowset.spi.SyncProviderException;
import org.javaee8recipes.chapter07.CreateConnection;

public class CachedRowSetExample {

    public static CachedRowSet crs = null;

    public static void main(String[] args) {
        boolean successFlag = false;
        CreateConnection.loadProperties();
        try(Connection conn = CreateConnection.getConnection();) {

    // Perform Scrollable Query
            queryWithRowSet(conn);
            updateData();
            syncWithDatabase(conn);
        } catch (java.sql.SQLException ex) {
            System.out.println(ex);
        }
    }
```

```
/**
 * Call this method to synchronize the data that has been used in the
 * CachedRowSet with the database
 */
public static void syncWithDatabase(Connection conn) {
    try {
        crs.acceptChanges(conn);
    } catch (SyncProviderException ex) {
    // If there is a conflict while synchronizing, this exception
    // will be thrown.
        ex.printStackTrace();
    } finally {
    // Clean up resources by closing CachedRowSet
        if (crs != null) {
            try {
                crs.close();
            } catch (SQLException ex) {
                ex.printStackTrace();
            }
        }
    }
}

public static void queryWithRowSet(Connection conn) {
    RowSetFactory factory;
    try {
    // Create a new RowSetFactory
        factory = RowSetProvider.newFactory();
    // Create a CachedRowSet object using the factory
        crs = factory.createCachedRowSet();
    // Alternatively populate the CachedRowSet connection settings
    // crs.setUsername(createConn.getUsername());
    // crs.setPassword(createConn.getPassword());
    // crs.setUrl(createConn.getJdbcUrl());
    // Populate a query that will obtain the data that will be used
        crs.setCommand("select id, chapter_number, title, description, book_id from
        chapter");
    // Set key columns
        int[] keys = {1};
        crs.setKeyColumns(keys);
    // Execute query
        crs.execute(conn);
    // You can now work with the object contents in a disconnected state
        while (crs.next()) {
            System.out.println(crs.getString(2) + ": " + crs.getString(3)
                    + " - " + crs.getString(4));
        }
    } catch (SQLException ex) {
        ex.printStackTrace();
    }
}
```

```
    public static boolean updateData() {
        boolean returnValue = false;
        try {

        // Move to the position before the first row in the result set
            crs.beforeFirst();
        // traverse result set
            while (crs.next()) {
        // If the chapter_number equals 1 then update
                if (crs.getInt("CHAPTER_NUMBER") == 1) {
                    System.out.println("updating Chapter 1");
                    crs.updateString("TITLE", "Subject to change");
                    crs.updateRow();
                }
            }
            returnValue = true;
        // Move to the position before the first row in the result set
            crs.beforeFirst();
        // traverse result set to see changes
            while (crs.next()) {
                System.out.println(crs.getString(2) + ": " + crs.getString(3));
            }
        } catch (SQLException ex) {
            returnValue = false;
            ex.printStackTrace();
        }
        return returnValue;
    }
}
```

Running this example code will display output that looks similar to the following code, although the text might vary depending on the values in the database. Notice that the database record for Chapter 1 has a changed description after the update of the CachedRowSet.

```
Successfully connected
 1: Getting Started with Java 7 - javax.sql.rowset.serial.SerialClob@5e7afcba
 2: Strings - javax.sql.rowset.serial.SerialClob@5c6647cb
 3: Numbers and Dates - javax.sql.rowset.serial.SerialClob@3ef38fd1
 4: Data Structures, Conditionals, and Iteration - javax.sql.rowset.serial.
    SerialClob@686702a0
 5: Input and Output - javax.sql.rowset.serial.SerialClob@42dd8bec
 6: Exceptions, Logging, and Debugging - javax.sql.rowset.serial.SerialClob@5f0d553f
 7: Object-Oriented Java - javax.sql.rowset.serial.SerialClob@6457cbd9
 8: Concurrency - javax.sql.rowset.serial.SerialClob@40084706
 9: Debugging and Unit Testing - javax.sql.rowset.serial.SerialClob@5f6efbc1
10: Unicode, Internationalization, and Currency Codes - javax.sql.rowset.serial.
    SerialClob@6f526cd9
updating Chapter 1
 1: Subject to change
 2: Strings
 3: Numbers and Dates
```

```
 4: Data Structures, Conditionals, and Iteration
 5: Input and Output
 6: Exceptions, Logging, and Debugging
 7: Object-Oriented Java
 8: Concurrency
 9: Debugging and Unit Testing
10: Unicode, Internationalization, and Currency Codes11-3: Handling SQL Exceptions - Using
    SQLException
```

How It Works

It is not possible to remain connected to the Internet 100% of the time if you are working on a mobile device and traveling. In such cases, solutions like the CachedRowSet object can come into play. The CachedRowSet is the same as a regular ResultSet object, except it does not have to maintain a connection to a database in order to remain usable. You can query the database, obtain the results, and place them into a CachedRowSet object; then you work with them while not connected to the database. If changes are made to the data at any point, those changes can be synchronized with the database at a later time.

There are a couple of ways to create a CachedRowSet. The solution to this recipe uses a RowSetFactory to instantiate a CachedRowSet. However, you can also use the CachedRowSet default constructor to create a new instance. Doing so would look like the following line of code:

```
CachedRowSet crs = new CachedRowSetImpl();
```

Once instantiated, you need to set up a connection to the database. There are also a couple of ways to do this. Properties could be set for the connection that will be used, and the solution to this recipe demonstrates this technique within comments. The following excerpt from the solution sets the connection properties using the CachedRowSet object's setUsername, setPassword, and setUrl methods. Each of them accepts a String value, and in the example, that string is obtained from the CreateConnection class:

```
// Alternatively populate the CachedRowSet connection settings
// crs.setUsername(createConn.getUsername());
// crs.setPassword(createConn.getPassword());
// crs.setUrl(createConn.getJdbcUrl());
```

Another way to set up the connection is to wait until the query is executed and pass a Connection object to the executeQuery method. This is the technique that is used in the solution to this recipe. But before we can execute the query, it must be set using the setCommand method, which accepts a String value. In this case, the string is the SQL query you need to execute:

```
crs.setCommand("select id, chapter_number, title, description, book_id from chapter");
```

Next, if a CachedRowSet will be used for updates, the primary key values should be noted using the setKeys method. This method accepts an int array that includes the positional indices of the key columns. These keys are used to identify unique columns. In this case, the first column listed in the query, ID, is the primary key.

```
int[] keys = {1};
crs.setKeyColumns(keys);
```

Finally, execute the query and populate the CachedRowSet using the execute method. As mentioned previously, the execute method optionally accepts a Connection object, which allows the CachedRowSet to obtain a database connection.

```
crs.execute(conn);
```

Once the query has been executed and the CachedRowSet has been populated, it can be used just like any other ResultSet. You can use it to fetch records forward and backward or by specifying the absolute position of the row you'd like to retrieve. The solution to this recipe demonstrates only a couple of these fetching methods, but the most often used ones are listed in Table 7-2.

Table 7-2. *CachedRowSet Fetching Methods*

Method	Description
first()	Moves to the first row in the set
beforeFirst()	Moves to the position before the first row in the set
afterLast	Moves to the position after the last row in the set
next()	Moves to the next position in the set
last()	Moves to the last position in the set

It is possible to insert and update rows within a CachedRowSet. To insert rows, use the moveToInsertRow method to move to a new row position. Then populate a row by using the various CachedRowSet methods (updateString, updateInt, and so on) that correspond to the data type of the column you are populating within the row. Once you have populated each of the required columns within the row, call the insertRow method, followed by the moveToCurrentRow method. The following lines of code demonstrate inserting a record for Chapter 11 into the CHAPTER table:

```
crs.moveToInsertRow();
crs.updateInt(1, sequenceValue); // obtain current sequence values with a prior query
crs.updateInt(2, 11);
crs.updateString(3, "Chapter 11 Title");
crs.updateString(4, "Description");
crs.updateInt(5, bookId);
crs.insertRow();
crs.moveToCurrentRow();
```

Updating rows is similar to using an updatable ResultSet. Simply update the values using the CachedRowSet object's methods (updateString, updateInt, and so on) that correspond to the data type of the column that you are updating within the row. Once you have updated the column or columns within the row, call the updateRow method. This technique is demonstrated in the solution to this recipe.

```
crs.updateString("TITLE", "Subject to change");
crs.updateRow();
```

To make any updates or inserts propagate to the database, the acceptChanges method must be called. This method can accept an optional Connection argument in order to connect to the database. Once called, all changes are flushed to the database. Unfortunately, because time might have elapsed since the data was last retrieved for the CachedRowSet, there could be conflicts. If such a conflict arises, a

SyncProviderException will be thrown. You can catch these exceptions and handle the conflicts manually using a SyncResolver object. However, resolving conflicts is out of the scope of this recipe, so for more information, see the online documentation at

http://download.oracle.com/javase/tutorial/jdbc/basics/cachedrowset.html

CachedRowSet objects provide great flexibility for working with data, especially when you are using a device that is not always connected to the database. However, they can also be overkill in situations where you can simply use a standard ResultSet or even a scrollable ResultSet.

7-13. Joining RowSet Objects When Not Connected to the Data Source

Problem

You want to join two or more RowSets while not connected to a database. Perhaps your application is loaded on a mobile device that is not connected to the database 100 percent of the time. In such a case, you are looking for a solution that will allow you to join the results of two or more queries.

Solution

Use a JoinRowSet to take data from two relational database tables and join them. The data from each table that will be joined should be fetched into a RowSet, and then the JoinRowSet can be used to join each of those RowSet objects based upon related elements that are contained within them. For instance, suppose that there were two related tables contained in a database. One of the tables stores a list of authors, and the other table contains a list of chapters that are written by those authors. The two tables can be joined using SQL by the primary and foreign key relationship.

■ **Note** A primary key is a unique identifier within each record of a database table, and a foreign key is a referential constraint between two tables.

The application will not be connected to the database to make the JOIN query, so it must be done using a JoinRowSet. The following class demonstrates one strategy that can be used in this scenario:

```
import com.sun.rowset.JoinRowSetImpl;
import java.sql.Connection;
import java.sql.SQLException;
import javax.sql.rowset.CachedRowSet;
import javax.sql.rowset.JoinRowSet;
import javax.sql.rowset.RowSetFactory;
import javax.sql.rowset.RowSetProvider;
import org.javaee8recipes.chapter07.CreateConnection;

public class JoinRowSetExample {

    public static CreateConnection createConn;
    public static CachedRowSet bookAuthors = null;
```

```
    public static CachedRowSet authorWork = null;
    public static JoinRowSet jrs = null;

    public static void main(String[] args) {
        boolean successFlag = false;
        CreateConnection.loadProperties();
        try(Connection conn = CreateConnection.getConnection();) {

        // Perform Scrollable Query
            queryBookAuthor(conn);
            queryAuthorWork(conn);
            joinRowQuery();
        } catch (java.sql.SQLException ex) {
            System.out.println(ex);
        } finally {

            if (bookAuthors != null) {
                try {
                    bookAuthors.close();
                } catch (SQLException ex) {
                    ex.printStackTrace();
                }
            }
            if (authorWork != null) {
                try {
                    authorWork.close();
                } catch (SQLException ex) {
                    ex.printStackTrace();
                }
            }
            if (jrs != null) {

                try {
                    jrs.close();
                } catch (SQLException ex) {
                    ex.printStackTrace();
                }
            }
        }
    }

    public static void queryBookAuthor(Connection conn) {
        RowSetFactory factory;
        try {
        // Create a new RowSetFactory
            factory = RowSetProvider.newFactory();
        // Create a CachedRowSet object using the factory
            bookAuthors = factory.createCachedRowSet();
        // Alternatively populate the CachedRowSet connection settings
        // crs.setUsername(createConn.getUsername());
```

```
    // crs.setPassword(createConn.getPassword());
    // crs.setUrl(createConn.getJdbcUrl());
    // Populate a query that will obtain the data that will be used
        bookAuthors.setCommand("SELECT ID, LAST, FIRST FROM BOOK_AUTHOR");
        bookAuthors.execute(conn);
    // You can now work with the object contents in a disconnected state
        while (bookAuthors.next()) {
            System.out.println(bookAuthors.getString(1) + ": " + bookAuthors.getString(2)
                    + ", " + bookAuthors.getString(3));
        }
    } catch (SQLException ex) {
        ex.printStackTrace();
    }
}

public static void queryAuthorWork(Connection conn) {
    RowSetFactory factory;
    try {

    // Create a new RowSetFactory
        factory = RowSetProvider.newFactory();
    // Create a CachedRowSet object using the factory
        authorWork = factory.createCachedRowSet();
    // Alternatively populate the CachedRowSet connection settings
    // crs.setUsername(createConn.getUsername());
    // crs.setPassword(createConn.getPassword());
    // crs.setUrl(createConn.getJdbcUrl());
    // Populate a query that will obtain the data that will be used
        authorWork.setCommand(
        "SELECT ID, AUTHOR_ID, BOOK_ID FROM AUTHOR_WORK");
        authorWork.execute(conn);
    // You can now work with the object contents in a disconnected state
        while (authorWork.next()) {
            System.out.println(authorWork.getString(1) + ": " + authorWork.getInt(2)
                    + " - " + authorWork.getInt(3));
        }
    } catch (SQLException ex) {
        ex.printStackTrace();
    }
}

public static void joinRowQuery() {
    try {
    // Create JoinRowSet
        jrs = new JoinRowSetImpl();
    // Add RowSet & Corresponding Keys
        jrs.addRowSet(bookAuthors, 1);
        jrs.addRowSet(authorWork, 2);
```

```
        // Traverse Results
            while (jrs.next()) {
                System.out.println(jrs.getString("BOOK_ID") + " - "
                        + jrs.getString("FIRST") + " "
                        + jrs.getString("LAST"));
            }

        } catch (SQLException ex) {
            ex.printStackTrace();
        }
    }
}
```

Running this class will result in output that resembles the following:

```
Successfully connected
21: JUNEAU, JOSH
22: DEA, CARL
23: BEATY, MARK
24: GUIME, FREDDY
25: JOHN, OCONNER
21: 21 - Java 7 Recipes
22: 23 - Java 7 Recipes
23: 22 - Java 7 Recipes
24: 24 - Java 7 Recipes
25: 21 - Java EE 7 Recipes
26: 22 - Java FX 2.0 - Introduction by Example
Java 7 Recipes - FREDDY GUIME
Java 7 Recipes - MARK BEATY
Java FX 2.0 - Introduction by Example - CARL DEA
Java 7 Recipes - CARL DEA
Java EE 7 Recipes - JOSH JUNEAU
Java 7 Recipes - JOSH JUNEAU
```

How It Works

A `JoinRowSet` is a combination of two or more populated `RowSet` objects. It can be used to join two `RowSet` objects based on key-value relationships, just as if it were a SQL `JOIN` query. To create a `JoinRowSet`, you must first populate two or more `RowSet` objects with related data, and then they can each be added to the `JoinRowSet` to create the combined result.

In the solution to this recipe, the two tables that are queried are named `BOOK_AUTHOR` and `AUTHOR_WORK`. The `BOOK_AUTHOR` table contains a list of author names, while the `AUTHOR_WORK` table contains the list of chapters in a book along with the `AUTHOR_ID` for the author who wrote the chapter. Following along with the `main` method, first the `BOOK_AUTHOR` table is queried, and its results are fetched into a `CachedRowSet` using the `queryBookAuthor` method. For more details regarding the use of `CachedRowSet` objects, see Recipe 7-12.

Next, another `CachedRowSet` is populated with the results of querying the `AUTHOR_WORK` table, when the `queryAuthorWork` method is called. At this point, there are two populated `CacheRowSet` objects, and they can now be combined using a `JoinRowSet`. To do so, each table must contain one or more columns that relate to the other table. In this case, the `BOOK_AUTHOR.ID` column relates to the `AUTHOR_WORK.AUTHOR_ID` column, so the `RowSet` objects must be joined on those column results.

The final method that is invoked within the main method is joinRowQuery. This method is where all the JoinRowSet work takes place. Note that the connection to the database can be null at this time. A new JoinRowSet is created by instantiating a JoinRowSetImpl object.

```
jrs = new JoinRowSetImpl();
```

■ **Note** You will receive a compile-time warning when using JoinRowSetImpl because it is an internal SUN proprietary API. However, the Oracle version is OracleJoinRowSet, which is not as versatile.

Next, the two CachedRowSet objects are added to the newly created JoinRowSet by calling its addRowSet method. The addRowSet method accepts a couple of arguments. The first is the name of the RowSet object that you want to add to the JoinRowSet, and the second is an int value indicating the position within the CachedRowSet, which contains the key value that will be used to implement the join. In the solution to this recipe, the first call to addRowSet passes the bookAuthorsCachedRowSet, along with the number 1 because the element in the first position of the bookAuthorsCachedRowSet corresponds to the BOOK_AUTHOR.ID column. The second call to addRowSet passes the authorWorkCachedRowSet, along with the number 2 because the element in the second position of the authorWork CachedRowSet corresponds to the AUTHOR_WORK.AUTHOR_ID column.

```
// Add RowSet & Corresponding Keys
jrs.addRowSet(bookAuthors, 1);
jrs.addRowSet(authorWork, 2);
```

The JoinRowSet can now be used to fetch the results of the join, just as if it were a normal RowSet. When calling the corresponding methods (getString, getInt, and so on) of the JoinRowSet, pass the name of the database column corresponding to the data you want to store.

```
while(jrs.next()){
System.out.println(jrs.getInt("CHAPTER_NUMBER") + ": " +
jrs.getString("CHAPTER_TITLE") + " - " +
jrs.getString("FIRST") + " " +
jrs.getString("LAST"));
}
```

Although a JoinRowSet is not needed for every project, it can be handy when performing work against two related sets of data. This especially holds true if the application is not connected to a database all the time or if you are trying to use as few Connection objects as possible.

7-14. Querying with a REF_CURSOR

Problem

Your database has implemented a REF_CURSOR data type, which holds a query cursor value. You would like to have the ability to call upon a REF_CURSOR from your application and use the results just like a standard query.

Solution

Utilize a CallableStatement to call upon the database function or procedure that returns a REF_CURSOR and register the returned value as Types.REF_CURSOR. The result will be returned as a ResultSet.class type, which can then be called upon like an ordinary query ResultSet to obtain the results. In the following example, a procedure named AUTHOR_PROC is called upon, which returns a REF_CURSOR. The results are then registered and parsed accordingly.

```
CallableStatement cstmt = conn.prepareCall("{AUTHOR_PROC(?)}");
cstmt.registerOutParameter(1, Types.REF_CURSOR);
cstmt.executeQuery();
ResultSet rs = cstmt.getObject(1, ResultSet.class);
while(rs.next()){
    System.out.println("Name="+ rs.getString(1));
}
```

How It Works

A REF_CURSOR is a database construct that allows one to generate a query string that can be passed by reference and called upon when needed. Oftentimes these constructs are returned from functions or procedures, and they allow for the ability to generate dynamic queries. As such, it can be quite useful to call upon a REF_CURSOR from within a Java application. The JDBC 4.2 release added the ability to call upon and work with REF_CURSORs.

In the solution to this recipe demonstrates how to call upon a REF_CURSOR and obtain a ResultSet. The ResultSet can then be used to obtain access to the record data that is returned. Return a CallableStatement to call upon the REF_CURSOR by invoking the Connection prepareCall method and passing a string containing the name of the database procedure or function that returns the REF_CURSOR using the following syntax:

```
CallableStatement cstmt = conn.prepareCall("{AUTHOR_PROC(?)}");
```

Once the CallableStatement has been generated, call upon the registerOutParameter method and pass the REF_CURSOR positional index, which in this case is 1, and the data type of the value being returned at that index. In this case, the data type is Types.REF_CURSOR.

```
cstmt.registerOutParameter(1, Types.REF_CURSOR);
```

Lastly, call upon the CallableStatement executeQuery method, which will execute the query and return the result. The CallableStatement getObject method can then be called upon, once again passing the position of the value being returned. In this case the position is 1 and the type is ResultSet.class, and this can be assigned to a ResultSet, which can then be used to return the results of the REF_CURSOR query. As you can see from the example, a String value is expected.

```
ResultSet rs = cstmt.getObject(1, ResultSet.class);
while(rs.next()){
    System.out.println("Name="+ rs.getString(1));
}
```

The support for REF_CURSOR is a great addition for the JDBC API with release 4.2. REF_CURSORs provide the ability to create dynamic queries within SQL, and with the addition of the JDBC support, these dynamic SQL statements can now be utilized from Java applications.

CHAPTER 8

Object-Relational Mapping

For years, the Java Database Connectivity API (JDBC) was the standard for working with databases both web or desktop Java applications alike. Over the years, techniques for obtaining access to data stores and working with data within applications has evolved, and many organizations began to develop their own strategies for working with data in a more convenient way. Developers often find it easier to work with Java objects rather than Structured Query Language (SQL) for relational data. Chapter 7 discusses some techniques that have been used in order to encapsulate SQL into separate utility classes and abstract it from developers so that they can work with Java objects rather than the SQL. Such strategies are known as *object-relational mapping* (ORM) strategies, and there are several well-known ORM strategies available from a multitude of organizations today.

Among the most well-known ORM strategies are Hibernate (`http://hibernate.org`), Oracle's TopLink (`www.oracle.com/technetwork/middleware/toplink/overview/index.html`), and EclipseLink (`http://wiki.eclipse.org/EclipseLink/UserGuide/JPA/Basic_JPA_Development`). In an effort to standardize the industry, the Java Persistence API (JPA) has been deemed the strategy to use for moving forward with Java Enterprise Edition. JPA includes many features that were introduced in ORM strategies, such as Hibernate and TopLink. In fact, some of the top representatives from many of the different ORM projects have come together to formulate the Java Specification Requests (JSRs) for Java EE, providing Java enterprise developers with a standard, efficient, and highly productive way to work with an underlying RDBMS from within Java applications. JPA allows developers to choose from a variety of Java persistence providers to utilize the configuration with which they are most comfortable, without the need to include multiple third-party libraries or customizations within the application. The possible providers are as follows:

- EclipseLink (JPA default)
- Hibernate
- TopLink Essentials
- KODO
- OpenJPA

Object-relational mapping is the process of mapping a Java object to a database table, such that each column of the database table maps to a single field or property within the Java object. Java objects that are used to map against database tables are referred to as *entity classes*, and this chapter focuses on the creation and use of entity classes. Recipes cover areas such as creating classes and performing standard database transactions. You will learn how to configure a connection against a database, how to utilize JPA to persist and retrieve objects without using SQL, and how to relate objects to one another in a meaningful and productive manner.

J. Juneau, *Java EE 8 Recipes*, https://doi.org/10.1007/978-1-4842-3594-2_8

Not only does ORM programming abstract the implementation details of working directly with a database from a developer, but it also provides a standard mechanism for deploying applications on databases from multiple vendors. JPA takes care of translating code into SQL statements, so once an application is written using JPA, it can be deployed using almost any underlying database. The Java EE 8 platform introduces JPA 2.2, which includes more benefits such as enhanced support for streams, repeatable annotations, and more.

■ **Note** The recipes in this chapter may or may not be available for your use depending on which JPA provider you choose. For instance, providers may include a different set of metadata annotations to use. Rather than list each annotation that is available for use in each recipe, I direct you to very good resources for learning about all of the possible annotations that can be used, along with each of the most widely used providers. While most of the annotations are common among all providers, there are a handful of custom annotations for each.

EclipseLink (Use 2.7+ with Java EE 8): `http://www.eclipse.org/eclipselink/api/2.7/org/eclipse/persistence/annotations/package-summary.html`

Hibernate (Use 5.3+ with Java EE 8): `https://docs.jboss.org/hibernate/orm/5.3/javadocs/`

Toplink JPA (Java Persistence API): `www.oracle.com/technetwork/middleware/ias/toplink-jpa-annotations-096251.html`

The sources for Chapter 8 reside in the `org.javaee8recipes.chapter08` package. To run the examples from Chapter 8, deploy the application to the application server and then visit the URL `http://localhost:8080/JavaEERecipes/faces/chapter08/home.xhtml`. It should be noted that the examples for Chapter 8 cannot be run within a web application without using other technologies such as Enterprise JavaBeans, which are covered in Chapter 9. For that reason, many of the examples in this chapter utilize stand-alone Java classes for testing purposes.

8-1. Creating an Entity

Problem

You want to create a Java object that can be mapped to a database table such that the class can be used for persistence, rather than using JDBC.

Solution

Create an entity class against a particular database table. Declare persistent fields or properties for each of the columns in the underlying data store table and use annotations to map the fields to a given column. Provide getters and setters for each of the persistent fields or properties that are declared within the entity so that other classes can access the contents.

The following code is an entity class named BookAuthor, which maps the BOOK_AUTHOR database table to a standard Java object for use in the application:

```
package org.javaee8recipes.chapter08.entity;

import java.io.Serializable;
import java.math.BigDecimal;
import javax.persistence.*;
import javax.validation.constraints.NotNull;
import javax.validation.constraints.Size;

/**
 * Chapter 8
 * Entity class for the BOOK_AUTHOR database table of the Acme Bookstore application
 * @author juneau
 */
@Entity
public class BookAuthor implements Serializable {
    private static final long serialVersionUID = 1L;
    @Id
    @Basic(optional = false)
    @NotNull
    @Column(name = "ID")
    private BigDecimal id;
    @Size(max = 30)
    @Column(name = "LAST")
    private String last;
    @Size(max = 30)
    @Column(name = "FIRST")
    private String first;
    @Lob
    @Column(name = "BIO")
    private String bio;

    public BookAuthor() {
    }

    public BookAuthor(BigDecimal id) {
        this.id = id;
    }

    public BigDecimal getId() {
        return id;
    }

    public void setId(BigDecimal id) {
        this.id = id;
    }
```

```
    public String getLast() {
        return last;
    }

    public void setLast(String last) {
        this.last = last;
    }

    public String getFirst() {
        return first;
    }

    public void setFirst(String first) {
        this.first = first;
    }

    public String getBio() {
        return bio;
    }

    public void setBio(String bio) {
        this.bio = bio;
    }

    @Override

    public int hashCode() {
        int hash = 0;
        hash += (id != null ? id.hashCode() : 0);        return hash;
    }

    @Override
    public boolean equals(Object object) {
        // TODO: Warning - this method won't work in the case the id fields are not set
        if (!(object instanceof BookAuthor)) {
            return false;
        }
        BookAuthor other = (BookAuthor) object;
        if ((this.id == null && other.id != null) || (this.id != null && !this.
        id.equals(other.id))) {
            return false;
        }
        return true;
    }

    @Override
    public String toString() {
        return "org.javaee8recipes.chapter08.entity.BookAuthor[ id=" + id + " ]";
    }

}
```

The entity itself cannot be used alone to access the database. Minimally, a persistence unit is required in order to connect with a database and perform transactions with the entity classes. To learn more about creating a persistence unit, refer to Recipe 8-3.

How It Works

As an object-oriented developer, it sometimes makes more sense to work with objects that represent data, rather than working with variables of data and writing SQL to work directly with the underlying data store. The concept of mapping objects to database tables is better known as *object-relational mapping*. The Java Persistence API utilizes ORM for storing and retrieving data from a database via the usage of object classes known as *entity classes*. An entity class is a Java object that represents an underlying database table.

■ **Note** Prior to EJB 3.0, XML files were used instead of annotations in order to manage metadata for entity classes. You can still use XML descriptors to manage metadata today, but I do not cover how to do so in this text. Most annotations can be used to selectively override default values in a class.

The entity class is usually named the same as the underlying database table, using camel-case lettering (capitalized first letters for all words) to separate different words within the table name. For instance, the BOOK_AUTHOR database table has a Java entity class named BookAuthor. The name of the entity can differ from the name of the underlying database table. However, it is a standard practice to name the entity class the same. In such cases where the name of the entity class has to differ from the database table, the @Table annotation can be used to annotate the entity class, providing the name of the underlying data table. Every entity class must be annotated as such by specifying the javax.persistence.Entity annotation. In the example, the BookAuthor entity class specifies only those annotations that are required. If the entity were to be named differently than the database table, the @Table annotation could be utilized as follows:

```
...
@Entity
@Table(name = "BOOK_AUTHOR")
...
```

An entity class must have a public or protected no-argument constructor. It is always a good idea to make an entity class Serializable by implementing the java.io.Serializable interface because doing so ensures that the entity class may be passed by value and persisted to disk, if needed. All entity classes must contain private or protected instance variables for each of the columns within the underlying database table, as well as variables for each relationship that the entity may have with other entities. (To read more about entity relationships, look at Recipes 8-6, 8-7, and 8-8.) All database tables that will be mapped to Java entity classes must contain a primary key field, and the corresponding instance variable within the entity class that maps to the primary key column must be annotated with @Id. Each of the instance variables that maps to a database column can be annotated with @Column, specifying the name of the underlying database column. However, if no @Column annotation is specified, the name of the variable should match the database column name exactly, using camel-case lettering to separate words within the column name. To signify that a particular database column and its mapped instance variable cannot contain a NULL value, the variable can be annotated with @NotNull.

Another annotation worth mentioning that is used in the example for this recipe includes `@Size`, which is used to specify the maximum size for a `String` variable. The size value should correspond to the database column size for the corresponding column. In addition, the `@Lob` annotation can be used to signify that the underlying database data type is a large object. There are other annotations that can be used to further customize an entity class; see the link in the introduction of this chapter for the JPA provider that you are using in order to learn more about all of the annotations that can be used. Table 8-1 summarizes the most commonly used annotations when creating an entity class. Those annotations are covered in the solution to this recipe.

Table 8-1. *Commonly Used Annotations for Creating Entity Classes*

Annotation	Description
`@Entity`	Designates a plain old Java object (POJO) class as an entity so that it can be used with JPA services
`@Table`	Specifies the name of the primary table associated with an entity (optional)
`@Id`	Designates one or more persistent fields or properties of the entity's primary key
`@Basic`	Configures the fetch type to `LAZY`
`@Column`	Associates a persistent attribute with a different name if the column name is awkward, is incompatible with a preexisting data model, or is invalid as a column name in your database

As mentioned in the solution for this recipe, an entity class cannot be used by itself. It is part of an overall solution for working with an underlying data source. Entity classes make it easy to map Java objects to database tables. They should be used in tandem with Enterprise JavaBeans (EJB) classes (Chapter 9), Contexts and Dependency Injection (CDI), or stand-alone with a persistence unit (Recipe 8-3) to perform database operations. A full Java EE solution utilizing the JSF framework can also use JSF managed beans to work directly with EJBs, or JAX-RS RESTful clients, which in turn, conduct work via the entity classes.

■ **Note** You may be wondering why the `hashCode()` and `equals()` methods are overridden in the example. The `equals()` method is present in every Java object, and it is used to determine object identity. Every entity class needs to contain an implementation of these methods in order to differentiate objects from one another. It is very possible for two entity objects to point to the same row in a database table. The `equals()` method can determine whether two entities point to the same row. Moreover, all Java objects that are equal to one another should contain the same `hashCode`. In entity classes, it is important to override these methods to determine whether objects represent the same database table row.

8-2. Mapping Data Types

Problem

You are interested in mapping database table columns with entity class fields, but you are unsure which data types to declare for the fields within the class.

■ **Note** Transient fields or properties cannot contain mapping annotations. A transient field or property is not persisted to the database.

Solution

Map database table column data types with their equivalent data type in the Java language specification when declaring instance variables for the columns within an entity class. The Java EE container will convert the database value accordingly so long as the database column data type matches a Java data type that will contain the specified column's value. To demonstrate data type mapping, an entity class will be written for the Acme Bookstore's CONTACT database table. The CONTACT table has the following description:

```
SQL> desc contact
 Name                                    Type
 -------------------------- ----------------------------
 ID                                  NOT NULL NUMBER
 FIRST                               VARCHAR2(50)
 LAST                                VARCHAR2(50)
 EMAIL                               VARCHAR2(150)
 PASSWORD                            VARCHAR2(30)
 DESCRIPTION                         CLOB
 OCCUPATION                          VARCHAR2(150)
 RECEIVENOTIFICATIONS                VARCHAR2(1)
 GENDER                              VARCHAR2(1)
```

The corresponding entity class is named Contact, and its class listing, shown next, demonstrates how to match each database column type to an appropriate Java data type:

```
package org.javaee8recipes.chapter08.entity;
...

@Entity
@Table(name = "CONTACT")
public class Contact implements Serializable {
    private static final long serialVersionUID = 1L;

    @Id
    @Basic(optional = false)
    @NotNull
    @Column(name = "ID")
    private BigDecimal id;
    @Size(max = 50)
    @Column(name = "FIRST")
    private String first;
    @Size(max = 50)
    @Column(name = "LAST")
    private String last;
    @Size(max = 150)
    @Column(name = "EMAIL")
    private String email;
```

```
    @Size(max = 30)
    @Column(name = "PASSWORD")
    private String password;
    @Lob
    @Column(name = "DESCRIPTION")
    private String description;
    @Size(max = 150)
    @Column(name = "OCCUPATION")
    private String occupation;
    @Size(max = 1)
    @Column(name = "RECEIVENOTIFICATIONS")
    private String receivenotifications;
    @Size(max = 1)
    @Column(name = "GENDER")
    private String gender;

    public Contact() {
    }

    ...

// getters and setters

    ...

    @Override
    public int hashCode() {
        ...
    }

    @Override
    public boolean equals(Object object) {
        ...
    }

    @Override
    public String toString() {
        return "org.javaee8recipes.chapter08.entity.Contact[ id=" + id + " ]";
    }

}
```

It is important to specify the correct mapping data types because errors can occur down the line if this is not done correctly. Such is often the case with numerical data types.

How It Works

To create a Java class that will be used to represent a database table, you must map each of the table's columns to a class instance variable. In doing so, the variable must be assigned a data type that corresponds to that database column's data type. In some cases, more than one Java data type will map to a single database column's data type. In other cases, however, a database column's data type must match a specific

Java data type. Table 8-2 lists the different Java data types and their associated Oracle database data types. If you are using another database for your work, see the documentation for the database to rectify any discrepancies between the data types from those used by Oracle.

Table 8-2. *Oracle Database and Java Data Type Mapping*

Oracle Data Type	Java Data Types
BINARY_INTEGER, NATURAL, NATURALN, PLS_INTEGER, POSITIVE, POSITIVEN, SIGNTYPE, INT, INTEGER	int
CHAR, CHARACTER, VARCHAR2 LONG, STRING, VARCHAR	java.lang.String
RAW, LONG RAW	byte[]
DEC, DECIMAL, NUMBER	java.math.BigDecimal
DOUBLE PRECISION, FLOAT	double
SMALLINT	int
REAL	float
DATE	java.sql.Timestamp java.sql.Date
TIMESTAMP (or derivative)	java.sql.Timestamp
BOOLEAN	boolean
CLOB	java.sql.Clob
BLOB	java.sql.Blob
VARRAY	java.sql.Array
REF CURSOR	java.sql.ResultSet

Mapping data types correctly is a very important step in the creation of an entity class because incorrect mapping can result in incorrect precision for numerical values and so forth. Utilizing the correct data types when mapping entity classes to the database table may vary depending on database vendor, but Table 8-2 should be easily translated from Oracle data types to the data types for the RDBMS of your choice.

8-3. Creating a Persistence Unit

Problem

You want to use an entity class to perform database transactions. Therefore, you need to configure your application's database connectivity.

Solution

Create a persistence unit to configure a database connection, and then use the persistence unit to perform transactions with a given entity class. A persistence unit can use a database connection pool configured in an application server, or it can utilize a local JDBC configuration in order to obtain a database connection. In this example, I demonstrate the use of the local JDBC configuration since the example will be run as a stand-alone application, rather than being deployed to an application server.

The following persistence unit is configured to create local JDBC connections, rather than using JPA for connections. However, you can learn more about configuring a persistence unit to work with database connection pools that are configured within an application server in the "How It Works" section of this recipe. The following code is from a file named `persistence.xml`, which is located in the `src\conf` directory for Chapter 8:

```
<?xml version="1.0" encoding="UTF-8"?>
<persistence version="2.0" xmlns="http://java.sun.com/xml/ns/persistence" xmlns:xsi="http://
www.w3.org/2001/XMLSchema-instance" xsi:schemaLocation="http://java.sun.com/xml/ns/
persistence http://java.sun.com/xml/ns/persistence/persistence_2_0.xsd">
    <persistence-unit name="JavaEERecipesLOCAL" transaction-type="RESOURCE_LOCAL">
        <class>org.javaee8recipes.chapter08.entity.BookAuthor</class>
        <properties>
            <property name="javax.persistence.jdbc.user" value="username"/>
            <property name="javax.persistence.jdbc.password" value="password"/>
            <property name="javax.persistence.jdbc.url" value="jdbc:oracle:thin:@
            hostname:port_number:dbname"/>
        </properties>
    </persistence-unit>
</persistence>
```

How It Works

To work with a database, an application needs to have the ability to connect. Usually a database connection pertains to a single user name/password in a database. The persistence context XML file is where the connection information for the Java Persistence API resides. A persistence context can contain configuration for more than one connection to the database. Each connection configuration is referred to as a *persistence unit*, and each has a unique name that is used to identify the connection from within the application classes. The `persistence.xml` file can be packaged as part of a web archive (WAR) or enterprise archive (EAR) file, or it can be packed into a JAR file, which is, in turn, packaged with a WAR or EAR. If it's packaged with an EAR file, it should reside within the `META-INF` directory. If using a WAR file, the `persistence.xml` file should be packaged in the `resources/META-INF` directory. Lastly, if you're packaging a JAR file, the JAR should reside in the `WEB-INF/lib` directory of a WAR or the library directory of an EAR.

As mentioned previously, each `persistence.xml` file can contain more than one database configuration, or persistence unit. Each persistence unit contains the type of JPA provider that will be used for the connection, the transaction type (`JTA` or `RESOURCE_LOCAL`), classes to be used for persistence (entity classes), and database connection specifics. In this section, I break down the persistence unit that is configured for the recipe solution and describe each piece.

At the root of each persistence unit is the `persistence-unit` element, which contains the `name` and `transaction-type` attributes. Each persistence unit has a name; in the case of the example, it is `JavaEERecipesLOCAL`, and this name is used to obtain a reference to the persistence unit from within application code. The `transaction-type` attribute of a persistence unit indicates whether Java Transaction API entity managers will be created (for use within an application server) or `Resource-Local` entity managers will be created (for use with stand-alone applications).

Next in the example you see a series of classes listed within separate `class` elements. Within the `persistence-unit` element, zero or more classes can be identified for use with the persistence unit. These classes are the entity classes that will be mapped to the underlying database table. If using the `RESOURCE_LOCAL` transaction type, each entity class must be listed within the persistence unit. If you're using JTA (deployed to an application server within a WAR or EAR file), then the container takes care of identifying the entity classes and they do not need to be listed in the persistence unit. If an entity class is not identified in the persistence unit and the transaction type is `RESOURCE_LOCAL`, then that entity class will not be available for use within the application.

■ **Note** A persistence unit may also include an `<exclude-unlisted-classes>` element, which should be set to a boolean value. This element is used to indicate whether classes must be listed using a `<class>` element within the persistence unit when using JTA, and it is `FALSE` by default. It may make sense to set this element to `TRUE` if two or more data sources are being used in an application and only specified entity classes should be used for each.

The `properties` element should contain sub-elements that identify the connection to the database. Specifically, the user, password, and database URL are identified in sub-properties of the properties element. For `RESOURCE_LOCAL` persistence units, the following points are true:

- The `javax.persistence.jdbc.username` property should be used to identify the database user name for the connection.
- The `javax.persistence.jdbc.password` property should identify the database user password for the connection.
- The `javax.persistence.jdbc.url` property should identify the database URL for the connection.

The properties for a Java Transaction API connection are different. In fact, for JTA, there can be no properties specified. Instead, an element named `jta-data-source` can be used to specify a JNDI name of a database connection that has been configured within the application server for use. For example, let's say the database connection is configured as `jdbc/OracleConnection` within the application server. Furthermore, let's assume you are deploying a WAR file to the GlassFish application server, and you will use `JTA` instead of `RESOURCE_LOCAL`. If this is the case, the persistence unit may look like the following:

```
<persistence-unit name="JavaEERecipesJTA" transaction-type="JTA">
    <jta-data-source>jdbc/OracleConnection</jta-data-source>
    <properties/>
</persistence-unit>
```

■ **Note** There are no classes listed in the JTA example because the application server automatically identifies the entity classes for use with the persistence unit. However, there are circumstances for which it may be useful to list classes, as mentioned in the preceding note.

To use a persistence unit, an `EntityManagerFactory` object must first be obtained. An `EntityManagerFactory` object can be obtained by calling the `Persistence.createEntityManagerFactory` method and passing the string-based name of the persistence unit for which you want to obtain a connection. Once an `EntityManagerFactory` object has been obtained, an `EntityManager` object can be created and used to begin a database transaction. Obtaining a connection via a persistence unit would look similar to the following:

```
...
EntityManagerFactory emf = Persistence.createEntityManagerFactory("JavaEERecipesLOCAL");
EntityManager em = emf.createEntityManager();
try {
```

```
    EntityTransaction entr = em.getTransaction();
    entr.begin();
    Query query = em.createNamedQuery("BookAuthor.findAll");
...
```

■ **Note** The preceding example uses `createNamedQuery` in order to substitute a named query rather than writing the Java Persistence Query Language (JPQL) inline. For more information, see Recipe 8-9.

The `persistence.xml` configuration file contains the database connection information that will be utilized by an application to work with databases. If you are working with JPA, you will become very familiar with creating a persistence unit, whether using local JDBC connections or an application server connection pool.

8-4. Using Database Sequences to Create Primary Key Values

Problem

Your database contains sequences that are used to generate primary key values for your database table records. Your application needs to use those database sequences in order to assign primary key values when creating and persisting objects.

Solution

Annotate an entity class's primary key field with a `SequenceGenerator` and then associate it with an entity `Generator` in order to utilize a database sequence for populating a database table column value. In the following example, the `BookAuthor` entity has been updated to utilize the `BOOK_AUTHOR_S` database sequence for creating primary key values. As such, the `id` field has been annotated accordingly.

```
package org.javaee8recipes.chapter08.entity;

import java.io.Serializable;
import java.math.BigDecimal;
import javax.persistence.*;
import javax.validation.constraints.NotNull;
import javax.validation.constraints.Size;

/**
 * Chapter 8
 * Entity class for the BOOK_AUTHOR database table of the Acme Bookstore application
 * @author juneau
 */
@Entity
@Table(name = "BOOK_AUTHOR")
public class BookAuthor implements Serializable {
    private static final long serialVersionUID = 1L;
```

```
    @Id
    @Basic(optional = false)
    @SequenceGenerator(name="book_author_s_generator",sequenceName="book_
    author_s",            initialValue=1, allocationSize=1)
    @GeneratedValue(strategy=GenerationType.SEQUENCE,
    generator="book_author_s_generator")
    @NotNull
    @Column(name = "ID")
    private BigDecimal id;

    @Size(max = 30)
    @Column(name = "LAST")
    private String last;
    @Size(max = 30)
    @Column(name = "FIRST")
    private String first;
    @Lob
    @Column(name = "BIO")
    private String bio;

    public BookAuthor() {
    }

    ...
```

When a new BookAuthor object is persisted to the database, the next sequence value for BOOK_AUTHOR_S will be used as the primary key value for the new database record. The org.javaee8recipes.chapter08.recipe08_04.SequenceTest.java class can be run to test the sequence-generated primary key once the persistence context has been configured for the local JDBC database connection (see Recipe 8-3 for details). The following excerpt is taken from the SequenceTest class, and it demonstrates how to add a new BookAuthor object to the database:

```
...
EntityManagerFactory emf = Persistence.createEntityManagerFactory("JavaEERecipesLOCAL");
EntityManager em = emf.createEntityManager();
try {
    EntityTransaction entr = em.getTransaction();
    entr.begin();
    BookAuthor author = new BookAuthor();
    author.setFirst("JOE");
    author.setLast("TESTER");
    author.setBio("An author test account.");
    boolean successful = false;
    try {
        em.persist(author);
        successful = true;
    } finally {
        if (successful){
            entr.commit();
```

```
            } else {
                entr.rollback();
            }
        }
        Query query = em.createNamedQuery("BookAuthor.findAll");
        List authorList = query.getResultList();
        Iterator authorIterator = authorList.iterator();
        while (authorIterator.hasNext()) {
            author = (BookAuthor) authorIterator.next();
            System.out.print("Name:" + author.getFirst() + " " + author.getLast());
            System.out.println();
        }
    } catch (Exception ex){
        System.err.println(ex);
    } finally {
        em.close();
    }
...
```

■ **Note** This example demonstrates the use of transactions. Transactions allow for an entire sequence of processes to be performed at once. If a failure occurs in one of the processes, then all processes in the transaction fail, and changes to the database are rolled back. Otherwise, if all processes in the transaction complete successfully, they are committed to the database. Transactions are very useful in situations where multiple database events depend on one another.

How It Works

In many cases, it makes sense to generate primary key values for database table records via a database sequence. Utilizing JPA allows you to do so by incorporating the use of the `@SequenceGenerator` and `@GeneratedValue` annotations into an entity class. Every database table that is mapped to an entity class must have a primary key value, and using database sequences to obtain those values makes sense for many reasons. For instance, in some cases an application administrator will need to know what the next number, current number, or last number used for a primary key value might be. By using a database sequence, gathering information regarding the next, current, or last numbers is just a query away.

The `@SequenceGenerator` annotation should be placed directly before the declaration of the primary key field or property within the entity class, or it can be placed before the entity class declaration. Note that other annotations may be placed between the `@SequenceGenerator` annotation and the actual variable declaration. The `@SequenceGenerator` annotation accepts values regarding the database sequence that is to be used for primary key generation. More specifically, the annotation accepts the following attributes:

- `name` (required): The name of the generator (this name can be an arbitrary value)
- `sequenceName` (optional): The name of the database sequence from which to obtain the primary key value
- `initialValue` (optional): The initial value of the sequence object
- `allocationSize` (optional): The amount of increment when allocating numbers from the sequence

The @GeneratedValue annotation provides for the specification of the primary key generation strategy for the entity. Similar to the @SequenceGenerator attribute, it can be placed before the declaration of the primary key field or property within the entity class, or it can be placed before the entity class declaration. It is used to specify the means for which the entity class primary key will be generated. The three options are as follows:

- The entity class will generate its own primary key value before inserting a new record.
- The entity class will use a database sequence for the key generation.
- The entity class will generate keys via some other means.

The attributes that can be specified for the @GeneratedValue annotation are as follows:

- generator (optional): This is the name of the primary key generator to use as specified by the @SequenceGenerator annotation. This must match the name attribute that was supplied for the @SequenceGenerator annotation unless you're using an @TableGenerator. This defaults to the ID generator supplied by the persistence provider.
- strategy (optional): This is the primary key generation strategy that will be used by the persistence provider to generate the primary key for the annotated field or entity class. This defaults to AUTO if not supplied.

The strategy attribute of @GeneratedValue can accept four javax.persistence.GenerationType Enum values.

- AUTO: Indicates that the persistence provider should choose an appropriate strategy for a particular database
- IDENTITY: Indicates that the persistence provider must assign primary keys for the entity using the database identity column
- SEQUENCE: Indicates that the persistence provider must assign primary keys for the entity using the database sequence column
- TABLE: Indicates that the persistence provider must assign primary keys for the entity using an underlying database table to ensure unique values are provided

In the example for this recipe, the BOOK_AUTHOR_S database sequence is specified for the sequenceName attribute of the @SequenceGenerator annotation, and the name of the generator is book_author_s_generator. Note that the @GeneratedValue name attribute matches that of the @SequenceGenerator annotation; this is very important! Once specified, the entity class will automatically obtain the next value from the database sequence when a new object is persisted.

■ **Note** There are other options for generating key values, such as AUTO, IDENTITY, and TABLE. Those strategies can be valid in different situations. For more information on using other options, refer to the online Java EE 8 documentation at https://javaee.github.io/.

8-5. Generating Primary Keys Using More Than One Attribute

Problem

A particular database table does not contain a primary key. Since use of the Java Persistence API (JPA) requires a primary key for mapping entity classes to database tables, you need to join the values of two or more of the table columns in order to create a primary key for each record.

Solution #1

Create a composite primary key by developing an embedded composite primary key class and denoting the composite key field within an entity using the `javax.persistence.EmbeddedId` and `javax.persistence.IdClass` annotations. Consider the `AUTHOR_WORK` database table that is used for the Acme Bookstore application. Suppose that the `AUTHOR_WORK` database table did not contain a primary key column. It would be possible to generate a primary key for each record based on its `BOOK_ID` and `AUTHOR_ID` columns. The following entity class is for the `AuthorWork` entity. Instead of using the `ID` column as a primary key, it uses the `bookId` and `authorId` columns together to formulate a composite primary key.

```
package org.javaee8recipes.chapter08.entity;

import java.io.Serializable;
import java.math.BigDecimal;
import java.math.BigInteger;
import javax.persistence.*;
import javax.validation.constraints.NotNull;
import org.javaee8recipes.chapter08.entity.key.AuthorWorkPKEmbedded;
import org.javaee8recipes.chapter08.entity.key.AuthorWorkPKNonEmbedded;

/**
 * Chapter 8 - Example of Embedded Primary Key
 * @author juneau
 */

@Entity
@Table(name = "AUTHOR_WORK")
//  (Named queries are covered in Recipe 8-9)
@NamedQueries({
    @NamedQuery(name = "AuthorWork.findAll", query = "SELECT a FROM AuthorWork a")})
public class AuthorWorkEmbedded implements Serializable {
    private static final long serialVersionUID = 1L;

    // You can use an embedded ID in-place of a standard Id if a table
    // contains more than one column to compose a primary key.  Comment
    // out along with the getters and setters to use a non-embeddable primary key.
    @EmbeddedId
    private AuthorWorkPKEmbedded embeddedId;

    public AuthorWorkEmbedded() {
    }
```

```
    public AuthorWorkEmbedded(BigInteger bookId, BigInteger authorId) {
        this.embeddedId = new AuthorWorkPKEmbedded(bookId, authorId);
    }

    /**
     * @return the embeddedId
     */
    public AuthorWorkPKEmbedded getEmbeddedId() {
        return embeddedId;
    }

    /**
     * @param embeddedId the embeddedId to set
     */
    public void setEmbeddedId(AuthorWorkPKEmbedded embeddedId) {
        this.embeddedId = embeddedId;
    }

}
```

To utilize an embedded primary key, you must create a class that contains the logic for mapping the primary key ID to the columns that are used to compose it. For this example, the `AuthorWorkPKEmbedded` class serves this purpose, which is shown here:

```
package org.javaee8recipes.chapter08.entity.key;

import java.io.Serializable;
import java.math.BigInteger;
import javax.persistence.Embeddable;

/**
 * Embeddable Primary Key class for AuthorWork
 *
 * @author juneau
 */
@Embeddable
public class AuthorWorkPKEmbedded implements Serializable {

    private BigInteger bookId;
    private BigInteger authorId;

    public AuthorWorkPKEmbedded() {
    }

    public AuthorWorkPKEmbedded(BigInteger bookId, BigInteger authorId){
        this.bookId = bookId;
        this.authorId = authorId;
    }
```

```
    /**
     * @return the bookId
     */
    public BigInteger getBookId() {
        return bookId;
    }

    /**
     * @param bookId the bookId to set
     */
    public void setBookId(BigInteger bookId) {
        this.bookId = bookId;
    }

    /**
     * @return the authorId
     */
    public BigInteger getAuthorId() {
        return authorId;
    }

    /**
     * @param authorId the authorId to set
     */
    public void setAuthorId(BigInteger authorId) {
        this.authorId = authorId;
    }

    public int hashCode() {
        return bookId.hashCode() + authorId.hashCode();
    }

    public boolean equals(Object obj) {
        if (obj == this) {
            return true;
        }
        if (!(obj instanceof AuthorWorkPKEmbedded)) {
            return false;
        }
        if (obj == null) {
            return false;
        }
        AuthorWorkPKEmbedded pk = (AuthorWorkPKEmbedded) obj;
        return (((bookId == ((AuthorWorkPKEmbedded) obj).getBookId()))
                && ((authorId == ((AuthorWorkPKEmbedded) obj).getAuthorId())));
    }
}
```

■ **Note** Although the preceding example is not an entity class, its member values are persisted. Even if the members are not designated as `@Basic`, they are still persisted.

Both the `hashCode()` and `equals()` methods must be present in composite key classes.

Solution #2

Create a composite primary key by developing a non-embedded composite primary key class and denote two or more of the columns within the entity class with the `@Id` annotation. Also, if using a non-embedded primary key class, the entity class must be designated as such by utilizing the `@IdClass` annotation and specifying the non-embedded primary key class.

Consider the `AUTHOR_WORK` database table that is used for the Acme Bookstore application. Suppose that the `AUTHOR_WORK` database table did not contain a primary key column. It would be possible to generate a primary key for each record based on its `BOOK_ID` and `AUTHOR_ID` columns since together they would formulate a unique value for each record. The following entity class is that for the `AuthorWork` entity. Instead of using the `ID` column as a primary key, it uses the `bookId` and `authorId` columns together to formulate a composite primary key:

```
package org.javaee8recipes.chapter08.entity;

import java.io.Serializable;
import java.math.BigDecimal;
import java.math.BigInteger;
import javax.persistence.*;
import javax.validation.constraints.NotNull;
import org.javaee8recipes.chapter08.entity.key.AuthorWorkPKEmbedded;
import org.javaee8recipes.chapter08.entity.key.AuthorWorkPKNonEmbedded;

/**
 * Chapter 8 - Example of Non-Embedded Primary Key
 * @author juneau
 */

@IdClass(AuthorWorkPKNonEmbedded.class)
@Entity
@Table(name = "AUTHOR_WORK_LEGACY")
@NamedQueries({
    @NamedQuery(name = "AuthorWork.findAll", query = "SELECT a FROM AuthorWork a")})
public class AuthorWorkNonEmbedded implements Serializable {
    private static final long serialVersionUID = 1L;

    @Id
    @Column(name = "BOOK_ID")
    private BigInteger bookId;
```

```
    @Id
    @Column(name= "AUTHOR_ID")
    private BigInteger authorId;

    public AuthorWorkNonEmbedded() {
    }

    public AuthorWorkNonEmbedded(BigInteger bookId, BigInteger authorId) {
        this.bookId = bookId;
        this.authorId = authorId;
    }

    public BigInteger getBookId() {
        return bookId;
    }

    public void setBookId(BigInteger bookId) {
        this.bookId = bookId;
    }

    public BigInteger getAuthorId() {
        return authorId;
    }

    public void setAuthorId(BigInteger authorId) {
        this.authorId = authorId;
    }

}
```

The associated non-embeddable primary key class is named AuthorWorkPKNonEmbedded. The code for this class is as follows:

```
package org.javaee8recipes.chapter08.entity.key;
import java.io.Serializable;
import java.math.BigInteger;

/**
 * Non-Embeddable Primary Key class for AuthorWork
 *
 * @author juneau
 */
public class AuthorWorkPKNonEmbedded implements Serializable {

    private BigInteger bookId;
    private BigInteger authorId;

    public AuthorWorkPKNonEmbedded() {
    }
```

```
    /**
     * @return the bookId
     */
    public BigInteger getBookId() {
        return bookId;
    }

    /**
     * @param bookId the bookId to set
     */
    public void setBookId(BigInteger bookId) {
        this.bookId = bookId;
    }

    /**
     * @return the authorId
     */
    public BigInteger getAuthorId() {
        return authorId;
    }

    /**
     * @param authorId the authorId to set
     */
    public void setAuthorId(BigInteger authorId) {
        this.authorId = authorId;
    }

    public int hashCode() {
        return bookId.hashCode() + authorId.hashCode();
    }

    public boolean equals(Object obj) {
        if (obj == this) {
            return true;
        }
        if (!(obj instanceof AuthorWorkPKEmbedded)) {
            return false;
        }
        if (obj == null) {
            return false;
        }
        AuthorWorkPKEmbedded pk = (AuthorWorkPKEmbedded) obj;
        return (((bookId == ((AuthorWorkPKEmbedded) obj).getBookId()))
                && ((authorId == ((AuthorWorkPKEmbedded) obj).getAuthorId())));
    }
}
```

■ **Note** Although the `AuthorWorkPKNonEmbedded` class is not an entity, its member values are persisted.

How It Works

There can be situations in which a database table may not contain a single primary key value to uniquely identify each row. Oftentimes this can be the case when working with legacy databases. In the Java Persistence API, all entity classes must contain a primary key that can be used to uniquely identify an object. To get around this obstacle when working with tables that do not contain a single primary key value, a composite primary key can be used to uniquely identify an object. A composite primary key is composed of two or more fields or properties in an entity class that can be combined together to create a unique identifier. Think in terms of performing a database query and attempting to return a record that matches only certain criteria. In such a case, you often need to include multiple relationships within the SQL WHERE clause. Creating a composite primary key within an entity class is basically the same concept in that you are telling JPA to use all of the fields or properties designated in the composite key in order to uniquely identify an object.

There are a couple of different techniques, embeddable and non-embeddable, that can be used to develop a composite primary key. The two techniques are similar in that they each require the creation of a separate class to compose the primary key, but they differ by the way in which the primary key is denoted in the entity class. In fact, the separate primary key class in both techniques can be created almost identically, except that an embeddable primary key class must be annotated using @Embeddable, as demonstrated in Solution #1 to this recipe. An entity with an embeddable primary key class should contain only a single primary key, and the data type for the primary key should be the same as the embeddable primary key class. That is, the primary key class should be declared within the entity using a private modifier, along with all of the other persistent properties and fields, and it should be annotated with @Id to indicate that it is the primary key. The following excerpt from Solution #1 shows how this is done:

```
@EmbeddedId
private AuthorWorkPKEmbedded embeddedId;
```

The entity class containing an embedded primary key should contain a constructor that accepts one parameter for each of the persistent fields or properties used for the primary key. Within the constructor, a new instance of the embeddable primary key class should then be instantiated using the passed-in arguments. The entity class using an embeddable primary key should contain accessor methods for the primary key field or property. However, unlike most entity classes, the hashCode() and equals() methods are not present because they are within the primary key class instead. Now that I've gone over the logistics of an entity class that uses an embeddable primary key, let's look at the embeddable primary key class itself to see how it works.

A primary key class that is used for creating an embeddable primary key should contain declarations for each of the persistent fields or properties that will be used to compose the primary key for the associated entity class. Of course, these fields or properties should be made private, and there should be corresponding getters and setters for accessing the fields. The embeddable primary key class should be annotated with @Embeddable. It can contain two constructors: one that accepts no arguments and another optional constructor that accepts an argument for each of the persistent fields or properties that compose the primary key. Remember how the entity class that uses the embeddable primary key contains no hashCode() method? That is because it resides in the primary key class. It simply adds together the hashCodes for each of the fields used to compose the primary key and returns the sum. The most important piece of the primary key class is the equals() method since it is used to determine whether an object or database record uniquely matches the associated primary key. The equals() method should accept an argument of type Object, which will be the object that is being compared against the current primary key object. The object is then compared to determine whether it is equal to the current primary key object, and if so, a true is returned. If it's not equal, then the object is compared to determine whether it is the same type of class as the embeddable primary key class, and a false is returned if it is not the same type. A false is also returned if the object is NULL. Finally, if a boolean has not yet been returned based on the conditionals that have been tested, then the object is casted into the same type of object as the primary key class, and each of its fields or properties is compared against those in the current primary key class. If they're equal, then a true is returned; if they're not equal, then a false is returned. The following lines of code demonstrate the equals() method:

```
public boolean equals(Object obj) {
    if (obj == this) {
        return true;
    }
    if (!(obj instanceof AuthorWorkPKEmbedded)) {
        return false;
    }
    if (obj == null) {
        return false;
    }
    AuthorWorkPKEmbedded pk = (AuthorWorkPKEmbedded) obj;
    return (((bookId == ((AuthorWorkPKEmbedded) obj).getBookId()))
            && ((authorId == ((AuthorWorkPKEmbedded) obj).getAuthorId())));
}
```

Solution #2 covers the use of a non-embedded primary key. The generation of a non-embeddable primary key is sometimes preferred over the use of an embedded primary key because some believe that the resulting entity class is easier to read. The overall construction of a non-embeddable primary key is basically the same, although there are a few subtle differences. For instance, when developing the primary key class for the non-embeddable primary key, there is no @Embeddable annotation on the class. The second difference that you may notice from the code in Solution #2 is that there is only one constructor used. Of course, an optional second constructor can still be created, accepting an argument for each of the persistent fields or properties that are used to compose the primary key.

Most differences take place within the entity class itself. To use a non-embedded composite primary key, the entity class must be annotated with @IdClass, naming the class that is used to construct the composite primary key. In the case of Solution #2, the @IdClass is as follows:

```
@IdClass(AuthorWorkPKNonEmbedded.class)
```

The second big difference in an entity class that uses a non-embeddable composite primary key is that instead of declaring one persistent field or property as an ID using the @Id annotation, the two or more fields or properties that are used to compose the primary key for the entity are declared directly in the entity, and each of them is annotated accordingly. The rest of the implementation is the same as an entity that uses an embedded composite primary key.

Which type of composite key you decide to use is completely a personal preference. Many people use a non-embeddable primary key to make the entity class easier to follow, in that it resembles a standard entity class more closely than an entity class using an embeddable composite primary key. In the end, they produce the same result and allow entity classes to be created for those database tables that do not contain a single primary key field.

8-6. Defining a One-to-One Relationship

Problem

A database table that is used by your application contains data that has a one-to-one reference with data records from another table. As such, you want to create a one-to-one relationship between two entity objects in your application.

Solution

Create an association between the two tables that have a one-to-one relationship by declaring each of the entity classes themselves as persistent fields or properties within each other using an "owned" relationship and annotate those fields with @OneToOne. For instance, let's say that each record in the AUTHOR database table can be associated with a record in another table named AUTHOR_DETAIL and vice versa. The AUTHOR_DETAIL table contains contact information for the author, so, in fact, these tables have a one-to-one relationship. To correlate them to each other from within the entity classes, specify the @OneToOne annotation on the field or property that is associated with the corresponding entity class. To have the ability to obtain the full author information from either table, a bidirectional one-to-one relationship needs to be created.

■ **Note** A one-to-one mapping could be unidirectional or bidirectional. A unidirectional mapping contains only an @OneToOne annotation on the owning entity for the corresponding entity class.

A relationship is referred to as *owned* if one entity contains a reference to another entity object referring to the entity itself. On the other hand, a relationship where an entity refers to another entity by primary key value is known as an *unowned* relationship.

In this solution, the Author entity would contain a @OneToOne reference for the AuthorDetail entity to create a bidirectional one-to-one mapping. In this code excerpt from the Author entity, the Author entity is the owning entity:

```
...
@Entity
@Table(name = "AUTHOR")

public class Author implements Serializable {

    private static final long serialVersionUID = 1L;
    @Id
    @Basic(optional = false)

    @SequenceGenerator(name="author_s_generator",sequenceName="author_s", initialValue=1,
    allocationSize=1)

    @GeneratedValue(strategy=GenerationType.SEQUENCE,
    generator="author_s_generator")
    @NotNull
    @Column(name = "ID")
    private BigDecimal id;
    @Size(max = 30)
```

```
    @Column(name = "LAST")
    private String last;
    @Size(max = 30)
    @Column(name = "FIRST")
    private String first;
    @Lob
    @Column(name = "BIO")
    private String bio;
    @OneToOne
    private AuthorDetail authorId;

    public Author() {
    }

    ...
```

An excerpt for the entity class for the AUTHOR_DETAIL table is shown next. Of course, it has the name of AuthorDetail, and it contains a reference to the Author entity class.

```
...
@Entity
@Table(name = "AUTHOR_DETAIL")

public class AuthorDetail implements Serializable {
    private static final long serialVersionUID = 1L;
    @Id
    @Basic(optional = false)
    @SequenceGenerator(name="author_detail_s_generator",sequenceName="author__detail_s",
    initialValue=1, allocationSize=1)
    @GeneratedValue(strategy=GenerationType.SEQUENCE,
    generator="author_detail_s_generator")
    @NotNull
    @Column(name = "ID")
    private BigDecimal id;
    @Size(max = 200)
    @Column(name = "ADDRESS1")
    private String address1;
    @Size(max = 200)
    @Column(name = "ADDRESS2")
    private String address2;
    @Size(max = 250)
    @Column(name = "CITY")
    private String city;
    @Size(max = 2)
    @Column(name = "STATE")
    private String state;
    @Size(max = 10)
    @Column(name = "ZIP")
    private String zip;
    @Column(name = "START_DATE")
    @Temporal(TemporalType.DATE)
    private Date startDate;
```

```
@Lob
@Column(name = "NOTES")
private String notes;
@OneToOne(optional=false, mappedBy="authorDetail")
private Author authorId;

public AuthorDetail() {
}
...
```

How It Works

It is not uncommon in the world of relational databases to have one table that depends on another. In the case where a record from a table has a one-to-one correspondence to a record from another table, an entity class for one table should be configured to have a one-to-one correspondence with the entity class for the other table. Working with objects is a bit different from working with database records, but the concept is basically the same. Within the database, a unique identifier is used to correlate one table to another. For instance, in the case of this example, the `AUTHOR_DETAIL` table contains a field named `AUTHOR_ID`, and it must contain an `ID` from the `AUTHOR` database table in order to map the two records together. Owned entity relationships work a bit differently in that the entity object itself is used to map to another entity, rather than an `ID` number.

When creating a bidirectional one-to-one relationship between entity classes, each entity class must declare the other entity class as a persistent field or property and then designate the type of relationship using the `@OneToOne` annotation. The `@OneToOne` annotation is used to designate a one-to-one relationship between the entities. The `@OneToOne` annotation contains the following optional attributes:

- `cascade`: The operations (e.g., delete) that must be cascaded to the target of the association. Default: no operations.
- `fetch`: Whether the association should be lazily loaded or must be eagerly fetched. Default: `EAGER`.
- `optional`: Whether the association is optional. For instance, can the entity be persisted without the association? Default: `true`.
- `mappedBy`: The field that owns the relationship. Default: `""`.

In the solution to this recipe, the `AuthorDetail` entity specifies the `@OneToOne` annotation prior to the declaration of the `Author` field specifying the `mappedBy` and `optional` attributes. The `mappedBy` attribute is set to `authorDetail`, because this will be the mapping field, and the optional attribute is set to `false`. On the other hand, the `Author` entity specifies the `@OneToOne` annotation prior to the declaration of the `AuthorDetail` field, and there are no attributes specified. In practice, when these entities are used, a bidirectional mapping will be enforced. This means that an `AuthorDetail` object cannot exist without a corresponding `Author` object.

8-7. Defining One-to-Many and Many-to-One Relationships

Problem

You want to associate two entity classes to each other, such that one entity object can contain a reference to many of the other entity objects.

Solution

Define a relationship between the two entities by specifying the @OneToMany annotation on a field or property referencing the other entity class within the owning object and by specifying the @ManyToOne annotation on a field or property referencing the owning object within the non-owning entity. For instance, let's say you allow an Author object to contain many different addresses or AuthorDetail objects. In fact, an Author can contain as many addresses as needed. That being the case, there would be one Author object for every AuthorDetail object. Likewise, there could be many AuthorDetail objects for every Author object.

In the following code listings, I demonstrate the one-to-many relationship between the Author and AuthorDetail objects. First, let's look at the Author object, which is otherwise referred to as the *owning* object. This entity class can contain a reference to many different AuthorDetail objects.

```
@Entity
@Table(name = "AUTHOR")

public class Author implements Serializable {

    private static final long serialVersionUID = 1L;
    @Id
    @Basic(optional = false)
    @SequenceGenerator(name="author_s_generator",sequenceName="author_s", initialValue=1,
    allocationSize=1)
    @GeneratedValue(strategy=GenerationType.SEQUENCE,
    generator="author_s_generator")
    @NotNull
    @Column(name = "ID")
    private BigDecimal id;
    @Size(max = 30)
    @Column(name = "LAST")
    private String last;
    @Size(max = 30)
    @Column(name = "FIRST")
    private String first;
    @Lob
    @Column(name = "BIO")
    private String bio;
    @OneToMany(mappedBy="author
    private Set<AuthorDetail> authorDetail;

    public Author() {
    }
...
```

Next, I'll show the non-owning object, also known as the AuthorDetail class. There may be many AuthorDetail objects in a single Author object.

```
public class AuthorDetail implements Serializable {
    private static final long serialVersionUID = 1L;
    @Id
    @Basic(optional = false)
```

```
    @SequenceGenerator(name="author_detail_s_generator",sequenceName="author__detail_s",
    initialValue=1, allocationSize=1)
    @GeneratedValue(strategy=GenerationType.SEQUENCE,
    generator="author_detail_s_generator")
    @NotNull
    @Column(name = "ID")
    private BigDecimal id;
    @Size(max = 200)
    @Column(name = "ADDRESS1")
    private String address1;
    @Size(max = 200)
    @Column(name = "ADDRESS2")
    private String address2;
    @Size(max = 250)
    @Column(name = "CITY")
    private String city;
    @Size(max = 2)
    @Column(name = "STATE")
    private String state;
    @Size(max = 10)
    @Column(name = "ZIP")
    private String zip;
    @Column(name = "START_DATE")
    @Temporal(TemporalType.DATE)
    private Date startDate;
    @Lob
    @Column(name = "NOTES")
    private String notes;
    @ManyToOne
    private Author author;

    public AuthorDetail() {
    }
...
```

■ **Note** To run the `org.javaee8recipes.chapter08.recipe08_07.RecipeTest.java` example, be sure to add both entity classes for this example to the `persistence.xml` context file. Also, be sure to comment out any other entities in the persistence context by the same name, because there cannot be duplicate entities in a single persistence context.

How It Works

The most common database table relationship is the one-to-many or many-to-one relationship, whereby a record in one table relates to one or more records in another table. Consider the scenario from the solution to this recipe, being that a single AUTHOR table record may have one or more address records in the AUTHOR_DETAIL table. Defining this relationship within the entity classes is easy, because annotations are used to indicate the relationship.

When creating a one-to-many relationship in an entity, the entity that corresponds to the table where one record can correlate to many in another table is known as the *owning* entity. The entity that correlates to the database table that may contain more than one record relating to the single record in the other table is known as the *non-owning* entity. The owning entity class should declare a persistent field or property for the entity to which it relates and may have more than one related object. Since there may be more than one non-owning entity object, the owning entity must declare a Set of the non-owning objects and indicate as such using the @OneToMany annotation. The mappedBy attribute of the @OneToMany annotation should be set to the name, which is used within the non-owning entity for declaration of the many-to-one relationship. In the example, the Author entity contains a one-to-many relationship with AuthorDetail. Therefore, the Author entity declares the relationship as follows:

```
@OneToMany(mappedBy="author")
private Set<AuthorDetail> authorDetail;
```

On the other end of the spectrum is the many-to-one relationship. In the example, more than one AuthorDetail object may relate to one Author object. Therefore, a many-to-one relationship should be defined in the AuthorDetail entity class for the Author entity. This is done by declaring a persistent field or property for the Author entity and signifying the relationship with the @ManyToOne annotation as follows:

```
@ManyToOne
private Author author;
```

When working with the entities, a Set containing one or more AuthorDetail objects should be persisted in a single Author object. The following code demonstrates how to use a one-to-many relationship in an application:

```
EntityManagerFactory emf = Persistence.createEntityManagerFactory("JavaEERecipesLOCAL");
EntityManager em = emf.createEntityManager();
try {
    em.getTransaction().begin();
    Author author = new Author();
    author.setFirst("JOE");
    author.setLast("TESTER");
    author.setBio("An author test account.");
    Set detailSet = new HashSet<AuthorDetail>();
    AuthorDetail detail = new AuthorDetail();
    detail.setAddress1("Address 1");
    detail.setAddress2("Address 2");
    detail.setCity("NoMansLand");
    detail.setState("ZZ");
    detail.setZip("12345");
    detail.setNotes("This is a test detail");
    detailSet.add(detail);
    AuthorDetail detail2 = new AuthorDetail();
    detail.setAddress1("Address 1");
    detail.setAddress2("Address 2");
    detail.setCity("NoMansLand");
    detail.setState("ZZ");
    detail.setZip("12345");
```

```
    detail.setNotes("This is a test detail");
    detailSet.add(detail2);
    em.persist(author);
    em.getTransaction().commit();
} catch (Exception ex){
    System.err.println(ex);
} finally{
            if (em != null){
                em.close();
            }
}
```

The @OneToMany annotation contains the following optional attributes:

- cascade: The operations (e.g., delete) that must be cascaded to the target of the association. Default: no operations.
- fetch: Whether the association should be lazily loaded or must be eagerly fetched. Default: EAGER.
- orphanRemoval: Whether to apply the remove operation to entities that have been removed from the relationship and to cascade the remove operation to those entities. Default: false.
- targetedEntity: The entity class that is the target of the association. Default: "".

The @ManyToMany annotation contains the following optional attributes:

- cascade: The operations (e.g., delete) that must be cascaded to the target of the association. Default: no operations.
- fetch: Whether the association should be lazily loaded or must be eagerly fetched. Default: EAGER.
- targetedEntity: The entity class that is the target of the association. Default: "".

8-8. Defining a Many-to-Many Relationship

Problem

There are tables in your database that contain cases where multiple records from one table may correlate to multiple records from another. You want to define entity relationships for these tables.

Solution

Create a many-to-many association between the two tables by declaring a field or property in each entity class for a Set objects corresponding to the entity class on the opposite end. Utilize the @ManyToMany annotation to specify the relationship and mark the owning side of the relationship by specifying a mappedBy attribute on the non-owning entity's @ManyToMany annotation. Therefore, the org.javaee8recipes.chapter08.recipe08_08.Book class is the entity class corresponding to the BOOK database table, and it will contain the @ManyToMany annotation on a declaration for a Set of BookAuthor objects. A mapping table in the database will be "automagically" populated with the associated mappings from the entities. Shown next is the partial code for the Book class, the "owning" entity:

```
@Entity
@Table(name = "BOOK")
@NamedQueries({
    @NamedQuery(name = "Book.findAll", query = "SELECT b FROM Book b"),
})
public class Book implements Serializable {

    private static final long serialVersionUID = 1L;
    @Id
    @Basic(optional = false)
    @SequenceGenerator(name="book_s_generator",sequenceName="book_s", initialValue=1,
    allocationSize=1)
    @GeneratedValue(strategy=GenerationType.SEQUENCE,
    generator="book_s_generator")
    @NotNull
    @Column(name = "ID")
    private BigDecimal id;
    @Size(max = 150)
    @Column(name = "TITLE")
    private String title;
    @Size(max = 500)
    @Column(name = "IMAGE")
    private String image;
    @Lob
    @Column(name = "DESCRIPTION")
    private String description;
    @ManyToMany
    private Set<BookAuthorMany> bookAuthors;
```

The BookAuthor class is mapped to the Book class using the same concept. The only difference is that it contains a mappedBy attribute in the @ManyToOne annotation to signify the owning table relation.

```
@Entity
@Table(name = "BOOK_AUTHOR")
@NamedQueries({
    @NamedQuery(name = "BookAuthor.findAll", query = "SELECT b FROM BookAuthor b"),
    @NamedQuery(name = "BookAuthor.findById", query = "SELECT b FROM BookAuthor b WHERE b.id
    = :id"),
    @NamedQuery(name = "BookAuthor.findByLast", query = "SELECT b FROM BookAuthor b WHERE
    b.last = :last"),
    @NamedQuery(name = "BookAuthor.findByFirst", query = "SELECT b FROM BookAuthor b WHERE
    b.first = :first")})
public class BookAuthorMany implements Serializable {

    private static final long serialVersionUID = 1L;
    @Id
    @Basic(optional = false)
```

```
@SequenceGenerator(name="book_author_s_generator",sequenceName="book_author_s",
initialValue=1, allocationSize=1)
@GeneratedValue(strategy=GenerationType.SEQUENCE,
generator="book_author_s_generator")
@NotNull
@Column(name = "ID")
private BigDecimal id;
@Size(max = 30)
@Column(name = "LAST")
private String last;
@Size(max = 30)
@Column(name = "FIRST")
private String first;
@Lob
@Column(name = "BIO")
private String bio;
@ManyToMany(mappedBy="bookAuthors")
private Set<Book> books;
```

■ **Note** The BookAuthor entity has been named BookAuthorMany so that there are no conflicting entity classes in the JavaEERecipes sources. No entities with duplicate names can exist in the same application.

How It Works

It is possible for databases to contain a many-to-many relationship between two or more different tables. In the case of the example in this recipe, a book may have many authors, and an author may have written many books. On that note, both the database table containing books and the database table containing authors are associated to each other via a many-to-many relationship. It is easy to associate entity classes to one another to form a many-to-many relationship via the use of the @ManyToMany annotation. The @ManyToMany annotation is used to signify that an entity contains a many-to-many association with the annotated persistent field or property.

To create the association, each entity within the many-to-many relationship should declare a field or property for a Set of the associated entity objects. In the case of the example, the Book entity should declare a Set of BookAuthor objects, and vice versa. That declaration is then annotated with @ManyToMany, using any attributes that are deemed necessary to make the association. The @ManyToMany annotation contains the following optional attributes:

- targetEntity: The entity class that is the target of the association. This is necessary only if the collection-valued relationship property is not defined using Java generics.
- cascade: The operations that must be cascaded to the target of the association.
- fetch: Whether the association should be lazily loaded or eagerly fetched. The default is javax.persistence.FetchType.LAZY.
- mappedBy: The field that owns the relationship. This is not required if the relationship is unidirectional.

As such, when creating an object of either type, one may persist a Set of the associated entity objects using the persistent field or property that has been annotated with @ManyToMany. The following example demonstrates how to create an entity with a many-to-many relationship (excerpt from the org.javaee8recipes.chapter08.recipe08_08.RecipeTest class):

```
EntityManagerFactory emf = Persistence.createEntityManagerFactory("JavaEERecipesLOCAL");
EntityManager em = emf.createEntityManager();
try {
    em.getTransaction().begin();
    Book book1 = new Book();
    book1.setTitle("New Book 1");
    Book book2 = new Book();
    book2.setTitle("New Book 2");

    BookAuthorMany author1 = new BookAuthorMany();
    author1.setFirst("JOE");
    author1.setLast("AUTHOR 1");

    BookAuthorMany author2 = new BookAuthorMany();
    author2.setFirst("MARYJJOE");
    author2.setLast("AUTHOR 2");

    Set authors = new HashSet();
    authors.add(author1);
    authors.add(author2);

    Set books = new HashSet();
    books.add(book1);
    books.add(book2);

    book1.setBookAuthor(authors);
    author1.setBooks(books);

    em.persist(author1);
    em.persist(book1);
    em.getTransaction().commit();
} catch (Exception ex){
    // Please use a logging framework, such as log4j in production
    System.err.println(ex);
} finally{
            if (em != null){
                em.close();
            }
}
```

When an entity object that contains a many-to-many association with another is created, a record is populated into a mapping table that contains the primary key from each associated table record. You can optionally specify the name of the mapping table by using the annotation @JoinTable and specifying the name of the table. If no @JoinTable annotation is used, then the mapping table name is derived from a concatenation of the two entity classes, beginning with the owning entity. Therefore, in the example, the mapping table name is BOOK_BOOK_AUTHOR, and it contains a field for storing the primary key from the associated records of each table.

8-9. Querying with Named Queries

Problem

Rather than issue SQL or Java Persistence Query Language (JPQL) queries to a persistence unit, you want to define one or more predefined queries for an entity class that can be called by name.

Solution

Specify a single named query or a group of named queries for an entity class. Provide a name for each of the named queries so that they can be called by that name. In this example, a group of named queries will be added to the BookAuthor entity class, and then a separate class may be used to query the entity class using the named queries. We will create an EntityManagerFactory and database connection based on a persistence.xml file that obtains a local JDBC connection to the database. The following excerpt is taken from the BookAuthor entity, and it demonstrates how to associate named queries with an entity class:

```
@Entity
@Table(name = "BOOK_AUTHOR")
@NamedQueries({
    @NamedQuery(name = "BookAuthor.findAll", query = "SELECT b FROM BookAuthor b"),
    @NamedQuery(name = "BookAuthor.findById", query = "SELECT b FROM BookAuthor b WHERE b.id
    = :id"),
    @NamedQuery(name = "BookAuthor.findByLast", query = "SELECT b FROM BookAuthor b WHERE
    b.last = :last"),
    @NamedQuery(name = "BookAuthor.findByFirst", query = "SELECT b FROM BookAuthor b WHERE
    b.first = :first")})
public class BookAuthor implements Serializable {

    private static final long serialVersionUID = 1L;
    @Id
    @Basic(optional = false)
    @SequenceGenerator(name="book_author_s_generator",sequenceName="book_author_s",
    initialValue=1, allocationSize=1)
    @GeneratedValue(strategy=GenerationType.SEQUENCE,
    generator="book_author_s_generator")
    @NotNull
    @Column(name = "ID")
    private BigDecimal id;
    @Size(max = 30)
    @Column(name = "LAST")
    private String last;
    @Size(max = 30)
    @Column(name = "FIRST")
    private String first;
    @Lob
    @Column(name = "BIO")
    private String bio;

    public BookAuthor() {
    }
...
```

In another class, the named queries that have been registered with the BookAuthor entity can be called by name. The following excerpt from the org.javaee8recipes.chapter8.recipe8_09.RecipeTest class demonstrates how to invoke a named query:

```
EntityManagerFactory emf = Persistence.createEntityManagerFactory("JavaEERecipesLOCAL");
EntityManager em = emf.createEntityManager();
try {
    EntityTransaction entr = em.getTransaction();
    entr.begin();
    Query query = em.createNamedQuery("BookAuthor.findAll");
    List authorList = query.getResultList();
    Iterator authorIterator = authorList.iterator();
    while (authorIterator.hasNext()) {
        BookAuthor author = (BookAuthor) authorIterator.next();
        System.out.print("Name:" + author.getFirst() + " " + author.getLast());
        System.out.println();
    }
} catch (Exception ex){
    System.err.println(ex);
}
```

How It Works

A named query is contained within an entity class, and it consists of a static JPQL query that is specified via metadata. A given entity class can include zero or more named queries or a group of named queries. A named query is expressed via the @NamedQuery annotation, which contains two attributes: name and query. The name attribute of the @NamedQuery annotation is used to specify a string-based name for the query, and the query attribute is used to specify the static JPQL query against the entity. If an entity contains a group of named query annotations, they can be grouped together using the @NamedQueries annotation. One or more @NamedQuery annotation specifications can exist within a single @NamedQueries annotation, separated by commas.

The JPQL within a named query can contain zero or more bind variables that can have values substituted when the named query is called. To utilize a named query, you must first obtain an active connection to the database. To learn more about obtaining an active connection to the database via an EntityManagerFactory, refer to Recipe 8-3. Once an active database connection has been obtained, the EntityManager object's createNamedQuery method can be called, passing the string-based name of the named query that you would like to issue. A Query object is returned from the call, and it can be used to obtain the query results.

In the example for this recipe, you can see that the BookAuthor entity is queried, returning a list of BookAuthor objects. A simple while loop is used to iterate through the list of objects, printing the first and last names from each BookAuthor object to System.out (the server log), although use of a logging framework such as Log4j is encouraged.

8-10. Performing Validation on Entity Fields

Problem

You want to specify validation rules for specific fields within an entity class to prevent invalid data from being inserted into the database.

Solution

Include bean validation constraints within an entity class. Bean validation constraints are annotations that are applied to persistent fields or properties of an entity class. The bean validation mechanism provides a number of annotations that can be placed on fields or properties in order to validate data in different ways. In the following example, the AuthorWork entity has been enhanced to include bean validation for the id, address1, state, and zip fields.

```
...
@Entity
@Table(name = "AUTHOR_DETAIL")

public class AuthorDetailBeanValidation implements Serializable {
    private static final long serialVersionUID = 1L;
    @Id
    @Basic(optional = false)
    @SequenceGenerator(name="author_detail_s_generator",sequenceName="author__detail_s",
    initialValue=1, allocationSize=1)
    @GeneratedValue(strategy=GenerationType.SEQUENCE,
    generator="author_detail_s_generator")
    @NotNull
    @Column(name = "ID")
    private BigDecimal id;
    @Size(max = 200)
    @Pattern(regexp="", message="Invalid Address")
    @Column(name = "ADDRESS1")
    private String address1;
    @Size(max = 200)
    @Column(name = "ADDRESS2")
    private String address2;
    @Size(max = 250)
    @Column(name = "CITY")
    private String city;
    @Size(max = 2)
    @Column(name = "STATE")
    @Pattern(regexp="^(?-i:A[LKSZRAEP]|C[AOT]|D[EC]|F[LM]|G[AU]|HI|I[ADLN]|K[SY]|LA|M[ADEHIN
    OPST]|N[CDEHJMVY]|O[HKR]|P[ARW]|RI|S[CD]|T[NX]|UT|V[AIT]|W[AIVY])$",
            message="Invalid State")
    private String state;
    @Size(max = 10)
    @Column(name = "ZIP")
    @Pattern(regexp="^\\d{5}\\p{Punct}?\\s?(?:\\d{4})?$",
            message="Invalid Zip Code")
    private String zip;
    @Column(name = "START_DATE")
    @Temporal(TemporalType.DATE)
    private Date startDate;
    @Lob
    @Column(name = "NOTES")
```

```
    private String notes;
    @ManyToOne
    private AuthorBeanValidation author;
...
```

In an attempt to insert a value that does not conform to the validation rules, the object will not be persisted, and the message correlating to the bean validation annotation will be displayed.

How It Works

It is always a good idea to utilize a data validation strategy when working with user input, especially if the data will be persisted into a database or other data store for later use. The Java Persistence API allows bean validation to occur within an entity class, whereby a developer can place validation rules directly on a persistent field or property. By default, the persistence provider automatically invokes validation processes on entities containing bean validation annotation constraints after the `PrePersist`, `PreUpdate`, and `PreRemove` lifecycle events occur. At that time, any value that does not adhere to the given validation constraint will cause the entity to stop persistence and display an associated message.

The details of bean validation are the same, whether it be on a plain old Java object (POJO) or an entity class. In the case of an entity class, either the persistent field or property can be annotated with the desired bean validation constraint. To see a list of possible bean validation constraint annotations, refer to Chapter 11.

In the example for this recipe, the `@NotNull` and `@Pattern` annotations are specified on persistent properties of the `AuthorDetail` entity. Specifically, the `id` field is annotated with `@NotNull`, and validation will fail in an attempt to enter a `NULL` value for that field. The `state` and `zip` fields contain a `@Pattern` annotation, along with a corresponding regular expression and failure message. If the values for those fields do not adhere to the regular expression that has been specified, then the message that is assigned to the message attribute of the `@Pattern` annotation will be displayed via a JSF view by the `h:message` component corresponding to the validated field. What if you want to apply a set of regular expression patterns to a given field or property? Such a feat can be done using the `@Pattern.List` syntax, whereby the list would contain a comma-separated list of `@Pattern` annotations. The following lines of code demonstrate this technique:

```
@Pattern.List({
    @Pattern(regexp=”regex-pattern”, message=”Error Message”),
    @Pattern(regexp=”another regex-pattern”, message(“Error Message 2”)
})
```

Bean validation is a good way to ensure that invalid data is not submitted to a data store. However, most advanced desktop or web applications today use a couple tiers of validation to make the user experience more convenient. Many times, web applications use JavaScript field validation first so that users do not have to submit a page in order to see their validation errors displayed on the screen. If using JSF or other web frameworks, some components allow direct access to bean validation, in which cases an Ajax submission of a given field or property will occur behind the scenes, allowing the bean validation to take place without page submission. Whatever tact you take, bean validation within entity classes is important and should become a handy tool to add to your arsenal.

8-11. Generating Database Schema Objects Automatically

Problem

You are developing an application and want to automatically have your entity classes generated into tables in the underlying database.

Solution

Use the automatic schema generation that was introduced in EJB 3.2. Schema generation is determined by the object-relational metadata of the `persistence.xml` unit, unless custom scripts are provided for the generation. The application developer can package scripts as part of the persistence unit or can supply URLs to the location of the scripts for schema generation. The execution of such scripts can be carried out by the container itself, or the container may direct the persistence provider to take care of script execution.

Table 8-3 in the "How It Works" section of this recipe lists the different `persistence.xml` or `EntityManagerFactory` properties that are used to configure schema generation. These properties are passed as a `Map` argument from the container to the `PersistenceProvider generateSchema` method or the `createContainerEntityManagerFactory` method.

To define the different objects that need to be generated, annotate entity classes accordingly. The standard entity class annotations (`@Table`, `@Id`, and so on) determine what objects are created and how they are structured. For more information regarding the specification of annotations in entity classes in order to generate schema objects, refer to the annotations listed in Table 8-4 in the "How It Works" section of this recipe.

How It Works

Schema generation refers to the creation of underlying database tables, views, constraints, and other database artifacts. Prior to the Java EE 7 release, schema generation had been automated only via the use of an IDE such as NetBeans or Eclipse. However, the EE 7 release took a step toward breaking this dependency on an IDE by allowing schema generation to become automated by configuring an appropriate `persistence.xml` file for an application.

Schema generation can be applied directly to the database, or it can generate SQL scripts that can be manually applied to the database (or both), depending on which options are configured for the application. Schema generation may occur prior to application deployment or when an `EntityManagerFactory` is created as part of the application deployment and initialization. To perform schema generation, the container may call the `PersistenceProvider generateSchema` method separately from and/or prior to the entity manager factory for the persistence unit. The `createContainerEntityManagerFactory` call can accept additional information to cause the generation of schema constructs to occur as part of the entity manager factory creation or initialization process. Furthermore, this information can determine whether the database is manipulated directly or whether SQL scripts are created, or both.

■ **Note** Schema generation is also available outside of a managed container (e.g., web application server) in Java SE environments. To perform schema generation in a Java SE environment, the application may call the `Persistence generateSchema` method separately from and/or prior to the creation of the entity manager factory or may pass information to the `createEntityManagerFactory` method to cause schema generation to occur as part of the entity manager factory creation.

Table 8-3 lists the different schema generation properties that can be specified in the persistence.xml file in order to automate schema generation.

Table 8-3. *Schema Generation Properties*

Property	Purpose
schema-generation-action	Controls the action to be taken by persistence provider with regards to object generation and destruction. Values: none, create, drop-and-create, drop.
schema-generation-target	Controls whether the schema is to be created within the database, whether DDL scripts are to be created, or both. Values: database, scripts, database-and-scripts.
ddl-create-script-target, ddl-drop-script-target	Controls target locations for writing scripts if the schema-generation-target specifies script generation. Writers are preconfigured for the persistence provider. Values: java.io.Writer (e.g., MyWriter.class) or URL strings.
ddl-create-script-source, ddl-drop-script-source	Specifies locations from which DDL scripts are to be read. Readers are preconfigured for the persistence provider. Values: java.io.Reader (e.g., MyReader.class) or URL strings.
sql-load-script-source	Specifies the file location of SQL bulk load script. Values: java.io.Reader (e.g., MyReader.class) or URL string.
schema-generation-connection	JDBC connection to be used for performing schema generation.
database-product-name, database-major-version, database-minor-version	Needed if scripts are to be generated. Values are those obtained from JDBC DatabaseMetaData.
create-database-schemas	Whether the persistence provider needs to create schema in addition to creating database objects such as tables, sequences, constraints, and so on. Values: true, false.

Programmatically, schema generation is determined by a series of annotations that are placed in entity classes. The @Table annotation denotes an entity mapping to an underlying database table. By default, a table is generated for each top-level entity and includes columns based on the specified attributes for that entity. Therefore, the @Column and @JoinColumn annotations are used for generating such columns for a table. Column ordering is not determined based on the ordering of @Column or @JoinColumn annotations. If column ordering is important, then a Data Definition Language (DDL) script must be supplied for generating the table. Other annotations and annotation attributes, such as @Id, also play important roles in schema generation. Table 8-4 lists the different annotations that are involved in schema generation, along with a brief description and the elements that can be populated for further control over the generated schema.

Table 8-4. *Schema Generation Annotations*

Annotation	Description	Elements
`@Table`	Used for generating tables. By default, the table name is generated from the entity name, and the entity name is defaulted from the class name.	
`@SecondaryTable`	A secondary table is created to partition the mapping of entity state across multiple tables.	
`@CollectionTable`	A collection table is created for mapping of an element collection. The `Column`, `AttributeOverride`, and `AssociationOverride` annotations may be used to override `CollectionTable` mappings.	
`@JoinTable`	Used in mapping of associations. By default, join tables are created for the mapping of many-to-many relationships and unidirectional one-to-many relationships.	
`@TableGenerator`	Used to store generated primary key values.	
`@Column`	Determines the name and configuration for a column within a table.	`unique`, `nullable`, `columnDefinition`, `table`, `length`, `precision`, `scale`, `name`
`@MapKeyColumn`	Specifies the mapping name of a key column of a map when the key is of basic type.	`unique`, `nullable`, `columnDefinition`, `table`, `length`, `precision`, `scale`
`@Enumerated`, `@MapKeyEnumerated`	Controls whether string- or integer-valued columns are generated for basic attributes of enumerated types and therefore impact the default column mapping of these types.	
`@Temporal`, `@MapKeyTemporal`	Controls whether date-, time-, or timestamp-value columns are generated for basic attributes of temporal types and therefore impact the default column mappings for these types.	
`@Lob`	Specifies that a persistent attribute is to be mapped to a database large object type.	

(*continued*)

Table 8-4. *(continued)*

Annotation	Description	Elements
@OrderColumn	Specifies the generation of a column that is used to maintain the persistent ordering of a list that is represented in an element collection, one-to-many, or many-to-many relationship.	name, nullable, columnDefinition
@DiscriminatorColumn	Generated for the SINGLE_TABLE mapping strategy and may optionally be generated by the provider for use with the JOINED inheritance strategy.	
@Version	Specifies the generation of a column to serve as an entity's optimistic lock.	
@Id	Specifies a database primary key column . Use of the @Id annotation results in the creation of a primary key, which consists of the corresponding column or columns.	
@EmbeddedId	Specifies an embedded attribute whose corresponding columns formulate a database primary key. Use of the @EmbeddedId annotation results in the creation of a primary key consisting of the corresponding columns.	
@GeneratedValue	Indicates a primary key that should have an automatically generated value. If a strategy is indicated, the provider must use it if it is supported by the target database.	
@JoinColumn	The @JoinColumn annotation is typically used for specifying a foreign key mapping.	name, referencedColumnName, unique, nullable, columnDefinition, table, foreignKey
@MapKeyJoinColumn	Specifies foreign key mappings to entities that are map keys in element collections or relationships that consist of map values.	name, referencedColumnName, unique, nullable, columnDefinition, table, foreignKey
@PrimaryJoinKeyColumn	Specifies that a primary key column is to be used as a foreign key. This annotation is used in the specification of the JOINED mapping strategy and for joining a secondary table to a primary table in a one-to-one relationship mapping.	

(continued)

Table 8-4. *(continued)*

Annotation	Description	Elements
@ForeignKey	Used within the JoinColumn, JoinColumns, MapKeyJoinColumn, MapKeyJoinColumns, PrimaryKeyJoinColumn, and PrimaryKeyJoinColumns annotations to specify or override a foreign key constraint.	
@SequenceGenerator	Creates a database sequence to be used for ID generation.	
@Index	Generates an index consisting of the specified columns.	
@UniqueConstraint	Generates a unique constraint for the given table.	

As per Table 8-4, there are a couple of annotations that have been created specifically to facilitate schema generation. The new annotations are @Index and @ForeignKey, where @Index is responsible for generating an index of the specified columns. @ForeignKey is used to define a foreign key on a table.

8-12. Mapping Date-Time Values

Problem

You want to utilize the Date-Time API to persist Java LocalDate values to the database.

Solution

Use JPA 2.2 support for the Date-Time API to work with the LocalDate. Since the JPA 2.2 maintenance release supports the Java Date-Time API, it is possible to use the new Java 8 date and time objects to persist without the need for the @Temporal annotation. The following entity class demonstrates how to achieve this feat.

```
public class Book implements Serializable {
    private static final long serialVersionUID = 1L;
    @Id
    @Basic(optional = false)
    @Column(name = "ID")
    private BigDecimal id;
    @Size(max = 150)
    @Column(name = "TITLE")
    protected String title;
    @Size(max = 500)
    @Column(name = "IMAGE")
    private String image;
    @Lob
```

```
    @Column(name = "DESCRIPTION")
    private String description;
    @Column(name = "PUBLISH_DATE")
    private LocalDate publishDate;
    @ManyToMany(mappedBy="books")
    private Set<BookAuthor> authors;
    @OneToMany(mappedBy="book", cascade=CascadeType.ALL)
    private List<Chapter> chapters = null;

    public Book() {
    }
. . .
}
```

As you can see, the entity class contains a `LocalDate` field that includes no special annotations.

How It Works

When Java 8 was initially released, Java EE and JPA did not have support for the updated Date-Time API. Therefore, in order to utilize the newer date and time objects, you had to develop a converter to perform automatic conversion between the new date and time objects and `java.util.Date`. Since JPA Maintenance Release 2.2, this issue has been mitigated, as the Java Date-Time API is officially supported, making it easier than ever before to persist fields that contain date and time values.

In order to map a database column that contains a date to a Java object, simply annotate the column with the `@Column` annotation, specifying the column name if you want. The `@Temporal` annotation is no longer required. Apply one of the following data types to the class field:

- `java.time.LocalDate`
- `java.time.LocalTime`
- `java.time.LocalDateTime`
- `java.time.OffsetTime`
- `java.time.OffsetDateTime`

It is as simple as that! The JPA Date-Time support has provided the ability to utilize the API in Java EE applications without needing a converter. It has also cut down on code because `@Temporal` is no longer required. Note that in order to use these features, you must use a Java EE 8 compatible JPA implementation, such as EclipseLink 2.7.0+.

8-13. Using the Same Annotation Many Times

Problem

You want to utilize the same annotation a number of different times within a given class. For instance, suppose that you would like to use more than one `@PersistenceContext` annotation in a single class.

Solution

Take advantage of the Java 8 repeatable annotation support that has been provided with JPA 2.2. This added support provides the ability to use repeatable annotations for a number of situations. In the following example, the @NamedQuery annotation is utilized more than one time in the same class. Prior to JPA 2.2, this would not work without first grouping the annotations together into a single container annotation.

```
@Entity
@Table(name = "EMPLOYEE")
@XmlRootElement

@NamedQuery(name = "Employee.findAll", query = "SELECT e FROM Employee e")
@NamedQuery(name = "Employee.findById", query = "SELECT e FROM Employee e WHERE e.id = :id")
@NamedQuery(name = "Employee.findByFirst", query = "SELECT e FROM Employee e WHERE e.first =
:first")
@NamedQuery(name = "Employee.findByLast", query = "SELECT e FROM Employee e WHERE e.last =
:last")
@NamedQuery(name = "Employee.findByAge", query = "SELECT e FROM Employee e WHERE e.age =
:age")
@NamedStoredProcedureQuery(name = "createEmp", procedureName = "CREATE_EMP")
public class Employee implements Serializable {

    private static final long serialVersionUID = 1L;
    // @Max(value=?)  @Min(value=?)//if you know range of your decimal fields consider using
       these annotations to enforce field validation
    @Id
    @Basic(optional = false)
    //@NotNull
    @Column(name = "ID")
    private BigDecimal id;
    @Size(max = 30)
    @Column(name = "FIRSTNAME")
    private String first;
    @Size(max = 30)
    @Column(name = "LASTNAME")
    private String last;
    @Column(name = "AGE")
    private BigInteger age;
    @ManyToOne(optional = false)
    @JoinColumn(name = "JOB_ID", nullable = false)
    private Jobs job;
    @Column(name = "STATUS")
    private String status;

    public Employee() {
    }

. . .
}
```

How It Works

Repeatable annotation support came to the Java platform with the release of Java 8. This enables you to utilize the same annotation more than once within a portion of code. Annotations are not repeatable by default; the annotation class must be designated as such with the `@Repeatable` annotation. Therefore, not all annotations will be usable more than once within a class. The following annotations have been made repeatable for the Java EE 8 release:

- `AssociationOverride`
- `AttributeOverride`
- `Convert`
- `JoinColumn`
- `MapKeyJoinColumn`
- `NamedEntityGraph`
- `NamedNativeQuery`
- `NamedQuery`
- `NamedStoredProcedureQuery`
- `PersistenceContext`
- `PersistenceUnit`
- `PrimaryKeyJoinColumn`
- `SecondaryTable`
- `SqlResultSetMapping`

As mentioned previously, annotations must be designated as repeatable by marking them with the `@Repeatable` annotation. Therefore, if you have created a custom annotation and you would like to make it repeatable, then you can do so.

CHAPTER 9

Enterprise JavaBeans

Enterprise JavaBeans were created in order to separate the view layer from the database access and business layers. EJBs are where all of the database (`EntityManager`) access and business logic can take place within a Java EE application, and they have become significantly easier to use over the past few releases. EJBs are used to coordinate database tasks with entities, and JSF managed beans (aka, controller classes) are used to interact directly with the JSF views or web pages. Managed beans are used to provide a façade between the view layer and the business layer.

EJBs are deployed to an application server container, which manages the bean lifecycle. The container also provides features such as transaction management and security for EJBs. EJBs are portable, meaning that they can be deployed to different application server containers. This adds benefit for EJB developers because a single EJB can be utilized across multiple applications. EJBs also alleviate the issue of modifying applications to work with multiple databases due to the use of Java Persistence Query Language (covered in Chapter 10) rather than routine SQL is used to perform database operations. Therefore, if an application is developed on one database, it can be ported to another without the need to rewrite any SQL.

There are three types of EJBs that can be used: stateless, stateful, and message-driven. This chapter covers the first two, and message-driven beans are covered in Chapter 12 where the Java Messaging Service (JMS) is covered. Stateless session beans are used most often, because they are used for quick transactions and do not maintain any conversational state. Stateful beans, on the other hand, are to be used in situations where a conversational state across multiple client requests is required.

This chapter includes recipes to familiarize you with stateful and stateless session beans. You learn how to access EJBs from a JSF managed bean client and display content within a JSF view or web page that the EJB has queried from the database. There are also recipes covering useful tactics such as using bean `Timers` and creating singleton session beans.

Note In recent times, EJBs may be considered older technology because CDI beans can now be used in their place. However, EJBs are a widely adopted technology and remain a viable option. At the time of this writing, EJB usage is still dominant full CDI replacement.

9.1. Obtaining an Entity Manager

Problem

You have created a persistence unit for your database connection, and you want to use it to obtain a connection for working with the database.

J. Juneau, *Java EE 8 Recipes*, https://doi.org/10.1007/978-1-4842-3594-2_9

Solution #1

Create an `EntityManagerFactory` object utilizing a local JDBC connection by calling the `javax.persistence.Persistence createEntityManagerFactory` method and passing the name of the `RESOURCE_LOCAL` persistence unit. Obtain an `EntityManager` object from the factory object that has been created, and then utilize the `EntityManager` object as needed to work with the database entities. The following lines of code demonstrate how to accomplish the creation of an `EntityManager` object using a local JDBC connection:

```
EntityManagerFactory emf = Persistence.createEntityManagerFactory("JavaEERecipesLOCAL");
 EntityManager em = emf.createEntityManager();
```

■ **Note** For further reference regarding the creation of a persistence unit, see Recipe 8-3.

Solution #2

Inject `EntityManager` into EJB when using a database connection within an environment utilizing the Java Naming and Directory Interface (JNDI), such as an application server. To do so, declare a private field of the `EntityManager` type and annotate it using `@PersistenceContext`. Pass the name of the relevant persistence unit to the `@PersistenceContext` annotation. The following lines of code demonstrate how this technique is performed. In an application, these lines of code would reside within an EJB for an entity class.

```
@PersistenceContext(unitName = "JavaEERecipes")
 private EntityManager em;
```

How It Works

Before an entity class can be used to persist an object or obtain query results, an entity manager must be created from the persistence unit database connection configuration. The way in which you achieve the creation of an entity manager will differ depending on the type of database connection you are using. For instance, if you are creating an entity manager from a local JDBC connection, then there is a little more work to be done because an `EntityManagerFactory` must be used to obtain the `EntityManager` object. On the other hand, if you are creating a container-managed entity manager from a database connection that is registered with an application server via JNDI, then much of the work is done for you behind the scenes via metadata annotations.

In the first solution to this recipe, a persistence unit pertaining to a local JDBC connection is used to obtain an `EntityManager` object. As mentioned previously, within an EJB, an `EntityManagerFactory` object must first be obtained by calling the `javax.persistence.Persistence` class's `createEntityManagerFactory` method and passing the string-based persistence unit name to the method. From there, an `EntityManager` object can be instantiated by invoking the `EntityManagerFactory`'s `createEntityManager` method.

In the second solution to this recipe, a container-managed `EntityManager` object instance is obtained. If an application is deployed to an enterprise application server container such as Oracle's GlassFish or Payara, this is the preferred way to obtain an `EntityManager`. Utilizing container-managed entity managers makes JPA development easier because a Java EE container manages the lifecycle of container-managed entity managers. Moreover, container-managed entity managers are automatically propagated to all application components within a single Java Transaction API (JTA) transaction. To obtain a container-managed entity manager, declare an `EntityManager` field within an EJB and simply annotate it with `@PersistenceUnit`, passing the string-based name of the persistence unit to the annotation. Doing so injects the entity manager into the application component.

After performing either of these solutions, the newly obtained EntityManager object is ready to be utilized. The most often used EntityManager methods are createQuery, createNamedQuery, and persist. You will learn more about utilizing the EntityManager in the following recipes. However, a handful of recipes in Chapter 8 also use EntityManager objects.

9.2. Developing a Stateless Session Bean

Problem

You want to create a class that can be used to perform tasks for a client, but the application does not require the bean to retain any state between transactions. Additionally, you want to have the ability to interact with a database from within the class.

Solution #1

Create a stateless session bean for the entity class for which you'd like to perform tasks. Create an EntityManager object from a persistence unit and initiate tasks against the database using the entity classes. In the following solution, a stateless session bean is created for working with the Book entity:

```
package org.javaee8recipes.chapter09.session;

import javax.ejb.Stateless;
import javax.persistence.EntityManager;
import javax.persistence.PersistenceContext;
import org.javaee8recipes.entity.Book;

/**
 * Stateless Session Bean for the Book entity
 * @author juneau
 */
@Stateless
public class BookFacade {
    @PersistenceContext(unitName = "JavaEERecipes")
    private EntityManager em;

    protected EntityManager getEntityManager() {
        return em;
    }

    public BookFacade() {

    }

    /**
     * Create a book object
     * @param book
     */
    public void create(Book book){
        em.persist(book);
    }
```

```
    /**
     * Update a book object
     * @param book
     */
    public void edit(Book book){
        em.merge(book);
    }

    /**
     * Remove a book object
     * @param book
     */
    public void remove(Book book){
        em.remove(book);
    }

    /**
     * Return a Book object based upon a given title. This assumes that there
     * are no duplicate titles in the database.
     * @param title
     * @return
     */
    public Book findByTitle(String title){
        return (Book) em.createQuery("select object(o) from Book o " +
                              "where o.title = :title")
                              .setParameter("title", title.toUpperCase())
                              .getSingleResult();
    }

}
```

In the example session bean, the create, edit, and remove methods can be called via a client to perform CRUD operations with the database. The findByTitle method can be called via a client to obtain a Book object from the database.

Solution #2

Create a stateless session bean for the entity class for which you'd like to perform tasks and extend an abstract class that encapsulates standard operations from the session bean. Create an EntityManager object from a persistence unit and initiate tasks against the database using the entity classes. In the following solution, a stateless session bean is created for working with the Book entity. It extends a class named AbstractFacade, which contains implementations for most of the commonly used tasks within EJBs.

First, let's look at the BookFacade class, the stateless session bean.

```
package org.javaee8recipes.chapter09.session;

import javax.ejb.Stateless;
import javax.persistence.EntityManager;
import javax.persistence.PersistenceContext;
import org.javaee8recipes.entity.Book;
```

```
/**
 * Stateless Session Bean for the Book entity
 * @author juneau
 */
@Stateless
public class BookFacade extends AbstractFacade<Book> {
    @PersistenceContext(unitName = "JavaEERecipes")
    private EntityManager em;

    @Override
    protected EntityManager getEntityManager() {
        return em;
    }

    public BookFacade() {
        super(Book.class);
    }

    /**
     * Return a Book object based upon a given title. This assumes that there
     * are no duplicate titles in the database.
     * @param title
     * @return
     */
    public Book findByTitle(String title){
        return (Book) em.createQuery("select object(o) from Book o " +
                              "where o.title = :title")
                              .setParameter("title", title.toUpperCase())
                              .getSingleResult();
    }

}
```

As you can see, there is only a single method implemented within the EJB, which is the `findByTitle` method. However, other CRUD functionality such as `create`, `update`, and `remove` for the Book entity, can also be performed via the `BookFacade` session bean because it extends `AbstractFacade`. The `AbstractFacade` class is an abstract class that implements the most commonly used EJB methods. It accepts an entity class type specified as a generic, and its implementation is as follows.

■ **Note** The following code was automatically generated via the Apache NetBeans IDE along with the `BookFacade` session bean after creating a stateless session bean for the `Book` entity class.

```
package org.javaee8recipes.chapter09.session;

import java.util.List;
import javax.persistence.EntityManager;
```

```
/**
 * Abstract Facade for Session Beans
 *
 * @author Netbeans 8.x
 */
public abstract class AbstractFacade<T> {
    private Class<T> entityClass;

    public AbstractFacade(Class<T> entityClass) {
        this.entityClass = entityClass;
    }

    protected abstract EntityManager getEntityManager();

    public void create(T entity) {
        getEntityManager().persist(entity);
    }

    public void edit(T entity) {
        getEntityManager().merge(entity);
    }

    public void remove(T entity) {
        getEntityManager().remove(getEntityManager().merge(entity));
    }

    public T find(Object id) {
        return getEntityManager().find(entityClass, id);
    }

    public List<T> findAll() {
        javax.persistence.criteria.CriteriaQuery cq = getEntityManager().
getCriteriaBuilder().createQuery();
        cq.select(cq.from(entityClass));
        return getEntityManager().createQuery(cq).getResultList();
    }

    public List<T> findRange(int[] range) {
        javax.persistence.criteria.CriteriaQuery cq = getEntityManager().
        getCriteriaBuilder().createQuery();
        cq.select(cq.from(entityClass));
        javax.persistence.Query q = getEntityManager().createQuery(cq);
        q.setMaxResults(range[1] - range[0]);
        q.setFirstResult(range[0]);
        return q.getResultList();
    }

    public int count() {
        javax.persistence.criteria.CriteriaQuery cq = getEntityManager().
        getCriteriaBuilder().createQuery();
        javax.persistence.criteria.Root<T> rt = cq.from(entityClass);
```

```
        cq.select(getEntityManager().getCriteriaBuilder().count(rt));
        javax.persistence.Query q = getEntityManager().createQuery(cq);
        return ((Long) q.getSingleResult()).intValue();
    }

}
```

All of the methods declared in AbstractFacade are available to BookFacade since it extends the class. One of the biggest benefits of using an abstract class to implement the standard CRUD functionality is that it can be applied across many different EJBs, rather than written from scratch each time.

How It Works

A Java class that is used to encapsulate the business logic and data access for an application is also known as a *session bean*. More specifically, session beans typically correspond to entity classes, whereas there is usually one bean per entity, although this is not a requirement and there are instances in which such an implementation does not work well. Any database transactions for an application should be encapsulated within a session bean class that is responsible for business process implementations, and clients should then make calls to the session beans in order to invoke those business processes.

A stateless session bean does not retain any state, meaning that variables within the bean are not guaranteed to retain their values across invocations. An application server container maintains a pool of session beans for use by its clients, and when a client invokes a bean, then one is taken from the pool for use. Beans are returned to the pool immediately after the client is finished with the invoking task. Therefore, stateless session beans are thread-safe, and they work very well within a concurrent user environment.

Stateless session beans should contain a no-argument constructor, and they are instantiated by an application server container at application startup. To signify that a session bean is stateless, the class should be annotated with @Stateless, optionally passing a string-based name parameter for the bean. If no name parameter is specified within the @Stateless annotation, then the name of the bean is used. A stateless session bean should not be final or abstract; therefore, all methods within the bean should contain an implementation. They can extend other session beans or POJOs in order to extend functionality. In pre–EJB 3.1 environments, there was a requirement for session beans to implement business interfaces that contained method signatures for those methods that were to be made public for client use. However, it is no longer a requirement for a session bean to implement a business interface, and indeed the solutions to this recipe do not demonstrate the use of business interfaces (see Recipe 9-4 for a concrete example).

Zero or more variables can be declared within a stateless session bean, although the contents of those variables are not guaranteed for retention across client calls. It is typical for a stateless session bean to contain at least one EntityManager connection, although it is possible for a bean to contain zero or more connections. For instance, in some cases session beans do not have a need to persist data, and in such cases no database connection would be needed. In other instances, there may be a need for a session bean to have the ability to work with multiple databases, in which case multiple database connections would be necessary. In the example for this recipe, a single database connection is declared as an EntityManager object, corresponding to the JavaEERecipes persistence unit. It is possible to use standard JDBC persistence units, as well as standard JDBC DataSource objects within a session bean. The use of a standard JDBC DataSource declaration may look like the following:

```
@Resource(name="jdbc/MyDataSource")
private DataSource dataSource;
```

As mentioned previously, stateless session beans can implement business interfaces, although it is not required. The business interfaces that can be implemented via a stateless session bean can be local, remote, or web service endpoints. A local business interface is designed for clients of stateless session beans that exist within the same container instance as the session bean itself. Designating a business interface with the `@Local` annotation specifies a local interface. Remote business interfaces are designed for use by clients that reside outside of the session bean's container instance. A remote business interface is denoted by the `@Remote` annotation.

Stateless session beans contain "callback methods" that will be invoked by the container automatically when certain lifecycle events occur. Specifically, stateless session beans can use two callbacks: `PostConstruct` and `PreDestroy`. After the container constructs a stateless session bean and resources have been injected, any method within the bean that is denoted with a `@PostConstruct` annotation will be invoked. Similarly, when the container decides that a bean should be removed from the pool or destroyed, then any method denoted with a `@PreDestroy` annotation will be invoked before the bean is destroyed. Callback methods can be very useful for instantiating database connections and so forth.

LIFECYCLE OF A STATELESS SESSION BEAN

Stateless session beans have the following lifecycle:

1. A container creates a stateless session bean using the default no-argument constructor.
2. Resources are injected as necessary (i.e., database connections).
3. A managed pool of beans is generated, and multiple instances of the session bean are placed into the pool.
4. An idle bean is taken from the pool when the invocation request is received from a client. If all beans in pool are currently in use, more beans are instantiated until the maximum specified amount of beans has been reached.
5. The business method invoked by the client is executed.
6. The bean is returned to the pool after the business method process is complete.
7. The bean is destroyed from the pool on an as-needed basis.

In the first solution to this recipe, a stateless session bean is listed that does not implement any interfaces or extend any other classes. Such a stateless session bean is very typical, and it is not uncommon to see in EJB 3.1+ applications. The bean in the solution declares an `EntityManager` object, and the application server container performs the creation of the `EntityManager` automatically and injects it into the bean since the `@PersistenceUnit` annotation is specified. The annotation must designate a persistence unit name to tell the container the type of `EntityManager` to inject. In the case where a bean needs access to multiple database connections, then more than one `EntityManager` objects may be declared, specifying different names for each persistence unit corresponding to the different connections that are required by the bean. A no-argument constructor is specified as per the guidelines for stateless session beans. The solution also contains one business method implementation, `findByTitle`, which accepts a `String` argument and queries the `Book` entity for the specified book title. If found, the matching `Book` object is returned to the caller. The `findByTitle` method demonstrates the typical usage of an `EntityManager` object for working with a database from within a session bean.

In the second solution to the recipe, the `BookFacade` stateless session bean extends a class named `AbstractFacade`. The `AbstractFacade` class contains a number of method implementations that are commonly used within session bean classes. For instance, the `create` method within `AbstractClass` can be used to persist an object (insert into the database), and the `edit` method can be used to update an object. Solution #2 demonstrates a good technique that can be used to encapsulate commonly used business logic into a separate class so that it can be extended to multiple different beans. Consider that the application may contain several different stateless session beans that corresponded to several different entity classes, and each of those beans would need to contain a create, edit, and remove method. It is much easier to simply extend a single class that contains this functionality, rather than rewriting in each separate session bean class.

Stateless session beans are highly performant objects that are used to encapsulate the business logic and data access corresponding to an application entity. While most times a single session bean is written for each entity class, this is not a mandatory rule. Stateless session beans should be considered first when deciding on which type of bean to use for encapsulating the logic for a particular application process. If a conversational state between the client and the bean are not required (no state needs to be maintained), then stateless session beans are the best choice since they provide the most concurrency and best performance. If, however, state is required, then consider using stateful session beans.

9.3. Developing a Stateful Session Bean

Problem

You want to develop a session bean that has the capability of maintaining a conversational state with the client. For instance, you want the client to have the ability to perform a multistep process without the state of the session bean being lost between requests.

Solution

Create a stateful session bean and implement the business logic pertaining to the entity class of your choice. Consider that a customer is browsing the pages of the Acme Bookstore application and wants to add a book to a shopping cart. The cart would need to be maintained within a stateful session bean since it would be required to maintain state until the customer decides to make a purchase, cancel an order, or close the browser.

The following class is that of `OrderFacade`, the stateful session bean that maintains a visitor's shopping cart and purchases:

```
package org.javaee8recipes.chapter09.session;

import java.util.concurrent.TimeUnit;
import javax.ejb.PostActivate;
import javax.ejb.PrePassivate;
import javax.ejb.Remove;
import javax.ejb.Stateful;
import javax.ejb.StatefulTimeout;
import org.javaee8recipes.chapter09.object.Cart;

@Stateful
@StatefulTimeout(unit = TimeUnit.MINUTES, value = 30)
public class OrderFacade {

    private Cart cart;

    @SuppressWarnings("unused")
    @PrePassivate
    private void prePassivate() {
        System.out.println("In PrePassivate method");
    }
```

```
    @SuppressWarnings("unused")
    @PostActivate
    private void postActivate() {
        System.out.println("In PostActivate method");
    }

    public Cart getCart() {
        if(cart == null)
            cart = new Cart();
        return cart;
    }

    public void setCart(Cart cart) {
        this.cart = cart;
    }

    public void completePurchase() {
        System.out.println("Not yet implemented..");
    }

    @Remove
    public void destroy() {
        System.out.println("Destroying OrderFacade...");
    }
}
```

A client can make calls to a stateful session bean in the same manner as with a stateless session bean (see Recipe 9-2). That is, a client can access the methods of the stateful session bean via a business interface or controller class/CDI bean. In this example, the `CartController` JSF CDI bean will access the stateful session bean. The following code for `CartController` demonstrates how to access the `OrderFacade`. The main point of access to the EJB takes place within the `getCart()` method.

```
@Named(name = "cartController")                    // Specifies a CDI bean
@SessionScoped                                     // Specifies a session scoped bean
                                                      (See Recipe 3-2)
public class CartController implements Serializable {

    private Item currentBook = null;

    @EJB         // Injects EJB
    OrderFacade orderFacade;

    @Inject      // Injects specified managed bean controller
    private AuthorController authorController;

    /**
     * Creates a new instance of CartController
     */
    public CartController() {
    }
```

```
public String addToCart() {
    if (getCart().getBooks() == null) {
        getCart().addBook(getAuthorController().getCurrentBook(), 1);
    } else {
        getCart().addBook(getAuthorController().getCurrentBook(),
                searchCart(getAuthorController().getCurrentBook().getTitle()) + 1);
    }
    FacesMessage facesMsg = new FacesMessage(FacesMessage.SEVERITY_INFO,
            "Successfully Updated Cart", null);
    FacesContext.getCurrentInstance().addMessage(null, facesMsg);
    return null;
}

/**
 * Determines if a book is already in the shopping cart
 *
 * @param title
 * @return
 */
public int searchCart(String title) {
    int count = 0;

    for (Item item : getCart().getBooks()) {
        if (item.getBook().getTitle().equals(title)) {
            count++;
        }
    }
    return count;
}

public String viewCart() {
    if (getCart() == null) {
        FacesMessage facesMsg = new FacesMessage(FacesMessage.SEVERITY_INFO,
                "No books in cart...", null);
        FacesContext.getCurrentInstance().addMessage(null, facesMsg);
    }

    return "/chapter09/cart";
}

public String continueShopping() {
    return "/chapter09/book";
}

public String editItem(String title) {
    for (Item item : getCart().getBooks()) {
        if (item.getBook().getTitle().equals(title)) {
            currentBook = item;
        }
    }
    return "/chapter09/reviewItem";

}
```

```
    public String updateCart(String title) {
        Item foundItem = null;
        if (currentBook.getQuantity() == 0) {
            for (Item item : getCart().getBooks()) {
                if (item.getBook().getTitle().equals(title)) {
                    foundItem = item;
                }
            }
        }
        getCart().getBooks().remove(foundItem);
        FacesMessage facesMsg = new FacesMessage(FacesMessage.SEVERITY_INFO,
                "Successfully Updated Cart", null);
        FacesContext.getCurrentInstance().addMessage(null, facesMsg);
        return "/chapter09/cart";
    }

    /**
     * @return the cart
     */
    public Cart getCart() {
        return orderFacade.getCart();
    }

    /**
     * @return the currentBook
     */
    public Item getCurrentBook() {
        return currentBook;
    }

    /**
     * @param currentBook the currentBook to set
     */
    public void setCurrentBook(Item currentBook) {
        this.currentBook = currentBook;
    }

    public void isBookInCart(ComponentSystemEvent event) {
        UIOutput output = (UIOutput) event.getComponent();
        if (getCart() != null) {
            if (searchCart(getAuthorController().getCurrentBook().getTitle()) > 0) {
                output.setValue("This book is currently in your cart.");
            } else {
                output.setValue("This book is not in your cart.");
            }
        } else {
            output.setValue("This book is not in your cart.");
        }
    }
```

```
    public void updateRowData(RowEditEvent e) {
        System.out.println("Perform editing logic here...");
        currentBook = (Item)e.getObject();
        // Call the updateCart method, passing the title of the current book.
        updateCart(((Item)e.getObject()).getBook().getTitle());
    }

    /**
     * @return the authorController
     */
    public AuthorController getAuthorController() {
        return authorController;
    }

    /**
     * @param authorController the authorController to set
     */
    public void setAuthorController(AuthorController authorController) {
        this.authorController = authorController;
    }
}
```

How It Works

A stateful session bean is a Java class that is used to encapsulate business logic for an application. In most cases, a stateful bean has a one-to-one correspondence with an entity class, in that the bean handles all of the database calls regarding one particular entity. Programmatically, a stateful session bean is very similar to a stateless session bean in that regard. However, stateful session beans are guaranteed to maintain a conversational state with a client, whereas a stateless session bean is not. That said, the application server container handles stateful session beans differently, and they have a much different lifecycle than stateless session beans. The application server container maintains a pool of the stateful session beans for client use, but there is a one-to-one mapping between a client and a bean in that when a client invokes a stateful bean, it will not release that bean back to the pool while it is still active. Therefore, stateful session beans can be less efficient than stateless, and they can take up a larger memory footprint than stateless session beans because if there are a large number of active sessions using a stateful bean, then there will be a large number of stateful beans retained in memory and remaining active for those sessions.

To make a stateful session bean, the class must be designated as such by annotating it with `@Stateful`. The optional name parameter of the `@Stateful` annotation can be used to specify a string-based name for the bean. Similar to stateless session beans, a stateful session bean can implement a business interface, but as of EJB 3.1, it is not mandatory. In the example to this recipe, no business interface is used; therefore, any method within the bean that has a public modifier will be available for use by a client. Any variables that are used to store conversational state must be Java primitive types or `Serializable`. When an instance variable is used to store data, it will be maintained throughout the lifecycle of the conversation.

Every stateful session bean must also contain a method that will be called when the bean client removes it. The state of the bean will be maintained until the `@Remove` method is called. The container will invoke the method annotated with `@Remove` when this occurs, and the bean will be removed after the `@Remove` method completes.

LIFECYCLE OF STATEFUL SESSION BEAN

Stateful session beans have the following lifecycle:

1. The container creates new bean instances utilizing the default constructor whenever a new client session is started.
2. Resources are injected into the bean.
3. The bean instance is stored in memory.
4. The method invoked by the client is executed.
5. The bean waits and executes any subsequent requests.
6. The bean is *passivated*, or removed from active memory into temporary storage, if the client remains idle for a period of time.
7. The client invocation of a passivated bean will bring it back into memory from temporary storage.
8. Failure of client to invoke a passivated bean instance for a period of time will cause the bean to be destroyed.
9. If a client requests the removal of a bean instance, then it is activated if necessary and then destroyed.

Stateful session beans are stored in memory for a period of time. If the client does not request a stateful bean for use again after a period of time, then the container passivates it. Passivation is the process of taking a stateful session bean out of active memory and storing it into a temporary location on disk. The container does this by serializing the entire bean instance and moving it into permanent storage on disk. A bean is then activated later if a client invokes it, and activation is the opposite of passivation.

Another way to passivate a stateful session bean on a timed basis is by annotating the class using @StatefulTimeout. This annotation allows the developer to choose how long to maintain the state of the bean. In the case of the example for this recipe, the state is maintained for 30 minutes before the bean is passivated.

```
@StatefulTimeout(unit = TimeUnit.MINUTES, value = 30)
```

Stateful session beans have more callback methods than stateless session beans. Callback methods can be used to perform operations at a certain point in the bean's lifecycle. Specifically, the following annotations can be placed before method signatures in order to mark them for execution when the given bean lifecycle event occurs: `@PostConstruct`, `@PrePassivate`, `@PostActivate`, and `@PreDestroy`. The `@PostConstruct` annotation denotes that the annotated method will be executed by the container as an instance is created. `@PrePassivate` denotes that the annotated method will be executed by the container before passivation occurs. `@PostActivate` denotes that the annotated method should be executed after activation or, in other words, once a bean becomes active again. Lastly, methods annotated with `@PreDestroy` will be executed by the container just before the bean is destroyed.

If your session bean needs the ability to retain state throughout a conversation, then you will need to use a stateful session bean. However, it is important to use stateful session beans sparingly since they are less efficient than stateless session beans and they require a larger memory footprint on the application server.

9.4. Utilizing Session Beans with JSF

Problem

You want to develop a web-based client for a session bean that resides within the same container as the session bean itself.

Solution

Write a Java client and work directly with the session bean of your choice. The following code demonstrates a JSF managed bean controller that interacts directly with a stateless session bean. The JSF CDI bean, named `BookController`, is the client class for the `BookFacade` EJB session bean. You will see from the code that the bean can interact directly with the EJB session bean public methods via the declaration of a property pertaining to the `BookFacade` class.

```
package org.javaee8recipes.chapter09.jsf;

import java.math.BigDecimal;
import java.util.List;
import java.util.Map;
import javax.ejb.EJB;
import javax.enterprise.context.SessionScoped;
import javax.inject.Inject;
import javax.inject.Named;
import org.javaee8recipes.entity.Book;
import org.javaee8recipes.entity.BookAuthor;
import org.javaee8recipes.chapter09.session.BookFacade;

@Named(value="bookController")
@SessionScoped
public class BookController implements java.io.Serializable {

    @EJB
    BookFacade ejbFacade;

    private List<Book> completeBookList = null;
    private List<Map> customBookList = null;
    private List<Book> booksByAuthor = null;
    private List<Book> nativeBookList = null;
    private List<Book> namedNativeBookList = null;

    @Inject
    private AuthorController authorController;

    public BookController(){

    }
```

```
    public List<Book> getCompleteBookList() {
        completeBookList = ejbFacade.findAll();
        return completeBookList;
    }

    public List<Map> getCustomBookList(){
        customBookList = ejbFacade.obtainCustomList();
        return customBookList;
    }

    public void setCompleteBookList(List<Book> completeBookList) {
        this.completeBookList = completeBookList;
    }

    public String populateBookList(BigDecimal bookId){
       String returnValue = authorController.populateAuthorList(bookId);
       return returnValue;
    }

    /**
     * Recipe 9-4
     * @param author
     * @return
     */
    public String findBooksByAuthor(BookAuthor author){
        setBooksByAuthor(ejbFacade.findBooksByAuthor(author));
        return "/chapter10/recipe10_2b.xhtml";
    }

    /**
     * @return the booksByAuthor
     */
    public List<Book> getBooksByAuthor() {
        return booksByAuthor;
    }

    /**
     * @param booksByAuthor the booksByAuthor to set
     */
    public void setBooksByAuthor(List<Book> booksByAuthor) {
        this.booksByAuthor = booksByAuthor;
    }

    /**
     * Recipe 9-4a: Using a Native Query
     */

    public List<Book> getNativeBookList() {
        nativeBookList = ejbFacade.obtainNativeList();
        return nativeBookList;
    }
```

```
    /**
     * @param nativeBookList the nativeBookList to set
     */
    public void setNativeBookList(List<Book> nativeBookList) {
        this.nativeBookList = nativeBookList;
    }

    /**
     * @return the namedNativeBookList
     */
    public List<Book> getNamedNativeBookList() {
        namedNativeBookList = ejbFacade.obtainNamedNativeList();
        return namedNativeBookList;
    }

    /**
     * @param namedNativeBookList the namedNativeBookList to set
     */
    public void setNamedNativeBookList(List<Book> namedNativeBookList) {
        this.namedNativeBookList = namedNativeBookList;
    }
}
```

As you can see from the example, it is also possible for one JSF managed bean client to work with another JSF managed bean client because the `BookController` class declares a variable for the `AuthorController` CDI managed bean and injects it into the class. The JSF view can interact directly with the methods within the bean, making it easy to form the complete cycle for a web view utilizing information from a database.

How It Works

An EJB is the class within an application that is used to work directly with database objects. JSF web views and desktop Java clients cannot work directly with EJB methods since they reside on the application server. For this reason, EJBs must provide a way for clients to communicate with their methods, whether that client resides within the same container as the EJB itself or in a remote location. Prior to the release of EJB 3.1, if an EJB was going to be exposed to a client within the same container, such as a JSF managed bean, the EJB would need to implement a business interface denoted as a local interface with the `@Local` annotation. On the other hand, if an EJB were to be made accessible to a client running within a remote environment under pre-EJB 3.1, then the EJB would need to implement a business interface denoted as a remote interface with the `@Remote` annotation. In the majority of Java EE applications that are developed in more recent days, a web framework such as JSF is used to work with the EJB in order to manipulate or read data from an RDBMS or other datasource. Such clients are local to the container in which the EJB pools reside, and therefore they would access the EJB via a local business interface.

■ **Note** At first, the concept of a local client may be difficult to understand, so I will try to explain in a bit more detail. A typical JSF application utilizes local clients, those being JSF CDI managed beans, to work directly with the EJBs. Although the user of the web application is sitting in a remote location from the EJB server container, they are working with HTML pages that are generated by JSF views within a browser, and those views interact directly with the JSF managed bean controllers. It is almost as if the JSF views are bound directly to the JSF managed bean controllers, which usually reside within the same container as the EJB. Figure 9-1 shows how this relationship works.

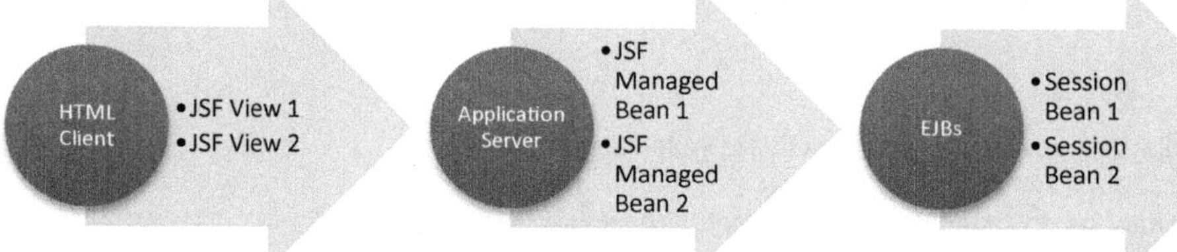

Figure 9-1. *HTML client (JSF view) to EJB relationship*

Since EJB 3.1+, it has been possible for local clients to utilize "no-interface" business views for access to public EJB methods, thereby alleviating the need for the EJB to implement an interface. Using the no-interface view technique enables developers to be more productive because there is one less Java file to maintain (no interface needed), and the workflow becomes easier to understand since the local client can interact directly with the EJB, rather than via an interface. Remote clients, such as Java classes running in a remote application server container, cannot use the no-interface view, and therefore a `@Remote` business interface is still needed in such situations.

The solution demonstrates the use of the no-interface view to allow JSF managed bean controllers to work with publicly declared EJB methods. To obtain a reference to the no-interface view of an EJB through dependency injection, use the `javax.naming.EJB` annotation, along with a declaration of the enterprise bean's implementation class. The following code excerpt taken from the managed bean in the solution demonstrates the dependency injection technique:

```
@EJB
BookFacade ejbFacade;
```

It is possible to use JNDI to perform a lookup on the EJB rather than using dependency injection, although such situations are rarely required. To do so, use the `javax.naming.InitialContext` interface's `lookup` method in order to perform the JNDI lookup as follows:

```
BookFacade ejbFacade = (BookFacade)
        InitialContext.lookup("java:module/BookFacade");
```

■ **Note** Many people still have a bad taste in their mouth because of the complexity of EJBs prior to the release of EJB 3.0. Development of EJB 2.*x* required much XML configuration, which made EJBs difficult to understand and maintain, even though they were still robust and very viable for the development of enterprise applications. Moreover, the container manages the lifecycle and resources for EJBs, which allows developers to focus on other application features rather than worry about lifecycle and resource handling.

9.5. Persisting an Object

Problem

You want to persist an object in your Java enterprise application. In other words, you want to create a new database record within one of the database tables used by your application.

Solution

Create an `EntityManager` object using one of the solutions provided in Recipe 9-1, and then call its `persist` method, passing the object you want to persist. The following lines of code demonstrate how to persist an object to the database using an `EntityManager`. In this case, a `Book` object is being persisted into the `BOOK` database table. This excerpt is taken from the `BookFacade` session bean.

```
...
@PersistenceContext(unitName = "JavaEERecipes")
    private EntityManager em;
...
em.persist(book);
...
```

How It Works

The persistence of entity objects takes place within EJB classes. To persist an object to the underlying data store and manage it, call the `EntityManager` object's `persist` method. You must pass a valid entity object to the `persist` method, and the object should not yet exist in the database, meaning that it must have a unique primary key.

A few different exceptions may be thrown when working with the `persist` method that will help you determine what issue(s) are occurring. The `EntityExistsException` is self-explanatory, and it is thrown if the primary key for the entity that you are persisting already exists. However, in some cases a `PersistenceException` will be thrown instead at flush or commit time, so you should catch each of these exceptions when issuing a call to persist. If the object that you are trying to persist is not an entity, then the `IllegalArgumentException` will be thrown. Lastly, the `TransactionRequiredException` will be thrown if invoked on a container-managed entity manager of type `PersistenceContextType.TRANSACTION`, and there is no transaction made.

9.6. Updating an Object

Problem

The contents of an entity object have been changed, and you want to persist the updates to the underlying datasource.

Solution

Create an EntityManager object using one of the solutions provided in Recipe 9-1, and then call the EntityManager object's merge method, passing a populated entity object that you want to update. The following lines of code demonstrate how to persist an object to the database using an EntityManager. In this case, a Book object is being updated in the BOOK database table. This excerpt is taken from the BookFacade session bean.

```
...
@PersistenceContext(unitName = "JavaEERecipes")
    private EntityManager em;
...
em.merge(book);
...
```

■ **Note** If the entity object (database record) being persisted does not already exist within the table, it will be stored as a newly persisted object rather than updated.

How It Works

The code implementation that is responsible for updating entity objects within the underlying data store resides within EJB classes. A valid EntityManager object must be available for use, and then the EntityManager's merge method can be called, passing a valid entity object for update within the underlying data store. When this is done, the state of the entity object will be merged into the data store, and the underlying data will be updated accordingly.

Two possible exceptions may be thrown when attempting to merge data. An IllegalArgumentException may be thrown if the instance being merged is not an entity (the database table does not exist) or is a removed entity. A TransactionRequiredException may be thrown if the merge method is invoked on a container-managed entity manager of type PersistenceContextType.TRANSACTION and there is no transaction.

9.7. Returning Data to Display in a Table

Problem

You want to display the contents of a database table via a JSF dataTable.

Solution #1

Return a list of entity objects from the underlying table containing the contents you want to display. Map a JSF dataTable component value to a managed bean controller property that contains a list of objects. In this case, the CDI managed bean property would be the list of the entity objects corresponding to the database table. Within the CDI managed bean, the list of entity objects can be obtained via an EJB call.

The following code excerpt is taken from the JSF managed bean controller named BookController. The managed bean property named completeBookList will be referenced from a dataTable component within a JSF view, displaying the data from the underlying table.

```
@Named(value="bookController")
@SessionScoped
public class BookController implements java.io.Serializable {

    @EJB
    BookFacade ejbFacade;

    private List<Book> completeBookList;

    @Inject
    private AuthorController authorController;

. . .

    public List<Book> getCompleteBookList() {
        completeBookList = ejbFacade.findAll();
        return completeBookList;
    }

    public void setCompleteBookList(List<Book> completeBookList) {
        this.completeBookList = completeBookList;
    }
. . .

}
```

Next, let's look at an excerpt from the EJB named BookFacade. It is a stateless session bean that contains the method, which is invoked by the BookController in order to obtain the list of entity objects.

■ **Note** The findAll() method that is called by BookController is inherited from the AbstractFacade class.

```
...
@Stateless
public class BookFacade extends AbstractFacade<Book> {
    @PersistenceContext(unitName = "JavaEERecipes")
    private EntityManager em;
```

```
    @Override
    protected EntityManager getEntityManager() {
        return em;
    }

    public BookFacade() {
        super(Book.class);
    }
...
```

In AbstractFacade, the findAll() method is implemented in a generic manner:

```
public abstract class AbstractFacade<T> {
    private Class<T> entityClass;

    public AbstractFacade(Class<T> entityClass) {
        this.entityClass = entityClass;
    }

    protected abstract EntityManager getEntityManager();

    public List<T> findAll() {
        javax.persistence.criteria.CriteriaQuery cq = getEntityManager().
getCriteriaBuilder().createQuery();
        Root<T> root = cq.from(entityClass);
        cq.select(root);
        return getEntityManager().createQuery(cq).getResultList();
    }
...
}
```

The List<Book> that is returned from the findAll() method in the EJB, which is contained in the AbstractFacade abstract class. This list is used to populate the completeBookList property in the BookController. Since the BookController communicates directly with the view layer, the JSF view will be able to utilize the completeBookList property to display the data.

Solution #2

Return a list of Map objects containing the results of a native SQL query against the underlying table. The JSF managed bean controller can contain a property that is a list of Map objects, and it can be referenced from within a JSF dataTable component. In this case, EJB method that is invoked by the managed bean controller will make a native SQL query against the database, returning certain columns of data from the table and populating map objects with those column values.

In the following excerpt, the BookController.getCustomBookList() method populates a managed bean property named customBookList via a call to the EJB method named obtainCustomList. Excerpts including both of these methods are shown next.

Here's the excerpt from `org.javaee8recipes.chapter09.BookController`:

```
...
public List<Map> getCustomBookList(){
        customBookList = ejbFacade.obtainCustomList();
        return customBookList;
    }
...
```

Here are the excerpts from `org.javaee8recipes.chapter09.session.BookFacade`:

```
...
    protected EntityManager getEntityManager() {
        return em;
    }
...
public List<Map> obtainCustomList(){

        List<Object[]> results = em.createNativeQuery(
                "select id, title, description " +
                "FROM BOOK " +
                " ORDER BY id").getResultList();

        List data = new ArrayList<HashMap>();

        if (!results.isEmpty()) {
            for (Object[] result : results) {
                HashMap resultMap = new HashMap();
                resultMap.put("id", result[0]);
                resultMap.put("title", result[1]);
                resultMap.put("description", result[2]);

                data.add(resultMap);
            }
        }
        return data;
    }
```

The `customBookList` property of the `BookController` class is populated by the EJB method, making the data available to the view.

How It Works

One of the most often required tasks of a web application is to display content. What's more, displaying database content is key to just about every enterprise application. Displaying content in table format provides the user with the ability to see the data because it is stored within the underlying table, in columnar format. The JSF `dataTable` component provides Java EE applications utilizing the JSF framework with an efficient and powerful way to display entity data in a table format.

The JSF dataTable component is capable of taking a list, DataModel, or Collection of objects and displaying them to the user. This recipe covers two different variations of retrieving data and storing it within a list for use in a dataTable component. The first solution is the most common situation. In both solutions, a CDI managed bean property is used to store the list of entity objects. However, the first solution stores a list of entity objects themselves, whereas the second solution stores a list of Map objects. Let's walk through each a little more closely.

In Solution #1 to this recipe, the completeBookList field within the BookController managed bean class is used to store the list of Book entities. The getCompleteBookList method populates the list by invoking the BookFacade session bean's findAll method to return all of the rows within the BOOK database table. Each database row is stored in a separate Book entity object, and in turn, each Book entity object is stored in the list. Finally, that list is returned to the BookController and assigned to the completeBookList field. In the end, the JSF dataTable component references the completeBookList to display the content.

■ **Note** To learn more about working with JSF dataTable components, refer to Recipe 3-12.

In Solution #2, the BookController field named customBookList is used to populate a JSF dataTable. The customBookList field is a list of Map objects. As far as the BookController method of population goes, the customBookList field is populated in much the same manner as the completeBookList in Solution #1. An EJB method is called, which returns the populated list of objects. In this case, the EJB named BookFacade returns a list of Map objects from a native SQL query. The BookFacade session bean class method obtainCustomList is responsible for creating the native SQL query and then storing the results within Map objects. In this case, the native query returns only a subset of the columns that are present within the BOOK database table in each row as a resultList and stores them into a List<Object[]>. A new ArrayList of HashMaps is then created and populated with the contents of the List from the database query.

To populate the ArrayList, the List<Object[]> is traversed using a for loop. A HashMap object is created for each object that is returned from the database. The HashMap object is populated with name-value pairs, with the name of the column being the first part, and the value from the entity object being the second part in each element. Each column that was retrieved via the query is stored into the HashMap, and the HashMap itself is then added to a list. In the end, the list of HashMap objects is returned to the managed bean and stored into the customBookList field. In the JSF view, the names that were associated with each of the database columns in the HashMap are used to reference the values for display within the dataTable.

Both of the solutions showcased in this recipe offer valid options for displaying database data JPA within a JSF dataTable component; I recommend using the first solution where possible because it is less error prone than Solution #2, which will require manual mapping of the database columns to map indices. There is also native SQL hard-coded into the EJB for Solution #2, which is okay when necessary but never the best option. It is always much better when you can utilize an EJB method, such as the findAll method that is available in AbstractFacade (Recipe 9-2), because if the underlying database table changes, then there is no need to alter the application code.

9.8. Creating a Singleton Bean

Problem

You want to develop a session bean in which all application clients will use the same. Only one instance of the bean should be allowed per application so that there is always a single site visitor counter for the number of visitors.

■ **Note** In this recipe, the counter is not cumulative. That is, it is not persisted across application startups. To create a cumulative counter, the current count must be persisted to the database before the application or server is restarted, and restored when the application is resumed.

Solution

Develop a singleton session bean that allows concurrent access by all application clients. The bean will keep track of the number of visitors who have been to the bookstore and display the number within the footer of the Acme Bookstore application. The following bean named `BookstoreSessionCounter` is a singleton session bean for the Acme Bookstore that is responsible for keeping track of an active session count:

```
package org.javaee8recipes.chapter09.session;

import javax.ejb.Singleton;
import javax.ejb.ConcurrencyManagement;
import static javax.ejb.ConcurrencyManagementType.CONTAINER;

@Singleton
@ConcurrencyManagement(CONTAINER)
public class BookstoreSessionCounter {

    private int numberOfSessions;
   /**
     * Initialize the Bean
     */
     @PostConstruct
     public void init(){
         // Initialize bean here
         System.out.println("Initializing bean...");
     }

    // Resets the counter on application startup
    public BookstoreSessionCounter(){
        numberOfSessions = 0;
    }

    /**
     * @return the numberOfSessions
     */
    public int getNumberOfSessions() {
        numberOfSessions++;
        return numberOfSessions;
    }
```

```
    /**
     * @param numberOfSessions the numberOfSessions to set.  This could be set
*  from the database if the current counter were persisted before the application
*  was shutdown
     */
    public void setNumberOfSessions(int numberOfSessions) {
        this.numberOfSessions = numberOfSessions;
    }
}
```

Next, let's look at the JSF managed bean controller that invokes the singleton session bean method for updating the site counter. The following excerpt is taken from a session-scoped managed bean named `BookstoreSessionController`, and the counter property is used to update the number of visitors within the EJB:

```
...
@Named("bookstoreSessionController")
@SessionScoped
public class BookstoreSessionController {

    @EJB
    BookstoreSessionCounter bookstoreSessionCounter;

    private int counter;
    private boolean flag = false;

    /**
     * @return the counter
     */
    public int getCounter() {
        if (!flag) {
            counter = bookstoreSessionCounter.getNumberOfSessions();
            flag = true;
        }
        return counter;
    }

    /**
     * @param counter the counter to set
     */
    public void setCounter(int counter) {
        this.counter = counter;
    }

}
```

Lastly, the counter is bound to a JSF EL expression within the Acme Bookstore Facelets template. The following line of code is excerpted from the template named `custom_template_search.xhtml`, which resides in the `chapter09/layout` directory of the book sources:

```
Number of Visitors: #{bookstoreSessionController.counter}
```

How It Works

A class that is specified as a singleton is created once per application. There is only one instance of a singleton class at any given time, and all client sessions interact with that same instance. To generate a singleton session bean, denote a bean as such by specifying the `javax.ejb.Singleton` annotation. Programmatically, the annotation specification is one of the main differences between the coding of a standard stateless session bean and a singleton session bean. However, functionally, the bean is treated much different by the container than a standard stateless session bean.

Singleton session beans are instantiated by the container at an arbitrary point in time. To force the instantiation of a singleton instance at application startup, the `javax.ejb.Startup` annotation can be specified. In the case of the example, there is no `@Startup` annotation specified, so the singleton instance could be instantiated by the container at any given point. However, a singleton will be started up before any of the application EJBs begin to receive requests. In the example, you can see that the `@PostConstruct` callback annotation is being used. This causes the method on which the annotation is specified to be executed directly after instantiation of the bean. Singletons share the same callback methodology as standard stateless session beans. To read more about callback methods, refer to Recipe 9-2.

■ **Note** If one or more singleton beans depend on other singleton beans for initialization, the `@DependsOn` annotation can be specified for the bean to denote which bean it depends on. A chain of dependencies can be set up using this annotation if needed.

By default, singletons are concurrent, meaning that multiple clients can access them at the same time (also known as *thread-safe*). There are two different ways in which to control concurrent access to singleton beans. The `@ConcurrencyManagement` annotation can be specified along with a given `ConcurrentManagementType` in order to tell the bean which type of concurrency to use. The two types of concurrency are `CONTAINER`, which is the default type if nothing is specified, and `BEAN`. In the example, the bean is annotated to specify container-managed concurrency. When container-managed concurrency is specified, the EJB container manages the concurrency. The `@Lock` annotation can be specified on methods of the singleton to tell the container how client access should be managed on the method. To use the `@Lock` annotation, specify a lock type of `LockType.READ` or `LockType.WRITE` (default) within the annotation to tell the container that many clients can access the annotated method concurrently or that the method should become locked to others when a client is accessing it.

The entire class can also be annotated with `@Lock`, in which case the designated lock type will be used for each of the methods within the class unless they contain their own lock type designation. For example, the following lines specify a method within a singleton class that should be locked when accessed by a client so that only one client at a time has access:

```
@Lock(LockType.WRITE)
public void setCounter(int counter){
this.counter = counter;
}
```

Bean concurrency is different in that it allows full concurrent, thread-safe locking access to all clients on all methods within the class. The developer can use Java synchronization techniques such as `synchronized` and `volatile` to help manage the state of concurrency within those singletons designated with bean-managed concurrency.

9.9. Scheduling a Timer Service

Problem

You want to schedule a task that performs database transactions on a recurring interval.

Solution #1

Use the Timer service to schedule a task within a bean using an automatic timer. The timer will specify a required interval of time, and the method used to perform the task will be invoked each time the interval of time expires. The following session bean is set up to create an automatic timer, which will begin upon application deployment. The following code is contained within the Java file named `org.javaee8recipes.chapter09.timer.TimerBean`:

```
import javax.ejb.Singleton;
import javax.ejb.Schedule;

/**
 * Recipe 9-9: The EJB Timer Service
 * @author juneau
 */
@Singleton
public class TimerBean {

@Schedule(minute="*/5", hour="*")
    public void automaticTimer(){
        System.out.println("*** Automatic Timeout Occurred ***");
    }
}
```

The automatic timer will begin when the class is deployed to the application server. Every five minutes, the `automaticTimer()` method will be invoked as will any processes that are performed within that method.

Solution #2

Create a programmatic timer and specify it to start when it is deployed to the application server. Configure an initialization method within the timer bean that will create the timer automatically when the bean is initialized. The following example class is named `org.javaee8recipes.chapter09.timer.ProgrammaticTimerExample`, and it will be automatically started when the application is deployed:

```
package org.javaee8recipes.chapter09.timer;

import javax.annotation.PostConstruct;
import javax.annotation.Resource;
import javax.ejb.Singleton;
import javax.ejb.Timer;
import javax.ejb.Timeout;
import javax.ejb.TimerService;
```

```
@Singleton
@Startup
public class ProgrammaticTimerExample {

    @Resource
    TimerService timerService;

    @PostConstruct
    public void createTimer(){
        System.out.println("Creating Timer...");
        Timer timer = timerService.createTimer(100000, "Timer has been created...");
    }

    @Timeout
    public void timeout(Timer timer){
        System.out.println("Timeout of Programmatic Timer Example...");
    }

}
```

After deployment, you should see the message in the server log indicating `Creating Timer`..., and then once the timer expires, the `Timeout of Programmatic Timer Example`... message will be displayed in the logs.

How It Works

Timer solutions make it easy to incorporate scheduled or timed tasks into an application process. The EJB Timer service helps make such solutions possible because it offers applications a method for scheduling tasks that will be performed by the application over a specified interval of time. There are two types of timers: programmatic and automatic. In Solution #1 to this recipe, an automatic timer is demonstrated. Although the solution does not perform any actual work, the method annotated with the `@Schedule` annotation is where the work takes place. An automatic timer is created when an EJB contains one or more methods that are annotated with `@Schedule` or `@Schedules`. The `@Schedule` takes a calendar-based timer expression to indicate when the annotated method should be executed.

■ **Note** One or more `@Schedule` annotations can be grouped within `@Scheduled{ ... }`, separating each `@Schedule` with a comma.

Calendar-based timer expressions can contain one or more calendar attributes paired with values to indicate a point in time for invocation of the method. Table 9-1 lists the different calendar-based timer expressions, along with a description of each.

Table 9-1. *Calendar-Based Timer Expressions*

Attribute	Description
dayOfWeek	One or more days in a week: (0 - 7) or (Sun, Mon, Tue, Wed, Thu, Fri, Sat)
dayOfMonth	One or more days in a month: (1 - 31) or (Last) or (1st, 2nd, 3rd, 4th, 5th, Last), along with any of the dayOfWeek values
month	One or more months in a year: (1 - 12) or month abbreviation
year	Four-digit calendar year
hour	One or more hours within a day: (0 - 23)
minute	One or more minutes within an hour: (0 - 59)
second	One or more seconds within a minute: (0 - 59)

When creating a calendar-based timer expression, the asterisk (*) can be specified as a wildcard. The forward slash (/) can be used to indicate an interval in time. An interval in time follows this pattern:

```
beginning time (larger unit) / frequency
```

Therefore, specifying `/5` in the example (`minute="*/5" hour="*"`) indicates that you want the timer to be executed every five minutes within the hour because the wildcard indicates which hour to begin the timer and the 5 indicates how often. Timer expression attributes can contain more than one value, and a comma should separate each value. To indicate that you want to execute a timer at 3 a.m. and again at 6 a.m., you could write the following:

```
@Schedule(hour="3,6")
```

A range of values can also be specified for timer attributes. To indicate that you want to have the timer executed every hour between the hours of 4 and 7 a.m., you could specify the following:

```
@Schedule(hour"4-7")
```

Multiple timer expressions can be combined to tune the timer in a more fine-grained fashion. For instance, to specify a timer schedule that will execute at 1 a.m. every Sunday morning, you could write the following:

```
@Schedule(dayOfWeek="Sun", hour="1")
```

Programmatic timers are the second option that can be used when developing a timed-process, as demonstrated in Solution #2. A programmatic timer is different from an automatic timer because there is no schedule involved. Rather, a client can invoke a timer, or it can be initialized with the construction of a bean. A programmatic timer contains one method that is denoted using the `@Timeout` annotation. The `@Timeout` method will be executed when the timer expires. The `@Timeout` method must return `void`, and it can optionally accept a `javax.ejb.Timer` object. A `@Timeout` method must not throw an application exception.

To create a programmatic timer, invoke one of the create methods of the `TimerService` interface. Table 9-2 indicates the different `create` methods that can be used.

Table 9-2. Programmatic Timer Create Methods

Method	Description
createTimer	Standard timer creation
createSingleActionTimer	Creates a timer that expires once
createIntervalTimer	Creates a timer that expires based on a given time interval
createCalendarTimer	Creates a timer based on a calendar

In Solution #2 of this recipe, a standard timer is created, passing an interval of 100,000 milliseconds. This means that the method annotated with @Timeout will be executed once after 100,000 milliseconds has passed. The following is another syntax that could be used to create a timer that has the same schedule:

```
long duration = 100000;
Timer timer = timerService.createSingleActionTimer(duration, new TimerConfig());
```

Similarly, a date can be passed to the create method in order to specify a given date and time when the timer should expire. The following timer will expire 30 days from the date in which the application is deployed:

```
Calendar cal = Calendar.getInstance();
cal.add(Calendar.DATE, 30);
Timer timer = timerService.createSingleActionTimer(cal.getTime(), new TimerConfig());
```

To create a programmatic calendar-based timer, you must create a new schedule using the ScheduleExpression helper class. Doing so will allow you to utilize the calendar-based expressions that are listed in Table 9-1 to specify the timer expiration date. The following example demonstrates a timer that will expire every Sunday at 1 a.m.:

```
ScheduleExpression schedule = new ScheduleExpression();
schedule.dayOfWeek("Sun");
schedule.hour("1");
Timer timer = timerService.createCalendarTimer(schedule);
```

Timers do not need to be created in singleton session beans; they can be used in stateless session beans as well. However, they cannot be specified in stateful session beans. Timers are a topic that cannot be discussed within the boundaries of a single recipe. However, this brief introduction to timers should give you enough to get started using this technology within your applications. To learn more about timers, refer to the online documentation at https://docs.oracle.com/javaee/7/tutorial/ejb-basicexamples004.htm.

■ **Note** All timers are persistent by default, meaning that if the server is shut down for some reason, the timer will become active again when the server is restarted. In the event that a timer should expire while the server is down, the timer will expire (or the @Timeout method will be called) once the server is functioning normally again. To indicate that a timer should not be persistent, call TimerConfig.setPersistent(false) and pass it to a timer-creation method.

9.10. Performing Optional Transaction Lifecycle Callbacks

Problem

You are interested in beginning a transaction when a bean is instantiated and ending the transaction when it is destroyed.

Solution

Choose to utilize the optional transaction lifecycle callbacks built into EJB. To begin a transaction during the `@PostConstruct` or `@PreDestroy` callbacks, annotate the methods accordingly with `@TransactionAttribute`, passing the `TransactionAttributeType.REQUIRES_NEW` attribute. In the following example, a transaction is started when the bean named `AcmeFacade` is created. Another transaction is started when the bean is being destroyed.

```
import javax.annotation.PostConstruct;
import javax.annotation.PreDestroy;
import javax.ejb.Stateful;
import javax.ejb.TransactionAttribute;
import javax.ejb.TransactionAttributeType;
import javax.persistence.EntityManager;
import javax.persistence.PersistenceContext;
import javax.persistence.PersistenceContextType;

@Stateful
public class AcmeFacade {

    @PersistenceContext(unitName = "JavaEERecipesPU", type = PersistenceContextType.
EXTENDED)
    private EntityManager em;

    @TransactionAttribute(TransactionAttributeType.REQUIRES_NEW)
    @PostConstruct
    public void init() {
        System.out.println("The Acme Bean has been created");
    }

    @TransactionAttribute(TransactionAttributeType.REQUIRES_NEW)
    @PreDestroy
    public void destroy() {
        System.out.println("The Acme Bean is being destroyed...");
        em.flush();
    }
}
```

How It Works

Session beans can contain callback methods that are invoked when certain stages of a bean's lifecycle occur. For instance, a method can be registered within a session bean via annotation to invoke after the bean is constructed (`@PostConstruct`), before it is destroyed (`@PreDestroy`), and so on. Sometimes it makes sense to start a new transaction when one of these events occurs. It is possible to specify the transactional status of an annotated lifecycle callback method within a session bean when using container-managed transactions.

The annotation accepts a transaction type as per the values listed in Table 9-3.

Table 9-3. *Container-Managed Transaction Demarcation*

Attribute	Description
`MANDATORY`	The container must invoke an enterprise bean method whose transaction is set to this attribute in the client's transaction context. The client is required to call with a transaction context.
`REQUIRED`	The container must invoke an enterprise bean method whose transaction is set to this attribute value with an unspecified transaction context.
`REQUIRES_NEW`	The container must invoke an enterprise bean method whose transaction is set to this attribute value with a new transaction context.
`SUPPORTS`	If the client calls with a transaction context, then the container treats it as `REQUIRED`. If the client calls without a transaction context, the container treats it as `NOT_SUPPORTED`.
`NOT_SUPPORTED`	The container invokes an enterprise bean method whose transaction attribute is set to this value with an unspecified transaction context.
`NEVER`	The container invokes an enterprise bean method whose transaction is set to this value without a transaction context defined by the EJB specification.

By default, the lifecycle callback methods are not transactional in order to maintain backward compatibility. By annotating the callback method with the `@TransactionAttribute` and the preferred demarcation type, the callback method has opted in to be transactional.

9.11. Ensuring a Stateful Session Bean Is Not Passivated

Problem

Rather than have your inactive stateful session bean passivated, you want to keep it in memory.

Solution

Specify to the container that the bean is not to be passivated by indicating as such within the `@Stateful` annotation. To opt out of passivation, set the `passivationCapable` attribute of the `@Stateful` annotation to `false`, as demonstrated in the following excerpt:

```
@Stateful(passivationCapable=false)
public class AcmeFacade {
    ...
}
```

How It Works

When a stateful session bean has been inactive for a period of time, the container may choose to passivate the bean in an effort to conserve memory and resources. Typically, the EJB container will passivate stateful session beans using a least recently used algorithm. When passivation occurs, the bean is moved to secondary storage and removed from memory. Prior to the passivation of a stateful session bean, any methods annotated with `@PrePassivate` will be invoked. When a stateful session bean that has been passivated needs to be made active again, the EJB container activates the bean, then calls any methods annotated with `@PostActivate`, and finally moves the bean to the ready stage.

In EJB 3.2, stateful session beans can opt out of passivation so that they will remain in memory instead of being transferred to secondary storage if inactive. This may be helpful in situations where a bean needs to remain active for application processes or if the bean contains a nonserializable field, since these fields cannot be passivated and are made `null` upon passivation. To indicate that a bean is not to be passivated, set the `passivationCapable` attribute of the `@Stateful` annotation to `false`, as per the solution to this recipe.

9.12. Denoting Local and Remote Interfaces

Problem

You want to explicitly designate a local or remote interface for an EJB.

Solution

A business interface cannot be made both the local and remote business interfaces for a bean. Therefore, the EJB specification contains an API to specify whether a business interface is intended as local or remote. The following rules pertain to business interfaces implemented by enterprise beans classes:

- The `java.io.Serializable`, `java.io.Externalizable`, and interfaces defined by the `javax.ejb` package are always excluded when determination of local or remote business interfaces are declared for a bean.
- If a bean class contains the `@Remote` annotation, then all implemented interfaces are assumed to be remote.
- If a bean class contains no annotation or if the `@Local` annotation is specified, then all implemented interfaces are assumed to be local.
- Any business interface that is explicitly defined for a bean that contains the no-interface view must be designated as `@Local`.
- Any business interface must be explicitly designated as local or remote if the bean class explicitly specifies the `@Local` or `@Remote` annotation with a nonempty value.
- Any business interface must be explicitly designated as local or remote if the deployment descriptor specifies as such.

How It Works

The release of EJB 3.0 greatly simplified development with EJBs because it introduced the no-interface view for making local business interfaces optional. The no-interface view automatically exposes all public methods of a bean to the caller. By default, a no-interface view is automatically exposed by any session bean that does not include an `implements` clause and has no local or remote client views defined. The EJB 3.2 provided further granularity for those situations where local and remote interfaces need to be explicitly specified.

Let's break down the rules that were defined within the solution to this recipe. First, if an EJB exposes local interfaces, then there is no need to explicitly denote a bean as such. For instance, the following bean contains a local interface, although it is not explicitly denoted:

```
@Stateless
public class AcmeSession implements interfaceA {
        ...
}
public interfaceA { ... }
```

If a bean class is annotated with @Remote, then any interfaces that it implements are assumed to be remote. For instance, the following bean class implements two interfaces, and both are assumed to be remote, although they do not contain any annotation to indicate as such.

```
@Remote
@Stateless
public class AcmeSession implements interfaceA, interfaceB {
        ...
}
```

If a bean class contains the @Local annotation, then any interfaces that it implements are assumed to be local. For instance, the following bean class implements two interfaces, and both are assumed to be local although they do not contain any annotation to indicate as such:

```
@Local
@Stateless
public class AcmeSession implements interfaceA, interfaceB {
        ...
}
```

If a bean class contains the @Local or @Remote annotation and specifies an interface name within the annotation, then the same designation is applied as the annotation specifies. For instance, the following bean is annotated to include a local business interface, and the name of the interface is specified in the annotation, thereby making the interface local.

```
@Local(interfaceA.class)
@Stateless
public class AcmeSession implements interfaceA {
        ...
}
```

These new designation rules make it easier to designate and determine the type of business interface that is implemented by a bean.

9.13. Processing Messages Asynchronously from Enterprise Beans

Problem

You want to have the ability to process messages from session beans in an asynchronous manner.

Solution

Develop a message-driven bean to perform the message processing for your application. To develop a message bean, create an EJB that is annotated with `@MessageDriven`, passing the appropriate configuration options. In the bean, code a method named `onMessage` that will perform all of the message processing. The following example, `org.javaee8recipes.chapter09.jsf.AcmeMessageBean`, demonstrates how to code a message-driven bean that processes messages from a `javax.jms.Queue` that has been configured in the application server container.

■ **Note** Prior to running these examples, you must create the JMS resources within GlassFish or Payara. Refer to Recipe 14-1 for more details.

```
@MessageDriven(mappedName="jms/Queue", activationConfig = {
    @ActivationConfigProperty(propertyName = "destinationType",
                              propertyValue = "javax.jms.Queue")
})
public class AcmeMessageBean implements MessageListener {

    public AcmeMessageBean(){

    }

    @Override
    public void onMessage(Message msg) {
        if(msg != null){
            performExtraProcessing();
            System.out.println("Message has been received: " + msg);
        } else {
            System.out.println("No message received");
        }
    }

    public void performExtraProcessing(){
        System.out.println("This method could perform extra processing");
    }

}
```

How It Works

Message-driven beans (MDBs) are Enterprise JavaBeans that are utilized for processing messages in an asynchronous manner. Most often MDBs are JMS message listeners, receiving messages and processing accordingly. A message-driven bean is created by annotating a bean with the `@MessageDriven` annotation and optionally implementing the `MessageListener` interface. When a message is received in the container queue, the container invokes the bean's `onMessage` method, which contains the business logic that is responsible for processing the message accordingly.

■ **Note** Any session bean can be used for processing messages, but only message-driven beans can do so in an asynchronous manner.

MDBs must be made public, and not static or final. An MDB must contain a public, no-argument constructor, and it must contain a method named `onMessage` that accepts a `javax.jms.Message` argument. The `onMessage` method is responsible for performing all message processing, and it can utilize other methods within the bean to help out, where needed.

Bean providers may provide special configurations for MDBs to the deployers, such as information regarding message selectors, acknowledgment modes, and so on, by means of the `activationConfig` element of the `@MessageDriven` annotation. A standard list of `activationConfig` properties exists to provide JMS 2.0 alignment. Table 9-4 lists the new properties along with a description of what they do.

Table 9-4. *JMS 2.0 Aligned activationConfig Properties*

Property	Description
`destinationLookup`	Provides advice to the deployer regarding whether the message-driven bean is intended to be associated with a `Queue` or `Topic`. Values for this property are `javax.jms.Queue` and `javax.jms.Topic`.
`connectionFactoryLookup`	Specifies the lookup name of an administratively defined `ConnectionFactory` object that will be used for a connection to the JMS provider from which a message-driven bean will send JMS messages.
`clientId`	Specifies the client identifier that will be used for a connection to the JMS provider from which a message-driven bean will send JMS messages.
`subscriptionName`	If the message-driven bean is intended to be used with a `Topic`, then the bean provider can specify the name of a durable subscription with this property and set the `subscriptionDurability` property to `Durable`.
`shareSubscriptions`	This property is only to be used when a message-driven bean is deployed to a clustered application server, and the value for this property can be either `true` or `false`. A value of `true` means that the same durable subscription name or nondurable subscription will be used for each instance in the cluster. A value of `false` means that a different durable subscription name or nondurable subscription will be used for each instance in the cluster.

CHAPTER 10

The Query API and JPQL

The Java Persistence API (JPA) utilizes a query language for communicating with underlying data stores. Although Java EE uses entities rather than SQL for database access, it provides a query language so that developers can obtain the required information via the entities. The Java Persistence Query Language (JPQL) does just that because it provides a facility for querying and working with Java EE entity objects. Although it is very similar to SQL, it is an object-relational query language, so there are some minor differences of which developers should be aware. Using JPQL along with Java EE entities allows developers to create versatile applications because JPQL is not database-specific and applications can be written once and deployed to run on top of a myriad of databases.

The release of Java EE 8 introduced with it a maintenance release of JPA 2.2, and that means added and enhanced features. Some of the improvements from the previous 2.1 release include support for stored procedures and built-in functions, downcasting support, and outer join support with `ON` conditions. The latest release includes new enhancements including support for the Java 8 Date-Time API, the ability to stream query results, and repeatable annotation support, to name a few. The recipes in this chapter do not attempt to cover all of the features that JPQL has to offer because there are many. However, the recipes contain enough information to introduce beginners to the world of JPQL and to get intermediate developers up to date with the latest that JPQL has to offer. To review the entire set of documentation for using JPQL, see the online resources available at `https://docs.oracle.com/javaee/7/tutorial/persistence-querylanguage002.htm#BNBRG`.

10-1. Querying All Instances of an Entity

Problem

You want to retrieve all the instances for a particular entity. That is, you want to query the underlying database table associated with the entity and retrieve all rows.

Solution #1

Call the `EntityManager`'s `createQuery` method and use JPQL to formulate a query that will return all instances of a given entity. In the following example, a JPQL query is used to return all objects within the `BookAuthor` entity:

```
public List<BookAuthor> findAuthor(){
        return em.createQuery("select object(o) from BookAuthor o").getResultList();
}
```

When the `findAuthor` method is called, a `List` containing all of the `BookAuthor` entity instances in the entity (all records in the underlying database table) will be returned.

J. Juneau, *Java EE 8 Recipes*, https://doi.org/10.1007/978-1-4842-3594-2_10

Solution #2

Create a `CriteriaQuery` object by generating a criteria builder from the `EntityManager` object and calling its `createQuery` method. Once a `CriteriaQuery` object has been created, generate a query by calling a series of the `CriteriaBuilder` methods against the entity that you want to query. Finally, call the `EntityManager`'s `createQuery` method, passing the query that you have previously built. Return the `ResultList` from the query to return all the rows from the table. In the following lines of code, you can see this technique performed:

```
javax.persistence.criteria.CriteriaQuery cq = getEntityManager().getCriteriaBuilder().
createQuery();
Root<BookAuthor> bookAuthor = cq.from(BookAuthor);
cq.select(bookAuthor);
return getEntityManager().createQuery(cq).getResultList();
```

How It Works

An entity instance can be referred to as a *record* in the underlying data store. That is, there is an entity instance for each record within a given database table. That said, sometimes it is handy to retrieve all of the instances for a given entity. Some applications may require all objects in order to perform a particular task against each, or perhaps your application needs to simply display all of the instances of an entity for the user. Whatever the case, there are a couple of ways to retrieve all of the instances for a given entity. Each of the techniques should occur within an EJB.

In Solution #1, the JPQL can be used to query an entity for all instances. To create a dynamic query, call the `EntityManager`'s `createQuery` method, to which you can pass a string-based query that consists of JPQL syntax, or a `javax.persistence.Query` instance. The `Query` interface has a sizable number of methods that can be used to work with the query object. Table 10-1 describes what these methods do.

Table 10-1. *javax.persistence.Query Interface Methods*

Method	Description
`executeUpdate`	Executes an `update` or `delete` statement
`getFirstResult`	Specifies the position of the first result the query object was set to retrieve
`getFlushMode`	Gets the flush mode in effect for the query execution
`getHints`	Gets the properties and hints and associated values that are in effect for the query instance
`getLockMode`	Gets the current lock mode for the query
`getMaxResults`	Specifies the maximum number of results the query object was set to retrieve
`getParameter`	Gets the parameter object corresponding to the declared positional parameter
`getParameters`	Gets the parameter objects corresponding to the declared parameters of the query
`getParameterValue(int)`	Returns the value bound to the named or positional parameter
`getResultList`	Executes a `SELECT` query and then returns the query results as an untyped list
`getSingleResult`	Executes a `SELECT` query and then returns a single untyped result
`isBound`	Returns a boolean indicating whether a value has been bound to the parameter

In the example, a query string is passed to the method, and it reads as follows:

```
select object(o) from BookAuthor o
```

To break this down, the query is selecting all objects from the BookAuthor entity. Any letter could have been used in place of the o character within the query, but o is a bit of a standard since JPQL is referring to objects. All queries contain a SELECT clause, which is used to define the types of entity instances that you want to obtain. In the example, the entire instance is selected from the BookAuthor entity, as opposed to single fields that are contained within the instance. Since the JPA works with objects, queries should always return the entire object; if you want to use only a subset of fields from the object, then you can call upon those fields from the instance(s) returned from the query. The object keyword is optional and is provided mainly for readability. The same JPQL could be written as follows:

```
select o from BookAuthor o
```

The FROM clause can reference one or more identification variables that can refer to the name of an entity, an element of a single-valued relationship, an element of a collection relationship, or a member of a collection that is the multiple side of a one-to-many relationship. In the example, the BookAuthor variable refers to the entity itself.

■ **Note** For more information regarding the full query language syntax, refer to the online documentation: https://javaee.github.io/tutorial/persistence-querylanguage.html#BNBTG

The example in Solution #2 demonstrates the use of the CriteriaQuery, which is used to construct queries for entities by creating objects that define query criteria. To obtain a CriteriaQuery object, you can call the EntityManager's getCriteriaBuilder method and, in turn, call the createQuery method of the CriteriaBuilder. The CriteriaQuery object allows you to specify a series of options that will be applied to a query so that an entity can be queried using native Java, without hard-coding any string queries. In the example, the CriteriaQuery instance is obtained by the chaining of subsequent method calls against the EntityManager and CriteriaBuilder instances. Once the CriteriaQuery is obtained, its from method is called, passing the name of the entity that will be queried. A javax.persistence.criteria.Root object is returned from the call, which can then be passed to the CriteriaQuery instance select method to return a TypedQuery object to prepare the query for execution, which can then return the ResultList of entity instances. In the example, the final line of code chains method calls again, so you do not see the TypedQuery object referenced at all. However, if the chaining were to be removed, the code would look as follows:

```
cq.select(bookAuthor);
TypedQuery<BookAuthor> q = em.createQuery(cq);
return q.getResultList();
```

Both the JPQL and CriteriaQuery techniques can provide similar results. Neither technique is any better than the other, unless you prefer that the JPQL be written in code that is more like native SQL, or that CriteriaQuery be written in native Java.

10-2. Setting Parameters to Filter Query Results

Problem

You want to query an entity and retrieve only a subset of its instances that match specified criteria.

Solution #1

Write a JPQL dynamic query and specify parameters that can be bound to the query using bind variables. Call the Query object's setParameter method to assign a parameter value to each bind variable. In the following example, a query is written to search the Book entity for all Book instances that were written by a specified author. The BookAuthor object in this example is a named parameter that will be bound to the query using a bind variable.

```
public List<Book> findBooksByAuthor(BookAuthor authorId){
        return em.createQuery("select o from Book o " +
                "where :bookAuthor MEMBER OF o.authors")
                .setParameter("bookAuthor", authorId)
                .getResultList();
    }
```

The matching Book instances for the given author will be returned.

Solution #2

Write a Criteria API query and specify parameters that can be bound to the query using bind variables.

```
public List<Book> findBooksByAuthorCriteria(BookAuthor authorId){
        CriteriaBuilder cb = em.getCriteriaBuilder();
        CriteriaQuery<Book> cq = cb.createQuery(Book.class);
        Root<Book> book = cq.from(Book.class);
        cq.where(book.get(Book_.bookAuthor).in(authorId));
        TypedQuery<Book> tq = em.createQuery(cq);
        return tq.getResultList();
}
```

As you can see, the Criteria API allows you to generate a statically typed query. This can be beneficial for helping to reduce errors in typing strings, and also for promoting efficiency, as Criteria API queries are not compiled each time they are executed.

How It Works

It is often desirable to return a refined list of results from a query, rather than returning the entire list of records within a database table. In standard SQL, the WHERE clause allows one or more expressions to be specified, which will ultimately refine the results of the query. Using JPQL, the WHERE clause works in the same manner, and the process of refining results of a query is almost identical to doing so with standard JDBC.

In the solution for this recipe, the JPQL technique is used to refine the results of a query against the Book entity such that only instances pertaining to books written by a specified author will be returned. The `findBooksByAuthor` method within the `org.javaee8recipes.chapter09.session.BookFacade` class accepts a `BookAuthor` object as an argument, and the argument will then be specified to refine the results of the query. As you'll see in the code, a single line of code (using the Effective Java builder pattern) within the `findBooksByAuthor` method performs the entire task. The `EntityManager`'s `createQuery` method is called, passing a string-based JPQL query that includes a bind variable named `:bookAuthor`. The JPQL string is as follows:

```
Select o from Book o where :bookAuthor MEMBER OF o.authors
```

After creating the query object, the `Query` interface's `setParameter` method can be called, passing the name of the bind variable for which you want to substitute a value, along with the value you want to substitute it with. In this case, the `String bookAuthor` is passed along with the `Author` object you want to match against for obtaining `Book` instances. If more than one parameter needs to be specified, more than one call to `setParameter` can be strung together so that each bind variable has a matching substitute. Finally, once all of the parameters have been set, the `getResultList` method can be called against the `Query`, returning the matching objects.

■ **Note** Two types of parameters can be used with JPQL: `named` and `positional`. The example in this recipe, along with many of the others in this book, uses named parameters. Positional parameters are written a bit differently in that they are denoted within JPQL using a question mark (`?`) character, and a positional number is used instead of passing the variable name to the `setParameter()` method. The same query that is used in this recipe can be rewritten as follows to use positional parameters:

```
return em.createQuery ("select o from Book o " +

        "where ? MEMBER OF o.authors")

        .setParameter (1, authorId)

                .getResultList();
```

Both named and positional parameters achieve the same results. However, I recommend against using positional parameters because it makes code harder to manage, especially if there are more than a handful of parameters in use. It is also easier to mistype the `setParameter()` calls, and if the wrong positional number is passed with an incorrect parameter value, issues can arise.

In Solution #2 to this recipe, the Criteria API is used to construct the same query and return the same results as those from Solution #1. To build the criteria query, first obtain a `CriteriaBuilder` from the entity manager. Next, use the `CriteriaQuery` to create a `CriteriaQuery<Object>` by calling upon the `createQuery` method and passing the entity class type.

10-3. Returning a Single Object

Problem

You have specified JPQL for a given query that will return exactly one matching entity instance, and you want to store it within a local object so that tasks can be performed against it.

Solution

Create a dynamic query, specifying the JPQL that is necessary for obtaining the entity instance that matches the given criteria. The JPQL will include a bind variable that will bind the parameter to the query in order to obtain the desired instance. The method in the following code excerpt can be found in the `org.javaee8recipes.chapter09.session.BookFacade` class within the sources:

```
public Book findByTitle(String title){
    return (Book) em.createQuery("select object(o) from Book o " +
                          "where o.title = :title")
                          .setParameter("title", title.toUpperCase())
                          .getSingleResult();
}
```

To invoke the method and return results, the previous method, which resides within an EJB, can be invoked from within a JSF managed bean controller. The method that is defined within the controller can subsequently be referenced from within a JSF view to display the results.

How It Works

A single entity instance can be retrieved by specifying a query, along with the necessary parameters to refine the possible matches to a single object. The `javax.persistence.Query` interface's `getSingleResult` method allows just one instance to be returned, given that there is only one instance that matches the given query specification. In the example to this recipe, assume that each `Book` instance has a unique name to identify it. Therefore, you can be sure that when a name is bound to the query it will return a single result.

Problems can arise if more than one instance matches the criteria. An attempt to call `getSingleQuery` using a query that returns more than one instance will result in a `NonUniqueResultException` being thrown. It is a good idea to catch this exception within your applications to avoid ugly error messages being displayed to the users if more than one matching instance exists. Another case to watch out for is when a query returns no result at all. If no result is returned, then a `NoResultException` will be thrown.

10-4. Creating Native Queries

Problem

The query you want to use against an entity contains some SQL functionality that pertains to the specific database vendor that your application is using, or you are more comfortable working with standard SQL than using JPQL. That said, you want to use standard SQL to query one of your entity objects.

■ **Note** When using native queries, you will be forced to work against database records, rather than Java objects. For this reason, it is recommended to use JPQL unless necessary.

Solution #1

Create a native query by calling the `EntityManager` object's `createNativeQuery` method. Pass a SQL query as the first parameter and pass the entity class that you want to return the results of the query into as the second parameter. Once the query has been created, call one of the corresponding `javax.persistence.Query` methods (see Table 10-1) to return the results. The following example taken from `org.javaee8recipes.chapter09.session.BookFacade` EJB demonstrates the use of a native query on the Book entity:

```
public List<Book> obtainNativeList(){
        Query query = em.createNativeQuery(
                "select id, title, description " +
                "FROM BOOK " +
                " ORDER BY id", org.javaee8recipes.entity.Book.class);
        return query.getResultList();

}
```

In the previous example, each of the database attributes will map to a field in the Book class.

Solution #2

Specify a `@NamedNativeQuery` within the entity class for the entity class that you want to query. Provide a name, query, and mapping class for the `@NamedNativeQuery` via the annotation. Within the EJB method, call the `EntityManager` object's `createNativeQuery` method and provide the name that was specified as a named native query rather than a SQL string. The following code excerpt demonstrates the creation of a named native query for the `org.javaee8recipes.entity.Book` entity:

```
...
@Entity
@Table(name="BOOK")
@NamedNativeQuery(
    name="allBooks",
    query = "select id, title, description " +
                "FROM BOOK " +
                "ORDER BY id",
    resultClass=Book.class)
...
```

Next, let's take a look at how the named native query is invoked from within the EJB. The following excerpt of code is taken from the org.javaee8recipes.chapter09.session.BookFacade bean, and it demonstrates the invocation of the allBooks named native query:

```
public List<Book> obtainNamedNativeList(){
        Query query = em.createNamedQuery(
                "allBooks", org.javaee8recipes.entity.Book.class);
        return query.getResultList();

    }
```

How It Works

Native queries provide a way to utilize native SQL code for retrieving data from an underlying data. Not only do they allow an inexperienced JPQL developer to write in native SQL, but they also allow native SQL syntax, such as Oracle-specific PL/SQL functions, or procedure calls to be made. On the downside, however, native queries do not return results in an entity-oriented manner, but rather as plain old objects. For this reason, the named native query provides the option to specify an entity class into which the results should be returned.

There are a handful of ways to work with native queries, and I've covered a couple of the most commonly used tactics in this recipe. A javax.persistence.Query is generated either by calling the EntityManager's createNativeQuery method or by calling the EntityManager's createNamedQuery method and passing a named native query. In Solution #1, a string-based SQL query is used to retrieve results into an entity class. For starters, the createNativeQuery method accepts a query in String format, or a named native query for the first parameter. In Solution #1, a query is used to obtain all the records from the BOOK database table. The second argument to the createNativeQuery method is an optional mapping class into which the results of the query will be stored. Solution #1 specifies Book.class as the second parameter, which will map the columns of the database table to their corresponding fields within the Book entity. Once the Query instance is created, then its methods can be invoked in order to execute the query. In this case, the getResultSet method is invoked, which will return a list of the matching records and bind each of them to a Book entity class instance.

In Solution #2, a named native query is demonstrated. Named native queries allow the SQL string to be specified once within the corresponding entity class, and then they can be executed by simply passing the string-based name that has been assigned to the named native query. To utilize a named native query, add the @NamedNativeQuery annotation to the entity class that you want to query, and then specify values for the three parameters of the annotation: name, query, and resultClass. For the name parameter of the @NamedNativeQuery annotation, a String-based name that will be used to reference the query must be specified, the query parameter must be the native SQL string, and the resultClass must be the entity class that the query results will be stored into. The @NamedNativeQuery also includes the resultSetMapping parameter that can be used to specify a SqlResultSetMapping for those queries involving more than one table. To execute the named native query, use the same technique as demonstrated in Solution #1, but instead call the EntityManager object's createNamedQuery method. Instead of specifying a SQL string, pass the name that was specified within the @NamedNativeQuery annotation for the respective query.

■ **Note** If the named query involves more than one database table, then a SqlResultSetMapping must be defined. See Recipe 10-5 for more details.

In some cases, using a native SQL query is the only solution for retrieving the data that your application requires. In all cases, it is recommended that JPQL be used, rather than native SQL, if possible. However, for those cases where native SQL is the only solution, then creating a native query using one of the techniques provided in this recipe is definitely the way to go. Which technique is better? Well, that depends on what you need to do. If you are trying to create a dynamic query, whereas the actual SQL string for the query may change dynamically, then the standard native query is the solution for you. However, if the SQL query that you are specifying will not change in a dynamic manner, then perhaps the named native query is the best choice for two reasons. First, the named native query allows SQL to be organized and stored within a single location, which is the entity class on which the SQL is querying. Second, named native queries can achieve better performance because they are cached after the first execution. Therefore, the next time the named native query is called, the SQL does not have to be recompiled. Such is not the case with a standard native query. Each time a standard native query is called, the SQL must be recompiled, which ultimately means that it will not be executed as fast.

10-5. Querying More Than One Entity

Problem

The JPQL or native SQL query being used references more than one entity or underlying database table. Since there are attributes from more than one table, the results cannot be stored in a single entity object.

Solution #1

Use a `SqlResultSetMapping`, which allows the specification of more than one entity class for returning query results. The `@SqlResultSetMapping` annotation can be specified in order to map a result set to one or more entities, allowing the joining of database tables to become a nonissue. In the following example, the `BOOK` and `BOOK_AUTHOR` database tables are joined together using a native SQL query, and the results are returned using a `SqlResultSetMapping`. The following `@SqlResultSetMapping` can be found in the `org.javaee8recipes.entity.BookAuthor` entity class:

```
@SqlResultSetMapping(name="authorBooks",
        entities= {
            @EntityResult(entityClass=org.javaee8recipes.entity.Book.class, fields={
                @FieldResult(name="id", column="BOOK_ID"),
                @FieldResult(name="title", column="TITLE")
            }),
            @EntityResult(entityClass=org.javaee8recipes.entity.BookAuthor.class, fields={
                @FieldResult(name="id", column="AUTHOR_ID"),
                @FieldResult(name="first", column="FIRST"),
                @FieldResult(name="last", column="LAST")
            })
        })
```

Next, let's look at how the SqlResultSetMapping is used. The following method is taken from the org.javaee8recipes.session.BookAuthorFacade session bean:

```
public List findAuthorBooksMapping(){

        Query qry = em.createNativeQuery(
                "select b.id as BOOK_ID, b.title as TITLE, " +
                "ba.id AS AUTHOR_ID, ba.first as FIRST, ba.last as LAST " +
                "from book_author ba, book b, author_work aw " +
                "where aw.author_id = ba.id " +
                "and b.id = aw.book_id", "authorBooks");

        return  qry.getResultList();
    }
```

The resulting list can then be referenced from within a JSF dataTable, or another client data iteration device, in order to display the results of the query.

Solution #2

Utilize a native query to return the necessary fields from more than one database table and return the results to a HashMap, rather than to an entity class. In the following method taken from the org.javaee8recipes.session.BookAuthorFacade session bean, this technique is demonstrated:

```
public List<Map> findAuthorBooks(){

        Query qry = em.createNativeQuery(
                "select ba.id, ba.last, ba.first, ba.bio, b.id, b.title, b.image,
                b.description " +
                "from book_author ba, book b, author_work aw " +
                "where aw.author_id = ba.id " +
                "and b.id = aw.book_id");

        List<Object[]> results = qry.getResultList();
        List data = new ArrayList<HashMap>();

        if (!results.isEmpty()) {
            for (Object[] result : results) {
                HashMap resultMap = new HashMap();
                resultMap.put("authorId", result[0]);
                resultMap.put("authorLast", result[1]);
                resultMap.put("authorFirst", result[2]);
                resultMap.put("authorBio", result[3]);
                resultMap.put("bookId", result[4]);
                resultMap.put("bookTitle", result[5]);
                resultMap.put("bookImage", result[6]);
                resultMap.put("bookDescription", result[7]);

                data.add(resultMap);
            }
```

```
        }
        return data;
    }
```

Using this solution, no SqlResultSetMapping is required, and the results are manually stored in a map that can be referenced from a client, such as a JSF view.

How It Works

The SqlResultSetMapping can come in handy when you need to map your ResultSet to two or more entity classes. As demonstrated in the first solution to this recipe, configure the mapping by specifying a @SqlResultSetMapping annotation on the entity class of which you are querying. SqlResultSetMapping is useful when working with native queries and joining underlying database tables.

In the example, the @SqlResultSetMapping annotation is used to create a mapping between the Book and BookAuthor entity classes. The @SqlResultSetMapping annotation accepts a few different parameters, as described in Table 10-2.

Table 10-2. *SqlResultSetMapping Parameters*

Parameter	Description
name	String-based name for the SqlResultSetMapping
entities	One or more @EntityResult annotations, denoting entity classes for the mapping
columns	One or more columns against which to map a resultSet, designated by @FieldResult or @ColumnResult annotations

To use a SqlResultSetMapping, simply specify its name rather than an entity class when creating the native query. In the following excerpt taken from the solution, the query results are mapped to the authorBooks SqlResultSetMapping:

```
Query qry = em.createNativeQuery(
                "select b.id as BOOK_ID, b.title as TITLE, " +
                "ba.id AS AUTHOR_ID, ba.first as FIRST, ba.last as LAST " +
                "from book_author ba, book b, author_work aw " +
                "where aw.author_id = ba.id " +
                "and b.id = aw.book_id", "authorBooks");
```

The list of results that is returned from this query can be utilized within a client, such as a JSF view, in the same manner as any list containing a single entity's results. The SqlResultSetMapping allows fields of an entity class to be mapped to a given name so that the name can then be specified in order to obtain the value for the mapped field. For instance, the following JSF dataTable source is taken from the chapter10/recipe10_05a.xhtml view, and it displays the list of results from the query in the solution:

```
<h:dataTable id="table" value="#{authorController.authorBooks}"
                                var="authorBook">
    <h:column>
        <f:facet name="header">
            <h:outputText value="Book ID"/>
        </f:facet>
```

```
        <h:outputText value="#{authorBook.id}"/>
    </h:column>
    <h:column>
        <f:facet name="header">
            <h:outputText value="Title"/>
        </f:facet>
        <h:outputText value="#{authorBook.title}"/>
    </h:column>

    <h:column>
        <f:facet name="header">
            <h:outputText value="Author"/>
        </f:facet>
        <h:outputText value="#{authorBook.first} #{authorBook.last}"/>
    </h:column>

</h:dataTable>
```

As mentioned previously, entity fields can be mapped to a specified field returned from the database within the native SQL query. You can do so by specifying either the @FieldResult or @ColumnResult annotation for the columns parameter of a @SqlResultSetMapping annotation. For instance, in the example, you return only the TITLE and BOOK_ID columns from the BOOK database table, as well as the AUTHOR_ID, FIRST, and LAST columns from the BOOK_AUTHOR table. You include the SQL in the native query to join the tables and retrieve the values from these columns and return a SqlResultSetMapping that corresponds the following:

```
@SqlResultSetMapping(name="authorBooks",
        entities= {
            @EntityResult(entityClass=org.javaee8recipes.entity.Book.class, fields={
                @FieldResult(name="id", column="BOOK_ID"),
                @FieldResult(name="title", column="TITLE")
            }),
            @EntityResult(entityClass=org.javaee8recipes.entity.BookAuthor.class, fields={
                @FieldResult(name="id", column="AUTHOR_ID"),
                @FieldResult(name="first", column="FIRST"),
                @FieldResult(name="last", column="LAST")
            })
        })
```

In Solution #2, no SqlResultSetMapping is used, and instead the results of the query are returned into a list of HashMap objects, rather than entity objects. The query returns a list of Object[], which can then be iterated over in order to make the data accessible to the client. As shown in the example, after the list of Object[] is obtained, a for loop can be used to iterate over each Object[], obtaining the data for each returned database record field and storing it into a HashMap. To access the field data, specify a positional index that corresponds to the position of the database field data that you want to obtain. The positional indices correlate to the ordering of the returned fields within the SQL query, beginning with an index of 0. Therefore, to obtain the data for the first field returned in the query, specify an index of 0 on the Object for each row. As the Object[] is traversed, each database record can be parsed, in turn, obtaining the data for each field in that row. The resulting data is then stored into the HashMap, and a string-based key that corresponds to the name of the returned field is specified so that the data can be made accessible to the client.

When accessing a HashMap of results from a client, such as a JSF view, the data can be accessed in the same manner as if a standard entity list were being used. This is because each HashMap element contains a key field that corresponds to the name of the data field. The following excerpt, taken from chapter10/recipe10_05b.xhtml, demonstrates how to use the results of a native query that have been stored into a HashMap using this technique.

```
<h:dataTable id="table" value="#{authorController.authorBooks}"
                                 var="authorBook">
    <h:column>
        <f:facet name="header">
            <h:outputText value="Title"/>
        </f:facet>
        <h:outputText value="#{authorBook.bookTitle}"/>
    </h:column>
    <h:column>
        <f:facet name="header">
            <h:outputText value="Author"/>
        </f:facet>
        <h:outputText value="#{authorBook.authorFirst} #{authorBook.authorLast}"/>
    </h:column>

</h:dataTable>
```

As of JPA 2.2 (Java EE 8), the SqlResultSetMapping is a repeatable annotation, so you may use more than one of them in the same entity class without encapsulating it within a container annotation. The SqlResultSetMapping makes it possible to use customized queries and joins into returning results via entity class objects. It is one more of the techniques that help complete the object-relational mapping (ORM) experience when using JPA.

10-6. Calling JPQL Aggregate Functions

Problem

You want to return the total number of records from a database table that match specified filtering criteria. For example, you want to return the total count of BookAuthor instances for a specified book.

Solution

Use the JPQL aggregate function COUNT to return the total number of objects that match the given query. The following method, which resides in the org.javaee8recipes.session.AuthorWorkFacade class, uses the COUNT aggregate function:

```
public Long findAuthorCount(Book book){
        Query qry = em.createQuery("select COUNT(o.authorId) from AuthorWork o " +
                "where o.bookId = :book")
                .setParameter("book", book.id);
        return (Long) qry.getSingleResult();
    }
```

The function will return a Long result, which will be the count of matching AuthorWork results.

How It Works

Aggregate functions can group values of multiple rows together on certain criteria to form a single value. Native SQL contains aggregate functions that can be useful for calculating the sum of all rows in a particular table, maximum values of a column, first values within a column, and so on. JPQL contains a number of aggregate functions that can be used within queries. In this recipe, the example demonstrates the use of the `COUNT` function, which returns the total number of rows in an underlying data store table. The value is calculated and returned as a `Long` data type, which can be cast from a call to the `javax.persistence.Query` object's `getSingleResult` method. However, there are a number of other functions at your disposal. Table 10-3 lists those functions and their return types.

Table 10-3. *JPQL Aggregate Functions*

Function	Description	Return Type
`COUNT`	Total number of records	`Long`
`MAX`	Record with largest numeric value	Same as field to which applied
`MIN`	Record with lowest numeric value	Same as field to which applied
`AVG`	Average of all numeric values in column	`Double`
`SUM`	Sum of all values in column	`Long` when applied to integral types; `Double` when applied to floating-point; `BigInteger` when applied to `BigInteger`; `BigDecimal` when applied to `BigDecimal`

If a particular database record contains a `NULL` value for a column to which an aggregate function is being applied, then that `NULL` value is eliminated before the function is applied. The `DISTINCT` keyword can be used to specify that any duplicate values should be eliminated before the function is applied. The following line of code demonstrates the use of `DISTINCT`:

```
Query qry = em.createQuery("select DISTINCT(COUNT(o.title)) from Book o");
```

The important thing to remember when using aggregate functions is that they are applied to the same field within all objects that satisfy the query. This is analogous to the function being applied to all values returned for a single column's results within a query.

10-7. Invoking Database Stored Procedures Natively

Problem

The application you are writing uses JPQL and relies on one or more database stored procedures to perform tasks on the data. You need to have the ability to call those stored procedures from within the business logic of your Java application code.

Solution

Create a native query and write a SQL string that executes the database stored procedure. Suppose you have a database procedure named `CREATE_USER` and it accepts two arguments: `username` and `password`. You can invoke the `CREATE_USER` procedure by calling it via a native SQL query. The following method, named createUser, accepts a user name and password as arguments and passes them to the underlying database procedure and executes it:

```
public void createUser(String user, String pass){
        Query qry = (Query) em.createNativeQuery(
         "select CREATE_USER('" + user + "','" + pass + "') from dual")
        .qry.getSingleResult();
    }
```

How It Works

Historically, the only way to work with database-stored procedures from JPA was to utilize a native query. The solution to this recipe demonstrates this tactic because a native query is used to invoke a database-stored procedure. In the example, a method named createUser accepts two parameters, username and password, which are both passed to the database stored procedure named CREATE_USER via the native query. The EntityManager's createNativeQuery method is called, and a SQL string that performs a SELECT on the stored procedure is passed to the method. In SQL, performing a SELECT on a stored procedure will cause the procedure to be executed. Notice that the DUAL table is being referenced in the SQL. The DUAL is a dummy table that can be used when you need to apply SELECT statements to different database constructs, such as a stored procedure.

Execution of native SQL is an acceptable solution for invoking stored procedures that have no return values or when you have only a limited number of SQL statements to maintain. However, in most enterprise situations that require an application with multiple stored procedure calls or calls that require a return value, the @NamedStoredProcedure solution in Recipe 9-10 can be advantageous.

10-8. Joining to Retrieve Instances Matching All Cases

Problem

You want to create joins between entities in order to return fields from more than one underlying database table.

Solution

Use JPQL to create a join between two entities that share a one-to-many and many-to-one relationship with each other. In this example, a one-to-many relationship is set up against the Book and Chapter entities such that one book can contain many chapters. The following excerpt from the org.javaee8recipes.entity.Book class demonstrates the one-to-many relationship declaration:

```
@OneToMany(mappedBy="book", cascade=CascadeType.ALL)
private List<Chapter> chapters = null;
```

The Chapter entity contains a many-to-one relationship with the Book entity, such that many chapters can be related to one book. The following excerpt from the org.javaee8recipes.entity.Chapter class demonstrates the many-to-one relationship:

```
@ManyToOne
@JoinColumn(name = "BOOK_ID")
private Book book;
```

Ultimately, the join query is contained within a method named `findBookByChapterTitle`, which resides in the `org.javaee8recipes.session.Chapter` session bean. The following code excerpt contains the lines of code that make up that method:

```
public List<Book> findBookByChapterTitle(String chapterTitle){
    return em.createQuery("select b from Book b INNER JOIN b.chapters c " +
       "where c.title = :title")
        .setParameter("title", chapterTitle)
        .getResultList();
}
```

■ **Note** To return several different properties within the `SELECT` clause, rather than an object, the result will be returned in an `Object[]`. To find out more about working with such a solution, refer to Solution #2 of Recipe 10-5.

How It Works

The most common type of database table join operation is known as an *inner join*. When performing an inner join, all of the columns from each table will be available to be returned as if it were a single, combined table. To create a join between two entities, they must be related to each other via a one-to-many relationship. This means that one of the entities could contain an instance that possibly contains many references to the other entity, whereas the other entity could have many instances that would reference only one instance of the other entity. In the example for this recipe, the `Book` entity has a one-to-many relationship with the `Chapter` entity. This means that a single book may contain many chapters.

The example for this recipe demonstrates a join between the `Book` and `Chapters` entities. The method `findBookByChapterTitle` contains a JPQL query that will return any `Book` objects that contain a matching chapter title. To generate an inner join query, invoke the `EntityManager` object's `createQuery` method, passing the string-based JPQL query that contains the join syntax. A JPQL string for performing an inner join should be written in the following format, where `INNER` is an optional (default) keyword:

```
SELECT a.col1, a.col2 from Entity1 a [INNER] JOIN a.collectionColumn b WHERE expressions
```

In the example, an entire `Book` instance will be returned for each `Book` entity that contains a `Chapter` instance, which has a title matching the parameter. Typically, the join occurs over a foreign key, and in the case of the one-to-many relationship, it occurs on the field that is a collection of the related entity's instances.

10-9. Joining to Retrieve All Rows Regardless of Match

Problem

You want to create joins between entities in order to produce results that will include all objects of the left entity listed and matching results or `NULL` values when there is no match from the right entity listed.

Solution

In this example, a one-to-many relationship is set up against the Book and Chapter entities such that one book can contain many chapters. The following excerpt from the org.javaee8recipes.entity.Book class demonstrates the one-to-many relationship declaration:

```
@OneToMany(mappedBy="book", cascade=CascadeType.ALL)
private List<Chapter> chapters = null;
```

The Chapter entity has a many-to-one relationship with the Book entity, such that many chapters can be related to one book. The following excerpt from the org.javaee8recipes.entity.Chapter class demonstrates the many-to-one relationship:

```
@ManyToOne
@JoinColumn(name = "BOOK_ID")
private Book book;
```

The code that contains the left outer join query resides within the findAllBooksByChapterNumber method, which is contained within the org.javaee8recipes.session.ChapterFacade class. The following excerpt taken from the class lists the method implementation:

```
public List<Book> findAllBooksByChapterNumber(BigDecimal chapterNumber){
        return em.createQuery("select b from Book b LEFT OUTER JOIN b.chapters c " +
                "where c.chapterNumber = :num")
                .setParameter("num", chapterNumber)
                .getResultList();
    }
```

How It Works

An outer join, otherwise known as a LEFT OUTER JOIN or LEFT JOIN, is not as common of an occurrence as an inner join. To explain an outer join in database terminology, all rows of the table listed on the left side of the JOIN keyword are returned in a LEFT SQL join, and only those matching rows from the table listed to the right of the keyword will be returned. In other words, an outer join enables the retrieval of a set of database records where a matching value within the join may not be present. In JPA terminology, all instances of the entity class to the left of the JOIN keyword will be returned.

Outer joins on entities usually occur between two related entities in which there is a one-to-many relationship, or vice versa. To form an outer join JPQL query, use the following format, where the [OUTER] keyword is optional:

```
SELECT a.col1, a.col2 FROM Entity1 a LEFT [OUTER] JOIN a.collectionColumn b WHERE expression
```

In the example, all Book objects would be returned, but only those Chapter objects that match the specified criteria would be included in the ResultSet.

10-10. Applying JPQL Functional Expressions

Problem

You want to apply functions within your JPQL strings to alter the results of the execution. For example, you are interested in altering strings that will be used in the WHERE clause of your JPQL query.

Solution

Utilize any of the built-in JPQL functions to apply functional expressions to your JPQL. To alter strings that are utilized within a JPQL query, develop the query containing string functions that will be applied within the WHERE clause of the query. In the following example, the UPPER function is utilized in order to change the case of the given text into all uppercase letters. In this case, a search page has been set up for users to enter an author's last name and search the database for a match. The string that the user enters is converted to uppercase and used to query the database.

The following lines of code are taken from the search view, which resides within the JSF view that resides in the chapter10/recipe10_10.xhtml file.

```
<ui:composition template="layout/custom_template_search.xhtml">
    <ui:define name="content">
        <h:form>
            <h2>Recipe 10-10: Using JPA String Functions</h2>
            <br/>
            <p>Enter an author's last name below to search the author database.</p>
            <br/>
            <h:outputLabel value="Last Name:"/>
            <h:inputText id="last" value="#{authorController.authorLast}" size="75"/>
            <br/>
            <br/>
            <h:commandButton value="Search" action="#{authorController.findAuthorByLast}"/>

        </h:form>
    </ui:define>
</ui:composition>
```

Next, the code for the CDI bean controller method, findAuthorByLast, is listed. This method resides in the org.javaee8recipes.jsf.AuthorController class. This code is responsible for populating the authorList and then directing navigation to the recipe10_10b.xhtml view.

```
public String findAuthorByLast(){
    authorList = ejbFacade.findAuthorByLast(authorLast);
    return "/chapter10/recipe10_10b.xhtml";
}
```

Lastly, the EJB method named findAuthorByLast(String) is contained in the org.javaee8recipes.session.BookAuthorFacade class. The method accepts the string value that the user entered into the web search form and uses it to query the database for a matching author.

```
public List<BookAuthor> findAuthorByLast(String authorLast){
    return em.createQuery("select o from BookAuthor o " +
    "where o.last = UPPER(:authorLast)")
    .setParameter("authorLast", authorLast).getResultList();
}
```

The resulting page will display any author names that match the text that was entered by the user.

How It Works

The JPA query language contains a handful of functions that can be used to manipulate strings, perform arithmetic, and make dates easier to work with. The functions can be specified within the `WHERE` or `HAVING` clause of JPQL query strings. JPQL contains a number of string functions. Table 10-4 lists the different string functions that are available, along with a description of what they do.

Table 10-4. *JPQL String Functions*

Function	Description
`CONCAT(string1, string2)`	Returns a concatenated string composed of the two arguments.
`SUBSTRING(string, expr1, expr2)`	Returns a substring of the specified string. The first position within the substring is denoted by `expr1`, and the length of the substring is denoted by `expr2`.
`TRIM([[spec][char]FROM]str)`	Trims a specified character (`spec`) from a string (`str`).
`LOWER(string)`	Returns the given string in all lowercase letters.
`UPPER(string)`	Returns the given string in all uppercase letters.

There are also a number of functions within JPQL to help perform arithmetic within queries. Table 10-5 lists the different arithmetic functions that are available, along with a description of what they do.

Table 10-5. *JPQL Arithmetic Functions*

Function	Description
`ABS(expr)`	Returns the absolute value. Takes a numeric argument and returns a number of the same type.
`SQRT(expr)`	Returns the square root value. Takes a numeric argument and returns a double.
`MOD(expr1, expr2)`	Returns the modulus value in integer format.
`SIZE(collection)`	Returns the total number of elements in the given collection in integer format. If the collection contains no elements, it evaluates to zero.

Working with dates from any programming language can sometimes be a bit tough. The JPQL contains a handful of helpful datetime functions to make it a bit easier. Table 10-6 lists the different datetime functions that are available, along with a description of what they do.

Table 10-6. *JPQL Datetime Functions*

Function	Description
CURRENT_DATE	Returns the current date
CURRENT_TIME	Returns the current time
CURRENT_TIMESTAMP	Returns the current timestamp

10-11. Forcing Query Execution Rather Than Cache Use

Problem

The default EntityManager is using cached results from a database query, and you want to force a query to be executed each time a table is loaded, rather than allowing the results of the cache to be displayed.

Solution

After the javax.persistence.Query instance is created, set a hint, javax.persistence.cache.retrieveMode, to bypass the cache and force the query to be executed. In the following lines of code, the Book entity is queried, and the cache is bypassed by setting the hint:

```
public List<Book> findAllBooks(){
    Query qry = em.createQuery("select o from Book o");
    qry.setHint("javax.persistence.cache.retrieveMode", CacheRetrieveMode.BYPASS);
    return qry.getResultList();
}
```

Upon execution, the query will be forced to execute, returning the most current results from the underlying database table.

How It Works

There are often occasions when an application requires the most current table data to be displayed or used for performing a given task. For instance, if you were to write a stock market application, it would not make sense to cache the current market results since stale data would not be very useful to investors. In such cases, it is imperative to force queries to be executed and bypass any caching. This is possible via the use of hints that can be registered with javax.persistence.Query instances.

By setting the javax.persistence.cache.retrieveMode hint to CacheRetrieveMode.BYPASS, the JPA is told to always force the execution of a query. When the query is executed, it will always return the most current results from the database.

10-12. Performing Bulk Updates and Deletes

Problem

You want to update or delete a group of entity objects.

Solution

Perform a bulk update or deletion using the Criteria API. The Criteria API allows the use of the Builder pattern for specifying entity operations. In the following example, a bulk update is performed on the `Employee` entity. The following example method resides in a session bean class for the `org.javaee8recipes.entity.Employee` entity. The session bean class name is `org.javaee8recipes.session.EmployeeSession.java`, and the following excerpt from that class shows how to perform a bulk update:

```
...
public String updateEmployeeStatusInactive() {
        String returnMessage = null;
        CriteriaBuilder builder = em.getCriteriaBuilder();
        CriteriaUpdate<Employee> q = builder.createCriteriaUpdate(Employee.class);
        Root<Employee> e = q.from(Employee.class);
        q.set(e.get("status"), "ACTIVE")
                .where(builder.equal(e.get("status"), "INACTIVE"));
        Query criteriaUpd = em.createQuery(q);
        int result = criteriaUpd.executeUpdate();
        if (result > 0){
            returnMessage = result + " records updated";
        } else {
            returnMessage = "No records updated";
        }
        return returnMessage;
    }
...
```

Similarly, the Criteria API can be used to perform a bulk deletion. The following method, also within the `EmployeeSession` bean, demonstrates how to do so:

```
...
    public String deleteEmployeeOnStatus(String condition) {
        CriteriaBuilder builder = em.getCriteriaBuilder();
        CriteriaDelete<Employee> q = builder.createCriteriaDelete(Employee.class);
        Root<Employee> e = q.from(Employee.class);
        q.where(builder.equal(e.get("status"), condition));
        return null;
    }
...
```

How It Works

The Criteria API has been enhanced to support bulk updates and deletions. As seen in earlier recipes, the Criteria API allows developers to utilize Java language syntax in order to perform database queries and manipulations, rather than JPQL or SQL. A javax.persistence.criteria.CriteriaUpdate object can be used to perform bulk update operations, and a javax.persistence.criteria.CriteriaDelete object can be used to perform bulk deletion operations. How do we obtain such objects? The Criteria API is dependent on the javax.persistence.criteria.CriteriaBuilder interface, which is used to return objects that can be used to work with specified Entity classes. In the JPA 2.1 release, the CriteriaBuilder was updated to include the methods createCriteriaUpdate and createCriteriaDelete, which will return the CriteriaUpdate or CriteriaDelete object, respectively.

To use the CriteriaBuilder, you first need to obtain a CriteriaBuilder from the EntityManager. You can then use the CriteriaBuilder to obtain the CriteriaUpdate or CriteriaDelete object of your choosing. In the following lines of code, a CriteriaUpdate object is obtained for use with an Employee entity:

```
CriteriaBuilder builder = em.getCriteriaBuilder();
CriteriaUpdate<Employee> q = builder.createCriteriaUpdate(Employee.class);
```

Once obtained, the CriteriaUpdate can be used to build a query and set values, as desired, for making the necessary updates or deletions. In the following excerpt, the CriteriaUpdate object is used to update all Employee objects that have a status of INACTIVE, changing that status to ACTIVE:

```
Root<Employee> e = q.from(Employee.class);
q.set(e.get("status"), "ACTIVE")
        .where(builder.equal(e.get("status"), "INACTIVE"));
```

Let's break this down a bit to explain what exactly is going on. First, the query root is set by calling the q.from method and passing the entity class for which you want to obtain the root, where q is the CriteriaUpdate object. Next, the q.set method is invoked, passing the Path to the Employee status attribute, along with the ACTIVE String. The q.set method is performing the bulk update. To further refine the query, a WHERE clause is added using a chained call to the .where method and passing the Employee objects that have a status of INACTIVE. The entire criteria can be seen in the solution for this recipe.

Finally, to complete the transaction, you must create the Query object and then execute it using the following lines of code:

```
Query criteriaUpd = em.createQuery(q);
criteriaUpd.executeUpdate();
```

The bulk deletion is very similar, except instead of using the CriteriaBuilder to obtain a CriteriaUpdate object, use it to obtain a CriteriaDelete object instead. To obtain a CriteriaDelete object, call the CriteriaBuilder createCriteriaDelete method, as follows:

```
CriteriaBuilder builder = em.getCriteriaBuilder();
CriteriaDelete<Employee> q = builder.createCriteriaDelete(Employee.class);
```

Once a CriteriaDelete object has been obtained, the conditions for deletion need to be specified by filtering the results using a call (or chain of calls) to the .where method. When using the bulk delete, all objects that match the specified condition will be deleted. For example, the following lines of code demonstrate how to delete all Employee objects that have the status attribute equal to INACTIVE:

```
Root<Employee> e = q.from(Employee.class);
q.where(builder.equal(e.get("status"), "INACTIVE"));
```

■ **Note** Both the `CriteriaUpdate` and `CriteriaDelete` examples demonstrated can be made more type-safe by using the MetaModel API. For each entity class in a particular persistence unit, a metamodel class is created with a trailing underscore, along with the attributes that correspond to the persistent fields of the entity class. This metamodel can be used to manage entity classes and their persistent state and relationships. Therefore, instead of specifying an error-prone `String` in the `Path` to obtain a particular attribute, you could specify the metamodel attribute instead, as follows: `e.get(Employee_.status)`.

For more information on using the MetaModel API to create type-safe queries, refer to the online documentation.

The Criteria API can be very detailed, and it is also very powerful. To learn more about the Criteria API, see the documentation online at `https://javaee.github.io/tutorial/persistence-criteria.html#GJITV`.

10-13. Retrieving Entity Subclasses

Problem

You want to obtain the data for an entity, along with all of the data from that entity's subclasses.

Solution

Utilize the downcasting feature of the JPA API. To do so, specify the `TREAT` keyword within the `FROM` and/or `WHERE` clause of a JPA query in order to filter the specified types and subtypes that you want to retrieve. In the following example, the query will return all `BookStore` entities that are from the IT book. The assumption is that the `ItCategory` entity is a subtype of the `BookCategory` entity. The method in the example, named `getBookCategories`, resides in the `org.javaee8recipes.chapter09.session.BookCategoryFacade` session bean.

```
public List getBookCategories(){
        TypedQuery<Object[]> qry = em.createQuery("select a.name, a.genre, a.description " +
               "from BookStore s JOIN TREAT(s.categories as ItCategory) a", Object[].class);

       List data = new ArrayList();
        if (!qry.getResultList().isEmpty()) {
             List<Object[]> tdata = qry.getResultList();
            for (Object[] t : tdata) {
                HashMap resultMap = new HashMap();
                resultMap.put("name", t[0]);
                resultMap.put("genre", t[1]);
                resultMap.put("categoryDesc", t[2]);
                data.add(resultMap);
            }
        }
        return data;
    }
```

When invoked, this query will return data from the ItCategory entity, which is a subclass of the BookCategory entity, as per the previous description. To better understand how to relate the entities, refer to the entire source code within the two entities, located within the org.javaee8recipes.entity.BookCategory.java and org.javaee8recipes.entity.ItCategory.java files in the book sources.

How It Works

The act of *downcasting* is defined as the casting of a base type or class reference to one of its derived types or classes. The Java EE platform introduced the concept of downcasting in JPA 2.1 by providing the ability to obtain a reference to a subclass of a specified entity within a query. In other words, you can explicitly query one or more entities and retrieve the attributes from each of the entities as well as any attributes from entities that are subclasses of those that are explicitly declared. To provide this ability, the TREAT keyword was added to JPA.

The use of the TREAT operator is supported for downcasting within path expressions in the FROM and WHERE clauses. The first argument to the TREAT operator should be a subtype of the target type; otherwise, the path is considered to have no value, attributing nothing to the end result. The TREAT operator can filter on the specified types and subtypes, as well as perform a downcast.

The syntax for use of the TREAT operator is as follows:

```
SELECT b.attr1, b.attr2
FROM EntityA a JOIN TREAT(a.referenceToEntityB as EntityBSubType) b
```

In the previous JPQL, the TREAT operation contains an attribute from the specified entity (EntityA) that relates to a joined entity (EntityB). The TREAT operation tells the container to treat the referenced entity (EntityB) as the type of EntityBSubtype. Therefore, the downcast takes place and allows access to those subtype entities. The following lines of code demonstrate this technique in action:

```
SELECT a.name, a.genre, a.description
FROM BookStore s JOIN TREAT(s.categories AS ItCategory) a
```

As mentioned previously, the TREAT operator can also be used in the WHERE clause in order to filter a query based on subtype attribute values. Downcasting support allows JPA to be even more flexible for developers to use, making more complex queries possible. This technique makes it easier to obtain values from related entities or subtypes, without the need to issue an extra query.

10-14. Joining with ON Conditions

Problem

You want to retrieve all the entities that match the specified criteria for joining two entities, along with each entity that does not match on the left side of an OUTER join.

Solution

Utilize the ON condition to specify a join of two or more entity classes based on the specified filtering criteria. The following method includes the JPQL for retrieving all Jobs entities, along with a count of the number of Employee entities that belong to those Jobs. This method, named obtainActiveEmployeeCount, utilizes the ON condition to filter the join based on the Employee status.

```
public List obtainActiveEmployeeCount() {
      TypedQuery<Object[]> qry = em.createQuery("SELECT j.title, count(e) "
              + "FROM Jobs j LEFT JOIN j.employees e "
              + "ON e.status = 'ACTIVE' "
              + "WHERE j.salary >= 50000 "
              + "GROUP BY j.title", Object[].class);

      List data = new ArrayList();
       if (!qry.getResultList().isEmpty()) {
            List<Object[]> tdata = qry.getResultList();
           for (Object[] t : tdata) {
               HashMap resultMap = new HashMap();
               resultMap.put("title", t[0]);
               resultMap.put("count", t[1]);
               data.add(resultMap);
           }
       }
       return data;

   }
```

How It Works

When writing JPQL queries, it is sometimes beneficial to join two or more database tables to acquire related information. Furthermore, it is usually helpful to filter information based on certain specified criteria so that the number of records returned can be manageable. JPQL joins typically include INNER, OUTER, and FETCH joins. To review, an INNER join allows retrieval from two tables such that records being returned contain at least one match in both tables. For instance, you may want to query an Employee entity and join it to the Jobs entity to return only those employees who have a specific job title. An OUTER join allows retrieval from two tables such that all of the records from one of the entities (left entity) are returned, regardless of whether they match with a record in the other entity. Lastly, a FETCH join enables the fetching of an association as a side effect of the query execution.

In JPA 2.1, JPQL was updated to include the ON condition, which allows you to perform an OUTER join and include a specified condition with the join. This capability has always been available with the WHERE clause of the JPQL query, but what about the cases when you want to return all matching records along with those that may not match, like with an OUTER join? JPA provides this functionality in a concise manner using ON conditions. Simply put, an ON condition modifies a join query such that it will incorporate better control over the data that is returned in a concise manner.

To demonstrate this new syntax, let's take a look at a SQL query, and then you will compare it to its JPQL counterpart. The following SQL will join the EMPLOYEE table with the JOBS table on the JOB_ID field. It will also limit the returned records to those that include a salary of greater than or equal to 50,000 with the specification in the WHERE clause.

```
SELECT J.TITLE, COUNT(E.ID)
FROM JOBS J LEFT JOIN EMPLOYEE E
   ON J.JOB_ID = E.JOB_ID and E.STATUS 'ACTIVE'
WHERE J.SALARY >= 50000
GROUP BY J.TITLE;
```

This SQL will return all of the JOB records and include a count of each job that contains an Employee whose status is ACTIVE. The method in the solution of this recipe contains the JPQL equivalent for this SQL, using the ON condition to perform the join. In the end, the ON condition helps make JPQL outer joins more concise and easy to use. Although the same capability has been available in previous versions of JPQL, the ON clause helps make record filtering with joins much easier.

10-15. Processing Query Results with Streams

Problem

You want to process the results of a JPA query using a concise functional style.

Solution

Utilize streams to process the results of a JPA query. In the following example, a stream is returned from a JPA query. The stream is then processed using the Stream API to retrieve the desired results. This particular example demonstrates a stream being used to process books by author.

```
public List<AuthorWork> performFindByAuthorStream(BookAuthor authorId){
    Stream<AuthorWork> awStream = em.createQuery("select object(o) from AuthorWork o")
        .getResultStream();

    return awStream.filter(
        ba -> authorId.equals(ba.getAuthorId()))
        .collect(Collectors.toList());

}
```

■ **Note** This particular example demonstrates filtering the results of an SQL query using streams, which may not be the most effective approach. Be sure to weigh the performance benefits of using standard JPQL versus using streams to ensure you choose the best option for your situation.

How It Works

Streams offer a powerful alternative to processing SQL results sets. The Stream API was introduced into the Java platform with the release of Java SE 8. The JPA 2.2 release has brought the API into alignment with Java SE 8, allowing JPA users to benefit from the use of the Stream API while processing results. The Stream API allows you to apply filters and functions to data in a functional way, making processing much more concise and easy to follow. JPA 2.2 features a new getResultStream method on the Query and TypeQuery interfaces, allowing you to return a stream of results, rather than a list or single object result. Once the stream has been returned, it can be processed accordingly.

Breaking down the recipe example, first the AuthorWork entity is queried without any filters. Note that instead of calling on getResultList, the getResultStream is called upon. This will return a stream of the objects that are being queried. Once the stream has been returned, it is processed by filtering the data to return only those records that have an authorId matching that which was passed into the method. Note the notation that's used for processing is as follows:

```
ba -> authorId.equals(ba.getAuthorId())
```

First, note that the syntax is very much like that of the lambda processing syntax. The ba -> portion is simply a local variable that is declared to represent the current object in the stream, and the arrow characters are used to note that the processing expression follows. Each object in the stream is iterated, and ba changes for each one. Next, the filter is applied, only retaining those records that have authorId equal to the one that is passed into the method. Next, we want to return a list of the results from that filtering process, so the Collectors utility is used to collect the filtered results into a list:

```
.collect(Collectors.toList())
```

It is important to keep in mind that if it is possible to filter queries in the traditional manner, via the SQL where clause, that may perform better than the stream alternative. The reason being that the default stream toResultStream implementation will fetch all of the data from the query into an in-memory list, and then process accordingly. This could be very bad if the result set is large. It is possible for different implementations of this process to be created. At the time of this writing, Hibernate provides something similar in the stream() method, whereby a scrollable ResultSet is returned, rather than the entire list of results. Such an implementation would be much better performing in a large dataset scenario.

10-16. Converting Attribute Data Types

Problem

You want to convert the data type of a particular entity class attribute when it is retrieved from the database. In turn, you want to convert back to the original data type when persisting data back to the database column.

Solution

Create an attribute converter to convert to/from different data types when retrieving and persisting data. Suppose that you want to convert between a boolean-based full employee status within a Java entity and a string-based ACTIVE or INACTIVE value in the database. Each time the attribute is accessed, the converter is used to automatically convert the values to/from the desired data types.

```
package org.javaee8recipes.converter;

import javax.persistence.AttributeConverter;
import javax.persistence.Converter;

@Converter
public class EmployeeStatusConverter implements

AttributeConverter<Boolean, String> {

    @Override
    public String convertToDatabaseColumn(Boolean entityValue) {
        if(entityValue){
            return "ACTIVE";
        } else {
            return "INACTIVE";
        }
    }
```

```
    @Override
    public Boolean convertToEntityAttribute(String databaseValue) {
        return databaseValue.equals("ACTIVE");
    }
}
```

The converter can be applied to a single entity class attribute, as follows:

```
@Column(name= "STATUS")
@Convert(converter=org.javaee8recipes.converter.EmployeeStatusConverter.class)
private boolean status;
```

In this example, when the `Employee` object is persisted to the database, a `true` would be converted to `"ACTIVE"`. Likewise, when an `Employee` object is retrieved, an `"INACTIVE"` status value is converted to `false`.

How It Works

Attribute converters allow for data type conversion to occur between the database column and an entity class attribute. Attribute converters can be created by annotating a class with `@Converter` and implementing `AttributeConverter`. The `AttributeConverter` type takes two arguments, those being the type of the entity class attribute and the type of the database column. When implementing `AttributeConverter`, two methods must be overridden. The `convertToDatabaseColumn` method should provide the implementation for conversion from the entity class attribute to the database column type. Similarly, the `convertToEntityAttribute` method should provide the opposite implementation, conversion from the database column type to the entity class attribute.

In the example for this recipe, the attribute converter is applied to a single entity class attribute. To do so, the `@Convert` annotation is applied to the attribute, passing the converter class as an argument. The converter could also be applied to all entity class attributes pertaining to the entity data type by changing the `@Converter` annotation on the attribute converter to the following: `@Converter(autoApply=true)`.

CHAPTER 11

Bean Validation

One of the most important pieces of any data-using application is data validation. It is imperative that one validates data before it is inserted into a database in order to maintain integrity. There are a number of reasons to validate, the most important being security purposes, data consistency, and proper formatting. Many web applications use validation in the presentation layer via JavaScript for validation of form data, and also in the persistence layer. However, sometimes JavaScript can become problematic in that the code can become unwieldy and there is also no guarantee that it will execute. It is oftentimes found to be a good idea to perform validation within the domain model, although this can cause code clutter.

In this chapter, we take a look at the Bean Validation API, which is used to apply validation to a JavaBean. In the context of Java EE, since JPA entity classes are Plain Old Java Objects (POJOs), this allows developers to use bean validation on entity classes and entity class attributes. A Java controller class may have validation logic to ensure that only specific data passes through to the database. The Bean Validation API is another means of performing data validation in either the domain model or presentation layer via metadata, using an annotation-based approach. To validate with this API, one simply applies validation constraint annotations the entity class attribute(s), as needed, and the constraint validators will automatically enforce the validation. Bean validation was introduced into Java EE platform with Java EE 6, and it has been given a face lift in Java EE 8, introducing a number of new features for the Bean Validation 2.0 release. Although this chapter focuses on the use of bean validation with Java EE, it can be used in JavaBeans across all different flavors of Java, be it Java FX, Java EE, or Java SE. Bean validation contains an API that can be used to manually invoke validation, but in most cases the validation occurs automatically because of the integration that has been made across the various Java EE specifications.

Bean validation annotation constraints can be applied on types, fields, methods, constructors, parameters, container elements, and other container annotations. Validation is applied not only to the object level, but it can also be inherited from super classes. Entire object graphs can be validated, meaning that if a class declares a field that has the type of a separate class containing validation, cascading validation can occur.

This chapter demonstrates examples of each validation type, explaining the strongholds for each of the different methodologies. In the end, you will have a good understanding of how the Bean Validation API works, and you should be able to apply bean validation strategies to your applications.

Note Bean validation allows one to declare constraints via XML, rather than annotations. For the purposes of brevity, this chapter will not cover this feature. For more information, see the Bean Validation 2.0 Specification.

J. Juneau, *Java EE 8 Recipes*, https://doi.org/10.1007/978-1-4842-3594-2_11

11-1. Validating Fields with Built-In Constraints

Problem

Imagine that you create a Chapter entity class, which will be used to store the contents regarding a book chapter. In doing so, you want to apply validation to specified fields of the entity class such that only compliant data is allowed to be inserted or updated in the database. In this case, suppose that there are a number of fields that must contain values, and you also want to be certain that strings of text are within the size limits of the underlying database field.

Solution #1

Apply the pertinent bean validation constraints to field(s) that you want to validate. In this example, the standard @NotNull and @Size constraint annotations are placed on specific fields of the Chapter entity. Namely, the id attribute is marked as @NotNull so that it must contain a value, and the title attribute is marked to have a maximum size of 150 characters.

```
@Entity
@Table(name = "CHAPTER")

public class Chapter implements Serializable {
    private static final long serialVersionUID = 1L;
    @Id
    @Basic(optional = false)
    @NotNull
    @Column(name = "ID")
    private BigDecimal id;
    @Column(name = "CHAPTER_NUMBER")
    private BigDecimal chapterNumber;
    @Size(max = 150)
    @Column(name = "TITLE")
    private String title;
    @Lob
    @Column(name = "DESCRIPTION")
    private String description;
. . .
```

Solution #2

Apply the pertinent bean validation constraint annotations to the getter methods (accessor methods) of the field(s) you want to validate. In this case, the following example shows the getChapterNumber() and getTitle() methods. Each of these accessor methods is annotated accordingly.

```
@NotNull
private BigDecimal getId(){
    return this.id;
}
. . .
```

```
@Size(max=150)
private String getTitle(){
    return this.title;
}
```

How It Works

The Bean Validation API provides a number of built-in constraint definitions that are ready to use. These standard constraints span the array of common use cases for data validation. Table 11-1 lists each of the standard validation constraint annotations along with a description of each.

Table 11-1. *Standard Built-In Constraints*

Annotation	Description
@Null	The annotated element must be null.
@NotNull	The annotated element must not be null.
@AssertTrue	The annotated element must be true.
@AssertFalse	The annotated element must be false.
@Min	The annotated element must be a number with a value that is higher or equal to the specified minimum.
@Max	The annotated element must be a number with a value that is lower or equal to the specified maximum.
@DecimalMin	The annotated element must be a decimal with a value that is higher or equal to the specified minimum.
@DecimalMax	The annotated element must be a decimal with a value that is lower or equal to the specified maximum.
@Negative	The annotated element must be a strictly negative number.
@NegativeOrZero	The annotated element must be a negative number or zero.
@Positive	The annotated element must be a strictly positive number.
@PositiveOrZero	The annotated element must be strictly positive or zero.
@Size	The annotated element size must fall within the specified boundaries.
@Digits	The annotated element must be a number in the accepted range.
@Past	The annotated element must be an instant, date, or time in the past.
@PastOrPresent	The annotated element must be an instant, date, or time in the past or present.
@Future	The annotated element must be an instant, date, or time in the future.
@FutureOrPresent	The annotated element must be an instant, date, or time in the future or present.
@Pattern	The annotated element must fall within the constraints of the specified regular expression.
@NotEmpty	The annotated element must not be empty or null.
@NotBlank	The annotated element must not be null and must contain at least one character.
@Email	The annotated string must be a well-formed email address.

To apply validation to a field, simply specify the built-in or custom bean validation annotation to the field declaration, along with the appropriate constraint attribute(s). You also have the option of annotating a field's corresponding getter method, rather than the field declaration itself. Any single field may have more than one annotation constraint applied to it. You are welcome to combine constraints to suit the requirement. If an annotated class extends another class that contains bean validation constraints, then those constraints are applied to all annotated fields, whether the field belongs to the extended class or the class that extends.

Attributes are used to associate metadata with the annotations for specifying information, such as the error message that is to be displayed should the validation fail, or the number of characters to be validated. Table 11-2 lists the common constraint annotation attributes that you'll find across each of the different constraints. These are all considered reserved names.

Table 11-2. *Common Constraint Annotation Attributes*

Attribute	Description
`message`	Allows a string for specifying an error message to display.
`groups`	Specifies processing groups with which the constraint declaration is associated.
`payload`	Specifies the payload with which the constraint declaration is associated.
`validationAppliesTo`	Used to specify which constraint targets a validation constraint will apply to.

Most of the constraint attributes are optional. However, in some cases, an attribute should be specified. For instance, when applying the `@Size` constraint, if the `max` attribute is not specified, the default is 2147483647. Therefore, given that someone will likely never enter a value that large, one should specify a maximum size using the `max` attribute. The group's attribute is used to specify if a particular annotation constraint is part of a processing group. A validation group defines a subset of constraints, and a group can simply be an empty interface. Groups are used to control the order of evaluation for constraints, or to perform partial state validation for a JavaBean. To learn more about applying groups, refer to Recipe 11-8.

The `payload` attribute is used to assign a payload to a validation annotation. Payloads are typically used by bean validation clients to associate some kind of metadata information. A payload is usually defined as a class that implements the Payload interface. Payloads can be seen in more detail with Recipe 11-9.

11-2. Writing Custom Constraint Validators

Problem

Your application requires a specific validation that is not provided among the built-in bean validation constraints. For example, you want to validate that a book title includes the word "Java" in the title.

Solution

Implement a custom constraint validator for the application. A custom constraint can be created by developing a constraint annotation along with a validator implementation class and a default error message. The example that follows demonstrates a custom constraint that is used to compare whether a string contains the text "Java". The annotation for such a constraint may resemble the following:

```
import java.lang.annotation.Documented;
import static java.lang.annotation.ElementType.ANNOTATION_TYPE;
import static java.lang.annotation.ElementType.FIELD;
```

```
import java.lang.annotation.Retention;
import static java.lang.annotation.RetentionPolicy.RUNTIME;
import java.lang.annotation.Target;
import javax.validation.Payload;

@Target({ FIELD, ANNOTATION_TYPE})
@Retention(RUNTIME)
@Documented
public @interface JavaBookTitle {

    String message() default "{org.javaee8recipes.annotation." +
            "message}";

    Class<?>[] groups() default { };

    Class<? extends Payload>[] payload() default { };

}
```

The implementation for the validator should look like that of the BookTitleValidator class:

```
import javax.validation.ConstraintValidator;
import javax.validation.ConstraintValidatorContext;

public class BookTitleValidator implements ConstraintValidator<JavaBookTitle, String> {

    @Override
    public void initialize(JavaBookTitle constraintAnnotation) {

    }

    @Override
    public boolean isValid(String title, ConstraintValidatorContext cvc) {
        if(title.toUpperCase().contains("JAVA")){
            return true;
        } else {
            return false;
        }
    }
}
```

Now that the constraint annotation has been created, it can be applied to a field as follows:

```
@JavaBookTitle(message = "Book Title Should Contain The Word Java")
@Column(name = "TITLE")
protected String title;
```

How It Works

Creating a custom validation constraint annotation is quite easy, although the implementation may look a bit daunting at first glance. A validation constraint consists of the following pieces:

- Constraint Annotation
- Validator Implementation Class
- Default Error Message

The constraint annotation is created just like any standard Java annotation. The annotation declaration is a standard Java interface. The interface must be annotated with `@Target`, passing a list in curly brackets, which specifies the types that the annotation can be applied to. The `@Retention` annotation can also be specified on the declaration, passing a value to specify how long the annotation will be retained. Valid values include `SOURCE`, `CLASS`, and `RUNTIME`. An annotation declaration may also include the `@Documented` annotation, which indicates whether an annotation declaration will be documented by JavaDoc by default.

Annotation declaration interfaces can contain elements to associate metadata to a validation constraint. A constraint annotation must contain three elements: a `message` element of type `String`, a `groups()` method, and a `payload()` method. Each of the elements can be declared WITHIN the annotation constraint with a default value, as seen in the example. The `message` element is used to create a default error message for the validator. The `message` may include String interpolation and it may also be loaded from a resource bundle to take advantage of features such as internationalization. The `groups()` method is used to specify any processing groups to which the constraint will belong. The `Default` group is declared if no group is specified and the array is empty. The `payload()` method is typically used to associate metadata with a given validation constraint. A `validationAppliesTo` element can be used to specify which targets the constraint associates against. Lastly, one may choose to declare a custom element to assist in the validation of values.

The second piece of required code is the constraint implementation class. This class should implement `CustomValidator<AnnotationType, Type>`. In doing so, this class must override the `initialize()` and `isValid()` methods. If there is any data that needs to be initialized prior to validation, then it should be done within the initialize method. The `isValid()` method should accept the data to be validated, along with `ConstraintValidatorContext` as arguments. The implementation of the method should validate the data and return a boolean to indicate whether the data complies with the constraint.

Once these pieces of code are in place, the annotation can be specified on the targets for validation. The annotation should specify additional elements to associate metadata, if needed. In the example, the annotation specifies the message element, which allows a default error message to be declared.

11-3. Validating at the Class Level

Problem

You want to validate some or all of the fields within an object to ensure that those fields of the object contain valid data as a whole. For instance, you must validate that a field declared as `numChapters` contains the same number of chapters as those in a field of type `List<Chapter>`.

Solution

Specify class-level constraints to perform the validation. In the example for this recipe, the `Book` entity contains a number of fields that must validate against one another in order to constitute a valid object.

```
@ValidNumChapters
public class Book implements Serializable {
    private static final long serialVersionUID = 1L;
    // @Max(value=?)  @Min(value=?)//if you know range of your decimal fields consider using
    these annotations to enforce field validation
    @Id
    @Basic(optional = false)
    @NotNull
    @Column(name = "ID")
    private BigDecimal id;
    @Size(max = 150)
    @Column(name = "TITLE")
    protected String title;
    @Size(max = 500)
    @Column(name = "IMAGE")
    private String image;
    @Column(name = "NUM_CHAPTERS")
    private int numChapters;
    @Column(name = "NUM_PAGES")
    private int numPages;
    @Lob
    @Column(name = "DESCRIPTION")
    private String description;
    @Column(name = "PUBLISH_DATE")
    private LocalDate publishDate;
    @ManyToMany(mappedBy="books")
    private Set<BookAuthor> authors;
    @OneToMany(mappedBy="book", cascade=CascadeType.ALL)
    private List<Chapter> chapters = null;
```

The `@ValidateNumChapters` annotation is used to validate that the `numChapters` value is greater than or equal to the chapters list. Following this logic, a `Book` may be in progress and more `Chapter` objects can be added to the list as completed, but there cannot be more `Chapter` objects than the `numChapters` value. As covered in Recipe 11-2, in order to create the `@ValidateNumChapters` annotation, there must be an annotation declaration class and a constraint implementation class. The following class is used to declare the annotation.

```
import java.lang.annotation.Documented;
import static java.lang.annotation.ElementType.ANNOTATION_TYPE;
import static java.lang.annotation.ElementType.TYPE;
import java.lang.annotation.Retention;
import static java.lang.annotation.RetentionPolicy.RUNTIME;
import java.lang.annotation.Target;
import javax.validation.Payload;

@Target({ TYPE, ANNOTATION_TYPE})
@Retention(RUNTIME)
@Documented
public @interface ValidNumChapters {
```

```
    String message() default "{org.javaee8recipes.annotation." +
            "message}";

    Class<?>[] groups() default { };

    Class<? extends Payload>[] payload() default { };

}
```

The annotation class contains the default error message as well as the declaration for the annotation itself. The following class is the constraint validation implementation for validating the number of chapters in the book.

```
public class NumChaptersValidator implements ConstraintValidator<ValidNumChapters, Book> {

    @Override
    public void initialize(ValidNumChapters constraintAnnotation) {

    }

    @Override
    public boolean isValid(Book book, ConstraintValidatorContext cvc) {
        if (book == null){
            return true;
        }
        return book.getChapters().size() <= book.getNumChapters();
    }
}
```

Once these classes have been created, the annotation can be placed onto the class(es) accordingly.

How It Works

The class-level validation constraint is one that can be quite powerful, as it can pose a validation on one or more fields of the class. Applying a validation constraint to the class level means that one or more of the fields must adhere to the validation constraint. In the cases where a built-in validation constraint is applied at the class level, all fields of the class must adhere to the constraint. For instance, if `@NotNull` were applied, then each field within the class must be populated for each instance. On the other hand, applying a constraint such as `@Size` at the class level would not work if the class contained fields that were of a type other than `String`. More often, class-level constraints are custom created and apply only to a specified subset of the class fields.

In the recipe example, the `@ValidNumChapters` constraint is placed at the class level, which means that this particular constraint has access to each of the fields within the class. However, the constraint implementation only actually validates the `numChapters` and `chapters` fields to determine if the number of `Chapter` objects within the array are less than or equal to the `numChapters` value. Recipe 11-2 covers the declaration of an annotation in detail, so I won't cover that here.

The important piece of the puzzle for this recipe is to look closely at the annotation implementation within the `NumChaptersValidator` class. To create this implementation, the class must implement `ConstraintValidator<A extends Annotation, T>`. The `ConstraintValidator` interface utilizes generics to specify the constraint along with an object that will be validated. In the signature of the interface, `A` must be the name of an annotation declaration class, so in this case: `ValidNumChapters.` `T` is any given object that must resolve to a non-parameterized type, or generic parameters of `T` must be unbounded wildcard types. In the example, the `Book` entity class is specified as `T`.

The interface enforces the implementation of the `initialize(A constraintAnnotation)` and `isValid(T value, ConstraintValidatorContext context)` methods. Many times, the initialize method can be empty, but if needed, it should contain code to initialize the validator in preparation for call to `isValid`. The `isValid` method contains the actual validation logic. The `Book` object that is passed into the method is first checked to ensure that it is not null. If it is null, then true is returned; otherwise, the number of `Chapter` objects in the chapters list is compared against the `numChapters` value to return a boolean result.

Class-level validation can be very powerful, as it allows validation of class fields in a custom manner. It is also very easy to implement, making it even more powerful when validating complex objects such as those that contain Lists of other objects.

11-4. Validating Parameters

Problem

You want to specify some preconditions on a method such that the parameters adhere to a specified constraint.

Solution

Apply validation constraint annotations to method parameter(s) such that the parameter(s) will be validated by either built-in or custom constraints. This will enforce constraint logic at the time of a method call such that only arguments that meet the specified constraints will be acceptable as parameters to a given method. In the following example, a method that accepts a parameter is demonstrated including a validation constraint.

```
public void submitEmailAddress(@Email String emailAddress){
    System.out.println("Do something with the address: " + emailAddress);
}
```

In this particular example, a single parameter is being validated. However, it is possible to include more than one parameter containing a validation constraint. It is also possible to include a cross-parameter constraint at the method level, which can be used to apply validation across all of the method parameters.

How It Works

Bean validation makes it possible to include validation constraints on non-static method parameters for the purposes of applying preconditions that will ensure invalid data cannot be passed into the method. Either built-in or custom validation constraints can be applied to method parameters. If an invalid value is passed into a method that contains a parameter constraint, a validation error will be thrown and the method will not be executed.

In the example, the `submitEmailAddress` method accepts a single parameter, `emailAddress`. If the `emailAddress` parameter does not adhere to a valid email format, as specified via the `@Email` validation constraint, the method call will fail. It is also possible to validate more than a single method parameter by applying a constraint validation on the method itself. Doing so is much the same as applying a class-level constraint (Recipe 11-3) in that the constraint can be either built-in or custom. Built-in constraints applied at the method level, such as `@NotNull`, would be applied to each of the parameters of the method. Custom constraints can be created in the same manner as previously shown in Recipe 11-3 whereby one or more parameters can be validated. Constraints that are placed at the method level must be configured within the `ConstraintValidator` implementation using the `@SupportedValidationTarget` annotation to indicate that the constraint is to be placed on the method level. This is because return type constraints are also placed at the method level, so the `@SupportedValidationTarget` helps to distinguish which validation type shall occur. The following code example demonstrates how to write a constraint validation implementation targeted for use at the method level.

```
@SupportedValidationTarget(value = ValidationTarget.PARAMETERS)
public class ValidEmployeeEmailValidator implements ConstraintValidator<ValidEmployeeEmail,
Object[]> {
    @Override
    public void initialize(final ValidEmployeeEmail constraintAnnotation) {
        // no-op
    }

    @Override
    public boolean isValid(final Object[] parameters, final ConstraintValidatorContext
    context) {
        // Ensure employee email is from our organization
        return parameters == null || parameters[0].toString().contains("@acme.com");
    }
}
```

11-5. Constructor Validation

Problem

You want to validate the instantiation of a class through the validation of constructor parameters.

Solution

Apply validation constraint annotations to the individual constructor parameters or at the constructor level itself to perform validation. In the following example, a constructor is annotated with `@NotNull` at the constructor level. Therefore, the `@NotNull` validation constraint is applied across each of the constructor parameters.

```
@NotNull
public ConstructorValidationController(String parameterOne,
                                       String parameterTwo){
    this.p1 = parameterOne;
    this.p2 = parameterTwo;
}
```

How It Works

In some cases, it makes sense to validate parameters that are passed into a class at the time of instantiation. Bean validation makes this easy by allowing one to apply constraint annotations to parameters of a class constructor, or to the constructor itself. When an annotation is placed on the parameters of a class constructor, the class cannot be instantiated if the validation(s) fail. Similarly, if a constraint annotation is placed on the constructor declaration itself, then it will be applied across all of the constructor parameters. As such a constraint that is applied at the constructor level is called a cross-parameter constraint.

In the example, a cross-parameter `@NotNull` annotation is applied to the constructor of a class. Each of the parameters of the constructor must contain a value, otherwise the validation will fail and the class will not be instantiated. As mentioned previously, if a custom annotation were placed on the constructor, it could validate one or more of the parameters, just like a method-level constraint.

■ **Note** Take special care to ensure that unintended behavior does not occur as a result of subtype constructor constraints. It is important to keep the object hierarchy in mind when applying validation constraints on a class or class constructor.

11-6. Validating Return Values

Problem

You want to validate return value of a method, such that the returning value must adhere to a constraint. If the return value does not adhere, then a validation exception shall be thrown.

Solution

Place a validation constraint on the return type of a method signature to ensure that the result will conform to the validation constraint. In the following example, the return type of the method is validated by the annotation that is placed at the method level. In this case, the returned value must be in an email address format.

```
@Email
public String getEmailAddress(){
    return emailAddress;
}
```

How It Works

Validation constraint annotations that are placed at the method level can be targeted toward return value validation. In doing so, a method must return a valid value per the constraint, otherwise a bean validation exception is thrown. In order to ensure that the constraint being placed at the method level is targeted toward a return type validation, the validator implementation must contain the `@SupportedValidationTarget` annotation, which specifies whether the validator applies to parameters or to the method itself. If a validation constraint implementation does not include this specification, there is no way for the Bean Validation API to determine where the validation should be applied. In this case, the implementation would specify the following:

```
@SupportedValidationTarget(value = ValidationTarget.ANNOTATED_ELEMENT)
```

As with many of the other validation types, return type validation can utilize both standard and custom constraints.

11-7. Defining a Dynamic Validation Error Message

Problem

You want to supply a dynamic error message containing information that is pertinent to the validated value for a constraint.

Solution

Utilize string interpolation within the bean validation message attribute. String interpolation allows one to place message parameters and message expressions into a message string, thereby creating a dynamic string-based message. In the following example, the actual length of the string value will be substituted into the message to provide more feedback:

```
@Size(max = 150, message="The title cannot exceed {max} characters, current title is
$'{validatedValue}'")
@Column(name = "TITLE")
protected String title;
```

How It Works

Providing a clear error message for the user can make or break the success of an application. Utilizing string interpolation within an error message can help you provide a specific message to the user to help indicate the cause of the validation failure. In much the same way that substitution variables work, an error message can contain zero or more variables that can be substituted.

■ **Note** String interpolation requires expression language libraries to be available within your project. If the expression language API and an implementation library are not added to the project, errors will be thrown at runtime. The following maven dependencies can be added to fulfill this requirement:

```
<dependency>
    <groupId>javax.el</groupId>
    <artifactId>javax.el-api</artifactId>
    <version>3.0.0</version>
</dependency>

<dependency>
    <groupId>org.glassfish.web</groupId>
    <artifactId>javax.el</artifactId>
    <version>2.2.6</version>
</dependency>
```

To utilize string interpolation, curly braces can be used to surround the variable that will be substituted with dynamic values. Constraint attributes can be interpolated by placing the attribute inside of curly braces. In the example, the `max` attribute will be substituted for the `{max}` string interpolation. The validated value or custom expression variables can be specified to substitute values within a message by utilizing the `EL` notation, thereby enclosing within curly braces and proceeded with a $. In the example, the `$'{validatedValue}'` variable is one such example. When the error message is produced, `$'{validatedValue}'` is replaced with the current validated value.

Message interpolation occurs in phases, outlined in the following order:

1. Resolve any message parameters using them as a key for a resource bundle named `ValidationMessages.properties`.
2. Resolve any message parameters using them as a key for a resource bundle that contains the standard error messages for built-in constraints.
3. Utilize a value constraint annotation member to substitute as the message parameter. As such, the message parameters will simply be replaced by the value constraint annotation member of the same name.
4. Resolve any message parameters using evaluations as expressions of the Unified Expression Language. This allows us to formulate error messages based on conditional logic and enables us to achieve advanced formatting.

The characters {, }, and $ are special characters for message descriptors. Therefore, if one wants to utilize one of these characters within a validation error message, it must be escaped by proceeding it with a \. Therefore, to escape a $, one would use \$.

It is possible to define a custom message interpolation algorithm, if needed, by plugging in a custom `MessageInterpolator` implementation. To develop a custom interpolator, implement the `javax.validation.MessageInterpolator` interface. The interpolator must be thread-safe, and it is recommended to delegate the final implementation to the default interpolator. The default interpolator is available by calling on `Configuration.getDefaultMessageInterpolator()`. For more information, refer to the bean validation specification.

11-8. Manually Invoking Validator Engine

Problem

You want to call on the bean validation validator engine programmatically, rather than relying on automatic invocation.

Solution

Utilize the Validator API to perform validation. The Validator API allows one to create an executable validator from a number of different validation types, those being parameter, return, class, etc. The following example demonstrates how to manually validate the data for a given entity class. In the following example, a `Book` entity class that is annotated with bean validation constraints is manually instantiated and validated using the Validator API.

```
ValidatorFactory factory = Validation.buildDefaultValidatorFactory();
Validator validator = factory.getValidator();
```

```
Book book = new Book();
book.setId(BigDecimal.ONE);
book.setTitle("The Best Java Book");

Set<ConstraintViolation<Book>> violations = validator.validate(book);

for(ConstraintViolation<Book> violation: violations){
    System.out.println(violation.getMessage());
}
```

How It Works

Bean validation is typically invoked automatically within a Java EE environment. For instance, if using JSF, the validation occurs during the “Process Validations” phase automatically when a form is submitted either synchronously or asynchronously via AJAX. In some cases, it is useful to have the option to call on the Validator API manually. This can be useful in a Java SE environment or perhaps when writing unit tests.

To invoke the Validator API, first create a `ValidatorFactory` by calling on `Validation.buildValidatorFactory()`. Next, use the factory to generate a validator. Lastly, validate a bean by calling on the validator’s `validate` method, passing the bean to be validated. This method will return a `Set` of `ConstraintValidation` objects. You can then iterate over each of the returned validation errors, obtaining each by calling on the `ConstraintViolation.getMessage()` method.

11-9. Grouping Validation Constraints

Problem

You want to group a number of validation constraints together, such that an entire group of validations can occur at the same time.

Solution

Groups can be applied to constraint annotations by specifying the group(s) to which the annotation belongs via the groups annotation attribute. Groups themselves are generated via Java interfaces. The following interface defines the BookGroup:

```
public interface BookGroup {

}
```

The BookGroup group can be applied to one or more constraint annotations by specifying the interface within the group’s annotation attribute, as seen in the following example:

```
. . .
@Entity
@Table(name = "BOOK")
@NamedNativeQuery(
    name="allBooks",
    query = "select id, title, description " +
                "FROM BOOK " +
                "ORDER BY id",
```

```
    resultClass=Book.class)
@NamedQueries({
    @NamedQuery(name = "Book.findAll", query = "SELECT b FROM Book b")})

@XmlRootElement
@ValidNumChapters
public class Book implements Serializable {
    private static final long serialVersionUID = 1L;
    @Id
    @Basic(optional = false)
    @NotNull
    @Column(name = "ID")
    private BigDecimal id;
    @JavaBookTitle(message = "Book Title Should Contain The Word Java")
    @Size(max = 150, message="The title cannot exceed {max} characters, current title is
    $'{validatedValue}'",
          groups={BookGroup.class})
    @Column(name = "TITLE")
    protected String title;
    @Size(max = 500)
    @Column(name = "IMAGE")
    private String image;
    @NotNull(groups={BookGroup.class})
    @Column(name = "NUM_CHAPTERS")
    private int numChapters;
    @Column(name = "NUM_PAGES")
    private int numPages;
    @Lob
    @NotNull(groups={BookGroup.class})
    @Column(name = "DESCRIPTION")
    private String description;
    @Column(name = "PUBLISH_DATE")
    private LocalDate publishDate;
    @ManyToMany(mappedBy="books")
    private Set<BookAuthor> authors;
    @OneToMany(mappedBy="book", cascade=CascadeType.ALL)
    private List<Chapter> chapters = null;

    public Book() {
    }. . .
```

Once the group has been put into place, validation can occur against a group, which would cause every constraint annotation that is assigned to that group to be validated. The following is a brief example of how one could utilize the Validation API to validate on a group basis:

```
ValidatorFactory factory = Validation.buildDefaultValidatorFactory();
Validator validator = factory.getValidator();
. . .
Set<ConstraintViolation<Book>> violations = validator.validate(book, "bookGroup");

for(ConstraintViolation<Book> violation: violations){
    System.out.println(violation.getMessage());
}
```

How It Works

Applying a group to a constraint annotation allows that annotation to become part of a grouping with other annotations to which the same group is applied. Formulating groups of annotations can be beneficial when performing tasks in which a specified set of constraints should always be validated. Validation can occur at the group level, thereby validating constraint groups as needed.

To create a group, one must utilize an interface. The Java interface should be empty and acts as a placeholder for the group. The group can be applied to a constraint annotation by specifying the annotation's groups attribute and pass a list of groups to it. The group attribute accepts one or more groups in the list. The example demonstrates a single group, named BookGroup, being applied to the annotation constraint.

```
@NotNull(groups={BookGroup.class})
@Column(name = "NUM_CHAPTERS")
```

To validate a group of constraints, pass the group or groups for validation to the `Validator validate()` method. In the example, the single BookGroup group is validated, but if there were more groups to be validated, the following syntax would come into play:

```
validator.validate(book, "group1", "group2");
```

CHAPTER 12

Java EE Containers

The GlassFish application server is the industry standard for Java EE. GlassFish 5 is the reference implementation for Java EE 8, so it contained more up-to-date features than any other Java application server available at time of Java EE 8 release. It is a fully featured and easy-to-manage application server, making it a powerful choice for deploying modern and robust Java EE applications. Although plenty of excellent application server choices are available, with many of them being Java EE 8 compliant or working in that direction, GlassFish will remain the best choice for those who want to utilize the most current implementations in the Java EE space since it is the reference implementation for the platform at the time of this writing. The downside to utilizing GlassFish is that there is currently no production support offered for the server, as it is open source and not a licensed vendor product.

Aside from GlassFish, there are a number of excellent Java EE-compliant application servers that do contain vendor support. Many of these options provide commercially licensed implementations, as well as open source or "free to use" releases. Some servers of this ilk are Payara Server, Apache TomEE, JBoss Wildfly, and Websphere Liberty or Open Liberty. Some of these options provide paid support, and all of these options are fully Java EE 7 compliant. Many of them are also Java EE 8 compliant or planning for compliancy soon.

Another realm for delivering Java EE applications and services is in the microservices and cloud space. Such applications and services in this space are not deployed to a traditional application server container, but instead deployed to micro-containers and cloud platforms. This chapter focuses on working with GlassFish 5, the reference implementation, and Payara 5, which is commercially supported. It also covers the basics of developing microservices with Java EE or EE4J and working with container solutions such as Docker.

12.1. Installing GlassFish 5 or Payara 5 and Starting Up

Problem

You want to install Oracle's GlassFish application server for Java EE 8 development on your machine. Once installed, you want to start the server so that you can begin to use it.

Solution #1: GlassFish

Download a GlassFish 5 ZIP archive from the site `https://javaee.github.io/glassfish/` and unzip the contents of the archive onto your operating system. If you are looking for the most current development releases of GlassFish, visit the download section of the project page. For the purposes of this recipe example, let's assume you are going to install the GlassFish 5 server into a directory named `/JAVA_DEV/GlassFish` on *nix systems or OS X, or named `C:\JAVA_DEV\GlassFish` on Windows.

J. Juneau, *Java EE 8 Recipes*, https://doi.org/10.1007/978-1-4842-3594-2_12

Once you have downloaded and unzipped the archive, you are ready to begin the installation process. The unzipped archive will be in a root directory named `glassfish`. Copy the `glassfish` directory and all of its contents into the `/JAVA_DEV/GlassFish` directory. You are now ready to start the server and or begin configuring your GlassFish application server.

Solution #2: Payara

Download the Payara server by visiting the `https://www.payara.fish` website and clicking on the Downloads menu option. Once there, click on the Payara Server Full release, which will also include a version number. This will provide you with the most recently released full version of the Payara server. Once you download the server, save it on your drive to a folder named `/Java_Dev/payara` on *nix systems or OS X, or to a folder named `C:\Java_Dev\Payara` on Windows. Once it's saved, unzip the contents of the archive.

Once the archive has been unzipped, the root directory will be named payara5. The server is now ready for startup and/or configuration.

How It Works

The GlassFish and Payara application servers can be installed by simply downloading the ZIP archive and unzipping it into the directory of your choice. Once this is completed, you are ready to begin configuring your server environment. The first step of configuring your environment should be to change the default administrator password, which is outlined in Recipe 12-3. However, if you are anxious to test your environment, you can traverse into the `<<glassfish or payara5>>/bin` directory and start the server using the following command:

*nix and OS X:

```
./asadmin start-domain domain1
```

Windows:

```
asadmin start-domain domain1
```

■ **Note** The first time you start the application server using this command, it will not contain an administrative password. It is not recommended to start the application server without first setting the administrator password unless you are on an operating system with a firewall configuration, as doing so can leave your system vulnerable. For more information on setting or changing the administrator user password, see Recipe 12-3.

12.2. Logging into the Administrative Console

Problem

You have started your GlassFish or Payara server domain, and you want to have the ability to configure your GlassFish or Payara environment using a graphical user interface (GUI).

Solution

Start your GlassFish or Payara server and then point your browser to the administrative console URL. By default, the URL is `http://localhost:4848`, but if you changed the settings within the `domain.xml` configuration file or have more than one server installed on your machine, then that port number may vary. Once you have opened the administrative console URL, you will be greeted with a login screen, as shown in Figure 12-1, if you have already set a password, but the first time you run the server there will be no password needed. However, you should set the administrative password as soon as possible. See Recipe 12-3 for more details on how to set or change the administrative password.

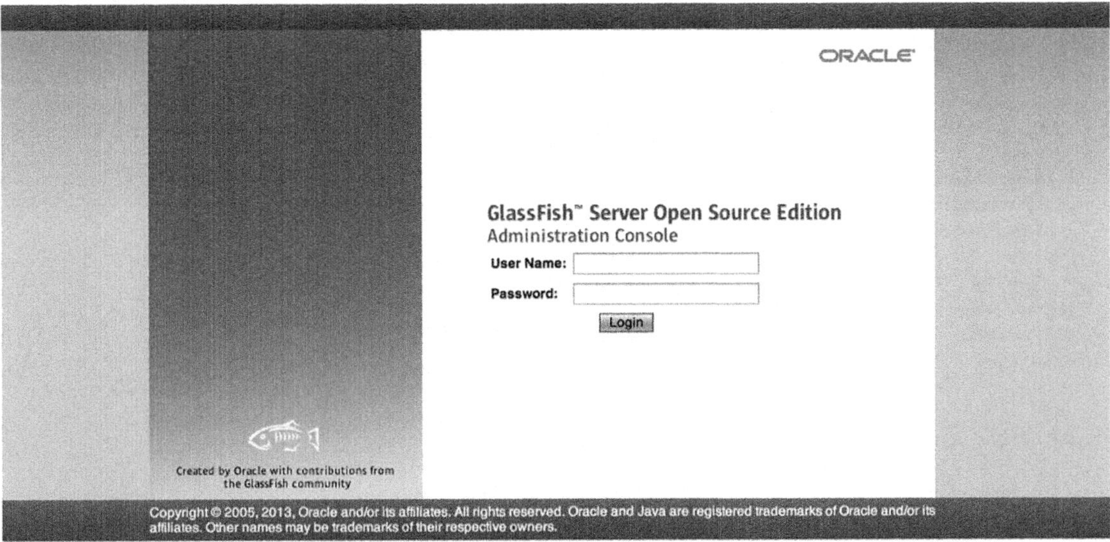

Figure 12-1. *GlassFish administrative console login if password is set*

If you have not yet set up a password, then you will be brought to the main GlassFish administrative console screen (see Figure 12-2), where you can select the specific area of the application server that you want to configure. As advised in the previous recipe, if you have no administrative password configured then you should proceed to Recipe 12-3 and set this up immediately in order to secure your environment.

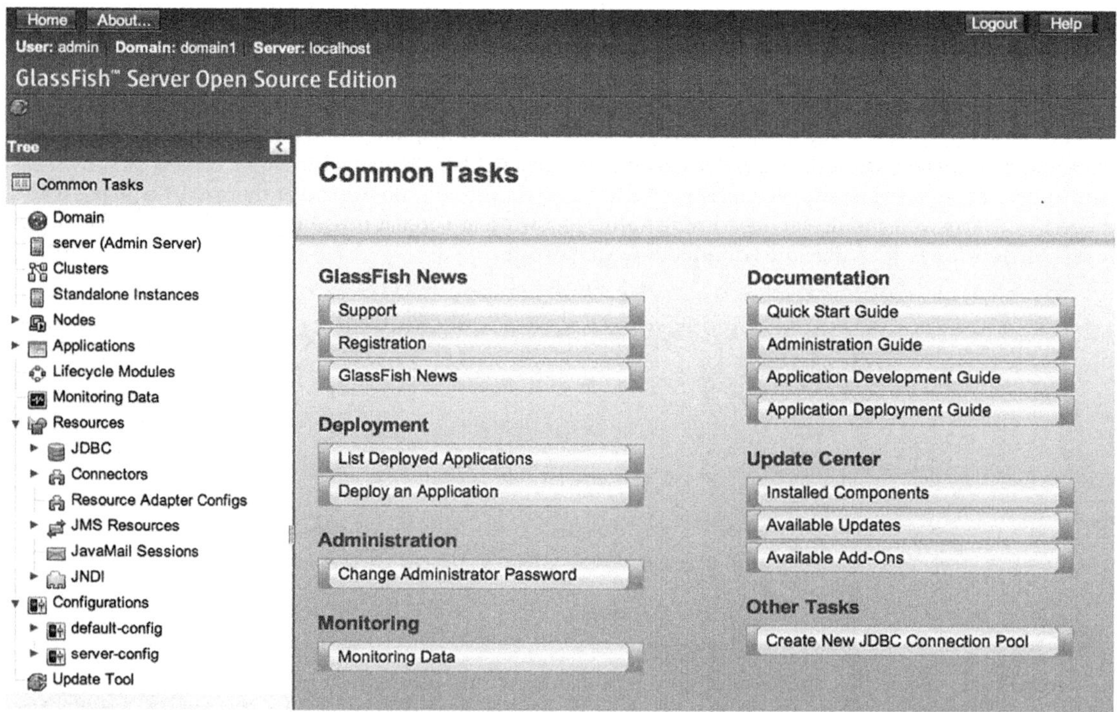

Figure 12-2. *GlassFish administrative console main screen*

How It Works

The first step in setting up an application server environment is to install it, which basically consists of unzipping it into a directory. The very next step after installing the server environment should be to configure some basic settings, such as setting the administrative user password and setting up database connection pools for your applications. The administration console is the hub of configuration for your GlassFish or Payara application server. Virtually all security, database, messaging, and application-specific configurations occur within the administration console or the command line interface. This section provides you with a brief overview of the most commonly used screens within the administrative console.

■ **Note** Payara 5 offers different options in the administrative console than GlassFish 5. This is because Payara 5 contains a superset of features above and beyond what GlassFish has to offer.

Once you enter the console, you will be greeted with a tree menu on the left side of the screen, which contains menu options for each of the console subsections. The right side of the screen will contain a Common Tasks panel (see Figure 12-3), which displays links for support, registration, and news, along with links to some of the most commonly used sub-forms within the console. You'll also see the option to view installed components and available updates and add-ons, which is a good panel to visit frequently to learn about possible updates and add-ons for the server. Of course, the documentation for GlassFish is extremely important, and you will also find links to the various pieces of documentation within the Common Tasks panel.

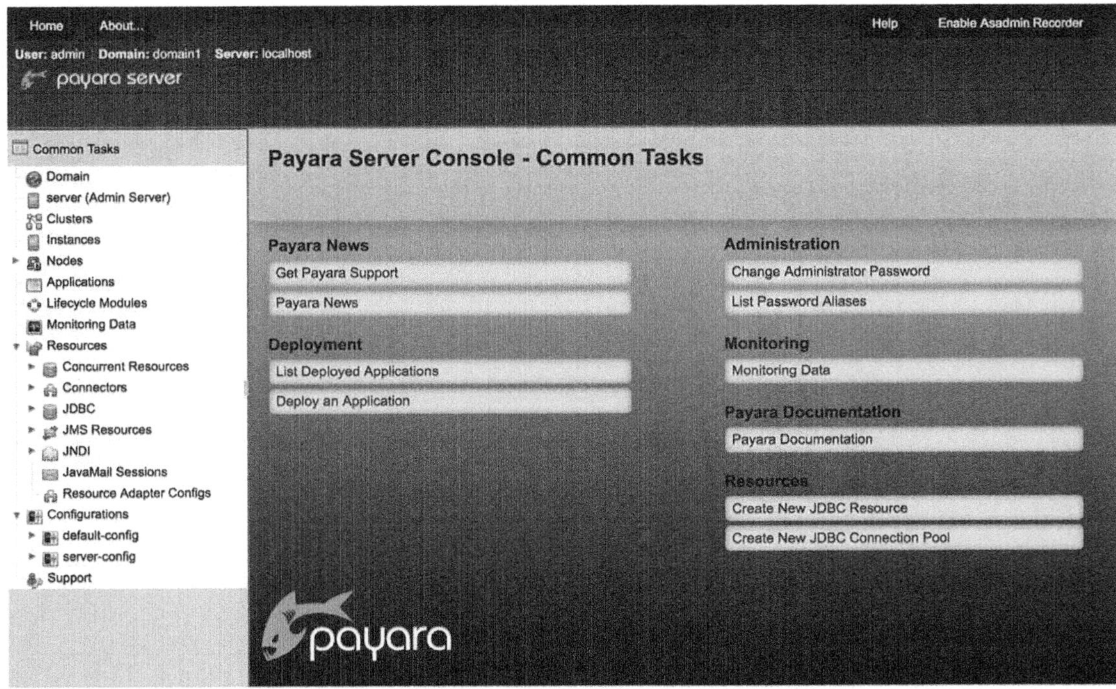

Figure 12-3. *Payara's Common Tasks panel*

The Domain menu option opens a panel that contains tabbed forms for making domain-level changes, as shown in Figure 12-4. When you install GlassFish, the default domain is known as `domain1`, but you can create domains by different names if you'd like. Configurations for how applications are auto-deployed, reloaded, and so on, can be found on the Applications Configuration tab of the Domain panel, and you can change the administrator password within that panel as well (see Recipe 12-3 for details). If you're using Payara server, there are a few more options than GlassFish, including HazelCast configuration.

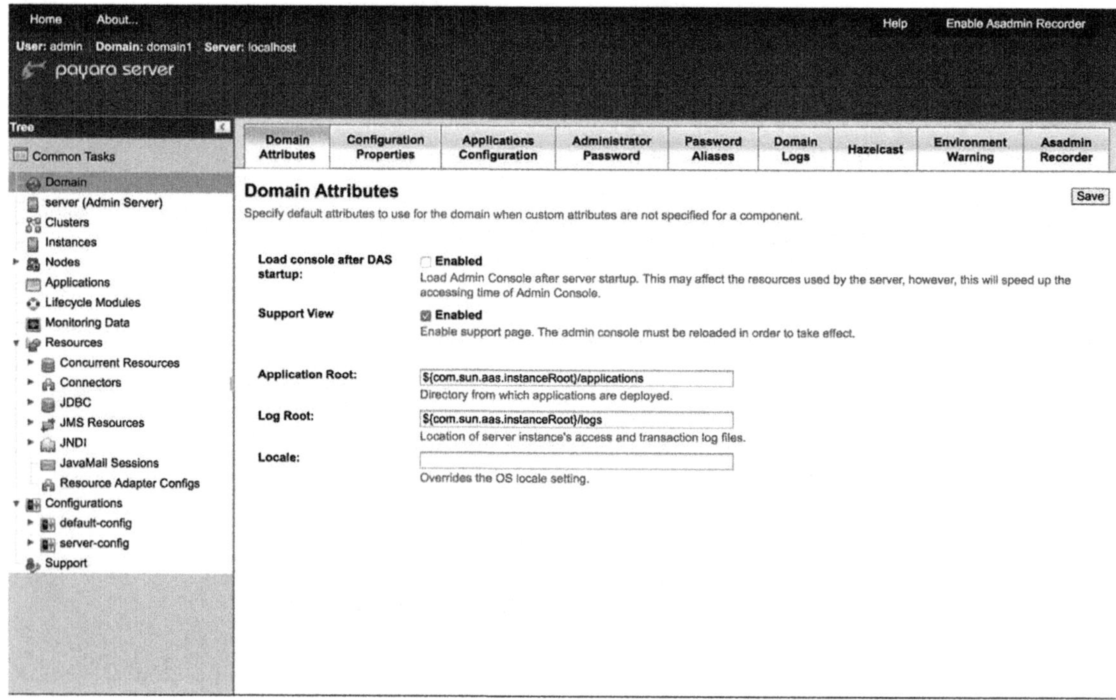

Figure 12-4. *Domain panel*

The Server (Admin Server) menu option is one of the most important options available. Clicking that menu option will open a tabbed panel containing information regarding your server, the JVM, resources, and properties. You can stop or restart the application server instance from this panel, and you can also view and manage the server logs from here. Figure 12-5 displays the General Information panel, which is displayed when clicking the Server menu option.

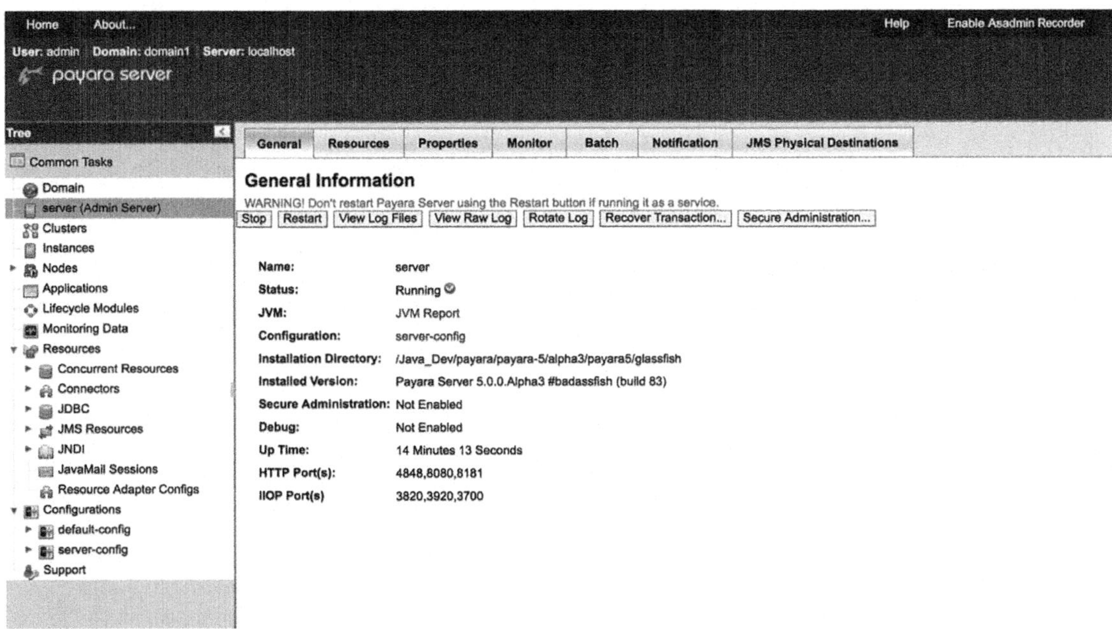

Figure 12-5. *General Information panel*

The Applications menu option allows you to view any applications that are currently deployed to the server. You can also deploy new applications from this panel, as well as un-deploy, enable, or disable existing applications. If there comes a need to re-deploy or reload an existing application, the panel also provides easy access to perform those activities. The Applications panel (shown in Figure 12-7) will most likely become one of the most commonly visited menu options as you work with GlassFish.

The Resources menu contains several submenu options that are useful for configuring resources that can be utilized by your applications. From database resources such as connection pools to Java Messaging and JavaMail sessions, the Resources section provides the ability to make enterprise features available to applications deployed within the server. You will learn more about configurations for these resources in later recipes.

The Configurations menu provides the ability to tweak the server's JVM settings, logging, web and EJB containers, security, network services, and more. This is the area of the administration console that allows customization of the server itself in order to provide the best settings for your environment. For instance, if you want to implement special options for the application server's JVM, this is the place to do that. If you want to set up authentication for your applications using JDBC or LDAP (se Recipe 12-6), then this can be done in the Configurations section as well. These servers provide the ability to fine-tune the application server, making it truly conform to the environment, and the console makes it easy to apply the customizations.

Although any of the features can be changed by manually updating XML configuration files, the administration console provides developers and administrators with an easy way to see the server configurations and change pieces to suit the needs of the environment. It also provides a central location for viewing information about the server, its applications, and the resources available for use by the server applications. The administration console is a one-stop shop for all of your configuration and tuning.

12.3. Changing the Administrator User Password

Problem

You want to add security to your newly installed GlassFish or Payara environment by changing the administrative user password.

Solution #1

Traverse into the server /bin directory within your terminal or command prompt and enter the following:

```
./asadmin change-admin-password
```

After issuing the command, follow the prompts accordingly to change the administrator password.

Solution #2

Log in to the administrative console to change the administrative user password. Once authenticated, click the Domain menu option within the tree menu on the left. This will bring you to a screen that includes several tabs, allowing different configurations for your application server domain. One of those tabs is named Administrator Password, and this is the tab you want to use for changing the password. Once you've clicked the tab, you will be presented with a form that will allow you to change the administrative password accordingly.

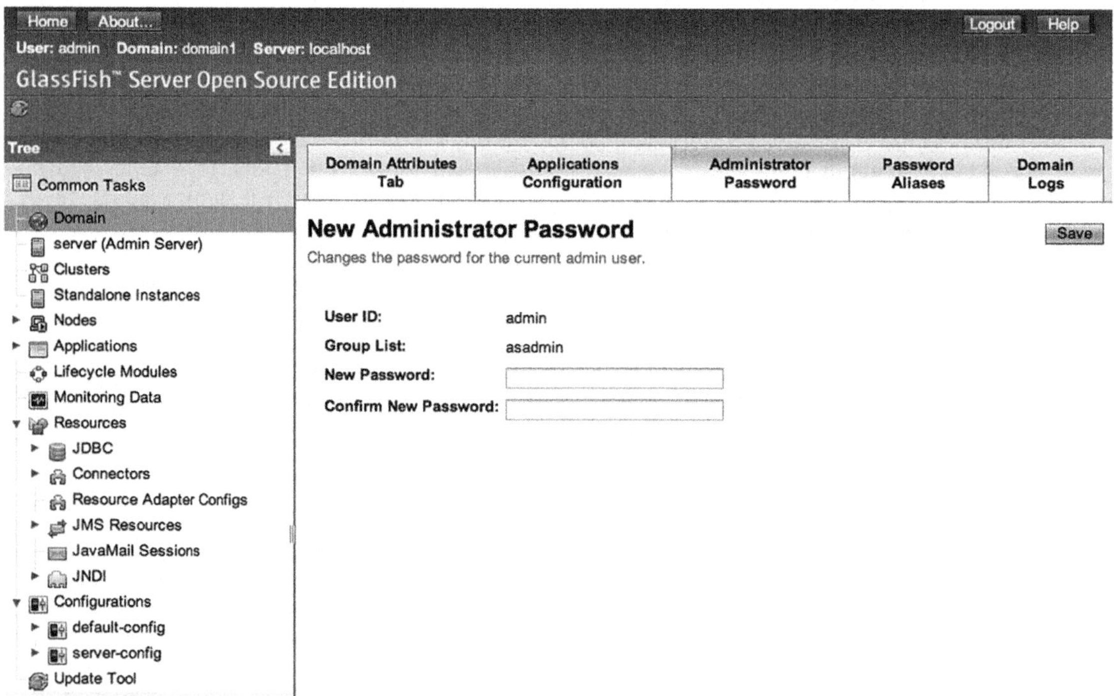

Figure 12-6. *The New Administrator Password form*

■ **Note** This should be your first configuration step after installing a new GlassFish/Payara application server environment. This is especially the case if you are running on an operating system that does not have a firewall installed, configured, and turned on. Leaving the server unsecured without a password leaves the environment vulnerable.

To that end, I recommend using Solution #1 to this recipe for changing the administrator password the first time. That way, your server doesn't need to be started before the password can be changed, making your server secure from the first startup. The Administrator Password form within the administration console is great for changing the password after it has been set.

How It Works

The most important configuration you can make to your newly installed GlassFish or Payara environment is to set the administrator password. If the server is left without a password, it opens up a major vulnerability because a hacker could gain access to your administration console and gain full access to your applications or the entire machine. Changing the password is very easy to do, and there are a couple of ways to do it. First, there is a special command that can be used to change the password without even starting the server. You will need to use the `change-admin-password` utility to set the administrator password before domain startup. Solution #1 demonstrates this technique, and the advantage of using it is that the domain does not have to be started in order to use it.

If you want to change the administrator password after you have already started the domain, you can do so by logging in to the administration console and going to the Domain panel. Once there, you will see an Administrator Password tab, which will allow you to change the password. This technique is outlined in Solution #2 to this recipe. It is a straightforward procedure, and using the administration console for changing the password provides an easy means of doing so after the server is up and running.

12.4. Deploying a WAR File

Problem

You want to deploy a WAR archive to the application server so that your web application will be available for use.

Solution #1

Log in to the administrative console and select the Applications menu option in the left menu, which will open the Applications panel (see Figure 12-7). The list of deployed applications will be displayed within the right panel. Click the Deploy button above the application list in order to begin the deployment process.

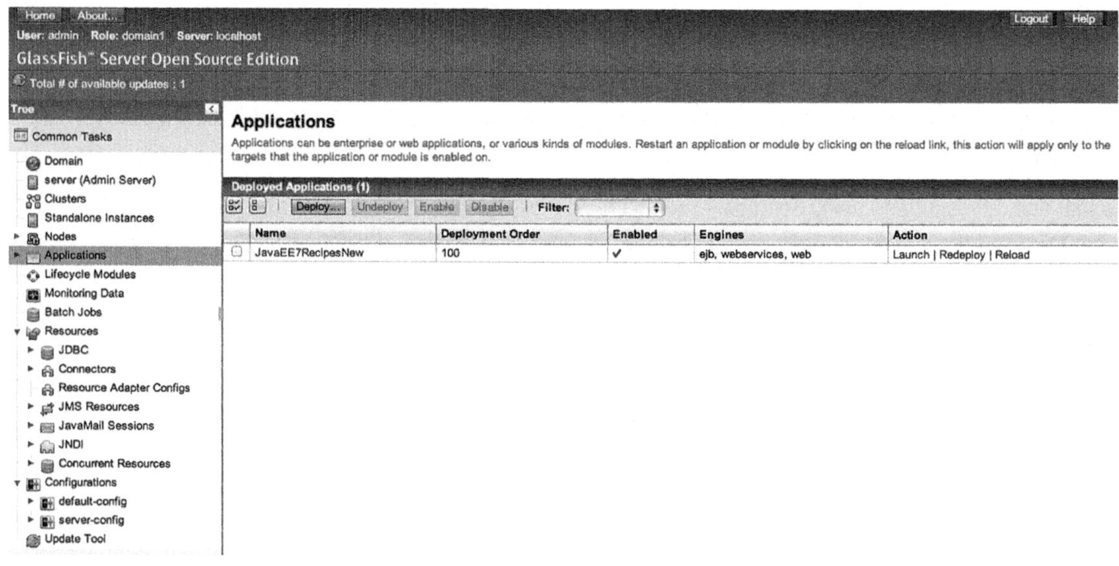

Figure 12-7. GlassFish administrative console Applications panel

Once you're within the Deploy Applications or Modules panel (see Figure 12-8), find the WAR archive that you want to deploy by selecting the Browse button and locating the WAR archive of your choice. The application name and context path will be auto-populated, but you can change them if you want. In many cases, you may leave all of the other default options selected.

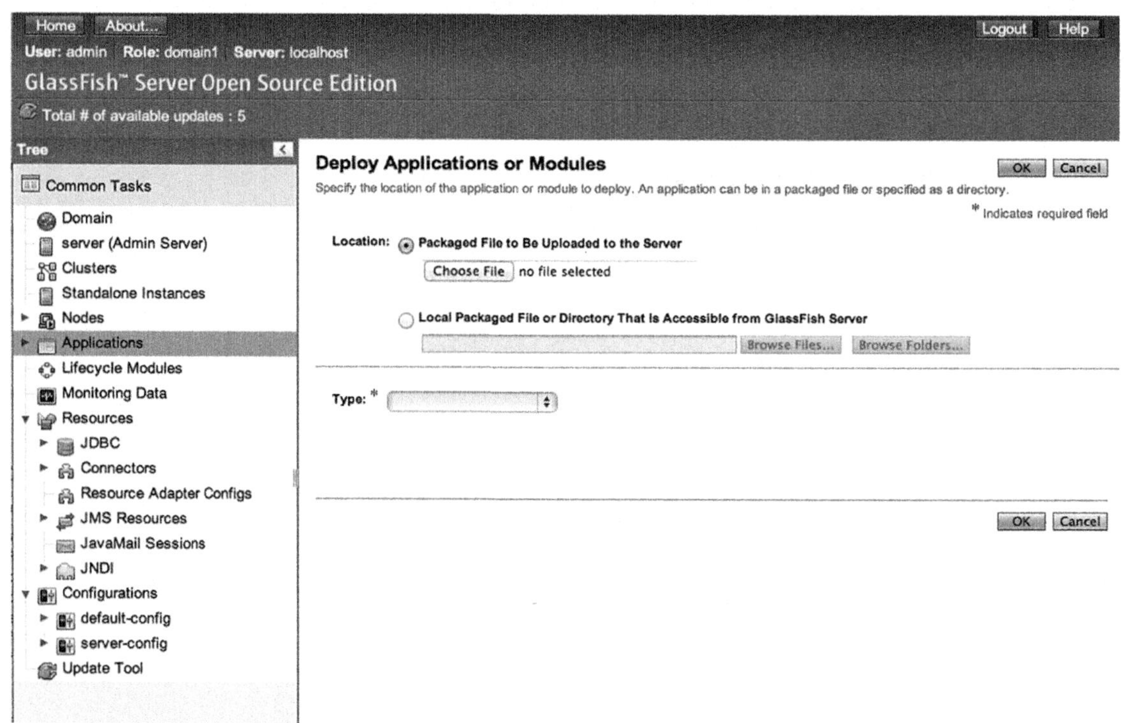

Figure 12-8. GlassFish administrative console: Deploy Applications or Modules

Next, click the Deploy button to initiate the application deployment. The application server will complete the deployment, assuming that there are no configuration issues with the application archive.

Solution #2

Utilize the GlassFish or Payara application server's auto-deployment option by logging in to the application server host machine if you haven't done so already. Browse the filesystem to find the WAR file that you want to deploy. Copy the desired WAR file. Locate the auto-deployment directory (path) and paste the WAR file inside it. The application server will complete the deployment, assuming that there are no configuration issues with the application archive.

How It Works

To make a web application accessible to users on the Web, it must be deployed to the application server. GlassFish and Payara have a couple of very easy techniques for deploying applications for use. Java web applications can be packaged in a few different ways before deploying. To further understand the deployment process, it helps to take a look at the variety of possible deployment scenarios for a Java enterprise application.

In the early days of Java EE, the most common package structure was an enterprise archive (EAR) file. An EAR file is an archive that consists of one or more modules, usually in Java archive (JAR) file format, along with XML deployment descriptors. The standard EAR structure contains two JAR files along with XML deployment descriptors. One of those JAR files contains the web sources, including the HTML, JSP, JSF, JavaScript, the `WEB-INF` directory, and other files used for displaying web content. This JAR file is known as the *web module*, and it corresponds to a web application as defined within the Java Servlet specification. The second JAR file contains the Java sources that are packaged and used for the business logic of the application. Together, the two packages can be combined into an EAR file and deployed to a Java application server, in which case the application server takes on the task of using the XML deployment descriptors to place the different modules into their proper locations within the application server. EAR files are still in use today, and most applications written using Java EE 5 and older are deployed using an EAR file format. Until recently, EAR files were the most common way to distribute and deploy Java EE applications.

Currently, the most common type of archive for Java web application deployment is the web archive (WAR). WAR files are archives that contain all of the web markup and Java sources together under the same archive module. Typically, those Java web applications that contained no enterprise application structures, such as EJBs, web services, or the like, could be deployed using the WAR file format. Since Java EE 6, all enterprise applications can be deployed in the WAR file format as well, which makes it much easier to package and deploy an application. Although if you're using a Java IDE, the work is done for you, so deployment of WAR files is much faster than that of the EAR file, and it is much easier to work with all of an application's source files within the same module, rather than using more than one.

Both the EAR and WAR file formats are simply ZIP files that contain either the `.ear` or `.war` extension. As a matter of fact, you can easily view the contents of these archives by renaming them with a `.zip` extension and unzipping them to your filesystem. The GlassFish application server makes it easy to deploy each file type, whether using the administration console or the auto-deploy technique. When the application server is deploying the archives, it un-packages the contents of the archives into the deployment directory, which is located in the `<GlassFish-Home>/glassfish5/ /domains/domain1/applications` directory.

■ **Note** It is possible to edit web files after an application has been deployed by updating the files that exist in the deployment directory. Any XHTML, HTML, JS, or other code files that do not need to be compiled, along with JSPs that are compiled on the fly, can be updated in place while the application is up and running. This can sometimes prove useful for making minor layout or JavaScript changes while in production. However, remember that if the application is undeployed or another application is deployed in place of an existing application, then all sources within the deployment directory are deleted.

12.5. Adding a Database Resource

Problem

Your application utilizes an underlying RDBMS, and you want to configure a database resource for this purpose.

Solution

Create a connection pool resource for the database to which you want to connect. After the connection pool has been created, define a new JDBC resource, which will be used to provide applications with a means to connect to the database. To perform these tasks, first log in to the GlassFish or Payara administration console and then expand the JDBC menu under the Resources option within the tree menu on the left, as shown in Figure 12-9.

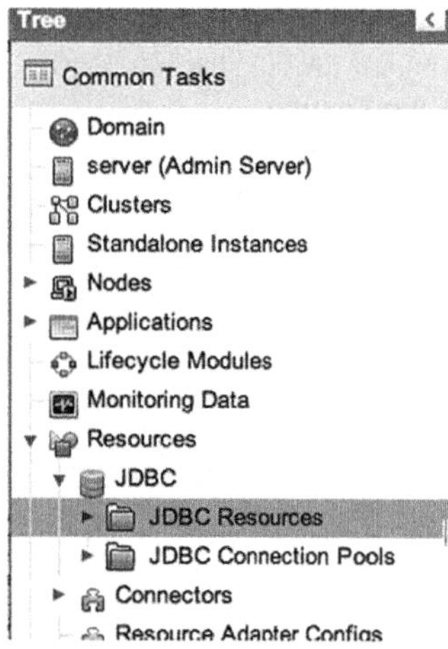

Figure 12-9. *GlassFish administration console: JDBC Resources*

Next, click the JDBC Connection Pools menu option, which will open the JDBC Connection Pools panel on the right side of the screen. Here you will be provided with a list of the current connection pools, as well as buttons to add new pools or delete existing pools. Click the New button to initiate the creation of a new connection pool. This will open the New JDBC Connection Pool (Step 1 of 2) panel, as shown in Figure 12-10. In this panel, specify the name of the pool you want to create, and then select a resource type and a database vendor from the selection lists.

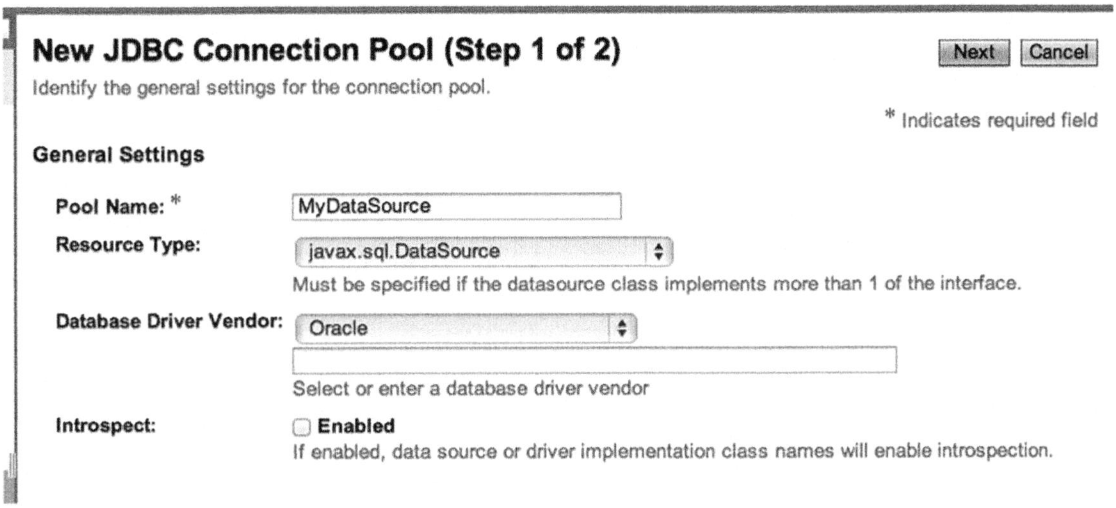

Figure 12-10. *New JDBC Connection Pool (Step 1 of 2) panel*

After clicking the Next button to continue, the second screen for creating a new JDBC connection pool will be displayed (see Figure 12-11), which contains a number of settings to help configure the connection pool. For instance, the datasource class name can be selected, pool settings can be adjusted, and transaction management options can be tweaked. I recommend retaining all of the default configurations unless it has been determined that something needs to be adjusted in order for application functionality. You can always revisit the connection pool settings and adjust them later if need be.

New JDBC Connection Pool (Step 2 of 2)

Previous Finish Cancel

Identify the general settings for the connection pool. Datasource Classname or Driver Classname must be specified for the connection pool.

* Indicates required field

General Settings

Pool Name: MyDataSource

Resource Type: javax.sql.DataSource

Database Driver Vendor: Oracle

Datasource Classname: oracle.jdbc.pool.OracleDataSource

Select or enter vendor-specific classname that implements the DataSource and/or XADataSource APIs

Driver Classname:

Select or enter vendor-specific classname that implements the java.sql.Driver interface.

Ping: **Enabled**

When enabled, the pool is pinged during creation or reconfiguration to identify and warn of any erroneous values for its attributes

Description:

Pool Settings

Initial and Minimum Pool Size: 8 Connections

Minimum and initial number of connections maintained in the pool

Maximum Pool Size: 32 Connections

Maximum number of connections that can be created to satisfy client requests

Pool Resize Quantity: 2 Connections

Number of connections to be removed when pool idle timeout expires

Idle Timeout: 300 Seconds

Maximum time that connection can remain idle in the pool

Max Wait Time: 60000 Milliseconds

Amount of time caller waits before connection timeout is sent

Transaction

Non Transactional Connections: **Enabled**

Returns non-transactional connections

Transaction Isolation:

Figure 12-11. *New JDBC Connection Pool (Step 2 of 2) panel*

At the bottom of the form you will find the Additional Properties table (see Figure 12-12), which is where you need to enter the specifics pertaining to the database connection you want to configure. While there are a number of properties listed in the table by default, you need to enter values only for a user, password, and URL in order to obtain a connection. Once you've entered this detail, you will be able to click the Finish button to create the pool.

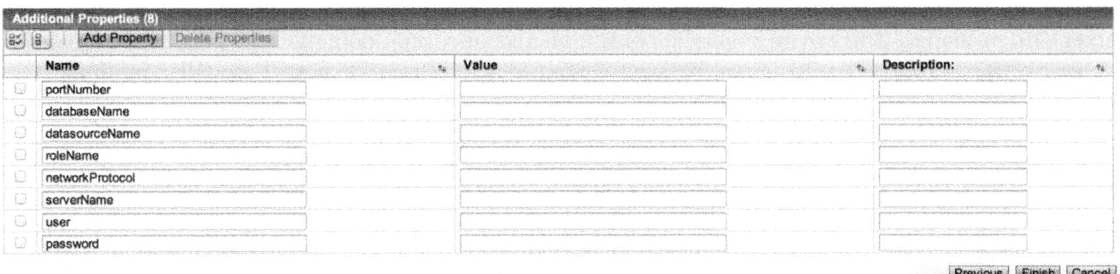

Figure 12-12. *Additional JDBC connection properties*

■ **Note** You must have the database driver (JAR file) for the database you want to use installed within the application server. To do so, simply copy the JAR file into the `<GlassFish-Home>/glassfish5 /domains/domain1/lib` directory. For instance, to enable the use of the Oracle database driver, download the JDBC driver file called `ojdbc7.jar` and use that.

Once the pool has been created, you can generate a JDBC resource for use from within your applications. The JDBC resource is basically a string identifier that references your database connection pool, and it is used from within a Java web application's `persistence.xml` unit to utilize an application server connection pool. To create the JDBC resource, click the JDBC Resources menu option from within the tree menu, which will open the JDBC Resources pane (see Figure 12-13), listing each of the existing resources. Click New in order to configure a new resource.

JDBC Resources

JDBC resources provide applications with a means to connect to a database.

Resources (3)

New... Delete Enable Disable

JNDI Name	Enabled	Connection Pool	Description
jdbc/DerbyConnection	✓	DerbyPool	
jdbc/__TimerPool	✓	__TimerPool	
jdbc/__default	✓	DerbyPool	

Figure 12-13. *JDBC Resources pane*

How It Works

Just about every enterprise application uses an underlying database to store and retrieve data. To connect to the database, you need to configure a database account for which to connect and code a connection utility that is responsible for opening and closing connections. Well, that is one way to do it; another way is to rely on the application server to manage the database connections. Utilizing an application server's database connection pool can be very useful because it takes away the burden of handing connections within the application's business logic, and it also helps the overall performance of an application by maintaining a number of open connections in a pool. When a process needs to work with the database, it grabs one of the open connection objects, uses it, and then places it back into the pool when finished. By maintaining this pool, the overhead of opening and closing connections for every single task is alleviated, helping your applications perform much faster. Another benefit to having the application server manage connections is that the user name and password used to obtain the connection are stored in only one place, the application server. User names and passwords do not need to be hard-coded into applications that use application server JDBC resources. This can be helpful not only from a security standpoint but also from a maintenance stance. Isn't it much easier to change the password in one location when it expires, rather than fumbling around with each of the applications that use it?

Configuring a datasource within the GlassFish and Payara application servers is straightforward because you can manage everything from within the administration console. However, there are a number of configurations that can be altered in order to change the way in which your connection pool manages connections. On the first New JDBC Connection Pool panel of the connection pool configuration, you need to determine which type of resource you want to create. Table 12-1 describes the different resource types.

Table 12-1. *JDBC Connection Pool Resource Types*

Resource Type	Description
`javax.sql.DataSource`	Suitable for local transactions
`javax.sql.XADataSource`	Suitable for global transactions
`javax.sql.ConnectionPoolDataSource`	Suitable for local transactions, possible performance improvements
`java.sql.Driver`	Standard driver

The Pool Settings section of the second New JDBC Connection Pool panel allows you to configure the number of connections that will be available for application use. By default, the number of open connections at application server startup will be eight. This means applications can grab and use eight connections from the pool without incurring any extra overhead, because the pool has already opened these connections.

The Maximum Pool Size option is set to 32 by default. When an application needs to use a connection, it goes to the pool and requests one. If there is a connection available in the pool, then it is given to the application. However, if no connection is available, then a new connection is made. The Maximum Pool Size value is the upper bound of connections that can possibly be made. So, by default, if there are 32 connections open and an application requests a new connection, then a database connection error will be thrown. Remember, when an application is finished using a connection, it is returned to the pool, so if an application is working properly and releases connections once it's finished using them, the maximum number of connections should be fairly difficult to reach in most environments.

A number of other configurations can be managed for your connection pool, such as determining when connections will time out and when to resize the pool. Adjust accordingly, if needed, after your application has been using the connection pool for a period of time. The transaction configuration for the pool makes it possible to set up an isolation level. It is recommended by Oracle to try to leave the isolation level alone if possible. If not, consider setting Isolation Level Guaranteed to false and make sure applications do not alter a connection's isolation level. The different isolation levels are listed in the following bullets, from best performing on top to worst-performing on bottom:

- `READ_UNCOMMITTED`
- `READ_COMMITTED`
- `REPEATABLE_READ`
- `SERIALIZABLE`

12.6. Adding Forms-Based Authentication

Problem

You want to configure authentication for your applications by utilizing a database table to hold user names and passwords, along with user groups for different access privileges.

Solution

Set up forms-based authentication within your GlassFish application server by creating the necessary database tables to contain user accounts and groups and then configuring the application server to use those tables for authentication. The first step to setting up forms-based authentication is to create the necessary database artifacts to support the authentication. To do so, create two database tables. One of the tables will contain the user names and passwords, and the second table will contain the groups, along with the users who have access to those groups.

The following lines of SQL can be used to generate these tables (Oracle syntax), along with the database sequences that will be used to populate the table primary key values:

```
create table users(
id number,
username varchar(150) not null,
password varchar(50) not null,
primary key (id));

create table groups(
id number,
username varchar2(150) not null,
groupname varchar2(100) not null,
primary key(id));

create sequence users_s
start with 1
increment by 1;

create sequence groups_s
start with 1
increment by 1;
```

For testing purposes, let's create a couple of user accounts along with a couple of different access groups. The following lines of SQL will insert these records:

```
insert into users values(
users_s.nextval,
'admin',
dbms_obfuscation_toolkit.md5(input=>utl_raw.cast_to_raw('javaeerecipes')));

insert into users values(
users_s.nextval,
'juneau',
dbms_obfuscation_toolkit.md5(input=>utl_raw.cast_to_raw('testpass')));
```

```
insert into groups values(
groups_s.nextval,
'admin', 'administrator');

insert into groups values(
groups_s.nextval,
'juneau','reader');
```

Now that the database has been set up for authentication, it is time to configure the database to use these tables for authentication purposes. To do so, log in to the GlassFish administrative console, navigate to the Configuration, server-config, Realms menu option, and click the New button. Doing so will open the New Realm panel, which is shown in Figure 12-14.

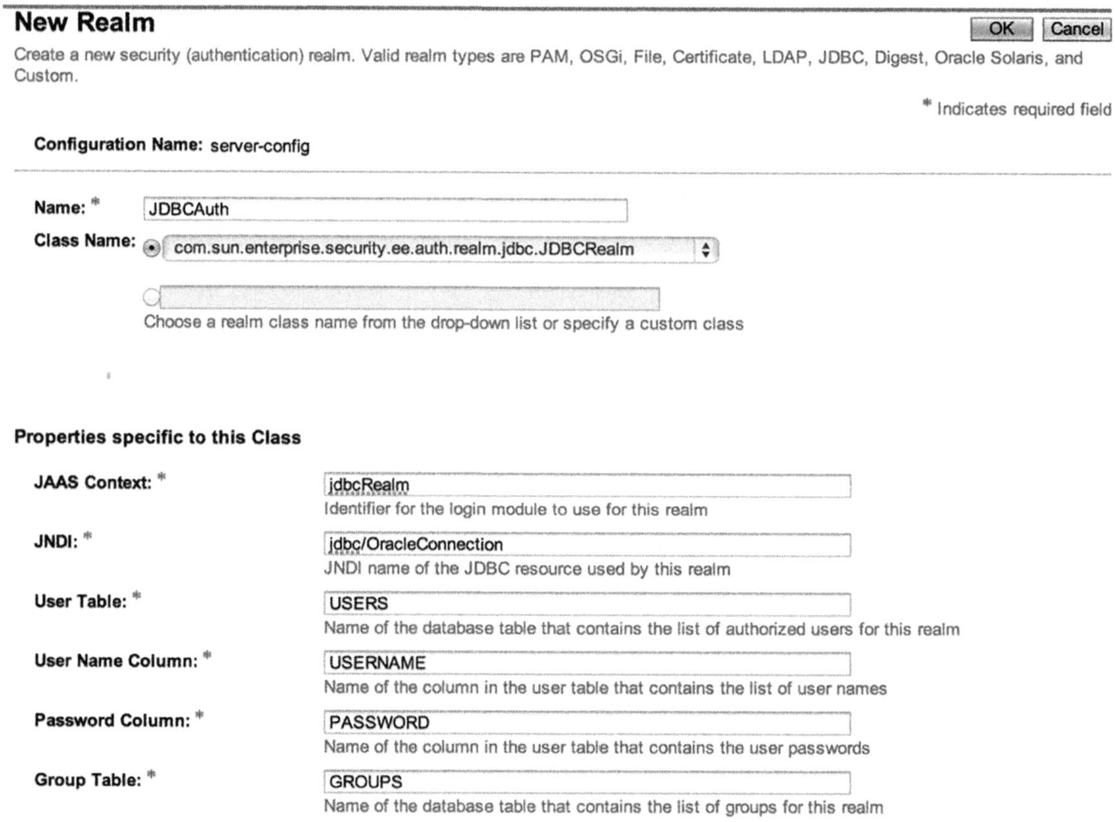

Figure 12-14. *Creating a new security realm for GlassFish*

Within the New Realm form, enter a name for the realm, which you will call `JDBCAuth` for this example. Next, for the class name, choose `com.sun.enterprise.security.auth.realm.jdbc.JDBCRealm` from the drop-down menu. Once you've completed this first section of the form, it is time to fill out the properties specific to the class. For this example, use the values shown in Table 12-2 to complete this form.

Table 12-2. *Properties Specific to JDBC Security Realm Class*

Property	Value
JAAS	`jdbcAuth`
JNDI	`jdbc/OracleConnection`
User Table	`users`
User Name Column	`username`
Password Column	`password`
Group Table	`groups`
Group Name Column	`groupname`
Password Encryption Algorithm	`MD5` (algorithm used in SQL insert statement)

Once you're finished, click OK to save the values and create the realm. The newly created realm should now appear in the Realms listing, as shown in Figure 12-15.

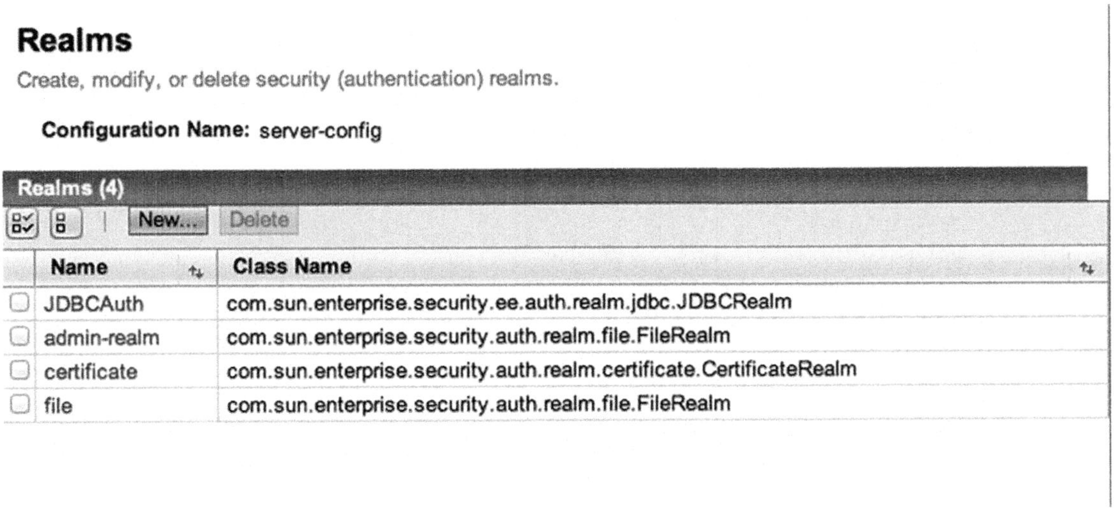

Realms

Create, modify, or delete security (authentication) realms.

Configuration Name: server-config

Realms (4)

New... Delete

Name	Class Name
JDBCAuth	com.sun.enterprise.security.ee.auth.realm.jdbc.JDBCRealm
admin-realm	com.sun.enterprise.security.auth.realm.file.FileRealm
certificate	com.sun.enterprise.security.auth.realm.certificate.CertificateRealm
file	com.sun.enterprise.security.auth.realm.file.FileRealm

Figure 12-15. *Realms listing in the GlassFish administration console*

That does it for the application server configuration. Now how do you actually use the new security realm? One way is to utilize the mature technique of creating a login view and making some configuration changes to your application's `web.xml` file in order to implement the authentication within your application. A more modern technique is to utilize the Java EE Security API, which was introduced to the platform in Java EE 8. This recipe covers the older technique, highlighting some differences between it and the newer Java EE Security API. To see a more modern example from start to finish, refer to Chapter 17. To begin, let's look at the changes that will need to be made to `web.xml` in order to configure the forms authentication. The following excerpt, taken from the `web.xml` configuration file in the `JavaEE8Recipes` sources, demonstrates the updates that need to be made:

```
<security-constraint>
        <display-name>Admin</display-name>
        <web-resource-collection>
            <web-resource-name>Admin Tools</web-resource-name>
            <description/>
            <url-pattern>/faces/admin/*</url-pattern>
            <http-method>GET</http-method>
            <http-method>POST</http-method>
            <http-method>HEAD</http-method>
            <http-method>PUT</http-method>
            <http-method>OPTIONS</http-method>
            <http-method>TRACE</http-method>
            <http-method>DELETE</http-method>
        </web-resource-collection>
        <auth-constraint>
            <description/>
            <role-name>admin</role-name>
        </auth-constraint>
    </security-constraint>
    <security-constraint>
        <display-name>User</display-name>
        <web-resource-collection>
            <web-resource-name>Protected Users Area</web-resource-name>
            <description/>
            <url-pattern>/faces/users/*</url-pattern>
            <http-method>GET</http-method>
            <http-method>POST</http-method>
            <http-method>HEAD</http-method>
            <http-method>PUT</http-method>
            <http-method>OPTIONS</http-method>
            <http-method>TRACE</http-method>
            <http-method>DELETE</http-method>
        </web-resource-collection>
        <auth-constraint>
            <description/>
            <role-name>user</role-name>
        </auth-constraint>
    </security-constraint>
```

```
<login-config>
        <realm-name>JDBCRealm</realm-name>
        <form-login-config>
            <form-login-page>/faces/loginForm.xhtml</form-login-page>
            <form-error-page>/faces/loginError.xhtml</form-error-page>
        </form-login-config>
    </login-config>
```

Next, the GlassFish server security role mapping needs to be added to the sun-web.xml configuration file, which maps application roles to database groups. The following excerpt demonstrates the mapping configuration:

```
<security-role-mapping>
<role-name>admin</role-name>
<group-name>administrator</group-name>
</security-role-mapping>
<security-role-mapping>
<role-name>user</role-name>
<group-name>reader</group-name>
</security-role-mapping>
```

Lastly, the views that the user will see must contain specific names for the user name and password input text fields, and the form action must be set to j_security_check, which will cause control to be passed to the application server for handling the authentication. The following login form demonstrates this process. You can see the sources within the login.xhtml form contained within the JavaEE8Recipes project.

```
<?xml version="1.0" encoding="UTF-8"?>

<!DOCTYPE html PUBLIC "-//W3C//DTD XHTML 1.0 Strict//EN" "http://www.w3.org/TR/xhtml1/DTD/
xhtml1-strict.dtd">
<html xmlns="http://www.w3.org/1999/xhtml"
      xmlns:f="http://xmlns.jcp.org/jsf/core"
      xmlns:h="http://xmlns.jcp.org/jsf/html">
    <h:head>
        <meta http-equiv="Content-Type" content="text/html; charset=UTF-8"/>
        <title>TODO supply a title</title>

    </h:head>
    <h:body>
        <p>
            <form method="POST" action="j_security_check">
                Username: <input type="text" name="j_username" />
                Password: <input type="password" name="j_password" />
                <br />
                <input type="submit" value="Login" />
                <input type="reset" value="Reset" />
            </form>
        </p>
    </h:body>
</html>
```

When users point their browsers to the login.xhtml view, they will be prompted to log in to the application.

How It Works

Securing an application is a vital step for any enterprise application. Adding the security of a user name and login is one of the most basic forms of security that can be put into place. The combination of GlassFish or Payara application server, the underlying database, and some basic Java EE application configurations make securing applications via user name and password an easy task. The solution to this recipe demonstrates how to configure a security realm within the application server that will utilize a database table for storing user name and password combinations. While some of the database code in this solution is specific to Oracle Database, the same technique can be applied to most RDBMSs with only minor modifications made to the code for securing the password within the database.

The first step toward configuring the security realm within GlassFish or Payara is to set up the underlying database table that will be used to contain the security credentials. It is of utmost importance to ensure that password stored within the table are encrypted; otherwise, they can be seen by anyone who has read-only access to the security table that is created for this solution. In the solution to this recipe, the Oracle database `dbms_obfuscation_toolkit.md5` function is used in order to hash the passwords. However, if you're using another database system, there should be similar tools to use for encryption purposes. When configuring the database, a table should be created to hold the user names and passwords, and another should be created to hold the groups, or security roles. This will allow applications using the realm to contain a high level of security configuration in that various levels of access can be granted to different users based on role.

Once the database objects have been created, the server must be configured to utilize the database for authentication purposes. This is done by logging in to the administrative console and setting up a new security realm. There are several pieces of information to fill out on the New Realm form that are used to map the realm to the appropriate database tables and columns. The name given to the realm can be any valid string, and the class name should be `com.sun.enterprise.security.auth.realm.jdbc.JDBCRealm`, since there are a number of different types of security realms that can be created, including LDAP realms, and so on. The remaining information on the form should be filled out according to the directions for each text field. It is important to be sure that the JDBC resource has been configured already and the name given for the JDBC resource matches the one that is provided for the JNDI field on the form.

To configure an application for use with a security realm, the security constraints and login configuration must be specified within the `web.xml` configuration file for the application. Security constraints are used to map designated web folders to different user roles for an application. This means that all of the administrative pages for an application can be placed into a folder, and a security constraint can be set up within the `web.xml` file to limit access to that folder, based on security credentials. If you look at the configuration example in the solution, you can see that there has been a security constraint configured with a display name of `Admin`. Any valid string identifier can be given to the `display-name`, `web-resource-name`, or `description` elements of the security constraint. The `url-pattern` element designates which folder should be protected by the constraint, and anything placed in that folder will be protected from unauthorized users. Each of the `http-method` elements lists the different HTTP methods that pertain to the resources within the given folder. The `auth-constraint` subelement contains the role mapping, which can be given a `description` along with the `role-name` that should be used for limiting access. The specified `role-name` should match one of the group values that was placed within the database table that was created to contain groups. Any user names that correspond to the given group or role will have access to the resources contained within the protected folder, provided that they are able to log in to the application successfully. The `sun-web.xml` configuration file must be updated to contain the mapping of roles to groups if you are deploying to GlassFish. This is done by adding `security-role-mapping` elements to the `sun-web.xml` file, and each of the elements must contain a `role-name` element along with a corresponding `group-name` element.

The final piece of the puzzle is to create a login form. The form must contain an action by the name of j_security_check because this will pass control of the authentication to the application server. The user name and password elements must contain the names of j_username and j_password, respectively. Doing so will allow these elements to be passed to the authentication mechanism properly. When the form is submitted, the user name and password are sent to the authentication mechanism, which is handled by the application server via the security realm you created. If an appropriate user name and password combination is used, the session is granted access to whichever resources have been designated for the authenticated user's role. If the given user's role does not permit access to certain areas of the application via the security-constraints that have been set up within the web.xml file, the user is denied access.

Configuring forms-based authentication is a good means of controlling access to an application. It allows each application to contain its own security infrastructure, providing the ability to limit certain areas of an application to designated roles. The only downside to the use of the JDBC realm is that the password must be stored in the database table. So as long as a good encryption algorithm is used to obfuscate the password, this should be a minimal risk.

■ **Note** To use LDAP authentication instead, set up a security realm using the com.sun.enterprise.security.auth.realm.ldap.LDAPRealm class. Specify a String value for the JAAS context, which will be used to reference the realm. Directory should be set to the URL for the LDAP server that you want to use for authentication. Base DN must be set to the base DN for the user who will be used for authenticating to the LDAP server (use a separate LDAP account for authentication that has read access to the LDAP directory). Additional properties that may be required for your LDAP configuration include search-bind-password, search-bind-dn, and/or search-filter. To learn more about LDAP configuration, reference the online documentation.

12.7. Deploying a Microservice to Payara Micro

Problem

You want to deploy a Java EE application to a lighter application server container that contains only a minimal set of specifications that are necessary to support the application. You also will develop the application that's targeted to provide a specific set of data via web services.

Solution

Develop a minimalistic application that is focused toward providing a set of web services for a targeted set of data. In the following example, a small Java EE web application to host a set of web services for providing book author data will be developed. This small web application will be configured to use only those Java EE 8 specifications that are required for the application functionality. The application will then be deployed to Payara Micro and packaged as an executable JAR file.

■ **Note** This example demonstrates the construction of the Java classes required for the solution. To see the entire solution, including configuration files, see the AuthorService project sources for this book.

To get started, create a new Maven web application named `AuthorService` and add the following dependencies:

- JAX-RS 2.1
- JPA 2.2
- Apache Derby JDBC
- Bean Validation 2.0
- EJB 3.2
- Eclipse Persistence 2.5.2

Once finished, the POM dependencies should look as follows:

```
<dependencies>
    <dependency>
        <groupId>javax.ws.rs</groupId>
        <artifactId>javax.ws.rs-api</artifactId>
        <version>2.1</version>
        <scope>provided</scope>
    </dependency>
    <dependency>
        <groupId>javax.persistence</groupId>
        <artifactId>javax.persistence-api</artifactId>
        <version>2.2</version>
        <scope>provided</scope>
    </dependency>
    <dependency>
        <groupId>javax.validation</groupId>
        <artifactId>validation-api</artifactId>
        <version>2.0.0.Final</version>
    </dependency>
    <dependency>
        <groupId>javax.ejb</groupId>
        <artifactId>javax.ejb-api</artifactId>
        <version>3.2</version>
        <type>jar</type>
    </dependency>
    <dependency>
        <groupId>org.eclipse.persistence</groupId>
        <artifactId>eclipselink</artifactId>
        <version>2.5.2</version>
    </dependency>
    <dependency>
        <groupId>org.eclipse.persistence</groupId>
        <artifactId>org.eclipse.persistence.jpa.modelgen.processor</artifactId>
        <version>2.5.2</version>
        <scope>provided</scope>
    </dependency>
```

```
        <dependency>
            <groupId>org.apache.derby</groupId>
            <artifactId>derbyclient</artifactId>
            <version>10.14.1.0</version>
        </dependency>
    </dependencies>
```

Next, add two Java packages: `org.javaee8recipes.authorservice.entity` and `org.javaee8recipes.authorservice.rest`. Create entity classes for the AUTHOR_WORK, BOOK, BOOK_AUTHOR, and CHAPTER database tables within the entity package. The sources for the `Author` entity class are as follows. Follow the same technique for generating the other entity classes:

```
package org.javaee8recipes.authorservice.entity;

import java.io.Serializable;
import java.math.BigDecimal;
import java.math.BigInteger;
import javax.persistence.*;
import javax.validation.constraints.NotNull;

@Entity
@Table(name = "AUTHOR_WORK")
@NamedQueries({
    @NamedQuery(name = "AuthorWork.findAll", query = "SELECT a FROM AuthorWork a")})
@XmlRootElement
public class AuthorWork implements Serializable {
    private static final long serialVersionUID = 1L;

    @Id
    @Basic(optional = false)
    @NotNull
    @Column(name = "ID")
    private BigDecimal id;
    @Column(name = "BOOK_ID")
    private BigDecimal bookId;
    @JoinColumn(name = "AUTHOR_ID", referencedColumnName = "ID")
    @ManyToOne(optional = false)
    private BookAuthor authorId;

= authorId;

// Getters and Setters

    @Override
    public int hashCode() {
        int hash = 0;
        hash += (id != null ? id.hashCode() : 0);
        return hash;
    }
```

```
    @Override
    public boolean equals(Object object) {
        // TODO: Warning - this method won't work if the id fields are not set
        if (!(object instanceof AuthorWork)) {
            return false;
        }
        AuthorWork other = (AuthorWork) object;
        if ((this.id == null && other.id != null) || (this.id != null && !this.
        id.equals(other.id))) {
            return false;
        }
        return true;
    }

    @Override
    public String toString() {
        return "org.javaee8recipes.entity.AuthorWork[ id=" + id + " ]";
    }

}
```

■ **Note** Remember to annotate each entity class with `@XmlRootElement`, as this is the annotation that enables the entity to be converted into XML format. One of the common web service formats is XML, so you will almost always want to enable this feature.

Next, create a web service class that will query the database return data to web service clients in an appropriate format. To do so, create a class named `BookAuthorFacadeREST` that will contain a number of methods that will query the entity classes and return data to callers in a JSON or XML format. To begin, annotate the class with `@javax.ejb.Stateless` so that the class can perform transactional queries using JPA. Next, annotate with `@javax.ws.rs.Path`, providing a path for which the REST services will be made available via the URI. Inject a `@PersistenceContext` that references the persistence context unit name of your application. Note, you'll need to create a persistence unit for your application, so refer to Recipe 8-3 for more details, if needed. The persistence unit is used to query the data via the JPA API. Since this application will be deployed to Payara Micro instead of a traditional application server, it is a good practice to define the datasource within the `web-xml`, and then refer to the defined datasource from within the `persistence.xml`. Therefore, create a `web.xml` deployment descriptor containing the following configuration:

```
<?xml version="1.0" encoding="UTF-8"?>

<web-app xmlns="http://xmlns.jcp.org/xml/ns/javaee"
         xmlns:xsi="http://www.w3.org/2001/XMLSchema-instance"
         xsi:schemaLocation="http://xmlns.jcp.org/xml/ns/javaee http://xmlns.jcp.org/xml/ns/
javaee/web-app_3_1.xsd"
         version="3.1">
    <session-config>
        <session-timeout>
            30
        </session-timeout>
    </session-config>
```

```
    <data-source>
        <name>java:global/DerbyDataSource</name>
        <class-name>org.apache.derby.jdbc.ClientDriver</class-name>
        <server-name>localhost</server-name>
        <port-number>1527</port-number>
        <url>jdbc:derby://localhost:1527/acme</url>
        <user>acmeuser</user>
        <password>yourpassword</password>
    </data-source>
</web-app>
```

Finally, write the methods that will be used to query the database and return the data in the appropriate format. In this case, the methods will return BookAuthor data. One of the methods will return all of the records in the BOOK_AUTHOR database table, while the other will return a BOOK_AUTHOR record that contains the matching ID.

```
package org.javaee8recipes.authorservice.rest;

import java.math.BigDecimal;
import java.util.List;
import javax.ejb.Stateless;
import javax.persistence.EntityManager;
import javax.persistence.NoResultException;
import javax.persistence.PersistenceContext;
import javax.ws.rs.GET;
import javax.ws.rs.Path;
import javax.ws.rs.PathParam;
import javax.ws.rs.Produces;
import javax.ws.rs.core.MediaType;
import org.javaee8recipes.authorservice.entity.BookAuthor;

@Stateless
@Path("bookAuthor")
public class BookAuthorFacadeREST {

    @PersistenceContext(unitName = "AuthorService_1.0PU")
    private EntityManager em;

    @GET
    @Path("{id}")
    @Produces({MediaType.APPLICATION_XML, MediaType.APPLICATION_JSON})
    public BookAuthor find(@PathParam("id") BigDecimal id) {
        BookAuthor bookAuthor = null;
        try {
            bookAuthor = (BookAuthor)
                    em.createQuery("select object(o) from BookAuthor o " +
                    "where o.id = :id")
                    .setParameter("id", id)
                    .getSingleResult();
        } catch (NoResultException ex){
```

```
            System.out.println("Error: "  + ex);
        }
        return bookAuthor;
    }

    @GET
    @Produces({MediaType.APPLICATION_XML, MediaType.APPLICATION_JSON})
    public List<BookAuthor> findAll() {
        List<BookAuthor> bookAuthors = null;
        try {
            bookAuthors = em.createQuery("select object(o) from BookAuthor o")
                    .getResultList();
        } catch (NoResultException ex){
            System.out.println("Error: "  + ex);
        }
        return bookAuthors;
    }

    protected EntityManager getEntityManager() {
        return em;
    }

}
```

Lastly for the application, create the `ApplicationConfig` class, which will be used to configure JAX-RS for the application.

```
@javax.ws.rs.ApplicationPath("rest")
public class ApplicationConfig extends Application {
    @Override
    public Set<Class<?>> getClasses() {
        Set<Class<?>> resources = new java.util.HashSet<>();
        resources.add(org.javaee8recipes.authorservice.rest.BookAuthorFacadeREST.class);
        return resources;
    }
}
```

The application should now be ready to deploy to an application server. As such, it is deployable to GlassFish 5 or Payara 5 and it should work without issue. However, for this solution we want to deploy via the sleek and compact Payara Micro server, which will package the application for use in a microservices environment. Follow these steps in order to deploy to Payara Micro:

1. Download the latest release of Payara Micro from the Payara website at `https://www.payara.fish/payara_micro`.

2. Place the Payara Micro JAR file into the directory of your choice on your machine and execute the file using your Java Runtime Environment:

```
java -jar payara-micro-4.1.2.174.jar --deploy AuthorService.war
```

The output will show the server start and, if everything is successful, a message similar to the following will be displayed:

```
Instance Configuration
Host: localhost
HTTP Port(s): 8080
HTTPS Port(s):
Instance Name: Amused-Rockfish
Instance Group: MicroShoal
Hazelcast Member UUID 810e3d71-ccdd-4d56-b668-90d7081af500
Deployed: AuthorService ( AuthorService war /AuthorService )

]]

[] [INFO] [] [PayaraMicro] [tid: _ThreadID=1 _ThreadName=main] [timeMillis: 1511931917617]
[levelValue: 800] [[

Payara Micro URLs
http://localhost:8080/AuthorService

'AuthorService' REST Endpoints
GET   /AuthorService/rest/bookAuthor
GET   /AuthorService/rest/bookAuthor/{id}

]]

 [] [INFO] [] [PayaraMicro] [tid: _ThreadID=1 _ThreadName=main] [timeMillis: 1511931917617]
[levelValue: 800] Payara Micro  4.1.2.174 #badassmicrofish (build 192) ready in 16,304 (ms)
```

The `bookAuthor` service will be available at `http://localhost:8080/AuthorService/rest/bookAuthor/`.

How It Works

The Payara Micro container is a convenient and minimalistic server for running Java EE applications. The Payara Micro container is less than 70MB. It automatically clusters with other Payara Micro instances, and it runs without any need for installation. On top of that, it is compatible with Eclipse Microprofile, which makes it easy to run standardized Java EE microservices.

In this recipe, a simple Java EE application "microservice" is created and deployed to Payara Micro. To create the minimalistic application, create a Maven web application and include only the Java EE APIs that are required for running the application as dependencies. In this case, those dependencies include JAX-RS, JPA, Bean Validation, and EJB. Two other dependencies are required for running the application, those being Apache Derby JDBC driver and the Eclipse Persistence JPA implementation. Payara Micro provides support for most of the Java EE specifications along with a good number of other commonly used APIs, including:

- Servlets, JSTL, EL, and JSPs
- WebSockets
- JSF
- JAX-RS

- EJB Lite
- JTA
- JPA
- Bean Validation
- CDI
- Interceptors
- JBatch
- Concurrency
- JCache
- JCA
- Configs (Microprofile Specific)
- Healthcheck (Microprofile)
- JWT - JSON Web Token (Microprofile)
- Fault Tolerance (Microprofile)

As seen in the example, to create the `SimpleService` application, include the `AuthorWork` entity class. Create a `web.xml` deployment descriptor for the application and define a `data-source` within it, which will be used to connect to the Apache Derby database. A persistence unit can then be created for use by the application JPA calls. Configuring the datasource within the deployment descriptor makes it easy to deploy on Payara Micro, as no server-side configuration is necessary.

This simple application contains a handful of entity classes, which map to database tables that are required for querying the `BOOK_AUTHOR` database table. The entity classes are then used to create RESTful services in the `BookAuthorFacadeREST` class. This class contains two simple REST services, each of them `@GET` services. This means that these services will be used to retrieve data. The `find()` method creates a service that allows you to query for a `BookAuthor` entity that matches a given ID. That ID can be specified within the URI when calling upon the service. The `findAll()` method simply returns all `BookAuthor` results in XML or JSON format. For more details on developing RESTful web services, refer to Chapter 15.

The `ApplicationConfig` class registers the JAX-RS classes with the API itself, so as to make the RESTful services available for use. The class extends the `Application` abstract class, which allows `getClasses()` to be overridden to return the list of JAX-RS resources for the application. In this case, the only JAX-RS resource is `org.javaee8recipes.authorservice.rest.BookAuthorFacadeREST.class`. The `@ApplicationPath` annotation provides the path that should be used within the URI to access the RESTful services.

Once the application has been compiled, it can be easily deployed to Payara Micro by invoking the Payara Micro JAR file with a local Java runtime and passing the `--deploy` flag with the invocation call, providing the complete path to the resulting WAR file from compilation of the application.

```
java -jar payara-micro-4.1.2.174.jar --deploy AuthorService.war
```

It is also possible to deploy an exploded WAR application to Payara Micro. An exploded WAR is simply the contents of a WAR file extracted into a folder. A WAR file can be extracted by simply changing the `.war` extension to `.zip` and extracting the contents. If you are using a Maven-based application, the project directory will contain a target directory after compilation. Inside of the target directory will be the exploded WAR, along with a number of other folders, including the WAR file itself. It is sometimes beneficial to deploy an exploded WAR if you want to change those files that do not require recompiling (XHTML, JS, CSS, HTML, JSP, etc.) without recompiling the war. To deploy to an exploded WAR, simply pass the path of the exploded WAR directory to the `--deploy` option.

```
java -jar payara-micro-4.1.2.174.jar --deploy /path-to-authorservice/AuthorService
```

Payara Micro makes it possible to deploy multiple applications at once by simply listing the `--deploy` option multiple times, once for each application being deployed:

```
java -jar payara-micro-4.1.2.174.jar --deploy AuthorService1.war --deploy AuthorService2.war
```

If you want to place a number of WAR files in the same directory, Payara Micro can also pick up all WARs within that directory and deploy them at once using the `--deploymentDir` option. Simply pass the path to the directory containing the WAR files using the `--deploymentDir` option.

Lastly, Payara Micro makes it possible to deploy directly from a Maven repository by specifying the `--deployFromGAV` option. To use this option, pass a comma-separated string containing the Maven repository's `groupId`, `artifactId`, and version attributes. You can also search for deployment artifacts in additional Maven repositories by specifying the `--additionalRepository` option and passing the URI to the repository.

Payara Micro provides a number of options for deploying Java EE applications and microservices. This server allows you to deploy applications with little to no configuration necessary. In many cases, microservices are deployed as JAR files. Payara Micro also makes this possible, and the next recipe covers more about this option.

12.8. Packaging a Web Application with Payara Micro as an Executable JAR

Problem

Not only do you want to run your Java EE application using a light application server container, but you also want to deploy it as an executable JAR file, rather than host via a web server.

Solution

Deploy your WAR file to Payara Micro using one of the options outlined in Recipe 12-7 and specify the `--outputUberJar` option, passing the name that you would like to specify for the resulting JAR file. If you're using the same example shown in Recipe 12-7, the following invocation of Payara Micro will create an Uber JAR named `BookAuthor.jar`:

```
java -jar payara-micro-4.1.2.174.jar --deploy AuthorService-1.0.war --outputUberJar
AuthorService.jar
```

Once the `AuthorService.jar` has been created, it can be executed using the following command from the command line or terminal:

```
java -jar AuthorService.jar
```

Once it's been executed, the application will start up just as if you were deploying the WAR file to Payara Micro, and once startup is complete you can invoke the web service using URLs or endpoints displayed from the output in the terminal. Here is an excerpt from the terminal after execution of the JAR file—the port number may vary depending on whether port 8080 is busy:

```
Payara Micro URLs
http://localhost:8080/AuthorService-1.0

'AuthorService-1.0' REST Endpoints
GET     /AuthorService-1.0/rest/bookAuthor
GET     /AuthorService-1.0/rest/bookAuthor/{id}
```

If you would like to deploy more than one WAR file to a single JAR file, then simply specify more than one `--deploy` option (one for each WAR), pointing to the respective WAR files that you want to package into the JAR. At JAR startup, the output in the terminal will indicate each of the different WAR files that have been started up inside of the container.

■ **Note** If you try to perform multiple deployments from separate terminals, you will need to run them on different ports using the `--port` option when executing the Uber JAR and specifying a different port for each.

How It Works

The Payara Micro server makes it easy to create executable JAR files that package the entire application server along with one or more applications. When the resulting JAR file(s) are executed, all of the WAR files deployed within the embedded container are started. This is a great way to deploy a number of services together at once.

The `--outputUberJar` deployment option makes it possible to generate an executable JAR file that contains the server, along with all applications that you deploy to it. As seen in the example, one or more applications can be deployed to a single JAR file. If you want to create multiple JAR files and execute them at the same time in the same environment, then the `--port` option can be used to indicate separate ports for each executable instance.

There are a number of options that can be passed to the Payara Micro JAR when you're deploying and creating an Uber JAR. Each of these options allows for customization of the container. For example, by default each instance is auto-clusterable, meaning that it will cluster with other running instances automatically. To disable this functionality, pass `--noCluster = true`.

12.9. Deploying Payara Micro Apps on Docker

Problem

You want to deploy your Java EE application to a portable container that can be deployed in almost any environment. You also want to ensure that your container is stable so that it will run exactly the same, regardless of the environment into which it is deployed.

Solution

Install Docker on your machine, then pull a Docker image of Payara Micro. Use the Payara Micro image to start up a Payara Micro container and deploy your Java EE applications to the container. This recipe covers the basics of running Payara Micro within a Docker container via the deployment of the AuthorService application that was generated for Recipe 12-7.

Perform the following steps to obtain an image of Payara Micro for Docker. From this point forward, it is assumed that Docker has been installed and configured on your machine. To get started, open a command line or terminal and issue the following command to pull the latest Payara Micro 5 image:

```
docker pull payara/micro:5-SNAPSHOT
```

Once the image has been downloaded, it can be started up by issuing the following command:

```
docker run -p 8080:8080 payara/micro java -jar /opt/payara/payara-micro.jar
```

Once the container is started, you can use it as a local application server. However, no applications are deployed by default. To stop the running container, determine the container ID by typing docker ps:

```
Juneau$ docker ps
CONTAINER ID        IMAGE               COMMAND                        CREATED
STATUS              PORTS
NAMES
b34de6907615        payara/micro        "java -jar /opt/pa..."
```

Use the container ID to stop the container by issuing docker stop <<container id>>. A new container can be started with a deployed Java EE application. In this case, we deploy the AuthorService application. This recipe covers one means for creating a docker container, configuring it accordingly, and deploying an application to it. Such orchestration can be achieved via a dockerfile. To create a dockerfile for the AuthorService application, either create a new text file and save it in the project directory, providing a name of Dockerfile without an extension. Place the following lines within the dockerfile:

```
# Using the Payara Micro 5 snapshot build (previously pulled)
FROM payara/micro:5-SNAPSHOT

# Downloads the Apache Derby JDBC JAR
RUN wget -O $PAYARA_PATH/derbyclient-10.14.1.0.jar http://central.maven.org/maven2/org/
apache/derby/derbyclient/10.14.1.0/derbyclient-10.14.1.0.jar

# Adds an application to be loaded
ADD AuthorService-1.0.war $PAYARA_PATH

ENTRYPOINT ["java", "-jar", "/opt/payara/payara-micro.jar", "--addJars", "/opt/payara/
derbyclient-10.14.1.0.jar", "--deploy", "/opt/payara/AuthorService-1.0.war"]
```

To execute the dockerfile, ensure that you have a terminal or command line open and traverse inside of the project directory so that you are in the same area as the dockerfile. Execute the following statement:

```
docker build -t authorservice_image .
```

Next, to run the container, issue the `docker run` command as follows:

```
docker run -i -t -p 8080:8080 authorservice_image
```

How It Works

Utilizing a container system such as Docker makes it possible to build a portable package, which can then be moved between different hosts. Docker is essentially a virtual machine repository, which allows you to create a container that runs an operating system such as Ubuntu, along with any service that you want to install within that container. The beauty of a system such as Docker is that the container can be created and destroyed very quickly, and the creation of a container can be scripted. By scripting the creation of a container, it enables the possibility for creating portable containers, deploying application servers to those containers, configuring accordingly, and lastly deploying applications to those containers. In the recipe example, one such script is demonstrated, which deploys a Payara Micro container, installs an Apache Derby database driver, and deploys a Java EE application.

■ **Note** This recipe covers only the very basics of running a Docker container. Refer to the online Docker documentation for a full tutorial at `https://docs.docker.com`.

To begin using Docker, install to your OS according to the online documentation found at `https://docs.docker.com/manuals/`. Once it's been installed, you can download or create images within the Docker repository. Docker images are essentially virtual machines or containers, which when started up, run a virtual environment within the host machine. In this recipe, it is assumed that Docker has been installed on the operating system. The next step after installation is to obtain a Payara Micro image that can be used to build a container. This is done using the `docker pull` command. The `pull` command tells Docker to obtain an image or repository from a registry. For example, the following command tells Docker to obtain the Payara Micro 5 snapshot and store it in the local repository.

```
docker pull payara/micro:5-SNAPSHOT
```

The image that has been obtained is a basic Payara Micro container. It can be used to create a fully configured container to which Java EE applications can be installed and executed. To simply run the image as-is, issue the `docker run` command as seen in the example for this recipe. If so desired, the container can be started and you can log in to the admin console and deploy applications. However, typically you need to script a container creation and configuration so that the script can be executed to recreate the container on demand. A dockerfile can be used to script the configuration and deployment of an application. In this recipe, a dockerfile is created that will pull from the Payara Micro 5 image, and it then downloads a copy of the Apache Derby JDBC driver JAR and places it into the Payara path.

Next, the dockerfile adds the WAR file for the Java EE application that is being deployed. Lastly, an `ENTRYPOINT` is generated, which uses the Java executable to start up Payara Micro. It then passes the `--addJars` option to add the Apache Derby JAR to the deployment and passes the `--deploy` option to specify the application that is to be deployed.

To build the image, traverse into the same directory as the dockerfile and issue `docker build`, along with any options that are required. In the example, the `-t` option is specified to provide the name of the image. Lastly to run the container, execute `docker run -i -t <<image name>>`. The `-i` is used to keep session as interactive, and the `-t` option is used to specify to allocate a `pseudo-TTY`. The `-p` option is used to map container ports to the host ports. Once issued, the container will start up and you should be able to open a browser and navigate to the application using the application name and specifying the port. In this case, navigate to `http://localhost:8080/AuthorService-1.0/`.

Utilization of a Docker container to deploy applications provides one of the most portable options for packaging. You only need Docker to be installed on a host in order to run the container. This recipe only covers the very minimum to get started with Docker. There are a number of other options, such as linking containers together using bridged networking. Such an option is useful when deploying multiple containers, such as a database server in one Docker container and a Java EE application in a different Docker container. The possibilities are endless, and when you mix Payara Micro with Docker, it makes the possibilities even more flexible.

CHAPTER 13

Contexts and Dependency Injection

One of the most important specifications in the Java EE platform is Contexts and Dependency Injection (CDI). As stated on the `cdi-spec.org` site, it is a suite of complementary services that can improve the overall structure and design of code. The specification provides the following features for Java EE and Java SE applications, as per the `cdi-spec.org`:

- Contextual objects with a well-defined lifecycle providing multiple scopes of availability
- Ability to bind directly between contextual objects and Unified Expression Language (EL)
- Dependency injection utilizing a type-safe system that is easy to use
- Binding of interceptors to contextual objects
- Event notification model
- Portable extension SPI

Mentioned in the listing, perhaps one of the most widely used features of CDI is the ability bind the web tier and the business logic or transactional tier of the Java EE platform together. CDI makes it easy to expose business objects for use within web views via EL so that developers can directly bind JSF view components to public JavaBean members and methods. Another widely used feature is the injection contextual classes and resources into other Java objects in a type-safe and efficient manner.

CDI is architected from two methodologies: contexts and dependency injection. *Contexts* provide the ability to bind the lifecycle and interactions of stateful components to well-defined but extensive contexts. In the Java EE 8 tutorial, *dependency injection* is defined as the ability to inject components into an application in a type-safe way, including the ability to choose at deployment time which implementation of a particular interface to inject. To use CDI, a developer should become familiar with a series of annotations that can be used to decorate objects and injected components. This chapter covers recipes that demonstrate such annotations and where they should be used.

Since CDI provides a high level of loose coupling, it is an important piece of any Java enterprise application. Those applications that use CDI the right way can become very efficient because CDI provides a decoupling of resources, as well as strong typing, eliminating the requirement to use string-based names for managed resources by using declarative Java. This chapter covers widely used features of this important specification, touching on a few new features, including asynchronous events, and an API for booting CDI in Java SE environments.

J. Juneau, *Java EE 8 Recipes*, https://doi.org/10.1007/978-1-4842-3594-2_13

13-1. Injecting a Contextual Bean or Other Object

Problem

You would like to utilize a contextual bean or other object from within another class to take advantage of the bean's state.

Solution

Utilize dependency injection to make the bean or object available from within another class. The following class represents an object that can be injected into another class:

```
package org.javaee8recipes.chapter13;
import javax.inject.Named;

@Named
public class CalculationBean {

    public int addNumbers(int[] numArray){
        int temp = 0;
        for(int x : numArray){
            temp = temp + x;
        }
        return temp;
    }

}
```

As you can see, the CalculationBean class represents a standard Java object. This object can be injected into another class by using the @Inject annotation. The following class, located in the same package as CalculationBean within the sources, demonstrates how to inject an object. Note that CalculationBean is never specifically instantiated; rather, it is injected.

```
package org.javaee8recipes.chapter13;

import javax.inject.Inject;

public class UsingClass {

    @Inject
    CalculationBean calcBean;

    public void performCalculation(){
        int[] intarr = new int[2];
        intarr[0] = 2;
        intarr[1] = 3;
        System.out.println("The sum of 2 + 3:" + calcBean.addNumbers(intarr));
    }

}
```

In the example, `@Default CalculationBean` is injected into the bean. Once the bean or resource is injected into another Java class, it can be referenced as if it were local to the class into which it was injected.

How It Works

The concept of dependency injection greatly reduces the amount of overhead that is necessary for a developer in order to gain reference to a contextual Java object from within another Java class. The Java EE stack makes it very easy to gain reference to just about any Java object from within another class. Dependency injection refers to the ability to inject components into an application in a type-safe manner, including the ability to choose at deployment time which implementation of a particular interface to inject. CDI allows almost any Java object to be injected into another with very little configuration. This ability increases the usability of resources since such resources can be referenced from any number of different classes and maintain the same state wherever they are being used. In reality, just about any object can be injected anywhere with CDI. The following are some Java objects that can be injected:

- Almost any Java class
- Session beans
- Java EE resources: data sources, JMS topics, queues, connection factories
- Persistence contexts
- Producer fields
- Objects returned by producer methods
- Web service references
- Remote EJB references

To inject a resource into another, the application module or JAR file must contain a `META-INF` directory that includes a `beans.xml` configuration file. The `beans.xml` file may be empty, or it can contain a descriptor to customize the way in which component scanning will occur within the application. As such, configuration within `beans.xml` may be slightly different depending on the bean discovery mode for the application. However, for the purposes of this example (and for most general CDI use cases), the `beans.xml` file specifies that bean discovery should occur for all classes within the application.

```
<?xml version="1.0" encoding="UTF-8"?>

<beans xmlns="http://xmlns.jcp.org/xml/ns/javaee"
       xmlns:xsi="http://www.w3.org/2001/XMLSchema-instance"
       xsi:schemaLocation="http://xmlns.jcp.org/xml/ns/javaee http://xmlns.jcp.org/xml/ns/
javaee/beans_1_1.xsd"
       version="1.1" bean-discovery-mode="all">
</beans>
```

The `bean-discovery-mode` attribute indicates how scanning will occur. A value of `all` indicates that all components are processed, `annotated` indicates that only those components containing a class-level annotation are processed, and none effectively disables CDI.

Next, the javax.inject.Inject annotation (@Inject) must be used to denote the class being injected by annotating a class member of the object type. For instance, if you want to inject a Java object of TypeA, you would declare a class variable of type TypeA and annotate it with @Inject, as follows:

```
@Inject
TypeA myTypeVar;
```

Note that the object used for injection (CalculationBean) contains an @Named annotation at the class level. This particular annotation doesn't need to be present in order to make the object available for injection unless the bean-discovery-mode="annotated". The @Named annotation allows one to provide a custom name for the object, and it also makes the object available for reference from within Unified Expression Language.

Once said injection is performed, the declared field can be utilized throughout the class because it is a direct reference to the original class of the specified Java type. By defining a specific scope to the injection bean (see Recipe 13-5), you can indicate whether an injected object will cause the instantiation of a new object of that type or whether it will look up an existing object of that type and reuse it. By far, one of the most convenient and useful cases for using CDI is the ability to inject a managed bean into another object and use its current state, as if its contents existed everywhere.

CDI provides type-safe injection because there is no need to specify a string-based name in order to instantiate or refer to another object. By maintaining declared variables that are used as points of injection, the variable name itself provides for strong typing and thus reduces the number of errors that may arise.

13-2. Binding a Bean to a Web View

Problem

You want to bind a JavaBean to a JSF view using Unified Expression Language (EL).

Solution

Annotate a class with the @Named annotation, and optionally specify a name for the class in String format. The String that is specified within the @Named annotation can be used to gain reference to the bean from within a JSF view. If no optional string is specified, then the class name with a lowercase first letter is used to gain reference. The following example demonstrates the binding of a bean field and method to a JSF view. The following Java class, named CalculationBean, is a CDI managed bean that contains the @Named annotation, specifying myBean as the bean reference name:

```
import javax.enterprise.context.RequestScoped;
import javax.inject.Named;

@Named("myBean")
@RequestScoped
public class CalculationBean implements java.io.Serializable{

    private int num1 = 1;
    private int num2 = 0;
    private int sum;

    public CalculationBean(){
    }
```

```
    public void addNumbers(){
        System.out.println("Called");
        setSum(getNum1() + getNum2());
    }

    //getters and setters ...

}
```

The bean is bound to the JSF view via the string-based name myBean, making a seamless binding between the web view and the backend business logic. The following JSF view contains three fields and a JSF commandButton component with an action that is bound to myBean via the JSF EL:

```
<html xmlns="http://www.w3.org/1999/xhtml"
      xmlns:f="http://xmlns.jcp.org/jsf/core"
      xmlns:h="http://xmlns.jcp.org/jsf/html">
    <h:head>
        <meta http-equiv="Content-Type" content="text/html; charset=UTF-8"/>
        <title>Recipe 13-2: Binding a Bean to a Web View</title>

    </h:head>
    <h:body>
        <p>
            <h:form>
            <h:inputText value="#{myBean.num1}"/>
            <br/>
            <h:inputText value="#{myBean.num2}"/>

            <br/><br/>
            Sum: <h:outputText id="sum" value="#{myBean.sum}"/>

            <br/><br/>
            <h:commandButton value="Calculate" type="submit" action="#{myBean.addNumbers}">

            </h:commandButton>
            </h:form>
        </p>
    </h:body>
</html>
```

As mentioned previously, when the @Named annotation is specified without providing a string-based name designation, a binding name will be derived from the class name, converting the first letter of the class name to lowercase. For the following example, assume that the class CalculationBean that was referenced in the previous example is going to be referenced from within a JSF view via EL, except there will be no string-based identifier specified within the @Named annotation. Since the @Named annotation does not specify a name, the EL would refer to the class name as such:

```
<html xmlns="http://www.w3.org/1999/xhtml"
      xmlns:f="http://xmlns.jcp.org/jsf/core"
      xmlns:h="http://xmlns.jcp.org/jsf/html">
```

```
    <h:head>
        <meta http-equiv="Content-Type" content="text/html; charset=UTF-8"/>
        <title>Recipe 13-2: Binding a Bean to a Web View</title>

    </h:head>
    <h:body>
        <p>
            <h:form>
            <h:inputText value="#{calculationBean.num1}"/>
            <br/>
            <h:inputText value="#{ calculationBean.num2}"/>

            <br/><br/>
            Sum: <h:outputText id="sum" value="#{ calculationBean.sum}"/>

            <br/><br/>
            <h:commandButton value="Calculate" type="submit" action="#{ calculationBean.
            addNumbers()}">

            </h:commandButton>
            </h:form>
        </p>
    </h:body>
</html>
```

@MANAGEDBEAN VS. @NAMED?

If the `@Named` annotation can be used to specify a binding name for a CDI bean, then what is the point of using the `@ManagedBean` annotation at all? The fact is, the `@ManagedBean` annotation has been carried over from previous versions of JSF. While it is still a capable mechanism of marking a bean as managed and providing a binding identifier to JSF, it is suggested for use only when CDI is not available for an application. If an application has full access to the entire Java EE stack, including CDI, then the `@ManagedBean` annotation is not a requirement.

In reality, the CDI technology is much more powerful than the use of `@ManagedBean`, which was a customized solution for JSF, and therefore CDI is the preferred technique to use. This is the preferred technique because CDI allows for a broader base of classes to be categorized as managed resources. CDI also carries with it many other bonuses such as transaction management and type-safe dependency injection, of which `@ManagedBean` is not capable. As of JSF 2.3, there are also certain capabilities that are only available when using CDI, and `@ManagedBean` has become a deprecated technology.

How It Works

One of the most widely used features of CDI is that it helps provide a seamless integration between the web views and the backend business logic for an application. Utilizing CDI, public bean members and methods can be made accessible to JSF views very easily. The `javax.inject.Named` annotation provides a facility for referencing a JavaBean class from within a JSF view, either by accepting a string that will be used to make the reference or by simply utilizing the JavaBean class name with a lowercase first letter. The solutions provided in this recipe demonstrate both techniques. From a technical standpoint, the example of not using a string to provide the reference is the most type-safe solution. However, sometimes it is necessary to provide a string for reference, as demonstrated in the first example, but that solution is recommended only on an as-needed basis.

■ **Note** Notice that the bean in the example, `CalculationBean`, contains an `@RequestScoped` annotation. This annotation specifies the scope for the bean state. For a fun trick, try to remove the `@RequestScoped` annotation and see what happens. As it turns out, the bean will still work as prescribed, but it will not return any results. This is because the bean will be reinitialized after each request. Therefore, the view will call the `getSum` method to read the current contents of the `sum` field, and it will have been reinitialized to a value of 0 before the request has been made. To learn more about bean scope, see Recipe 13-4.

By annotating a class with `@Named`, it becomes available for use by JSF views within the same application. Any public class member or method can be called upon from within a JSF view by specifying the name of the class with a lowercase first letter, along with the public member or method that is needed. For instance, the following JSF EL expression calls upon a method named `myMethod` that is contained within a class named `MyClass`. Note that this EL expression works if the class is named `MyClass` and includes an empty `@Named` annotation and if the class is named something different and includes the `@Named("myClass")` annotation.

```
#{myClass.myMethod}
```

As mentioned in the sidebar for this recipe, the `@ManagedBean` and `@Named` annotations play similar roles in that they both make Java classes available for use within a web view. However, it is safe to acknowledge that the `@Named` annotation is preferred over using `@ManagedBean`; read the sidebar for more information.

13-3. Allocating a Specific Bean for Injection

Problem

You have more than one JavaBean that implements a particular API, and you want to specify which of the beans you want to inject.

Solution

Utilize a qualifier for the injection. To alleviate the issues of referencing a duplicate class, add a qualifier to each of the classes to differentiate them from one another. In the following code example, two classes, named `PaperbackController` and `EbookController`, each implement the `Book` interface. To allow client bean developers to specify which of the bean classes should be injected, qualifiers are used. In the first listing, let's take a look at the `Book` interface, which is being implemented by at least two JavaBeans in the example.

```
public interface Book {
    public String title = null;
    public String description = null;
}
```

The class PaperbackController uses a qualifier @Paperback in order to differentiate it from other beans that implement the Book interface. The following listing is that of the PaperbackController class. Note that the Paperback interface (source shown next) must already exist in order to utilize the @Paperback annotation in this example.

```
package org.javaee8recipes.chapter13.recipe13_03;

import javax.inject.Named;
import javax.enterprise.context.SessionScoped;
import java.io.Serializable;

@Named(value = "paperbackController")
@SessionScoped
@Paperback
public class PaperbackController implements Serializable, Book {

    /**
     * Creates a new instance of PaperbackController
     */
    public PaperbackController() {
    }
...
}
```

Another JavaBean, named EbookController, also implements the Book interface. It contains a different qualifier, @Ebook, in order to differentiate it from other classes implementing the Book interface. The EbookController class looks like the following:

```
package org.javaee8recipes.chapter13.recipe13_03;

import javax.inject.Named;
import javax.enterprise.context.SessionScoped;
import java.io.Serializable;

@Named(value = "ebookController")
@SessionScoped
@Ebook
public class EbookController implements Serializable, Book {

    /**
     * Creates a new instance of EbookController
     */
    public EbookController() {

    }
...
}
```

Lastly, let's see what the @Paperback and @Ebook binding annotations actually look like. The following two code listings show the contents of the org.javaee8recipes.chapter13.recipe13_03.Paperback and org.javaee8recipes.chapter13.recipe13_03.Ebook interfaces, which are used to create the two annotations:

```
import java.lang.annotation.*;
import javax.inject.Qualifier;

@Qualifier
@Retention(RetentionPolicy.RUNTIME)
@Target({ElementType.TYPE, ElementType.METHOD, ElementType.FIELD, ElementType.PARAMETER})
public @interface Paperback {}

import java.lang.annotation.*;
import javax.inject.Qualifier;

@Qualifier
@Retention(RetentionPolicy.RUNTIME)
@Target({ElementType.TYPE, ElementType.METHOD, ElementType.FIELD, ElementType.PARAMETER})
public @interface Ebook {}
```

When a client wants to use one or the other, it simply needs to call on the qualifier as follows:

```
@Paperback PaperbackController paperback;
@Ebook EbookController ebook;
```

How It Works

When there are two or more classes that implement the same Java interface, CDI needs some help to determine which of them is going to be used at an injection point. If an application that uses CDI is deployed and an attempt is made to perform injection on a class that implements the same interface as another class, then Weld will throw an ambiguous dependency error. This means that it cannot determine what bean to use for the given injection point. When CDI attempts to determine which bean should be used at an injection point, it takes all class types into account, and it also uses qualifiers. A qualifier is an annotation that can be applied at the class level to indicate the type of a bean. Qualifiers can also be used to annotate methods, or other areas of code, to help CDI determine what kind of bean needs to be injected.

■ **Note** Weld is the reference implementation for CDI. Therefore, you will see references to Weld within the server logs when utilizing CDI within a Java EE application. For more information regarding Weld, see the online documentation at http://seamframework.org/Weld.

Every bean without an explicit qualifier automatically becomes annotated with the @Default qualifier. This qualifier is not needed when another qualifier type is used. In the solution to this recipe, two qualifiers are created in order to mark two different beans of the Book type: the @Paperback and @Ebook qualifiers. To create a qualifier, generate a Java interface and annotate that interface with @Qualifier, Retention(RetentionPolicy.RUNTIME), and @Target({ElementType.TYPE, ElementType.METHOD, ElementType.FIELD, ElementType.PARAMETER}). All qualifiers are created in the same manner, and once created, they can be used to annotate beans for differentiation. As you can see from the example, both the

PaperbackController and EbookController classes have been annotated with their respective qualifiers. This makes for an easy way to allow CDI to determine which bean to inject since each of the two beans are different implementations of the Book type.

The CDI API provides a handful of qualifiers out of the box that can be used in your bean classes. I have already discussed the @Default qualifier, which is added to any bean that does not explicitly contain a qualifier. Other qualifiers that are provided by CDI include @Named and @Any. The @Named qualifier is used to mark a bean as EL-injectable. If a bean contains an @Named qualifier, then it can be referenced within a JSF view. The @Any qualifier is also included on all beans, and it allows an injection point to refer to all beans or events of a certain bean type. For instance, to refer to all of the beans of type Book, you could declare a member as follows:

```
@Inject @Any Instance<Book> anyBook;
```

Qualifiers are not used in everyday code, but they are a feature of Java EE that come in handy on occasions where ambiguous bean injection is possible.

13-4. Determining the Scope of a Bean

Problem

You want to ensure that the scope of a particular bean within your application will be available for a user's entire session.

Solution

Define the scope of the bean that you want to make available by annotating the bean accordingly. The org.javaee8recipes.chapter13.recipe13_03.PaperbackController and org.javaee8recipes.chapter13.recipe13_03.EbookController that are listed in Recipe 13-3 are examples of request-scoped beans since they are annotated as such. To make a bean available within a different scope, annotate using one of the other scope-based annotations. For example, let's create a bean that has a session scope, meaning that it will retain its state for multiple HTTP requests for the life of a web session. To create a session-scoped bean, annotate the class using @SessionScoped. The following class, named CartBean, is a CDI session-scoped JavaBean that contains an integer field, which will be adjusted when a user invokes either the addItem or removeItem method:

```
package org.javaee8recipes.chapter13.recipe13_04;

// Import and change to @RequestScoped to see a functional difference
//import javax.enterprise.context.RequestScoped;
import javax.enterprise.context.SessionScoped;
import javax.inject.Named;

@Named
@SessionScoped
public class CartBean implements java.io.Serializable {

    private int orderList = 0;

    public CartBean(){}
```

```
    public void addItem(){
        setOrderList(getOrderList() + 1);
    }

    public void removeItem(){
        setOrderList(getOrderList() - 1);
    }

    /**
     * @return the orderList
     */
    public int getOrderList() {
        return orderList;
    }

    /**
     * @param orderList the orderList to set
     */
    public void setOrderList(int orderList) {
        this.orderList = orderList;
    }

}
```

■ **Note** The comment within the `CartBean` class indicates that if you change the scope to `@RequestScoped`, you will see a functional difference. The difference is that the `orderList` field will retain its state for only one HTTP request. Therefore, the number will never increase more than 1, and it will never decrease below -1.

What fun would this bean be if you did not use it within a JSF view? Well, let's take a look at a JSF view, named `recipe13_04.xhtml`, which utilizes the `CartBean` class to display the `orderList` field. The view contains two buttons, each of which is bound to different methods that reside within the `CartBean` class. One button will increase the size of the `orderList int`, and the other button will decrease it.

```
<html xmlns="http://www.w3.org/1999/xhtml"
      xmlns:f="http://xmlns.jcp.org/jsf/core"
      xmlns:h="http://xmlns.jcp.org/jsf/html">
    <h:head>
        <meta http-equiv="Content-Type" content="text/html; charset=UTF-8"/>
        <title>Recipe 13-4: Determining the Scope of a Bean</title>

    </h:head>
    <h:body>
        <p>
            <h:form>
            <h:outputText value="#{cartBean.orderList}"/>
            <br/>
```

```
            <br/><br/>
            <h:commandButton value="Add Order" type="submit" action="#{cartBean.
            addItem()}"/>

            <h:commandButton value="Remove Order" type="submit" action="#{cartBean.
            removeItem()}"/>
            </h:form>
        </p>
    </h:body>
</html>
```

How It Works

Depending on an application's requirement, some beans may need to retain state longer than others. Sometimes it makes sense for each user of an application to have its own version of a particular bean, whereas the state of the bean lives and dies with the user's session. Other times it makes more sense for a bean to share its state among all users of an application, and still other times it makes sense for a bean's state to live and die with each user request. To specify the amount of time that a bean will retain its state, annotate the bean class with one of the CDI scope annotations. Table 13-1 describes the different scope annotations.

Table 13-1. *CDI Bean State Annotations*

Annotation	Description
`@RequestScoped`	Per user and retains state for a single HTTP request.
`@SessionScoped`	Per user and retains state across multiple HTTP requests.
`@ApplicationScoped`	Shared state across all user interactions within an application.
`@Dependent`	Object exists to serve one client bean and contains the same lifecycle as the bean. (This is the default scope if none is specified.)
`@ConversationScoped`	Per user scope and is utilized within servlet-based application, such as one that utilizes JSF. Boundaries of the scope are controlled via a developer and extend the scope across multiple invocations of the servlet lifecycle. All long-running conversations are scoped to a particular servlet session and may not cross session boundaries.

While it is easy to define a particular scope for a bean, sometimes it takes some practice and testing to determine the correct scope for a particular application requirement. Moreover, as an application evolves, it makes sense to review the different scopes that have been applied to various beans to ensure that the assigned scope is still desirable.

■ **Note** One of the most common mistakes when working with the scope annotations is importing the wrong annotation for use within the bean. Remember that JavaServer Faces has its own set of scope-based annotations for use within managed beans (only available for backwards compatibility as of JSF 2.3). Always be sure to import from the `javax.enterprise.context.*` package when working with CDI scope or you will achieve erroneous results.

13-5. Injecting Non-Bean Objects

Problem

You want to inject an object that is not a bean into another Java class.

Solution

Use producer fields to inject objects that are not beans, objects that require custom initialization, or objects that may have varying values at runtime. To create a Producer field, annotate a public class field with the javax.injection.Produces annotation and return the field you want to inject. In most cases, you will also need to annotate a producer method with a CDI qualifier so that CDI will know what to inject when called upon.

In this example, a JavaBean named InitalValueController contains a producer field that will be called upon to assign an initial value to CDI bean fields. The following source listing is that of the IntialValueController class, which contains the producer field implementation:

```
package org.javaee8recipes.chapter13.recipe13_05;

import javax.enterprise.inject.Produces;

public class InitialValueController implements java.io.Serializable {

       @Produces @InitValue public int initialValue = 1000;

}
```

The producer field in the class listing contains a qualifier annotation of @InitValue. The qualifier implementation is as follows:

```
package org.javaee8recipes.chapter13.recipe13_05;

import java.lang.annotation.*;
import javax.inject.Qualifier;

@Retention(RetentionPolicy.RUNTIME)
@Target({ElementType.TYPE, ElementType.METHOD, ElementType.FIELD, ElementType.PARAMETER})
@Qualifier
public @interface InitValue {}
```

The producer field can be called upon from anywhere. In this case, it is injected into a CDI bean in order to initialize a bean field value. In the following listing, the CDI bean field named ProducerExample demonstrates how to inject the producer field and use it:

```
package org.javaee8recipes.chapter13.recipe13_05;

import javax.enterprise.context.SessionScoped;
import javax.inject.Inject;
import javax.inject.Named;
```

```
@Named
@SessionScoped
public class ProducerExample implements java.io.Serializable {

    @Inject
    @InitValue
    private int initial;

    private int orderList = -1;

    public ProducerExample(){

    }

    public void addItem(){
        setOrderList(getOrderList() + 1);
    }

    public void removeItem(){
        setOrderList(getOrderList() - 1);
    }

    /**
     * @return the orderList
     */
    public int getOrderList() {
        if (orderList == -1)
            orderList = initial;
        return orderList;
    }

    /**
     * @param orderList the orderList to set
     */
    public void setOrderList(int orderList) {
        this.orderList = orderList;
    }

}
```

When the `orderList` field is added to a JSF view, the `getOrderList` method will be invoked upon the loading of the view because the `orderList` property is called upon from the view. This will, in turn, cause the `orderList` field value to become initialized the first time the JSF view is loaded. The following code demonstrates the use of the field within a JSF view. To see the sources, look at the `chapter13/recipe13_05.xhtml` file.

```
<html xmlns="http://www.w3.org/1999/xhtml"
      xmlns:f="http://xmlns.jcp.org/jsf/core"
      xmlns:h="http://xmlns.jcp.org/jsf/html">
```

```
    <h:head>
        <meta http-equiv="Content-Type" content="text/html; charset=UTF-8"/>
        <title>Recipe 13-5: Injecting Non-Bean Objects</title>

    </h:head>
    <h:body>
        <p>
            <h:form>
            <h:outputText value="#{producerExample.orderList}"/>
            <br/>

            <br/><br/>
            <h:commandButton value="Add Order" type="submit" action="#{producerExample.
            addItem()}"/>

            <h:commandButton value="Remove Order" type="submit" action="#{producerExample.
            removeItem()}"/>
            </h:form>
        </p>
    </h:body>
</html>
```

How It Works

Situations may arise when it makes sense to inject an object other than a CDI managed bean or resource. Objects such as fields, methods, and the like, can become injection targets if they are declared as producers. In some cases, it may make sense to declare a class field as an injectable object. To do so, annotate the field with `javax.enterprise.inject.Produces` (`@Produces`), and the EE container will then treat the field as a getter method for the field. In most cases, a CDI qualifier annotation should also be created and used to annotate the field so that the field can be referenced via the qualifier at the injection point.

In the solution to this recipe, a field that will be used to initialize values is declared within a Java class named `IntitialValueController`. The field name is `initialValue`, and it will return an `int` type, being the number that will be used for initialization. Looking at the code, you can see that a qualifier named `@ InitValue` is also placed at the field declaration. This will allow the injection point to simply refer to the qualifier to gain a handle on the injection target. To use the `initialValue` field, it is injected into a CDI managed bean as follows:

```
@Inject
@InitValue
private int initial;
```

Once injected, the field can be utilized as if it were part of the class into which it was injected. In the case of this example, it is used to initialize the value of the `orderList` field, which is then displayed via a JSF view named `chapter13/recipe13_05.xhtml`.

It is also possible to create producer methods, which can return values that are injectable to a bean or non-Java (JSF) context. In doing so, the `@Produces` annotation is used to annotate the method in the same manner that a field producer is declared. For example, the following method demonstrates the declaration of a producer method that would be used to inject an object of the `Book` type. The method can be called upon in order to return the desired `Book` object type, depending on the type that is passed to it.

```
@Produces @BookQualifier public Book getBook(Book book){

        if(book.equals(EbookController.class))
            return new EbookController();
        else
            return new PaperbackController();
    }
```

In this case, the method also uses a qualifier named @BookQualifier. The producer method result can then be injected into a bean or non-Java context. The injection point references the qualifier in order to make the injection possible, and the producer method is called by the container to obtain the desired instance object as follows:

```
@Inject
@BookQualifier
Book getBook(ebookController);
```

Producers can be a great way to develop injectable objects. With a bit of practice, they can also become valuable for creating sophisticated object factories via the use of a producer method.

13-6. Ignoring Classes

Problem

You want to mark a class as ignored by CDI.

Solution #1

Denote the class with the @Veto annotation. Any class containing the @Veto annotation will be ignored by CDI. The following example demonstrates the use of @Veto:

```
@Veto
public class OrderBean implements java.io.Serializable {

    public OrderBean(){

    }

    // Class Implementation
}
```

Solution #2

Denote the class with the @Requires annotation to mark the class as ignored by CDI if it does not meet the specified requirements. The following example demonstrates how to utilize the @Requires annotation:

```
@Requires("javax.persistence.EntityManager")
public class EmployeeFacade {
    ...
```

```
    @Produces
    public EntityManager getEntityManager(){
        ...
    }
    ...
}
```

In this example, the @Requires annotation has a string containing javax.persistence.EntityManager passed to it. As such, if the specified class is not available and/or the class is unable to fulfill the specified dependency, then it will be ignored by CDI.

How It Works

To veto a bean means to mark it as ignored by CDI. Therefore, if a bean contains the @Veto annotation, it cannot be processed by CDI. A vetoed class will not contain the lifecycle of a contextual instance, and it cannot be injected into other classes. In fact, if a session bean contains the @Veto annotation, it cannot be considered a session bean at all. In some cases, it makes sense to mark a bean as such to ensure that it cannot become managed by CDI. The following code demonstrates how to apply the @Veto annotation to a class.

The @Veto annotation can also be placed on a package declaration, which will prevent all of the beans that are contained within that package from being processed via CDI.

```
@Veto
package org.javaee8recipes.chapter13.*;
...
```

Any of the following definitions on a vetoed type will not be processed:

- Managed beans, session beans, interceptors, decorators
- Observer methods, producer methods, producer fields

The @Requires annotation can be used to conditionally mark a class to be ignored by CDI if it does not meet the specified required criteria. The @Requires annotation accepts a string-based fully qualified class name of the dependency or dependencies. If the object is able to fulfill its dependencies, then it will be managed by CDI. Similar to @Veto, the @Requires annotation can be placed on a package as well. If that package is unable to fulfill the dependency that is denoted by @Requires, then all classes contained within that package will be unmanaged by CDI.

13-7. Disposing of Producer Fields

Problem

Your application uses a producer field, and you want the producer field to be destroyed once it is no longer required for use.

Solution

Mark the producer field with the @Disposes annotation to indicate that it should be removed once it is no longer in use. The following code excerpt demonstrates a producer field that will be removed once it is no longer required for use:

```
...
    @Produces @Disposer
    List<Book> books;
...
```

How It Works

A producer method can be used to generate an object that needs to be removed once it is no longer needed. Much like a finalizer for a class, an object that has been injected via a producer method can contain a method that is invoked when the injected instance is being destroyed. Such a method is known as a *disposer method.* To declare a method as a disposer method, create a method defined within the same class as the producer method. The disposer method must have at least one parameter, with the same type and qualifiers as the producer method. That parameter should be annotated with @Disposes. As of CDI 1.1, this technique can be applied to producer fields.

13-8. Specifying an Alternative Implementation at Deployment Time

Problem

You want to have the ability to code different implementations of an interface and then choose which implementation to utilize when an application is deployed.

Solution

Create a default implementation for an interface, and then create any alternative implementations for that interface and denote them with the @Alternative annotation. Specifying the javax.enterprise.inject.Alternative annotation flags a class as an alternate, and if that class is noted in the beans.xml file, then it will be loaded at deployment time, rather than the default interface implementation.

The following code excerpt demonstrates the use of an alternative class implementation. For the purposes of this demonstration, let's assume that there is already a default implementation for the OrderType interface named BookstoreOrderBean.

```
@Alternative
public class WarehouseOrderBean implements OrderType {
...
}
```

To specify the use of the alternative implementation rather than the default, modify the beans.xml file by listing the alternative class. The following is an example excerpt from the beans.xml file that designates the use of the WarehouseOrderBean:

```
<beans ... >
    <alternatives>
        <class>org.javaee8recipes.chapter13.WarehouseOrderBean</class>
    </alternatives>
</beans>
```

How It Works

Sometimes it makes sense to create two or more implementations of a class for use in different environments. However, it can become a cumbersome nightmare to remove or rename classes in order to build and distribute the correct implementation for each environment. The use of the javax.enterprise.inject.Alternative annotation allows more than one implementation of an interface to be used, and the appropriate implementation can be specified by altering the file before deployment.

13-9. Injecting a Bean and Obtaining Metadata

Problem

You want to acquire metadata information about a bean from within your application classes.

Solution

Inject the interface of a bean into the classes that need to utilize the metadata. Once it's injected, call upon the bean methods to retrieve the required metadata. In the following example, a bean named OtherBean has its metadata injected:

```
@Named("OtherBean")
public class OtherBean {
    @Inject Bean<Order> bean;

    public String getBeanName(){
        return bean.getName();
    }

    public Class<? extends Annotation> getBeanScope(){
        return bean.getScope();
    }
}
```

How It Works

If you need to use bean metadata, you can easily obtain it by injecting the target bean's metadata. To do so, specify the `@Inject` annotation, followed by the `Bean` class of the target bean type. Once the bean interface has been injected, methods can be called upon it to obtain the desired information. Table 13-2 describes the different methods that can be called upon the `Bean` class to obtain metadata.

Table 13-2. *Bean Metadata*

Method	Description
`getName`	Returns the name of the bean
`getBeanClass`	Returns the bean class
`getInjectionPoints`	Returns a `Set` of `InjectionPoint` objects for the bean
`getQualifiers`	Returns a `Set` of qualifier annotations for the bean
`getScope`	Returns the scope of the bean
`getStereotypes`	Returns a `Set` of stereotype data (common metadata) for a bean
`getTypes`	Returns a `Set` of the bean types
`isAlternative`	Returns a boolean to specify whether the bean is an alternative
`isNullable`	Returns a boolean to specify whether a bean can be nullable

13-10. Invoking and Processing Events

Problem

You want to invoke an action when a particular event occurs within your application.

Solution

Process the event in a synchronous or asynchronous manner by creating a CDI event, an optional qualifier, observer, and event handling method. In this scenario, a bookstore wants to send an alert to the book publisher each time a sale occurs. If an online sale occurs, the publisher will receive an alert to indicate as such. Similarly, if an in-store sale occurs, the publisher will receive a different alert to indicate a store sale has occurred. First, create a book event object to contain data elements that need to be made available at event invocation. In this case, some simple data regarding the book, store of sale, number of books, and price will be included in the event object. The source of the `BookEvent` class is as follows:

```
package org.javaee8recipes.chapter13.event;

import java.math.BigDecimal;
import java.time.LocalDate;
import java.util.List;

public class BookEvent {
    private BigDecimal book;
    private String storeName;
    private BigDecimal price;
```

```
    private int numBooks;
    private LocalDate date;
    private List<String> notifyList;

    // accessor methods (getters and setters)

}
```

Next, create a qualifier for each type of book event that can occur. The qualifier is an optional step, as it is only necessary when there will be more than one event of the same type. In this case, an online sale event or a store sale event can occur. The qualifier source for the `OnlineSale` is as follows, with the qualifier for the `StoreSale` being the same with only a different name:

```
package org.javaee8recipes.chapter13.qualifier;

import static java.lang.annotation.ElementType.TYPE;
import static java.lang.annotation.ElementType.FIELD;
import static java.lang.annotation.ElementType.METHOD;
import static java.lang.annotation.ElementType.PARAMETER;
import java.lang.annotation.Retention;
import static java.lang.annotation.RetentionPolicy.RUNTIME;
import java.lang.annotation.Target;

import javax.inject.Qualifier;

@Qualifier
@Retention(RUNTIME)
@Target({METHOD, FIELD, PARAMETER, TYPE})
public @interface OnlineSale {
}
```

Next, an observer needs to be used to listen for the event invocation and act upon it once made. In this case, two observers will need to be generated, one for the `@OnlineSale` and another for `@StoreSale`. The observers reside within a class named `BookEventHandler`.

```
public class BookEventHandler {

    @Inject
    private BookController bookController;

    public BookEventHandler(){

    }

    public void  notifyPublisherOnline (@Observes @OnlineSale BookEvent event) {
        for (String s : event.getNotifyList()) {
            System.out.println("Sending Notification to Publisher: " + s + " purchase of
            book online: "
                    + bookController.findById(event.getBook()).getTitle() + " from store: "
                    + event.getStoreName()
```

```
                    + " purchase price: $" + event.getPrice()
                    + " on: " + event.getDate());
        }
    }

    public void notifyPublisherInStore (@Observes @StoreSale BookEvent event) {
        for (String s : event.getNotifyList()) {
            System.out.println("Sending Notification to Publisher: " + s + " purchase of
            book in store: "
                    + bookController.findById(event.getBook()).getTitle() + " from store: "
                    + event.getStoreName()
                    + " purchase price: $" + event.getPrice()
                    + " on: " + event.getDate());
        }
    }
}
```

Lastly, create an event handling method that will invoke the CDI event when a sale is made. For this example, a simple JSF user interface will be used to invoke a sale event, so the event handling method will be placed into a JSF controller class.

```
@Named
@RequestScoped
public class BookstoreSaleController {

    @Inject
    @OnlineSale
    private Event<BookEvent> onlineSaleEvent;

    private BookEvent currentEvent;

    public BookstoreSaleController() {

    }

    /**
     * Fires synchronous CDI event BookEvent.
     */
    public void onlineSaleAction() {
        onlineSaleEvent.fire(currentEvent);
    }

    /**
     * Fires asynchronous CDI event BookEvent.
     */
    public void storeSaleAction() {
        onlineSaleEvent.fireAsync(currentEvent)
                .whenComplete((event, throwable) -> {
                    if (throwable != null) {
```

```
                    FacesContext.getCurrentInstance().addMessage(null, new FacesMessage(
                            FacesMessage.SEVERITY_ERROR, "FAIL", "Error has occurred " +
                            throwable.getMessage()));
                } else {
                    FacesContext.getCurrentInstance().addMessage(null, new FacesMessage(
                            FacesMessage.SEVERITY_INFO, "SUCCESS", "Successful Brick-
                            and-Mortar Store Sale Processing..."));
                }
            });
    }

    /**
     * @return the currentEvent
     */
    public BookEvent getCurrentEvent() {
        return currentEvent;
    }
}
```

When a sale is invoked, either an online or in-store sale type is chosen. Given the selected sale type, the respective JSF controller method is invoked.

How It Works

CDI events allow for decoupled event handling to occur among a number of beans. The bean classes do not have any binding to one another, but context can be passed between them, allowing beans to invoke contextual events without explicit binding. To orchestrate events, only a few annotations need to be placed, as there is no additional configuration. In the example, a book store is able to complete two types of sales, those being online and in-store. Therefore, when a book is sold, an event is to be invoked to notify the publisher and indicate which type of sale has been made.

To begin, a contextual object is used to contain data about each event. Therefore, a bean named `BookEvent` is generated as a simple Plain Old Java Object (POJO). Next, event qualifiers are coded for differentiation between the two types of possible events. An event qualifier is simply an annotation that can be placed on an event handler and it is also used to create an event of the specified type. In the example, both an online and in-store event qualifier are created. As seen in the code for the qualifier, the annotation declaration is marked with the `javax.inject.Qualifier` annotation, and it is targeted for use with the following: `METHOD, FIELD, PARAMETER, TYPE.`

When an event is fired, an event handler is used to process the event. Event handlers are also known as observers, and they are simply classes that contain at least one method that can be used to contain the processing for the event. In the example, the `BookEventHandler` class contains two methods that are used to perform the actions of the events. Event handling methods must accept an event (simply an object) that is annotated with an optional qualifier and the `@Observes` annotation. The `@Observes` annotation signifies that the method is observing events of the type that is passed into the method. In the example, the `BookEvent` object is used as a parameter and it is annotated with the qualifier annotation for each of the respective methods. Therefore, the method named `notifyPublisherOnline` observes events of type `@OnlineSale`, and `notifyPublisherInStore` observes `@StoreSale` event types.

Lastly, the event initiation occurs within a CDI controller class in this example, although some other class type could also invoke an action. In the example, the BookstoreSalesController contains an injected Event<BookEvent> object, which is used for firing events of type BookEvent. The controller contains methods for firing online sales and also in-store sales. The online sale method action method fires a synchronous event by calling upon the injected event fire() method and passing the current BookEvent object. The fire() method initiates a synchronous event call, so once the event processing is completed, control is returned to the caller.

The in-store sale action method fires an asynchronous event by calling upon the injected event fireAsync() method and passing the current BookEvent object. In this case, since the fireAsync() method initiates an asynchronous event call, the processing must be handled when the event has completed is processing. However, in this scenario, once the fireAsync() method is initiated, control is passed back to the caller and the event is processed in the background. The fireAsync() method was introduced with the release of CDI 2.0 in Java EE 8.

The CDI event model can be harnessed to provide super powerful solutions for applications of all kinds. Since events can be called upon with a loosely coupled architecture, it makes event invocation easy to achieve in new applications and easy to add into existing applications.

13-11. Intercepting Method Invocations

Problem

You want to intercept a method invocation in an application, such that each time the method is called upon, special functionality will occur.

Solution

Utilize a CDI interceptor to invoke special functionality each time a specified method, or all methods within a specified class, are called upon. In the following scenario, an interceptor will be utilized to send an email to an administrator each time certain methods of an application are called upon. In this example, each time a book order is canceled then the email is invoked.

To begin, an annotation must be generated for the interceptor. The interceptor annotation in this case is named Notified, and the sources are as follows:

```
package org.javaee8recipes.chapter13.interceptor;

import static java.lang.annotation.ElementType.METHOD;
import static java.lang.annotation.ElementType.TYPE;
import java.lang.annotation.Inherited;
import java.lang.annotation.Retention;
import static java.lang.annotation.RetentionPolicy.RUNTIME;
import java.lang.annotation.Target;
import javax.interceptor.InterceptorBinding;

@Inherited
@InterceptorBinding
@Retention(RUNTIME)
@Target({METHOD,TYPE})
public @interface Notified {
}
```

Next, the interceptor class can be created. The interceptor class is annotated with @Interceptor and it contains a method which is annotated with @AroundInvoke. This annotated method will be invoked whenever some method that is annotated with @Notified or a method contained within a class that is annotated with @Notified is invoked. In this case, the interceptor class is named NotificationInterceptor and its implementation is as follows:

```
package org.javaee8recipes.chapter13.interceptor;

import java.util.Date;
import java.util.Properties;
import javax.interceptor.AroundInvoke;
import javax.interceptor.Interceptor;
import javax.interceptor.InvocationContext;
import javax.mail.Message;
import javax.mail.Session;
import javax.mail.Transport;
import javax.mail.internet.InternetAddress;
import javax.mail.internet.MimeMessage;

@Interceptor
@Notified
public class NotificationInterceptor {

    @AroundInvoke
    public Object emailNotification(InvocationContext ctx) throws Exception {
        String smtpServer = "mysmtpserver.com";
        String email = "publisherEmail@publisher.com";
        Properties props = System.getProperties();
        props.put("mail.smtp.host", smtpServer);
        Session session = Session.getInstance(props, null);
        sendEmail(session,
                  email,
                  "Method invocation",
                  "Entering method: " + ctx.getMethod().getName());

        return ctx.proceed();
    }

    protected void sendEmail(Session session, String toEmail, String subject, String body) {
        try {
            MimeMessage msg = new MimeMessage(session);
            //set message headers
            msg.addHeader("Content-type", "text/HTML; charset=UTF-8");
            msg.addHeader("format", "flowed");
            msg.addHeader("Content-Transfer-Encoding", "8bit");
            msg.setFrom(new InternetAddress("no_reply@javaee8recipes.com", "NoReply"));
            msg.setReplyTo(InternetAddress.parse("no_reply@javaee8recipes.com", false));
            msg.setSubject(subject, "UTF-8");
            msg.setText(body, "UTF-8");
            msg.setSentDate(new Date());
            msg.setRecipients(Message.RecipientType.TO, InternetAddress.parse(toEmail, false));
            Transport.send(msg);
```

```
        } catch (Exception e) {
            e.printStackTrace();
        }
    }
}
```

Lastly, a class or method(s) must be designated for interception. In this example, we want to notify the administrator each time someone logs in to the administrative console.

```
@Notified
@Named
@RequestScoped
public class AdminConsoleController {

    public AdminConsoleController(){

    }

    public void login(){
        System.out.println("This is an action method which would allow one to log into an"
                + "administrative console");
    }

}
```

In the example code, the `login()` method would be used to authenticate an individual to the administrative console for the bookstore. However, since this is for demo purposes only, it merely displays a message in the system log. In order to enable this interceptor, the following lines must be added to the `beans.xml` configuration:

```
<interceptors>
    <class>org.javaee8recipes.chapter13.interceptor.NotificationInterceptor
    </class>
  </interceptors>
```

How It Works

Interceptors allow cross-cutting functionality to be introduced into a new or existing application without explicitly modifying the code of specified classes or methods. An interceptor allows the functionality to be executed due to an invocation of the specified methods or due to invocation of a method within a specified class. As such, interceptors are very similar to CDI events, except they do not require an explicit call to `fire()` or `fireAsync()` for invocation.

An interceptor solution requires an interceptor binding type annotation and an implementation class. The interceptor binding type annotation is a standard annotation declaration containing the `@Inherited` and `@InterceptorBinding` annotations. The `@Inherited` annotation denotes that the annotation can be inherited from superclasses. The interceptor binding type annotation should contain a target of `METHOD` and `TYPE`.

The interceptor implementation class can contain methods annotated with `@AroundInvoke`, `@PostConstruct`, `@PreDestroy`, `@PrePassivate`, `@PostActivate`, and `@AroundTimeout`. These annotations are used to specify when the interceptor method will be invoked. When a class or a method is annotated with the interceptor binding, the interceptor implementation will be invoked based on the specified implementation. `@AroundInvoke` specifies that the implementation will be executed when the intercepted method is being invoked. The lifecycle callback annotations (@PostConstruct, @PreDestroy, @PrePassivate, and @PostActivate) specify that the interceptor implementation will be invoked when the intercepted method or class enters the specified state. Lastly, the @AroundTimeout annotation is used to indicate that the implementation will be invoked when the intercepted method has an EJB timeout occur.

The @AroundInvoke annotation carries with it a couple of requirements. If an implementation method is annotated as such, it must accept a javax.interceptor.InvocationContext argument, and it must call upon that argument's proceed() method. The invocation of the proceed() method causes the target to be invoked.

An interceptor implementation class can contain one or more methods annotated with the aforementioned annotations. However, only one of each type can be specified within a given implementation class. In order to enable an interceptor, it must be specified within the beans.xml, as indicated in the example.

Interceptors can be a great way to add functionality to a process without modifying the existing code. They work well for performing actions such as logging each time a method is accessed. Typically an interceptor can be reused in multiple circumstances because the functionality is generic and not bound to a specific line of business logic. To learn more about adding more specific business logic functionality to existing methods, refer to Recipe 13-13 covering decorators.

13-12. Bootstrapping Java SE Environments

Problem

You want to utilize the capabilities of CDI in a Java SE environment, outside of a Java EE container.

Solution

Bootstrap the Java SE application using the SeContainerInitializer. In this example, a standard Java SE application named SeCDIExample has been created. A beans.xml file is added to the application's META-INF folder using the CDI 2.0 references:

```
public class BootstrapExample {

    public static void main(String[] args) {
        SeContainerInitializer initializer = SeContainerInitializer.newInstance();

        try (SeContainer container = initializer.initialize()) {
            /**
             * work with CDI
             */
            BookstoreBean storeBean = container.select(BookstoreBean.class).get();
            storeBean.setStoreName("Java Gurus");
            storeBean.printStore();

        }
    }
}
```

When this block of code is executed, the SeContainer can be used to work with CDI capabilities.

How It Works

There are oftentimes situations where a standard Java SE application would benefit from using the utilities that CDI has to offer. The CDI 2.0 release has made this possible with the addition of the bootstrapping API. In order to bootstrap, you must include the CDI dependencies in the application. You must also include a `beans.xml` file to indicate that CDI will be utilized. If you're using a maven project, use coordinates for the `cdi-core` dependency as seen here (update version as needed):

```
<dependency>
    <groupId>org.jboss.weld.se</groupId>
    <artifactId>weld-se-shaded</artifactId>
    <version>3.0.0.Final</version>
</dependency>
```

The `beans.xml` file should contain the CDI configuration information. The following `beans.xml` source provides the minimum configuration:

```
<?xml version="1.0" encoding="UTF-8"?>
<beans xmlns="http://xmlns.jcp.org/xml/ns/javaee" xmlns:xsi="http://www.w3.org/2001/
XMLSchema-instance"
    xsi:schemaLocation="http://xmlns.jcp.org/xml/ns/javaee http://xmlns.jcp.org/xml/ns/
    javaee/beans_2_0.xsd"
    bean-discovery-mode="all" version="2.0">
</beans>
```

The `SeContainerInitializer` class can be used to return an instance of itself. It can be used to configure the CDI container for your application by calling on its many customization methods. See the online documentation for full details (`http://docs.jboss.org/cdi/api/2.0/`). The `SeContainerInitialize` class should be utilized following the builder pattern for configuring options, and the last method to call upon should be its `initialize()`, as seen in the example. The `SeContainerInitializer` is auto-closable, so it works well within a `try-with-resources` block. All of the CDI usage can occur within the `try` block. In the example, a contextual bean is obtained and used.

While this example is brief, it shows how easy it is to bootstrap a CDI configuration for a Java SE application.

13-13. Enhancing Business Logic of a Method

Problem

You would like to enhance the functionality of an existing method, including the ability to integrate with a bean's business logic.

Solution

Utilize a decorator to implement an enhancement of functionality for an existing method. In the following example, a decorator is generated for an existing method in order to enhance functionality by logging to a database. In this particular example, a registration form is used to register for a bookstore event. The decorator will be used to enhance the registration process by adding the registrant into a different database table for entry into a drawing.

To begin, each registrant must enter a first, last, and email address. This information will go into a `Registration` object. The object code is as follows:

```
public class Registration {

    private String first;
    private String last;
    private String email;

    public Registration(){

    }
// . . . Getters and Setters
}
```

Next, an interface must be generated for the registration type. In this case, each registration type must contain a method `register()` that accepts a `Registration` object:

```
public interface BookstoreRegistration {
    public String register(Registration registration);
}
```

Now create a decorator, which is a public abstract class that takes the interface that was created earlier as an injection point.

```
package org.javaee8recipes.chapter13.decorator;

import javax.decorator.Decorator;
import javax.decorator.Delegate;
import javax.enterprise.inject.Any;
import javax.inject.Inject;
import org.javaee8recipes.chapter13.recipe13_13.BookstoreRegistration;
import org.javaee8recipes.chapter13.recipe13_13.Registration;

@Decorator
public abstract class RegistrationDecorator implements BookstoreRegistration {

    @Inject
    @Delegate
    @Any
    private BookstoreRegistration bookstoreRegistration;

    @Override
    public String register(Registration registration){
        // Submit to registration database table
        // Submit to promotional database table
        return registration.getEmail() + " has been entered into the giveaway";
    }
}
```

Lastly, we need to invoke the register method to initiate the decorator functionality. In this example, we invoke via a JSF controller class method.

```
@Named
@ViewScoped
public class BookstoreRegistrationController implements BookstoreRegistration, Serializable
{

    @Inject
    private Registration current;

    public BookstoreRegistrationController(){

    }
// Getters and Setters

    public String register(){
        return register(current);
    }

    @Override
    public String register(Registration registration) {
        // Persist current registration
        return "chapter13/recipe13_13.xhtml";
    }
}
```

When the `register()` method is invoked, the enhanced decorator functionality will also be invoked to add the registrant to the giveaway database table.

How It Works

Decorators are another powerful component of CDI. Much like interceptors, decorators add enhanced functionality to existing methods. These two constructs differ from each other in that decorators enhance functionality and have access to bean fields and methods for which the enhanced functionality is occurring. Interceptors, on the other hand, do not have access to bean fields and methods and therefore provide a more generic functionality in addition to the standard functionality of an existing method.

To create a decorator, you must utilize an interface as an injection point, and one or more of the interface methods will be enhanced via implementation that is added to the decorator class. In the example, a standard bookstore account registration is enhanced by adding the registrant into a sweepstakes giveaway. Although the example does not actually demonstrate the database persistence, etc., if the code is executed, you can see the decorator being invoked.

The decorator class must be denoted with a `@Decorator` annotation, and it must implement an interface and contain at least one method implementation. However, the decorator class can be made abstract so that it does not have to implement each of the methods contained within the interface. A decorator must contain a delegate injection point, which is annotated with `javax.decorator.Delegate`. This injection point can be a field, constructor parameter, or initializer method parameter of the decorator class.

In order to enable a decorator, it must be added to the beans.xml file. The following beans.xml file demonstrates the addition of RegistrationDecorator.

```
<decorators>
    <class>org.javaee8recipes.chapter13.decorator.RegistrationDecorator</class>
</decorators>
```

An application can contain more than one decorator, of course. To manage the order in which the decorators are fired, use the beans.xml file and list in the order of priority. Another way to manage priority is to annotate a decorator with the @Priority annotation. Interceptors take precedence over decorators, so if a method contains both an interceptor and a decorator, the interceptor will be fired first.

CHAPTER 14

Java Message Service

The Java Message Service is an API that allows software to create, edit, read, and send messages between other software applications or components. The API allows resources to be created within an application server that facilitates messaging capability in various contexts. The application server houses connection factory and destination resources, and these resources are created and maintained by the application server. That said, different application server implementations might have minor differences in their JMS implementations.

In addition to the basic messaging facilities, JMS also provides the ability to send messages to destinations and publish messages to subscriptions. This chapter contains recipes that focus on basic concepts of JMS, as well as some advanced techniques and additions that were made to the Java EE platform with the release of Java EE 7. When following along with the examples in this chapter, note that JMS could be used in various situations for creating many different types of messages. For brevity, this chapter covers essential concepts and uses `TextMessage` objects only. The examples are invoked using JSF view actions, although in real-life applications, there are many different ways to implement the sending and receiving of messages. From internal message invocation, to scheduled tasks via an EJB timer or `ManagedExecutorService`, and even implementation of JMS messaging with EJB message driven beans, JMS can be utilized in many different contexts. After reading through the recipes, you should be able to apply the strategies utilized within the recipes in order to create the messaging system of your needs.

JMS 2.0 revamped the API with a simplified technique for sending and receiving messages. In this chapter, you see both the legacy standard API and the simplified API so that the differences can be compared. The updated API also included enhancements to message subscriptions, delivery delay, and more. The breadth of JMS is far too large for complete coverage in this single chapter. To learn about all of the features, refer to the JMS 2.0 specification.

Note The examples in this chapter focus on working with JMS resources within a GlassFish application server environment. Some of the recipes demonstrate the use of the NetBeans IDE for producing and working with JMS resources. However, although the focus is on GlassFish, the main concepts and techniques can be carried forth to just about every Java EE compliant application server environment. For more specific details on working with another application server or IDE, see the documentation that is specific to the corresponding environment.

J. Juneau, *Java EE 8 Recipes*, https://doi.org/10.1007/978-1-4842-3594-2_14

14-1. Creating JMS Resources

Problem

You would like to provide the ability to create a JMS resource to deploy within a GlassFish application server environment.

Solution #1

The easiest technique for creating JMS resources is to utilize an IDE, such as NetBeans. In this example, a standard JMS connection factory will be created for an application project utilizing the NetBeans IDE.

1. Right-click the project within the NetBeans Projects navigator menu, choose New and then Other. The New File wizard will open, from which you will select the GlassFish menu option from the Categories select list, followed by the JMS Resource file type (see Figure 14-1).

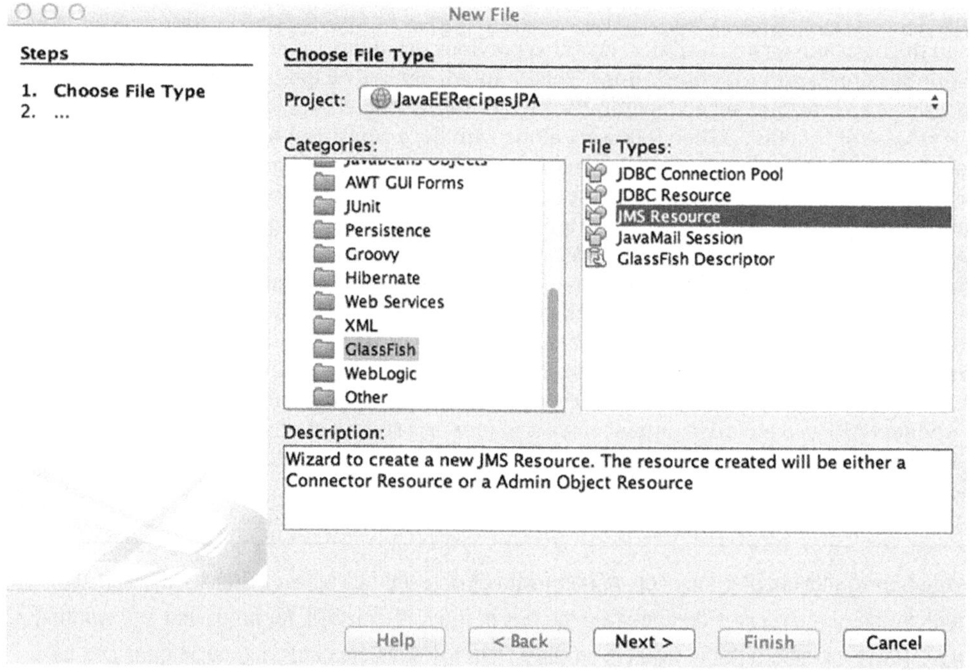

Figure 14-1. *Create JMS Resource file from within NetBeans*

2. Within the New JMS Resource wizard, enter a JNDI Name (using the `jms/` prefix) and a description. If you would like to enable the resource, be sure to do so within this wizard screen as well. Next, select the resource type that you want to create. In this example, we demonstrate the creation of a connection factory, as seen in Figure 14-2.

New JMS Resource

Steps

1. Choose ...
2. General Attributes - JMS Resource
3. Properties

General Attributes - JMS Resource

Enter the configuration information for the JMS Resource. Fields with an * mar k are required.

JNDI Name:* jms/javaEERecipesConnectionFactory

Enabled: true

Description: Connection Factory for use with the Jav

Choose Resource Type:*

Admin Object Resource

javax.jms.Queue

javax.jms.Topic

Connector Resource

javax.jms.QueueConnectionFactory

javax.jms.TopicConnectionFactory

javax.jms.ConnectionFactory

Help | < Back | Next > | Finish | Cancel

Figure 14-2. *New JMS Resource wizard*

3. Click Finish, and a file named `glassfish-resources.xml` will be created within your project if it does not already exist. When you deploy the application project to the server, the resource will be automatically created for you, as shown in Figure 14-3.

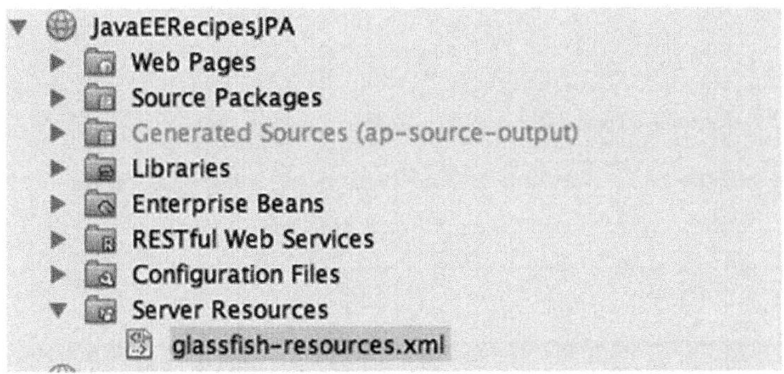

Figure 14-3. *The glassfish-resources.xml file within a NetBeans project*

■ **Note** You can utilize the same steps to create `javax.jms.TopicConnectionFactory` and `javax.jms.QueueConnectionFactory` resources.

Solution #2

Create a new JMS resource from within the GlassFish or Payara application server administrative console. In this recipe example, we create a JMS destination resource. Specifically, we walk through the creation of a `javax.jms.Queue` resource. Follow these steps to create the resource:

1. Log into the GlassFish or Payara administrative console by navigating to `https://localhost:4848`. Expand the Resources the JMS Resources menu in the navigation tree to expose the Destination Resources menu option (see Figure 14-4).

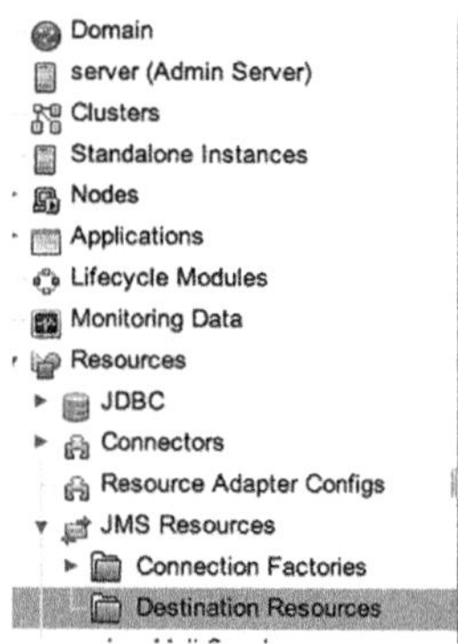

Figure 14-4. *GlassFish and Payara administration console Destination Resource menu*

2. Click the New button within the JMS Destination Resource window to open the New JMS Destination Resource window (see Figure 14-5). Enter a JNDI name (beginning with `jms/`), followed by a unique name for the Physical Destination Name field. Finally, choose the Resource Type that you want to create.

New JMS Destination Resource

OK Cancel

The creation of a new Java Message Service (JMS) destination resource also creates an admin object resource.

JNDI Name: * jms/Queue
A unique name of up to 255 characters; must contain only alphanumeric, underscore, dash, or dot characters

Physical Destination Name * javaeeRecipesQueue
Destination name in the Message Queue broker. If the destination does not exist, it will be created automatically when needed.

Resource Type: * javax.jms.Queue

Description:

Status: ✓ **Enabled**

Additional Properties (0)

Add Property Delete Properties

Name	Value	Description:
No items found.		

OK Cancel

Figure 14-5. *GlassFish administration console for new JMS destination resource*

3. Click OK to create the destination.

■ **Note** The GlassFish/Payara `asadmin create-jms-resource` command can also be used to create JMS-administered objects from the command line. The `asadmin` tool can also be used to perform other tasks. For more information, refer to the documentation at `http://docs.oracle.com/cd/E19798-01/821-1751/giobi/index.html`.

How It Works

The JMS API utilizes administrative resources in order to create and consume messages. We refer to these resources as JMS resources. There are a couple of different types of JMS resources that can be created—connection resources and destination resources. The connection resources are used to create connections to a provider. There are three types of connection resources that can be created:

- `ConnectionFactory`: Instance of the `javax.jms.ConnectionFactory` interface. Can be used to create JMS Topics and JMS Queue types.
- `TopicConnectionFactory`: Instance of the `javax.jms.TopicConnectionFactory` interface.
- `QueueConnectionFactory`: Instance of the `javax.jms.QueueConnectionFactory` interface.

JMS connection factory resources are very similar to JDBC connection factories in that they provide a pool of connections that an application can use in order to connect and produce a session. There are many attributes that can be provided when creating connection factory resources:

- *Initial and Minimum Pool Size*: The initial and minimum number of connections that will be created and maintained by the connection pool.
- *Maximum Pool Size*: The maximum number of connections that can be created within the pool.
- *Pool Resize Quantity*: The number of connections that will be removed when the pool idle timeout expires.
- *Idle Timeout*: The maximum amount of time that connections can remain in the pool if they are idle (seconds).
- *Max Wait Time*: The maximum amount of time that a caller will wait before a connection timeout is sent (milliseconds).
- *On Any Failure*: If set to `true` (checked), all connections would be closed and reconnected on failure.
- *Transaction Support*: The level of transaction support (`XATransaction`, `LocalTransaction`, or `NoTransaction`). The default is empty.
- *Connection Validation*: If set to `true`, then connections will need to be validated.

Solution #1 to this recipe demonstrates how to create a connection factory resource using the NetBeans IDE. This step-by-step procedure makes it easy to create such objects and deploy them to your GlassFish or Payara application server for use. You can also create connection factory objects using the

GlassFish or Payara administrative console by following the steps that are provided in Solution #2 to this recipe and choosing the Connection Factories submenu rather than the Destination Resources submenu in Step 1. `ConnectionFactory` objects are registered automatically with JNDI once created, and they can then be injected into Java classes and used. The following lines of code demonstrate how to inject a `ConnectionFactory` resource into a class:

```
@Resource(name = "jms/MyConnectionFactory")
private static ConnectionFactory connectionFactory;
```

Destination resources can also be created in a similar fashion to connection resources. Destination resources act as targets that receive or consume messages that are produced. Destination resources can be one of two types: `javax.jms.Queue` (Queue) or `javax.jms.Topic` (Topic). A Queue is a destination resource that consumes messages in a point-to-point (PTP) manner, much like a one-way line of traffic. When a producer sends a message to a queue, the message will stay in the queue until it is consumed. A topic is a destination that is used in a pub/sub scenario, whereas messages sent to a `Topic` may be consumed by multiple receivers. One or more receivers can subscribe to a `Topic`.

Solution #2 demonstrates how to create a destination resource within a GlassFish or Payara application server, using the administrative console. The console provides a wizard that can be used to easily create a destination resource. The most important piece of information to provide when creating a destination is the name. As with any JMS resource, the JNDI name should begin with the `jms/` prefix. When creating a destination resource, a unique name must also be provided for the Destination Resource Name, although other Java EE application servers may or may not make this a mandatory specification. Destination resources can be injected into Java classes in the same manner as `ConnectionFactory` resources. The following lines of code demonstrate the injection of a `Topic` resource.

```
@Resource(name="jms/myTopic")
private Topic myTopic;
```

14-2. Creating a Session

Problem

You would like to create a JMS session so that you can send or consume messages.

Solution

Create a connection so that you can subsequently create one or more sessions, which in turn, can send messages to destinations or consume messages. In order to create a connection, obtain a `ConnectionFactory` object by injection via the `@Resource` annotation and call its `createConnection` method as demonstrated in the following line of code:

```
Connection connection = connectionFactory.createConnection();
```

After you have created a connection, you need to start a session. In order to do so, call the connection objects `createSession` method as follows:

```
Session session = connection.createSession(false,
     Session.AUTO_ACKNOWLEDGE);
```

■ **Note** If you are using the simplified JMS API, which is covered in more detail in Recipe 14-3, you do not need to manually create a JMS session. The creation of a JMS session is only required when utilizing the standard API.

Running the Example

If you take a look at the sources that can be found in the `JavaEERecipes` project within the `org.javaee8recipes.chapter14` package, you can see a full demonstration for creating a JMS session. To see the example in action, deploy the `JavaEERecipes` project to your application server after setting up a JMS connection factory (see Recipe 14-1) and visit the following URL:

```
http://localhost:8080/JavaEERecipes/faces/chapter14/recipe14_02.xhtml
```

How It Works

Before you can begin to send or consume messages, you must obtain a JMS connection so that you can start a session. A session can be used to create JMS resources such as Message Consumers, Message Producers, Messages, Queue Browsers, and Temporary Queues and Topics. A session can be created using a `Connection` object. To create a session, call a `Connection` object's `createSession` method and pass the appropriate arguments depending on your application's needs. The `createSession` syntax is as follows:

```
createSession(boolean isTransacted, int acknowledgementType)
```

The first argument to the `createSession` method is a boolean value to indicate if transactions should take place within the session. If a session is created as transacted (set to `true` for the first argument to `createSession`), acknowledgment occurs once the entire transaction is successfully committed. If for some reason the transaction is not committed, the entire transaction is rolled back, and all messages are redelivered. However, if a session is not transacted, one must indicate which type of acknowledgment must be received to consider a message successfully sent. The second argument to the `createSession` method indicates the acknowledgment type. Table 14-1 lists the different acknowledgment types along with a description of each.

Table 14-1. *JMS Session Message Acknowledgment*

Acknowledgment Type	Description
`Session.AUTO_ACKNOWLEDGE`	The session automatically acknowledges a client's receipt of a message, either when the client has successfully returned from a call to receive or when the `MessageListener` it has called to process the message has successfully returned.
`Session.CLIENT_ACKNOWLEDGE`	The client acknowledges the receipt of a message by calling the message's acknowledge method.
`Session.DUPS_OK_ACKNOWLEDGE`	Lazy acknowledgment of messages, allowing duplicates to be received.

In the solution to this recipe, the session that is created is non-transactional, and the receipt type is `Session.AUTO_ACKNOWLEDGE`. This is the most common type of JMS session that is created. Once the session has been created, then it can be used to create JMS resources.

14-3. Creating and Sending a Message

Problem

You want to create and send a JMS message.

Solution #1

Use the standard API to create and send a message. To do so, create a Message object with respect to the type of message you want to send, and then create and use a message producer in order to send messages to a destination. To create a message, first decide on the type of message that you want to send. Once decided, create the appropriate message object from the JMS session. In this example, we demonstrate the creation of a text message. The following lines of code demonstrate how to create a text message, including a string.

```
TextMessage message  = session.createTextMessage();
message.setText("Java EE 8 Is the Best!");
```

Next, to create a MessageProducer and send the message, call a JMS session's createProducer method and pass the object type of the destination to which you want to send a message. The following lines of code demonstrate how to create a message producer and send the text message that was created in the previous lines. The first lines of code demonstrate how to inject the destination resource, and then the actual creation of the message producer and sending of the message follows.

```
@Resource(name="jms/javaEERecipesQueue")
private Queue myQueue;
...
    public void sendMessage() {
        if (connection != null) {
            System.out.println("Creating Session");
            try(Session session = connection.createSession(false, Session.AUTO_ACKNOWLEDGE);
                ) {
                myQueue = (Queue) getContext().lookup("jms/javaEERecipesQueue");
                MessageProducer producer = session.createProducer(myQueue);
                TextMessage message = session.createTextMessage();
                message.setText("Java EE 8 Is the Best!");

                producer.send(message);
                producer.close();
                setConnectionString("Message Successfully Sent to Queue");

            } catch (NamingException | JMSException ex) {
                System.out.println(ex);
                setConnectionString("Session not created and message not sent");
            }
        } else {
            setConnectionString("No connection available");
        }
    }
```

Solution #2

Use the simplified API to create and send a message. To utilize the simplified API, create a `JMSContext` object, and then utilize it to create a `MessageProducer` and send the message to the appropriate destination. In the following example, a simple `String`-based message is sent to a `Queue` using the simplified API. This technique provides the same result as Solution #1.

```
@Resource(name = "jms/javaEERecipesConnectionFactory")
    private ConnectionFactory connectionFactory;
    @Resource(lookup = "jms/javaEERecipesQueue")
    Queue inboundQueue;
...
    public void sendMessageNew() {
        try (JMSContext context = connectionFactory.createContext();) {
            StringBuilder message = new StringBuilder();
            message.append("Java EE 8 Is the Best!");
            context.createProducer().send(inboundQueue, message.toString());
        }
    }
```

Running the Examples

An example that can be run from within a JSF view has been created for this recipe. The code found at `org.javaee8recipes.chapter14.Example14_03.java` contains a managed bean that includes a `sendMessage` method that utilizes the standard API implementation, and a `sendMessageNew` method that utilizes the simplified API. Both methods are responsible for creating a message and sending it to a destination Queue. By running the example, you can look at the server log to see the output from the method. Deploy the `JavaEERecipes` project and visit the following URL to run the example: `http://localhost:8080/JavaEERecipes/faces/chapter14/recipe14_03.xhtml`.

How It Works

The reason that any application uses JMS is to incorporate the ability to send or receive messages. Therefore, it is no surprise that the JMS API has been developed to make these tasks very easy for the developer. In Java EE 7, things were made even easier using the simplified JMS API. Let's begin by discussing the steps that are needed to utilize the standard API for sending a JMS message. To send a JMS message using the standard API, you need to create a resource destination for your message and obtain a connection and a JMS session, as seen in Recipes 14-1 and 14-2. Once you have obtained a JMS session, the next step is to create a `MessageProducer` using the `Session createProducer` method, passing the destination as an argument. After this legwork has been completed, the message can be constructed. You can create a message by calling the `javax.jms.Session` method that corresponds to the type of message that you want to create. To see all of the available methods, refer to the online documentation at `https://javaee.github.io/javaee-spec/javadocs/javax/jms/Session.html`. In the example for this recipe, a text message is created by calling the `session.createTextMessage()` method. The text is then set by calling the `TextMessage` object's `setText` method.

Once a message has been created, a `MessageProducer` must be created in order to facilitate the sending of the message. Again, `javax.jms.Session` comes to the rescue here as we can call its `createProducer` method, passing the destination resource for which we'd like to create the `MessageProducer`. Once created, the producer's `sendMessage` method can be invoked, passing the message that you want to send.

As mentioned previously, the `javax.jms.Session` can be used to generate different message types. Table 14-2 lists the different message types that can be created, along with a description.

Table 14-2. *JMS Message Types*

Message Type	Creation Method
`StreamMessage`	The message body contains a stream of primitive values in the Java programming language. Filled and read sequentially.
`MapMessage`	Message body contains a set of name/value pairs that are formed from `String` objects and Java primitives. May be accessed sequentially or randomly by name, and the order of entries is undefined.
`TextMessage`	Message body contains a `String` object. Able to be used for plaintext as well as XML messages.
`ObjectMessage`	Message body contains a `Serializable` Java object.
`BytesMessage`	Message body contains a stream of uninterpreted bytes.

When utilizing the simplified API that was introduced with Java EE 7, there are a few shortcuts that can be made. To compare Solution #1 with Solution #2, you can see that there are fewer lines of code in the second solution. The simplified API enables developers to produce the same results as the standard API with much less code. A `JMSContext` object is obtained via a call to the `ConnectionFactory`'s `createContext` method, and it can be used to begin a chain of method invocations that will result in the sending of a message in just one line of code. To break it down a bit, after the `JMSContext` has been obtained, its `createProducer` method can be called, chaining a call to the send method, passing the `Queue` and the message to be sent.

JMS message implementations may vary between the different application server products. However, all JMS messages types share some common characteristics. For instance, all JMS messages implement the `javax.jms.Message` interface. Messages are composed of a header, properties, and a body. The header of a message contains values that are utilized by clients and providers for routing and identification purposes, properties provide message filtering, and the body portion of the message carries the actual message content. The message header is used for linking messages to one another, and a field named the `JMSCorrelationID` contains this content. Message objects contain the ability to support application-defined property values. The properties can be set via a construct known as *message selectors*, and they are responsible for filtering messages. For more-detailed information regarding message properties, see the online documentation at `https://javaee.github.io/javaee-spec/javadocs/javax/jms/Message.html`. The body varies across the different message types, as listed in Table 14-2.

It can be useful to add properties and headers to a particular message in order to allow message consumers to have filtering capabilities via JMS message selectors. To learn more about using JMS message selectors, refer to Recipe 14-5.

14-4. Receiving Messages

Problem

You would like to receive messages that have just been sent by a JMS producer.

Solution #1

Use the standard JMS API to create a message consumer. Using the JMS session, create the message consumer by calling the `createConsumer` method, passing the type of message consumer that you would like to create. Once the message consumer object has been created, invoke the `start` method on the JMS connection object, and then call the consumer object's `receive` method to receive a message. In the following example managed bean controller, a message consumer will be created and set up to receive the message that was sent by the producer in Recipe 14-3.

The following code excerpt is taken from the `org.javaee8recipes.chapter14.recipe14_04.Example14_04.java` source file. The method named `receiveMessage` is responsible for consuming messages from a specified destination point `Queue`. Note that the code assumes that the messages within the queue would eventually end and that there would not be a continuous stream of incoming messages.

```
public void receiveMessage() {
        boolean stopReceivingMessages = false;
        if(connection == null){
            createConnection();
        }
        try(Session session = connection.createSession(false, Session.AUTO_ACKNOWLEDGE);) {
            createConnection();
            myQueue = (Queue) getContext().lookup("jms/javaEERecipesQueue");
            try (MessageConsumer consumer = session.createConsumer(myQueue)) {
                connection.start();

                while (!stopReceivingMessages) {
                    Message inMessage = consumer.receive();
                    if (inMessage != null) {
                        if (inMessage instanceof TextMessage) {
                            String messageStr = ((TextMessage) inMessage).getText();
                            setDisplayMessage(messageStr);
                        } else {
                            setDisplayMessage("Message was of another type");
                        }
                    } else {
                        stopReceivingMessages = true;
                    }
                }
                connection.stop();
            }
        } catch (NamingException | JMSException ex) {
            Logger.getLogger(Example14_04.class.getName()).log(Level.SEVERE, null, ex);
        } finally {
            if (connection != null){
                closeConnection();
            }
        }
    }
```

Solution #2

Utilize the simplified API to create a message consumer. Utilize a `JMSContext` object to create the `JMSConsumer` in an efficient and simplified manner. The following example method resides in a managed bean controller. The message consumer in this example is created and set up to receive the message that was sent by the producer in Recipe 14-3.

```
public String receiveMessageNew() {
    try (JMSContext context = connectionFactory.createContext()) {
        JMSConsumer consumer = context.createConsumer(myQueue);
        return consumer.receiveBody(String.class);
    }
}
```

Running the Example

The `JavaEERecipes` project contains a working example for this recipe that demonstrates the sending and receiving of JMS messages. To view the example, you need to deploy the project to your application server and then visit the following URL:

```
http://localhost:8080/JavaEERecipes/faces/chapter14/recipe14_04.xhtml
```

How It Works

The receiving client of a message is also known as the *message consumer*. Message consumers can be created using the standard or the simplified JMS API. We compare these two approaches in this section to give you an idea of the differences between the two.

Using the standard API, a consumer is created from JMS `Session` objects in the same manner that producers are created (see Recipe 14-3), calling the `createConsumer` method of JMS `Session` and passing the destination object from which the consumer will listen for and accept messages. Message consumers have the ability to consume messages that are waiting within a queue, and they listen indefinitely for new incoming messages.

To set up a consumer, call the JMS `Session` object's `createConsumer` method and pass the destination object that you want to consume from. The next step is to call the JMS `Connection start` method. This will tell JMS that the consumer is ready to begin receiving messages. After invoking the `connection.start()` method, a consumer can receive a message by calling the `Consumer` object's `receive` method, optionally passing time in milliseconds for the consumer to listen for messages. If no time limit is specified, the consumer will listen indefinitely.

As you can see from the example in this recipe, once the `receive` method is called, a `Message` object is retrieved. Once the message is received, the application can glean whatever it needs by calling the `Message` object's getter methods accordingly.

Now let's take a look at using the simplified API. As you can see from Solution #2, there are fewer lines of code required to produce the same result achieved from Solution #1. The `JMSContext` object aids in producing less code by calling its `createConsumer` method and passing the resource from which the application will need to consume messages. This method call will return a `JMSConsumer`, which has a similar API to `MessageConsumer`, with the ability to receive messages both synchronously and asynchronously. In the example, a `String` message is consumed synchronously.

■ **Note** It is possible to create an asynchronous consumer by registering a `MessageListener` with the `MessageConsumer`. After a listener has been registered for the consumer, the listener's `onMessage()` method will be called each time a message has been delivered. For instance, the following code could be used to register a listener to the consumer that was created within the example for this recipe.

```
javax.jms.MessageListener javaEERecipesListener = new MyMessageListener();

consumer.setMessageListener(javaEERecipesListener);
```

14-5. Filtering Messages

Problem

You would like to provide properties for your messages that will make it easier for consumers to filter through and find messages of their choice.

Solution

Utilize message selectors in order to filter the messages that are being consumed. Message selectors are `String`-based expressions that can be assigned to consumers upon creation, and they are generally used to filter the types of messages that a consumer will receive. In the following example, both the `sendMessage1` and `sendMessage2` methods create JMS messages. The `sendMessage1` method sets a property named `TYPE` with a value of `JAVAEE` on the message. After setting this property, a `MessageProducer` is created and the message is sent. The `sendMessage2` method sets a property named `TYPE` with a value of `JAVASE` on the message. Just like `sendMessage1`, the `sendMessage2` method then creates a `MessageProducer` and sends the message. The `receiveMessage` method sets up a `MessageConsumer` with a selector specified to only consume messages with a property of `TYPE` that include a value of `JAVAEE`.

The following excerpt has been taken from the class named `org.javaee8recipes.chapter14.recipe14_05.Example14_05.java`.

```
public void sendMessage1() {
        if (connection != null) {
            try (Session session = connection.createSession(false, Session.AUTO_
            ACKNOWLEDGE);
                    MessageProducer producer = session.createProducer(myQueue);) {
                TextMessage message = session.createTextMessage();
                message.setText("Java EE 8 Is the Best!");
                message.setStringProperty("TYPE", "JAVAEE");
                producer.send(message);

            } catch (JMSException ex) {
                System.out.println(ex);

            }
        }

    }
```

```
    public void sendMessage2() {
        if (connection != null) {
            try (Session session = connection.createSession(false, Session.AUTO_ACKNOWLEDGE);
                    MessageProducer producer = session.createProducer(myQueue);) {

                System.out.println("Creating message");
                TextMessage message2 = session.createTextMessage();
                message2.setText("Java SE 9 Is Great!");
                message2.setStringProperty("TYPE", "JAVASE");
                producer.send(message2);

            } catch (JMSException ex) {
                System.out.println(ex);

            }
        }

    }

    public void receiveMessage() {
        boolean stopReceivingMessages = false;
        String selector = "TYPE = 'JAVAEE'";
        try(Connection connection = connectionFactory.createConnection();
            Session session = connection.createSession(false, Session.AUTO_ACKNOWLEDGE);
            MessageConsumer consumer = session.createConsumer(myQueue, selector);) {

            connection.start();

            while (!stopReceivingMessages) {
                Message inMessage = consumer.receive();
                if (inMessage != null) {
                    if (inMessage instanceof TextMessage) {
                        String messageStr = ((TextMessage) inMessage).getText();
                        setDisplayMessage(messageStr);
                    } else {
                        setDisplayMessage("Message was of another type");
                    }
                } else {
                    stopReceivingMessages = true;
                }

            }
            connection.stop();

        } catch (JMSException ex) {
            System.out.println(ex);
        }
    }
```

Running the Example

If you deploy the `JavaEERecipes` project, you can run the example by pointing your browser to the following URL: `http://localhost:8080/JavaEERecipes/faces/chapter14/recipe14_05.xhtml`. You can click the Receive Messages button to start the consumer. Then click on the Send EE Message and Send SE Message buttons to send messages, which contain different property values. Watch the server log to see output pertaining to the browsed messages.

How It Works

Message selectors are string-based expressions that can be assigned to consumers upon creation. To create a selector, form a string that contains an expression with syntax based on a subset of the SQL 92 conditional expression syntax. The expression string should formulate the filter that you want to use when consuming messages. An expression will look very much like the `WHERE` clause of a database query. In the example for this recipe, the selector is set to the following string:

```
TYPE = 'JAVAEE'
```

This selector causes the consumer to filter all messages that are received and only consume those messages containing a property named `TYPE` that is assigned a value of `JAVAEE`. Standard SQL 92 can be used to combine filters and build an expression that will provide the filtering capability that is required by the consumer.

To assign the selector to a consumer, pass it to the JMS session `createConsumer` method. After doing so, any messages received by the created consumer will be filtered based on the selector expression.

14-6. Inspecting Message Queues

Problem

Your application uses a JMS queue and you would like to browse through each of the messages within the queue without removing them.

Solution

Create a `QueueBrowser` object and use it to browse through each of the messages that are contained in the queue.

In the following excerpt from Java class `org.javaee8recipes.chapter14.Example14_06.java`, the `browseMessages()` method connects to a JMS session, creates a browser queue, and traverses the messages within the queue.

```
public void browseMessages() {

        try(Connection connection = connectionFactory.createConnection();
            Session session = connection.createSession(false, Session.AUTO_ACKNOWLEDGE);
            QueueBrowser browser = session.createBrowser(myQueue);) {

            Enumeration msgs = browser.getEnumeration();
```

```
            if(!msgs.hasMoreElements()){
                System.out.println("No more messages within the queue...");
            } else {
                while(msgs.hasMoreElements()){
                    Message currMsg = (Message)msgs.nextElement();
                    System.out.println("Message ID: " + currMsg.getJMSMessageID());
                }
            }

        } catch (JMSException ex) {
            System.out.println(ex);
        }
    }
```

Running the Example

If you deploy the JavaEERecipes project, you can run the example by pointing your browser to the following URL: http://localhost:8080/JavaEERecipes/faces/chapter14/recipe14_06.xhtml. You can click the Send Message button within the view several times, and then click on the Browse Through Messages button, and watch the server log to see output pertaining to the browsed messages.

How It Works

There are times when it is important to have the ability to search through messages in order to find the one that you would like to read. In circumstances such as these, message queue browsers come to the rescue. A QueueBrowser object provides the ability for an application to search through each message within a queue and display the header values for each of them. This capability can be important if the message header contains important information that helps to differentiate each type of message that is sent by a particular application. The JMS QueueBrowser object makes it easy to sift through messages in order to find the one you would like, using similar semantics as those that are used to create other JMS objects.

To create a QueueBrowser, you must first have an open JMS session object. You can then call the Session object's createBrowser method, passing the JMS destination type as an argument. Therefore, if you want to browse messages in a queue that is named jms/myQueue, you would pass the injected resource for jms/myQueue to the createBrowser method. Once you have created a browser object, simply iterate over the messages and browse through them using the Enumeration that is returned from the call to the browser.getEnumeration() method.

14-7. Creating Durable Message Subscribers

Problem

You would like to ensure that an application receives all published messages, even when the subscriber is not active.

Solution

Create a durable subscriber for the Topic destination that will be used to send and receive messages. Once created, messages can be published to the topic using the standard message publishing techniques, as demonstrated in Recipe 14-3, sending to the Topic destination that contains the subscription. The messages can then be consumed via a message consumer that has been created using said Topic and subscription.

In this example, a durable message subscriber is created, the message is created and published to the Topic destination, and finally, the message is consumed.

The Topic Connection

Topic connections are a bit different than Queue connections in that they utilize an object named TopicConnection, rather than a standard Connection object. Moreover, a TopicConnectionFactory must be injected into an object in order to create a TopicConnection. The following lines of code demonstrate how to create a connection factory to generate TopicConnections for working with subscriptions.

```
@Resource(name = "jms/javaEERecipesConnectionFactory")
    private TopicConnectionFactory connectionFactory;
TopicConnection connection = (TopicConnection) connectionFactory.createConnection();
connection.setClientID("durable");
```

Creating the Initial Durable Subscriber

When creating a durable subscriber, an initial durable subscriber must be created prior to sending any messages to the Topic. This initial subscriber will initialize the subscription and make it available for publishing and receiving purposes. The following code excerpt, taken from org.javaee8recipes.chapter14.recipe14_07.Example14_07.java, demonstrates the creation of a durable subscriber.

```
public void createTopicSubscriber(){
        try {
            createConnection();
            TopicSession session = connection.createTopicSession(false, Session.AUTO_
            ACKNOWLEDGE);
            myTopic = (Topic) getContext().lookup("jms/javaEERecipesTopic");
            TopicSubscriber subscriber = session.createDurableSubscriber(myTopic,
            "javaEERecipesSub");
            connection.close();
        } catch (javax.naming.NamingException | JMSException ex) {
            Logger.getLogger(Example14_07.class.getName()).log(Level.SEVERE, null, ex);
        }
    }
```

For the demonstration application, a JSF h:commandButton component invokes this method so that you can watch the output occurring within the server log.

Creating and Publishing a Message

Creating and publishing a message to a Topic is much like publishing messages to a Queue. However, instead of creating a Producer, a Publisher is generated. The following code excerpt, taken from org.javaee8recipes.chapter14.recipe14_07.Example14_07.java, demonstrates the creation of a Message and then it is published to the durable subscriber.

```
public void sendMessage() {
        try {
            createConnection();
```

```
            System.out.println("Creating session");
            TopicSession session = connection.createTopicSession(false, Session.AUTO_
            ACKNOWLEDGE);
            System.out.println("Creating message");
            TextMessage message  = session.createTextMessage();
            message.setText("Java EE 8 Is the Best!");
            message.setStringProperty("TYPE", "JAVAEE");

            System.out.println("Creating producer");
            myTopic = (Topic) getContext().lookup("jms/javaEERecipesTopic");
            TopicPublisher publisher = session.createPublisher(myTopic);
            System.out.println("Sending message");
            publisher.publish(message);

            System.out.println("Message sent, closing session");
            publisher.close();
            session.close();
            connection.close();

        } catch (NamingException | JMSException ex) {
            Logger.getLogger(Example14_07.class.getName()).log(Level.SEVERE, null, ex);

        }
```

This method is also bound to an `h:commandButton` component for our example view, and you can see more output generated from the actions that take place within the method.

Receiving the Message

Each message created and published to the `Topic` is later consumed by subscriber(s) to the `Topic`. The method demonstrates how to create a durable subscriber and receive messages from it.

```
public void receiveMessage() {
        boolean stopReceivingMessages = false;
        try {
            createConnection();
            System.out.println("Creating session to receive message");
            TopicSession session = connection.createTopicSession(false, Session.AUTO_
            ACKNOWLEDGE);
            myTopic = (Topic) getContext().lookup("jms/javaEERecipesTopic");
            System.out.println("Setting up consumer");

            String selector = "TYPE = 'JAVAEE'";
            TopicSubscriber subscriber = session.createDurableSubscriber(myTopic,
            "javaEERecipesSub");
            connection.start();

            while (!stopReceivingMessages) {
                System.out.println("Receiving message");
                Message inMessage = subscriber.receive();
```

```
            if (inMessage != null) {
                System.out.println(inMessage);
                if (inMessage instanceof TextMessage) {
                    String messageStr = ((TextMessage) inMessage).getText();
                    System.out.println(messageStr);
                    setDisplayMessage(messageStr);
                } else {
                    System.out.println("Message was of another type");
                    setDisplayMessage("Message was of another type");
                }
            } else {
                stopReceivingMessages = true;
            }

        }
        connection.stop();
        subscriber.close();

        session.close();
        closeConnection();
    } catch (NamingException | JMSException ex) {
        Logger.getLogger(Example14_07.class.getName()).log(Level.SEVERE, null, ex);
    }
}
```

The receiveMessage method is bound to an h:commandButton component within the JSF view in the example program, and you can follow along with the output that can be seen in the server log.

Unsubscribing from the Subscription

It is important to unsubscribe from a subscriber when you're finished using it because subscribers use up additional resources, as discussed in the "How It Works" section. The following method demonstrates how to unsubscribe.

```
public void unsubscribe(){
        try {
            createConnection();
            TopicSession session = connection.createTopicSession(false, Session.AUTO_
            ACKNOWLEDGE);
            // close subscriber if open, then unsubscribe
            session.unsubscribe("javaEERecipesSub");
            connection.close();
        } catch (JMSException ex) {
            Logger.getLogger(Example14_07.class.getName()).log(Level.SEVERE, null, ex);
        }
    }
```

Running the Example

An example that binds all the methods shown in this recipe to JSF views can be executed by deploying the JavaEERecipes project to your GlassFish/Payara server and visiting the following URL:

http://localhost:8080/JavaEERecipes/faces/chapter14/recipe14_7.xhtml

How It Works

A message subscription is a JMS consumer that retains a durable connection to a specified topic destination. Message subscriptions cannot be made for Queue destinations, only for Topics, because they utilize publish/subscribe messaging. By default, a durable subscriber remains persistent, because the delivery mode is PERSISTENT by default. Subscriptions are stored in a server cache so that they can be retrieved in the event of a server failure. Because durable message subscribers retain messages in a cache, they take up a larger memory footprint. Therefore, it is important that subscribers remain subscribed only as long as necessary, and then unsubscribe to release the memory.

■ **Note** Durable subscriptions can have only one subscriber at a time.

To work with message subscribers, a special set of connection and session objects must be used. To start, you must inject a TopicConnectionFactory into any object that will use Topics. A TopicConnection can be created by calling the createTopicConnection method. A TopicSession must be created, in turn, from the TopicConnection. The TopicSession object can be used to create durable message subscribers and message publishers.

When creating a subscriber, one must invoke the JMS session method, createDurableSubscriber, and pass the Topic destination, along with a string that is used to identify the subscriber. The String identifier is important because this is the identifier that will be used by consumers to subscribe to the messages being published to the Topic. A TopicSubscriber object is generated from the createDurableSubscriber method, and it is important to create the initial durable subscriber in order to create the Topic subscription. Once the initial durable subscriber has been created, messages can be sent to the subscription, and consumers can subscribe to it.

To create a message and send it to a subscription, the JMS session createPublisher method must be invoked, passing the Topic destination object as an argument. The call to createPublisher will generate a TopicPublisher object, which can be utilized for publishing messages to a Topic subscription. Any type of message can be sent to a Topic. To learn more about the different types of messages that can be sent, refer to Recipe 14-3. Any number of messages can be sent to a Topic, and if a consumer has subscribed to the subscriber, it will receive the messages. New subscribers will begin receiving messages that are sent to the subscription after the time when they've subscribed.

In order to subscribe to a Topic, a TopicSubscriber object should be created by calling the JMS session createDurableSubscriber method, passing the Topic destination object and the string-based identifier that was originally used to establish the subscriber. Once the TopicSubscriber has been created, messages can be consumed as usual, invoking the TopicSubscriber receive method for each message that will be consumed. Typically, an application will set a boundary limit to the number of messages that will be consumed and perform a loop to receive that number of messages from a subscribed Topic.

Since a durable subscription creates a memory footprint, it is essential for consumers to unsubscribe when they're finished with the Topic. If a consumer does not unsubscribe, the application server will starve other subscriber resources and will eventually run out of usable memory. To unsubscribe a consumer, invoke the JMS session unsubscribe method, passing the string-based name of the subscriber. I told you that the string you use for identifying the subscriber was important!

It is sometimes useful to create message subscriptions for certain circumstances. Pertinent situations for using a subscriber may include a subscription for client consumers to receive messages regarding application errors, or for an alert system so that administrators can subscribe to alerts that they want to receive. In any case, durable subscriptions can be useful, so long as they are used sparingly and maintained in an appropriate manner.

14-8. Delaying Message Delivery

Problem

You would like to delay a message that is being sent.

Solution

Set the time of delay in milliseconds by calling the producer's `setDeliveryDelay(long)` method. In the following example, the message sending will be delayed by 1000 milliseconds.

```
TopicPublisher publisher = session.createPublisher(myTopic);
publisher.setDeliveryDelay(1000);
```

How It Works

In JMS 2.0, it is possible to delay the delivery of a message. The JMS API provides a method, `setDeliveryDelay`, for producers. This method can be called, passing the delay time in milliseconds, prior to sending the message. Once the delay has been set, this will cause all subsequent message deliveries by that producer to be delayed.

CHAPTER 15

RESTful Web Services

Java Web Services can play a vital role in enterprise application development. A web service can be described as a client and server application that communicates over HTTP, which provides a standard means for communication and interoperability between different applications. There are many different web service implementations available across each of the different programming platforms. A web service is made accessible via an endpoint implementation. Clients and servers transmit messages to exchange information between various web services. Entire applications can be implemented using web services that transmit messages and data to and from each other. The two main web service implementations that have been part of Java EE over the past few releases are the Java API for XML Web Services (JAX-WS) and the Java API for RESTful Web Services (JAX-RS). In the most recent release, Java EE 8, JAX-WS was not updated and it is no longer deemed as a "current" technology. Therefore, most recipes in this chapter cover JAX-RS. However, a handful of JAX-WS recipes have been added for complete coverage.

JAX-WS utilizes XML messages following the Simple Object Access Protocol (SOAP) standard. SOAP is an XML language that defines messages. JAX-WS utilizes a Web Services Description Language (WSDL) file to describe each of the various operations of a particular web service, and clients can use the WSDL file to obtain a proxy to the service. Recipes in this chapter demonstrate how to use JAX-WS to serve content via web services.

JAX-RS is the Java API for Representational State Transfer (REST) web services. REST services are useful for performing operations via HTTP without the need for a WSDL or XML messages. REST services do not follow the SOAP standard. REST service implementations are stateless, and they provide a smaller footprint for bandwidth than SOAP services, making them ideal for HTTP on mobile devices.

Although both SOAP and REST support SSL, JAX-WS provides WS-Security, which provides enterprise-related security. JAX-WS provides a very formal transaction process over a service, whereas REST is limited by HTTP. In most cases, it is recommended to use REST services over JAX-WS when possible. However, the use of JAX-WS has its merits, especially in very secure enterprises and for use with applications requiring transaction security, such as banking services. However, newer security APIS such as JSON Web Tokens (JWT) have been introduced, providing JAX-RS services with levels of security that can be achieved with JAX-WS.

Over the next several recipes, you will be shown how to develop both JAX-WS and JAX-RS web services. You'll learn how to configure your environment to work with each type of service, and how to code a client to use the services.

J. Juneau, *Java EE 8 Recipes*, https://doi.org/10.1007/978-1-4842-3594-2_15

SETTING UP A REST ENVIRONMENT

There are a couple of options that can be utilized for creating and utilizing REST services. In this chapter, we focus on using the JAX-RS reference implementation for REST services on the Java EE platform, based upon Jersey. If you are using GlassFish 5, the API JARs are provided with the distribution, so you do not need to download any additional libraries in order to add REST functionality to your applications. However, if you are utilizing another application server, such as Tomcat, you will need to download Jersey from the home page at `https://jersey.dev.java.net/` and add the JAR files to your application server installation or application `WEB-INF/lib` directory.

In order for JAX-RS to handle REST requests, you have to configure a REST servlet dispatcher in the application's `web.xml` configuration file or in a Java class. The following excerpt from the `web.xml` configuration file demonstrates how to set up JAX-RS for an application:

```
<servlet>
        <servlet-name>javax.ws.rs.core.Application</servlet-name>
        <load-on-startup>1</load-on-startup>
    </servlet>
    <servlet-mapping>
        <servlet-name>javax.ws.rs.core.Application</servlet-name>
        <url-pattern>/rest/*</url-pattern>
    </servlet-mapping>
```

You can also use an annotation within a Java class to configure JAX-RS and forget about the `web.xml` configuration. To do so, add the `@ApplicationPath` annotation to a class, which extends `javax.ws.rs.core.Application`, as follows:

```
@javax.ws.rs.ApplicationPath("rest")
public class ApplicationConfig extends Application {
    @Override
    public Set<Class<?>> getClasses() {
        Set<Class<?>> resources = new java.util.HashSet<>();
        resources.add(org.javaee8recipes.authorservice.rest.BookAuthorFacadeREST.class);
        return resources;
    }
}
```

Additionally, if you would rather utilize Jersey so that you can use the newest features in REST, you can bundle Jersey JARs in your application and configure for Jersey utilization instead. The following configuration demonstrates a Jersey servlet dispatcher that will look for REST service classes in the `org.javaee8recipes.chapter15.rest` package.

```
<!-- REST Configuration -->
    <servlet>
        <servlet-name>Jersey REST Service</servlet-name>
        <servlet-class>com.sun.jersey.spi.container.servlet.ServletContainer
        </servlet-class>
```

```
        <init-param>
            <param-name>com.sun.jersey.config.property.packages</param-name>
            <param-value>org.javaee8recipes.chapter15.rest</param-value>
        </init-param>
        <load-on-startup>1</load-on-startup>
    </servlet>
    <servlet-mapping>
        <servlet-name>Jersey REST Service</servlet-name>
        <url-pattern>/rest/*</url-pattern>
    </servlet-mapping>
    <!-- End of REST -->
```

The tact you decide to take depends on the application you are developing. If you need to use the Java standard for RESTful web services, then choose JAX-RS, but if you want to work with the latest and greatest features in REST, choose Jersey. The material covered in the REST recipes for this chapter work with JAX-RS and Jersey.

15-1. Creating a JAX-WS Web Service Endpoint

Problem

You would like to develop a JAX-WS web service that can be called upon from a desktop or web-based client application.

Solution #1

To develop a web service endpoint solution, create an endpoint interface that exposes any public methods of the service that will be implemented. In the interface, annotate method definitions that will be exposed as web service endpoints with the `javax.jws.WebMethod` annotation. Create a class that implements the interface, and annotate it with the `javax.jws.WebService` annotation. In the following example, we develop a web service endpoint solution that exposes a single method to a client application.

The following interface is a web service endpoint interface, which declares one method, named `obtainContactList`, that will be implemented by the web service implementation class.

```
package org.javaee8recipes.chapter15.recipe15_01.endpointinterface;

import java.util.List;
import javax.jws.WebMethod;
import javax.jws.WebService;
import javax.jws.soap.SOAPBinding;
import javax.jws.soap.SOAPBinding.Style;

/**
 * Bookstore Web Service Endpoint Interface
 * @author juneau
 */
```

```
@WebService
@SOAPBinding(style=Style.DOCUMENT)
public interface BookstoreEndpoint {
    @WebMethod String obtainCompleteContactList();
}
```

Next, let's look at the web service implementation class, which implements the web service endpoint interface. The following class, `org.javaee8recipes.chapter15.recipe15_01.endpoint.BookstoreService`, defines a web service method that calls an EJB that will return the list of `Contacts` that are stored in the Acme Bookstore database.

```
package org.javaee8recipes.chapter15.recipe15_01.endpoint;

import java.util.List;
import javax.ejb.EJB;
import javax.jws.WebMethod;
import javax.jws.WebService;
import javax.xml.ws.WebServiceClient;
import org.javaee8recipes.chapter15.recipe15_01.endpointinterface.BookstoreEndpoint;
import org.javaee8recipes.entity.Contact;
import org.javaee8recipes.chapter09.session.ContactFacade;

@WebService(endpointInterface="org.javaee8recipes.chapter15.recipe15_01.endpointinterface.
BookstoreEndpoint")
public class BookstoreService implements BookstoreEndpoint {

    @EJB
    ContactFacade contactFacade;

    public void BookstoreService(){

    }

    @Override
    public String obtainCompleteContactList(){
        StringBuilder sb = new StringBuilder();
        sb.append("Here is the new JAX-WS Web Service\n");
        List<Contact> contacts = contactFacade.findAll();
        for(Contact contact: contacts){
            sb.append(contact.getEmail() + "\n");
        }
        return sb.toString();
    }
}
```

Now that the web service endpoint interface and service implementation has been created, it is time to deploy so that clients can consume the service. Refer to Recipe 15-2 for more details on deployment.

■ **Note** When annotating a class with `@WebService`, the endpoint interface is optional. However, it has been shown in this solution to demonstrate its use. In Solution #2, you will see that the interface is optional.

Solution #2

Use an IDE, such as NetBeans, to develop a web service endpoint class. The following steps walk you through the process of developing a web service endpoint using NetBeans 8.x IDE.

1. Create a new Maven Web application that will be used to host the web service, or add a web service to an existing application. Once the new application has been created, or you've chosen which of your existing Java EE applications to add the web service into, create the web service by right-clicking the NetBeans project and choosing New ➤ Web Services ➤ Web Service (see Figure 15-1). Click Next after completing the form.

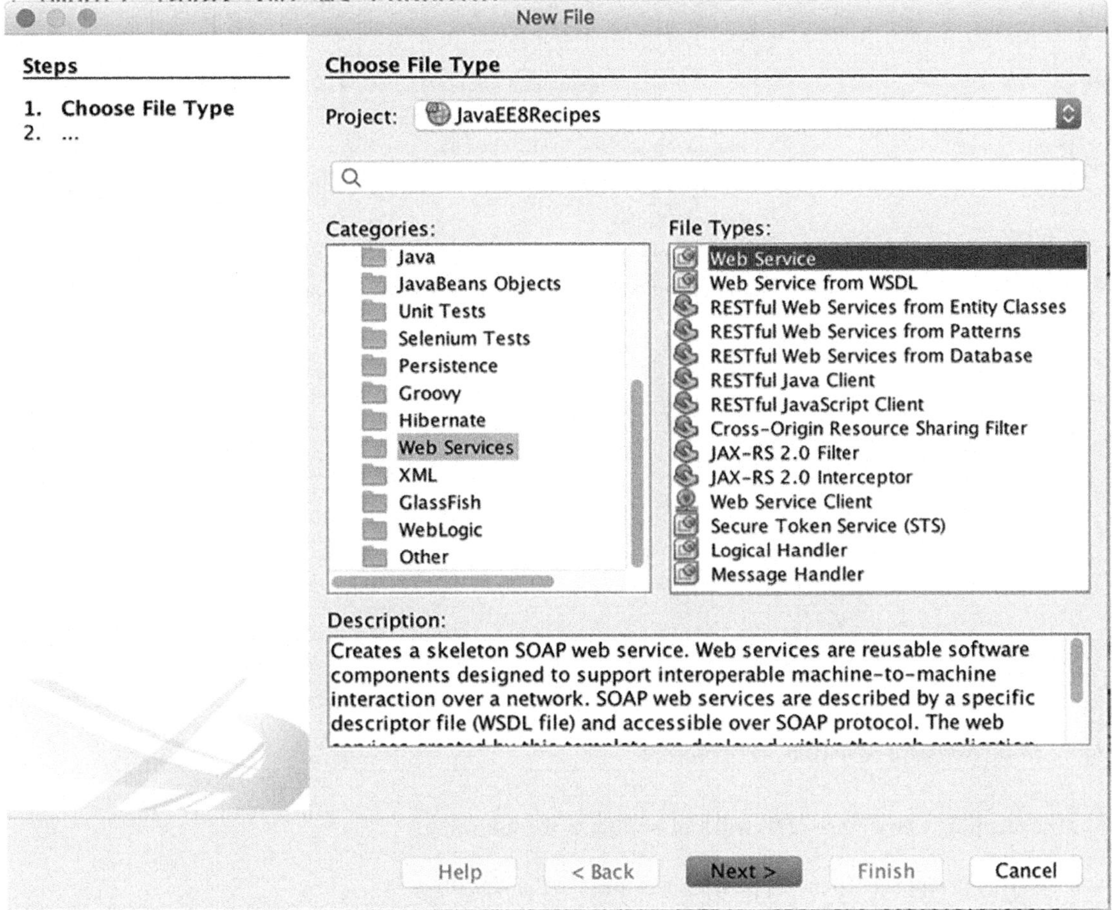

Figure 15-1. *Creating a new web service within NetBeans*

2. Complete the New Web Service form by entering a service name, location, and package in which to create the service class. For this example, leave the location as Source Packages and leave the Create Web Service from Scratch option selected (see Figure 15-2). Click Finish to create the service.

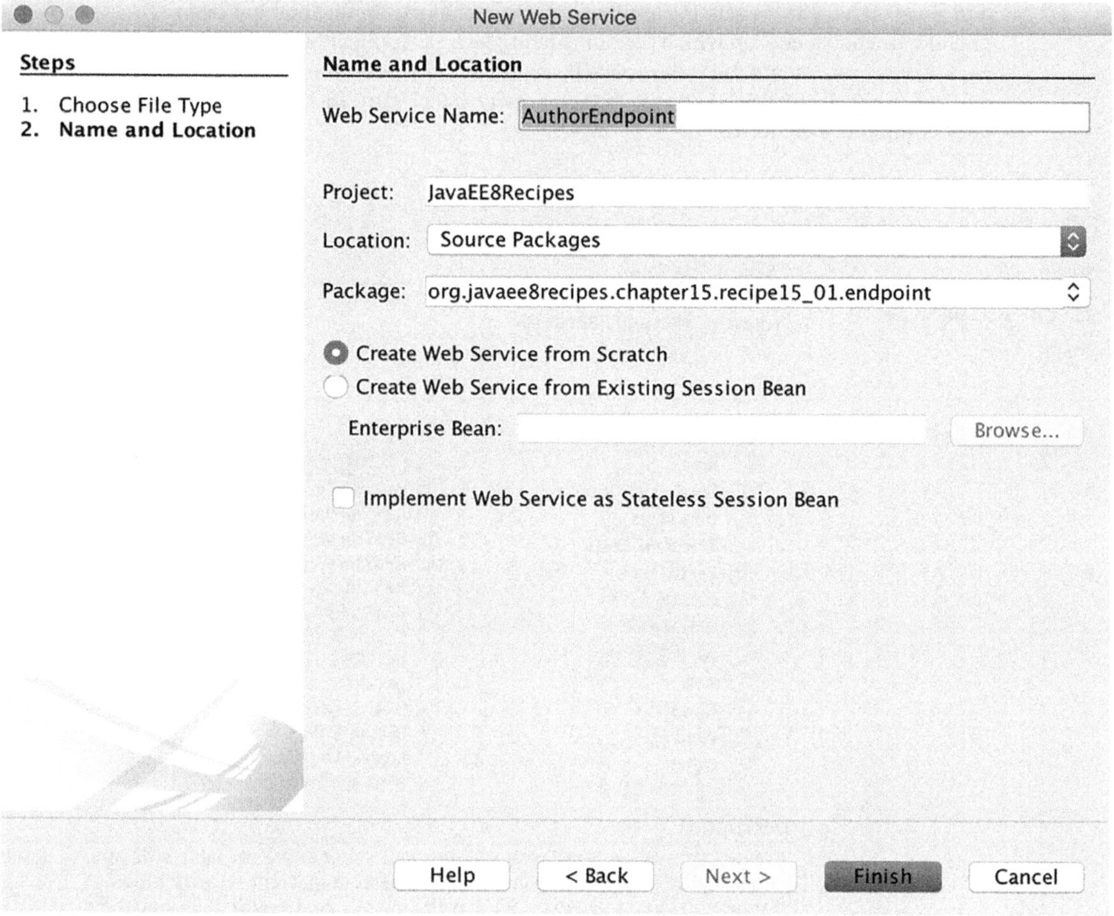

Figure 15-2. *NetBeans New Web Service form*

The resulting web service class will look similar to the following:

```
package org.javaee8recipes.chapter15.recipe15_01.endpoint;

import javax.jws.WebService;
import javax.jws.WebMethod;
import javax.jws.WebParam;

/**
 * JAX-WS service implementation class, generated by NetBeans
 * @author juneau
```

```
 */
@WebService(serviceName = "AuthorEndpoint")
public class Author {

    /**
     * This is a sample web service operation
     */
    @WebMethod(operationName = "hello")
    public String hello(@WebParam(name = "name") String txt) {
        return "Hello " + txt + " !";
    }
}
```

■ **Note** Notice that NetBeans does not generate a service endpoint interface. This is because when annotating a class with `@WebService`, an interface is optional.

How It Works

There are a few different ways to produce a JAX-WS web service, either by coding directly or by using an IDE. Perhaps the easiest way to develop a JAX-WS web service is using an IDE, such as NetBeans. However, it is important to understand the web service that you are developing before using automated tools to produce a solution. Therefore, Solution #1 shows how to develop a complete web service, which uses a web service endpoint interface. In many situations, an interface is no longer required for the development of a web service implementation class. However, some clients still necessitate coding against an interface (see Recipe 15-3 for details). Solution #2 covers the easier technique for generating web services, that is, utilizing an IDE.

When writing a service endpoint interface, which is optional with newer releases of Java EE, create a standard Java interface that contains signatures for any public methods that will be exposed. A service interface differs from a standard interface because it is annotated with `@WebService`. It may also contain an optional `@SOAPBinding` interface to specify the style of the service that is to be created. By default, the `@SOAPBinding` style attribute is set to `Style.DOCUMENT`, but `Style.RPC` can also be specified to create an RPC-style service. Any methods that are declared within the interface should be annotated with `@WebMethod`.

The service implementation class should implement the service endpoint interface if there is one. In the example for Solution #1, the class does implement the service endpoint interface, and therefore, it is annotated with `@WebService`, and the `endpointInterface` attribute of the annotation contains the fully qualified name of the endpoint interface in `String` format. Being that the service implementation class in this example implements the interface, it needs to implement the method(s) contained within the interface. Since the endpoint interface designates the `obtainCompleteContactList` method with a `@WebMethod` annotation, it will be exposed via the service. After the service implementation class and its endpoint interface are deployed, the service will be identified by the specified `serviceName` attribute of the `@WebService` annotation. If this attribute is not specified, the application server will append the word `Service` to the end of every web service class name to create a default identifier for the service.

It is possible to construct the same web service without the need for a service endpoint interface. However, some clients require the use of an interface to work properly. If you're developing a web service implementation class without the service endpoint interface, omit the `endpointInterface` attribute of the `@WebService` annotation and mark any methods that will be exposed with the `@WebMethod` annotation. The following source listing is the same `BookstoreService` class shown in Solution #2, but it does not use a service endpoint interface.

```
@WebService
public class BookstoreService implements BookstoreEndpoint {

    @EJB
    ContactFacade contactFacade;

    public void BookstoreService(){
    }

    @WebMethod
    public String obtainCompleteContactList(){
        StringBuilder sb = new StringBuilder();
        sb.append("Here is the new JAX-WS Web Service\n");
        List<Contact> contacts = contactFacade.findAll();
        for(Contact contact: contacts){
            sb.append(contact.getEmail() + "\n");
        }
        return sb.toString();
    }
}
```

Table 15-1 lists the different optional elements of the `@WebService` annotation.

Table 15-1. *@WebService Elements*

Element	Description
`endpointInterface`	The complete name of the service endpoint interface.
`name`	The name of the web service.
`portName`	The port name of the web service.
`serviceName`	The service name of the web service.
`targetNamespace`	Used for the namespace for the `wsdl:portType`.
`wsdlLocation`	The location of a predefined WSDL describing the service.

Table 15-2 lists the different optional elements of the `@WebMethod` annotation.

Table 15-2. *@WebMethod Elements*

Element	Description
`action`	The action for this operation.
`exclude`	Marks a method to NOT be exposed as a web method.
`operationName`	Name of the `wsdl:operation` matching this method.

When using an IDE to develop a web service, there is usually very little coding involved. Most IDEs, such as NetBeans, include a wizard to help developers create web services. Solution #2 walks you through the process of creating a JAX-WS web service using the NetBeans IDE. By default, the wizard does not create a service endpoint interface, so the entire web service solution is contained within a single class.

WHAT IS A WSDL DOCUMENT?

When a web service is deployed, it produces what is known as a WSDL document. A *WSDL document* is constructed of XML elements that describe the web service so that it can be consumed. A WSDL file uses the following elements to describe web services:

- `<binding>`: Specifies data protocol and binding for each particular port type.
- `<message>`: Contains `<part>` subelements that define the data elements for the service.
- `<portType>`: Defines a web service, the operations it can perform, and the messages it contains.
- `<types>`: Defines the datatypes that are used by the web service.

The following XML is an excerpt of the WSDL that is generated by the `BookstoreService` web service created in this recipe:

```
<!--
Published by JAX-WS RI at http://jax-ws.dev.java.net. RI's version is Metro/2.1
(branches/2.1-6728; 2011-02-03T14:14:58+0000) JAXWS-RI/2.2.3 JAXWS/2.2.
-->
<!--
Generated by JAX-WS RI at http://jax-ws.dev.java.net. RI's version is Metro/2.1
(branches/2.1-6728; 2011-02-03T14:14:58+0000) JAXWS-RI/2.2.3 JAXWS/2.2.
-->
<definitions xmlns:wsu="http://docs.oasis-open.org/wss/2004/01/oasis-200401-wss-
wssecurity-utility-1.0.xsd" xmlns:wsp="http://www.w3.org/ns/ws-policy"

    xmlns:wsp1_2="http://schemas.xmlsoap.org/ws/2004/09/policy"
    xmlns:wsam="http://www.w3.org/2007/05/addressing/metadata"
    xmlns:soap="http://schemas.xmlsoap.org/wsdl/soap/"
    xmlns:tns="http://endpoint.recipe15_01.chapter15.javaee8recipes.org/"
    xmlns:xsd="http://www.w3.org/2001/XMLSchema"
    xmlns="http://schemas.xmlsoap.org/wsdl/"
    targetNamespace="http://endpoint.recipe15_01.chapter15.javaee8recipes.org/"
    name="BookstoreServiceService">
<import namespace="http://endpointinterface.recipe15_01.chapter15.javaee8recipes.org/"
    location="http://localhost:8080/JavaEERecipes/BookstoreServiceService?wsdl=1"/>
<binding xmlns:ns1="http://endpointinterface.recipe15_01.chapter15.javaee8recipes.org/"
    name="BookstoreServicePortBinding" type="ns1:BookstoreEndpoint">
<soap:binding transport="http://schemas.xmlsoap.org/soap/http" style="rpc"/>
<operation name="obtainCompleteContactList">
<soap:operation soapAction=""/>
<input>
<soap:body use="literal"
    namespace="http://endpointinterface.recipe15_01.chapter15.javaee8recipes.org/"/>
</input>
<output>
<soap:body use="literal" namespace="http://endpointinterface.recipe15_01.chapter15.
javaee8recipes.org/"/>
</output>
```

```
</operation>
</binding>
<service name="BookstoreServiceService">
<port name="BookstoreServicePort" binding="tns:BookstoreServicePortBinding">
<soap:address location="http://localhost:8080/JavaEERecipes/BookstoreServiceService"/>
</port>
</service>
</definitions>
```

15-2. Deploying a JAX-WS Web Service

Problem

You have implemented a JAX-WS web service endpoint and you want to deploy it to a Java EE container so that clients can begin to consume it.

Solution #1

A JAX-WS web service can be deployed in a number of ways. First, be sure that the Java EE application to which the web service belongs has been fully developed, including all necessary configuration, and is ready for deployment. Once the application is ready to be deployed, it can be compiled into a WAR file, and then deployed to the application server container. The WAR file can be deployed to an application server container, such as GlassFish or Payara, via the standard means of deploying any type of Java web application. To that end, deploy the project via the GlassFish administrative console, manually copy the WAR into the GlassFish `autodeploy` directory, or utilize the GlassFish command-line interface. Refer to Chapter 12 for more details on deploying an application to GlassFish 5 or Payara 5 application server.

Solution #2

If using an IDE to develop your web service, it is typically very easy to deploy the service from directly within the development environment. In this case, we will assume that Apache NetBeans is the IDE of choice. To deploy a fully developed Java EE project that contains a web service, perform the following steps:

1. Ensure that your Apache NetBeans project appears in the left-side Projects menu.
2. Right-click your Apache NetBeans project and choose Deploy from the contextual menu.

■ **Note** In order to deploy an application from within Apache NetBeans, your project must be associated with an application server. To learn more about setting up an application server for use via Apache NetBeans, refer to Appendix A.

Solution #3

Create an endpoint publisher, which is a stand-alone application that will publish the service to a specified URL. To create a publisher, develop a stand-alone application that contains a main method and invoke the `javax.xml.ws.Endpoint` object's `publish` method from within the main method. Pass the URL to which you would like to publish the web service, along with an instance of the web service implementation class to the `publish` method. The following stand-alone application demonstrates the use of an `Endpoint` publisher. The sources for this publisher can be found at `org.javaee8recipes.chapter15.recipe15_02.endpoint.publisher.BookstorePublisher`.

```
package org.javaee8recipes.chapter15.recipe15_02.endpoint.publisher;

import javax.xml.ws.Endpoint;
import org.javaee8recipes.chapter15.recipe15_01.endpoint.BookstoreService;

//Endpoint publisher
public class BookstorePublisher{
    public static void main(String[] args) {
           Endpoint.publish("http://localhost:8080/JavaEERecipes/BookstoreServicePub", new
           BookstoreService());
    }
}
```

When the publisher class is started, the web service will become available at the specified URL.

How It Works

To deploy an application that contains a web service, use the same procedures that would be used to deploy any Java EE Application or Apache NetBeans project. Both Solution #1 and Solution #2 to this recipe show how to deploy an application or Apache NetBeans project to the GlassFish application server.

Once the service is deployed using one of the techniques mentioned, the WSDL for the service can be viewed by using the following URL within your browser: `http://localhost:8080/JavaEERecipes/BookstoreService?wsdl`.

The third solution to this recipe demonstrates the use of a publisher class to deploy a web service. The publisher class is a stand-alone application that can be executed in order to make the web service available for use.

15-3. Consuming a JAX-WS Web Service via WSDL

Problem

You would like to consume a published JAX-WS web service using its WSDL file.

Solution

In order for a client to gain reference to a web service implementation class, the artifacts must be generated via the Java compiler by using the `wsimport` utility. To generate the artifacts for clients to use, run the `wsimport` utility, passing the URL to the web service WSDL file. The following lines from the terminal or command line demonstrate how to use the `wsimport` tool to produce the artifacts for the JAX-WS web service that was created in Recipe 15-1.

```
wsimport -keep -verbose http://localhost:8080/JavaEERecipes/BookstoreServiceService?wsdl
parsing WSDL...

Generating code...

org/javaee8recipes/chapter15/recipe15_01/endpoint/BookstoreEndpoint.java
org/javaee8recipes/chapter15/recipe15_01/endpoint/BookstoreServiceService.java
```

Once the artifacts have been generated, they can be copied into the correct Java packages (if the `wsimport` tool was not run within the correct package already), and a client application can be coded to use the web service implementation classes.

How It Works

When a Java web service is created and deployed, the Java environment creates service implementation artifacts on the fly, which enable service discovery by the client applications. A client application can use `wsimport` to generate the client-side artifacts/classes that can be used to access the web service. The `wsimport` tool ships with the JDK, and therefore, resides in the `<JDK_Home>/bin` directory. To utilize the tool, open a command prompt or terminal window, and then traverse into the directory in which the resulting classes should be written. Optionally, you can specify the directory into which the files should be generated by passing the `-d` flag. The `wsimport` tool accepts the URL to the WSDL file of the web service for which you want to create the artifacts. In the example to this solution, there are a couple of optional flags specified as well. Table 15-3 lists the different flags that can be used along with the `wsimport` tool.

Table 15-3. *wsimport Command Flags*

Flag	Description
`-d <directory>`	Specifies where to place the generated output files.
`-b <path>`	Specifies an external JAX-WS or JAXB binding file.
`-B <jaxbOption>`	Passes this option to the JAXB schema compiler.
`-catalog`	Specifies a catalog file to use for resolving external entity references.
`-extension`	Allows vendor extensions to be utilized.
`-help`	Displays the help for `wsimport`.
`-httpproxy:<host>:<port>`	Specifies an HTTP proxy server.
`-keep`	Tells the tool to keep the generated files.
`-p`	Specifying a target package via this command-line option overrides any `wsdl` and schema binding.
`-s <directory>`	Specifies where to place the generated source files.
`-verbose`	Causes output messages explaining the steps taken by the compiler.
`-version`	Prints information regarding the tool version.
`-wsdllocation <location>`	Specifies the location to the WSDL file.
`-target`	Generates code as per the given JAX-WS specification version.
`-quiet`	Suppresses any output.

15-4. Consuming a JAX-WS Web Service via a Stand-Alone Application Client

Problem

You have written a JAX-WS web service and you would like to consume it using a stand-alone Java client application.

Solution

Develop a stand-alone application that will reference the WSDL of the web service that it will consume, then generate a service based on the WSDL and qualified name of the web service implementation. The following Java source is a stand-alone client application that consumes the JAX-WS web service that was developed in Recipe 15-1.

```
package org.javaee8recipes.chapter15.recipe15_01.endpoint.appclient;

import java.net.URL;
import java.util.List;
import javax.xml.namespace.QName;
import javax.xml.ws.Service;
import org.javaee8recipes.chapter15.recipe15_01.endpoint.BookstoreService;
import org.javaee8recipes.chapter15.recipe15_01.endpointinterface.BookstoreEndpoint;
import org.javaee8recipes.entity.Contact;

/**
 *
 * @author juneau
 */
public class BookstoreClient {

    public static void main(String[] args) {
        List<Contact> contacts = obtainList();
    }

    public static List<Contact> obtainList() {
        try {
            URL url = new URL("http://localhost:8080/JavaEERecipes/BookstoreService?wsdl");

            QName qname = new QName("http://endpoint.recipe15_01.chapter15.javaee8recipes.
            org/", "BookstoreServiceService");
            Service service = Service.create(url, qname);
            BookstoreEndpoint bookstore = service.getPort(BookstoreEndpoint.class);
            System.out.println(bookstore.obtainCompleteContactList());
        } catch (Exception e) {
            System.out.println("Exception: "+ e);
        }
        return null;
    }
}
```

Running this application will invoke the BookstoreService and display the entire list of contacts that are stored in the Acme Bookstore's CONTACT database table.

How It Works

A client that is going to consume a JAX-WS web service must have the ability to obtain information regarding the web service. This information can be obtained from the web service WSDL document. There are a couple of ways that a client can obtain a reference to and parse a WSDL in order to obtain a proxy to a web service. In the solution to this example, we assume that a web service endpoint interface has been coded, and therefore, the code makes use of the interface to call upon the exposed methods.

In the solution to this example, the client application creates a URL object that points to the web service WSDL file and uses it to invoke the service methods that have been exposed to clients. The next step the client application needs to take is to construct the qualified name of the web service in the form of a QName object. Once the client has both the URL to the WSDL and the QName, those can be passed to the javax.xml.ws.Service class create method to create a Service instance, which is the client view of the service. The service proxy can then be used to obtain a proxy to the service by calling the getPort method of the Service instance. The proxy returns the service endpoint interface, which can then be used to call upon the methods of the service.

As mentioned previously, it is possible to obtain a reference to the WSDL document and obtain a service proxy in different ways as well. If a web service does not contain a service endpoint interface

(@WebService and @WebMethod annotations exist within service implementation class), then you don't need to create URL and QName objects. In fact, a client application can simply call upon the Service getPort method to obtain a proxy to the service and return the service endpoint interface that is automatically generated by the container. The WSDL reference can also be injected into a client class to alleviate the need for URL and QName objects via the @WebServiceRef annotation. The following example client demonstrates these techniques to call the BookstoreService method.

```
import javax.xml.ws.WebServiceRef;

public class BookstoreClient {
    @WebServiceRef(wsdlLocation =
      "META-INF/wsdl/localhost_8080/JavaEERecipes/BookstoreServiceService.wsdl")
    private static BookstoreService service;

    /**
     * @param args the command line arguments
     */
    public static void main(String[] args) {
       System.out.println(sayHello("world"));
    }

    private static String obtainContacts() {
        org.javaee8recipes.chapter15.recipe15_1.BookstoreService port = service.get
        BookstoreServicePort();
        return port.obtainCompleteContactList();
    }
}
```

The @WebServiceRef annotation is used to define a reference to a web service and optionally an injection target for it. Table 15-4 lists the different (optional) elements of the @WebServiceRef annotation.

Table 15-4. *@WebServiceRef Elements*

Attribute	Description
lookup	A portable JNDI lookup name that resolves to the target web service reference.
mappedName	A product-specific name that this resource should be mapped to.
name	A JNDI name of the resource.
type	The Java type of the resource.
value	The service class, always a type extending javax.xml.ws.Service.
wsdlLocation	A URL pointing to the WSDL document for the web service.

15-5. Integrating JAX-WS Web Services into a Java EE Project

Problem

You want to expose methods as web services to be consumed via JSF views on an enterprise application.

Solution

Designate an EJB as a web service using the @WebService annotation and specify methods of the EJB to be exposed via the web service using the @WebMethod annotation. Once the EJB has been made into a web service, deploy it and use the wsimport tool to create artifacts from the resulting WSDL. Finally, reference the web service from a managed bean controller to use it.

EJB as a Web Service

The following excerpt, taken from org.javaee8recipes.chapter09.session.ChapterFacade, demonstrates how to expose an EJB as a web service using only a couple of annotations.

```
package org.javaee8recipes.chapter09.session;

import java.math.BigDecimal;
import java.util.List;
import javax.ejb.Stateless;
import javax.jws.WebMethod;
import javax.jws.WebService;
import javax.persistence.EntityManager;
import javax.persistence.PersistenceContext;
import org.javaee8recipes.entity.Book;
import org.javaee8recipes.entity.Chapter;

@WebService
@Stateless
public class ChapterFacade extends AbstractFacade<Chapter> {
    @PersistenceContext(unitName = "JavaEERecipesPU")
    private EntityManager em;
```

```
    @Override
    protected EntityManager getEntityManager() {
        return em;
    }

    public ChapterFacade() {
        super(Chapter.class);
    }

    @WebMethod
    public List<Book> findBookByChapterTitle(Chapter chapter){
        return em.createQuery("select b from Book b INNER JOIN b.chapters c " +
                "where c.title = :title")
                .setParameter("title", chapter.getTitle())
                .getResultList();
    }

    public List<Book> findAllBooksByChapterNumber(BigDecimal chapterNumber){
        return em.createQuery("select b from Book b LEFT OUTER JOIN b.chapters c " +
                "where c.chapterNumber = :num")
                .setParameter("num", chapterNumber)
                .getResultList();
    }

}
```

When the application that contains the annotated EJB is deployed, the ChapterFacade Service/ChapterFacade web service will be deployed and made available for use to client applications, including JSF-managed bean controllers.

Coding the JSF Client

A JSF CDI-managed bean can be a web service client, just as a servlet or stand-alone Java application can. Before writing the managed bean client, the wsimport tool (covered in Recipe 15-3) must be used to create the artifacts from the resulting WSDL file that was generated when the web service was deployed. Once the wsimport tool has run, the web service can be referenced via utilization of the @WebServiceRef annotation, and its methods can be invoked.

The ChapterController JSF CDI bean class of the Acme Bookstore application, found in the JavaEERecipes project at org.javaee8recipes.chapter09.jsf.ChapterController, has been modified to use the ChapterFacadeService. The following excerpt, taken from the class, demonstrates how to reference a web service implementation class and call the service methods from within a managed bean controller.

```
...
@Named (value = "chapterController")
@SessionScoped
public class ChapterController implements Serializable {

    @EJB
    ChapterFacade ejbFacade;
```

```
    // Uncomment after running wsimport utility and placing the compiled
    ChapterFacadeService class
    // into the CLASSPATH

  @WebServiceRef(wsdlLocation="http://localhost:8080/ChapterFacadeService/
  ChapterFacade?wsdl")
    ChapterFacade chapterService;

    private List<Book> booksByChapterTitle;
    private List<Chapter> completeChapterList;
    private List<Book> booksByChapterNumber;

    /**
     * Creates a new instance of ChapterController
     */
    public ChapterController() {
    }

    /* Uncomment after running wsimport utility and placing the compiled
    ChapterFacadeService class
     * into the CLASSPATH
     */
    public List<Book> loadAllChapters(){
        return chapterService.findAll();
    }
    ...
```

How It Works

Many enterprise applications utilize EJBs or CDI beans to retrieve data from an underlying database. In most cases, the data provided by these same queries residing within the EJB are necessary for use via remote clients. In such cases, it makes sense to make the entire EJB into a fully functional web service. Doing so is easy by decorating an EJB class and methods with the `@WebService` and `@WebMethod` annotations. By creating web services from EJB classes, enterprise applications can reduce the amount of redundant code that is required by coding separate web services, and increase performance since fewer resources are required when fewer classes are querying the underlying data store.

The `@WebService` annotation can be used to decorate an EJB class to denote it as a web service. The `@WebService` annotation accepts the (optional) elements that are listed in Table 15-1. If a class is designated as a web service, then all public methods will be made available to clients. The `@WebMethod` annotation can be placed before any public method within an EJB to expose it via the web service. In the solution to this example, the `@WebMethod` annotation is placed before the first method as a demonstration only. Since the class has been designated as a web service using the `@WebService` annotation, all public methods will be exposed, even if they are not decorated with `@WebMethod`. To deploy the web service, simply deploy the Java EE application that contains the annotated EJB to a compliant Java EE application server container, such as GlassFish or Payara.

In the end, JAX-WS web services can be easy to generate from existing entity classes. Once generated, JSF-managed bean controllers can use the web service to provide data or content from the web service to JSF views within the application.

15-6. Developing a RESTful Web Service

Problem

You would like to create a JAX-RS web service that will be exposed over the Internet to handle operations on data.

■ **Note** Prior to performing the solutions to this recipe, you must be sure that your environment is configured for using REST services. For more information, see the introduction to this chapter.

Solution #1

Create a RESTful (Representational State Transfer) web service by creating a root resource class (POJO) and adding resource methods to the class. To designate a class as a root resource class, annotate it with `@Path` or create at least one method in the class that is annotated with `@Path` and a request method designator (`@GET`, `@PUT`, `@POST`, or `@DELETE`). The following example demonstrates how to create a RESTful web service that simply displays a `String` or HTML to a client. The sources for this code can be found in the `JavaEE8Recipes` project in the `org.javaee8recipes.chapter15.SimpleRest.java` file.

```
package org.javaee8recipes.chapter15.rest;

import javax.ws.rs.GET;
import javax.ws.rs.Produces;
import javax.ws.rs.Path;

// Set the PATH to http://host:port/application/rest/simplerest/
@Path("/simplerest")
public class SimpleRest {

    @GET
    // Produces plaintext message
    @Produces("text/plain")
    public String getPlainMessage() {
        return "Hello from a simple rest service";
    }

    @GET
    // Produces plaintext message
    @Produces("text/html")
    public String getHTMLMessage() {
        return "<P>Hello from a <b>simple</b> rest service</P>";
    }
}
```

Assuming that you have configured your environment to work with JAX-RS, you can deploy the `JavaEE8Recipes` application and then visit the following URL to see the results produced from the REST service: `http://localhost:8080/JavaEERecipes/rest/simplerest`.

Solution #2

Utilize an IDE, such as NetBeans, to create a RESTful web service. The NetBeans IDE includes wizards for developing web services of different types. By right-clicking a project and choosing New ➤ Other from the contextual menu, the New File dialog will open, and you can choose Web Services from the selection list, as seen in Figure 15-1. Proceed with the following directions to generate a REST web service from an entity class.

1. Choose the RESTful Web Service from Entity Classes option from the New File menu.

2. Select one or more classes from the Available Entity Classes list and click the Add button. In this example, we'll choose the `org.javaee8recipes.entity.Book` entity, as shown in Figure 15-3. Choose Next.

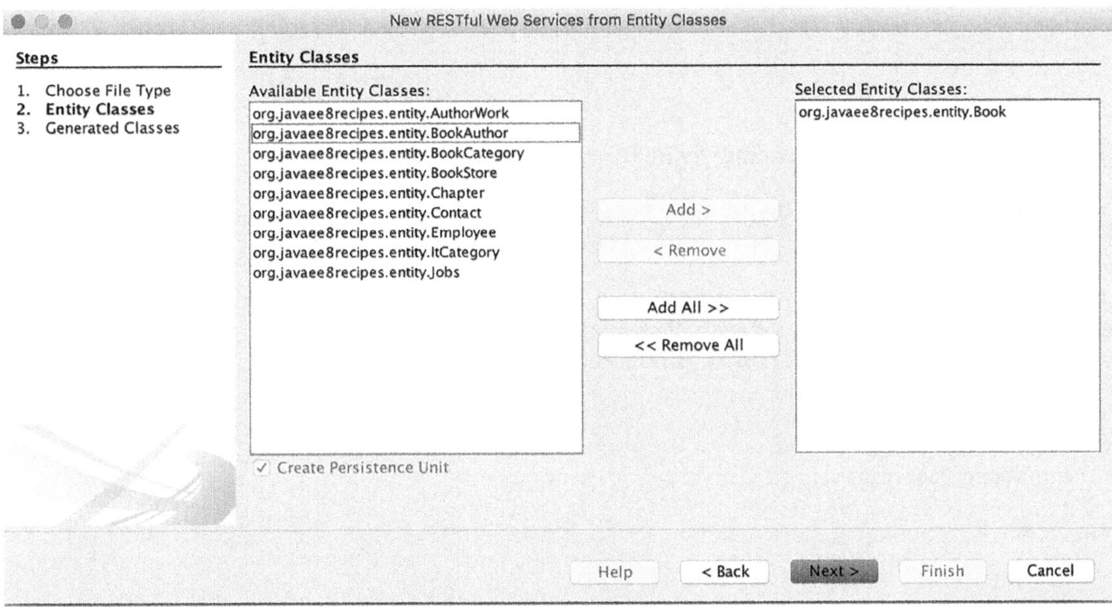

Figure 15-3. *Select entity classes for RESTful web services within NetBeans*

3. List the package into which the REST service class will be generated, along with a package location (see Figure 15-4). Click Finish.

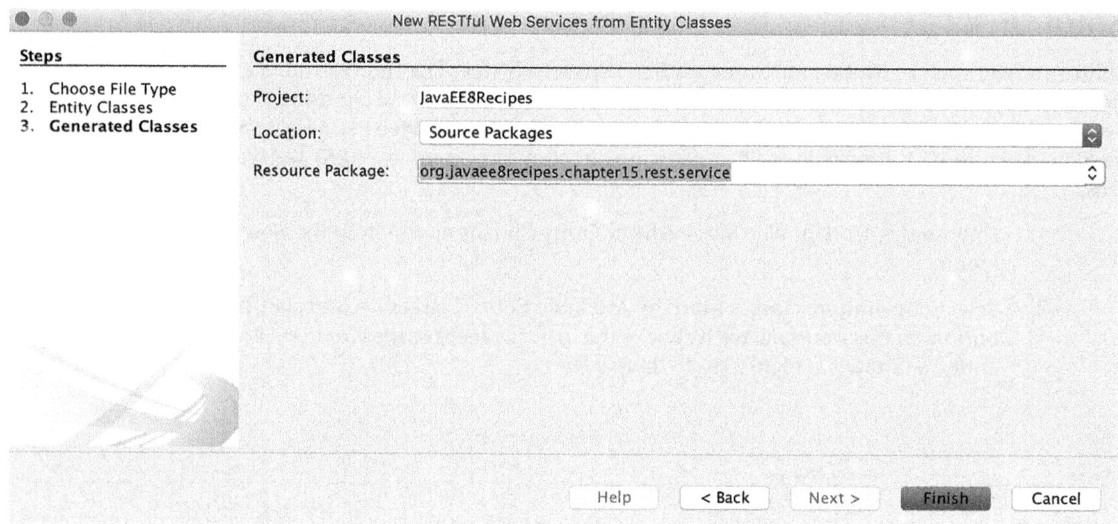

***Figure 15-4.** Choose a resource package for REST service class within NetBeans*

A REST service class that is similar to the following class is generated after performing these steps.

```
@Stateless
@Path("org.javaee8recipes.entity.book")
public class BookFacadeREST extends AbstractFacade<Book> {
    @PersistenceContext(unitName = "JavaEERecipesPU")
    private EntityManager em;

    public BookFacadeREST() {
        super(Book.class);
    }

    @POST
    @Override
    @Consumes({"application/xml", "application/json"})
    public void create(Book entity) {
        super.create(entity);
    }

    @PUT
    @Override
    @Consumes({"application/xml", "application/json"})
    public void edit(Book entity) {
        super.edit(entity);
    }

    @DELETE
    @Path("{id}")
    public void remove(@PathParam("id") BigDecimal id) {
        super.remove(super.find(id));
    }
```

```
    @GET
    @Path("{id}")
    @Produces({"application/xml", "application/json"})
    public Book find(@PathParam("id") BigDecimal id) {
        return super.find(id);
    }

    @GET
    @Override
    @Produces({"application/xml", "application/json"})
    public List<Book> findAll() {
        return super.findAll();
    }

    @GET
    @Path("{from}/{to}")
    @Produces({"application/xml", "application/json"})
    public List<Book> findRange(@PathParam("from") Integer from, @PathParam("to") Integer to) {
        return super.findRange(new int[]{from, to});
    }

    @GET
    @Path("count")
    @Produces("text/plain")
    public String countREST() {
        return String.valueOf(super.count());
    }

    @Override
    protected EntityManager getEntityManager() {
        return em;
    }

}
```

How It Works

RESTful web services are easy to develop, and they have the ability to produce and consume many different types of media. In most cases, REST web services are encouraged for services that will be sending and receiving information over the Internet. Before an application can support REST services, it must be properly configured to do so. In this book, the JAX-RS REST implementation is utilized, which is based on Jersey, the standard REST implementation for the industry. See the introduction to this chapter for more information on configuring JAX-RS (or Jersey, which is the Reference Implementation) in your application.

A Java class that is a REST service implementation contains a myriad of annotations. Table 15-5 lists the possible annotations that may be used to create a REST service.

Table 15-5. *REST Service Annotations*

Annotation	Description
@POST	Request method designator that processes HTTP POST requests.
@GET	Request method designator that processes HTTP GET requests.
@PUT	Request method designator that processes HTTP PUT requests.
@DELETE	Request method designator that processes HTTP DELETE requests.
@HEAD	Request method designator that corresponds to the HTTP HEAD method. Processes HTTP HEAD requests.
@Path	The value of this annotation should correlate to the relative URI path that indicates where the Java class will be hosted. Variables can be embedded in the URIs to make a URI path template.
@PathParam	A type of parameter that can be extracted for use in the resource class. URI path parameters are extracted from the request URI, and the parameter names correspond to the URI path template variable names specified in the @Path class-level annotation.
@QueryParam	A type of parameter that can be extracted for use in the resource class. Query parameters are extracted from the request.
@Consumes	Used to specify the MIME media types of representations that a resource can consume.
@Produces	Used to specify the MIME media types of representations that a resource can produce.
@Provider	Used for anything that is of interest to the JAX-RS runtime, such as a MessageBodyHeader and MessageBodyWriter.

To designate a class as a REST service, the @Path annotation must be placed prior to the class, or before at least one of the class method signatures. The @Path annotation is used to indicate the URI that should correspond to the service. The full URI includes the host name, port number, application name, and REST servlet name, followed by the path designated with the @Path annotation. In the example, the @Path annotation specifies "/simplerest" as the service path, so the URL http://localhost:8080/JavaEERecipes/rest/simplerest will invoke the web service. It is possible to include variables within a URL by enclosing them within brackets using the syntax: {var}. For example, if each user had his or her own profile for a particular site, the @Path designation could be as follows:

```
...
@Path("/simplerest/{user}")
...
```

In such a case, the URL could look like the following: http://localhost:8080/JavaEERecipes/rest/simplerest/Juneau.

The @Path annotation can also be specified before any methods that are marked with @GET, @POST, @PUT, or @DELETE in order to specify a URI for invoking the denoted method. Moreover, variables can be placed within the path in order to accept a more dynamic URL. For instance, suppose a method was added to the class in Solution #1 that would return a greeting for the user that is specified as a parameter within the URL. You may do something like the following in order to make the URL unique:

```
@Path("{user}")
@GET
@Produces("text/html")
```

```
public String getUserMessage(@PathParam("userv) String user){
    return "Greetings " + "<b>" + user + "</b>";
}
```

In this case, the `getUserMessage` method would be invoked if a URL like the following were placed into the browser: `http://localhost:8080/JavaEERecipes/rest/simplerest/josh`. If this URL were specified, then the method would be invoked, passing `josh` as the user variable value, and the message would be displayed as:

```
Hello josh
```

■ **Note** It is very important to create URIs that are readable and provide intuitive information about your web service. URIs that are based on these standards help to reduce errors within client applications and make the web service more functional.

Designate methods with the `@GET`, `@POST`, `@PUT`, or `@DELETE` designator to process the type of web service request that is desired. Doing so will generate web service functionality. If more than one method exists in a REST web service implementation and `@Path` is only specified at the class level and not at the method level, the method that returns the MIME type the client requires will be invoked. If you want your method to display content, designate a method with `@GET`. If you want to create a method for adding or inserting an object, designate the method as `@POST`. If you are creating a method for inserting new objects only, designate it with `@PUT`. Finally, if you are creating a method for removing objects, designate it with `@DELETE`. For more information regarding these annotations, refer to Recipe 15-8.

REST services can become fairly complex if they constitute many different methods and paths. Entire applications exist based on REST services, where all CRUD (Create, Retrieve, Update, Delete) manipulations are invoked via web service calls. This recipe provides only the foundation for developing with JAX-RS, as the topic is far too involved for a handful of recipes or a chapter in itself.

15-7. Consuming and Producing with REST

Problem

You would like to produce different types of content with a RESTful web service. Moreover, you would like the web service to consume content as well.

Solution

Create methods within the web service implementation class that are annotated with `@GET` for generating output, and optionally along with `@Produces` for specifying the type of output. Annotate methods with `@POST` or `@PUT` for updating or inserting data. The following sections provide examples utilizing these solutions.

Producing Output

Use the `@Produces` annotation to specify the type of content you want to produce from a decorated method. The following excerpt, taken from the `JavaEERecipes` project source at `org.javaee8recipes.chapter15.rest.SimpleRest`, demonstrates the use of `@Produces`.

```
    @GET
    // Produces an XML message
    @Produces("application/xml")
    public MessageWrapper getXMLMessage() {
        // Pass string to MessageWrapper class, which marshals the String as XML
        return new MessageWrapper("Hello from a simple rest service");
    }
```

Producing List Output

Use the @Produces annotation to specify the type of content you want to produce from a decorated method. The following excerpt, taken from the JavaEERecipes project source at org.javaee8recipes.chapter15.rest.SimpleRest, demonstrates the use of @Produces and returns an object that contains a list of results.

```
@GET
// Produces an XML message
@Path("all")
@Produces("application/xml")
public MessageWrapperList getXMLMessageList() {
    ArrayList<String> messageList = new ArrayList<>();
    messageList.add("String 1");
    messageList.add("String 2");
        return new MessageWrapperList(messageList);
}
```

In this case, the MessageWrapperList object sources are as follows, but this example could be changed to accept lists of any object type...not just strings.

```
package org.javaee8recipes.chapter15.recipe15_07;

import java.util.ArrayList;
import java.util.Collection;
import java.util.List;
import javax.xml.bind.annotation.XmlElement;
import javax.xml.bind.annotation.XmlRootElement;
import javax.xml.bind.annotation.XmlSeeAlso;

@XmlRootElement(name="messageWrapperList")
@XmlSeeAlso(String.class)
public class MessageWrapperList extends ArrayList<String> {
    private static final long serialVersionUID = 1L;

    public MessageWrapperList(){
        super();
    }

    public MessageWrapperList(Collection<? extends String> message){
        super(message);
    }
```

```
    @XmlElement(name="messageList")
    public List<String> getMessageList() {
        return this;
    }

    public void setMessageList(List<String> messages) {
        this.addAll(messages);
    }
}
```

Accepting Input

Annotate methods within a web service class with @PUT to indicate that some content is being passed to the method. To specify the type of content being passed, annotate the same method with @Consumes(content-type). The following excerpt, taken from the JavaEERecipes project source at org.javaee8recipes.chapter15.rest.SimpleRest.java, demonstrates the use of @Consumes.

```
@PUT
@Path("add")
@Consumes("text/plain")
public String add(@QueryParam("text") String text){
    this.message = text;
    return message;
}
```

To input a new message stating JavaEERecipes, you would reach the following URL in your browser, which passes the new message to the text variable: http://localhost:8080/JavaEERecipes/rest/simplerest/add?text=Javaee8recipes.

How It Works

Create a web service class by following the procedures outlined in Recipe 15-7, and then designate methods within the web service as producers or consumers by annotating them appropriately. Methods that will be generating some type of output should be annotated with @Produces, which should subsequently specify the type of output generated. Moreover, the methods that are generating output should also be annotated with @GET, which indicates that the method is a reading resource. Methods that will be accepting input should be annotated with @PUT or @POST. The @PUT annotation indicates that a new resource will be created, and the @POST annotation indicates that an existing resource will be updated or a new resource will be created. Incidentally, the methods that accept input should also be annotated with @Consumes, which should subsequently specify the type of content that is being consumed. Overall, @Produces annotations should coincide with the @GET annotated methods. That is, a method that is decorated with @GET will return some content to the client. @Consumes annotations should coincide with either @PUT or @POST annotated methods.

In the solution to this recipe, two types of methods are demonstrated. The first example demonstrates a REST method that produces XML content, and the @Produces("application/xml") annotation indicates it as such. Within the method, a string is passed to a class named MessageWrapper. The MessageWrapper class is responsible for marshaling the string as XML using JAXB. For more information, refer to the sources located at org.javaee8recipes.chapter15.recipe15_07.MessageWrapper.java and see the JAXB documentation online at https://javaee.github.io/tutorial/jaxrs-advanced007.html#GKKNJ. The beauty of JAX-RS is that just about any content type can be produced. A client application can visit the URL that corresponds to a web service's @GET method, and content will be returned in a format that will work for that client. For instance, if a client is a web browser, it will look for a method that produces "text/html" content within the web service, and then invoke that method.

The second example in the solution to this recipe demonstrates a REST method that consumes String content. The @PUT annotation indicates that either a new object will be generated, or an existing object will be updated with the request. In this case, the string-based message field is updated to the content that is passed into the web service via the text variable. The @Path annotation has been placed above the method signature to indicate a path following the format /add should be used to access this method. Lastly, the @Consumes annotation indicates that the method will consume plaintext.

If one were interested in returning a list of values, then a wrapper class for consuming the list of returned entity objects and storing into a local list is likely one of the best approaches. In the example, a List<String> is returned from the getXMLMessageList() service. This is facilitated by utilizing a wrapper object named MessageWrapperList, which extends ArrayList<String>, therefore accepting a list of strings, and returns that list when the getMessageList() method is called upon. Using a wrapper object such as this makes it easy to send lists of data to and from a web service.

The REST service in this example is very brief, and in real-world scenarios, many methods producing and consuming different types of content are utilized within REST service implementations.

15-8. Writing a JAX-RS Client

Problem

You want to create a JAX-RS client application to consume a RESTful web service.

Solution

Use the new JAX-RS Client API to build a client application. The following example demonstrates how to create a very basic client using the JAX-RS Client API.

```
import java.util.concurrent.ExecutionException;
import java.util.logging.Level;
import java.util.logging.Logger;
import javax.ws.rs.client.Client;
import javax.ws.rs.client.ClientBuilder;
import javax.xml.ws.Response;

/**
 *
 * @author Juneau
 */
public class RestClient {

    public static void main(String[] args){
        // Obtain an instance of the client
        Client client = ClientBuilder.newClient();

        Response res = (Response) client.target("http://localhost:8080/JavaEERecipes/rest/
        simplerest")
                .request("text/plain").get();
```

```
        try {
            System.out.println((String) res.get());
        } catch (InterruptedException ex) {
            Logger.getLogger(RestClient.class.getName()).log(Level.SEVERE, null, ex);
        } catch (ExecutionException ex) {
            Logger.getLogger(RestClient.class.getName()).log(Level.SEVERE, null, ex);
        }
    }
}
```

To test the client, first deploy and run the JavaEERecipes application so that the simplerest REST web service is available. Once it's deployed, run the RestClient class to see the result in the server log.

How It Works

Historically, it has always been no small task to test web services. That is because in order to test a web service, a separate web application either had to make a call to the web service, or custom client tests would have to be built to accommodate the testing. In the JAX-RS 2.0 release, a client API was introduced, allowing developers to follow a standard API for developing test clients and so forth.

To use the client API, obtain an instance of the javax.ws.rs.client.Client by either injecting the resource, or calling the javax.ws.rs.client.ClientBuilder newClient method. Once a Client instance is obtained, it can be configured by setting properties, or registering Provider and/or Feature classes. Properties are simply name-value pairs that can be passed to the client via the setProperty method. Features are Providers that implement the Feature interface. A Feature can be used for grouping-related properties and Providers into a single unit, making configuration even easier.

In the solution to this recipe, the client has been built to access the simplerest web service. After a client instance is obtained, properties can be set against it by calling the Client setProperty method, passing the property-value pair.

```
client.setProperty("property", "value");
```

Web Resource Targets

The first step toward invoking a web resource is to make a call to a target. This can be done in a couple of different ways. The previous example demonstrated the use of the Client target method, which accepts a URI and returns a WebTarget.

```
WebTarget myTarget = client.target("http://somehost.com/service");
```

Once the target has been obtained, a number of things can be done with it. A request can be made against it, as in the RestClientOne example, by invoking the target's request method. A target can also be further qualified by calling its path method and passing the next sequence in a URI path.

```
WebTarget myTarget =
    client.target("http://somehost.com/service").path("one");
```

A path can also contain dynamic content in the form of URI template parameters. To include a template parameter, wrap the dynamic portion of the path in curly brackets { }, and then add a call to the pathParam method, passing the name-value pair of the parameter. One could also send a query parameter via adding a call to queryParam using a similar format.

```
WebTarget myTarget =
  client.target("http://somehost.com/service").path("one").path("{code}")
  .pathParam("code","100375");
```

■ **Note** Path parameters and query parameters differ in the way that they are sent to the web service. A path parameter is chained to the end of the URI using the following format:

```
http://web-service/path-param1/path-param2
```

A query parameter is chained to the end of the URI using the following format:

```
http://web-service?query-param1&query-param2
```

WebTarget objects are immutable, in that methods for altering WebTargets, such as path, return new instances of WebTarget. WebTargets can also be configured by registering features or providers via a call to the target's register method, passing either type of class.

```
client.register(Feature.class)
client.register(Provider.class)
```

Obtaining a Response

The example at the beginning of this section demonstrated a simple client that returns a plaintext response. However, it is possible to return different response types by passing different Strings or MediaType fields to the Client target request method. Table 15-6 lists the different MediaType fields that can be used. All fields listed in the table that contain a _TYPE suffix are of type MediaType, whereas the others are static String types.

Table 15-6. MediaType Fields

Field	String
APPLICATION_ATOM_XML	"application/atom+xml"
APPLICATION_ATOM_XML_TYPE	
APPLICATION_FORM_URLENCODED	"application/x-www-form-urlencoded"
APPLICATION_FORM_URLENCODED_TYPE	
APPLICATION_JSON	"application/json"
APPLICATION_JSON_TYPE	
APPLICATION_OCTET_STREAM	"application/octet-stream"
APPLICATION_OCTET_STREAM_TYPE	
APPLICATION_SVG_XML	"application/svg+xml"
APPLICATION_SVG_XML_TYPE	
APPLICATION_XHTML_XML	" application/xhtml+xml"
APPLICATION_XHTML_XML_TYPE	
APPLICATION_XML	" application/xml"
APPLICATION_XML_TYPE	
MEDIA_TYPE_WILDCARD	"*"
MULTIPART_FORM_DATA	"multipart/form-data"
MULTIPART_FORM_DATA_TYPE	
TEXT_HTML	"text/html"
TEXT_HTML_TYPE	
TEXT_PLAIN	"text/plain"
TEXT_PLAIN_TYPE	
TEXT_XML	"text/xml"
TEXT_XML_TYPE	
WILDCARD	"*/*"
WILDCARD_TYPE	

To obtain a requested resource, call the `get` method, which will return a `javax.ws.rs.core.Response` object. The returned `Response` can be used to process the results accordingly, depending on what you are trying to do within the client. In the example, the `Response` object's `readEntity` method is called, which simply returns the results in the requested format. In the example, a `String.class` is passed to the `readEntity` method, implying that a response should be returned in `String` format. To see a complete list of methods that can be called against a `Response` object, refer to the online documentation (`https://javaee.github.io/javaee-spec/javadocs/javax/ws/rs/core/Response.html`), as the list is quite lengthy.

It is possible to filter a response by chaining methods, as needed, to specify headers, cookies, and so forth, off of the request method. Each of these chained method calls returns a Builder object, which can be further built upon. The following methods can be chained to further build the request:

- cookie(Cookie)
- cookie(String, String)
- header(String, Object)
- headers(MultivaluedMap<String, Object>)
- register

Returning Entities

Sometimes there is a requirement to return a type other than Response from a web resource. In these cases, it is possible to obtain an entity type by passing the entity class to the get call. The following lines of code demonstrate how to return an Employee entity, rather than a standard Response object.

```
Response res = client.target("http://localhost:8080/JavaEERecipes/rest/employeeSearch")
                .request("application/xml").get(Employee.class);
```

In cases where entities are being returned, the request type is required to be "application/xml" or APPLICATION_XML_TYPE.

Invoking at a Later Time

There are cases when it makes sense to obtain a request and prepare it for execution, but not invoke that request until a later time. In such cases, one can prepare an Invocation that can be executed at a later time. In the following lines of code, an Invocation is created by making a request to a WebTarget, and then calling the buildGet method.

```
Invocation inv1 = client.target("http://localhost:8080/JavaEERecipes/rest/simplerest")
                .request("text/plain").buildGet();
// Some time later...
Response res = inv1.invoke();
```

If we were posting a response, the buildPost method could be called against the WebTarget instead, as follows:

```
Invocation inv1 = client.target("http://localhost:8080/JavaEERecipes/rest/makeithappen")
                .request("text/plain").buildPost(order);
 Response res = inv1.invoke();
```

■ **Note** To asynchronously execute an Invocation, call the invocation submit method, rather than the invoke method.

Invocation objects can be configured similarly to WebTarget and Client objects. Filters, interceptors, properties, features, and providers can be configured on an Invocation by calling the register method and passing the appropriate configuration instance, as demonstrated in the following.

```
// Assume that inv1 is an Invocation instance
String result = inv1.register(MyInterceptor.class).invoke(String.class);
```

■ **Note** To learn more about filters and interceptors, read Recipe 15-9, which follows in this chapter.

WebTarget Injection

A WebTarget can be injected into any JAX-RS managed resource by specifying the @Uri annotation and passing the WebTarget URI. In following example, a WebTarget resource is injected into a JAX-RS resource to demonstrate this concept.

```
@Path("/orderservice")
public class OrderService {
    @Uri("order/{id}")
    WebTarget orderId;

    //...
}
```

15-9. Filtering Requests and Responses

Problem

You want to perform some activity against a web service request before it has been delivered to the network, or to a web service response before it has been sent back to the client.

Solution

Apply a filter or interceptor to the web service request or response to perform the desired activity. The following example filter is used to write alerts to the system log before an incoming request has been processed and before a response is sent back to the client.

```
import java.io.BufferedReader;
import java.io.IOException;
import java.io.InputStream;
import java.io.InputStreamReader;
import javax.annotation.Priority;
import javax.ws.rs.Priorities;
import javax.ws.rs.container.ContainerRequestContext;
import javax.ws.rs.container.ContainerRequestFilter;
import javax.ws.rs.container.ContainerResponseContext;
import javax.ws.rs.container.ContainerResponseFilter;
import javax.ws.rs.ext.Provider;
import org.javaee8recipes.chapter15.rest.interfaces.Alerter;
```

```
@Provider
@Alerter
public class AlertFilter implements ContainerRequestFilter,
        ContainerResponseFilter {

    @Override
    public void filter(ContainerRequestContext requestContext)
            throws IOException {
        alert(requestContext);
    }

    @Override
    public void filter(ContainerRequestContext crc, ContainerResponseContext crc1) throws
    IOException {
        alert(crc);
    }

    public void alert(ContainerRequestContext context) {

        try(InputStream in = context.getEntityStream();) {
            if (in != null) {
                InputStreamReader inreader = new InputStreamReader(in);
                BufferedReader reader = new BufferedReader(inreader);
                String text = "";

                while ((text = reader.readLine()) != null) {
                    System.out.println(text);

                }

            }
        } catch (IOException ex) {
            // Error handling
        }
    }
}
```

How It Works

The concept of filters and interceptors is analogous to the post office processing your mail before it comes to your address. Rather than a message being delivered directly from point A to point B, it is first routed to one or more postal offices, where it is further processed before reaching point B. Web resource filters and interceptors apply that same concept to requests or responses that are being processed via a web service. If a filter or interceptor is bound to a web resource, then it will be invoked at some point in the lifecycle of a request or response to that web resource. The type of filter or interceptor determines at what point in the lifecycle it is applied. Interceptors (otherwise known as entity interceptors) wrap around a method invocation at a specified extension point. Filters, on the other hand, execute code at a specified extension point, but they are not wrapped around methods. In the next few sections, you will take a closer look at each and how they are used.

Filters

An extension point is an interface that includes a method, which is responsible for filtering or intercepting the request or response. Filters have four such extension point interfaces, those being: `ClientRequestFilter`, `ClientResponseFilter`, `ContainerRequestFilter`, and `ContainerResponseFilter`. The name of the extension point helps to describe what a filter is applied to and at what point. `ClientRequestFilter` and `ClientResponseFilter` are used with the JAX-RS Client API. `ClientRequestFilter` is applied before an HTTP request is delivered to the network. A `ClientResponseFilter` is applied when a server response is received and before control is returned to the application. `ContainerRequestFilter` and `ContainerResponseFilter` classes are used with the JAX-RS Server API. Similar to the client-side filters, a `ContainerRequestFilter` is applied upon receiving a request from a client, and a `ContainerResponseFilter` is applied before the HTTP response is delivered.

Entity Interceptors

As mentioned in the previous section, an extension point is an interface that includes a method, which is responsible for filtering or intercepting the request or response. Entity interceptors have two such extension points, those being `ReaderInterceptor` and `WriterInterceptor`. An entity interceptor class must implement one or both of these extension points. Also mentioned previously, entity interceptors wrap calls to methods. More specifically, `MessageBodyWriter` implementations wrap calls to the `writeTo` method, whereas `MessageBodyReader` implementations wrap calls to the `readFrom` method.

Binding Filters and Interceptors

Filters and interceptors must be associated to application classes or methods, and this process is also known as *binding*. The default type of binding is global binding, and any filter or interceptor that does not include annotations is bound globally. Global binding associates the filter or interceptor with all resource methods in an application. That said, any time a resource method is invoked, all globally bound filters and interceptors are processed as well.

Filters and interceptors can be registered manually via `Application` or `Configuration`, or they can be registered dynamically. To indicate that a filter or interceptor should be registered dynamically, it should be annotated with `@Provider`. If a filter or interceptor is not annotated as such, it must be registered manually.

To manually bind a filter or interceptor to a resource method, the filter or interceptor class must be denoted with a `@NameBinding` annotation. A `@NameBinding` annotation can be coded just as a standard annotation would, but it should also include the `@NameBinding` annotation in its interface. The following annotation code could be used to create an `@NameBinding` annotation that might be placed on a filter that is responsible for firing alerts.

```
@NameBinding
@Target({ ElementType.TYPE, ElementType.METHOD })
@Retention(value = RetentionPolicy.RUNTIME)
public @interface Alerter { }
```

To associate the `@NameBinding` with a filter or interceptor, simply annotate the filter or interceptor class with it. The following `AlertFilter` class is a filter implementation that is denoted with the `@Alerter` annotation.

```
@Provider
@Alerter
class AlertFilter implements ContainerRequestFilter,
        ContainerResponseFilter {

...

}
```

That filter can now be bound to a resource method by annotating the resource method with the same `@NameBinding` as the filter class, as demonstrated in the following.

```
@GET
@Produces("text/html")
@Alerter
public String  getJobs(){
    ...
}
```

■ **Note** This same concept can be applied to `Application` subclasses in order to globally bind the filter or interceptor.

Setting Priorities

As mentioned in previous sections, filters and interceptors can be chained. Chains of filters or interceptors invoke individual filters or interceptors based on a given priority. To assign priority to a filter or interceptor, denote the implementation class with the `@BindingPriority` annotation. Integer numbers are used to associate priorities. The higher the integer, the higher the priority. Therefore, the filter or interceptor that has the highest priority integer assigned to it will be invoked first, and the lowest priority integer will be invoked last.

15-10. Processing Long-Running Operations Asynchronously

Problem

Your server-side JAX-RS method contains a long-running operation, and you would like to avoid blocking while waiting for the event to complete.

Solution

Perform asynchronous processing so that the resource method containing the long-running operation can inform JAX-RS that a response is not yet readily available, but will be produced at some point in the future. In the following example, a JAX-RS service named `AsyncResource` contains a resource method named `asyncOperation`. The `asyncOperation` method contains a long-running task, which is handed off to a `ManagedExecutorService` for processing.

```
import javax.annotation.Resource;
import javax.enterprise.concurrent.ManagedExecutorService;
import javax.ws.rs.GET;
import javax.ws.rs.Path;
import javax.ws.rs.container.AsyncResponse;
import javax.ws.rs.container.Suspended;

/**
 * Recipe 15-10: Asynchronous Processing
 * @author Juneau
 */
@Path("/asynchronous/asyncResource")
public class AsyncResource {

    @Resource(name = "concurrent/__defaultManagedExecutorService")
    ManagedExecutorService mes;

    @GET
    public void asyncOperation(@Suspended final AsyncResponse ar){
        mes.submit(
                new Runnable() {
                    public void run(){
                        // Perform long running operation
                        longRunningOperation();
                        ar.resume("Performing asynchronous operation");
                    }
                });
    }

    public void longRunningOperation(){
        // This is a method that contains a long-running operation
        System.out.println( "Performing long running task...");
    }

}
```

■ **Note** To learn more about ManagedExecutorService, see Chapter 18.

How It Works

The JAX-RS 2.0 API introduced the ability to hand long-running tasks off to a ManagedExecutorService for processing. This allows a server-side resource to return control back to a client, and avoid problematic blocks. The API also includes a way to register a timeout handler in case the asynchronous process does not return within a specified amount of time, along with client-side asynchronous capabilities. To begin, the server-side asynchronous implementation will be described, followed by the others.

To perform asynchronous processing within a JAX-RS resource, the resource method that contains long-running operations must accept an instance of AsyncResponse via the utilization of the @Suspended annotation. The AsyncResponse class provides a means for resuming operations and returning control to the client. A ManagedExecutorService (see Chapter 18 for more information) must be made available within the class, and it must be called upon to submit a new Runnable containing the long-running operation and a call to AsyncResponse.resume() to return control back to the client once the long-running process is completed. When the ManagedExecutorService submit method is called, the Runnable is passed to the server for further processing, forking a thread to execute the task and returning immediately. When the long-running task has completed, it will be passed back to the application, invoking the AsyncResponse resume method.

In order to avoid long-running operations that never return and cause a suspended connection to wait indefinitely, it is possible to specify a timeout value. The timeout value can be specified by setting a timeout handler via the AsyncResponse.setTimeoutHandler() method, passing a new instance of TimeoutHandler. After the setTimeoutHandler has been invoked, the timeout can be set by calling the AsyncResponse.setTimeout() method, passing any unit of type java.util.concurrent.TimeUnit. For instance, the following lines demonstrate how to set a timeout of 30 seconds for the long-running operation contained in the resource shown in the solution to this recipe:

```
...
@GET
    public void asyncOperation(@Suspended final AsyncResponse ar){
        ar.setTimeoutHandler(new TimeoutHandler() {
            public void handleTimeout(AsyncResponse ar){
                ar.resume("Timed out");
            }
        });
        ar.setTimeout(30, SECONDS);
        mes.submit(
                new Runnable() {
                    public void run(){
                        // Perform long running operation
                        longRunningOperation();
                        ar.resume("Performing asynchronous operation");
                    }
                });
    }
...
```

■ **Note** JAX-RS implementations will generate a ServiceUnavailableException with a status of 503 when a timeout value is reached and no timeout handler is present.

As mentioned at the beginning of this section, the asynchronous JAX-RS API has been extended to the client API as well. By default, invocations from a client to a target are executed in a synchronous fashion, but they can be changed to asynchronous by calling the async method and optionally registering an instance of InvocationCallback. For example, the following lines of code demonstrate a client call to the web service resource that was presented in the solution to this recipe:

```
Client client = ClientBuilder.newClient();
Target target = client.target("http://localhost:8080/JavaEERecipes/rest/asynchronous/
asyncResource");
Target.request().async().get();
```

For more information regarding the client API and asynchronous operations, refer to the JAX-RS documentation online.

15-11. Pushing One-Way Asynchronous Updates from Servers

Problem

You want to push one-way messages from a server to one or more clients.

Solution

Utilize Server Sent Events (SSE) to push messages from a server to one or more clients. The JAX-RS 2.1 API introduced the concept of SSE, which allows you to push messages from a server to subscribed clients. It also allows for subscription events to perform server actions. The following example contains sources for a JAX-RS class that contains a send() method, which allows a client to connect to the server obtain messages from a server that have been broadcasted via Server Sent Events.

```
package org.javaee8recipes.chapter15.rest.service;

import javax.ws.rs.GET;
import javax.ws.rs.Path;
import javax.ws.rs.Produces;
import javax.ws.rs.core.Context;
import javax.ws.rs.core.MediaType;
import javax.ws.rs.sse.Sse;
import javax.ws.rs.sse.SseEventSink;

@Path("sse")
public class SSEEventResource {

    @Resource(name = "DefaultManagedExecutorService")
    ManagedExecutorService executor;

    public SSEEventResource() {

    }

    @GET
    @Path("send")
    @Produces(MediaType.SERVER_SENT_EVENTS)
    public void send(@Context SseEventSink eventSink,
            @Context Sse sse) {
        executor.execute(() -> {
            try (SseEventSink sink = eventSink) {
                eventSink.send(sse.newEvent("Welcome to the List!"));
                eventSink.send(sse.newEvent("Message One!"));
                eventSink.send(sse.newEvent("SERVER-NOTIFICATION", "Message Two!"));
                eventSink.send(sse.newEventBuilder()
                        .comment("Nice Test")
                        .name("SERVER-TEST")
                        .data("Some data...could be an object")
```

```
                    .build());
            eventSink.close();
        }
    });
  }
}
```

You can visit the following URL and see the resulting messages broadcast: `http://localhost:8080/JavaEERecipes/rest/sse/send`.

To broadcast to multiple clients simultaneously, you can use `SseBroadcaster` to register multiple `SseEventSink` instances and send messages. The following example demonstrates how to construct a JAX-RS class that allows clients to register and the server to broadcast events to those registered clients.

```
package org.javaee8recipes.chapter15.rest.service;

import java.util.UUID;
import javax.annotation.PostConstruct;
import javax.ejb.Singleton;
import javax.ws.rs.GET;
import javax.ws.rs.POST;
import javax.ws.rs.Path;
import javax.ws.rs.PathParam;
import javax.ws.rs.Produces;
import javax.ws.rs.core.Context;
import javax.ws.rs.core.MediaType;
import javax.ws.rs.sse.Sse;
import javax.ws.rs.sse.SseBroadcaster;
import javax.ws.rs.sse.SseEventSink;

@Path("/")
@Singleton
public class SSEEventBroadcaster {

    @Context
    private Sse sse;

    private volatile SseBroadcaster sseBroadcaster;

    public SSEEventBroadcaster() {
    }

    @PostConstruct
    public void init() {
        sseBroadcaster = sse.newBroadcaster();
    }

    @GET
    @Path("register")
    @Produces(MediaType.SERVER_SENT_EVENTS)
    public void register(@Context SseEventSink eventSink) {
        eventSink.send(sse.newEvent("Thanks for registering!"));
        sseBroadcaster.register(eventSink);
    }
```

```
    @POST
    @Path("send/{message}")
    public void broadcast(@PathParam("message") String message) {
        sseBroadcaster.broadcast(sse.newEventBuilder()
                .mediaType(MediaType.APPLICATION_JSON_TYPE)
                .id(UUID.randomUUID().toString())
                .name("SSEEventBroadcaster Message")
                .data(message)
                .build()
        );
    }
}
```

How It Works

The JAX-RS 2.1 release introduced support for Server Sent Events (SSE). Server Sent Events make it possible to push messages from a server to multiple clients at a time over HTTP or HTTPS. The connection from the client to the server can remain open and messages can continue to be sent until the client disconnects. The API contains a number of interfaces that are used for sending messages to clients, registering connections, etc., and each of them resides within the `javax.ws.rs.sse` package. The `Sse` interface is the server-side entry point for creating `OutboundSseEvent` and `SseBroadcaster`. It can be injected into a field or used as a parameter to a method or constructor. The `SseEventSink` interface is used to actually send a stream of messages, and it can be acquired by injecting as a resource method parameter. `SseEvent` is the base event class, which defines properties such as ID, Name, and Comment. The `OutboundSseEvent` is used by the server to package an `SseEvent`, and `SseBroadcaster` is used to manage multiple `SseEventSink` objects. The `SseBroadcaster` enables the server to send events to all registered clients and provides facilities for handing exceptions.

In the first example, a simple JAX-RS class is used to demonstrate how a server can use a single method to register a client and send one or more events. In the example, the class is registered as a RESTful web service at the path "`sse`", and the method `send()` is registered at the path "`sse/send`". The `send()` method produces the type `MediaType.SERVER_SENT_EVENTS`. It accepts `@Context` parameters of type `SseEventSink` and `Sse`, which are used to register a client and push events. The class also injects a `ManagedExecutorService` instance, which is a server-side concurrency utility that is used to perform concurrent processes. You can learn more about the `ManagedExecutorService` in Chapter 18. Inside the method, a `try-with-resources` clause is used to open an `SseEventSink` identified as `eventSink`. The `eventSink` is used to send a number of `SseEvent` instances. Once completed, the `eventSink` is closed. The entire process is sent to the `ManagedExecutorService` so that it can be queued up in the server and executed in a concurrent manner.

The next example demonstrates how to construct a JAX-RS class that can be used to register clients and broadcast events. The class is registered as a singleton, meaning that only one instance of the class will be constructed and utilized by all sessions. An `Sse` context is registered with the class, as it can be used to create new `SseBroadcaster` objects, new `SseEvent` objects, and new event builder objects. An `SseBroadcaster` is declared as volatile, meaning that it will be stored in main Java memory and not in a cache. There is an `init()` method which is annotated with `@PostConstruct` so that it will be executed immediately after construction. The `init()` method contains a call to `sse.newBroadcaster()`, thereby obtaining a new `SseBroadcaster` instance. Clients can register by calling upon the register web service method, which produces `MediaType.SERVER_SENT_EVENTS`. An `SseEventSink Context` parameter is passed in as a parameter to the register method, and in the implementation a new `SseEvent` is sent via the `eventSink`. The `SseEventSink` is then registered to the `SseBroadcaster` instance. The broadcast method accepts a string as a path parameter, and inside the method the SseBroadcaster broadcast() is used to send an event. The method demonstrates the use of the SseEvent builder. As you can see, calling upon sse.newEventBuilder() allows for the construction of an SseEvent utilizing the builder pattern. In the example, the media type is set as MediaType.APPLICATION_JSON_TYPE, which indicates JSON.

```
sseBroadcaster.broadcast(sse.newEventBuilder()
    .mediaType(MediaType.APPLICATION_JSON_TYPE)
    .id(UUID.randomUUID().toString())
    .name("SSEEventBroadcaster Message")
    .data(message)
    .build()
);
```

In the next recipe, I demonstrate how to register a client to an SseBroadcaster and how to listen for events on the client.

15-12. Receiving Server Sent Events as a Client

Problem

You want create a client that subscribes to an SseBroadcaster on which messages are pushed from a server, and you'd like to have the client perform an action when a message is received.

Solution

Utilize Server Sent Events (SSE) to push messages from a server to one or more clients. The JAX-RS 2.1 API introduced the concept of SSE, which allows a server to broadcast messages to registered clients. In the following example, a JSF client is used to call a JAX-RS SSE broadcaster and register. The client then listens to broadcasted messages for 1000 milliseconds.

```
@Named
@RequestScoped
public class SseClient {

    private Client client;

    @PostConstruct
    public void init() {
        client = ClientBuilder.newClient();
    }

    public void listen() {
        WebTarget target = client.target("http://localhost:8080/JavaEERecipes/rest/
        ssebroadcaster/register");
        try (SseEventSource source = SseEventSource.target(target).build()) {
            source.register(System.out::println);
            source.open();
```

```
            Thread.sleep(1000); // Consume events for 1000 ms
            source.close();
        } catch (InterruptedException e) {

        }
    }
}
```

A JSF commandButton could be linked to the #{sseClient.listen} method, which would then invoke the client when pressed.

How It Works

A JAX-RS client can be used to register to a SSE broadcaster by simply calling on the broadcaster's registration method. Once registered, the SseEventSource can be opened for a defined amount of time (one should not leave an SseEventSource open without bound), and then it can be closed when finished listening for messages.

In the example, the SseEventSource is set to the target of the broadcaster URL. Next, it registers the output from the incoming message to be written to System.out.println(). Therefore, each message received will be written to the system log. After the registration, the source is opened for incoming messages. In the example, a thread is hard-coded to sleep for 1000 milliseconds. This is simply to keep the client open for messages for 1000 milliseconds, and would likely not be coded this way for a production application. Lastly, the SseEventSource is closed, which ends the client session.

CHAPTER 16

WebSockets and JSON

The Java EE 8 platform aims to provide a common ground for developing Java Enterprise solutions that incorporate HTML5 and other modern web technologies. As such, there are a few core features that were added to Java EE 7, allowing for better bidirectional support of HTML5. The Java EE 7 platform introduced communication between the client and the server via a technology named WebSockets, enabling more parity with the HTML5 standard. WebSockets is a full-duplex communication mechanism that allows both textual and binary messages to be sent between clients and servers, without the HTTP request/response lifecycle. WebSockets allow either the client or the server to send a message at any time, providing an asynchronous solution for working with data while the user is performing a task.

HTML5 has become the mainstream markup language for developing content that can be presented via the World Wide Web. It defines a standard, which can be used to produce both HTML and XHTML documents. Along with standardization, HTML5 also brings forth semantic features that were previously only possible on desktop application platforms. For example, elements such as `<video>` and `<audio>` allow media content to be embedded directly in web pages, without the need to embed a media player solution. There is no doubt that HTML5, the fifth revision of the HTML standard, has opened the doors to new possibilities in web application development.

The universally supported JSON (JavaScript Object Notation) object has become a widely adopted solution for sending data between points. HTML5-based web applications can utilize JSON to transport data, using WebSockets, Ajax, or other transport technologies. The Java EE 8 platform provides the JSON Processing (JSON-P) API, which introduces utilities that make it easier to build and work with JSON objects within the Java language. It also added enhancements to JSON-P, allowing the abilities to point to a specific location within a JSON document, and patch existing JSON documents. The JSON Binding (JSON-B) API was also introduced in Java EE 8, providing a convenient API for mapping JSON to Java objects.

This chapter focuses on recipes that demonstrate these HTML5 APIs. You learn how to use WebSockets, JSON-P, and JSON-B so that your application's client-server communication can become seamless, whether the user interface is written with HTML5, JSF, or another markup language.

16-1. Creating a WebSocket Endpoint

Problem

You want to create a WebSocket endpoint that can be used to receive messages asynchronously.

Solution

Create a WebSocket endpoint by annotating a server-side POJO class and a method within that class, accordingly. In the following example, a simple POJO class, named `org.javaee8recipes.chapter16.recipe16_01.BookChatEndpoint`, is annotated to indicate that it should be accessible via the web as a

J. Juneau, *Java EE 8 Recipes*, https://doi.org/10.1007/978-1-4842-3594-2_16

WebSocket endpoint. The class contains a method named messageReceiver, which is annotated to make it accessible to a client as a callable message consumer.

```
import javax.websocket.OnMessage;
import javax.websocket.server.ServerEndpoint;
...
@ServerEndpoint(path="/bookChatEndpoint")
public class BookChatEndpoint {

 @OnMessage
 public String messageReceiver(String message) {
     return "Message Received: " + message;
 }
}
```

The WebSocket endpoint will be accessible to clients at the URL ws://localhost:8080/JavaEERecipes/bookChatEndpoint. When a message is sent from a client to the endpoint, it is sent to the messageReceiver method, where it is processed accordingly. In this case, a simple String message is returned to the client.

How It Works

A server-side class can accept messages from clients by configuring it as a WebSocket endpoint. To develop a WebSocket endpoint, create a Java POJO and annotate it with @ServerEndpoint. The @ServerEndpoint annotation accepts a string-based path attribute, which is used to indicate the URI at which the server is available to accept client messages. Therefore, when the server is started, the value of the path attribute would be appended to the end of the context path and application name in which the WebSocket resides. By initiating a call to that URL, one method, annotated with @OnMessage, will be invoked to process the message that is sent.

In the example, a class named BookChatEndpoint is annotated as a WebSocket, so it is accessible to clients as an endpoint for receiving messages and returning a response. When initiating communication with the WebSocket endpoint, the client must utilize a URL that contains a URI scheme of ws rather than http. The ws URI scheme was introduced by the WebSocket protocol, and as such, indicates that the URL is used for communication with a WebSocket. In this example, a client can send a message to the server via the bookChatEndpoint WebSocket, and the server can send a message back at the same time, because WebSockets allow for full-duplex communication. *Full-duplex communication* is an HTML5 standard, rather than standard HTTP, which utilizes a request-response communication.

16-2. Sending Messages to a WebSocket Endpoint

Problem

You would like to send a message from a client to a WebSocket endpoint that is available on a server.

Solution

Engineer a JavaScript solution that can be used to send messages from a client browser to a WebSocket endpoint. Invoke the JavaScript function via an action event that is bound to an HTML input tag within the view. In the following example, a button contains an onclick attribute that will invoke a JavaScript function named bookChatRelay. The bookChatRelay function is responsible for opening a session with a WebSocket endpoint so that messages can be sent. The following listing is an excerpt from the recipe16_02.xhtml JSF view, which is located within the web/chapter16 directory of the JavaEERecipes source bundle.

```
...
<html>
    <head>
        <script type="text/javascript">
            var ws;
            function bookChatRelay()
            {
                if ("WebSocket" in window)
                {
                    alert("WebSocket is supported by your Browser!");

                    if (ws == null){
                        alert("Creating new websocket connection");
                        ws = new WebSocket("ws://localhost:8080/JavaEERecipes/
                        bookChatEndpoint");
                    } else {
                        ws.send("Another message");
                    }
                    ws.onopen = function()
                    {
                        // Web Socket is connected, send data using send()
                        ws.send("Message to send");
                        alert("Message is sent...");
                    };
                    ws.onmessage = function (evt)
                    {
                        var received_msg = evt.data;
                        alert("Message from server: " + received_msg);
                    };
                    ws.onclose = function()
                    {
                        // websocket is closed.
                        alert("Connection is closed...");
                    };
                }
                else
                {
                    // The browser doesn't support WebSocket
                    alert("WebSocket NOT supported by your Browser!");
                }
            }
            function closeConnection(){
                if (ws !== null){
                    ws.close();
                    ws = null;
                }
            }
```

```
        </script>
    </head>
    <body>

        <input id="wsRelay" type="button" value="WebSocket Test Message"
               onclick="bookChatRelay();"/>
        <input id="closeConn" type="button" value="Close Connection"
               onclick="closeConnection();"/>
    </body>

</html>
```

When the button is pressed, the message will be sent from the browser client to the WebSocket endpoint, and a message will be returned from the endpoint to the client.

■ **Note** The JavaScript code in this test creates a new WebSocket connection each time the button on the page is pressed. This is okay for testing purposes, but in a real-life scenario, you will want to retain and reuse the connection, if possible.

How It Works

The ability to asynchronously send messages (text or binary) from a client to a server defines the foundation of Ajax and HTML5 capability. The WebSockets API allows developers to send messages to the server via JavaScript calls to a WebSocket endpoint. Conversely, the API allows clients to receive messages and process them accordingly via a series of JavaScript functions. The example for this recipe demonstrates how to send a message to a WebSocket endpoint by clicking on a button in a web page. When the button is clicked, a JavaScript function named `bookChatRelay` is invoked, which embodies the processing implementation.

To send a message to a WebSocket endpoint via a JavaScript function, the first task is to confirm whether the user's browser is capable of working with WebSockets (HTML5 compliant). This confirmation can be performed using a conditional statement to verify if the `"WebSocket"` object is available within the client via the following `if` statement:

```
if("WebSocket" in window){
...
} else {
...
}
```

If the client browser is capable of working with WebSockets, then the implementation inside the `if` block is invoked; otherwise, the implementation within the `else` block is invoked. To process the WebSocket message, a new WebSocket object must be instantiated to establish the server connection, which is done by passing the URL to the WebSocket endpoint to a new WebSocket object.

```
var ws = new WebSocket("ws://localhost:8080/JavaEERecipes/bookChatEndpoint");
```

The constructor for creating a WebSocket takes either one or two parameters. The first parameter is the URL of the server to which the WebSocket will connect, and the optional second parameter is a `String` of protocols that can be used for message transmission. The WebSocket object contains a handful of events that are utilized to help implement message processing. Table 16-1 lists the different events that can occur in the lifecycle of a WebSocket object, along with a description of what they do.

Table 16-1. *JavaScript WebSocket Object Events*

Event	Handler Method	Description
`open`	`onOpen`	Occurs when the WebSocket connection is established.
`close`	`onClose`	Occurs when the WebSocket connection is closed.
`error`	`onError`	Occurs when there is a communication error.
`message`	`onMessage`	Occurs when data is received from the server.

After the WebSocket object has been instantiated successfully, a connection to the server will be established, which will cause the open event to occur. To process this event, assign a function to the `onOpen` handler and process events accordingly within that function. Messages are usually sent to the server when the open event occurs, and this is demonstrated within the example.

```
ws.onopen = function()
{
   // Web Socket is connected, send data using send()
   ws.send("Message to send");
   alert("Message is sent...");
};
```

Similarly, you can listen for any other events to occur, and then process tasks accordingly when they do. In the example, when a message is received from the server, it is printed within an `alert` dialog. Also in the example, when the WebSocket is closed, an `alert` dialog is presented to the user.

The example does not demonstrate all the possible ways that the WebSocket object in JavaScript can be utilized. For instance, you could send messages to the server by invoking the `send()` method and passing the data that you want to send as a parameter. The `close()` method can be called on a WebSocket to manually terminate the existing connection. WebSocket objects also contain the helpful attributes, `readyState` and `bufferedAmount`, which can be used for obtaining information about a connection. The `readyState` attribute will advise the current state of the WebSocket connection via a returned number, and the `bufferedAmount` attribute value represents the number of bytes of UTF-8 text that have been queued using the `send()` method. Table 16-2 displays the different possible values for the `readyState` attribute, along with a description of each.

Table 16-2. *JavaScript WebSocket readyState Values*

Value	Description
`0 WebSocket.CONNECTING`	Connection not yet established.
`1 WebSocket.OPEN`	Connection established, and communication is possible.
`2 WebSocket.CLOSING`	Connection going through closing handshake.
`3 WebSocket.CLOSED`	Connection closed and cannot be opened.

16-3. Building a JSON Object

Problem

You would like to build a JSON object that can be passed from a client to a server, or vice versa.

Solution

Use the `JsonObjectBuilder` to build a JSON object using Java code. The following example demonstrates how to utilize a `JsonObjectBuilder()` instance to create a new `JsonObject`. In this example class, multiple `JsonObjects` are created from reading the contents of a database table. Once the object is built, the sections of the object assigned to a string that will eventually be displayed or persisted.

```
import java.io.IOException;
import java.io.StringWriter;
import java.util.List;
import javax.ejb.EJB;
import javax.faces.bean.ManagedBean;
import javax.json.Json;
import javax.json.JsonObject;
import javax.json.JsonObjectBuilder;
import javax.json.JsonWriter;
import org.javaee8recipes.entity.BookAuthor;
import org.javaee8recipes.chapter09.session.BookAuthorFacade;

@Named(name = "jsonController")
public class JsonController {

    @EJB
    BookAuthorFacade bookAuthorFacade;
    private String authorJson;

    public void buildAuthors() {
        List<BookAuthor> authors = bookAuthorFacade.findAll();
        JsonObjectBuilder builder = Json.createObjectBuilder();
        StringBuilder json = new StringBuilder();
        try (StringWriter sw = new StringWriter();) {
            for (BookAuthor author : authors) {
                System.out.println("author" + author.getLast());
                builder.add("author", Json.createObjectBuilder()
                        .add("authorId", author.getId())
                        .add("first", author.getFirst())
                        .add("last", author.getLast())
                        .add("bio", author.getBio()));

            }
            JsonObject result = builder.build();
```

```
            try (JsonWriter writer = Json.createWriter(sw)) {
                writer.writeObject(result);
            }
            json.append(sw.toString());
            authorJson = json.toString();
        } catch (IOException ex) {
            System.out.println(ex);
        }
    }
...
```

Once created, the JsonObject can be passed to a client for processing, or in this case, it can be persisted to disk.

How It Works

The JavaScript Object Notation (JSON-P) API was added to the Java Enterprise platform as of the release of Java EE 7. JSON-P, also referred to as "JSON with padding," has become the standard way to build JSON objects using Java. The JSON-P API includes a helper class that can be used to create JSON objects using the builder pattern. Using the JsonObjectBuilder class, JSON objects can be built using a series of method calls, each building on each other—hence, the builder pattern. Once the JSON object has been built, the JsonObjectBuilder build method can be called to return a JsonObject.

In the example to this recipe, you construct a JSON object that provides details regarding book authors. The JsonObjectBuilder.beginObject() method is used to denote that a new object is being created. The add method is used to add more name/value properties, much like that of a Map. Therefore, the following line adds a property named authorId with a value of author.getId():

```
.add("authorId", author.getId())
```

Objects can be embedded inside of each other, creating a hierarchy of different sections within one JsonObject. In the example, after the first call to add(), another object named author is embedded inside the initial JsonObject by calling beginObject() and passing the name of the embedded object. Embedded objects can also contain properties, so to add properties to the embedded object, call the add() method within the embedded object. JsonObjects can embody as many embedded objects as needed. The following lines of code demonstrate the beginning and end of an embedded object definition:

```
.beginObject("author")
.add("first", "Josh")
.add("last", "Juneau")
.endObject()
```

It is also possible that a JsonObject may have an array of related subobjects. To add an array of subobjects, call the beginArray() method, passing the name of the array as an argument. Arrays can consist of objects, and even hierarchies of objects, arrays, and so forth. In the example to this recipe, the book object has a couple of arrays defined, one being an array of editor objects, and the other being an array of technicalReviewer objects.

Once a `JsonObject` has been created, it can be passed to a client. WebSockets work well for passing `JsonObjects` back to a client, but there are a bevy of different technologies available for communicating with JSON.

16-4. Writing a JSON Object to Disk

Problem

You would like to write a JSON object to the file system.

Solution

Utilize the JSON-P API to build a JSON object, and then store it to the file system. The `JsonWriter` class makes it possible to create a file on disk and then write the JSON to that file. In the following example, the `JsonObject` that was generated in Recipe 16-3 is written to disk using this technique.

```
public void writeJson() {
        try {
            JsonObject jsonObject = jsonController.buildAuthorsJson();

            javax.json.JsonWriter jsonWriter = Json.createWriter(new FileWriter("Authors.
            json"));

            jsonWriter.writeObject(jsonObject);
            jsonWriter.close();

            FacesContext.getCurrentInstance().addMessage(null, new FacesMessage(
                FacesMessage.SEVERITY_INFO, "JSON Built",
                "JSON Built"));
        } catch (IOException ex) {
            System.out.println(ex);
        }
    }
```

How It Works

The `JsonWriter` class can be utilized to write a `JsonObject` to a Java writer object. A `JsonWriter` is instantiated by passing a `Writer` object as an argument. Instantiating a `JsonWriter` will write to the `Writer` object that had been passed as an argument, using JSON format. After that `Writer` has been created, the `JsonWriter writeObject()` method can be invoked, passing the `JsonObject` that is to be written. Once the `JsonObject` has been written, the `JsonWriter` can be closed by calling its `close()` method. These are the only steps that are necessary for writing a JSON object to a Java `Writer` class type.

16-5. Reading JSON from an Input Source

Problem

You would like read a JSON object that has been built or persisted to a file.

Solution

Obtain a JSON object that you would like to read, and then read it using the `javax.json.Json createReader` utility. In the following example, a JSON file is read from disk, and then parsed to determine the hierarchy of events within it. Each of the events is printed to the server log as the JSON is being parsed.

```
public String readObject() {
        InputStream in = new ByteArrayInputStream(controller.buildAndReturnAuthors().
        getBytes());
         // or
        //Reader fileReader = new InputStreamReader(getClass().getResourceAsStream("Author
          Object.json"));
        //JsonReader reader = Json.createReader(fileReader);
        JsonReader reader = Json.createReader(in);
        JsonObject obj = reader.readObject();
        return obj.toString();

    }
```

How It Works

Once a JSON object has been persisted to disk, it will later need to be read back in for utilization. The `JsonReader` object takes care of this task. To create a `JsonReader` object, call the `Json.createReader()` method, passing either an `InputStream` or `Reader` object. Once a `JsonReader` object has been created, it can produce a `JsonObject` by calling its `readObject` method.

Parsing Content

In order to perform some tasks, a JSON object must be searched to find only the content that is desired and useful for the current task. Utilizing a JSON parser can make jobs such as these easier, as a parser is able to break the object down into pieces so that each different piece can be examined as needed, to produce the desired result.

The `javax.json.Json` class contains a static factory method, called `createParser()`, that accepts a bevy of input and returns an `iterable JsonParser`. Table 16-3 lists the different possible input types that are accepted via the `createParser()` method.

Table 16-3. *createParser Method Input Types*

Input Type	Method Call
`InputStream`	`createParser(InputStream in)`
`JsonArray`	`createParser(JsonArray arr)`
`JsonObject`	`createParser(JsonObject obj)`
`Reader`	`createParser(Reader reader)`

Once a `JsonParser` has been created, it can be made into an `Iterator` of `Event` objects. Each `Event` correlates to a different structure within the JSON object. For instance, when the JSON object is created, a `START_OBJECT` event occurs, adding a name\value pair will trigger both a `KEY_NAME` and `VALUE_STRING` event. These events can be utilized to obtain the desired information from a JSON object. In the example, the event names are merely printed to a server log. However, in a real-life application, a conditional would most likely test each iteration to find a particular event and then perform some processing. Table 16-4 lists the different JSON events, along a description of when each occurs.

Table 16-4. *JSON Object Events*

Event	Occurrence
`START_OBJECT`	Start of an object.
`END_OBJECT`	End of an object.
`START_ARRAY`	Start of an array.
`END_ARRAY`	End of an array.
`KEY_NAME`	Name of a key.
`VALUE_STRING`	Value of a name\value pair in string format.
`VALUE_NUMBER`	Value of a name\value pair in numeric format.
`VALUE_TRUE`	Value of a name\value pair in boolean format.
`VALUE_FALSE`	Value of a name\value pair in boolean format.
`VALUE_NULL`	Value of a name\value pair as NULL.

16-6. Converting Between JSON and Java Objects

Problem

You have obtained a list of Java objects in a response from a web service, and you want to convert the list to JSON.

Solution

Utilize the JSON-Binding (JSON-B) API to bind the Java objects elements to JSON format. In the following example, an XML response is received from a web service and converted into Java objects, and the JSON-B API is used to convert the objects into JSON. A JAX-RS client is used to obtain a response that will include a number of `Employee` objects, and each of them will be converted into a Java `Employee` object.

```
public String fetchJson(){
    WebTarget target = ClientBuilder.newClient().target("http://localhost:8080/
    JavaEERecipes/rest/org.javaee8recipes.entity.employee");

        employees = (target.request(javax.ws.rs.core.MediaType.APPLICATION_XML)
                .get(
                new GenericType<List<Employee>>() {
        }));
    System.out.println("Items: " + employees);
    Jsonb jsonb = JsonbBuilder.create();
    String result = null;

    result = jsonb.toJson(employees);

    return result;
}
```

Similarly, the JSON-B API can be used to convert from JSON to Java. In the following method, a JSON string is returned from a web service call, and it is converted into a Java `Collection`.

```
public List<Employee> fetchJavaFromJson(){
    WebTarget target = ClientBuilder.newClient().target("http://localhost:8080/
JavaEERecipes/rest/org.javaee8recipes.entity.employee");

        String employeesJson = (target.request(javax.ws.rs.core.MediaType.APPLICATION_JSON)
                .get(
                new GenericType<String>() {
        }));
    System.out.println("Items: " + employeesJson);
    Jsonb jsonb = JsonbBuilder.create();
    List<Employee> employees = new ArrayList();
    employees = jsonb.fromJson(employeesJson, ArrayList.class);
    return employees;
}
```

In the example, a JSF view is used to display the contents of the `Employee` JSON. The view markup sources are as follows:

```
<h:body>
    <p:panel header="JSON Representation of Employees">
        <h:outputText value="#{employeeJsonController.fetchJson()}"/>
    </p:panel>
    <p:panel header="Java Representation of Employees JSON">
        <p:dataTable value="#{employeeJsonController.fetchJavaFromJson()}" var="emp">
            <p:column>
                #{emp.last}
            </p:column>
        </p:dataTable>
    </p:panel>
</h:body>
```

The output would look similar to the output in Figure 16-1:

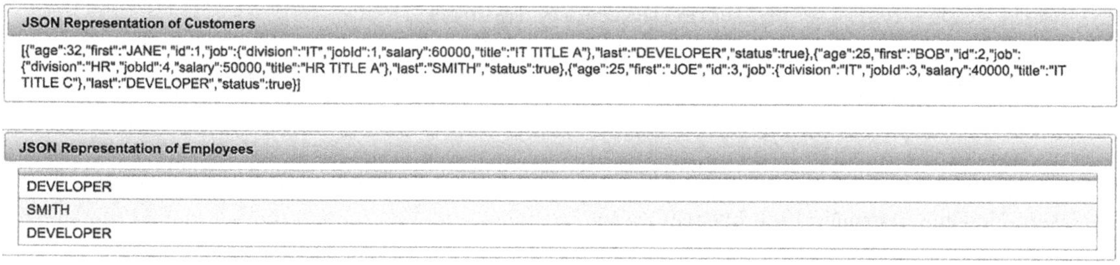

JSON Representation of Customers

[{"age":32,"first":"JANE","id":1,"job":{"division":"IT","jobId":1,"salary":60000,"title":"IT TITLE A"},"last":"DEVELOPER","status":true},{"age":25,"first":"BOB","id":2,"job":{"division":"HR","jobId":4,"salary":50000,"title":"HR TITLE A"},"last":"SMITH","status":true},{"age":25,"first":"JOE","id":3,"job":{"division":"IT","jobId":3,"salary":40000,"title":"IT TITLE C"},"last":"DEVELOPER","status":true}]

JSON Representation of Employees

DEVELOPER
SMITH
DEVELOPER

Figure 16-1. *Sample Output*

How It Works

The JSON-B API can be used to convert between JSON and Java seamlessly. In the release of Java EE 7, the transition between JSON and Java was missing. Therefore, this conversion had to take place manually and it was a bit painstaking. In Java EE 8, this gap has been closed and it is now possible to convert seamlessly between JSON and Java.

■ **Note** To view all documentation on the JSON-B website, visit `http://json-b.net/`.

The key piece of the JSON-B API is the `Jsonb` interface, which provides an abstraction over the JSON binding operations. The `JsonbBuilder` can be used to obtain a `Jsonb` object, which in turn is used to convert between Java and JSON. To create the `Jsonb` object, call on the `JsonBuilder create()` method. Once the `Jsonb` object has been obtained, it can be used to convert to JSON and `Serialize` by passing the Java object to the `toJson()` method.

```
Jsonb jsonb = JsonbBuilder.create();
    String result = null;

    result = jsonb.toJson(employees);
```

To go in the opposite direction and deserialize from JSON back to Java, use the `Jsonb fromJson()` method, passing the JSON string as the first argument and the Java type to which the JSON will be converted as the second argument.

```
Jsonb jsonb = JsonbBuilder.create();
List<Employee> employees = new ArrayList();
employees = jsonb.fromJson(employeesJson, ArrayList.class);
```

This technique is only one way to convert back to a `Collection` type. If you want to convert in a type-safe manner, back to the generic type `List<Employee>`, it can be done as follows:

```
employees = jsonb.fromJson(employeesJson, new ArrayList<Employee>(){}
                                    .getClass().getGenericSuperclass());
```

The Jsonb object can also convert back to a single Java object by passing the Java object type as the second argument to the fromJson() utility method, as follows:

```
Jsonb jsonb = JsonbBuilder.create();
Employee employee = new Employee;
employee = jsonb.fromJson(singleEmployeeJson, Employee.class);
```

This recipe covers the basics of converting JSON to Java and vice versa. For more information regarding customizations, see Recipe 16-7.

16-7. Custom Mapping with JSON-B

Problem

You want to change the JSON property names when converting to a Java class, or perform custom mapping for circumstances such as converting specific date formats or marking specified fields as transient.

Solution

Utilize a JsonbConfig to create a custom runtime configuration for the JSON mapping. There are also a handful of annotations that can be applied at the Java class level, field level, or getter/setters to customize some configurations. In the following scenario, a custom configuration is created to create a property naming strategy that includes lowercase with underscores.

```
JsonbConfig config = new JsonbConfig()
    .withPropertyNamingStrategy(PropertyNamingStragegy.LOWER_CASE_WITH_UNDERSCORES);
Jsonb jsonb = JsonbBuilder.create(config);
```

As mentioned previously, there are also a handful of annotations that can be applied to customize mapping. In the following scenario, the dog color property is marked as transient. This means that the color property will not be serialized into JSON when converting.

```
public class Dog {

    private String name;

    private int age;

    private String gender;

    @JsonbTransient
    private String color;
}
```

How It Works

The JsonbConfig class makes it easy to create a custom runtime configuration for your JSON mapping and formatting. Annotations can be used to create a custom compile-time configuration. Such customizations can include things like changing from the default property naming convention, or specifying a particular property ordering. To create a new configuration, simply create a new JsonbConfig class and pass the configuration to the JsonbBuilder.create() method, as such:

```
JsonbConfig config = new JsonbConfig();
Jsonb jsonb = JsonbBuilder.create(config);
```

The JsonbConfig class can be used to specify the runtime configurations contained in Table 16-5. In the example for this recipe, the .withPropertyNamingStrategy() option was specified to configure a property naming strategy that is lowercase with underscores.

Table 16-5. *JsonbConfig Options*

Option	Description
.withFormatting(boolean)	Create custom configuration with formatting.
.withPropertyNamingStrategy(strategy)	Provide strategy for constructing property names. Accepts a strategy of type PropertyNamingStrategy (IDENTITY, LOWER_CASE_WITH_DASHES, LOWER_CASE_WITH_UNDERSCORES, UPPER_CAMEL_CASE, UPPER_CAMEL_CASE_WITH_SPACES, CASE_INSENSITIVE).
.withPropertyOrderStrategy(strategy)	Provide strategy for ordering properties. Accepts a strategy of type PropertyOrderStrategy (LEXICOGRAPHICAL, ANY, REVERSE).
.withNullValues(boolean)	Change the default NULL handling. Global configuration.
.withDateFormat("format")	Change the default date format. Global configuration.
.withBinaryDataStrategy(strategy)	Provide strategy for binary data encoding. Default is BYTE encoding. Accepts BinaryDataStrategy (BYTE, BASE_64, BASE_64_URL).
.withAdapters(CustomAdapter)	Assign a CustomAdapter to a Jsonb configuration. (See JSON-B documentation for more on adapters.)
.withSerializers(JsonbSerializer)	Assign a JsonbSerializer to a Jsonb configuration.
.withDeserializers(JsonbDeserializer)	Assign a JsonbDeserializer to a Jsonb configuration.
.withStrictIJSON(boolean)	Provide support for the I-JSON restricted profile of JSON.

As previously mentioned, configurations can also be made at compile time by specifying annotations on Java classes, fields, or getters and setters. Table 16-6 lists the annotations that can be placed on a Java class, field, or accessor method.

Table 16-6. *Annotation Configurations*

Annotation	Description
`@JsonbProperty("name")`	Field and getter/setter level. Change name of a particular property. Placed on getter: the new name will be serialized when writing to JSON. Placed on a setter: the new name will be expected when reading during deserialization. Placed on field: the new name will be applied on both serialization and deserialization.
`@JsonbPropertyOrder(strategy)`	Class level. Customizes the order of serialized properties. Accepts a `PropertyOrderStrategy` (`LEXICOGRAPHICAL`, `ANY`, `REVERSE`).
`@JsonbTransient`	Field and getter/setter level. Indicates that an annotated field should be ignored by the JSON binding engine. Placed on field: the property is ignored during serialization and deserialization. Getter: the property is ignored during serialization. Setter: the property is ignored during deserialization.
`@JsonNillable(boolean)`	Class and field level. Indicates if `NULL` values are to be serialized. Default is false.
`@JsonbCreator`	Constructor level. Allows one to annotate a custom constructor with parameters or a static factory method used to create a class instance.
`@JsonbDateFormat("format")`	Field level. Customize date format for a specified property.
`@JsonbNumberFormat("format")`	Field level. Customize number format for a specified property.

16-8. Replacing a Specified Element in a JSON Document

Problem

You want to replace values of a JSON document that match a given pattern.

Solution

Utilize the JSON-P patch capability to replace the values within the JSON document. In the following example, a string of text is taken in from a JSF form and used to create a JSON pointer to the matching last name in the JSON string. The JSON `Replace` functionality is then used to replace the matching JSON string value with the string value of "`JsonMaster`".

```
public void findEmployeeByLast() {
    setSearchResult(null);
    String text = "/" + this.lastSearchText;
    JsonObject json = Json.createObjectBuilder().build();
    JsonValue object = json.getJsonObject(fetchJson());
    if (lastSearchText != null && object != null) {
        JsonPointer pointer = Json.createPointer(text);
        System.out.println("text: " + text + pointer);
        System.out.println("json: " + object);
        JsonValue result = pointer.getValue(object.asJsonArray());
```

```
        // Replace a value
        JsonArray array = (JsonArray) pointer.replace(object.asJsonArray(),
                          Json.createValue("JsonMaster"));
        setSearchResult(array.toString());
    }

}
```

The following markup shows the JSF form that is used to send the search text and display the resulting output.

```
<h:form id="jsonPointerForm">
    <p:panel header="Employee Search By Address">
        <p:outputLabel for="lastSearchText" value="Pointer String:"/>
        <p:inputText id="lastSearchText" value="#{employeeJsonController.lastSearchText}"/>
        <br/><br/>
        <p:commandButton id="searchButton"
                         action="#{employeeJsonController.findEmployeeByLast}"
                         update="searchResult" value="Find Value"/>
    </p:panel>
    <br/>
    <h:outputText id="searchResult" value="#{customerController.searchResult}"/>
</h:form>
```

How It Works

The JSON-P 1.1 API added the ability to point to a specified JSON value and to replace values of a JSON document. The JSON Pointer ability allows you to identify a specific value within a JSON document. To utilize the JSON Pointer functionality, you must first obtain a `JsonObject` by calling on the appropriate `Json` interface method for working with the JSON that is to be used. In the solution to this recipe, the `Json.createObjectBuilder().build()` methods are called on to return a `JsonObject`. The `JsonObject` can then be used to perform a JSON Patch operation. The `fetchJson()` method in the example returns a JSON String.

```
JsonObject json = Json.createObjectBuilder().build();
JsonValue object = json.getJsonObject(fetchJson());
```

The `JsonPointer` object is obtained by calling on the `Json` interface `createPointer()` method, passing the string of text to find in the JSON. The following excerpt from the solution shows the process of obtaining the JSON pointer:

```
JsonPointer pointer = Json.createPointer(text);
```

The JSON Patch functionality provides the ability to add, remove, or replace a portion of a JSON document or string that has been obtained via a JSON pointer. In the solution, the replace functionality is used to replace the last name that is pointed to with the string "`JsonMaster`". This is done by calling on the `JsonPointer replace()` method and passing the JSON object as the first argument. The `Json` that will replace the original JSON as the second argument.

```
JsonArray array = (JsonArray) pointer.replace(object.asJsonArray(),
                              Json.createValue("JsonMaster"));
```

The JsonPointer object also contains the methods add() and replace(). The add() method can be used to add a value into a JSON object or insert a value into an array. The add() method accepts a JsonObject as the first argument, and the Json value to add as the second argument. The remove() method allows you to remove a JsonPointer value from a JSON document.

CHAPTER 17

Security

One of the most important components to an enterprise-level application is security. It is a fact that enterprise applications must be rock solid and secure so that data and application functionality cannot fall into the wrong hands. Utilizing a combination of application server security and application-level security can help secure applications from thugs who are targeting enterprise data.

The release of Java EE 8 introduced the Security API, which for the first time provides the Java EE platform with a standard API that can be used for securing applications. In previous releases, security was certainly possible, but there was no standard API, so there were variations of homegrown authentication solutions and third-party APIs that were used throughout the applications that use the platform. In this chapter, I touch upon techniques that may have been used in previous releases for securing applications, and I outline similar solutions utilizing the new standard security API.

Three different types of security can be applied to enterprise-level applications: declarative, programmatic, and transport security. *Declarative* security occurs within an application's deployment descriptor or via annotations that are added to classes and methods within the application. Declarative security is used to provide the application server container with the ability to guard access to certain application features via the use of user authentication and roles. *Programmatic* security occurs when the developer manually codes the authentication methods, customizing the requirements for authentication into an application. *Transport* security occurs between the client and the server, and it is responsible for securing information as it is passed between the two.

This chapter touches on each of these three levels of security. It contains recipes that cover application server configurations utilizing GlassFish and Payara server for setting up database and LDAP (Lightweight Directory Access Protocol) authentication for applications that are deployed within the container. You will also learn how to utilize XML configuration, annotations, and JSF EL to secure portions of your applications. Lastly, the chapter touches on how to secure transport via SSL and certificates. Since the GlassFish and Payara administration is very similar, assume that when GlassFish is referenced in this chapter, the same holds true for Payara, unless otherwise noted. This chapter also touches on the new Java EE Security API, which provides a standardized solution that enables developers to produce portable applications and package security implementations within the application, rather than in the container.

J. Juneau, *Java EE 8 Recipes*, https://doi.org/10.1007/978-1-4842-3594-2_17

17-1. Setting Up Application Users and Groups in GlassFish

Problem

You want to create users, groups, and roles within your application server container for use with applications that are deployed to the container.

Solution

Log into the GlassFish or Payara administrative console to add users to the File security realm. You can then add the users to groups by specifying the group names when creating the users. This example will walk you through the configuration of a new user within the GlassFish application server.

1. Log in to the administrative console by navigating to `http://localhost:4848` and then logging in as an administrative user.

2. Use the tree menu on the left side of the screen to navigate to the Configurations ➤ server-config ➤ Security ➤ Realms menu. Once you click the Realms menu option, the Realms form will appear (see Figure 17-1).

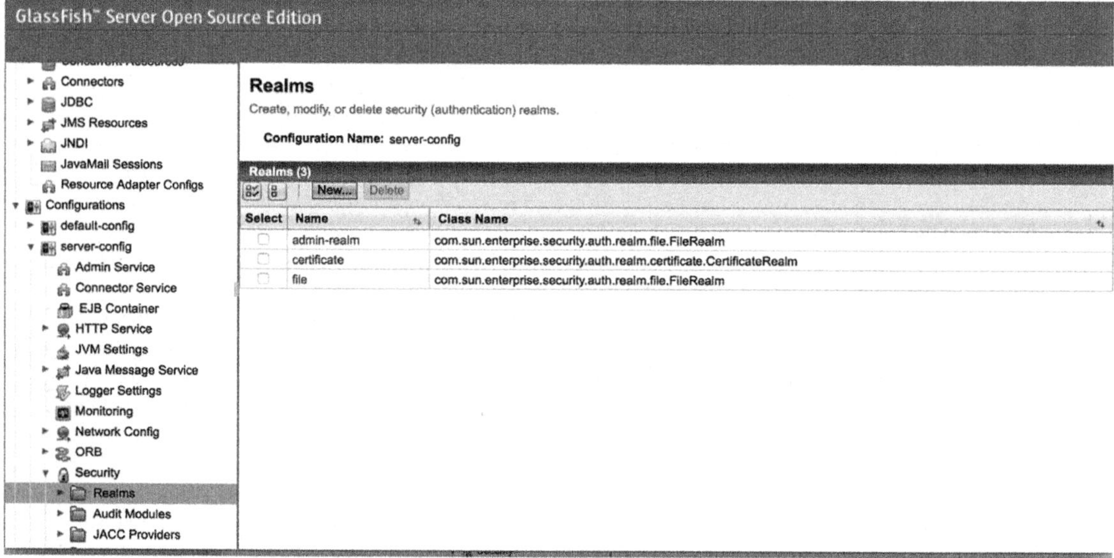

Figure 17-1. *GlassFish Realms form*

3. Click the File realm link to enter the Edit Realm form, as shown in Figure 17-2.

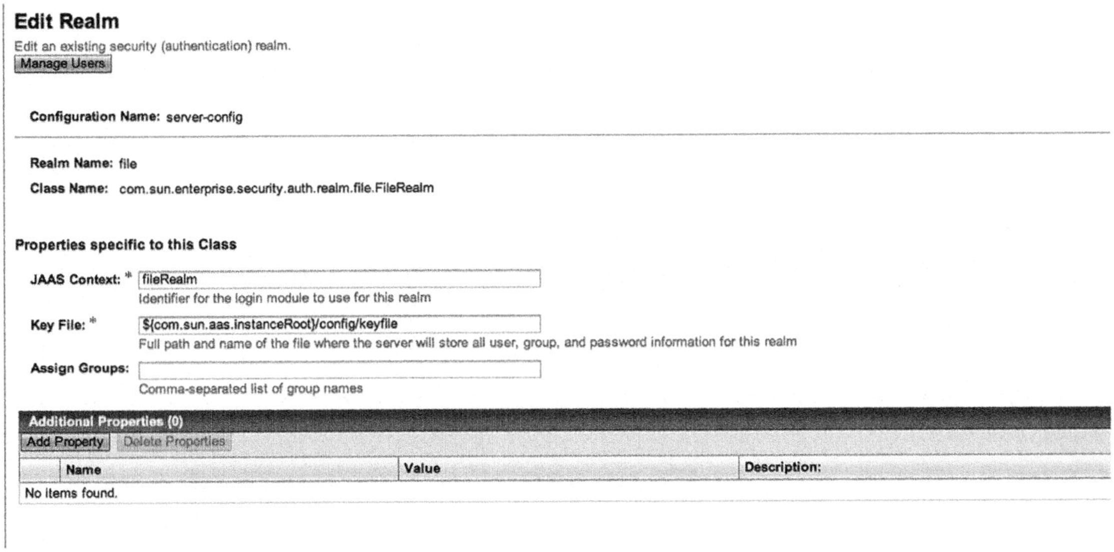

Edit Realm

Edit an existing security (authentication) realm.

Manage Users

Configuration Name: server-config

Realm Name: file

Class Name: com.sun.enterprise.security.auth.realm.file.FileRealm

Properties specific to this Class

JAAS Context: * fileRealm
Identifier for the login module to use for this realm

Key File: * ${com.sun.aas.instanceRoot}/config/keyfile
Full path and name of the file where the server will store all user, group, and password information for this realm

Assign Groups:
Comma-separated list of group names

Additional Properties (0)

Add Property Delete Properties

	Name	Value	Description:
No items found.			

Figure 17-2. GlassFish Edit Realm form

4. Click the Manage Users button on the Edit Realm form to open the File Users form, and then click the New button on the File Users form (see Figure 17-3) to enter the New File Realm User form (see Figure 17-4).

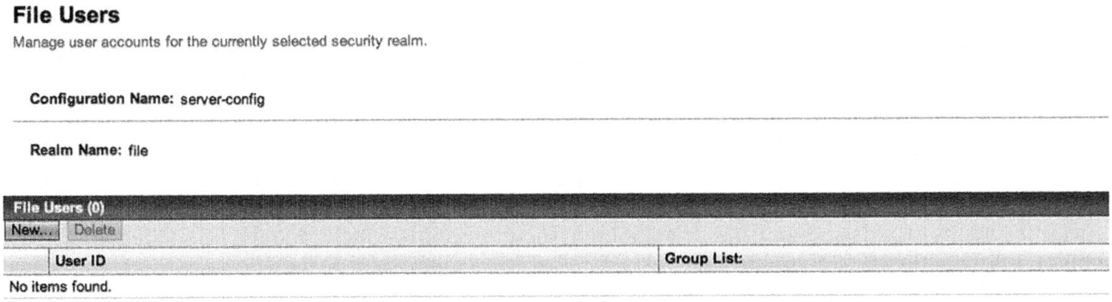

File Users

Manage user accounts for the currently selected security realm.

Configuration Name: server-config

Realm Name: file

File Users (0)

New... Delete

	User ID	Group List:
No items found.		

Figure 17-3. GlassFish File Users form

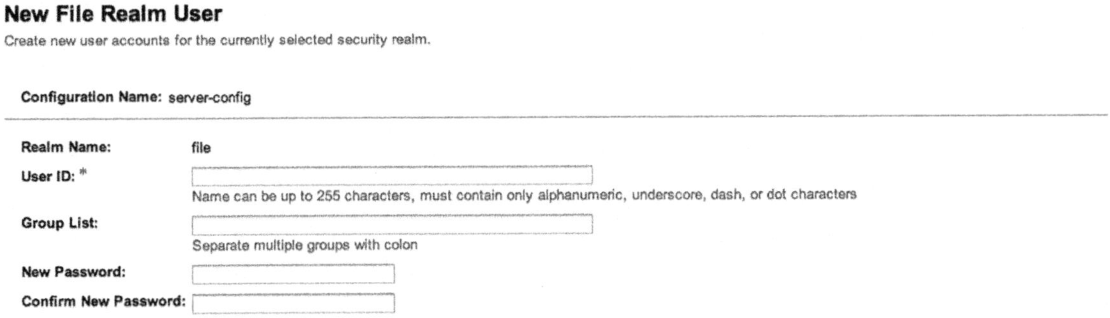

New File Realm User

Create new user accounts for the currently selected security realm.

Configuration Name: server-config

Realm Name: file

User ID: *
Name can be up to 255 characters, must contain only alphanumeric, underscore, dash, or dot characters

Group List:
Separate multiple groups with colon

New Password:

Confirm New Password:

Figure 17-4. GlassFish New File Realm User form

5. Fill in a user ID and the password information to complete the New File Realm User form and optionally add a group name to the Group List field. Click the Save button to add the user to the File Users list (see Figure 17-5).

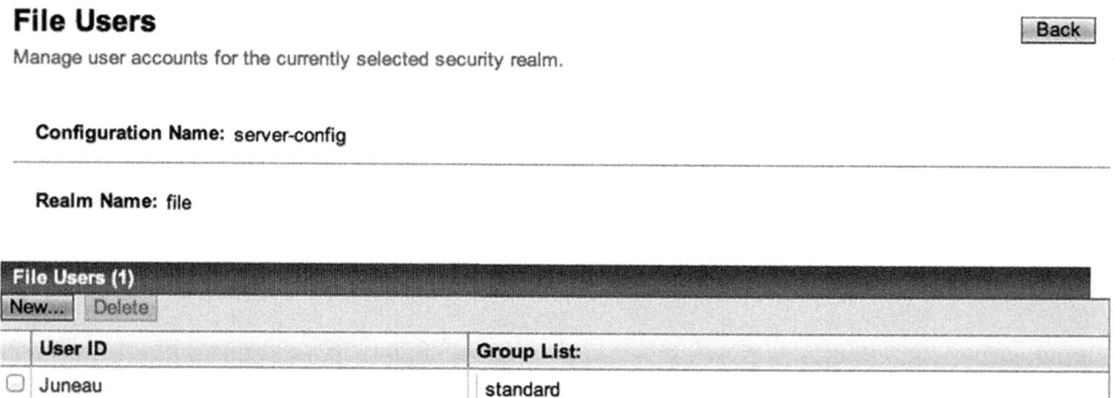

Figure 17-5. *File Users list*

Once they're created, users within GlassFish/Payara realms can be used for application authentication purposes. To learn more about configuring your applications to utilize application server container user authentication, refer to Recipe 17-2.

How It Works

Adding an authentication prompt to allow user access to secured areas can be one of the best forms of protection for any application. Fortunately, the Java platform makes authentication easy for you to add to your applications, albeit there was no formal standard introduced until the release of Java EE 8. Most application servers have some mechanism for adding user accounts that can be used to access applications that are deployed in the one of the server domains. GlassFish and Payara are no exception because they provide the ability to add users and groups to different security realms, which can then be applied to applications for authentication purposes.

■ **Note** Most application server containers also allow for connectivity with LDAP servers or databases, which enables authentication to occur against user accounts within the LDAP server or stored within a database table, rather than within the container itself. For an example of LDAP authentication, read the recipes later in this chapter.

When adding users to GlassFish, they must be incorporated with a security realm. The File security realm is available for use with the default installation, although more security realms can be created if desired. Adding users to realms is a fairly simple process, and individual users can be added by following the steps noted in the solution to this recipe. When creating a user, one of the options that can be specified is a *group*. You can think of a GlassFish user group as a role, in that more than one user can belong to a group. GlassFish does not contain a mechanism for managing the groups themselves; in fact, a group is merely a string value to GlassFish. However, if you follow through the steps in Recipe 17-2, you will see that groups can be mapped to roles at the application level. Therefore, if UserA belongs to a group named standard, then UserA can also belong to a group named admin. The application can then grant access to UserA for different portions of the application, depending on which groups or roles the user belongs to.

Users in GlassFish are simplistic in that they are used for authentication and access purposes within the deployed applications only. Users can be managed only on a per-server installation basis, so they are a bit cumbersome since they cannot be shared across servers to provide a single sign-on solution. For those reasons, it is recommended that GlassFish/Payara users be used for smaller applications/environments or testing purposes only. For a more substantial and enterprise authentication solution, either database or LDAP user accounts would be a better choice.

■ **Note** To learn about configuring form-based authentication within the GlassFish or Payara application server and utilizing a database to store user credentials, see Recipe 12-6.

17-2. Performing Basic Web Application Authorization

Problem

You have established users and associated them with groups within the application server container. Now you want to assign users to particular roles based on the access levels that they require for the application and apply a basic authentication mechanism for access to specified application views.

Solution #1

Configure forms-based security using basic authentication within the web application deployment descriptor. Map roles to groups within the glassfish-web.xml deployment descriptor, if needed. The following excerpt was taken from the web.xml deployment descriptor of the JavaEERecipes NetBeans project sources. It demonstrates how to secure all of the views that reside within the chapter17 folder (determined by the url-pattern element within web.xml) such that a user name and password combination is required for access. The auth-method tag within web.xml specifies the type of authentication that will be used for the application. In the example, you'll use BASIC authentication. Only those user names and passwords that have been configured in the GlassFish file realm with the appropriate group will be granted access; in this case, it is the users role.

```
<security-constraint>
        <web-resource-collection>
            <web-resource-name>secured</web-resource-name>
            <url-pattern>/faces/chapter14/*</url-pattern>
            <http-method>GET</http-method>
            <http-method>POST</http-method>
        </web-resource-collection>

        <auth-constraint>
            <role-name>users</role-name>
        </auth-constraint>
```

```
        <user-data-constraint>
        <transport-guarantee>CONFIDENTIAL</transport-guarantee>
        </user-data-constraint>
    </security-constraint>

    <login-config>
        <auth-method>BASIC</auth-method>
        <realm-name>file</realm-name>
    </login-config>

    <security-role>
        <role-name>users</role-name>
    </security-role>
```

If role names specified in the web.xml deployment descriptor are the same as the group names that have been associated with users in GlassFish, then you are done. Users will be granted access to those areas of the application that have been secured, based on the group association. However, if a role name differs from those groups that have been associated to users, you can manually map role names to group names by specifying a security-role-mapping in the glassfish-web.xml file for the application. The following excerpt, taken from the glassfish-web.xml configuration file for the JavaEERecipes NetBeans application, demonstrates how to do map roles to GlassFish users. In this case, the role standard that was specified for the account in Recipe 17-1 is mapped to the users role. The users role has access to the /faces/chapter17/* url-pattern.

```
<security-role-mapping>
  <role-name>users</role-name>
  <group-name>standard</group-name>
</security-role-mapping>
```

Once everything has been configured, access will be granted according to the configurations that have been placed in the web.xml deployment descriptor. To test the authentication mechanism, deploy the JavaEERecipes WAR file to your GlassFish/Payara application server and visit the following URL:

```
http://localhost:8080/JavaEERecipes/faces/chapter17/index.xhtml
```

Solution #2

Use annotations on classes and class methods to declare roles within an application for access to secured pages as deemed necessary. To implement access control on a particular class or method, annotate using @DeclareRoles and/or @RolesAllowed, specifying the roles that can be used to access them. Those users who are authenticated belonging to one of the specified roles will be granted access to the content.

In the example corresponding to this recipe, the chapter17/recipe17_02.xhtml JSF view contains two command buttons that invoke actions within a managed bean. Each of the buttons invokes a different action in the bean. One of the buttons invokes a method that is secured via the @RolesAllowed annotation, and the other does not. The following excerpt is taken from the class org.javaee8recipes.chapter17.recipe17_02.Recipe17_02b, which is the managed bean controller that contains the two methods being called from the command buttons:

```
public class Recipe17_02b implements Serializable {

    public Recipe17_02b() {
    }
```

```
    public String unsecuredProcess(){
        return "recipe17_02_1.xhtml";
    }

    @RolesAllowed("users")
    public String securedProcess(){
        return "recipe17_02_2.xhtml";
    }
}
```

When the commandButton that invokes the securedProcess method is clicked, users will be prompted to authenticate if they have not already done so.

How It Works

There are a couple of ways to secure an application using basic application server authentication. Commonly, applications provide basic authentication security via the use of XML configuration within the web.xml deployment descriptor along with optional configuration within the glassfish-web.xml deployment descriptor. It is also possible to add basic authentication security into an application using code only, via declarative security. Declarative security is based on the use of annotations for declaring roles for access to application classes and methods. While both of these techniques are very similar in concept, each of them has its own set of bonuses in certain situations.

In Solution #1 to this recipe, XML configuration is used to secure access to all web views that reside within a specific folder in the application. To add security via XML configuration files, the web.xml deployment descriptor needs to have the security-constraint, login-config, and security-role elements added to it for mapping application roles to GlassFish users and groups. The security-constraint element encompasses a handful of subelements that are used to tell the application server container which areas of the application to secure and which accounts are able to access those secured areas. First, a web-resource-collection element is used to declare the locations of the application to secure and which HTTP methods to secure. The following elements should be embedded within a web-resource-collection element:

- web-resource-name: This is an optional name that can be specified for the secured location. In the recipe solution, the name secured is specified.
- url-pattern: This is the URL pattern that will be used to determine which areas of the application are to be secured. An asterisk (*) is used as a wildcard. In the recipe solution, chapter14/* specifies that all views contained within the chapter14 folder should be secured. If you want to secure a specific page, then utilize the URL pattern to that page, including the page name.
- http-method: This is used to specify which HTTP methods should be secured for access to the locations specified by the url-pattern element.

Another subelement that can be declared within the security-constraint element is the auth-constraint element. This element lists the different security roles that are used to secure the locations specified by the url-pattern via adding role-name subelements. In the recipe solution, the users role is declared for the application. A user-data-constraint element can also be included as a subelement to the security-constraint element in order to specify the type of protection that will be applied when data is transported between the client and the server. In the example, this has been set to CONFIDENTIAL. The values that can be specified for the transport guarantee are as follows:

- NONE: Data requires no transport security.
- INTEGRAL: Data cannot be changed in transit between the client and the server.
- CONFIDENTIAL: Outside entities are unable to observe the contents of the transmission. Secure Sockets Layer (SSL) will be used in this case, and it must be configured within the web server.

The security-role XML element lists the different roles that can be used for securing access to the application pages. Add the role-name subelement to the security-role for each role specification. The login-config XML element is used to specify the method of authentication that is to be used for securing the application. The auth-method should be set to BASIC for most cases, but all possible values are BASIC, DIGEST, FORM, and CLIENT-CERT.

Adding the designated elements to the web.xml deployment descriptor, as described in this section, provides sufficient ability for applications to be secured via a user name/login to specified secure locations. In some cases, it makes sense to use annotations to declare roles from within the application code itself. For such cases, the @DeclareRoles and @RolesAllowed annotations can be specified on a class or method. The following annotations can be used to specify security within a class. For each of the annotations, either a single role or a list of roles can be specified.

- @DeclareRoles: This is specified at the class or method level, and each role that is allowed to access the class should be indicated within the annotation. For instance, one or more roles can be specified for access to the class using the following syntax:
- Class level:

```
@DeclareRoles("users")
public class MyClass {
  ...
}
```

- Method level:

```
public class MyClass {
  ...
     @DeclareRoles({"role1", "role2"})
     public void calculatePay(){
          ...
     }
...
}
```

- @RolesAllowed: This is specified at either the class or method level. A list of roles that are allowed to access the class or method should be indicated within the annotation. The syntax is the same as with that of @DeclareRoles.
- @PermitAll: This is specified at the class or method level. It indicates that all roles are allowed access.
- @DenyAll: This is specified at the class or method level. It indicates that no roles are allowed access.

When the @DeclareRoles and @RolesAllowed annotations are used in the same class, the combination of the roles listed within each are allowed to access that class. The roles specified for access on a particular method using @RolesAllowed override the roles that are listed to access the entire class.

It is possible to programmatically check to see which roles an authenticated user belongs to by calling the SessionContext isCallerInRole method. This allows you to permit access to particular features of an application using conditional logic, as demonstrated by the following lines of code:

```
@DeclareRoles({"role1", "role2, "role3"}
public class MyClass {

    ...
    @RolesAllowed("role2")
    public void calculatePay(){
        ...
    }

    @PermitAll
    public void calculatePay(){
        if (ctx.isUserInRole("role1")) {
            ...
        } else if (ctx.isUserInRole("role3")){
            ...
        }
    }
    ...
}
```

17-3. Developing a Programmatic Login Form with Custom Authentication Validation

Problem

You want to secure your JSF application to a specified group of users. Furthermore, you want to create a custom login view, which will be used to pass user credentials to the appropriate business objects for authentication.

Solution

Develop a login form that consists of user name and password inputText fields, along with a commandButton to invoke a programmatic login action that resides within a managed bean controller. Develop logic within the managed bean controller to authenticate users. In the following example, a login form is generated using JSF and Facelets, utilizing a managed bean for authentication control.

Creating the Login Form

A login form is basically the same as any other form, except it accepts a user name and a password as arguments and passes them to a JavaBean that utilizes the information to accept or deny the authentication request. The login form also utilizes a standard HTML form element that passes the user name (`j_username`) and password (`j_password`) field values to an action named `j_security_check`. The following code is used to comprise the `login.xhtml` form for a JSF authentication mechanism:

```
<?xml version="1.0" encoding="UTF-8" ?>
<!DOCTYPE html PUBLIC "-//W3C//DTD XHTML 1.0 Transitional//EN" "http://www.w3.org/TR/xhtml1/
DTD/xhtml1-transitional.dtd">
<html xmlns="http://www.w3.org/1999/xhtml"
      xmlns:ui="http://xmlns.jcp.org/jsf/facelets"
      xmlns:h="http://xmlns.jcp.org/jsf/html"
      xmlns:f="http://xmlns.jcp.org/jsf/core"
      xmlns:p="http://primefaces.org/ui">

    <ui:composition template="/layout/custom_template.xhtml">
        <ui:define name="title">
            <h:outputText value="Welcome to the Acme Bookstore"></h:outputText>
        </ui:define>
        <ui:define name="content">

                        <h:form id="login">
                            <center>
                                <p align="center" class="sub_head_sub"><br />
                                    <strong>Acme Bookstore Application</strong>
                                </p>
                                <span class="normal">
                                    You must authenticate to gain access to this application.
                                </span>
                                <br/>
                                <span class="error">
                                    <h:messages errorStyle="color: red" infoStyle="color: green"
                                    globalOnly="true"/>
                                </span>
                                <div>
                                    <p:panel rendered="#{authenticationController.
                                    authenticated}">

                                        <a href="/index.xhtml">Authenticated successfully...go
                                        to Application</a>
                                    </p:panel>

                                    <p:panel rendered="#{!authenticationController.authenticated}">
                                        Username: <h:inputText id="j_username"

                                                              value="#{authentication
                                                              Controller.username}"/>

                                        <br/><br/>
```

```
                                        Password: <h:inputSecret id="j_password"

                                                              value="#{authenticationController.
                                                              password}"/>
                                        <br/>
                                        <br/>
                                        <h:commandButton id="login" action="#{authenticationCon
                                        troller.login}"
                                                             value="Login"/>
                                    </p:panel>

                                    <br/>
                                </div>

                            </center>
                        </h:form>

                </ui:define>

        </ui:composition>

</html>
```

■ **Note** The inputSecret component used in this example will display a series of asterisks, rather than plain text, when input is typed into the text box.

Once loaded, the login form will resemble Figure 17-6 when using the Acme Bookstore template.

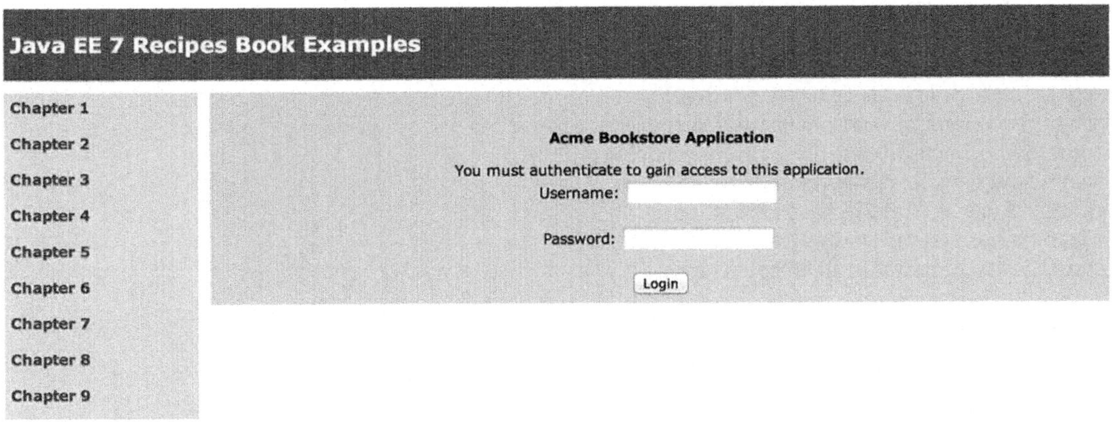

Figure 17-6. *Login form example*

Coding the Authentication Backend

The authentication backend is responsible for performing the authentication and maintaining state for a user session. The backend logic consists of an EJB for maintaining the authentication logic and a JSF controller that is used for binding view methods and fields to backend logic. The managed bean controller should be session scoped so that the user state can be managed for an entire session. Lastly, if you're using a database table to contain all of the user names that have access to the application, then an entity class will be required for that database table.

In this section, I introduce a custom technique as a non-standard solution, which utilizes an EJB to authenticate an individual's credentials. The authentication occurs calling on the `HttpServletRequest login()`, passing authentication off to the application server container. This is container-specific, meaning that it will work only if the application has been configured, as has been done with the first recipe in this chapter.

The second approach uses the Java EE Security API, which was introduced in Java EE 8, using servlet-based authentication within an `HttpAuthenticationMechanism` (HAM). To see more specifics regarding the Security API, see Recipe 17-4.

EJB (Custom Solution)

The Enterprise JavaBean that is used for this custom authentication backend is a stateless session bean that contains a `login` method, which makes calls to the application server container authentication mechanism. The following code is from the class `org.javaee8recipes.chapter17.recipe17_03.AutheticationBean.java` file in the `JavaEERecipes` NetBeans project.

```
package org.javaee8recipes.chapter17.recipe17_03;

import java.io.Serializable;
import javax.ejb.Remove;
import javax.ejb.Stateless;
import javax.faces.application.FacesMessage;

import javax.persistence.CacheRetrieveMode;

import javax.faces.context.FacesContext;
import javax.persistence.EntityManager;
import javax.persistence.NoResultException;
import javax.persistence.PersistenceContext;
import javax.persistence.Query;
import javax.servlet.ServletException;
import javax.servlet.http.HttpServletRequest;
import javax.servlet.http.HttpSession;

@Stateless
public class AuthenticationBean implements Serializable  {

    @PersistenceContext(unitName = "JavaEERecipesPU")
    private EntityManager em;
    private boolean authenticated = false;
    private String username = null;
    private String password = null;
    HttpSession session = null;
    User user;
```

```
public AuthenticationBean() {
}

public void findUser() {
    try {
        em.flush();

        getUser();
        Query userQry = em.createQuery(
                "select object(u) from User u "
                + "where u.username = :username").setParameter("username", getUser().
                getUsername().toUpperCase());

    // Enable forced database query
        userQry.setHint("javax.persistence.cache.retrieveMode", CacheRetrieveMode.BYPASS);
        setUser((User) userQry.getSingleResult());

        FacesContext.getCurrentInstance().addMessage(null, new
        FacesMessage(FacesMessage.SEVERITY_INFO, "Successfully Authenticated", ""));
    } catch (Exception e) {

        FacesContext.getCurrentInstance().addMessage(null, new
        FacesMessage(FacesMessage.SEVERITY_ERROR, "Invalid username/password", ""));
        setUser(null);

    }

}

public HttpSession getSession() {
    FacesContext context = FacesContext.getCurrentInstance();
    HttpServletRequest request = (HttpServletRequest) context.getExternalContext().
    getRequest();
    session = request.getSession(false);
    return session;
}

public boolean login() {

    HttpSession session = getSession();
    HttpServletRequest request = null;
    Query userQry = null;
    System.out.println("In the login method..." + getUser().getUsername());
    try {
        FacesContext context = FacesContext.getCurrentInstance();
        request = (HttpServletRequest) context.getExternalContext().getRequest();
        request.login(getUser().getUsername(), this.password);

        session.setMaxInactiveInterval(1800);
        session.setAttribute("authenticated", new Boolean(true));

        em.flush();
```

```
            userQry = em.createQuery(
                    "select count(u) from User u "
                    + "where u.username = :username").setParameter("username", getUser().
                    getUsername().toUpperCase());
            userQry.setHint("javax.persistence.cache.retrieveMode", CacheRetrieveMode.BYPASS);
            Long count = (Long)userQry.getSingleResult();
            if (count > 0){

                userQry = em.createQuery(
                        "select object(u) from User u "
                        + "where u.username = :username").setParameter("username",
                        getUser().getUsername().toUpperCase());

                // Enable forced database query
                userQry.setHint("javax.persistence.cache.retrieveMode", CacheRetrieveMode.
                BYPASS);
                setUser((User) userQry.getSingleResult());
                System.out.println("Setting  User, user exists in database with role ->" +
                user.getSecurityRole());
                setAuthenticated(true);
            } else {
               // User cannot authenticate successfully...do something
            }

            FacesContext.getCurrentInstance().addMessage(null, new
FacesMessage(FacesMessage.SEVERITY_INFO, "Successfully Authenticated", ""));

            return authenticated;
        } catch (NoResultException| ServletException ex) {
            setUser(null);
            setAuthenticated(false);
            session = getSession();
            session.setAttribute("authenticated", new Boolean(false));
            if(request != null){
                try {
                    request.logout();
                } catch (ServletException ex1) {
                    System.out.println("AuthBean#login Error: " + ex);
                }
            }
            FacesContext.getCurrentInstance().addMessage(null, new
            FacesMessage(FacesMessage.SEVERITY_ERROR, "Invalid username/password", ""));
            return false;

        } finally {
            setPassword(null);
        }
    }
```

```
/**
 * @return the isAuthenticated
 */
public boolean isAuthenticated() {

    if (getSession().getAttribute("authenticated") != null) {
        boolean auth = (Boolean) getSession().getAttribute("authenticated");
        if (auth) {
            authenticated = true;
        }
    } else {
        authenticated = false;
    }
    return authenticated;
}

/**
 * @param isAuthenticated the isAuthenticated to set
 */
public void setAuthenticated(boolean isAuthenticated) {
    this.authenticated = isAuthenticated;
}

@Remove
public void remove() {
    System.out.println("Being removed from session...");
    setUser(null);
}

/**
 * @return the username
 */
public String getUsername() {
    try {
        System.out.println("The current username is: " + user.getUsername());
        username = getUser().getUsername();
    } catch (NullPointerException ex) {
    }
    return username;
}

/**
 * @param username the username to set
 */
public void setUsername(String username) {
    getUser().setUsername(username);
    System.out.println("Just set the username to : " + getUser().getUsername());
    this.username = null;
}
```

```
    /**
     * @return the password
     */
    public String getPassword() {
        return this.password;
    }

    /**
     * @param password the password to set
     */
    public void setPassword(String password) {
        this.password = password;
    }

    /**
     * @return the user
     */
    public User getUser(){
        if (this.user == null) {
            user = new User();
        }
        return user;
    }

    /**
     * @param user the user to set
     */
    public void setUser(User user) {
        this.user = user;
    }
}
```

JSF Controller

The controller is responsible for coordinating authentication efforts between the JSF view and the EJB. It also has a session scope so that the user's state can be maintained throughout the life of the application session. The following code is taken from the `org.javaee8recipes.chapter17.recipe17_03.AuthenticationController.java` file that is contained within the JavaEERecipes NetBeans project:

```
import javax.servlet.http.HttpSession;

@Named("authenticationController")
@SessionScoped
public class AuthenticationController implements Serializable {

    @EJB
    private AuthenticationBean authenticationFacade;
    private String username;
    private User user;
    private boolean authenticated = false;
```

```
private HttpSession session = null;
private String userAgent;

/**
 * Creates a new instance of AuthenticationController
 */
public AuthenticationController() {

}

public HttpSession getSession() {
    // if(session == null){
    FacesContext context = FacesContext.getCurrentInstance();
    HttpServletRequest request = (HttpServletRequest) context.getExternalContext().
    getRequest();
    session = request.getSession();

    return session;
}

/**
 * @return the username
 */
public String getUsername() {
    this.username = getUser().getUsername();
    return this.username;
}

/**
 * @param username the username to set
 */
public void setUsername(String username) {
    this.username = username;
    getUser().setUsername(username);
}

/**
 * @return the password
 */
public String getPassword() {
    return authenticationFacade.getPassword();
}

/**
 * @param password the password to set
 */
public void setPassword(String password) {
    authenticationFacade.setPassword(password);
}
```

```
    public User getUser() {
        if (this.user == null) {
            user = new User();
            setUser(authenticationFacade.getUser());
        }

        return user;
    }

    public void setUser(User user) {
        this.user = user;
    }

    public String login() {
        authenticationFacade.setUser(getUser());
        boolean authResult = authenticationFacade.login();

        if (authResult) {
            this.authenticated = true;

            setUser(authenticationFacade.getUser());

            return "SUCCESS_LOGIN";
        } else {
            this.authenticated = false;
            setUser(null);
            return "BAD_LOGIN";
        }

    }

    public String logout() {
        user = null;
        this.authenticated = false;
        FacesContext facesContext = FacesContext.getCurrentInstance();
        ExternalContext externalContext = facesContext.getExternalContext();
        externalContext.invalidateSession();
        return "SUCCESS_LOGOUT";
    }

    /**
     * @return the authenticated
     */
    public boolean isAuthenticated() {
        try {
            boolean auth = (Boolean) getSession().getAttribute("authenticated");
            if (auth) {
                this.authenticated = true;
```

```
            } else {
                authenticated = false;
            }
        } catch (Exception e) {
            this.authenticated = false;
        }

        return authenticated;
    }

    public void setAuthenticated(boolean authenticated) {
        this.authenticated = authenticated;
    }
}
```

User Entity

For any application, it is a good idea to maintain a list of users who have the ability to access the application pages. Furthermore, if an application requires fine-grained access control, it is important to assign roles to each user to indicate which privilege level each user should have for the application. A database table can be used for this purpose, and the table should contain a field for the user name of each person who has access to the application, as well as a field for the user role. The following SQL is used for creating the USER database table in an Oracle database:

```
create table users(
id number,
username varchar(150) not null,
password varchar(50) not null,
primary key (id));
```

The following class listing is that for the `org.javaee8recipes.chapter17.recipe17_03.User.java` file, which is an entity class within the JavaEERecipes NetBeans project:

```
import java.io.Serializable;
import java.math.BigDecimal;
import javax.persistence.Column;
import javax.persistence.Entity;
import javax.persistence.Id;
import javax.persistence.Table;

/**
 * Entity class User
 */
@Entity

@Table(name = "USER")

public class User implements Serializable {
```

```
    @Id
    @Column(name = "USER_ID", nullable = false)
    private BigDecimal userId;

    @Column(name = "USERNAME")
    private String username;

    @Column(name = "SECURITY_ROLE")
    private String securityRole;

    /** Creates a new instance of User */
    public User() {
    }

    /**
     * Creates a new instance of User with the specified values.
     * @param userId the userId of the User
     */
    public User(BigDecimal userId) {
        this.userId = userId;
    }

    /**
     * Gets the userId of this User.
     * @return the userId
     */
    public BigDecimal getUserId() {
        return this.userId;
    }

    /**
     * Sets the userId of this User to the specified value.
     * @param userId the new userId
     */
    public void setUserId(BigDecimal userId) {
        this.userId = userId;
    }

    /**
     * Gets the username of this User.
     * @return the username
     */
    public String getUsername() {
        return this.username;
    }

    /**
     * Sets the username of this User to the specified value.
     * @param username the new username
     */
```

```
    public void setUsername(String username) {
        this.username = username;
    }

    /**
     * Gets the securityRole of this User.
     * @return the securityRole
     */
    public String getSecurityRole() {
        return this.securityRole;
    }

    /**
     * Sets the securityRole of this User to the specified value.
     * @param securityRole the new securityRole
     */
    public void setSecurityRole(String securityRole) {
        this.securityRole = securityRole;
    }

    /**
     * Returns a hash code value for the object.  This implementation computes
     * a hash code value based on the id fields in this object.
     * @return a hash code value for this object.
     */
    @Override
    public int hashCode() {
        int hash = 0;
        hash += (this.userId != null ? this.userId.hashCode() : 0);
        return hash;
    }

    /**
     * Determines whether another object is equal to this User.  The result is
     * <code>true</code> if and only if the argument is not null and is a User object that
     * has the same id field values as this object.
     * @param object the reference object with which to compare
     * @return <code>true</code> if this object is the same as the argument;
     * <code>false</code> otherwise.
     */
    @Override
    public boolean equals(Object object) {
        return false;
        }
        User other = (User)object;
        if (this.userId != other.userId && (this.userId == null || !this.userId.
        equals(other.userId))) return false;
        return true;
    }
}
```

How It Works

The HTTP request login method can be used to programmatically authenticate users for an application when the application server form-based authentication has been configured. A JSF form can pass parameters to a managed bean controller, which can pass them to the HTTP request login method to perform programmatic authentication using the credentials.

As demonstrated in the login form that is listed in the solution to this recipe, a standard JSF view can be coded that passes values from the `inputText` components to a corresponding managed bean controller. The corresponding fields, `username` and `password`, are bound to properties within the managed bean controller. The user name is then set into the `username` property of a new `User` entity object, and the `password` value is passed directly into the EJB for later use. The `password` is not stored in the managed bean controller at all, and therefore, it is not stored into the session.

Let's take a moment to discuss the methods within the managed bean controller. In the example, a `commandButton` is contained within the view, which is bound to the managed bean controller's `login` method. Once invoked, the `login` method invokes a method within the EJB, which is responsible for performing the actual authentication against the application server container and JPA data store user table. In this case, the EJB method is also named `login`, and when it is invoked, then the `User` entity object is passed to the EJB so that the `username` property that is stored in the object can be used for authentication purposes. The `login` method within the managed bean controller invokes the EJB `login` method, which passes back a boolean value to indicate whether the credentials have successfully authenticated the user. Depending on the outcome, the user is then granted or denied access to the application. Also within the managed bean controller is a `logout` method. This method invalidates the current session by obtaining the external context, which is the application server context, and then by invoking its `invalidate` method.

The `login` method within the EJB is where the real activity occurs because it is where the application server HTTP request `login` method is invoked to verify the credentials. First, the `HttpServletRequest` object is obtained from the external context, and then its login method is called. This method accepts the user name and password values, initiates the application server authentication mechanism, and raises an exception if the credentials are invalid. Otherwise, if the credentials are valid, then a time limit is set on the `HttpSession` object. The value passed to the `session.setMaxInactiveInterval` method indicates how long a user session can be inactive before the application server automatically invalidates the session. The remainder of this method is used for performing application-specific authentication using the `User` entity object. In the example, the entity manager is flushed, and then a query is issued that counts the number of `User` entity objects matching the user name that has been entered via the login form. When querying the entity, a hint is set that forces the database to be queried each time the request is initiated. The following line of code is an excerpt from the EJB login method that demonstrates how to set this hint:

```
user.setHint("javax.persistence.cache.retrieveMode", CacheRetrieveMode.BYPASS);
```

If there are zero matching entity objects for a given user name, then the user is not authenticated to the application, and a `false` value is returned to the managed bean controller to indicate invalid credentials. Otherwise, if there is a matching entity object for the given user name, then the matching entity object is obtained, and a session attribute is set to indicate that the user was successfully authenticated.

■ **Note** Applications can contain their own set of users, one that is separate from those users who are managed by the GlassFish application server or database. One way of doing so is to create a separate database table for each application, which will be used to store user names and roles for those users who may access the application. The login logic that is contained within the managed bean controller can then perform a query on the application-specific table to see whether the user name specified within the login view is contained within the table. If the user name is in the table, then the user can be granted access to the application; otherwise, no access will be granted. This approach adds two steps into the authentication process: application server forms-based authentication and authentication at the database table level.

17-4. Authenticating with the Security API Using Database Credentials

Problem

You are interested in utilizing a standard solution for integrating forms-based authentication into your application, using a database to store credentials.

Solution

Utilize the Java EE Security API to authenticate a user using the same form authentication as demonstrated in Recipe 17-3. However, this solution will utilize credentials saved in a database, although one could also utilize LDAP authentication, or another custom means via the security API. Configuration for the database takes place via an annotation within the application, so no application server configuration is necessary.

To configure the application, annotate an `@ApplicationScoped` bean to indicate the authentication identity store that will be used for the application. In this case, the `@DatabaseIdentityStoreDefinition` annotation is used to configure the database as an identity store for the application.

```
import javax.enterprise.context.ApplicationScoped;
import javax.inject.Named;
import javax.security.enterprise.identitystore.DatabaseIdentityStoreDefinition;
import javax.security.enterprise.identitystore.Pbkdf2PasswordHash;

@DatabaseIdentityStoreDefinition(
        dataSourceLookup = "${'jdbc/acmedb'}",
        callerQuery = "#{'select password from caller_store where name = ?'}",
        groupsQuery = "select group_name from caller_groups where caller_name = ?",
        hashAlgorithm = Pbkdf2PasswordHash.class,
        priorityExpression = "#{100}",
        hashAlgorithmParameters = {
            "Pbkdf2PasswordHash.Iterations=3072",
            "${applicationConfig.hash}"
        } // just for test / example
)
```

```
@ApplicationScoped
@Named
public class ApplicationConfig {

    public String[] getHash() {
        return new String[]{"Pbkdf2PasswordHash.Algorithm=PBKDF2WithHmacSHA512",
        "Pbkdf2PasswordHash.SaltSizeBytes=64"};
    }
}
```

A singleton can be used to configure a database connection. This code will be run once each time the application starts, and it will load the database configuration and populate the security database for testing purposes. In real life, this class would only be used to configure the datasource, as the security database would likely be populated by an administrator. The following excerpt is from the sources to the Singleton EJB:

```
import java.sql.Connection;
import java.sql.PreparedStatement;
import java.sql.SQLException;
import java.util.HashMap;
import java.util.Map;

import javax.annotation.PostConstruct;
import javax.annotation.PreDestroy;
import javax.annotation.Resource;
import javax.annotation.sql.DataSourceDefinition;
import javax.ejb.Singleton;
import javax.ejb.Startup;
import javax.inject.Inject;
import javax.sql.DataSource;
import javax.security.enterprise.identitystore.Pbkdf2PasswordHash;

@DataSourceDefinition(
    name = "java:global/JavaEE8Recipes/acmedb",
    className = "org.apache.derby.jdbc.ClientDataSource",
    serverName="localhost",
    databaseName="acme",
    user = "acmeuser",
    password = "databasepassword"
)
@Singleton
@Startup
public class LoadDatabase {

    @Resource(lookup="java:global/JavaEE8Recipes/acmedb")
    private DataSource dataSource;

    @Inject
    private Pbkdf2PasswordHash passwordHash;

    @PostConstruct
    public void init() {
```

```
        Map<String, String> parameters= new HashMap<>();
        parameters.put("Pbkdf2PasswordHash.Iterations", "3072");
        parameters.put("Pbkdf2PasswordHash.Algorithm", "PBKDF2WithHmacSHA512");
        parameters.put("Pbkdf2PasswordHash.SaltSizeBytes", "64");
        passwordHash.initialize(parameters);

        executeUpdate(dataSource, "CREATE TABLE caller_store(name VARCHAR(64) PRIMARY KEY,
        password VARCHAR(255))");
        executeUpdate(dataSource, "CREATE TABLE caller_groups(caller_name VARCHAR(64),
        group_name VARCHAR(64))");

        executeUpdate(dataSource, "INSERT INTO caller_store VALUES('juneau', '" +
        passwordHash.generate("eerecipes".toCharArray()) + "')");

        executeUpdate(dataSource, "INSERT INTO caller_groups VALUES('juneau', 'group1')");
        executeUpdate(dataSource, "INSERT INTO caller_groups VALUES('juneau', 'group2')");

    }

    @PreDestroy
    public void destroy() {
        try {
                executeUpdate(dataSource, "DROP TABLE IF EXISTS caller_store");
                executeUpdate(dataSource, "DROP TABLE IF EXISTS caller_groups");
        } catch (Exception e) {
                 // silently ignore, concerns in-memory database
        }
    }

    private void executeUpdate(DataSource dataSource, String query) {
        try (Connection connection = dataSource.getConnection()) {
            try (PreparedStatement statement = connection.prepareStatement(query)) {
                statement.executeUpdate();
            }
        } catch (SQLException e) {
           // do nothing
        }
    }

}
```

The same JSF login form from Recipe 17-3 can be used for the authentication UI in this case, with the exception of passing credentials and invoking `SecurityContext.authenticate()`. This is a different form-based scenario, which utilizes the `@CustomFormAuthenticationMechanismDefinition` annotation. The following excerpt is taken from the JSF login form, containing a PrimeFaces `commandButton` component that binds to a CDI controller action to perform the validation.

```
<html xmlns="http://www.w3.org/1999/xhtml"
      xmlns:f="http://xmlns.jcp.org/jsf/core"
      xmlns:h="http://xmlns.jcp.org/jsf/html"
```

```
        xmlns:ui="http://xmlns.jcp.org/jsf/facelets"
        xmlns:p="http://primefaces.org/ui">
    <h:head>
        <meta http-equiv="Content-Type" content="text/html; charset=UTF-8"/>
        <title>Java EE 8 Recipes = Chapter 17 Examples</title>
    </h:head>
    <h:body>
        <ui:composition template="layout/custom_template_search.xhtml">
            <ui:define name="content">
                <h1>Login Form for Java EE 8 Recipes Application</h1>
                <h:form id="loginForm">
                    <p:messages id="messages"/>
                    <p:panelGrid columns="2">
                        <p:outputLabel for="username" value="Username: "/>
                        <p:inputText id="username" value="#{standardizedAuthenticationCont
                        roller.username}"/>

                        <p:outputLabel for="password" value="Password "/>
                        <p:password id="password" value="#{standardizedAuthenticationContro
                        ller.password}"/>

                    </p:panelGrid>
                    <br/>
                    <p:commandButton id="loginAction" action="#{standardizedAuthentication
                    Controller.login}"
                                     value="Login"
                                     update="messages"/>
                </h:form>
            </ui:define>
        </ui:composition>
    </h:body>
</html>
```

Lastly, the code for the authentication CDI controller bean is as follows. The @RequestScoped controller contains properties for passing the user name and password, along with the logic for authenticating the credentials that have been supplied by the user.

```
import javax.enterprise.context.RequestScoped;
import javax.faces.application.FacesMessage;
import javax.faces.context.FacesContext;
import javax.inject.Inject;
import javax.inject.Named;
import javax.security.enterprise.credential.Credential;
import javax.security.enterprise.credential.Password;
import javax.security.enterprise.credential.UsernamePasswordCredential;
import javax.security.enterprise.identitystore.CredentialValidationResult;
import javax.security.enterprise.identitystore.IdentityStoreHandler;
import javax.servlet.http.HttpServletRequest;
import javax.servlet.http.HttpServletResponse;
import javax.validation.constraints.NotNull;
```

```
/**
 *
 * @author Juneau
 */
@Named
@RequestScoped
public class StandardizedAuthenticationController {

    @Inject
    private IdentityStoreHandler identityStoreHandler;

    @NotNull
    private String username;
    @NotNull
    private String password;

    public void login() {

        FacesContext context = FacesContext.getCurrentInstance();
        Credential credential = new UsernamePasswordCredential(username, new
        Password(password));

        CredentialValidationResult cres = identityStoreHandler.validate(credential);
        if (cres.getStatus().equals(CredentialValidationResult.Status.VALID)) {
            context.responseComplete();
            context.addMessage(null,
                    new FacesMessage(FacesMessage.SEVERITY_INFO, "Authentication
                    Successful", null));
        } else if (cres.getStatus().equals(CredentialValidationResult.Status.INVALID)) {
            context.addMessage(null,
                    new FacesMessage(FacesMessage.SEVERITY_ERROR, "Authentication Failure",
                    null));
        }

    }

    private static HttpServletResponse getResponse(FacesContext context) {
        return (HttpServletResponse) context
            .getExternalContext()
            .getResponse();
    }

    private static HttpServletRequest getRequest(FacesContext context) {
        return (HttpServletRequest) context
            .getExternalContext()
            .getRequest();
    }
```

```
    /**
     * @return the username
     */
    public String getUsername() {
        return username;
    }

    /**
     * @param username the username to set
     */
    public void setUsername(String username) {
        this.username = username;
    }

    /**
     * @return the password
     */
    public String getPassword() {
        return password;
    }

    /**
     * @param password the password to set
     */
    public void setPassword(String password) {
        this.password = password;
    }
}
```

How It Works

The Java EE Security API defines a set of annotations that can be used to configure an application identity store and HttpAuthenticationMechanism for an application, among other security configurations. These standardized annotations are available as part of the Java EE Security API across all Java EE 8 compliant containers, which means security configuration can now be packaged as part of an application without additional XML configuration requirements. This makes it possible to create portable applications that contain security in which the same security configuration can be used across a number of containers.

An identity store typically holds a list of callers and caller groups, as well as security credentials for authenticating the caller. The API defines the following set of standard identity store annotations, which supply an abstraction of an identity store.

- @LdapIdentityStoreDefinition: Supports a caller that is stored in an external LDAP server.
- @DatabaseIdentityStoreDefinition: Supports a caller that is stored in an external database, which is accessible via a JNDI-bound datasource.

The identity store annotations must be defined within a CDI bean that is marked as @ ApplicationScoped, so that they are configured one time per application startup. An identity store is stateless, and it should include the information required to authenticate a caller into an application. The caller should not interact directly with an identity store. Instead, an HttpAuthenticationMechanism, which will be explained shortly, should perform the interaction. An identity store contains two methods that can be implemented by an authentication mechanism in order to validate a caller's credentials and return a caller's security groups. Those methods are validate() and getCallerGroups(), respectively. An identity store can implement one or both of these methods, and calling on the identity store's validationTypes() method returns a set of values that indicate which methods are implemented via the VALIDATE and PROVIDE_GROUPS values.

The validate() method takes a Credential object, which is a portable object that contains a user name/password that has been supplied by a caller. The validate() method returns a CredentialValidationResult, indicating the validation status. The CredentialValidationResult can be used to obtain information such as the resulting validation status, and if it's successful, then it also contains the identity store ID, caller principal, caller's unique ID within the identity store, and the caller's groups. The getStatus() method of CredentialValidationResult will return one of the following status values:

- VALID: Validation succeeded and caller groups can be obtained, if any are available.
- INVALID: Validation failed.
- NOT_VALIDATED: Validation was not attempted due to invalid Credential type.

More than one identity store can be configured for an application by setting a priority. Identity stores can also be programmed by implementing the IdentityStore interface, or they can be injected via the use of the identity store annotations outlined previously. These topics, as well as more in-depth analysis of the identity store concept, are covered in detail in the JSR 375 specification, available on javaee.github.io at https://javaee.github.io/security-spec/.

HttpAuthenticationMechanism is used by the Security API to validate a user's credentials. There must be three HttpAuthenticationMechanisms supplied by a Java EE 8 compliant application server container, those being:

- BASIC (@BasicAuthenticationMechanismDefinition): Authenticates according to the HTTP basic authentication semantics.
- FORM (@FormAuthenticationMechanismDefinition): Authenticates according to the form-based authentication semantics.
- Custom FORM (@CustomFormAuthenticationMechanismDefinition): Authenticates according to the form-based authentication semantics, however, does not occur via posting back to j_security_check. Instead, SecurityContext.authenticate() is invoked with passed-in credentials.

An HttpAuthenticationMechanism can be coded by implementing the HttpAuthenticationMechanism interface, or it can be injected using one of the aforementioned annotations. To implement, you must code the validateRequest() method, which is invoked before the doFilter() method of a servlet filter or service() method of any servlet. The validateRequest() method is also called upon in response to code calling the HttpServletRequest authenticate() method. There are two methods that are part of the HttpAuthenticationMechanism which are not required for implementation: secureResponse() and cleanSubject().

The validateRequest() method is used to allow the caller to authenticate. The secureResponse() method is provided to allow for post processing on the response that is generated by a servlet or servlet filter. The cleanSubject() method is provided to allow for cleanup after the caller is logged out.

Since a compliant container must provide default implementations of the HttpAuthenticationMechanism, it is possible for an application to simply use the mechanism without coding or supplying an annotation. The example in this recipe does just that. When the caller inserts credentials into the login screen and presses the button, the StandardizedAuthenticationController login() method is called. This controller class contains an injected IdentityStoreHandler, which is used to hook into the HttpAuthenticationMechanism that is provided by the container. In the login() method, the caller's user name and password are passed into a UsernamePasswordCredential object to return a credential. The credential is then passed into the IdentityStoreHandler.validate() method, returning a CredentialValidationResult object. This object can be used to glean the success or failure of the authentication attempt. The resulting success or failure can be tested by calling upon the CredentialValidationResult.getStatus() method.

The Java EE Security API helps to bring standardization to an area of the platform that has been very non-standardized in the past. While many containers will likely retain their proprietary security APIs and techniques, any Java EE 8 compliant container must also adhere to the standards of the new Security API.

■ **Note** There are dozens of examples that can be found on the Java EE Security API (Soteria) GitHub project page at https://github.com/javaee/security-soteria. It is also a great idea to read through the specification, which is less than 50 pages, and it can be found at https://javaee.github.io/security-spec/.

17-5. Managing Page Access Within a JSF Application

Problem

You have set up authentication for your JSF application, specifying access to a limited user base via a user name and password combination. You want to limit certain views within your application such that only members of a particular role will be granted permission access.

Solution

Authenticate a user to an application and store a boolean indicating that the user has been successfully authenticated. Utilize that boolean to perform conditional logic within JSF views to render forms that should be accessed only via authenticated users. If a user is successfully authenticated, then the form is rendered, and if the user is not successfully authenticated, then the form will provide an error message indicating that authentication is required for access.

The following JSF view demonstrates the use of conditional logic for displaying portions of the page that require controlled access:

```
<?xml version="1.0" encoding="UTF-8" ?>
<!DOCTYPE html PUBLIC "-//W3C//DTD XHTML 1.0 Transitional//EN" "http://www.w3.org/TR/xhtml1/
DTD/xhtml1-transitional.dtd">
<html xmlns="http://www.w3.org/1999/xhtml"
      xmlns:ui="http://xmlns.jcp.org/jsf/facelets"
      xmlns:h="http://xmlns.jcp.org/jsf/html"
      xmlns:f="http://xmlns.jcp.org/jsf/core"
      xmlns:p="http://primefaces.org/ui">

    <ui:composition template="/layout/template.xhtml">
        <ui:define name="title">
            <h:outputText value="Java EE 8 Recipes Controlled Access"></h:outputText>
        </ui:define>
```

```
        <ui:define name="body">
            <h:panelGroup id="messagePanel" layout="block">
                <h:messages errorStyle="color: red" infoStyle="color: green" layout="table"/>
            </h:panelGroup>
            <p:panel rendered="#{authenticationController.authenticated}">
                <h:form>

                    This portion of the view contains secret content!

                </h:form>
            </p:panel>
            <p:panel rendered="#{!authenticationController.authenticated}">
                Please <a href="#{request.contextPath}/faces/chapter17/recipe17_03.
                xhtml">authenticate</a> to use this form.

            </p:panel>
        </ui:define>
    </ui:composition>

</html>
```

How It Works

The rendered attribute of JSF components can be used to perform conditional rendering. If you bind the rendered attribute to a managed bean property that returns a boolean indicating whether a user is authenticated, then this technique can be used to control access to certain components. In this example, this technique is demonstrated using a PrimeFaces `panel` component. The `panel` contains information that should be secured, and it is rendered only if the authenticated property returns a `true` value. If the authenticated property contains a `false` value, then a different `panel` component is rendered, which displays a message to the user indicating that authentication is required.

The managed bean controller that is used for programmatic authentication within a JSF application should contain a boolean value that can be bound to the conditional logic within the JSF view to indicate whether the current user has successfully authenticated. For this example, the managed bean controller, `org.javaee8recipes.chapter17.recipe17_03.AuthenticationController`, contains a boolean field named `authenticated`. The following excerpt from the class shows the `isAuthenticated` method, which is called when the `authenticated` property is accessed from a JSF view:

```
public boolean isAuthenticated() {
    try {
        boolean auth = (Boolean) getSession().getAttribute("authenticated");
        if (auth) {
            this.authenticated = true;

        } else {
            authenticated = false;
        }
    } catch (Exception e) {
        this.authenticated = false;
    }

    return authenticated;
}
```

This same technique can be used to hide or show individual components based on a user's authentication. Furthermore, fine-grained access control can be used to provide boolean values to the rendered attribute by utilizing JSF EL conditional expressions. For instance, if some components should be accessed only by users who belong in certain security roles, then a conditional expression can be used to render a component if the user belongs to a specified role. The following line of code demonstrates how to render an `outputText` component if a user belongs to the `ADMIN` security role:

```
<h:outputLink rendered="${authenticationController.user.securityRole eq 'ADMIN'}" value="#"
onclick="dialog.show()">Delete Property</h:outputLink>
```

Although the `rendered` attribute may not allow you to secure every part of an application, when used along with other security measures such as annotating methods (see Recipe 17-2), it can help provide a very secure environment.

17-6. Configuring LDAP Authentication Within GlassFish

Problem

You want to authenticate users to your application based on a centrally located LDAP server for your organization's enterprise.

Solution

Create a security realm for GlassFish/Payara from within the administrative console utility and set it up as a `com.sun.enterprise.security.auth.realm.ldap.LDAPRealm`. To create an LDAP security realm within GlassFish/Payara, use the following procedure:

1. Log in to the GlassFish/Payara administrative console.
2. Traverse to the Realms form by expanding the left tree menu Configurations ➤ Security ➤ server-config ➤ Realms.
3. Click the New button on the Realms form to create a new security realm.
4. Within the New Realm form, provide a name for the security realm. Next, select `com.sun.enterprise.security.auth.realm.ldap.LDAPRealm` from the Class Name pull-down menu. This will open the configurations for setting up an LDAP realm (see Figure 17-7).

New Realm OK Cancel

Create a new security (authentication) realm. Valid realm types are PAM, OSGi, File, Certificate, LDAP, JDBC, Digest, Oracle Solaris, and Custom.

* Indicates required field

Configuration Name: server-config

Name: *

Class Name: com.sun.enterprise.security.auth.realm.ldap.LDAPRealm

Choose a realm class name from the drop-down list or specify a custom class

Properties specific to this Class

JAAS Context: *
Identifier for the login module to use for this realm

Directory: *
LDAP url for your server

Base DN: *
LDAP base DN for the location of user data

Assign Groups:
Comma-separated list of group names

Additional Properties (0)

Add Property | Delete Properties

Name	Value	Description:
No items found.		

OK Cancel

Figure 17-7. *New LDAP security realm*

5. Complete the properties specific to the class in order to connect to an LDAP server of your choice.

6. Add the following additional properties by clicking the Add Property button and providing the name-value information for each:

   - `search-bind-dn`: Enter the fully qualified DN for your LDAP host, directory, and the LDAP account to which you will authenticate. For example:

     ```
     CN=account-name,OU=AccountGroup,DC=dc1,DC=dc2,DC=dc3
     ```

   - `search-bind-password`: Enter the password for the account name you specified previously.

   - `search-filter`: Type the following as the value for this property: `(sAMAccountName=%s)`.

7. Restart the application server.

How It Works

Perhaps the most efficient way to authenticate to applications is to utilize an LDAP account. Using an LDAP account for authentication can provide a single sign-on solution across all of an organization's servers and applications. LDAP authentication also provides a single point of maintenance for account information and still allows individual applications to maintain their own fine-grained security via roles. The solution to this recipe enumerates the steps that are involved in setting up an LDAP security realm within the GlassFish and Payara application servers. However, you can follow similar procedures for setting up an LDAP security realm in other application server containers.

Once you have LDAP authentication set up within the application server, you can configure your applications to use it. To configure an application to use LDAP authentication, add the following configurations to the web.xml deployment descriptor:

```
<login-config>
        <auth-method>FORM</auth-method>
        <realm-name>REALM-NAME</realm-name>
        <form-login-config>
            <form-login-page>/faces/login.xhtml</form-login-page>
            <form-error-page>/faces/loginError.xhtml</form-error-page>
        </form-login-config>
    </login-config>
```

In the previous excerpt from web.xml, the realm-name element should be the same as the name given to the LDAP security realm you created within GlassFish/Payara. The form-login-page and form-error-page values should reference the views that are to be used for logging into an application and the view that is displayed when there is a login error, respectively. Authenticating into an LDAP security realm is the same as that covered in Recipe 17-3. Simply call the HttpRequest object's login method to authenticate using the credentials provided by the user via the login view.

17-7. Configuring Custom Security Certificates Within GlassFish/Payara

Problem

You want to utilize custom certificates for securing access via SSL within your GlassFish/Payara environment.

Solution

Obtain a certificate from a certified certificate authority, and then install it into the GlassFish application server container. Once installed, route requests via a secured port that utilizes SSL and force users to accept the security certificate to proceed. To install a certificate that has been obtained from a valid certificate authority, follow these steps:

1. Copy the trusted root certificate from your certified authority to your server. Issue the following command from the command line or the terminal:

   ```
   keytool -import -alias root -keystore keystore_name.keystore -trustcacerts -file
   trustedcarootcertificate.crt
   ```

2. Next, import the trusted certificate:

```
keytool -import -alias cert_alias -keystore keystore_name.keystore -trustcacerts
-file certificate.crt
```

3. Adjust SSL settings from within the GlassFish administrative console. To adjust the settings, go to Configuration ➤ Network Config- ➤ Network Listeners ➤ http-listener-2 in order to open the secured HTTP listener page. Once it's open, select the SSL tab and enter the certificate nickname and keystore that match the ones you used in Step 2.

4. Restart your server and then access your applications securely using this URL:

```
https://localhost:8181/your_application_context
```

■ **Note** In the previous numbered list, `keystore_name.keystore` represents the name of a keystore, and `trustedcarootcertificate.crt` and `certificate.crt` represent the name of certificates.

How It Works

GlassFish comes with a self-signed security certificate that is suitable for test environments. However, when utilizing GlassFish as a production application server solution, it is imperative that a certificate from a verified authority be put in place in order to secure application transport. This recipe demonstrates how to install a security certificate for use with SSL in order to achieve secure transport.

Before you can install a verified certificate, you need to obtain it. You will need to choose from one of the many certificate authorities and then send a certificate request, which includes the key from your application server. A keystore will need to be created in order to generate a certificate request. Issue the following command from the command line or the terminal to create the keystore:

```
keytool -keysize 2048 -genkey -alias -keyalg RSA -dname "CN=yourdomain.org,O=company_
name,L=city,S=state,C=country" - keypass glassfish_master_password -storepass glassfish_
master_password -keystore choose_keystore_name.keystore
```

Once the keystore has been created, a certificate signing request that will be sent to the certificate authority can be generated. To generate the certificate signing request (CSR), issue the following command from your server:

```
keytool -certreq -alias -keystore chosen_keystore_name.keystore -storepass glassfish_master_
password -keypass glassfish_master_password -file csrname.csr
```

■ **Note** To change the GlassFish master password, issue the following command when your GlassFish domain is stopped: `asadmin change-master-password -savemasterpassword=true`.

Once you submit your CSR to the certificate authority, the certificate authority will send back a valid security certificate that can be installed into your server. Follow the steps in the solution to this recipe to install the certificate into GlassFish. Once the certificate is installed, your server will be verified secure via the certificate authority, and users should see a message indicating as such (usually a green lock) in their browsers when they visit your secured sites.

CHAPTER 18

Concurrency and Batch Applications

The Java Enterprise platform had been missing a few key features upon its inception. Those features included standard techniques for processing tasks concurrently, and standardization for batch application processing. In the release of Java EE 7, these two missing features were addressed with the addition of the Java Concurrency Utilities and Batch Processing APIs.

Each of the two APIs is quite large, and they include proven solutions that have been used by various enterprise projects for years. Using Java SE concurrency utilities such as `java.util.concurrent` and `java.lang.Thread` in Java EE applications has been problematic in the past, since the application server container was unable to work with such resources. Extensions of the `java.util.concurrent` API enabled application servers and other EE containers to become aware of these concurrency resources. The extensions allow enterprise applications to appropriately utilize asynchronous operations via the `java.util.concurrent.ExecutorService` resources that are made available within the EE environment.

The API for batch processing provides a fine-grained experience for developers, which enables them to produce and process batch applications in a variety of different ways. Enterprise applications no longer need to utilize customized classes for performing batch processing, allowing enterprise applications to adhere to an adopted standard.

As mentioned previously, the scope of these additional APIs is quite large, and this chapter will not attempt to cover each feature. However, the recipes contained within should provide enough information to get a developer up-and-running using some of the most frequently required pieces of each API. For more in-depth information regarding the details of the Concurrency Utilities for Java EE, refer to the JavaDoc located at `https://github.com/javaee/concurrency-ee-spec`. The recipes for this chapter work in both GlassFish 5 or Payara 5. Other Java EE 7-compliant application servers also contain similar solutions for the problems.

J. Juneau, *Java EE 8 Recipes*, https://doi.org/10.1007/978-1-4842-3594-2_18

18-1. Creating Resources for Processing Tasks Asynchronously in an Application Server

Problem

You would like to register a `ManagedExecutorService` resource within your application server environment.

Solution #1

Create a new `ManagedExecutorService` using the GlassFish or Payara `asadmin create-managed-executor-service` utility. To utilize concurrent utilities such as reporter tasks, the application server must be configured to utilize a `ManagedExecutorService`. To create a `ManagedExecutor` service in GlassFish, run the following command at the command prompt:

```
<path-to-glassfish>/bin/asadmin create-managed-executor-service concurrent/BatchExecutor
```

In the preceding command-line action, the name of the `ManagedExecutorService` that is being created is `concurrent/BatchExecutor`. However, this could be changed to better suit the application. To see all of the options available for the `create-managed-executor-service` command, issue the `--help` flag. The following shows the results of doing so:

```
bin/asadmin create-managed-executor-service --help
NAME
     create-managed-executor-service

SYNOPSIS
     Usage: create-managed-executor-service [--enabled=true] [--con
     textinfo=contextinfo] [--threadpriority=5] [--longrunningt
     asks=false] [--hungafterseconds=hungafterseconds] [--corepool
     size=0] [--maximumpoolsize=2147483647] [--keepaliveseconds=
     60] [--threadlifetimeseconds=0] [--taskqueuecapacity=2147483
     647] [--description=description] [--property=property] [--tar
     get=target] jndi_name

OPTIONS
     --enabled

     --contextinfo

     --threadpriority

     --longrunningtasks

     --hungafterseconds

     --corepoolsize

     --maximumpoolsize

     --keepaliveseconds
```

```
     --threadlifetimeseconds

     --taskqueuecapacity

     --description

     --property

     --target

OPERANDS
     jndi_name
```

Solution #2

Create a ManagedExecutorService using the GlassFish or Payara Server Administration Console. To do so, authenticate successfully into the administrative console and navigate to the Concurrent Resources ➤ Managed Executor Services administration panel using the left-side tree menu (see Figure 18-1).

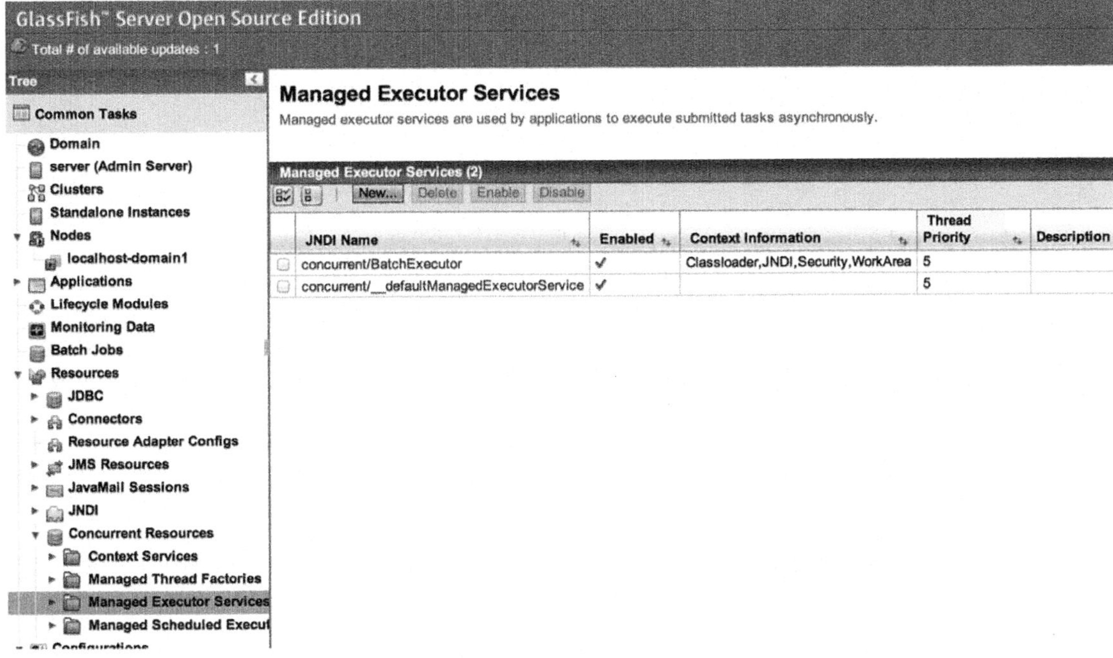

Figure 18-1. *GlassFish Managed Executor Services panel*

Once you've opened the panel, click the New button to create a new service. This will open the New Managed Executor Service panel, in which you will be required to populate a JNDI Name for your new service (see Figure 18-2).

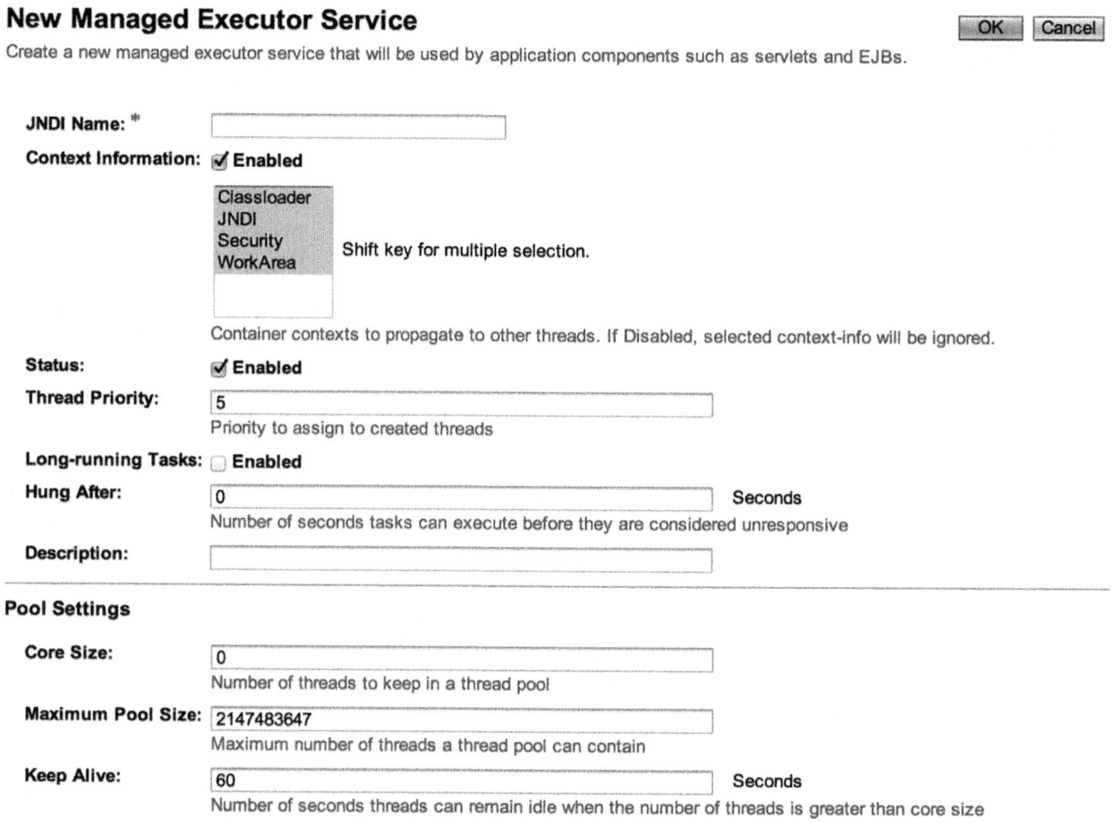

New Managed Executor Service

OK Cancel

Create a new managed executor service that will be used by application components such as servlets and EJBs.

JNDI Name: *

Context Information: ☑ Enabled

Classloader
JNDI
Security
WorkArea

Shift key for multiple selection.

Container contexts to propagate to other threads. If Disabled, selected context-info will be ignored.

Status: ☑ Enabled

Thread Priority: 5

Priority to assign to created threads

Long-running Tasks: ☐ Enabled

Hung After: 0 Seconds

Number of seconds tasks can execute before they are considered unresponsive

Description:

Pool Settings

Core Size: 0

Number of threads to keep in a thread pool

Maximum Pool Size: 2147483647

Maximum number of threads a thread pool can contain

Keep Alive: 60 Seconds

Number of seconds threads can remain idle when the number of threads is greater than core size

Figure 18-2. *New Managed Executor Service panel*

This panel offers quite a few options for the creation of the service. However, the only option that is required is the JNDI Name, as all others are populated with default values. The JNDI name that is specified should follow the format of `concurrent/YourExecutorServiceName`, where `YourExecutorServiceName` is a custom name of your choice.

How It Works

In Java EE 7, the `ManagedExecutorService` was introduced, adding the ability to produce asynchronous tasks that are managed by an application server. Although there is a default `ManagedExecutorService` available for use, application server administrators can create `ManagedExecutorService` resources within an application server that can be utilized by one or more applications, much like a Java Message Service (JMS) `Topic` or `Queue`. To create a service, issue the `asadmin create-managed-executor-service` command at the command prompt, passing the name that you would like to use to identify the service. There are a bevy of options that can be used to customize the service in different ways. For instance, the service can be configured to let tasks run for a specified amount of time, pools can be configured, and so forth, allowing you to generate a `ManagedExecutorService` that will best suit the application requirements.

For those who would prefer to work within the GlassFish or Payara administration console, there are been a few administration panels to make creation and management of concurrent resources easier. The Managed Executor Service panel can be used to create new application server `ManagedExecutorService` resources, as well as manage those that already exist.

■ **Note** GlassFish and other Java EE 7–compliant application servers come preconfigured with a default `ManagedExecutorService` resource that is named `java:comp/DefaultManagedExecutorService`.

18-2. Configuring and Creating a Reporter Task

Problem

You would like to create a long-running task that will communicate with a database and generate a report in the end.

Solution

Once the application server has been configured and the `ManagedExecutorService` has been created, an application can be written to utilize the newly created service. Within an application, you can choose to configure the application to use the `ManagedExecutorService` via XML, or a `@Resource` annotation can be used to inject the resource. To configure via XML, add a `<resource-env-ref>` element to the `web.xml` deployment descriptor. In this case, you need to configure a resource of type `javax.enterprise.concurrent.ManagedExecutorService`, as shown in the following excerpt from the `web.xml`:

```
<resource-env-ref>
 <description>
This executor is used for the application's reporter task. This executor has the following
requirements:
Run Location: NA
Context Info: Local Namespace
 </description>
    <resource-env-ref-name>
        concurrent/BatchExecutor
    </resource-env-ref-name>
    <resource-env-ref-type>
        javax.enterprise.concurrent.ManagedExecutorService
    </resource-env-ref-type>
</resource-env-ref>
```

In the XML configuration, the resource has been assigned to a reference name of `concurrent/BatchExecutor`, but you could name the reference to best suit your application. If you would rather utilize an annotation, then the following `@Resource` annotation can be specified to inject a `ManagedExecutorService` into a class for use. You will see an example of this in use later on.

```
@Resource(name = "concurrent/BatchExecutor")
ManagedExecutorService mes;
```

Once the configuration is complete, you can create a report task class, which is a class that implements `Runnable` and is responsible for running the actual reports. The following class, `org.javaee8recipes.chapter18.recipe18_02.ReporterTask`, is an example.

```
import java.util.List;
import javax.ejb.EJB;
import org.javaee8recipes.entity.Book;
import org.javaee8recipes.entity.BookAuthor;
import org.javaee8recipes.chapter09.session.BookAuthorFacade;
import org.javaee8recipes.chapter09.session.BookFacade;

/**
 * Example of a Reporter Task
 * @author Juneau
 */
public class ReporterTask implements Runnable {

    String reportName;
    @EJB
    private BookAuthorFacade bookAuthorFacade;
    @EJB
    private BookFacade bookFacade;

    public ReporterTask(String reportName) {
        this.reportName = reportName;
    }

    public void run() {
// Run the named report
        if ("AuthorReport".equals(reportName)) {
            runAuthorReport();

        } else if ("BookReport".equals(reportName)) {
            runBookReport();
        }
    }

    /**
     * Prints a list of authors to the system log.
     */
    public void runAuthorReport() {
        List<BookAuthor> authors = bookAuthorFacade.findAuthor();
        System.out.println("Author Listing Report");
        System.out.println("=====================");

        for (BookAuthor author : authors) {
            System.out.println(author.getFirst() + " " + author.getLast());
        }
    }

    /**
     * Prints a list of books to a file
     */
    void runBookReport() {
        System.out.println("Querying the database");
        Path reportFile = Paths.get("BookReport.txt");
```

```
        try (BufferedWriter writer = Files.newBufferedWriter(
                reportFile, Charset.defaultCharset())) {
            Files.deleteIfExists(reportFile);
            reportFile = Files.createFile(reportFile);
            writer.append("Book Listing Report");
            writer.newLine();
            writer.append("===================");
            writer.newLine();
            List<Book> books = bookFacade.findAllBooks();
            for (Book book : books) {
                writer.append(book.getTitle());
                writer.newLine();
            }
            writer.flush();
        } catch (IOException exception) {
            System.out.println("Error writing to file");
        }

    }
}
```

Lastly, the report needs to be invoked by the `ManagedExecutorService` that was configured within the `web.xml`. In this example, the `ManagedExecutorService` is injected into a servlet, which is then used to invoke the report, as seen in the following code:

```
@WebServlet(name = "BookReportServlet", urlPatterns = {"/BookReportServlet"})
public class ReportServlet extends HttpServlet implements Servlet { // Cache our executor
instance

    @Resource(name = "concurrent/BatchExecutor")
    ManagedExecutorService mes;

    protected void processRequest(HttpServletRequest request, HttpServletResponse response)
            throws ServletException, IOException {
        response.setContentType("text/html;charset=UTF-8");
        PrintWriter out = response.getWriter();
        try {

            out.println("<html>");
            out.println("<head>");
            out.println("<title>Book Report Invoker</title>");
            out.println("</head>");
            out.println("<body>");
            out.println("<h2>This servlet initiates the book report task. Please look " +
                    "in the server log to see the results.</h2> <br />" +
                    "Updating the web page is not run asynchronously, however," +
                    "the report generation will process independently.");
            out.println("<br/><br/>");
            ReporterTask reporterTask = new ReporterTask("BookReport");
            Future reportFuture = mes.submit(reporterTask);
            while( !reportFuture.isDone() )
```

```
                out.println("Running...<BR>");
            if (reportFuture.isDone()){
                out.println("Report Complete");
            }
            out.println("</body>");
            out.println("</html>");
        } finally {
            out.close();
        }
    }
...
}
```

When the servlet is visited, the reporter task will be initiated and it will begin to produce results.

How It Works

After the ManagedExecutorService has been created, it can be utilized by one or more applications to perform concurrent operations. An application must be either configured via XML to allow access to the ManagedExecutorService resource in the application server container, or the resource can be injected via the @Resource annotation. In the example for this recipe, each of these options is demonstrated. For the purposes of the example, it is assumed that the @Resource annotation is utilized to inject the service into the servlet.

To run a task concurrently using the service, you must create the task in a separate class that implements java.util.Runnable so that it can be invoked as a separate process, much like a standard Java Thread. In the example, a class named ReporterTask implements Runnable, and within the run method, the reporter task performs the tasks that we want to run in an asynchronous manner. In this example, a couple of methods are invoked from within the run method. The Runnable class that has been generated can then be passed to the ManagedExecutorService to be run concurrently while other tasks are being performed by the application. To use the ManagedExecutorService, register it with the application via XML or by resource injection. In the example for this recipe, resource injection is utilized, making the ManagedExecutorService available from within the Java servlet. To inject the resource, specify the name of it to the @Resource annotation.

```
@Resource(name = "concurrent/BatchExecutor")
ManagedExecutorService mes;
```

The ManagedExecutorService can then be invoked by calling the submit method and passing an instance of the Runnable task that we'd like to submit for processing. In this case, the ReporterTask class is instantiated, and an instance of it is then passed to the service, returning a java.util.concurrent.Future object.

```
ReporterTask reporterTask = new ReporterTask("BookReport");
Future reportFuture = mes.submit(reporterTask);
```

Once submitted, the Future object that was returned can be periodically checked to see if it is still running or if it has been completed by calling its isDone method. It can be cancelled by calling the cancel method, and a canceled task can be checked by calling its isCanceled method.

The reporter task is a long-running task that queries the database to obtain data for generation of a report. Having the ability to run such a task asynchronously fills a gap in the Java enterprise ecosystem that developers have been dealing with in enterprise solutions since the inception of Java EE.

18-3. Running More Than One Task Concurrently

Problem

You require the ability to run two or more tasks concurrently within your application. For instance, the application you are writing needs the ability to connect a database and retrieve data from two or more tables to obtain results at the same time. You want to have the results aggregated before returning them to the user.

Solution

Create a builder task that can be used to run two different tasks in parallel. Each of the tasks can retrieve the data from the different sources, and in the end, the data will be merged together and aggregated to formulate the result. To utilize a builder task, the application server environment must first be configured with a ManagedExecutorService, as per Recipe 18-1. Once the resource has been configured, an application can be configured to use the resource via XML or annotation. To utilize XML configuration, add a <resource-env-ref> element to the web.xml deployment descriptor. In this case, you need to configure a resource of type javax.enterprise.concurrent.ManagedExecutorService, as shown in the excerpt from the web.xml in Recipe 18-2, and repeated as follows:

```
<resource-env-ref>
 <description>
This executor is used for the application's builder tasks. This executor has the following
requirements:
Run Location: Local
Context Info: Local Namespace, Security
 </description>
    <resource-env-ref-name>
        concurrent/BuilderExecutor
    </resource-env-ref-name>
    <resource-env-ref-type>
        javax.enterprise.concurrent.ManagedExecutorService
    </resource-env-ref-type>
</resource-env>
```

In this example, the ManagedExecutorService resource in the application is configured to work with a resource that has been registered with the application server container and identified by the JNDI name of concurrent/BuilderExecutor. If you would rather utilize an annotation, then the following @Resource annotation can be specified to inject a ManagedExecutorService into a class for use within the Runnable.

```
@Resource(name = "concurrent/BuilderExecutor")
ManagedExecutorService mes;
```

Once the application has been configured to work with the ManagedExecutorService resource, you can create task classes for each of the different tasks that you want to run. Each task class must implement the javax.enterprise.concurrent.ManagedTask interfaces. The following code is from the file org.javaeereipes.chapter18.recipe18_03.AuthorTask.java, and it shows what a task class should look like.

```
public class AuthorTask implements Callable<AuthorInfo>, ManagedTask {
    // The ID of the request to report on demand.
    BigDecimal authorId;
```

```
    AuthorInfo authorInfo;
    Map<String, String> execProps;

    public AuthorTask(BigDecimal id) {
        this.authorId = id;
        execProps = new HashMap<>();

        execProps.put(ManagedTask.IDENTITY_NAME, getIdentityName());
    }

    public AuthorInfo call() {
// Find the entity bean and return it to the client.
        return authorInfo;
    }

    public String getIdentityName() {
        return "AuthorTask: AuthorID=" + authorId;
    }

    public Map<String, String> getExecutionProperties() {
        return execProps;
    }

    public String getIdentityDescription(Locale locale) {
        // Use a resource bundle...
        return "AuthorTask asynchronous EJB invoker";
    }

    @Override
    public ManagedTaskListener getManagedTaskListener() {
        return new CustomManagedTaskListener();
    }

}
```

One or more of such task classes can be implemented, and then they can be processed via the builder task using the `ManagedExecutorService` resource that has been registered with the application server container. The following servlet uses a `ManagedExecutorService` to coordinate the invocation of two task classes. In this case, the task class names are `AuthorTask` and `AuthorTaskTwo`.

```
@WebServlet(name = "BuilderServlet", urlPatterns = {"/builderServlet"})
public class BuilderServlet extends HttpServlet implements Servlet {
    // Retrieve our executor instance.

    @Resource(name = "concurrent/BuilderExecutor")
    ManagedExecutorService mes;
    AuthorInfo authorInfoHome;
    BookInfo bookInfoHome;

    protected void processRequest(HttpServletRequest req, HttpServletResponse resp) throws
ServletException, IOException {
```

```
        try {
            PrintWriter out = resp.getWriter();
            // Create the task instances
            ArrayList<Callable<AuthorInfo>> builderTasks = new ArrayList<Callable<AuthorIn
            fo>>();
            builderTasks.add(new AuthorTask(BigDecimal.ONE));
            builderTasks.add(new AuthorTaskTwo(BigDecimal.ONE));

            // Submit the tasks and wait.
            List<Future<AuthorInfo>> taskResults = mes.invokeAll(builderTasks);
            ArrayList<AuthorInfo> results = new ArrayList<AuthorInfo>();
            for(Future<AuthorInfo> result: taskResults){
                results.add(result.get());
                out.write("Processing Results...");
            }
        } catch (InterruptedException|ExecutionException ex) {
            Logger.getLogger(BuilderServlet.class.getName()).log(Level.SEVERE, null, ex);
        }
    }
...
}
```

How It Works

After the ManagedExecutorService has been created, it can be utilized by one or more applications to perform concurrent operations. An application must be either configured via XML to allow access to the ManagedExecutorService resource in the application server container, or the resource can be injected via the @Resource annotation. In the example for this recipe, each of these options is demonstrated. For the purposes of the example using the servlet, it is assumed that the @Resource annotation is utilized to inject the service into the servlet and no XML configuration has been made.

To coordinate the processing of tasks in an asynchronous manner via a ManagedExecutorService, the tasks that need to be processed should be contained in separate classes or multiple instances of the same task class. Each of the task classes should implement the java.util.concurrent.Callable and javax.enterprise.concurrent.ManagedTask interfaces. A task class should include a constructor that enables a caller to pass arguments that are required to instantiate the object, and should implement a call method, which returns the information that is needed to construct the report to the client. Two or more such task classes can then be invoked via the ManagedExecutorService in order to process all results into the required format.

To assemble the tasks for processing, create an ArrayList<Callable> and add instances of each task to the array. In the example, the array is named builderTasks, and instances of two different task types are added to that array.

```
ArrayList<Callable<AuthorInfo>> builderTasks = new ArrayList<Callable<AuthorInfo>>();
builderTasks.add(new AuthorTask(BigDecimal.ONE));
builderTasks.add(new AuthorTaskTwo(BigDecimal.ONE));
```

Next, pass the array that has been constructed to the ManagedExecutorService, returning a List<Future<object>>, which can then be used to process the results.

```
List<Future<AuthorInfo>> results = mes.invokeAll(builderTasks);
AuthorInfo authorInfo = (AuthorInfo) results.get(0).get();
// Process the results
```

Utilizing this technique, a series of tasks can be concurrently processed, returning results that can be later used to formulate a response. In this example, a report is constructed by calling two task classes and returning the results of queried information. This same technique can be applied to an array of different tasks, allowing an application to process the results of multiple task invocations in one central location.

18-4. Utilizing Transactions Within a Task

Problem

You would like to manage a transaction within an application task that will be processed using a ManagedExecutorService resource.

Solution

Use the javax.transaction.UserTransaction to create and manage a transaction. The following example demonstrates how to use the UserTransaction interface to demarcate transactions within a task class that will be processed by a ManagedExecutorService.

```
public class UserTransactionTask implements Runnable {

    @Resource
    SessionContext ctx;

    @EJB
    private BookAuthorFacade bookAuthorFacade;
    UserTransaction ut = ctx.getUserTransaction();

    public void run() {
        try {
            // Start a transaction ut.begin();
            ut.begin();
            List<BookAuthor> authors = bookAuthorFacade.findAuthor();
            for (BookAuthor author : authors) {
                // do something
            }
            ut.commit();
        } catch (NotSupportedException | SystemException | RollbackException
                | HeuristicMixedException | HeuristicRollbackException ex) {
            Logger.getLogger(UserTransactionTask.class.getName()).log(Level.SEVERE, null, ex);
        }
    }
}
```

The previous class can then be processed by ManagedExecutorService by implementing a solution similar to the following.

```
@WebServlet(name = "UserTransactionServlet", urlPatterns = {"/userTransactionServlet"})
public class UserTransactionServlet extends HttpServlet implements Servlet {

    @Resource(name = "concurrent/BatchExecutor")
    ManagedExecutorService mes;

    protected void processRequest(HttpServletRequest request, HttpServletResponse response)
            throws ServletException, IOException {
        response.setContentType("text/html;charset=UTF-8");
        PrintWriter out = response.getWriter();
        try {

            // servlet output...
            UserTransactionTask utTask = new UserTransactionTask();
            Future utFuture = mes.submit(utTask);
            while( !utFuture.isDone() )
                out.println("Running...<BR>");
            if (utFuture.isDone()){
                out.println("Report Complete");
            }
            out.println("</body>");
            out.println("</html>");
        } finally {
            out.close();
        }
    }
...
```

How It Works

In some cases, an application may require transaction coordination within a task that will be processed via a ManagedExecutorService. Transactions can be carried out within these tasks via utilization of the javax.transaction.UserTransaction interface. The UserTransaction can be obtained by calling the SessionContext.getUserTransaction() method. The SessionContext resource can be injected into a bean using the @Resource annotation.

Once the UserTransaction has been obtained, the transaction can begin by calling the UserTransaction begin method. The transaction can be ended by calling the UserTransaction commit method. The transaction encompasses any tasks that are performed after the call to begin, and before the call to commit. If one of the tasks within the transaction fails, then all work performed within the transaction is halted and values go back to what they were prior to the beginning of the transaction. This helps to ensure that all processes required for a task are completed if successful or rolled back in the event of a failure.

18-5. Running Concurrent Tasks at Scheduled Times

Problem

The application that you are utilizing needs to have the ability to periodically perform a task on a timed interval.

Solution

Use the ManagedScheduleExecutorService to create a scheduled task within your application. Before an application can use the service, it must be created within the application server container. To create a ManagedScheduleExecutorService instance within GlassFish, issue the following command from the command line:

```
bin/asadmin create-managed-scheduled-executor-service concurrent/name-of-service
```

In this command, name-of-service can be whatever name you choose. The create-managed-scheduled-executor-service command has many options that can be specified. To see and learn more about each option, invoke the command help by issuing the --help flag after the command, rather than providing the name of the service to create. Optionally, you could create the service using an application server resource, such as the GlassFish administration console.

Once the service has been created within the container, it can be utilized by an application. To utilize this type of service, the environment must be configured via XML or annotation. To utilize XML configuration, add a <resource-env-ref> element to the web.xml deployment descriptor. In this case, you need to configure a resource of type javax.enterprise.concurrent.ManagedScheduledExecutorService, as shown in the excerpt from the following web.xml:

```
<resource-env-ref>
 <description>Prints alerts to server log, if warranted, on a periodic basis</description>
<resource-env-ref-name>
concurrent/__defaultScheduledManagedExecutorService
</resource-env-ref-name>
 <resource-env-ref-type>
javax.enterprise.concurrent.ManagedScheduledExecutorService
 </resource-env-ref-type>
</resource-env-ref>
```

If you want to use annotations rather than XML, the @Resource annotation can be used in client code to inject the ManagedScheduledExecutorService, as shown in the following lines. In this case, the injected resource references a ManagedScheduledExecutorService that is identified by the name concurrent/__defaultManagedScheduledExecutorService.

```
@Resource(name="concurrent/ScheduledAlertExecutor")
ManagedScheduledExecutorService mes;
```

To write the task that you want to have scheduled, create a Java class that implements Runnable. As such, the class will contain a run method, which will be invoked each time the scheduled task is initiated. The following example demonstrates how to construct a task that can be used for logging. In this example, the BookAuthor entity is queried on a periodic basis to determine if new authors have been added to the database.

```
public class ScheduledLoggerExample implements Runnable {

    CreateConnection createConn = null;

    @Override
    public void run() {
        queryAuthors();
    }

    public void queryAuthors(){
        createConn = new CreateConnection();
        String qry = "select object(o) from BookAuthor o";
        createConn.loadProperties();
        try (Connection conn = createConn.getConnection();
                Statement stmt = conn.createStatement();
                ResultSet rs = stmt.executeQuery(qry);) {
            while (rs.next()) {
           // if new author, then alert
            }
        } catch (SQLException e) {
            e.printStackTrace();
        }
    }
}
```

To periodically invoke the task, utilize the `ManagedScheduledExecutorService` resource. The following JSF managed bean class demonstrates how to invoke this type of service.

```
@Named
public class ScheduledTaskClient {
    Future alertHandle = null;

    @Resource(name="concurrent/__defaultManagedScheduledExecutorService")
    ManagedScheduledExecutorService mes;

    public void alertScheduler() {

        ScheduledAuthorAlert ae = new ScheduledAuthorAlert();
        alertHandle = mes.scheduleAtFixedRate(
                ae, 5L, 5L, TimeUnit.MINUTES);
        FacesMessage facesMsg = new FacesMessage(FacesMessage.SEVERITY_INFO,
                "Task Scheduled", "Task Scheduled");
                FacesContext.getCurrentInstance().addMessage(null, facesMsg);

    }

}
```

How It Works

To schedule a task to run at specific times, utilize the javax.concurrent.ManagedScheduledExecutorService interface. This interface extends the java.util.concurrent.ScheduledExecutorService and javax.enterprise.concurrent.ManagedExecutorService interfaces. The ManagedScheduleExecutorService can be used to execute a Runnable task according to a specified schedule.

As mentioned previously, a ManagedScheduleExecutorService can be used to schedule Runnable tasks. That is, any class that implements java.lang.Runnable can be invoked via the service. The code that is contained within the task class's run method is invoked each time the task is initiated. In the example for this recipe, the run method executes another method within the class that is used to query an entity and perform some work against the results.

To use a ManagedScheduledExecutorService, one can be created within the application server container. This can be done by issuing the asadmin create-managed-scheduled-executor-service command, as demonstrated in the example for this recipe. However, any Java EE 7-compliant application server should contain a default ManagedScheduledExecutorService for use. Once the resource has been created in the application server, an application can use it. To enable an application to access the service, XML configuration within the web.xml deployment descriptor can be used, or a @Resource annotation can be used to inject the resource. In the example for this recipe, both techniques are demonstrated. However, in the class that is used to initiate the example task, the @Resource annotation is used to inject the application server's default ManagedScheduledExecutorService, which can be identified by the name of concurrent/__defaultManagedScheduledExecutorService.

```
@Resource(name=" concurrent/__defaultManagedScheduledExecutorService ")
    ManagedScheduledExecutorService mes;
```

To schedule the task, create an instance of the task class and then pass the instance to one of the ManagedScheduledExecutorService scheduler methods that are made available via the ScheduleExecutorService interface. The methods that can be used to schedule tasks are shown in Table 18-1.

Table 18-1. *ScheduleExecutorService Methods*

Method	Description
schedule(Callable<V> callable, long delay, TimeUnit unit)	Creates and executes a ScheduledFeature object. The object becomes available after the specified delay period.
schedule(Runnable command, long delay, TimeUnit unit)	Creates and executes a one-time task that becomes available after the specified delay.
scheduleAtFixedRate(Runnable command, long initialDelay, long period, TimeUnit unit)	Creates and executes a periodic task that becomes available after the initial specified delay period. Subsequent executions are then scheduled in increments of the specified period after the initial delay.
scheduleWithFixedDelay(Runnable command, long initialDelay, long delay, TimeUnit unit)	Creates and executes a periodic task that becomes available after the initial delay period. Subsequent executions are then scheduled with the specified delay period in between each execution.

In the example for this recipe, the `scheduleAtFixedRate` method is called, passing the task class, along with the initial delay period of five minutes, and then the task is executed every five minutes thereafter.

18-6. Creating Thread Instances

Problem

Your application requires the ability to perform tasks in the background while other tasks are executing.

Solution

Create thread instances to run tasks in the background by using a `ManagedThreadFactory` resource. Before an application can use the service, it must be created within the application server container. To create a `ManagedThreadFactory` instance within GlassFish, issue the following command from the command line:

```
asadmin create-managed-thread-factory concurrent/myThreadFactory
```

In this command, name-of-service can be whatever you choose. The `create-managed-thread-factory` command has many options that can be specified. To see and learn more about each option, invoke the command `help` by issuing the `--help` flag after the command, rather than providing the name of the service to create.

To utilize a `ManagedThreadFactory`, the environment must be configured via XML or annotation. To utilize XML configuration, add a `<resource-env-ref>` element to the `web.xml` deployment descriptor. In this case, you need to configure a resource of type `javax.enterprise.concurrent.ManagedThreadFactory`, as shown in the excerpt from the following `web.xml`:

```
<resource-env-ref>
 <description>
</description>
<resource-env-ref-name>
concurrent/AcmeThreadFactory
</resource-env-ref-name>
 <resource-env-ref-type>
javax.enterprise.concurrent.ManagedThreadFactory
 </resource-env-ref-type>
</resource-env-ref>
```

To utilize annotations rather than XML configuration, the `ManagedThreadFactory` can be injected using an annotation such as the following:

```
@Resource(name="concurrent/AcmeThreadFactory");
ManagedThreadFactory threadFactory;
```

In this example, a ManagedThreadFactory will be injected into an EJB so that a logging task can be used to print output to the server log when the EJB is created or destroyed. The following code demonstrates how to create a task that can be utilized by the ManagedThreadFactory:

```
public class MessagePrinter implements Runnable {

    @Override
    public void run() {
        printMessage();
    }

    public void printMessage(){
        System.out.println("Here we are performing some work...");
    }
}
```

To initiate the threading, call the ManagedThreadFactory, which can be injected into a using class via the @Resource annotation. The ManageThreadFactory newThread method can then be invoked to spawn a new thread, passing the Runnable class instance for which the thread should process. In the following servlet context listener example, when a thread context is initialized, then a Runnable class that was listed in the previous code listing, MessagePrinter, is instantiated and passed to the ManagedThreadFactory to spawn a new thread.

```
public class ServletCtxListener implements ServletContextListener {
    Thread printerThread = null;

    @Resource(name ="concurrent/AcmeThreadFactory")
    ManagedThreadFactory threadFactory;

    public void contextInitialized(ServletContextEvent scEvent) {

        MessagePrinter printer = new MessagePrinter();
        printerThread = threadFactory.newThread(printer);
        printerThread.start();
    }

    public void contextDestroyed(ServletContextEvent scEvent) {
        synchronized (printerThread) {
            printerThread.interrupt();
        }
    }
}
```

How It Works

Until the release of Java EE 7, multithreaded enterprise applications were very customized. In fact, until the release, there was no formal framework to utilize for spawning threads within an enterprise Java application. In both Java EE 7 and Java EE 8, which include the Concurrency utilities, thread processing has been formalized. To utilize threading within an enterprise application, you should create ManagedThreadFactory resource(s) within the application server container, and utilize those resources within application(s), as needed.

To create a ManagedThreadFactory resource within the GlassFish or Payara application server, invoke the asadmin create-managed-thread-factory command from the command prompt. At a minimum, the desired name for the resource should be included with the invocation of the command. However, there are a number of different options that can be specified to customize the resource. To learn more about those options, see the online documentation at https://concurrency-ee-spec.java.net/javadoc/.

As mentioned in the example, an application can use a ManagedThreadFactory resource by configuring XML within the web.xml deployment descriptor, or by injecting via the @Resource annotation within the classes that need to use the resource. Once that resource has been injected, calls can be made against it to spawn new threads using the newThread method. The newThread method returns a Thread instance, which can then be utilized as needed, by calling the Thread instance methods, as needed. In the solution to this recipe, the thread is started by calling the thread's start method, and when the context is destroyed, the thread's interrupt method is invoked.

The addition of a formal threading framework into Java EE has been very much welcomed. By adhering to the use of ManagedThreadFactory API, your enterprise applications can be made multithreaded using an accepted standard solution.

18-7. Creating an Item-Oriented Batch Process

Problem

You would like to create a job that runs in the background and executes a task.

Solution

Use the Batch Applications for the Java Platform API, introduced in Java EE 7, to create a job that handles item-oriented processing. Batch processing that is item-oriented is also known as "chunk" processing. In this example, a batch process is created to read text from a file, process that text accordingly, and then write out the processed text. To begin, construct an XML file to define the job. The XML file for this example will be called acmeFileProcessor.xml. We will break down the lines of this file, as well as discuss the different options for writing job XML, in the "How It Works" section. For now, let's take a look at what a job process looks like. The following lines are from the acmeFileProcessor.xml file.

```
<?xml version="1.0" encoding="UTF-8"?>

<job id="myJob" xmlns="http://batch.jsr352/jsl">
    <step id="readingStep" >
        <chunk item-count="2">
            <reader ref="acmeReader"></reader>
            <processor ref="acmeProcessor"></processor>
        </chunk>
    </step>
    <step id="writingStep" >
        <chunk item-count="1">
            <writer ref="acmeWriter"></writer>
        </chunk>
    </step>
</job>
```

There are three tasks being performed in this particular job: acmeReader, acmeProcessor, and acmeWriter. These three tasks can be associated with Java class implementations within the batch.xml file, which is located within the META-INF directory. The following code shows what the batch.xml looks like.

```
<?xml version="1.0" encoding="UTF-8"?>
<batch-artifacts xmlns="http://jcp.org.batch/jsl">
    <ref id="acmeReader" class="org.javaee8recipes.chapter18.recipe18_07.AcmeReader"/>
    <ref id="acmeProcessor" class="org.javaee8recipes.chapter18.recipe18_07.AcmeProcessor"/>
    <ref id="acmeWriter" class="org.javaee8recipes.chapter18.recipe18_07.AcmeWriter"/>
</batch-artifacts>
```

Next, let's take a look at each of these class implementations. We will begin by looking at the following AcmeReader class implementation. This class is responsible for reading a file and creating a new WidgetReportItem object for each line of text.

```
package org.javaee8recipes.chapter18.recipe18_07;

import java.nio.charset.Charset;
import java.nio.file.Files;
import java.nio.file.Path;
import java.nio.file.Paths;
import java.util.List;
import javax.batch.api.AbstractItemReader;

/**
 * Example of a file reading task
 *
 * @author Juneau
 */
public class AcmeReader extends AbstractItemReader<WidgetReportItem> {

    public AcmeReader() {
    }

    /**
     * Read lines of report and store each into a WidgetReportItem object.  Once
     * all lines have been read then return null to trigger the end of file.
     * @return
     * @throws Exception
     */
    @Override
    public WidgetReportItem readItem() throws Exception {
        Path file = Paths.get("widgetFile.txt");
        List<String> fileLines;
        Charset charset = Charset.forName("US-ASCII");
        fileLines = Files.readAllLines(file, charset);
        for(String line:fileLines){
            return new WidgetReportItem(line);
        }
        return null;

    }
}
```

Next, let's take a look at the AcmeProcessor class. This class is responsible for processing each WidgetReportItem accordingly. In this case, if the line of text that is contained in the object has the text "Two" in it, then it will be added to a WidgetOutputItem object (see the following code for WidgetReportItem and WidgetOutputItem).

```
package org.javaee8recipes.chapter18.recipe18_07;

import javax.batch.api.ItemProcessor;

/**
 *
 * @author Juneau
 */
public class AcmeProcessor implements ItemProcessor<WidgetReportItem, WidgetOutputItem> {

    public AcmeProcessor(){}

    /**
     * Write out all lines that contain the text "Two"
     * @param item
     * @return
     * @throws Exception
     */
    @Override
    public WidgetOutputItem processItem(WidgetReportItem item) throws Exception {
        if(item.getLineText().contains("Two")){
            return new WidgetOutputItem(item.getLineText());
        } else {
            return null;
        }
    }

}
```

Lastly, let's see what the AcmeWriter class looks like. This class is responsible for writing the WidgetOutputItem objects that have been processed by AcmeProcessor.

```
package org.javaee8recipes.chapter18.recipe18_07;

import java.util.List;
import javax.batch.api.AbstractItemWriter;

/**
 *
 * @author Juneau
 */
public class AcmeWriter extends AbstractItemWriter<WidgetOutputItem> {

    @Override
    public void writeItems(List<WidgetOutputItem> list) throws Exception {
        for(WidgetOutputItem item:list){
```

```
                System.out.println("Write to file:" + item.getLineText());
            }
        }

}
```

The WidgetReportItem and WidgetOutputItem objects are merely containers that hold a string of text. The following is the implementation for WidgetReportItem; other than the name, the WidgetOutputItem object is identical.

```
package org.javaee8recipes.chapter18.recipe18_07;

public class WidgetReportItem {
    private String lineText;

    public WidgetReportItem(String line){
        this.lineText = line;
    }

    /**
     * @return the lineText
     */
    public String getLineText() {
        return lineText;
    }

    /**
     * @param lineText the lineText to set
     */
    public void setLineText(String lineText) {
        this.lineText = lineText;
    }
}
```

When this batch job is executed, the text file is read, processed, and then specific lines of text are written to the system log. The read and process tasks are performed as part of the first step, and then the write is processed as the second step.

How It Works

Prior to the inclusion of Batch Applications for Java EE API, organizations and individuals had to write their own custom procedures for processing batch jobs. Utilizing the Batch API, developers can create batch jobs using a combination of XML for defining a job, and Java for programming the implementation. In the solution for this recipe, a simple batch job reads text from a file, processes it using a comparison, and then writes out the processed text. The example batch program is simplistic, but the API makes it easy to write very complex jobs.

Let's begin the explanation by first taking a brief look at the API from a high level. A job consists of one or more steps, and each step has exactly one ItemReader, ItemWriter, and ItemProcessor. A JobOperator is responsible for launching a job, and a JobRepository is used to maintain metadata regarding the currently running job. Jobs are defined via XML, and the <Job> element is at the root of the job definition. Thus, a <Job> is the foundational element, which consists of one or more <step> elements, and also defines other specifics of the job, such as the job name and if it is restartable or not. Each `<step>` of a job consists of one or more chunks or batchlets. In this recipe, which covers item-oriented processes, each step has just one chunk, although in general steps could encompass one or more chunks. To learn more about batchlets, see the specification or online documentation at https://javaee.github.io/javaee-spec/javadocs/javax/batch/api/Batchlet.html.

As expected, each chunk of a step is defined within the XML using a `<chunk>` element. A `<chunk>` element defines the reader, writer, and processor pattern of a batch job. A chunk runs within the scope of a transaction, and it is restartable at a checkpoint if it does not complete. The `<reader>` element is a child element of `<chunk>`, and it is used to specify the reader for that chunk. The `<reader>` element can accept zero or more name/value pair properties using a `<properties>` element. The `<processor>` element is also a child element of `<chunk>`, which specifies the processor element for that chunk. Like a `<reader>` element, a `<processor>` element can accept zero or more name/value pair properties using a `<properties>` element. The `<writer>` element is a child element of `<chunk>` as well, which specifies the writer for the chunk step. Again, like the reader and processor, the `<writer>` element can accept zero or more name/value pair properties using a `<properties>` element.

The XML configuration for a job resides in an XML file that should be named the same as the batch job to which it belongs. This file should reside within a folder named `batch-jobs`, which in turn resides in the `META-INF` folder. An XML file named `batch.xml` should also reside within the `META-INF` folder. This file contains the mapping for the item reader, writer, and processor elements using `<ref>` elements and mapping the item names to a Java implementation class.

```
<batch-artifacts xmlns="http://jcp.org.batch/jsl">
    <ref id="acmeReader" class="org.javaee8recipes.chapter18.recipe18_07.AcmeReader"/>
    <ref id="acmeProcessor" class="org.javaee8recipes.chapter18.recipe18_07.AcmeProcessor"/>
    <ref id="acmeWriter" class="org.javaee8recipes.chapter18.recipe18_07.AcmeWriter"/>
</batch-artifacts>
```

The implementation classes should either extend abstract classes (reader and writer) or implement an interface (processor). The `ItemReader` implementation class, in this case `AcmeReader`, extends the `AbstractItemReader` and accepts an object into which the read items will be stored. In the example for this recipe, that object class is named `WidgetReportItem`. As such, the class should implement the `readItem` method, which is responsible for performing the reading. The method should return the object to which the items are read, or return a `null` when there are no more items to read.

```
public class AcmeReader extends AbstractItemReader<WidgetReportItem> {
...
@Override
    public WidgetReportItem readItem() throws Exception {
        Path file = Paths.get("widgetFile.txt");
        List<String> fileLines;
        Charset charset = Charset.forName("US-ASCII");
        fileLines = Files.readAllLines(file, charset);
        for(String line:fileLines){
            return new WidgetReportItem(line);
        }
        return null;

    }
...
```

The ItemProcessor class implementation, in this case AcmeProcessor, is responsible for performing processing for the chunk, and it should implement the ItemProcessor interface, accepting both the object containing the read items and an object to which the processed items will be stored. The ItemProcessor implementation class should implement a processItem method, which is responsible for performing the processing.

The ItemWriter class implementation, in this case AcmeWriter, is responsible for performing the writing for the chunk. The class implementation should extend the AbstractItemWriter class and accept the object to which the processed items will be written. This implementation must contain the writeItems method, which is responsible for performing the writing.

As mentioned in the introduction to this chapter, the Batch Applications for Java EE API is very detailed, and this recipe barely scratches the surface of how to write batch jobs.

APPENDIX A

Java EE Development with Apache NetBeans IDE

Developing applications on the JVM can be a fun job, however, it can also become cumbersome if you constantly need to be concerned with Java environment details. When developing an application using only a text editor and the command line or terminal, you need to constantly maintain the `CLASSPATH` in mind to ensure that all required libraries are available to your application. Moreover, organization can be difficult if you are working on multiple applications at one time, and you need to maintain some method of application separation. These are only a couple of reasons why development can become cumbersome if you are not working within a development environment. The Apache NetBeans Integrated Development Environment (IDE) aims to ease the load on developers by abstracting the requirement to maintain `CLASSPATH`, organizing code effectively, and providing a plethora of features to make enterprise development much easier.

Note This appendix covers NetBeans release 8.2, which was the most recent release at the time. However, Apache NetBeans 9.0 is the first official release of NetBeans under Apache, and it will also work with Java EE and Jakarta EE development.

A-1. Configuring Application Servers Within NetBeans

Before you can associate application projects with a server for deployment and testing, you need to register one or more application server containers for use within NetBeans. Even if you are developing microservices that will be deployed to a container, such as Payara Micro, you'll still need to register a server with the IDE for development purposes. Note that it is a good practice to only configure those application servers that are used for development purposes (not for production) within NetBeans.

To add a local or remote server to NetBeans, perform the following tasks.

1. Navigate to the Services window and right-click the Servers menu selection. Click Add Server, as shown in Figure A-1.

J. Juneau, *Java EE 8 Recipes*, https://doi.org/10.1007/978-1-4842-3594-2_19

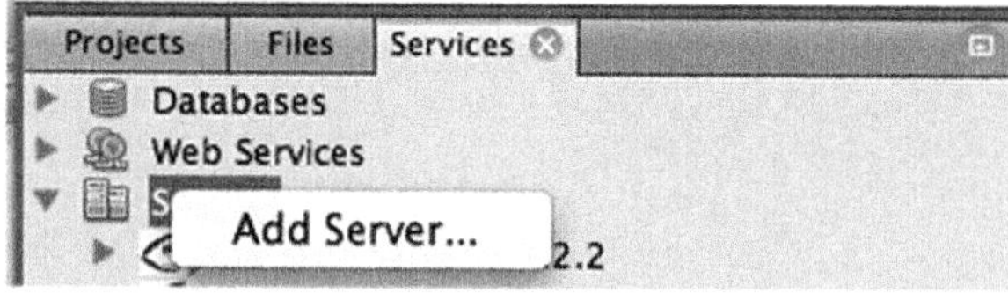

Figure A-1. Add Server to NetBeans IDE

2. When the Add Server Instance dialog appears, choose the server type that you want to add (see Figure A-2).

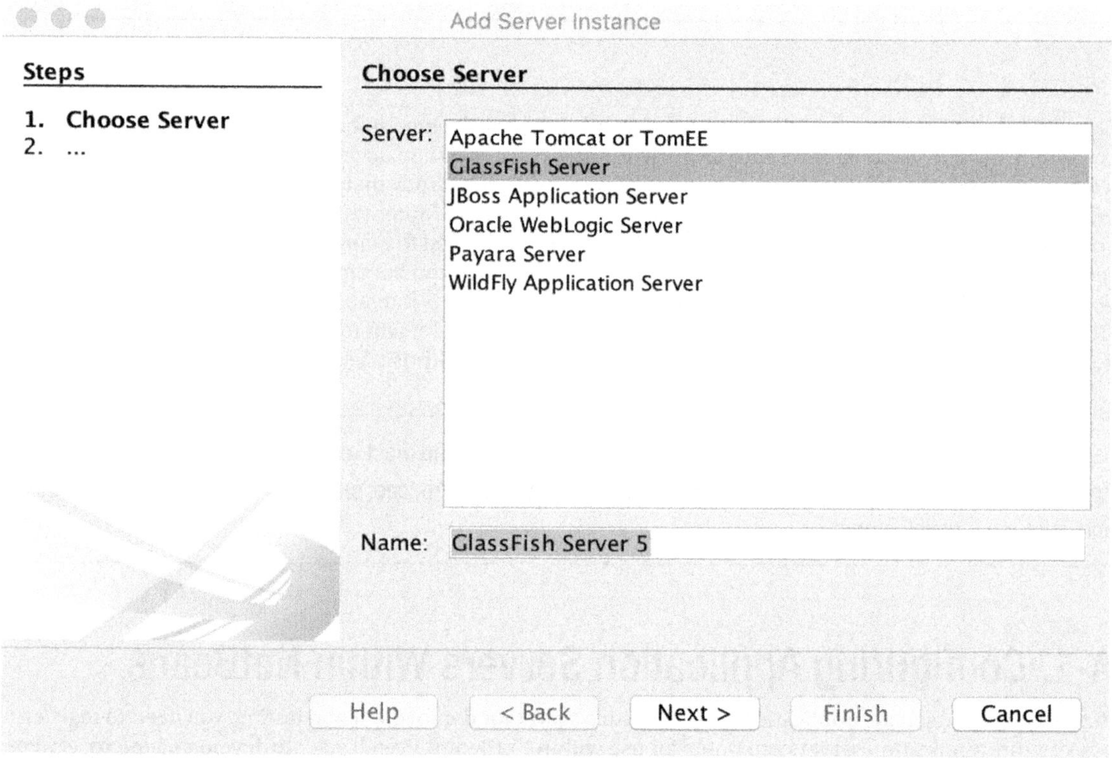

Figure A-2. Add Server Instance

3. On the next screen, enter the path to the application server installation that you would like to configure within NetBeans (see Figure A-3). Once you have chosen the location, click the Finish button.

Add Server Instance

Steps

1. Choose Server
2. **Server Location**
3. Domain Name/Location

Server Location

Installation Location:

/system-path/glassfish5 Browse...

Local Domain Remote Domain

Download Now... I have read and accept the license agreement... (click)

Figure A-3. *Set Server Location*

4. You can now deploy applications to the server by registering it with a given project from within the project properties. Note: You can also perform some basic application server tasks by selecting the application server from within the Servers window in NetBeans, as demonstrated in Figure A-4.

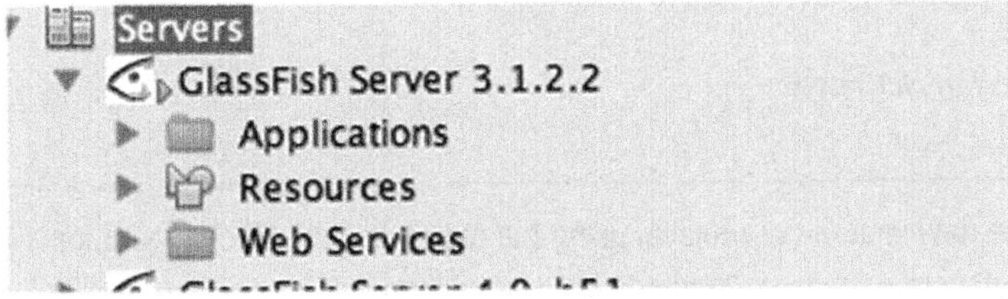

Figure A-4. *Expand and administer server in NetBeans*

Developing Java Web or Enterprise Applications

The NetBeans IDE makes it easy to develop Java Web or Enterprise applications. To begin, you first create a Java EE project within the IDE, and subsequently use the IDE to configure the project accordingly. NetBeans not only makes it easy to configure your application projects, but it also eases development with the aid of such features as autocompletion, syntax highlighting, autoformatting, and so forth. This section will cover how NetBeans can help Java EE developers with some of the most commonly performed Java EE development tasks.

A-2. Creating a NetBeans Java Web Project

There are a few different configurations to choose from for the creation of a Java Enterprise project within NetBeans. This book covers the creation Java Web application projects within NetBeans, which is the standard project selection for development of Java EE applications.

To begin the creation of a new project, open the New Project dialog by choosing File ➤ New Project. In the New Project dialog, you will see all of the different Java project categories listed in the left-side list box. Selecting one of the categories will display the project types for the selected category within the right-side list box. To create a Java EE project, select the Java Web category, and then select Web Application as the project type (see Figure A-5).

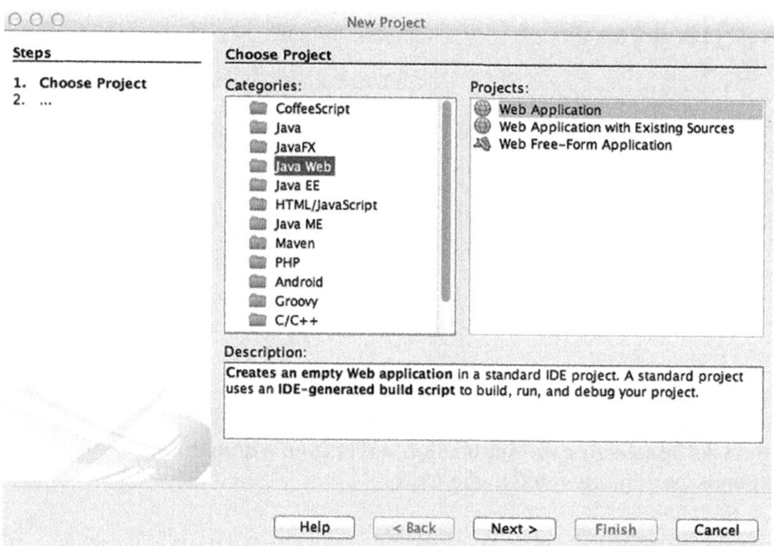

Figure A-5. *Creating a new Java EE project in NetBeans*

■ **Note** The Java EE category allows the development of projects using the old-style Java EE configuration. That is, project types within the Java EE category adhere to standards for developing with Java EE 5 or earlier. In such projects, separate Web (WAR) and EJB (JAR) projects are created, rather than a single project that deploys to a single distributable WAR file.

After selecting the project type, the New Web Application dialog will open. Enter a project name and location, as shown in Figure A-6. Once you're finished, choose Next.

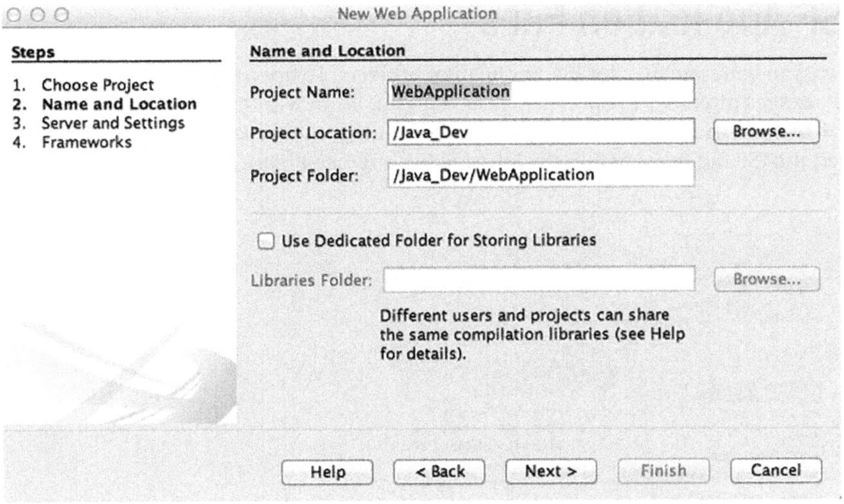

Figure A-6. *New Web Application: Name and Location*

In the Server and Settings screen, choose the application server that you want to use for deployment (see Configuring Application Servers in NetBeans), along with the Java EE version that you want to use. If you plan to use Contexts and Dependency Injection, then select the designated check box (see Figure A-7).

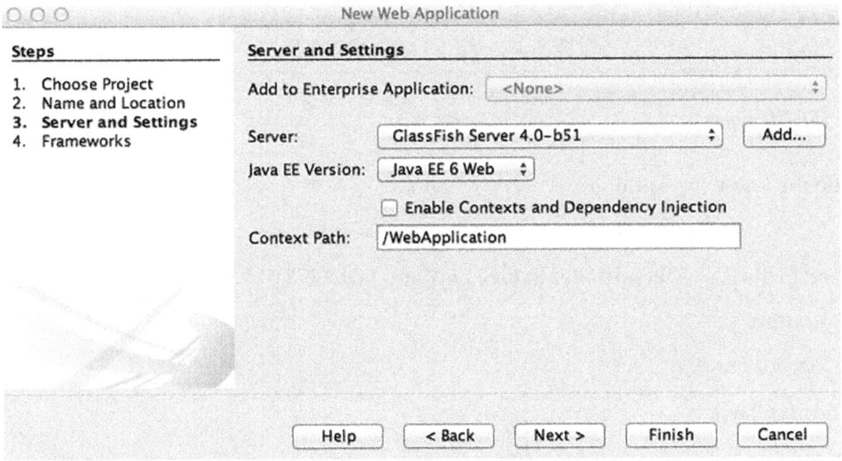

Figure A-7. *New Web Application: Server and Settings*

A-3. Creating JSF Application Files

The NetBeans IDE makes it easy to generate files for JSF application projects. To open the JSF menu, right-click an application Source Packages directory to open the context menu. From within the context menu, choose New and then Other... to open the New File dialog. Within the dialog, choose JavaServer Faces from the Categories list box to open the JSF file types within the left-side list box (see Figure A-8).

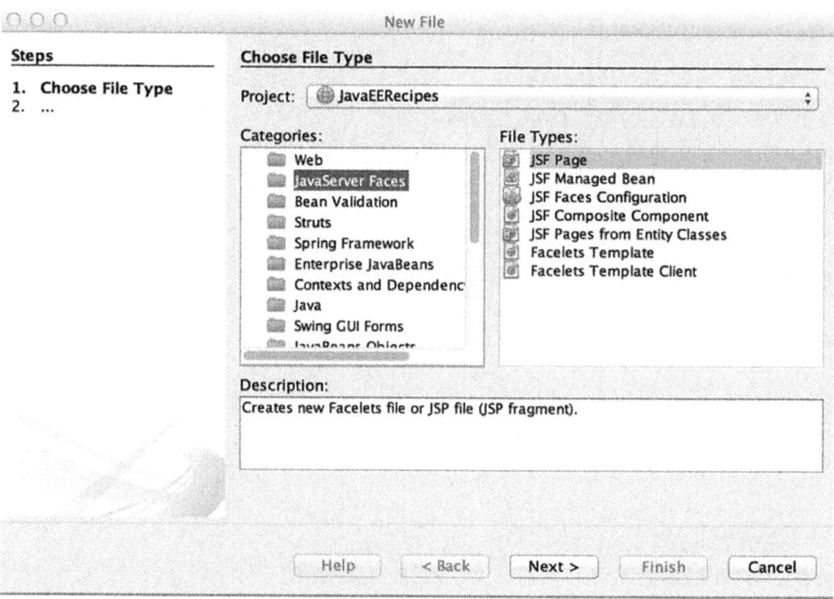

Figure A-8. *New File menu: JSF file types*

The JSF file types include the following options:

- JSF Page
- JSF Managed Bean (This is a CDI controller in Java EE 7 and Java EE 8)
- JSF Faces Configuration
- JSF Composite Component
- JSF Pages from Entity Classes
- Faces Template
- Faces Template Client

The JSF Page file selection opens a dialog that can be used to generate a new JSF page (see Figure A-9). The dialog allows you to choose a file location and name, and it also contains the ability to apply different options for the page type. The option choices for page type are Facelets (default), JSP File, or JSP Segment. The examples throughout this book feature the Facelets page type.

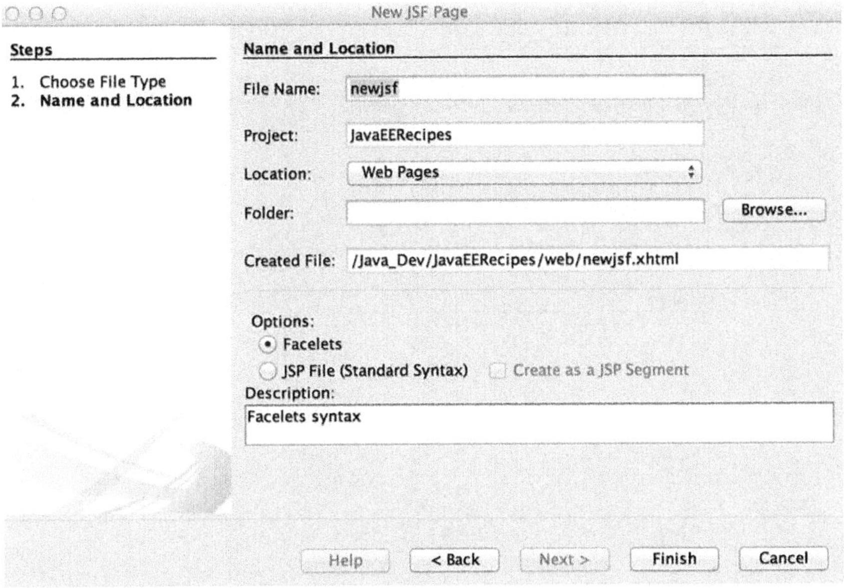

Figure A-9. *New JSF Page dialog*

The JSF Managed Bean file selection opens a dialog that allows you to generate a JSF CDI Bean controller class (see Figure A-10). The dialog provides the ability to choose to add the bean data to the `faces-config` file, as well as to choose the scope of the bean.

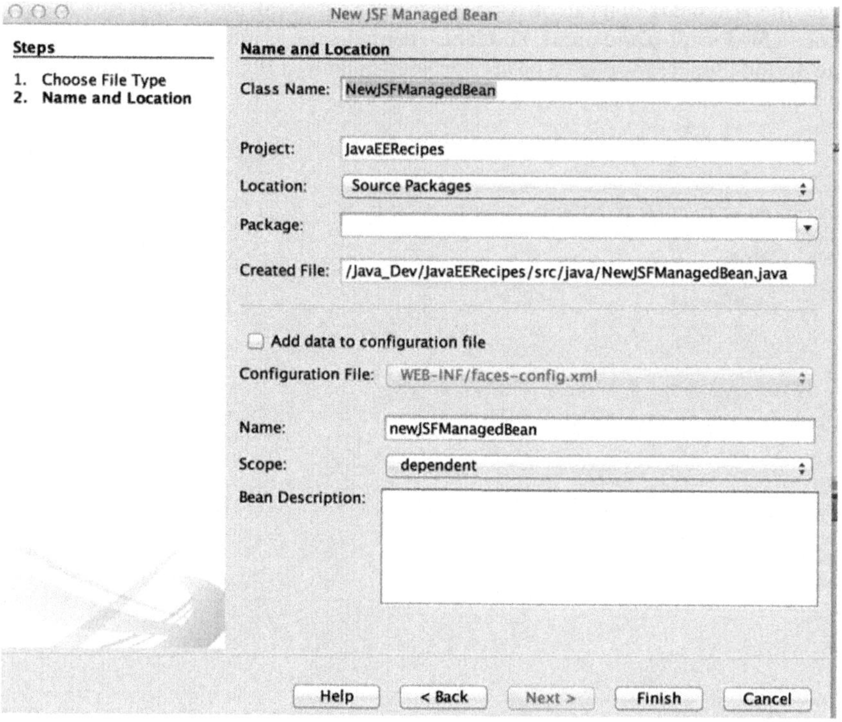

Figure A-10. *New JSF Managed/CDI Bean dialog*

The JSF Faces Configuration File selection is used to create a `faces-config.xml` file for a project. However, this option is not required if you choose to create a JSF project within the NetBeans Project Creation wizard.

The JSF Composite Component file selection opens a dialog that can be used to create a composite component file. The dialog does not provide many options other than the ability to choose a file location and name. The generated file contains the skeleton of a composite component, as listed in the following lines:

```
<?xml version='1.0' encoding='UTF-8' ?>
<!DOCTYPE html PUBLIC "-//W3C//DTD XHTML 1.0 Transitional//EN" "http://www.w3.org/TR/xhtml1/
DTD/xhtml1-transitional.dtd">
<html xmlns="http://www.w3.org/1999/xhtml"
xmlns:cc="http://xmlns.jcp.org/jsf/composite">

    <!-- INTERFACE -->
    <cc:interface>
    </cc:interface>

    <!-- IMPLEMENTATION -->
    <cc:implementation>
    </cc:implementation>
</html>
```

The JSF Pages from Entity Classes file selection can be quite powerful in that it allows you to choose an Entity Class from which to generate a JSF page, and then the resulting JSF page will be bound to the entity class upon generation. In order to use this option, the project must contain at least one entity class.

A-4. Developing Entity Classes

The NetBeans IDE provides facilities to help develop Entity Bean classes, either manually or based on a selected database table. To access the entity class wizards, right-click a project's Source Packages folder to open the context menu, and then choose New ➤ Other to open the New File dialog. Once it's open, choose the Persistence category from the left-side list box to display the file types in the right-side list box (see Figure A-11).

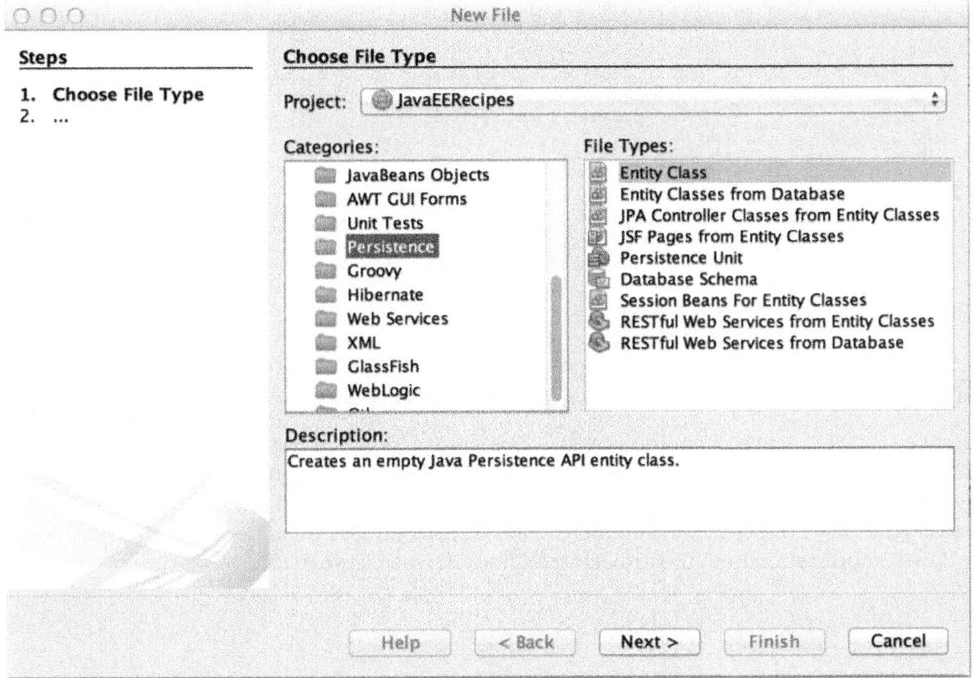

Figure A-11. *New File, Persistence*

The Entity Class option allows you to generate a blank entity class, and the Entity Classes from Database option allows you to generate an entity class from a selected database table. In doing so, all of the requisite code for mapping the entity class to the selected database table is automatically generated for you.

A-5. Using JPQL

NetBeans includes a feature that allows you to query a database using JPQL syntax. This can be quite helpful for those who are using JPQL in their EJB session beans. To access the JPQL query tool, expand a NetBeans web project that contains a `persistence.xml` configuration file in the project Configuration Files directory. Then perform the following steps:

1. Right-click the `persistence.xml` configuration file to open the context menu.
2. Click Run JPQL Query to open the tool (see Figure A-12), type in your query, and click the Run button on the upper-right side of the query editor.

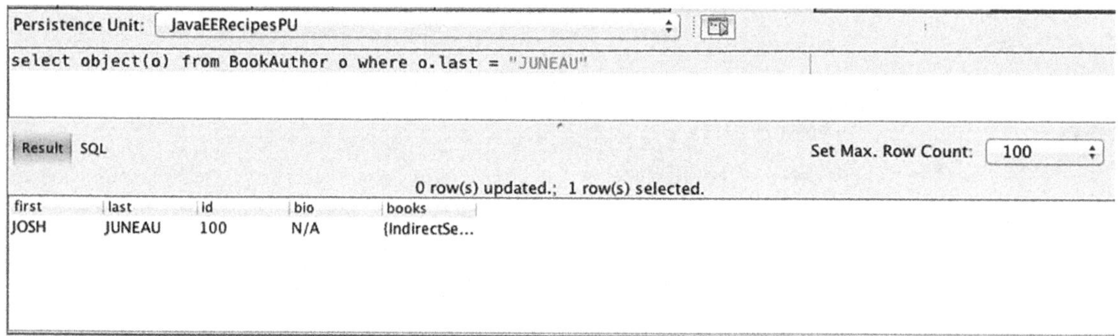

Figure A-12. *JPQL tool*

A-6. Using HTML5

Many applications use HTML5. The Java community has taken note of that and has made it easy to begin working with HTML5 within NetBeans itself. NetBeans has an HTML5 project option, which enables developers to debug HTML5 pages using a Chrome web browser plug-in. To create an HTML5 project from within the IDE, select the New Project option and then choose HTML/JavaScript in the Categories selection list, followed by HTML5 Application from the Projects selection list (see Figure A-13).

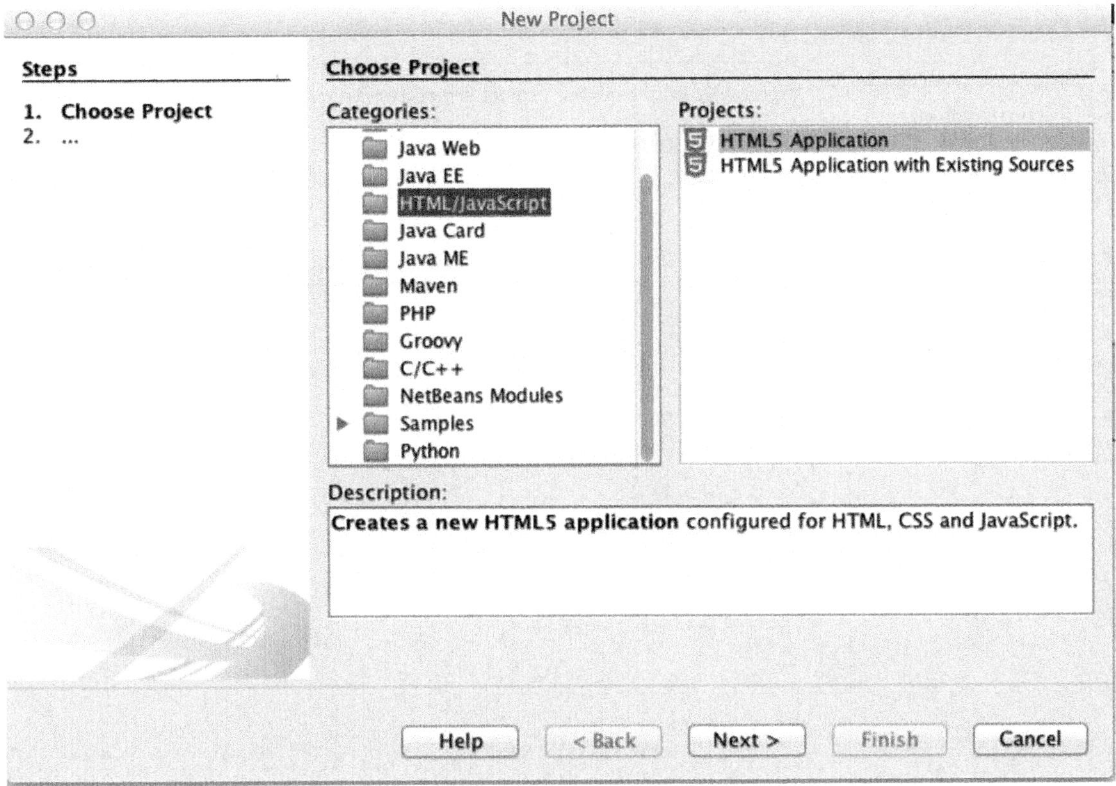

Figure A-13. *Create new HTML5 application*

Next, you are given the option to choose No Site Template, or you can select a template that you provide, or use one that you can download, as seen in Figure A-14.

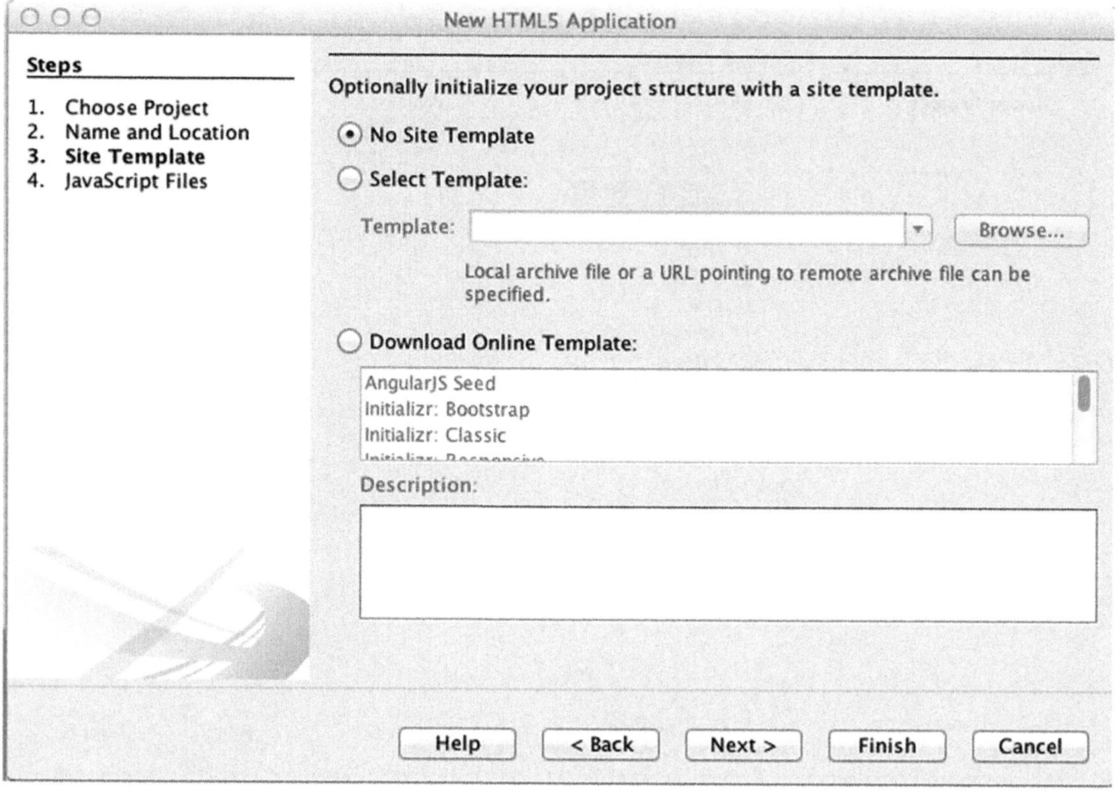

Figure A-14. *Choose site template*

Lastly, choose any libraries that you want to add to your HTML5 project (see Figure A-15), then click Finish.

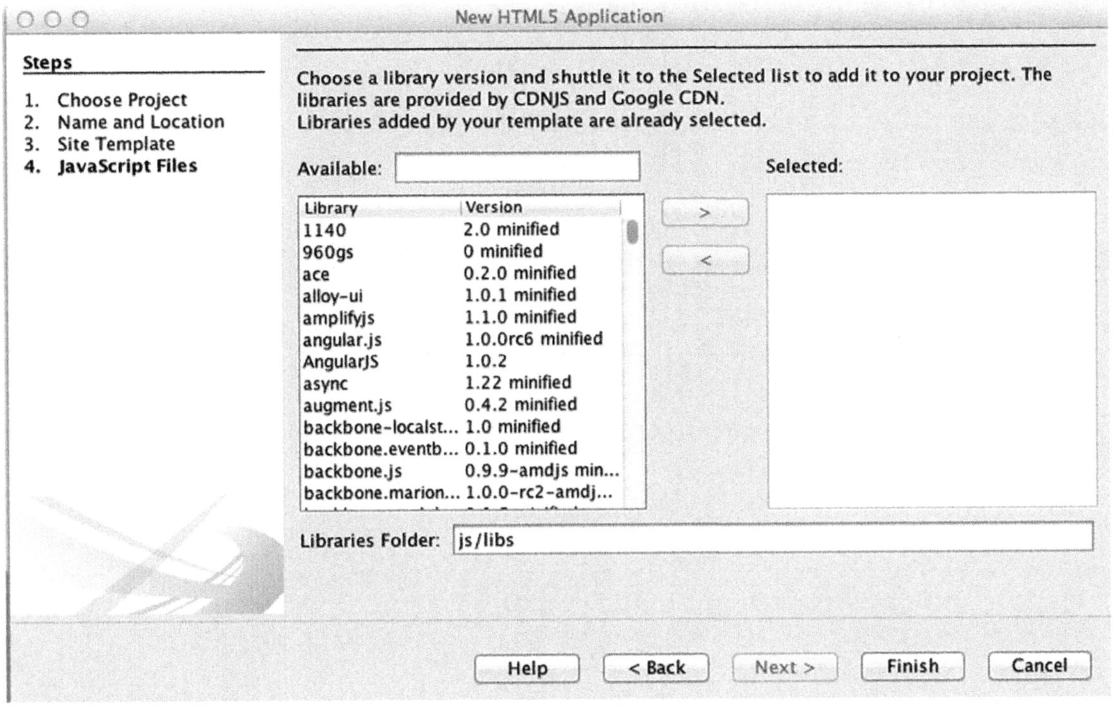

***Figure A-15.** Add libraries to project*

Once the project has been created, you can choose Run to have it opened within Chrome, assuming that you have installed the Chrome plug-in. If you have not yet installed the Chrome plug-in, you will be prompted to do so.

Index

A

B

J. Juneau, *Java EE 8 Recipes*, https://doi.org/10.1007/978-1-4842-3594-2

C

F

G

H

I

J, K

L

M

N

Q

R

S

T

U

V

W, X, Y, Z

Printed by Printforce, the Netherlands